BOTTOM LINE

health's

COMPLETE BOOK OF

SIMPLE

SOLUTIONS

2,354 Faster, Easier, Better Cutting-Edge Cures

By Michael Castleman

Bottom Line
Books
www.BottomLineSecrets.com

Bottom Line Health's Complete Book of Simple Solutions

Bottom Line® Books, First Edition
Published by arrangement with Rodale Inc.

Bottom Line® Books is a registered trademark of
Boardroom® Inc.
281 Tresser Blvd.
Stamford, CT 06901

ISBN 0–88723–266–3

10   9   8   7   6   5   4   3   2   1

The medical symptoms questionnaire (pages 32 and 33) is copyrighted © HealthComm International, Inc., and Immuno Laboratories, Inc. Permission to reprint by the Functional Medicine Research Center (FMRC), a division of HealthComm International, Inc.

The Amsler grid (page 452) is reprinted with permission of the American Academy of Ophthalmology.

The benign prostatic hypertrophy questionnaire (page 542) is adapted from "The AUA Symptom Index for Benign Prostatic Hyperplasia," an article by Barry, M. J., et al, that originally appeared in the *Journal of Urology* (1992, 148: 1549–57). Reprinted with permission.

Various visualization exercises in part 3 of this book are adapted from *Healing Visualizations* by Gerald Epstein. © 1989 by Gerald Epstein. Used by permission of Bantam Books, a division of Random House, Inc.

Notice: This book is intended as a reference volume only, not as a medical manual. The information given here is designed to help you make informed decisions about your health. It is not intended as a substitute for any treatment that may have been prescribed by your doctor. If you suspect that you have a medical problem, we urge you to seek competent medical help.

Printed in the United States of America

This one is for my children,
Maya and Jeff.

Simple Solutions Board of Advisors

In researching and writing *Simple Solutions*, I was extremely fortunate to be able to turn to an advisory board of distinguished experts who were extraordinarily generous with their time, experience, and wisdom. Much of the advice in this book is based upon their expert recommendations. To give them full credit, their academic and professional credentials, location, practice, and selected publications are given in full below.

Alan P. Brauer, M.D. A psychiatrist, Dr. Brauer is the founder and director of the TotalCare Medical Center, a complementary medicine center in Palo Alto, California. He is a clinical assistant professor in the department of psychiatry and behavioral medicine at Stanford University. He is also the author of *Mind as Healer* and *The New Promise of Pleasure for Couples in Love*.

James A. Duke, Ph.D. Until he retired in 1997, Dr. Duke was, for many years, the chief medical herbalist for the U.S. Department of Agriculture. He has traveled worldwide studying medicinal plants, and several times a year, he teaches workshops in Peru on rain-forest medicinal herbs under the auspices of the Amazon Center for Environmental Education and Research based in Helena, Alabama. He is the author of several books, including *The Green Pharmacy*, *The CRC Handbook of Medicinal Herbs*, *Medicinal Plants of China*, and *Medicinal Plants of the Bible*. He is a longtime consultant to the American Botanical Council, a leader in medicinal herb education based in Austin, Texas. He maintains a lush, 6-acre herb garden at his home in Fulton, Maryland, which includes many rare plants he has collected during his travels.

David Frawley, O.M.D. Dr. Frawley is a practitioner and teacher of Ayurvedic medicine in Santa Fe, New Mexico. He is the author of several books, including *Ayurvedic Healing: A Comprehensive Guide*, *The Yoga of Herbs* (with Dr. Vasant Lad), and *From the River of Heaven: Hindu and Vedic Knowledge for the Modern Age*. A Sanskrit scholar, he is a member of the International Advisory Committee of the Interdisciplinary School of Ayurvedic Medicine at the University of Poona, India. He is also the director of the American Institute of Vedic Studies in Santa Fe.

Alan Gaby, M.D. Dr. Gaby is a professor of nutrition at Bastyr University, the naturopathic medical school in Kenmore, Washington. A past president of the American Holistic Medical Association, he is medical editor of the *Townsend Letter for Doctors and Patients* and has served as an advisor to the National Institutes of Health Office of Alternative and Complementary Medicine. He is the author of *Preventing and Reversing Osteoporosis* and B_6: *The Natural Healer*.

Michael Reed Gach Gach is the founder and director of the Acupressure Institute in Berkeley, California. He is the author of several books, including *Acupressure's Potent Points*, *The Bum Back Book*, and *Arthritis Relief at Your Fingertips*.

Efrem Korngold, O.M.D., L.Ac., and Harriet Beinfield, L.Ac. A husband-and-wife team, Dr. Korngold and Beinfield are licensed acupuncturists and founders of Chinese Medicine Works, a Chinese medicine clinic in San Francisco. Dr. Korngold earned his O.M.D. in China at the Shanghai College of Traditional Chinese Medicine and at the Kunming Traditional Chinese Medicine Research Institute. He earned his O.M.D. at the San Francisco College of Acupuncture and Oriental Medicine, where he was a professor for 8 years. Dr. Korngold and Beinfield both serve on the faculty of the American College of Traditional Chinese Medicine in San Francisco and on the advisory board of *Natural Health* magazine. They are the authors of *Between Heaven and Earth: A Guide to Chinese Medicine* and *The Chinese Modular Solutions Handbook for Health Professionals*.

Shari Lieberman, Ph.D. Dr. Lieberman is a professor of nutrition at the University of Bridgeport School of Human Nutrition in Connecticut. She is the author (with Nancy Bruning) of *The Real Vitamin and Mineral Book*. She maintains a private practice in clinical nutrition in New York City.

Joseph Pizzorno Jr., N.D. Dr. Pizzorno is a founder and president of Bastyr University, the naturopathic medical school in Kenmore, Washington. He is the author (with Michael T. Murray, N.D.) of *A Textbook of Natural Medicine* and *The Encyclopedia of Natural Medicine*. He is a member of the Seattle–King County Board of Health, the senior medical advisor for the *Journal of Alternative and Complementary Therapies*, and a member of the Alternative Health Care Advisory Committee for Blue Cross of Washington and Alaska.

Martin L. Rossman, M.D. Dr. Rossman is a general practitioner and board-certified acupuncturist who is founder and director of the Collaborative Medicine Center, a blended-medicine clinic in Mill Valley, California. He is a clinical associate in the department of medicine at the University of California, San Francisco, Medical Center; an adjunct faculty member of the California School of Professional Psychology in San Francisco; and co-director of the Academy for Guided Imagery in Mill Valley. He is the author of *Healing Yourself: A Step-by-Step Program for Better Health through Imagery* and the producer of many visualization tapes through the Academy for Guided Imagery.

Anne Simons, M.D. Dr. Simons is an assistant clinical professor of family and community medicine at the University of California, San Francisco, Medical Center. She is working to establish a complementary therapies program within the San Francisco Department of Public Health. She is the author (with Bobbie Hasselbring and Michael Castleman) of *Before You Call the Doctor: Safe, Effective Self-Care for More Than 300 Common Medical Problems*.

Dana Ullman Ullman is the founder and director of Homeopathic Educational Services in Berkeley, California. He is the author of several books, including *The Consumer's Guide to Homeopathy*, *Discovering Homeopathy*, and *Homeopathic Medicines for Children and Infants*. He serves on the advisory boards of three magazines: *Natural Health*, *Healthy Living*, and *Let's Live*. He is also an advisor to the Alternative Medicine Center at Columbia University's College of Physicians and Surgeons and Harvard Medical School's Center to Assess Alternative Therapies for Chronic Illness.

Contents

PART THREE

**Simple Solutions for Treating
Conditions from Acne to
Yeast Infection**

RESOURCES

Acknowledgments

The love and companionship of Anne Simons and Jeff and Maya Castleman are my best-choice therapies for all of life's challenges.

Ed Claflin and Susan Berg, my editors at Rodale, deserve highest praise for their editorial guidance, hard work, and good humor. For their respective roles in ensuring the accuracy, consistency, and clarity of the text, my thanks go to assistant research manager Jane Unger Hahn; lead researcher Kathryn Piff; editorial researchers Grete Haentjens, Lois Guarino Hazel, Molly Donaldson Brown, Deborah Pedron, and Mary S. Mesaros; and senior copy editor Karen Neely. Thanks also to Debora Yost, vice president and editorial director, and Pat Corpora, president of Rodale's Book Division, for their support. A special note of homage to Robert Rodale, an early visionary supporter of blended medicine.

Michael Bear Schiesser, M.D., primary-care physician at the Marino Center for Progressive Health in Cambridge, Massachusetts, gave the manuscript a thorough and careful medical review. Thank you.

For 22 years, I have enjoyed outstanding representation by my literary agents, Katinka Matson and John Brockman, at Brockman, Inc., in New York.

I would also like to thank my advisory board and the many editors and friends who, over the years, have contributed to my appreciation of blended medicine: Anne Alexander; Harriet Beinfield, L.Ac.; Mark Blumenthal; Alan Brauer, M.D.; Mark Bricklin; Deke Castleman; Mildred and Louis Castleman; Sandy Close; Louanne Cole-Weston, Ph.D.; Richard Day, M.D.; Diane DiCostanzo; Jim Duke, Ph.D.; Nancy Evens; Donna Farhi; Alice Feinstein; David Fenton; Mark Fenton; Tom Ferguson, M.D.; Steven Foster; Neshama Franklin; David Frawley, O.M.D.; Alan Gaby, M.D.; Michael Reed Gach; Heather Gilberts; Peter Goggin; Joe and Teresa Graedon, Ph.D.; Kathleen Halloran; Martyn Harmon; Ben Kallen; Wayne Kalyn; Jeremy Katz; Jim Keough; Jon King; Jeffrey Klein; Marty Klein, Ph.D.; Jan Knight; Efrem Korngold, O.M.D. L.Ac.; Michael Lerner, Ph.D.; Fred Levine; Amy Levinson; Paul Libassi; Shari Lieberman, Ph.D.; Linda Ligon; Jean Maguire; Matthew Naythons, M.D.; Rachel Newman; Tricia O'Brien; Dean Ornish, M.D.; James Petersen; Carole Pisarczyk; Joe Pizzorno Jr., N.D.; Dana Points; Mark Powelson; Ted Rand; Tom Rawls; Amy Rennert; Marty Rossman, M.D.; Ellen Sanok; Emma Segal; Matt Segal; Dawn Sheggeby; Steve Slon; David Sobel, M.D.; Linda Sparrowe; Annie Stine; Barbara Tannenbaum; Trisha Thompson; Bill Thomson; Wallace Turner; Dana Ullman; and Patti Wolter.

Introduction:
Now You Can Blend the Best

These days, many of us have greater choice in health care than we've ever had before. We can try home remedies, we can call our family doctor. And, as many of us now know, we can select from more than two dozen alternative, or complementary, therapies.

Among the healing therapies now available are acupuncture, aromatherapy, biofeedback, bodywork, Chinese herbal medicine, chiropractic, homeopathy, hypnotherapy, massage, meditation, music therapy, naturopathy, nutritional therapies, qigong, tai chi, visualization, Western herbal medicine, and yoga. In addition, of course, we have access to all the forms of medicine that we consider more conventional—over-the-counter (OTC) drugs that we can find in any pharmacy, prescription drugs prescribed by physicians, plus all the high-tech medical procedures and surgical techniques that are available in clinics and hospitals.

Some people choose just one healing method and stick with it. Others start with one approach, but if that doesn't work after a while, they switch to another. Some combine two or more approaches at the same time. But few of us are experts at this selection process. The wide range of choices is likely to have most of us wondering "Which method should I try now?" and "Which works best?"

Thirty years ago, Americans had little medical freedom. Until well into the 1970s, the vast majority of people who got sick would immediately call an M.D., get a prescription, or have surgery, and that was that. There were few other accessible alternatives. Aside from a few chiropractors, the only other full-time practitioners of natural and alternative medicine seemed to be representatives of a bygone era—such as homeopathic doctors, naturopaths, herbalists, and a few doctors of oriental or Chinese medicine.

As a result, most of us have relied heavily on conventional Western medicine—what doctors call allopathic methods of healing. We are far less familiar with methods of alternative and natural healing. Yet, as we now realize, these other healing methods present an opportunity to try something that we haven't done before. And when we can wisely combine alternative medicine with all that conventional medicine has to offer, we have the best opportunity of all for good health and safe, effective cures.

There's a chance that unconventional methods will work much better than conventional medicine. But there's also a very good possibility that the best results of all come from a combination—quite literally, a blend—of conventional, alternative, and natural approaches.

How can we get the *most* benefit from blended medicine? To answer that question, there are many practical things that we need to know about this new form of personal health care. For instance:

◆ There are so many different therapies. How can I choose intelligently among them?

◆ Which approaches work best for what?

◆ Which *combinations* of approaches work well together?

◆ What about safety considerations? Do alternative therapies have any side effects or other dangers?

◆ Which therapies can I do at home? Which require professional practitioners?

◆ If professional practitioners are necessary, how can I find good ones?

◆ What are the specific benefits that I can get only from allopathic medicine—and what are the possible drawbacks or side effects if I use the conventional approach?

◆ If my family physician or M.D. can't help me with alternative and complementary therapies, where should I go for help? And what should I tell my physician?

◆ How do I know when I have an emergency situation that needs immediate attention?

Simple Solutions answers all these questions—and more. It discusses the real benefits and possible risks of the enormous range of therapies available today. *Simple Solutions* discusses which combination of approaches works best for more than 100 diseases and health conditions.

This book combines the expertise of a wide range of medical advisors, including medical doctors, herbalists, acupuncturists, doctors of oriental medicine, plus practitioners from a wide range of other specialties.

Many times, these experts let you know exactly how to use the blended-medicine approach at home. But they also tell you when it's best to seek professional care, whether from a medical doctor, a doctor of oriental medicine, or another well-qualified practitioner.

Should you need a professional, the information in this book will help you find one who is skilled and compassionate. You'll learn what each kind of practitioner will do for you.

Now, more than ever, the power to control your health and health care is yours. Use this important power with new wisdom and confidence.

PART ONE

Healing for the
Twenty-First Century

Chapter 1

Blending Medicines: The Best of All Worlds

Julie Brand awoke in the middle of the night with severe pain shooting down her right leg. The 30-year-old software developer thought she had strained a muscle during a weekend hike. She took aspirin, but it didn't help. So after a few days, she went to see her doctor, Leslie Vensel, M.D., at the Spence Center for Women's Health, a primary-care clinic near her home in Boston.

Dr. Vensel diagnosed sciatica—a pinched or compressed sciatic nerve, which causes lower-back and leg pain. She prescribed stronger pain relievers and a week of bed rest. They didn't help either. So Dr. Vensel referred Brand to Tammy Martin, M.D., the Spence Center's staff orthopedist. A magnetic resonance imaging test (MRI) ordered by Dr. Martin showed a herniated disk, which was putting pressure on the sciatic nerve. Dr. Martin prescribed additional anti-inflammatory and pain medication plus physical therapy.

"The treatments helped somewhat. I became more mobile," Brand recalls. "But after 5 months, I was still hurting. I hated it. One day I was a healthy person, and the next I was looking at a lifetime of chronic pain and disability. It was very depressing."

Then Brand's cousin, a nurse, suggested that she try acupuncture. "I was never into alternative medicine, but some of my friends had gotten good results from acupuncture," Brand says. "So I figured, why not? I had nothing to lose."

But how could she find someone qualified to administer the ancient Chinese needle therapy? She decided to consult Dr. Vensel. "When I told her about my interest in acupuncture, she said, 'Funny, I was just about to suggest it to you,'" Brand says. "Then she blew my mind by referring me to the Spence Center's own staff acupuncturist—Yao Zhang, D.O.M., a doctor of oriental medicine from China. I couldn't believe they had an acupuncturist right there."

In the Spence Center's acupuncture treatment room, Brand lay on her left side as Dr. Zhang inserted a dozen slim, sterile needles into her feet, thighs, buttocks, and back. "It was like getting a vaccination," Brand says. "The needles smarted, but only for a second." And any momentary discomfort was far outweighed by the results: She felt less pain the morning after her first treatment.

Brand received acupuncture treatments twice a week for a month. Her pain subsided, and she cut back on her medication. After the sciatica seemed gone for good, she continued getting treatments once a week for a few months to prevent a recurrence. After that, she went in for an acupuncture "tune-up" once every few months. Today, she sees Dr. Zhang only on those rare occasions when twinges of pain resurface.

What first attracted Brand to the Spence Center was its convenient location and its inclusion on her HMO's list of approved providers. But until her referral to Dr. Zhang, she had no idea that the clinic offered alternative therapies—acupuncture, chiropractic, nutrition counseling, massage therapy, and Chinese herbal medicine—in addition to a broad range of mainstream therapies.

Now Brand is sold on acupuncture for sciatic pain—and on the Spence Center's blending of mainstream and alternative medicine. "All of the practitioners work closely together. They talk to each other all the time. That means better-coordinated care," she says. "And all of my records are right there. Everything is under one roof. I think everyone should have access to this kind of medical care."

Spence Center founder Rina Spence would likely agree. The former president and chief executive officer of Emerson Hospital in Concord, Massachusetts, Spence says she opened her clinic because she believes that the best medical care comes from blending mainstream medicine and alternative therapies.

A Glimpse at the Future of Health Care

Blended medicine is still the exception, not the rule. But over the past few years, it has quietly found a niche in American health care.

According to a widely publicized Harvard Medical School survey, 42 percent of Americans used alternative therapies in 1997, spending more than $21 billion. But even before this survey made headlines, other, largely unpublicized studies revealed a changing attitude toward alternative medicine within the mainstream medical community itself. A growing number of mainstream physicians were open to alternative therapies, and many would consider referring their own patients to alternative practitioners.

Mainstream medicine's growing acceptance of alternative therapies raises a curious question: If alternative therapies go mainstream, are they still alternative?

"Increasingly, they are not—and I'm quite pleased about it," says Alan P. Brauer, M.D. "When people get mainstream therapies in one office, chiropractic in another, and nutrition counseling, biofeedback, and Chinese medicine elsewhere, their care is fragmented. Each practitioner sees only a small portion of

The Old School Tackles New Subjects

Alternative medicine remains on the periphery of medical education. But at least 75 medical schools—among them Harvard, Yale, Columbia, Johns Hopkins, Tufts, Stanford, Ohio State, the University of North Carolina, and the University of California, Los Angeles—now offer courses on alternative therapies.

"Not long ago, I was invited to address a medical meeting at Columbia," says Joseph Pizzorno Jr., N.D. "As far as I know, I was the first naturopath to receive such an invitation. I spoke about herbal medicine, and my talk was well-received. The conventional medical schools are definitely changing in a more inclusive direction."

At Dartmouth College in Hanover, New Hampshire, former surgeon general C. Everett Koop, M.D., is developing a medical center that combines mainstream and alternative medicine. "My experience as a doctor has taught me that a mix of different approaches is often necessary to achieve success," he notes. "We need to be flexible and adaptable.

"Drugs and surgery are useful tools, but I would like to see us broaden our range of approaches," Dr. Koop adds. "This is an opportune time to take a look at alternative treatments—not to offer them blindly but to research them scientifically, (always remembering) that while these treatments may look 'alternative' to us, they have long been part of the medical mainstream in their cultures of origin."

the overall therapeutic picture. Having everyone under one roof improves communication and continuity of care."

For years, Dr. Brauer was a medical iconoclast who experienced professional ostracism because he included alternative therapies in his practice. "Initially, I got a lot of criticism from other doctors in my area," he recalls. "But physicians are much more accepting today, now that so many unconventional therapies are being shown to have a sound basis in science."

"Mainstream medicine doesn't have all the answers," says Anne Simons, M.D. "Good research shows that for many conditions, alternative therapies can help. When I have a cold, I often take echinacea because several studies show that it's an antiviral immune stimulant. I think doctors should prescribe whatever works best. If what works best is a safe alternative treatment, it's fine with me."

From "Alternative" to "Complementary"

Of course, many mainstream physicians are still leery of alternative therapies—and some still call them worthless. But many more have come to realize that their brand of medicine doesn't have a monopoly on healing and that alternative approaches often are quite valuable. Today's medical rallying cry is "Whatever works best," and many of those promoting blended medicine have dropped the term *alternative* in favor of the term *complementary*. "*Complementary* says that these therapies do not replace mainstream medicine," Dr. Brauer explains. "Rather, they complete it, expanding it to include areas it has undervalued or overlooked—diet, exercise, traditional healing arts, and mind-body therapies."

"If I'm involved in a serious auto accident, I want the ambulance to take me to the nearest high-tech trauma center. Mainstream medicine is definitely the way to go for serious injuries," says Andrew T. Weil, M.D., director of the program in integrative medicine at the University of Arizona College of Medicine in Tucson. "But let's say I developed chronic pain as a result of the accident. Beyond narcotics, mainstream medicine doesn't have much to offer. But several complementary therapies can help. I might try chiropractic, acupuncture, yoga, massage, or visualization therapy."

"I'm not opposed to medical technology," adds Deepak Chopra, M.D., creative director and cofounder of the Chopra Center for Well-Being in La Jolla, California. "Technological medicine is unsurpassed in diagnosing disease and in treating serious injuries and infections. But it does not treat chronic illness—for example, arthritis and heart disease—very effectively, and it undervalues the

Who Pays for Alternative Therapies?

The clear trend in health care is away from fee-for-service medicine and toward lower-cost managed care. But the transition has been rocky. People complain that in order to cut costs, managed-care companies often cut corners on quality. Much of this criticism is true.

Ironically, the rise of managed care has also given a major boost to the blending of mainstream and alternative medicine. If the rallying cry of blended medicine is "whatever works best," the emerging mantra of the managed-care industry—and the health insurers intimately involved with it—is "whatever works best most cost-effectively." For many conditions, the treatment that fills this bill is an alternative one.

"For years, studies have shown that garlic can help control blood pressure and cholesterol. But few mainstream M.D.'s recommended it, even though it is cheaper than the pharmaceuticals and causes fewer side effects," says Alan P. Brauer, M.D. "Then an HMO we belong to sent me new guidelines for treating mildly elevated blood pressure. The guidelines *require* doctors to try garlic before prescribing drugs. When I read that, I did an honest-to-God double take."

The vast majority of health insurers still don't cover alternative therapies, but a growing number do. To locate an insurer that offers such coverage, ask agents or contact companies directly. Both are listed in the Yellow Pages under "Insurance."

connection between the mind and body. That's where the complementary therapies excel."

Meanwhile, as mainstream medicine has softened its once-steadfast opposition to anything unorthodox, alternative practitioners have tempered their criticism of many mainstream approaches. "I'm not totally opposed to pharmaceutical drugs or technological medicine," says Joseph Pizzorno Jr., N.D., president of Bastyr University in Kenmore, Washington, which is the nation's only accredited medical school that focuses on alternative therapies. "When the body's self-healing systems have been overwhelmed by injury or infection, conventional approaches save lives. But in my opinion, pharmaceuticals are over-prescribed. Their power is impressive in life-or-death situations. For everyday ailments, I prefer nonpharmaceutical therapies that support the body's self-healing mechanisms. These therapies are gentler. They often work just as well. And they don't breed resistance like antibiotics do."

The term *alternative medicine* is unlikely to disappear in the near future, but *complementary medicine* is clearly the coming concept. In late 1996, the National Institutes of Health's Office of Alternative Medicine changed its name to the Office of Complementary and Alternative Medicine.

People Like It, People Want It

One reason why more and more mainstream M.D.'s are open to blended medicine is that for the first time, mainstream medical journals are publishing studies showing that alternative therapies have real value. (Until recently, most journals published only dire warnings about the dangers of these therapies.) Another reason is high-profile advocates with mainstream medical backgrounds, such as Dr. Weil and Dr. Chopra.

But the people really driving the blending of mainstream and alternative approaches don't have any initials after their names. They're consumers like you. "People *like* alternative therapies," says Mark Blumenthal, founder and executive director of the American Botanical Council, an herbal education and research organization based in Austin, Texas. "No one is being forced to use them. A big— possibly the biggest—reason for their popularity is good word-of-mouth support. People tell their friends that their doctors couldn't relieve their menstrual cramps or shoulder tendinitis, but that an acupuncturist or homeopath or hypnotherapist or herbalist did."

Chapter 2

The Tapestry of Healing

A t first glance, mainstream and alternative medicine appear quite different from one another. Yet surprisingly, their various therapies have a good deal in common.

Take mainstream cardiology and Chinese medicine. On the surface, the two seem like polar opposites. They're based on philosophies so different that practitioners of one often have no idea what practitioners of the other are talking about. In addition, cardiology is high-tech. It relies on sophisticated machinery (such as stress tests and echocardiograms) and often involves surgery (angioplasty, coronary artery bypass, and heart transplants). By comparison, Chinese medicine is low-tech. It uses virtually no machinery (other than the occasional connection of acupuncture needles to low-power electrical stimulation devices) and resists surgery.

But dig a little deeper, and you'll discover that cardiology and Chinese medicine have almost as many similarities as differences. Both therapies view heart problems in the context of the whole body. Both rely on professional practitioners who interview and examine patients, make diagnoses, prescribe treatments, and provide follow-up care. Both incorporate medicines derived from plants (though most American cardiologists prescribe pharmaceutical versions of plant compounds). Both advocate therapeutic dietary modifications (though cardiology has been doing so only for the last few decades). And both have had success in dealing with a variety of heart problems.

The point is that all healing arts, no matter how distinct they seem, are like the individual threads in fabric. Woven together, they create a tapestry of healing—and a seamless approach to health care.

The chapters ahead provide an overview of the many alternative therapies that make up the tapestry of healing. While they may espouse different philosophies and practices, they have been proven to work through research and observation. Blended together and used properly, they establish a continuum of care that's the most direct route to optimum health.

The Health-Promoting Quartet

The tapestry of healing has four critical corners: sound nutrition, regular moderate exercise, stress management, and a feeling of connectedness to others and to the natural world. These factors constitute what Michael Lerner, Ph.D., refers to as the health-promoting quartet.

"If you eat well, get regular moderate exercise, and work on your psychological well-being by dealing with stress and embracing connections to the world beyond yourself, you become healthier," explains Dr. Lerner, cofounder of the Commonweal Cancer Help Program, an organization based in Bolinas, California, that sponsors weeklong retreats for people with cancer. "Even if you have an illness, you're healthier than other people with the same illness who don't focus on these dimensions of well-being. In my experience, cancer patients who embrace the health-promoting quartet often enjoy better outcomes: better responses to treatment, better quality of life, and—in some cases—longer, disease-free survival."

But the health-promoting quartet is not just for those who are already ill. "It's also an elegant prescription for a long, healthy life," says Alan P. Brauer, M.D.

Each component of the health-promoting quartet is fundamental to most alternative therapies. Each one has become well-incorporated into mainstream medicine over the past 25 years or so. And each one lends itself to home care through an array of therapies and practices, including the following:

♦ Nutrition: Low-fat eating, vegetarianism, supplementation, and elimination diets
♦ Exercise: walking, tai chi, qigong, and yoga
♦ Stress management: meditation, visualization, biofeedback, massage, and music therapy
♦ Connectedness: relationships and support groups

You'll learn more about each of these approaches—as well as practical ways to make them part of your self-care program—in chapters 3 through 15.

Herbs: The Original Medicines

Medicinal herbs are central to the alternative therapies. Practitioners of Chinese medicine and Ayurveda, India's traditional healing system, often prescribe herbal formulas. Many of the microdose medicines used in homeopathy come from plants. In fact, it was experiments with cinchona bark—the first effective treatment for malaria—that laid the groundwork for the development of homeopathy. Plants also provide the basis for Western herbal medicine, a cross-cultural blend of age-old European, Asian, African, Middle Eastern, and Native American herbal traditions.

What many people don't realize is that medicinal herbs are a key link between the alternative therapies and mainstream medicine. For much of the pharmaceutical industry's 130-year history, researchers have focused on extracting medicinal constituents from plants and repackaging them as drugs. An estimated 25 percent of all pharmaceuticals still come from plant sources.

Chapter 16 presents Western herbal medicine as a separate entity—in part because it lends itself to home care, in part because the herbs it employs are widely available in health food stores, pharmacies, supplement centers, and even some supermarkets. The chapters on homeopathy, Chinese medicine, Ayurveda, and naturopathy also touch on medicinal herbs, because herbs figure prominently in these alternative healing systems.

Healing Systems: Different Perspectives on Health

Mainstream medicine is a healing system. It has a distinct philosophy that lays the groundwork for a particular approach to diagnosis and treatment. Its proponents say that it can treat an enormous range of illnesses. And it relies on professional practitioners who use standard examination procedures and treatment protocols.

Three alternative therapies—homeopathy, Chinese medicine, and Ayurveda—meet these same criteria and so are considered healing systems. They're discussed in part 2, along with other alternative therapies that are close to being healing systems: naturopathy, which is fast becoming an umbrella term for an amalgam of alternative therapies; and the manipulation therapies (chiropractic, osteopathy, and some schools of bodywork), which focus on musculoskeletal problems but may also have value for other conditions.

Making the Best Choice

Chapter 24 asks the question "Which therapy works best for what?" As you'll see, the answer has a lot to do with your own circumstances, preferences, and experience. But I'll offer some advice for blending mainstream and alternative remedies—some of which require professional intervention, but many of which you can use at home.

In fact, home care is always an important component of healing, no matter what therapy you're using. For an enormous number of minor ailments (such as colds, constipation, and headaches), the do-it-yourself approach can be just as effective as a physician-administered treatment. And often home remedies are cheaper, more convenient, and more empowering.

Of course, more serious health problems (such as heart disease, cancer, and diabetes) require a doctor's attention. But even in these cases, home care has its place.

PART TWO

A Practical Guide to the
Healing Therapies

Chapter 3

Nutrition:
The Wisdom of a Low-Fat Lifestyle

Eating high-fat foods is a lethal habit, second only to smoking in terms of the number of lives it claims. According to one study, a high-fat diet is responsible for some 300,000 deaths each year.

Like smoking, a high-fat diet kills by directly contributing to a host of serious health problems. The strongest evidence links dietary fat to heart disease, stroke, high blood pressure, cancer, and diabetes. And, of course, there's obesity, which is a risk factor for many of these diseases.

Research has also identified a high-fat diet as a risk factor for chronic health problems such as hearing loss, osteoarthritis, and—in men—impotence. "Most Americans who have chronic health problems would not have those problems if they ate a low-fat diet," says Neal D. Barnard, M.D., president of the Washington, D.C.–based Physicians Committee for Responsible Medicine.

Adding Carbs, Subtracting Fat

In recent years, Americans have trimmed a little fat from their diets. But total fat consumption is still at near-record levels. Not surprisingly, so is obesity.

For years, carbohydrates were vilified as fattening. As it turns out, carbs are actually your friends, your body's main source of energy.

What's more, carbohydrates supply fewer calories than fat—4 calories per gram versus 9 calories per gram. So you can actually eat *more* carbohydrates than fat for the same number of calories. "Fat calories really sneak up on you," observes Ron Goor, Ph.D., coauthor (with his wife, Nancy) of the *Eater's Choice* low-fat cookbooks. "A few handfuls of potato chips has the same number of calories as two medium-size baked potatoes topped with nonfat yogurt and steamed vegetables."

"If you reduce your fat consumption from the typical 35 to 40 percent of calories to the 10 percent recommended in my program, you can eat one-third more food without increasing your total calorie intake," adds Dean Ornish, M.D., president of the Preventive Medicine Research Institute in Sausalito, California, whose ultra low fat diet has been shown to reverse heart disease. "You'll feel full and satisfied but still lose weight. And you'll reduce your risk of fat-related diseases."

No wonder the American Heart Association, the American Cancer Society, and the Center for Science in the Public Interest—a Washington, D.C.–based consumer nutrition organization—urge all Americans to reduce their dietary fat intakes. In a joint report, these groups estimated that if every person cut his fat consumption by one-third (to approximately 20 percent of calories), the nation's health-care bill would plummet by $17 billion a year.

Guidelines for Healthful Eating

To our credit, we Americans are consuming less meat, eggs, and whole milk these days. But in exchange, we're chowing down on a lot more pizza, french fries, and other fast-food items loaded with hidden fat.

You *can* take steps to pare down your dietary fat intake and reap the many health benefits of low-fat eating. The process begins with reading nutrition labels.

As a general rule, you're much better off if you select foods that derive no more than 20 percent of calories from fat per serving. But beware: The serving size may be smaller than what you actually eat, so your fat intake is higher than what's listed on the label. And don't be fooled by the percent Daily Value. This figure tells you how much of a day's worth of fat a food provides. But because it's based on a hypothetical 2,000-calorie-a-day diet, not on the number of calories in the food itself, it often misrepresents actual fat content.

You can get a more accurate read on a food's fat content by doing the math yourself. Simply multiply the number of grams of fat per serving by 9, then divide that figure by the number of calories per serving. If the answer is 0.20 (20 percent) or less, then the food is acceptable.

Also, scan labels for the words *low-fat* or *nonfat*. They can be used only on foods that meet certain criteria for fat content. (A low-fat food supplies 3 grams or less of fat per serving; a nonfat food, less than 0.5 gram per serving.) Super-

Eat Out without Bulging Out

Even if you stick with a low-fat diet at home, you may have a hard time passing up high-fat foods in restaurants. Those little splurges add up. If you go out for lunch at work every day and grab take-out for dinner a few nights a week, more than one-third of your meals come from restaurants.

"Low-fat restaurant dining requires a few adjustments," says Hope S. Warshaw, R.D., a registered dietitian in Newton, Massachusetts. "But with a little forethought, you can eat out without bulging out."

Some cuisines are naturally low in fat: Chinese, Indian, Thai, Vietnamese, Cambodian, Middle Eastern, and Japanese (except for deep-fried tempuras). In these cuisines, even the beef and pork dishes use relatively small portions of meat, which helps keep the fat content low.

On the other hand, steak houses, pizza parlors, barbecue and burger joints, delis, and French, German, Italian, Mexican, and Cajun restaurants all tend to serve up high-fat fare. But even in these danger zones, you can enjoy tasty low-fat dishes.

If you know that you're going to be eating out, a little forethought can spare you a lot of fat.

◆ Never arrive at a restaurant feeling ravenous. Take the edge off your hunger beforehand with a healthy low-fat snack: an apple, a banana, a pretzel, or a cup of nonfat yogurt.

◆ Beware buffets and all-you-can-eat specials. They're setups for losing control.

◆ When perusing the menu, look for items described as broiled, grilled, baked, boiled, roasted, poached, or steamed. Steer clear of anything fried, sautéed, creamed, breaded, batter-dipped, au gratin, en croute, or phyllo-wrapped; in a puff pastry, pot pie, or croissant; or with gravy, béarnaise, béchamel, beurre blanc, or crème fraîche.

Finally, if you catch yourself thinking, "Oh, what the heck . . . ," stop a moment, close your eyes, take a few deep breaths, and ask yourself if you *really* want that food.

markets now carry literally hundreds of low-fat and nonfat foods. What you see—and taste—just might surprise you.

With some foods, switching from the full-fat to the low-fat or nonfat variety can take some getting used to. For example, people who trade in whole milk for nonfat (skim) milk often complain that the latter tastes thin and watery. But after about 6 months of drinking nonfat milk, it tastes fine—and whole milk tastes too rich. "If you keep your fat intake down," notes John Foreyt, Ph.D., director of the Nutrition Research Clinic at Baylor College of Medicine in Houston, "your fat cravings and preferences for fatty foods eventually decline."

But as with full-fat foods, you must be careful not to overindulge in low-fat and nonfat foods. A study by Barbara J. Rolls, Ph.D., professor of nutrition and biobehavioral health at Pennsylvania State University in University Park, found that people often consume substantially larger amounts of foods that they know are low-fat or nonfat. And that means lots of extra calories—and eventually extra pounds.

Chapter 4

Vegetarianism: Eat Your Way to Better Health

Meat is expensive at the supermarket or butcher shop. But when experts analyze what the meat-centered American diet costs the nation's health-care system, the price goes sky-high: $29 billion to $61 billion a year. These figures come from a report issued by Neal D. Barnard, M.D., and other members of the Physicians Committee for Responsible Medicine, a Washington, D.C.–based organization that promotes health through nutrition.

As mind-boggling as these figures are, Dr. Barnard insists that they are conservative, because his team limited its findings to diseases for which the data are strongest. "Undoubtedly," he says, "meat costs the health-care system even more."

"If you look carefully at the data, the optimum amount of meat you should eat is zero," concurs Walter Willett, M.D., Dr.P.H., chairperson of the department of nutrition at the Harvard School of Public Health in Boston.

Research has linked meat consumption to colon, lung, prostate, and ovarian cancers as well as to non-Hodgkin's lymphoma, a type of lymph cancer. In fact, when researchers in New Zealand compared the health of 5,015 meat eaters and 6,115 vegetarians, they found that the vegetarians were 39 percent less likely to experience any form of cancer.

The same study showed that the vegetarians were 28 percent less likely to develop heart disease, the number one cause of death in the United States. That's no coincidence. Meat is a major source of dietary fat. Fat consumption is strongly associated with obesity, diabetes, and elevated cholesterol and blood pressure—all risk factors for heart disease.

In a landmark study comparing 25,000 Seventh-Day Adventists (whose religion espouses vegetarianism) to typical meat-eating Americans, researchers at

Loma Linda University in California discovered that the Adventists had 40 percent fewer heart attacks. What's more, their heart attacks occurred an average of 10 years later in life.

When people have a meatless or almost-meatless diet, they also seem to have a lower risk of stroke, which is the number three cause of death in the United States. When John Lynch, M.D., a neurology fellow at Yale University School of Medicine in New Haven, Connecticut, tracked the health of 6,500 stroke-free men over 10 years, he found that 12 percent of those who ate meat daily ended up having strokes. By comparison, just 5.4 percent of those who ate meat one to three times a month had strokes.

Meat delivers a double whammy to your health. It not only can be high in fat—especially saturated fat, the kind with strong ties to heart disease and cancer—it also tends to displace fruits and vegetables in the diet. That's not good. Fruits and vegetables are rich in fiber and nutrients that help prevent America's top three killers: heart disease, cancer, and stroke.

The Myths of Going Meatless

Clearly, building your diet around fruits, vegetables, and other plant-derived foods has a lot to offer, health-wise. Yet as recently as the mid-1970s, most nutritionists called vegetarianism a one-way ticket to malnutrition.

How things have changed. Today we know that eating healthfully is easier as a vegetarian than as a meat eater, largely because most vegetarians consume less fat than the typical omnivore. Even the American Dietetic Association now endorses vegetarianism as nutritionally sound. Nonetheless, the old arguments still crop up. Here's what those arguments sound like—and the reasons why they don't hold water.

Vegetarians can't get enough protein. For years, protein was the star nutrient in the American diet, and meat was its primary source. So experts assumed, quite logically, that vegetarians would develop protein deficiencies.

That thinking has shifted, for two reasons. First, nutritionists now realize that Americans eat way more protein than they actually need. Second, the kind of protein that comes from meat is accompanied by an unhealthy amount of fat.

The Daily Value for protein is 50 grams. You can easily meet this requirement by consuming plant-derived foods. A cup of lentils contains 15 grams of protein; 4 ounces of tofu, 9 grams; 2 tablespoons of peanut butter, 8 grams; a cup of cooked oat bran, 7 grams; a cup of pasta, 7 grams; and ½ cup of millet, 4 grams.

"Protein has become a nonissue," says Suzanne Havala, R.D., a registered

The Joy of Juicing

Juicing is a quick, convenient way to broaden your vegetarian horizons while enjoying tasty, satisfying, nutritious beverages. Supermarkets are selling more and more juices, and juice bars are springing up all over the country.

You can easily make your own juices. All you need is a juicer, an appliance similar to a blender but specifically designed to extract the liquid from fruits and vegetables. The liquid contains most of the food's vitamins, minerals, and other nutrients. What's left over is fiber. Of course, the body needs fiber for good digestion, and many Americans don't get enough. But vegetarians seldom have to worry about fiber deficiency. A good vegetarian diet provides plenty of fiber.

Juices pack incredible nutritional punch. One pint of mixed vegetable juice contains the vitamin and mineral equivalent of two meal-size salads. One pint of fresh carrot juice contains 20,000 international units of beta-carotene, which your body converts to vitamin A.

Juicers are sold in department stores and some health food stores. You can also purchase them through mail order, from companies that advertise in vegetarian publications.

dietitian in Charlotte, North Carolina. "If you eat a reasonable variety of foods, you won't have a problem getting enough protein. In fact, as long as you consume enough calories to meet your energy needs, you'd have to work hard to devise a protein-deficient diet."

Vegetarians can't get enough iron. Yes, you can—as long as you're also getting enough vitamin C. Plant-derived foods provide plenty of iron. The catch: It's nonheme iron, which isn't as well-absorbed as heme iron, the kind found in meat. You can easily improve the absorption rate by pairing a nonheme iron source with a vitamin C source. At breakfast, for example, have a glass of orange juice (which is rich in vitamin C) with a bowl of hot wheat cereal (which supplies 9 milligrams of nonheme iron, or 50 percent of the Daily Value).

Vegetarians can't get enough calcium. Dietitians recommend that Americans consume 1,200 to 1,500 milligrams of calcium a day. You can get all the calcium you need from low-fat or nonfat milk, cheese, yogurt, and other dairy

Should You Buy Organic Produce?

Many environmentally conscious Americans are nervous about pesticide residues on their fruits and vegetables—and with some reason. According to a study of 15,000 produce samples by the Environmental Working Group, a Washington, D.C.–based consumer organization, pesticide residues contaminate a large portion of the American fruit and vegetable supply. The dirtiest dozen: apples, apricots, bell peppers, cantaloupe, celery, cherries, cucumbers, grapes, green beans, peaches, spinach, and strawberries.

To minimize pesticide exposure, which some research has linked to increased cancer risk, more Americans are opting for organic produce. Organic produce is grown without the aid of chemical pesticides. It usually costs more, too.

Is it worth the higher price? Well, that's up to you.

"Don't let fear of pesticide residues stop you from eating fruits and vegetables," advises Gladys Block, Ph.D., professor of epidemiology and director of the nutrition program in the School of Public Health at the University of California, Berkeley. She notes that in her review of studies correlating diet with rates of certain cancers, every study used nonorganic

products that are rich in the mineral. But what if you eliminate dairy products, as some vegetarians do? In that case, many fruits and vegetables can make a contribution to your calcium intake. Among those highest in calcium are collard greens (290 milligrams per cup, cooked), bok choy (250 milligrams per cup, cooked), tofu (244 milligrams per cup), dried figs (161 milligrams in six figs), and kale (148 milligrams per cup, cooked).

Vegetarians risk neurological damage from vitamin B$_{12}$ deficiency. Because vitamin B$_{12}$ is found primarily in meats and other animal-derived foods, vegetarians often have low levels of the nutrient. The risk of not getting enough B$_{12}$ is of particular concern to the strictest vegetarians, called vegans (pronounced "VEE-guns"). These people forgo all animal products, including dairy foods like milk and cheese.

But even vegans can get as much vitamin B$_{12}$ as they need through sup-

fruits and vegetables. Still, those who ate the most produce had the lowest incidence of cancer.

If you decide to go organic, look for fruits and vegetables that carry an "organic" seal. Currently, several regional monitoring organizations grant these seals. The federal government is in the process of developing nationwide guidelines for their use.

If you opt to stick with conventionally grown produce, you can still minimize pesticide exposure. Just follow this advice.

◆ Wash all fruits and vegetables in a solution of dishwashing liquid and water. Use a vegetable brush.

◆ Peel apples, cucumbers, eggplants, and any other produce that has a wax coating. Pesticides can be sealed in with the wax.

◆ Discard the outer leaves of cabbage and lettuce.

◆ Chop spinach, broccoli, cauliflower, and celery before washing.

◆ Buy produce in season.

◆ Petition your supermarket to stock locally grown produce, which is less likely to be waxed and treated with post-harvest pesticides during transport and storage.

plementation. In fact, some nutritionists recommend that all vegetarians take a daily B_{12} supplement, just to be on the safe side. You need just 6 micrograms (that's six-millionths of a gram) to match the Daily Value. And you can probably get by with even less for a few months, since your body stores up to a 2-year supply.

Vegetarianism stunts children's growth. Several studies have shown that this simply isn't true. In one study, Kay L. Stanek, R.D., Ph.D., associate professor of nutritional sciences at the University of Nebraska in Lincoln, compared the body measurements and nutrient intakes of omnivorous children ages 10 to 12 with children of the same age who had been ovo-lactovegetarians from birth. (Ovo-lactovegetarians eat eggs and dairy products but no meat.) Neither group showed any nutritional deficiencies, and both had similar height ranges.

Chapter 5

Vitamin and Mineral Supplements:
Crucial Nutritional Extras

Everyone knows what vitamins and minerals are: They're in those little pills that you take with your morning orange juice. But what are they, really?

Vitamins and minerals are organic compounds that your body needs to function properly and stay healthy. Unlike foods, vitamins and minerals do not provide calories and energy. But they do play key roles in regulating metabolism and many other biochemical reactions.

You need only tiny quantities of vitamins and most minerals, which is why supplement manufacturers can pack so many different nutrients into multivitamin/mineral pills. Some supplements are natural, meaning that their vitamins and minerals have been extracted from plants—for example, vitamin C from rose hips. Others are synthetic laboratory creations.

Until the 1990s, mainstream medicine scoffed at supplements. Critics insisted that a balanced diet would supply all of the nutrients that a person could need. They charged that except for preventing vitamin-deficiency diseases (such as scurvy, rickets, and beriberi), supplements were medically worthless and a waste of money.

There are still a handful of naysayers who offer the media an "I told you so" whenever the occasional study raises questions about some supplement's safety or effectiveness for some condition. But by and large, mainstream medicine has come around to what a few M.D.'s and alternative practitioners have been saying—and documenting—for decades: Vitamin and mineral supplements are key elements in optimum health.

The evidence has become almost impossible to ignore, as a growing body of research substantiates the value of supplementation. Various studies have suggested that supplements of one kind or another can prevent heart attacks, boost immunity, enhance mental function, alleviate depression, and slow the progression of Alzheimer's disease and osteoarthritis. And that's just the beginning.

As scientists learn more about the health benefits of supplementation, public interest has blossomed, too. An estimated 150 million Americans take supplements, with sales topping $4 billion a year.

How Much Is Enough?

Time was when you could find certain supplements only in health food stores. These days, even supermarkets carry a mind-boggling array of brands and doses from which to choose. And many consumers have been left to wonder, "What should I take? And how much?"

The "how much" part is a matter of considerable controversy. To understand the debate, you need to know a little bit of nutrition history.

In 1943, the National Academy of Sciences Food and Nutrition Board established the first guidelines for nutrient intakes. These Recommended Dietary Allowances, or RDAs, were set at levels sufficient to prevent deficiency diseases, such as beriberi and scurvy. Each RDA was tailored to a specific age group or gender.

As ongoing nutrition research revealed important information about various vitamins and minerals, the Food and Nutrition Board continued tinkering with the RDAs. The board raised the values 10 times, most recently in 1989.

But by the early 1990s, board members had become bitterly divided. Traditionalists believed that the RDAs should stay true to their original mission of preventing deficiency diseases. Progressives argued that the RDAs should be raised to reflect mounting evidence that much larger amounts of nutrients could help prevent and treat an array of diseases. When the board convened in 1993, the two sides nearly came to blows.

Needless to say, that meeting quickly adjourned. The Food and Nutrition Board later asked several distinguished nutrition experts to submit their views in writing. One was supplement advocate Gladys Block, Ph.D., professor of epidemiology and director of the nutrition program in the School of Public

Health at the University of California, Berkeley. She argued that the RDAs should be raised.

"Take vitamin C," Dr. Block wrote. "The RDA is 60 milligrams a day. But to prevent cancer, the National Cancer Institute recommends eating five servings of fruits and vegetables a day. Anyone who does that can easily consume up to 500 milligrams of vitamin C a day, just from foods. In effect, the National Cancer Institute is recommending a vitamin C intake that's eight times higher than what the Food and Nutrition Board considers the maximum safe amount."

Around the time all this was going on, the Food and Drug Administration released its own nutritional guidelines. Called Daily Values, they're essentially averages of the RDAs for each nutrient. The Daily Values are what appear on food and supplement labels.

After considering the opinions of Dr. Block and others, the Food and Nutrition Board decided to completely replace the RDAs with new values called Dietary Reference Intakes (DRIs). The first DRIs were released in 1997. They're much higher than the RDAs, an indication that the Food and Nutrition Board has changed its opinion on what constitutes adequate nutrition.

Supplement critics still warn that raising the old RDAs will encourage people to take potentially hazardous overdoses. But that seems unlikely. In the 2 most recent years for which complete statistics are available, no American adult has died from a supplement overdose, says Rose Ann Soloway, R.N., administrator of the American Association of Poison Control Centers in Washington, D.C.

"Megadoses of some vitamins and minerals can cause problems," Soloway explains. "For example, vitamins A and D can be harmful in amounts higher than three to four times the recommended intakes. But few people take a large enough dose for a long enough time to become sick." You're much more likely to be struck by lightning than to be killed by vitamin or mineral supplements.

A Shopper's Guide to the Supplement Aisle

The debate over recommended vitamin and mineral intakes will likely continue, as ongoing research turns up more information about the relationship between supplementation and disease prevention. But at least many nutrition experts agree on some basic guidelines for buying and using supplements. Here's their advice.

First and foremost, eat healthfully. They're called supplements for a reason: They're intended to support a nutritious diet, not replace it. They can't undo the damage caused by poor eating habits.

Fruits and vegetables supply an abundance of disease-fighting nutrients. Yet only 20 percent of Americans consume even five servings of produce a day, the recommended minimum. "Fill your shopping cart with fruits and vegetables—and eat them," advises Elizabeth Somer, R.D., author of *Age-Proof Your Body*. "Then if you want a little extra nutritional insurance, take a supplement."

Invest in an insurance formula. A multivitamin/mineral supplement, or insurance formula, contains some combination of vitamins and minerals. They're economical and convenient. And they're better for you than single-nutrient supplements. "Few people understand that vitamins and minerals work synergistically," explains clinical nutritionist Shari Lieberman, Ph.D. "Nature packages nutrients together in foods. They should be taken the same way in supplements. I always advise people to start with an insurance formula and to take additional supplements as necessary to prevent or treat specific conditions."

Check for selenium and chromium. Not all multivitamin/mineral supplements contain selenium and chromium. Make sure that yours does. Both minerals may play important roles in disease prevention. One long-term study found that large doses of selenium may significantly reduce the risk of lung, colon, breast, prostate, and esophageal cancers. Other studies suggest that people who are deficient in chromium may have an increased risk of developing diabetes.

Consider single supplements. Multivitamin/mineral supplements have breadth, but they may not have the depth you need. For example, if you're a woman, nutrition experts recommend that you consume 1,000 to 1,500 milligrams of calcium a day. You can't get that much of the mineral in an insurance formula. So you may need a separate calcium supplement to make up the difference. (You can also get extra calcium from Tums 500 chewables.)

Likewise, people with certain health problems may require additional supplements, as may competitive athletes and women who are pregnant or menopausal. When in doubt, consult a nutrition professional. (For help in finding one, refer to How to Find What You Need on page 668.)

Get vitamin A as beta-carotene. Large doses of vitamin A can cause fatigue, nausea, vomiting, dizziness, and blurred vision. But as Somer notes, you really don't need to take supplemental vitamin A. Instead, take beta-carotene, which your body converts to A on an as-needed basis.

Avoid unnecessary extras. "Even if your diet is less than perfect, you almost certainly get enough biotin, vitamin K, phosphorus, potassium, and sodium," Somer says. "You don't need to take supplements of them." But if your insurance formula contains these nutrients, that's okay, too.

Choose bargains over brands. In terms of quality, most supplements are created equal. Major retail brands are manufactured by some of the same companies that make many of the national brands. "Only about a half-dozen drug companies actually manufacture supplements," says Sheldon Saul Hendler, M.D., Ph.D., author of *The Doctor's Vitamin and Mineral Encyclopedia*. "They supply all of the companies that distribute supplements. So when you buy an expensive brand, what you're paying for is packaging and advertising. Personally, I get the cheapest supplements that I can find. They're just as good as the expensive brands."

In fact, the Center for Science in the Public Interest, a Washington, D.C.–based nutrition advocacy organization, says that you shouldn't be spending more than $10 a month on supplements.

Weigh the need for natural. With a few exceptions, natural supplements work no better or worse than synthetic ones. Chemically, there's no difference between the vitamin C found in an orange and the vitamin C synthesized in a laboratory. In fact, "natural" supplements often contain just a tiny amount of natural nutrient combined with a large amount of synthetic nutrient. So what are the exceptions?

◆ Calcium: Some natural sources of calcium, such as bonemeal and dolomite, may be contaminated with lead. A laboratory creation called calcium carbonate is the way to go. It's found in Tums 500 chewables and Children's Mylanta liquid and chewables.

◆ Folic acid: Synthetic is better absorbed than natural.

◆ Vitamin E: The natural form (d-alpha-tocopherol) is better absorbed than the synthetic form (dl-alpha-tocopherol). But be careful: If the label says made *with* d-alpha, you may get a tiny amount of natural vitamin mixed with lots of synthetic vitamin. Look for a supplement that contains only d-alpha.

Ignore other hype. Don't pay extra for chelated (pronounced "KEY-lated") minerals. Chelation combines minerals with other substances, often amino acids. Proponents claim that chelation promotes absorption, but ordinary minerals get absorbed just fine.

Also, don't pay extra for vitamins that claim to be sugar- or starch-free. Unless you're seriously allergic, a little sugar or starch won't hurt you.

Timing Is Everything

When and how you take your supplements can definitely influence their effectiveness. A once-a-day insurance formula, or multivitamin, is better than nothing. But Somer recommends choosing a multi that you can take in small doses several times a day. And steer clear of timed-release supplements: They seldom provide a steady stream of nutrients. Taking a few pills a day is better—and almost always cheaper.

Also, take your supplements with meals whenever possible. Food stimulates the release of the digestive enzymes necessary for vitamin and mineral absorption. The one exception to this rule is iron, which is better absorbed on an empty stomach.

So what can you expect from supplementation? More energy? Less stress? Sexual bliss? A longer life? Some supplements promise to do all this and more—everything, it seems, but raise the dead.

Biochemically, vitamins and minerals play key roles in virtually every body system. So, yes, they are involved in energy production, stress responses, sexual enjoyment, and myriad other bodily functions. "But by themselves, supplements won't turn your life around," Somer explains. "They work with good nutrition and a healthy lifestyle. They're valuable, but they won't make all your dreams come true."

Chapter 6

Elimination Diet: Pinpoint the Source of Symptoms

W hen nutrition researcher Jeffrey S. Bland, Ph.D., needed volunteers to follow an elimination diet—that is, to avoid certain foods with the goal of improving health—he found 106 willing participants in the Seattle area. The group consisted of 92 women and 14 men, ranging in age from 28 to 55. All were considered healthy, meaning that physical examinations and mainstream medical tests had turned up nothing out of the ordinary.

Yet these people didn't feel well. They reported an array of vague, chronic symptoms: fatigue, muscle aches, joint pains, digestive upsets, headaches, sleep disturbances, and lapses in memory and concentration that several described as brain fog.

Mainstream physicians are not well-equipped to help people with such complaints. When standard exams and tests find nothing abnormal enough to qualify as disease, most conventionally trained doctors are at a loss. They may admit as much. Or they may decide that patients with vague, chronic symptoms are hypochondriacs. Or they may suggest that these people see psychiatrists. Meanwhile, the patients bounce from one doctor to the next, looking for answers and getting increasingly frustrated with the health-care system.

But the group from Seattle was lucky enough to capture the attention of Dr. Bland, founder and chief executive officer of HealthComm International in Gig Harbor, Washington. First, he had the group members complete a questionnaire in which they rated the severity of their symptoms. Then he administered six tests, including one that measures the liver's ability to remove potentially harmful substances from the blood and another that measures the "leakage" of certain molecules from the digestive tract. These tests are seldom

Elimination Diet for MSG Intolerance

Back in 1968, in a letter to the *New England Journal of Medicine*, a doctor described experiencing "2 hours of numbness, weakness, and heart palpitations" after eating in a Chinese restaurant. The doctor speculated that his symptoms were caused by monosodium glutamate (MSG), a food additive used in many Asian cuisines.

At least one study suggests that about 30 percent of Americans experience reactions after consuming just 5 grams of MSG, while a full 90 percent experience reactions after consuming 10 grams.

To assess your sensitivity to MSG, add a teaspoon or two of a seasoning that contains a concentrated amount of MSG to a bowl of homemade soup or a serving of fresh vegetables. (The seasoning Accent, for instance, contains about 6 grams per teaspoon.) Pay close attention to how you feel for several hours afterward. If you develop any of the symptoms mentioned above, you may be MSG-intolerant.

The best way to avoid MSG reactions is to eliminate the additive from your diet. "Unfortunately, that's easier said than done," says George R. Schwartz, M.D., a specialist in emergency medicine and toxicology in Santa Fe, New Mexico. "Food labels don't necessarily list MSG. Instead, they might list textured protein, hydrolyzed protein, hydrolyzed vegetable protein, yeast food, sodium or calcium caseinate, or natural flavors—all of which contain significant amounts of MSG. And watch out for any foods that come with flavor packets. They usually contain MSG, too."

So read labels carefully. Steer clear of processed foods and fast food, instead building your diet around whole grains and fresh fruits and vegetables. And if you know you'll be eating in an Asian restaurant, call ahead and ask if they use MSG.

used in mainstream medicine, but they are considered standard by naturopathic physicians, who are more nutrition-oriented.

Next, all 106 study participants began an elimination diet. They gave up dairy products, beef, pork, veal, alcohol, caffeine, and foods containing gluten,

(continued on page 34)

Food Intolerance Survey

The following questionnaire, developed by Jeffrey S. Bland, Ph.D., founder and chief executive officer of HealthComm International in Gig Harbor, Washington, can help determine whether or not you have a food intolerance. Read through the list of symptoms and rate each one on the following scale:

0   Never or almost never have the symptom.
1   Occasionally have it; effect is not severe.
2   Occasionally have it; effect is severe.
3   Frequently have it; effect is not severe.
4   Frequently have it; effect is severe.

At the end of the questionnaire, add up your score. A total of more than 50 suggests that you have a food intolerance, which may respond to an elimination diet. If your total is 200 or more, consult your physician promptly.

HEAD
____ Headache
____ Faintness
____ Dizziness
____ Insomnia

EYES
____ Watery or itchy eyes
____ Swollen, red, sticky eyelids
____ Bags or dark circles under eyes
____ Blurred or tunnel vision unrelated to near- or farsightedness

EARS
____ Itchy ears
____ Earaches or ear infections
____ Drainage from ear
____ Ringing in ears, hearing loss

NOSE
____ Stuffy nose
____ Sinus problems
____ Hay fever
____ Sneezing attacks
____ Excessive mucus formation

MOUTH
____ Canker sores
____ Swollen and discolored lips, gums, or tongue

THROAT
____ Sore throat, hoarseness, or loss of voice
____ Gagging or frequent need to clear throat
____ Chronic coughing

SKIN
____ Acne
____ Hives, rashes, or dry skin

___ Hair loss
___ Flushing or hot flashes
___ Excessive sweating

___ Compulsive eating
___ Water retention
___ Underweight

HEART

___ Irregular or skipped heartbeat
___ Rapid or pounding heartbeat
___ Chest pain

LUNGS

___ Chest congestion
___ Asthma or bronchitis
___ Shortness of breath
___ Difficulty breathing

DIGESTIVE TRACT

___ Nausea or vomiting
___ Diarrhea
___ Constipation
___ Bloated feeling
___ Belching or gas
___ Heartburn
___ Intestinal/stomach pain

JOINTS

___ Pain or aches
___ Arthritis
___ Stiffness or limitation of movement

MUSCLES

___ Pain or aches
___ Weakness or fatigue

WEIGHT

___ Binge eating or drinking
___ Food cravings
___ Excessive weight

ENERGY/ACTIVITY

___ Fatigue or sluggishness
___ Apathy or lethargy
___ Hyperactivity
___ Restlessness

MIND

___ Poor memory
___ Confusion or poor comprehension
___ Poor concentration
___ Poor physical coordination
___ Difficulty making decisions
___ Stuttering or stammering
___ Slurred speech
___ Learning disabilities

EMOTIONS

___ Mood swings
___ Anxiety, fear, or nervousness
___ Anger, irritability, or aggressiveness
___ Depression

OTHER

___ Frequent illness
___ Frequent or urgent urination
___ Genital itch or discharge

TOTAL [   ]

the protein that gives bread products their spongy elasticity. They were allowed to eat rice and corn but not wheat, oats, rye, or barley. In addition, 84 of the participants took a multivitamin/mineral supplement.

After 10 weeks, Dr. Bland had the entire group fill out the symptom questionnaire a second time. Those on the diet-only regimen recorded a 22 percent improvement in symptoms. That figure jumped to 52 percent among those on the diet-plus-supplement regimen. These people also showed significant improvement on three of the six tests of digestive and liver function.

Confusion over Food Allergies

Some people benefit from an elimination diet because they have food allergies. In a true allergy, exposure to an offending substance—called an allergen—triggers a quick, predictable response. In hay fever, for example, exposure to pollen kicks in a massive release of histamine, a compound that in turn produces nasal congestion, runny nose, and itchy, watery eyes.

According to the American Academy of Allergy and Immunology, an estimated 2 percent of adults and 5 percent of children experience this type of reaction to foods. In a true food allergy, eating even a morsel of an offending food—peanuts, for example—quickly produces symptoms. Your tongue will likely swell or itch, and you'll get a rash on your skin. You may also develop a headache, stomach cramps, extreme flatulence, and diarrhea. In rare cases, an allergic reaction may result in anaphylaxis, a potentially life-threatening condition in which blood pressure drops, the throat swells shut, and breathing becomes difficult.

But the vast majority of people who experience problems when they eat certain foods don't have true food allergies. Jonathan Brostoff, M.D., director of the allergy clinic at Middlesex Hospital in London, estimates that up to 10 percent of the general population has food intolerances, in which vague symptoms usually develop gradually and unpredictably.

Scientists aren't sure why some people develop food intolerances. The leading theory is that human genes have not had time to adapt to the modern diet. Our prehistoric ancestors ate only a small fraction of the foods that we eat: mostly wild fruits and vegetables; occasionally meat and eggs; never grains, dairy products, or junk food. That's a far cry from the burgers, fries, and soft drinks that pass for meals these days.

Even though tens of thousands of years separate us from our prehistoric ancestors, that's just a blink of an eye in evolutionary terms. Human genetic makeup has changed very little. No wonder the foods most likely to cause intolerances include gluten (derived from grains), dairy products, and eggs. Our genes aren't fully equipped to handle them.

Food Intolerance? Eliminate the Possibilities

If you suspect that you have a food intolerance, you may benefit from an elimination diet. But before you try one on your own, Anne Simons, M.D., suggests pursuing a blended-medicine approach. Start with a visit to your primary-care physician to rule out other potential health problems—for example, an ulcer or colitis. Then consult an allergist or immunologist, who can test you for allergies. If you don't have any, you can follow an elimination diet to help pinpoint the source of your symptoms. Your doctor or practitioner can guide you through the steps.

Chapter 7

Exercise:
Major Health Gains
Are No Sweat

A century ago, no one "worked out." Yet people then were more physically fit than most Americans today. How did they do it? Simple: They led physically active lives. They walked a great deal. They gardened, chopped wood, pumped water, churned butter, and washed their clothes largely by hand.

Today's modern conveniences are touted as labor-saving, but those savings carry a high price: less physical activity. According to a survey by the Centers for Disease Control and Prevention (CDC) in Atlanta, fewer than one-third of Americans are active enough for good health. Sixty percent don't exercise regularly, and 25 percent don't exercise at all.

But despite what those health club ads may lead you to think, you don't have to spend half your life sweating buckets with a personal trainer to reap major physical and emotional benefits from exercise. All you have to do is imitate your great-grandparents by incorporating more physical activity into your daily routine. You hardly have to break into a sweat.

"We made a mistake years ago when we told everyone that they had to engage in strenuous 20-minute aerobic workouts at least three times a week to obtain health benefits from exercise," says Steven N. Blair, P.E.D., director of research and director of epidemiology and clinical applications at the Cooper Institute of Aerobics Research in Dallas. "Regular moderate exercise is enough."

What exactly is "moderate exercise"? Brisk walking, bicycling, swimming, dancing—even gardening and housework, if you put effort into them. And what's "regular"? About 30 minutes every day. But that 30 minutes doesn't have to be all at once, Dr. Blair points out. Short-duration activities that add up to 30

When Working Out Hurts

It's normal to feel some muscle soreness 12 to 48 hours after exercising, especially if you're not in great shape. Soreness feels like a dull ache. You don't need to be concerned about it, but you might want to take aspirin, ibuprofen, or acetaminophen for relief. Wait until you feel better before you resume your workouts. Over time, as you become more fit, the soreness should stop—unless you increase the duration or intensity of your workout.

On the other hand, if any physical activity causes sharp pain, stop doing it. Pain is your body's way of telling you that something is wrong. If it persists, see your doctor.

minutes work just as well. So taking two 10-minute walks and mopping the kitchen floor are about enough.

The nation's health and fitness experts officially embraced the nonstrenuous approach to exercise in 1995. That's when the CDC and the American College of Sports Medicine issued a joint report stating, "If sedentary Americans would adopt a more active lifestyle, there would be enormous benefits to public health and individual well-being. An active lifestyle does not require a regimented, vigorous exercise program. Instead, small lifestyle changes that increase daily activity reduce risk of chronic disease and enhance quality of life."

The following year, the nation's highest-ranking health official joined the chorus. The first Surgeon General's Report on Physical Activity and Health urged all Americans to do something—anything—physical for 30 minutes a day.

According to Harold Elrick, M.D., director of the Foundation for Optimal Health and Longevity in Bonita, California, America's seven leading killers are heart disease, cancer, stroke, high blood pressure, chronic obstructive pulmonary disease, diabetes, and osteoporosis. These conditions are responsible for 70 percent of the deaths that occur in the United States every year. And we can help prevent or treat every one of them with regular moderate exercise.

Regular moderate exercise supports good health. It helps you lose weight faster, sleep better, and think more clearly. It boosts your immune system, eases osteoarthritis and back pain, minimizes menopausal discomforts, and combats

How Fit Are You Now?

Whether you're just starting an exercise program or you're already leading an active lifestyle, this simple self-test by Bryant A. Stamford, Ph.D., director of the Health Promotion and Wellness Center at the University of Louisville in Kentucky, can help you assess your current fitness level. Select the answers that best describe you, then tally your points and check your score below.

1. How many flights of stairs do you typically climb each day?

| None | 0 points | 6–9 | 2 points |
| 1–5 | 1 point | 10+ | 3 points |

2. If your job requires you to be on your feet and moving, how many hours a day does this amount to?

| 1 | 2 points | 3 | 4 points |
| 2 | 3 points | 4+ | 6 points |

3. If you have a desk job, how many times an hour do you get up to attend meetings, run errands, and the like?

| 6+ | 1 point |

4. How many hours a week do you spend doing household chores such as cooking, cleaning, and vacuuming?

| Each hour up to 5 | 1 point |

5. If you have a preschooler, what portion of the day do the two of you spend together? (If you have two preschoolers, multiply your points by 1.5. If you have three preschoolers, double your points.)

| Full-time day care | 1 point | With you all day | 5 points |
| Part-time day care | 3 points | | |

depression and anxiety. In fact, if you look at all of the research to date, you'd be hard-pressed to think of even one aspect of your health that exercise *doesn't* benefit.

Clearing the Hurdles

By now nearly all of us know that we should exercise—but obstacles often get in the way. Here's some advice for getting started at any age, from fitness trainer Joan Price, author of *Joan Price Says, Yes, You Can Get in Shape!*

6. How many miles do you walk each day?

<1	0 points	3	6 points
1	2 points	4+	10 points
2	4 points		

7. Do you have trouble opening jars?

Often	0 points	Rarely	2 points
Sometimes	1 point		

8. How many hours a week do you engage in light recreational activities such as leisurely strolling?

1	1 point	4	4 points
2	2 points	5+	6 points
3	3 points		

9. How many hours a week do you engage in moderate aerobic activities such as tennis, basketball, volleyball, or brisk walking?

1	1 point	3	3 points
2	2 points	4	4 points

10. How many hours a week do you engage in vigorous aerobic activities such as running, rowing, bicycling, or lap-swimming?

1	2 points	3	6 points
2	4 points	4+	10 points

SCORING

0 to 4: You need to become more active starting now.

5 to 10: You're moderately active, but you'd reap major health rewards by picking up your pace.

11 and over: Congratulations! Even if you don't have a formal exercise program, you're getting enough activity to add to your health and well-being.

◆ Be realistic. For every year that you've been out of shape, you need about a month to get back *in* shape.

◆ Start slowly and don't overdo it. You should be able to carry on a conversation while exercising. If you become breathless, you are pushing yourself too hard.

◆ During the first 6 months of your exercise program, expand your workouts slowly—if at all. Increase your sessions by no more than 5 minutes per month.

◆ Vary your activities, so you don't get bored.

◆ Recruit an exercise buddy. Work out together and give each other encouragement and support.

Leading an Active Life

The better your exercise program fits into your lifestyle, the better your chances of sticking with it. In fact, you don't even need to set up a formal program, if that doesn't work for you. Simply look for ways to put more oomph into everyday activities. Some suggestions:

◆ Park your car a few blocks farther from your workplace and walk the extra distance.

◆ Stash a pair of walking shoes in your desk or locker and walk at lunch and on breaks.

◆ Take the stairs instead of the elevator.

◆ Instead of calling coworkers, walk to their offices.

◆ Get a cordless phone for your home and pace or stretch while making calls.

◆ Instead of meeting friends for lunch, plan "active" dates for hiking, bicycling, or dancing.

◆ Clean out the attic, basement, or garage. All that lifting and carrying are good for you.

◆ Trade in your power mower for a push model.

◆ Tend a garden. Weeding, digging, raking, cutting, and hauling build stamina, strength, and flexibility.

◆ Play tag or hopscotch with your kids or grandkids.

◆ Walk your dog—if you don't have one, consider adopting one. Dogs are great exercise companions.

Chapter 8

Walking:
Step Up to Better Health

Along with a large brain, thumbs, and language ability, walking upright on two legs is on the short list of attributes that separate human beings from other animals. Indeed, you could say that walking is humankind's original exercise.

But because it's so fundamental, walking has long been taken for granted. When the ancient Greeks convened the first Olympics, foot races meant running, not walking. The same mindset was still in place more than 2,000 years later, when the fitness movement started gaining momentum in the mid-1970s. Among the first fitness bestsellers was Jim Fixx's *The Complete Book of Running*, not walking.

But over the last decade or so, walking has finally gained the respect it has long deserved, thanks to an avalanche of research on the health benefits of moderate exercise. In fact, most of the studies of moderate exercise use walking as their trial activity.

"Walking is one of the best ways to get fit and healthy—and stay that way," says Glenn Gaesser, Ph.D., associate professor of exercise physiology at the University of Virginia in Charlottesville. "It requires no special training or equipment. It's low-impact, so it minimizes the risk of injury. It's fun to do either indoors or outdoors, solo or with friends. And it's low-cost—even free, if you already own a good pair of walking shoes."

Such qualities have helped to make walking America's most popular fitness activity—five times more popular than running. But perhaps the biggest reason for walking's broad appeal is its utter simplicity. "You're already good at it," observes Mark Fenton, a five-time member of the U.S. National Race-walking Team and editor-at-large for *Walking* magazine. "If you approach it in a more organized way, you can make it very healthful, too."

These Shoes Are Made for Walking

Walking is easy on the budget. It requires no special equipment other than sturdy, supportive shoes and sensible socks.

Walking shoes have evolved into "systems" designed to make putting one foot in front of the other as comfortable and enjoyable as possible. "There are many qualities to consider," Fenton says. "But the four most important are fit, roll, weight, and flexibility."

Fit. Above all else, make sure the shoe fits. Your arch should rest on the shoe's arch. Your heel should be held firmly but comfortably in the heel counter (the curved insert at the back of the shoe). Make sure that your toes don't press up against the front and that your foot isn't rubbed at the sides.

Roll. The front and rear of the outsole (the bottom of the shoe) should be rounded to encourage a smooth, rolling heel-to-toe stride. Running shoes often have outsoles with flat, flared heels and toes to absorb the shock of a runner's footstrikes. Walking shoes don't need this extra shock absorption and shouldn't have it.

Weight. The lighter, the better. Hold different models of shoes in your hands to compare their weights.

Flexibility. Walking shoes should not feel stiff or restrict foot flexing. Stiff shoes make for sore feet and may contribute to muscle strains.

Consider shape and construction, too. The best shoe has a squarish toebox for comfort and "wiggle room," a notched collar (the opening of the shoe), and a firm heel counter for support and stability. It should feel well-cushioned but not spongy, with plenty of padding around heel and ankle and on the tongue. Check where your old shoes are worn, and make sure that your new shoes are extra-strong in those areas.

Do your shoe shopping in the afternoon, since your feet swell over the course of a day. And try on both shoes, not just one. Your feet may be different sizes, in which case you'll need to buy two different-size pairs to fit each foot properly. Some retailers will discount the second pair, so call around and ask before you make your purchase.

Keep in mind that walking shoes are designed to fit the average foot—but many people don't have average feet. That's why their feet hurt even after they have splurged on good shoes. If this happens to you, try orthotics. These shoe inserts not only provide extra support but also reshape the feet by adjusting balance and the demands on some foot muscles. "This reshaping takes time," says David B. Alper, D.P.M., a podiatrist in Belmont, Massachusetts. "Start by wearing orthotics for 2 to 3 hours, then add an hour a day until your feet adapt to them."

You can buy ready-made orthotics in many drugstores, shoe stores, and shoe repair shops. "Ready-made orthotics are inexpensive and often effective," Dr. Alper says. "Even if they don't help, they won't cause any harm."

If your feet continue to hurt, however, you'll need to consult a podiatrist for custom-made orthotics. They typically cost around $300, Dr. Alper says. In most cases, that's a one-time expenditure—unless you wear out your orthotics over many years of wear or your feet change because of significant weight loss or gain.

Socks Are Important, Too

Socks are an afterthought in many people's wardrobes. Color is often the main consideration. But once you become a walker, good socks become a necessity. Here's what to look for.

Foot fit. Too tight, and socks are constricting. Too loose, and they bunch up, causing irritation and blisters. In general, your socks should be one to two sizes larger than your shoes.

Leg fit. Crew socks extend to midcalf. Anklets come up over the ankles. Foot socks cover just the feet and barely protrude from your shoes. One style is as good as another. Wear what you find most comfortable.

Fabric. Cotton and wool are fine for people whose feet don't perspire much. But Orlon, polypropylene, and other synthetic materials do a better job of wicking away moisture. They keep sweaty feet dry and comfortable, which helps prevent blisters and odor. Blended-fiber socks are also available.

Extras. Some walking socks have extra padding on the soles, or slightly flared toes, or extra stitching across the toes and heels for added strength. Examine the wear patterns on your "regular" socks, then choose walking socks with reinforcement in all the right places.

It's All in Your Technique

Sure, you've been walking since you were a toddler. But you're never too old to fine-tune your technique. The following tips will help keep your constitutionals pleasurable, healthful, and injury-free.

Do it, but don't overdo it. Walk at a pace that feels comfortable. Don't dawdle, but don't become winded. Fenton recommends checking your intensity with what he calls the talk test. "You should be able to talk comfortably while walking," he says. "If you find yourself gasping for air when you talk, you're pushing yourself too hard."

Warm up beforehand. Why warm up? First, it makes walking easier by increasing the flow of oxygen-rich blood to your muscles. The extra oxygen enables your muscles to produce energy when you need it. Second, it stretches the muscles, tendons, and ligaments, preparing them for the upcoming workout and reducing your risk of injury. Third, it allows you to shift emotional gears so that you're in the right frame of mind to enjoy walking.

Pay attention to posture. The American Physical Therapy Association offers the following pointers for good walking posture: Stand up straight and look forward, not down. Keep your head erect, your chin pulled in toward your neck, your back straight, and your stomach and buttocks tucked in. Don't lean forward, except when walking uphill. Leaning increases the risk of back strain.

Set the right stride. Walk heel to toe, letting your feet gently roll forward through each step. This allows you to develop a comfortable, flowing, rhythmic stride.

Bend your elbows. As you walk, swing your arms, keeping your elbows bent at 90-degree angles and close to your trunk. Avoid straight-arm striding, which slows you down and makes your fingers swell uncomfortably. And don't thrust your elbows out to your sides, like chicken wings. This disrupts your rhythm and causes upper-body discomfort.

Keep your hands free. With your arms swinging unencumbered, you can stride more comfortably for a longer period of time without feeling winded. "If you need to carry anything, use a backpack," Fenton advises. "Carrying things in your hands is tiring and interferes with the natural rhythm of walking."

Expect to feel good. A good walking workout will leave you with a combination of fatigue, invigoration, and mood elevation. The fatigue should pass within an hour, but the invigoration and mood elevation will last much longer. And as your physical condition improves, you'll feel less fatigue and a greater sense of well-being after each workout.

Chapter 9

Tai Chi and Qigong:
Moving Meditations

Imagine if every one of the 60 million men, women, and children living in the western United States suited up each morning for 20 to 40 minutes of low-impact, no-sweat exercise. That's what happens in China, where an estimated 60 million people—particularly the elderly—start their days with routines that look just as elegant and graceful as ballet.

They're practicing either the slow, beautifully choreographed *tai chi chuan* (pronounced "tie chee chwan") or the more subtle, less dancelike *qigong* (pronounced "chee gong"). Both disciplines combine a series of fluid movements with meditative attention to the breath and body.

And while both have existed for thousands of years, they're relative new-comers to the United States. Tai chi chuan (also known as tai chi) has gradually gained popularity over the past 25 years as a gentle, relaxing form of physical activity and as a way to cope with a variety of illnesses. Qigong (sometimes spelled "chi gong" or "chi kung") has taken root in this country more recently, although for similar reasons.

Qi: The Key to Healing

In Chinese medicine, *chi* or *qi* is life energy, a vital force not formally recognized by mainstream M.D.'s. Qigong—the word means "cultivation of qi"—originated about 3,500 years ago, as Chinese physicians realized that a combination of low-impact movements and meditative focus could move qi around inside the body. Qigong exercises inspired all of the martial arts, including tai chi.

Tai chi was developed by Chang San-Feng, a semi-mythical Taoist monk and qigong practitioner who is said to have lived around A.D. 1400. One night, the story goes, he dreamed of a snake and a crane fighting. He was so fascinated by the animals' movements that he decided to combine them—as well as the combative movements of deer, tigers, bears, and monkeys—with qigong. This modified version of qigong became known as tai chi.

The phrase *tai chi chuan* is variously translated as "supreme boxing" or "optimal fist fighting." It is considered a martial art—but unlike karate and kung fu, with their hard punches and kicks, tai chi emphasizes fluidity of movement. According to tai chi masters, this gentle dance fosters the flexibility of a child, the strength of a lumberjack, and eventually the wisdom of a sage.

Tai Chi: Taking the "Work" Out of Workout

Because tai chi is more popular than qigong in the West, it has been subjected to more extensive research in the United States and Europe. The majority of studies have found that tai chi offers significant and surprising health benefits.

One reason it's so therapeutic is that it provides a deceptively intense workout. Canadian researchers reached this conclusion after monitoring a small group of men who had been taught a 20-minute tai chi routine. The men's heart rates rose to about 50 percent of their age-specific maximums—not high enough to qualify as a strenuous aerobic workout, but sufficient to reduce the men's risk of heart disease, high blood pressure, diabetes, arthritis, osteoporosis, and obesity.

This is the sort of exercise that physicians typically recommend for people over age 55. No wonder other researchers have since endorsed tai chi as a good all-around activity for seniors as well as for those with chronic medical conditions.

Tai chi also appears to have a positive effect on a variety of specific health problems and concerns. Studies show that it can help people who have high blood pressure, rheumatoid arthritis, and multiple sclerosis.

Research has shown that tai chi can also help improve balance and prevent falls. At Emory University in Atlanta, researcher Steven L. Wolf, M.D., divided 200 people (average age 76) into three groups. One group received tai chi instruction for 15 weeks, another received biofeedback balance training for 15 weeks, and the third attended seminars about fall prevention but received no physical training. All of the participants reported their falls over a 4-month period. Those who practiced tai chi went an average of 48 percent longer without a fall than those in the other two groups.

Qigong: Proving Its Worth

Qigong has never been as popular outside China as the many martial arts it inspired. But that's slowly changing as research—most of it from Asia—confirms the profound health benefits of qigong's subtle, meditative movements. So far, studies indicate that qigong can help people who suffer from heart disease, stroke, or respiratory problems.

It may also help with chronic pain and stress. In fact, people who practice qigong generally agree that the exercises enhance their ability to manage stress. When researchers at the Chinese Institute of Aviation Medicine in Beijing trained 18 jet fighter pilots in qigong, the pilots were better able to perform under stressful flying conditions.

A Taste of Tai Chi

Most teachers of tai chi say that learning one of the 50-move "short forms" popular in the United States takes about a year—and truly mastering the discipline takes a lifetime. The best way to train in tai chi is to enroll in a class. To find one, look in the Yellow Pages under "Tai Chi" or "Martial Arts" or ask for referrals from yoga or martial arts instructors.

To get just an idea of what tai chi is like, try these first five moves from the form that Terry Dunn demonstrates in his video *Tai Chi for Health*.

To test the effects of tai chi on people with high blood pressure, cardiologists at Royal Hallamshire Hospital in Sheffield, England, assigned 126 heart attack survivors (average age 56) to one of three groups. The first practiced tai chi once or twice a week; the second engaged in aerobic exercise once or twice a week; and the third participated in a support group that met once a week. After 8 weeks, the tai chi group registered the greatest drops in blood pressure, surpassing even the aerobic exercise group. The support group's blood pressure readings remained unchanged.

Other research has shown the benefits of tai chi for people who have rheumatoid arthritis, a potentially crippling inflammatory joint disease. At Charlotte Rehabilitation Hospital in North Carolina, 20 people with rheumatoid arthritis practiced tai chi for 1 hour twice a week. Over the course of 10 weeks, none of the participants experienced any aggravation of their symptoms. This is important because many doctors are reluctant to advise people with rheumatoid arthritis to exercise, fearing that overexertion will trigger joint inflammation. Apparently, tai chi poses no risk of inflammation.

Preparation: Stand with your heels together and your toes pointing outward at about a 20-degree angle. Place your arms at your sides (1). Focus on your breathing. Bend both knees and slowly shift all of your weight onto your right leg.

When there's no weight on your left leg, move the leg to the left so that your feet are shoulder-width apart. In a low seated position, slowly shift all of your weight to your left leg, keeping your back straight (2).

When there's no weight on your right leg, turn your right foot, pivoting on your heel until your feet are parallel. Shift your weight so that it's equally distributed between both legs. With your feet firmly planted on the ground, slowly rise up, straightening your legs. Rotate your elbows outward. Then flex your wrists upward until they are at a 45-degree angle with the plane of your shoulders (3).

Beginning: In this sequence, your torso is still and erect. Only your arms and shoulders move. Stand in the ending Preparation position. Inhale. Imagine that strings are tied around your wrists, pulling them upward in front of you. Allow your fingers and hands to dangle in a relaxed state as you

slowly bring your wrists up to shoulder level (4). When your wrists are at shoulder level, exhale and lift your fingers. Straighten your hands so that your palms are facing slightly forward (5). With your legs firmly planted on the ground and knees slightly bent, project your energy from the tips of your fingers.

Inhale. Drop your elbows to a position over your hips and draw your hands back to your shoulders. Gently lift your palms, then your fingers (6). While maintaining your wrists and hands in this position, allow your arms to slide down the length of your body until they are at your sides. Return to the ending Preparation position.

Ward Off Left: Begin in the ending Preparation position. Shift your weight to your left leg and pivot 90 degrees on your right heel. As you turn, raise your right hand to shoulder level with your palm down, and move your left hand to a position over your right hip with your palm up (7). Imagine that your hands are holding a large ball. Square your shoulders and hips to the right, keeping your knees bent and your weight in your seat and legs.

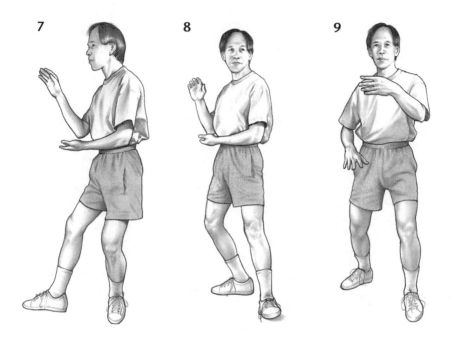

7 8 9

While keeping your back straight, shift your weight forward to your right leg and bend your right knee so that it is positioned over your right foot. Look left over your shoulder and step out with your left heel along the line of your left shoulder. Plant your left heel about 24 inches out, then step down with your toes so that your left foot is flat (8).

As you set your toes down, shift all of your weight to your left leg and turn your torso left from your waist. As you turn, raise your left forearm across your chest and drop your right arm so that your right hand is over your right hip, palm facing down. Pivot your right foot 45 degrees (9).

Ward Off Right: This sequence follows from Ward Off Left. Bring your right hand, palm up, to your waist level and your left hand, palm down, to the level of your left shoulder, as though you were holding a large ball. At the same time, rise up on your right toes. Shift your weight to your left leg. Keeping your back straight, sink your weight into your left hip (10).

While keeping your hands in position, step out with your right leg about 24 inches, along the line of your right shoulder. Plant your right heel, then your toes as you shift your weight forward to your right leg (11). Your knee should be

bent and over your right toes. As you do this, raise your hands to throat level in front of you, with your right hand in front of your left and your palms facing each other. Imagine that you're holding a medium-size ball. Keeping your back straight and your knees bent, pivot your left foot 45 degrees (12).

Grasp the Bird's Tail: This sequence follows from the Ward Off Right position. With your right knee over your right toes in Ward Off Right (13), turn your torso to the right at your waist. Do this while keeping your arms in the same position within the frame of your shoulders (14). Move your right palm forward so that the fingers point outward, and move your left palm back, in an upward position, so that the fingers point toward your right elbow (15).

Slowly shift your weight and turn left. At the same time, allow your left hand to swing down with the force of gravity and then back up so that it's in line with your left shoulder. Your right arm should remain bent, with your fingers up, as your forearm is brought across your chest. Your elbows should have a slight bend, as though you were holding a ball at chest level (16).

With your weight on your left leg, turn right and shift your weight onto

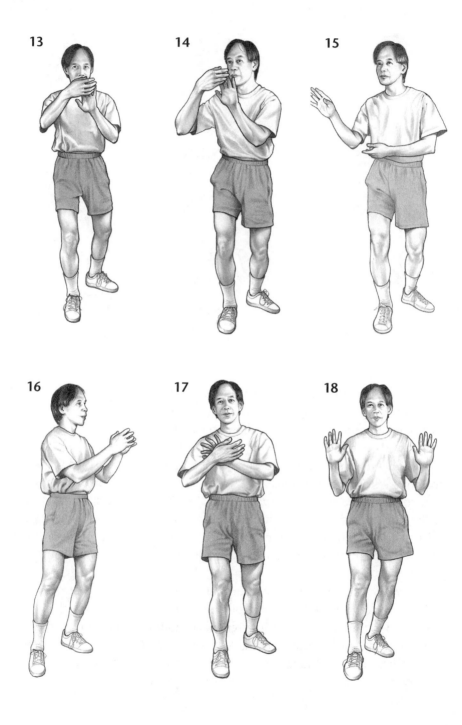

19

your right leg. As you turn, bring your left arm across your chest, with your palm facing to your right. Bring the palm of your right hand up so that your palms meet and press together over your right knee, which is in line with your right toes. Your hips and shoulders should be squared to the right (17).

Without turning your waist or shoulders, shift your weight back onto your left leg. Separate your palms, pull your hands back to your shoulders, and point your fingers up and your palms forward (18). Shift your weight to your right leg and extend your palms forward until your elbows are almost straight, as if you were pushing something (19).

A Qigong Sampler

Because qigong is only now becoming popular in the United States, teachers may be hard to find. Ask tai chi, yoga, or martial arts instructors in your area for recommendations. To get a sense of how qigong differs from tai chi, try these three exercises offered by qigong master Ching Tse Lee, Ph.D., psychology professor at Brooklyn College.

The Rejuvenator: Stand with your feet parallel and shoulder-width apart. Keeping your upper body straight and relaxed and your arms at your sides, slowly bend your knees about 45 degrees into a quarter-squat position (20). Slowly raise your arms in front of you about 35 degrees, with your elbows slightly bent and your palms facing each other (21). Bring your palms closer until you feel qi (characterized by sensations of tingling, throbbing, trembling, cold, heat, or electricity). Once you feel qi, stay with it and become familiar with it. The sensations may come and go. Practice this exercise for 3 to 10 minutes, or as long as you can comfortably maintain the bent-knee position. This exercise should leave you feeling refreshed and rejuvenated.

The Calmer: Begin by doing the Rejuvenator. After you've experienced qi for 5 to 10 minutes, observe your breathing—the natural expansion of your body as you inhale and the contraction as you exhale. Merge into the moment meditatively. Next, observe how your palms move farther apart when you in-

20

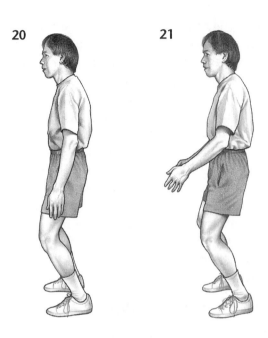

21

hale and closer together when you exhale. Once you've appreciated your breathing and body expansion and contraction, feel the energy all around you. Does one part of your body feel lighter or heavier? Warmer or colder? If you practice daily, you'll eventually feel the energy around you as even and balanced. This exercise produces a sense of profound calm.

22   **23**   **24**

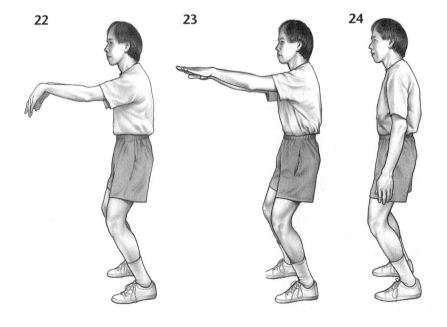

The Energizer: This exercise enhances the circulation of qi around your body. Begin by doing the Rejuvenator. Then relax and observe your breathing for a few minutes, feeling the expansion and contraction of your body, as in the Calmer. While inhaling, let your arms float up to shoulder height, with your elbows slightly bent (22). While exhaling, let your arms stretch out effortlessly (23). Inhale and let your arms bend and slowly descend until your thumbs touch the sides of your legs. Exhale and let your arms straighten out along your sides (24). Repeat this exercise for 3 to 5 minutes. As you do, focus on the qi flowing around you. You may feel it circulate from your back to your hands as you complete each cycle. Empty your mind meditatively. Become one with the exercise. Even if you don't notice qi movement at first, you will eventually—sometimes when you least expect it.

Chapter 10

Yoga: Stretch Yourself Healthy

From childhood through his late thirties, Robin Munro, Ph.D., of Cambridge, England, struggled to cope with chronic asthma and bronchitis. Then he discovered yoga, the 4,000-year-old Indian exercise discipline. As he practiced the gentle stretches and postures, his respiratory symptoms diminished and eventually disappeared. He hasn't had an asthma attack or bout of bronchitis since he became a yoga devotee.

Dr. Munro's experience led him to found the Yoga Biomedical Trust. The Trust polled 3,000 British yoga students, asking if yoga had helped them with any health problems. Indeed it had: In varying numbers, students reported that yoga had relieved arthritis, back pain, and migraines; minimized premenstrual and menopausal discomforts; lowered blood pressure; and supported weight loss and smoking cessation. Like Dr. Munro, some of the students noticed that their respiratory problems subsided, producing fewer asthma attacks and bronchitis flare-ups.

Of course, the participants were very subjective in reporting yoga's benefits, so the findings of the survey aren't scientific. But they do confirm what many practitioners have also observed: Yoga can be amazingly therapeutic.

Exercise from the East

Yoga is not only the world's most ancient exercise-based health regimen, it is also the first non-Western alternative therapy to gain popularity in the United States. Yoga master Swami Vivekananda first demonstrated his amazing flexibility at the 1893 Chicago World's Fair. Since then, yoga has become as American as the YMCA, which sponsors hundreds of yoga classes around the country.

The word *yoga* comes from the Sanskrit *yuga*, meaning "to join." It refers to the joining of body, mind, and spirit in a disciplined union. To appreciate what yoga is, you should know what yoga is *not*. It's not a religion, though it developed from Hinduism. It's not calisthenics, though it works up a sweat and tones and strengthens the muscles and joints as well as—or better than—most other forms of exercise. And it's not meditation, though its slow pace, deep breathing, and focus on the moment open a door to meditative relaxation.

So just what is yoga? "It's an exercise path to physical and emotional well-being," says Nashville pathologist Mary Pullig Schatz, M.D., author of *Back Care Basics*. "Not to mention that it cured my bad back."

There are several styles of yoga. The one most commonly practiced in the United States is hatha yoga, a collection of stretches and postures that Indian yoga masters call asanas. *Hatha* means "forceful"—an ironic choice of words, considering that hatha yoga is known for its gentleness. The most popular school of hatha yoga was developed by B. K. S. Iyengar, who modified the classic hatha asanas for the comfort of Western students.

Beyond the Yoga Biomedical Trust survey, many carefully controlled scientific studies have demonstrated yoga's health benefits. Most of the research comes from India, where yoga is practiced in conjunction with both Western medicine and Ayurveda, India's traditional medicine. But American and European researchers have also put yoga under the microscope, publishing their findings in leading Western scientific journals. Their studies show that yoga can help with heart disease, high blood pressure, diabetes, asthma, and back pain.

Poses to Practice

Yoga is quite safe for the vast majority of people. Still, anyone over age 60 or with a disability or a chronic health problem should consult a doctor before beginning a yoga program (or any exercise program, for that matter).

The best way to learn yoga is in a class with a qualified, experienced instructor. Yoga classes abound in every metropolitan area—and they're cropping up in small towns, too. To find one, ask friends, inquire at gyms or aerobics studios, or look in the Yellow Pages under "Yoga." In addition, *Yoga Journal* publishes a directory of yoga teachers around the country.

If you have a specific health problem, talk to your prospective instructor before enrolling in a class. Ask whether there are some postures that you should modify or not attempt at all. Most Iyengar yoga teachers will adapt postures for those with disabilities, chronic illnesses, or other special needs.

Most yoga sessions involve 15 to 30 postures. Here are 5 for you to try. The instructions have been provided by two longtime teachers of Iyengar yoga: Donna Farhi, a contributor to *Yoga Journal* and teacher of yoga workshops around the world; and Patricia Walden, a yoga teacher in Somerville, Massachusetts, and star of the *Yoga for Beginners* video.

Mountain pose: The mountain pose serves as the basis for all standing poses. It also teaches correct posture, which is important to your health and well-being even when you're not practicing yoga. Stand with your feet together—big toes touching and heels slightly apart—and your arms hanging at your sides. (If you feel unstable with your feet together, separate them a bit.) Evenly distribute your weight between your two feet and between the ball and heel of each foot (1).

Create a strong foundation with your feet and legs by separating and lengthening your toes. Tense your leg muscles to bring your kneecaps upward.

Focus on centering your pelvis over your legs. Try not to tuck your pelvis in to your tailbone (which pushes the pelvis forward) or overarch your back (which pushes the pelvis backward). Feel your body rise upward from your feet. Stretch your entire body from your inner heels through your legs and upward to your groin.

Relax your diaphragm and extend your spine upward from your pelvis. Open your chest. Breathe deeply and slowly from your diaphragm. Drop your shoulders and relax your face and eyes. Your shoulders, hips, and heels should be in line. Hold for up to 1 minute.

Jumping to the wide-leg standing pose: Jumping is a pose in itself as well as an elegant transition from the mountain pose to the other standing poses. Practice on a nonslip surface. If you have hip, knee, or back problems, avoid this pose.

Begin in the mountain pose, then inhale and bend your knees slightly. As you raise your arms to shoulder height, bend them at the elbows so that your middle fingers touch in front of your throat (2). Keep your chest raised and breathe. As you inhale, jump your feet outward and extend your arms straight out to the sides, palms facing down. The movement should be silent and graceful; you needn't jump high. Land with your feet parallel, 3 to 4 feet apart and pointing forward (3).

To return to the mountain pose, reverse the sequence.

Triangle pose: You may need a prop block to do this pose. A prop block is a piece of wood about the size of two bricks. It supports you throughout the pose, enabling you to bend without exceeding your comfort zone. If you don't

1

have a prop block, a stack of books will do. Be sure to practice this pose on a nonslip surface.

Begin in the mountain pose, then jump to the wide-leg standing pose. Pivot on your heels, turning your left foot inward 60 degrees and your right foot out 90 degrees. The arch of your left foot should be in line with the heel of your right foot. Slide the prop block or pile of books behind your right ankle.

Evenly distribute your weight between your feet and between the ball and heel of each foot. Spread and lengthen your toes. Do not overextend your knees. Use your front thigh muscles to draw your knees upward. Inhale, then as you exhale, bend from your hips to the right and extend your torso over your right leg. Place your right hand on the block or books. (Or place your hand on the floor, if you can comfortably reach it.)

Inhale and raise your left arm over your head,

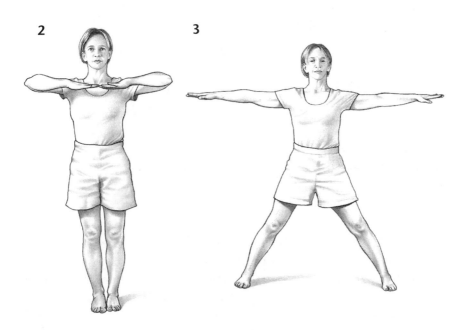

2

3

palm forward. On exhaling, turn your head and look up at your left hand (4). Feel the floor beneath your feet. Relax into lengthening your legs, spine, and arms. If your neck begins to ache, look forward. Hold the pose for up to 30 seconds, then repeat the sequence on the opposite side. Return to the wide-leg standing pose, then jump to the mountain pose.

Side stretch pose. Stand on a nonslip surface. Begin in the mountain pose, then jump so that your feet are 4 to 4½ feet apart. Turn your left foot in and your right foot out.

Keeping your left leg strong and planted, bend your right knee so that your thigh and lower leg form a right angle. Your right knee should be directly above your right ankle (5). Breathe deeply and bend from the hips, extending your torso over your right thigh. Place your right hand on a prop block (or on the floor) behind your right foot. Gently stretch both sides of your spine evenly.

4

Next, bring your left shoulder back and away from your right shoulder, as if you were moving toward an imaginary wall behind you. Turn your left palm to face your head. Reach up with your left arm (6) and lower it until it is parallel to your ear. On exhaling, gently turn your head and look up at the ceiling. All the while, remember to keep your legs strong. This makes it easier to move your upper body. Hold the pose for up to 1 minute, then repeat the sequence on the opposite side. Return to the wide-leg standing pose, then jump to the mountain pose.

Proud warrior pose. Begin in the mountain pose, then jump to the wide-leg standing pose. Land so that your feet are directly under your wrists. Lift your rib cage and bring your shoulders down, keeping your arms extended through

5

6

7

your hands. Imagine a line from the top of your head down through the center of your torso to your tailbone. Maintain an awareness of this line as you turn your left foot in and your right foot out. When you exhale, bend your right knee so that your thigh and lower leg form a right angle. Your right knee should be directly over your right ankle. Inhale.

While you are exhaling, turn your head and look at your right hand. Press your feet into the floor and feel your spine lengthen (7). Hold this position for about 30 seconds. Return to the wide-leg standing pose, then jump to the mountain pose. Repeat the sequence, this time turning to the left.

Chapter 11

Meditation: Stress Relief and So Much More

Ageneration ago, mere mention of the word *meditation* evoked exotic images of Indian gurus wearing turbans and sitting cross-legged for hours on end. Today, meditation is as mainstream as the meditation room at Pittsburgh International Airport. The 1,000-square-foot room, painted with soothing images of clouds, provides a tranquil sanctuary from the hustle and bustle of modern air travel.

Meditation was one of the first alternative therapies to enter Americans' health consciousness. But unlike yoga, which took root a century ago and gradually gained popularity, meditation arrived with a decidedly nonmeditative bang in 1975. That's when pioneering researcher Herbert Benson, M.D., now director of the Mind-Body Medical Institute at Harvard Medical School, published his bestseller *The Relaxation Response*. The book, which documents the therapeutic powers of meditation, is considered by many experts to be the watershed in mind-body research.

The Mind-Body Breakthrough

Dr. Benson didn't set out to study meditation. Back in 1968, he was more interested in biofeedback, a then-new therapy that had just emerged from high-tech Western medical laboratories. Specifically, he wanted to figure out whether biofeedback had any potential as a treatment for high blood pressure. He used monkeys as his test subjects.

At the time, most of Dr. Benson's peers in the medical profession viewed biofeedback as bogus because it suggested that the mind could somehow influence physical processes considered beyond conscious control. Such a concept seemed ridiculous to the medical mainstream. Nevertheless, Dr. Benson's work attracted media coverage, which in turn captured the attention of students of transcendental meditation (TM). TM had been brought to the United States a few years earlier by Maharishi Mahesh Yogi, one-time guru to the Beatles.

Some of the students visited Dr. Benson and told him that they could substantially lower their blood pressures without biofeedback, simply by meditating. It was a startling claim. After all, mainstream medicine simply didn't believe that a person could exert voluntary control over involuntary physical processes such as blood pressure. And despite his interest in biofeedback, Dr. Benson was a thoroughly mainstream physician. To him, the TM students' claim sounded ridiculous. When they offered to participate in his studies and undergo testing, Dr. Benson turned them down, opting to continue his work with monkeys.

The students persisted, and eventually, Dr. Benson relented. Much to his surprise, he discovered that the students could indeed lower their blood pressures by practicing TM. They could also slow their metabolic rates—that is, the rate at which the body burns calories for energy. And they could reduce their rates of oxygen consumption to levels usually achieved only in the deepest stages of sleep or during animal hibernation.

Dr. Benson became intrigued by Asian meditation—particularly TM, which is among the easiest meditative disciplines to learn. TM instructors give their students a word or phrase, called a mantra. Then the students sit quietly with their eyes closed and repeat the mantra over and over for 20 minutes at a time, once or twice a day. When distracting thoughts intrude, the students are instructed to observe them, accept them, and gently return their attention to the mantra. (Some meditators concentrate on their inhalations and exhalations instead of a mantra, a practice known as breath meditation.)

As Dr. Benson studied TM, he realized that the physical changes it invokes could also be achieved through other deep relaxation techniques—most notably progressive muscle relaxation (in which the muscles are sequentially tensed and released) and autogenic training (in which the body is given verbal instructions to relax). Dr. Benson also concluded that the state of profound calm induced by meditation is in fact a natural human reaction. It is the physiological opposite of the fight-or-flight response, which prepares the body to defend itself or flee from danger.

The fight-or-flight response increases blood pressure, heart and breathing rates, metabolism, and blood flow to the muscles. But as Dr. Benson observed, TM and other deep relaxation techniques lower blood pressure and slow heart and breathing rates, metabolism, and blood flow to the muscles. Dr. Benson dubbed this the relaxation response.

An Emotional Vaccine

In his book *The Relaxation Response*, Dr. Benson presents a case for the physical and emotional benefits of deep relaxation that appeals to Western scientific sensibilities. He describes the relaxation response as a physiological gift that anyone can use to calm down, cope with stress, and—for the spiritually inclined—feel one with God or the universe.

What's more, those who evoke the relaxation response on a regular basis experience something "extra" over time: a feeling of well-being and wholeness that lasts all day long. Mind-body physicians view this phenomenon as a kind of emotional vaccine that immunizes against anxiety, tension, and distress.

Soon after *The Relaxation Response* appeared, people who had once ridiculed meditation were themselves chanting mantras—and cultivating a deep respect for mind-body medicine. Today, meditation is among the most mainstream of the alternative therapies. And no wonder: Its benefits have been documented in dozens of studies.

"Meditation helps people with a wide range of medical disorders and life challenges," agrees Jon Kabat-Zinn, Ph.D., director of the stress reduction clinic at the University of Massachusetts Medical Center in Worcester. "During our 8-week meditation classes, we see improvement in the majority of people, regardless of their diagnoses."

Beyond helping people cope with illness, meditation appears to enhance immune function and lower risk of disease. When researchers drew blood from 225 meditators and 211 nonmeditators to analyze their erythrocyte sedimentation rates (ESRs)—an accepted measure of health status—the meditators had significantly lower ESRs. This suggests that the meditators were less likely to become sick.

For those concerned about health-care costs, meditation offers more good news. Canadian researchers tracked the medical expenses of 677 people who practiced TM for 20 minutes twice a day over the course of 3 years. Their medical expenses dropped by about 6 percent a year.

Meditation Made Easy

The deep relaxation and present-moment focus that characterize meditation play important roles in other alternative therapies, including tai chi and

Meditation + Imagination = Visualization

One of the hallmarks of meditation is its focus on just one thing, such as a mantra, with passive acceptance of any thoughts that happen to intrude. Visualization has the same focus. But instead of a mantra, it uses a storylike image to invoke the relaxation response. In fact, visualization is sometimes called imagery or guided imagery.

Like meditation, visualization can effectively treat a surprising array of medical conditions. According to Martin L. Rossman, M.D., visualization techniques may help people with many of the problems for which they see primary-care physicians.

How does visualization work? Scientists still aren't certain, but some studies have found that visualization used for pain relief stimulates the release of endorphins, the body's natural painkillers. In addition, a relatively new imaging technology called positron emission tomography (PET) has shown that some parts of the brain become activated whether a person actually performs an activity or just vividly imagines it.

One of the beauties of visualization is that it's perfectly suited to self-care. Some people follow written instructions, while others listen to prerecorded or self-recorded audiotapes. Still others seek professional guidance through visualization exercises. All three methods produce similar results, so choose the one that you're most comfortable with.

What's most important is creating a vivid, convincing image. As Dr. Rossman describes it, a visualization is "a flow of thoughts that you can see, hear, feel, smell, and taste. It's a window into your inner world, a current of daydreams, memories, plans, and possibilities. It's the language of the arts, the emotions, and—most important—the deeper self."

qigong, yoga, biofeedback, and massage. As you explore these other therapies, remember the words of Swami Satchidananda, who inspired Dean Ornish, M.D., president of the Preventive Medicine Research Institute in Sausalito, California, to develop his all-alternative program for reversing heart disease: "No one can calm the ocean's waves. But by using [meditative relaxation techniques], you can learn to surf."

The key to "surfing," of course, is the ability to invoke the relaxation response. It's easy, but it does take some practice. Just follow these steps.

1. Find a quiet place with a comfortable chair. Sit with your eyes closed.

2. Think of a single word or phrase, such as *one*, *peace*, or *tranquillity*.

3. Silently repeat the word or phrase over and over again. While doing so, try to empty your mind of all other thoughts.

4. When a distracting thought enters your mind, notice it, accept it, and let it go. Return to focusing on your word or phrase.

5. At first, meditate for just a minute or two once or twice a day. Gradually work up to 20 to 30 minutes once or twice a day.

If you're not comfortable reciting a word or phrase, use breath meditation to invoke the relaxation response. As explained earlier, breath meditators concentrate on inhaling and exhaling deeply rather than on repeating a mantra. All the other steps remain the same.

Chapter 12

Biofeedback: Wired for Deep Relaxation

S ometimes accomplishing the "impossible" requires only that someone believes it's possible.

Until the early 1960s, psychologists believed that animals could not learn complex tasks. Then came pioneering behaviorist B. F. Skinner, Ph.D., who devised a simple system of rewards and punishments that he called operant conditioning. He used operant conditioning to teach pigeons to peck a button only when certain combinations of lights flashed. He also trained mice to build towers out of plastic blocks.

Dr. Skinner thought operant conditioning might also help with toilet training children and performing other human tasks. But Neal Miller, Ph.D., then head of the Laboratory of Physiological Psychology at Rockefeller University in New York City, believed the technique had more profound implications.

Dr. Miller was fascinated by reports that Indian yoga masters and Japanese Zen masters could voluntarily control pulse, blood pressure, and metabolic rate—bodily functions that physiologists had long considered completely involuntary. He speculated that the yogis and Zen masters might be using a form of internal operant conditioning to alter their physiology.

In a classic series of experiments, Dr. Miller used a Skinnerian system of rewards and punishments to teach rats to raise and lower their heart rates, blood pressures, ear temperatures, kidney functions, and intestinal muscle contractions. When his research was published in a 1969 issue of *Science*, the nation's top research journal, it forever changed how Western scientists viewed learning. They realized that "involuntary" biological processes could be voluntarily modified with the right rewards, or feedback—hence the name *biofeedback*.

Your Mind Speaks, Your Body Listens

By the late 1970s, biofeedback had become an industry. Manufacturers developed simple, inexpensive biofeedback devices to monitor breathing, pulse rate, finger temperature, muscle tension, or minute changes in perspiration. By regulating these bodily functions, the theory goes, people can make their bodies relax. And that enables them not only to manage stress but also to treat specific medical conditions.

"Biofeedback is not a cure-all," says Francine Butler, Ph.D., executive director of the Association for Applied Psychophysiology and Biofeedback in Wheat Ridge, Colorado. "But it helps treat stress-related health problems." Among those problems are tension headaches, migraines, asthma, and incontinence. There's also evidence that biofeedback can help with temporomandibular disorder (TMD) and congestive heart failure.

TMD is a condition characterized by chronic pain around the temporomandibular joint, which connects the jaw to the skull. It has several possible causes, including chronic tension in the jaw muscles. Studies by Leonard Hukzinski, Ph.D., director of biofeedback services in the department of psychiatry at the Ochsner Medical Foundation in New Orleans, have shown that biofeedback provides effective long-term relief from tension-related TMD.

This therapy may also help people who have congestive heart failure. Researchers gave biofeedback training to 20 people with congestive heart failure, theorizing that biofeedback could improve circulatory efficiency. And they were right: The patients showed significant increases in the diameter of their blood vessels, which enhanced circulation and boosted their hearts' blood output.

One Therapy, Many Forms

Today, several thousand certified biofeedback therapists teach the necessary skills to tens of thousands of people every year. Thousands more people learn biofeedback on their own, using small home devices and the instruction books that come with them. (Home biofeedback equipment is available in some department stores and through some health-oriented mail-order catalogs.)

Just how does a biofeedback machine work? Well, suppose that you're feeling tense. Anxiety causes the tiny blood vessels in your hands to constrict, and, in turn, the skin temperature of your hands drops a few degrees. The biofeedback machine has a temperature-sensitive pad that's attached to a thermometer. When you touch the pad, the thermometer displays your skin temperature and, depending on the model, emits a high-pitched tone.

Then as you relax, the number on the thermometer goes higher, while the tone goes lower.

Biofeedback neophytes often have trouble adjusting their skin temperatures. But with a little coaching, they learn to breathe deeply and to notice small but important changes in the thermometer reading and tone. Pretty soon, they can warm their hands at will—and as they do, they feel more relaxed.

Not all biofeedback machines monitor skin temperature. As mentioned earlier, various models can track an assortment of bodily functions, including temperature, pulse, breathing, muscle tension, and brain waves. One type of biofeedback even tests the electrical conductivity of the skin, or galvanic skin response (GSR). This type of biofeedback is used to treat anxiety, insomnia, obesity, and chemical dependencies like drug addiction. It's also helpful for controlling overactive sweat glands (a condition called hyperhydrosis). Home biofeedback devices typically measure GSR.

Chapter 13

Massage: Your Hands Have the Power to Heal

Whenen a bruise or muscle strain causes pain, what's the first thing that most people do? Before they even say, "Ouch," they grab the injured area and rub it. Instinctively, folks know that massage makes them feel better.

Massage is certainly among the oldest forms of medicine. It's depicted in 15,000-year-old cave paintings discovered in the Pyrenees mountains. And 3,000 years ago, it was being prescribed by Chinese and Ayurvedic physicians for an array of ailments. Even Hippocrates, the father of Western medicine, once said, "The physician must be experienced in many things, but most assuredly in rubbing."

With the birth of Christianity, the use of massage and therapeutic touch took on religious overtones. The New Testament says that Jesus cured the blind by touching their eyes, and the lame by touching their legs: "He laid his hands on them one by one and healed them" (Luke 4:40). Later, priests began laying their hands on the sick. When the practice fell from favor in the Church, it was adapted by the kings of France and England, who used "the Royal Touch" to treat ailing supplicants.

The Rebirth of an Ancient Healing Art

Despite its history of healing, massage didn't seem to fit amid the science and technology of modern Western medicine. But that began to change in the mid-1970s with the pioneering work of Tiffany Field, Ph.D., professor of psychology, pediatrics, and psychiatry at the University of Miami School of Medicine.

Dr. Field became interested in medical care for premature infants when her

(continued on page 74)

Beyond Massage: The Many Schools of Bodywork

To some people, bodywork is what's done to fix a dent in a car. But the term also applies to an ever-broadening—and often-bewildering—group of alternative therapies.

Each of the approximately two dozen styles of bodywork has passionate promoters, yet many of the styles overlap so extensively that they can be difficult to differentiate. Generally, they fall into three categories: massage-based deep-tissue manipulation, exercise-based movement re-education, and combinations of the two.

Here's a rundown of some of the better-known schools of bodywork. The medical literature contains no reports of injuries from any of these therapies. Still, if you have a chronic medical condition, check with your physician first and proceed prudently.

DEEP-TISSUE MANIPULATION

The best-known styles of deep-tissue manipulation are Rolfing and myotherapy.

Rolfing. Developed by Ida Rolf, Ph.D., a Swiss biochemist, Rolfing involves the application of intense pressure to stretch and realign tendons and ligaments. The pressure can be quite painful, but many who have been through a typical 10-session program say the discomfort is worth it.

Myotherapy. Myotherapists use their fingers, knuckles, or elbows to press tender spots (called trigger points) and reduce chronic pain in these areas. The pressure is less intense than in Rolfing but deeper than in shiatsu massage. Myotherapists also teach gentle stretching exercises to help prevent trigger points from becoming painful again.

MOVEMENT RE-EDUCATION

The most popular schools of movement re-education are Alexander Technique, Feldenkrais, and Trager work.

Alexander Technique. When chronic hoarseness threatened to end his theater career, Shakespearean actor F. M. Alexander took matters into his own hands. He had noticed that the hoarseness grew worse when he held his head a certain way, so he tried making modest changes in his posture and movement—lifting his head, stretching his neck and shoulders, lengthening his spine. Over time, his hoarseness disappeared, his breathing deepened, and he moved more efficiently and gracefully.

Alexander died in 1955, but the Alexander Technique is now taught around the world. Instructors in the Alexander Technique show you how to make subtle postural changes as you sit, stand, walk, move, and rise from a seated or reclining position.

Feldenkrais. Feldenkrais combines Functional Integration (FI) and Awareness through Movement (ATM). FI involves gentle manipulations designed to improve breathing, posture, and the alignment of the musculoskeletal system. ATM—which is taught in a class format rather than individually—uses gentle, nonaerobic floor exercises to show people how their bodies move most effortlessly and efficiently.

Trager work. Trager work is based on the premise that chronic tension collects in the major muscle groups and impairs their function. A session begins with "hookup," in which the practitioner and client together enter a meditative state—the former to marshal healing energy, the latter to receive it. Then the practitioner gently rocks, shakes, and jiggles the client's body and coaxes the client's limbs through their range of motion. The client also receives instruction in mentastics, gentle, nonimpact, nonaerobic moves similar to tai chi.

COMBINATION BODYWORK

Better-known combination schools include Aston patterning and Hellerwork.

Aston patterning. Aston patterning combines manipulation that's less intense than Rolfing with movement re-education that's focused on everyday tasks—for example, standing up and sitting down.

Hellerwork. Hellerwork involves 11 sessions; each is 90 minutes long and focuses on a different part of the body in a prescribed sequence. A portion of each session involves deep-tissue manipulation to relieve tension and realign body parts in a manner akin to Rolfing. The rest of the session is devoted to psychotherapeutic conversation, focusing on the personal issues unearthed by deep-tissue manipulation, such as any chronic stress that's contributing to neck pain.

own daughter was born prematurely. Because preemies have underdeveloped immune systems, they are kept in special isolation cribs called Isolettes to protect them from infection—especially infection spread by human contact. Seeing her daughter in an Isolette bothered Dr. Field. She was familiar with research involving infant monkeys that showed impaired growth and other problems when they were deprived of maternal contact. She became so concerned that a lack of human contact might retard her daughter's development that she launched a study to find out.

Aromatherapy: A "Scents-ible" Companion to Massage

A good massage includes oil or lotion. Many such products are scented with essential oils, compounds that give plants their fragrances. Essential oils consist of small molecules that quickly reach the brain either by inhalation or through skin penetration. Using essential oils for medicinal purposes is a discipline known as aromatherapy.

Few researchers have investigated the health effects of aromatherapy massage. But according to the studies that have been done, combining aromatherapy and massage makes sense. Together they help relieve headache pain and reduce anxiety as well as control behavior problems among Alzheimer's patients.

Even without massage, aromatherapy appears to be helpful. In studies, essential oils have been used successfully to control compulsive eating, minimize menopausal discomfort, restore sound sleep, ease depression, and boost productivity.

Essential oils are highly concentrated and, therefore, need to be diluted before use. Add just 5 or 6 drops of an essential oil to an ounce of unscented lotion or a carrier oil (such as vegetable oil). Pour about a tablespoon of the mixture into the palm of one hand. Rub your hands together to warm the lotion or oil. Then massage it onto your skin.

You can buy essential oils in bath-and-body shops, most health food stores, and many department stores. Store them in a cool, dark place. And never taste or swallow essential oils: Even small amounts are toxic.

In consultation with the hospital staff, Dr. Field divided the preemies in Isolettes into two groups. One group received gentle massage for 15 minutes three times a day, while the other group did not. The results were dramatic: The babies who were given massages gained 47 percent more weight and went home 6 days sooner than the babies who weren't. "Everyone benefited," she recalls. "The children became healthier faster, and the hospital saved $10,000 per child in preemie care."

Dr. Field's personal interest quickly became her professional passion. She founded the Touch Research Institute at the University of Miami, the nation's leading center for research into the health benefits of massage. "We don't fully understand the biochemistry of touch, but we do know that human beings need it," she explains. "Medicine is just beginning to rediscover the tremendous power of massage."

Good for Body and Mind

Studies at the Touch Research Institute and elsewhere have revealed some amazing information about the health benefits of massage. For starters, massage has shown promise as an excellent immune booster. When a small group of senior volunteers got 10-minute back rubs, they showed significant increases in their levels of immunoglobulin A (IgA), an immune system protein. IgA acts as the body's first line of defense against the common cold.

Then, too, massage has been identified as an effective treatment for scores of common health problems and concerns, ranging from tension headaches and childbirth pain to anxiety, depression, and cancer pain.

One Therapy, Many Styles

Therapeutic massage takes many forms. In the United States, the word *massage* typically refers to some variation of Swedish massage. This particular style was developed about 150 years ago by Peter Ling, a Swede who integrated ancient Asian massage arts with a Western understanding of anatomy and physiology. Swedish massage came to the United States around the turn of the twentieth century and has served as the massage touchstone, so to speak, ever since.

Swedish massage combines long, gliding strokes using the whole hand or the heel of the palm with kneading strokes using the fingers. Depending on the preferences of the giver and the receiver, the strokes vary in pressure. Some people prefer light, feathery strokes that gently push on the major muscle groups. Others enjoy deeper strokes with firm, rolling pressure resembling the kneading of bread.

Less well-known in the United States, but building a loyal following, is shiatsu. In Japanese, the word *shiatsu* means "finger pressure." This style of massage is a Japanese adaptation of acupuncture. Like acupuncture, it's based on the idea that life energy (called *ki* in Japanese, *qi* in Chinese) circulates throughout the body along pathways called meridians. When this energy is blocked, shiatsu experts believe, people become ill. Applying finger pressure at specific points along the meridians frees blocked energy and reestablishes healthy flow.

Shiatsu practitioners must learn two things: where the pressure points are located and how they should be stimulated. Finding the points requires a good shiatsu chart—and lots of practice. The massage technique is relatively easy. It involves moving the thumb or forefinger in a penetrating circular pattern for about 30 seconds. Manipulating the points in this way produces tenderness, tingling, or mild discomfort, but without pain.

How to Give a Good Massage

If you're seriously interested in learning massage, your best bet is to take a class or watch an instructional video. The American Massage Therapy Association (AMTA) can refer you to a massage class in your area. And video stores carry an assortment of instructional massage videos. (For video recommendations or to contact the AMTA, see How to Find What You Need on page 668.)

But to self-treat your everyday aches and pains with massage, you don't need extensive training. Just follow these basic guidelines adapted from the video *Massage Your Mate* by Rebecca Klinger, a licensed massage therapist in New York City.

- ◆ Find a warm, quiet room with no phone.
- ◆ Play soft, soothing music to create a relaxing atmosphere.
- ◆ Wear loose clothing that doesn't restrict movement.
- ◆ Remove eyeglasses and all jewelry.
- ◆ Keep small pillows or rolled-up towels handy, in case you need them for support or cushioning.
- ◆ Relax by breathing deeply.
- ◆ Pour a little oil—any vegetable oil will do—into the palm of one hand. Rub your hands together to warm them and focus healing energy in them. Have a towel close by to blot up any excess oil. (Never pour oil directly on the body part that you're massaging. It's messy, and it feels jarring.)

◆ Begin the massage with light strokes, applying deeper pressure only after the muscles have relaxed and warmed up.

◆ Never apply pressure directly on the eyes, Adam's apple, or kneecaps.

As beneficial as massage can be, it must be used cautiously—if at all—by those with certain medical conditions. Do not give or receive a massage (especially deep-pressure manipulation) if you're acutely ill or feverish or if the pressure feels painful.

For women who are pregnant, light Swedish massage is okay. But it must be administered by a professional who has been trained in massage therapy for moms-to-be.

Even if you aren't able to receive a formal massage—or if you simply prefer not to—you can cultivate many of the same health benefits simply by exchanging touch with those you love. So hug your children or grandchildren. Embrace your friends. Cuddle with your spouse while you watch TV. You'll feel calmer, and you'll be better able to cope with stress.

Chapter 14

Music:
Sounds That
Soothe the Soul

In Greek mythology, Apollo was not only the god of medicine but also the god of music. The Greek philosopher Pythagoras advised daily singing and instrumental music to cleanse the emotions of worry, sorrow, and fear. And in the Bible, young David plucked a harp to soothe the troubled soul of King Saul (who, modern psychologists speculate, probably had depression).

Through the ages, music has played a prominent role in healing. The first scientific study of music as medicine—specifically, as a treatment for insomnia—was published in the *Medical Record* in 1899, just 22 years after Thomas Edison invented the phonograph. But as mainstream medicine grew more scientific, those who practiced it gradually lost interest in music's almost magical hold on the psyche.

Fortunately, music never entirely disappeared from medicine. In 1929, as radio became popular, Duke University Hospital in Durham, North Carolina, made headphones available to all of its patients. During and shortly after World War II, veterans hospitals across the United States used music to improve morale among injured, depressed, and shell-shocked soldiers. Around the same time, dentists became leading proponents of music as medicine, providing headphones that simultaneously relaxed patients and, to some extent, masked the whine of the drills.

Soon music therapy programs were established in the psychology departments of several American universities. And in 1950, the National Association for Music Therapy formed. Today, the United States boasts more than 5,000 certified music therapists. Music therapists also practice in many other countries, including Canada, Great Britain, France, Sweden, and New Zealand.

Despite its widespread acceptance and use, music therapy has remained outside the realm of mainstream medicine. But that's finally beginning to change. Today, the federal Health Care Financing Administration even includes music therapy among the services covered by Medicare.

"If you were to poll physicians at random, they'd likely say that they've never heard of music therapy or, if they have, that it's a fringe thing," says music therapist Bryan Hunter, Ph.D., associate professor at Nazareth College in Rochester, New York. "But among physicians who have worked with good music therapists, you'd find strong support for music therapy."

Melodies to Mend By

Opinions vary as to why music has such a profound effect on humans. At least some of its therapeutic power comes from its ability to trigger the release of endorphins, the powerful opiate-like chemicals produced in the brain that induce euphoria and relieve pain. In fact, researchers have discovered that if they administer drugs that block the production of endorphins, they significantly blunt a person's enjoyment of music, according to David S. Sobel, M.D., director of patient education and health promotion for Kaiser Permanente Northern California, a health maintenance organization.

Music triggers other positive changes, too. It reduces levels of stress hormones such as adrenaline. It has a calming effect on the limbic system, a group of structures within the brain that regulates emotions. And it boosts levels of immunoglobulin A (IgA), the body's first line of defense against colds and other infections.

Of course, music is no cure-all. But it can do some very remarkable things for the body and mind. It has been shown to help heart attack and surgical recovery, chronic-pain management, stroke rehabilitation, Alzheimer's care, and alleviation of depression.

In one study of people who had suffered heart attacks, eighty people—all newly admitted to hospital coronary care units—were divided into three groups. One group listened to a 20-minute audiotape of calming music; another practiced breathing and meditation to invoke a sense of calm, called the relaxation response; and the third received only standard care. The patients in the music and relaxation response groups showed significant reductions in heart rate and levels of stress hormones, compared with the patients in the standard care group. But the folks who listened to music were the least stressed, suggesting that music is even more relaxing than meditation.

Another study showed the effectiveness of using music for management of

Recommended Selections

If you'd like to try a little music therapy for yourself, consider one of the following selections recommended by Janet D. Cook, a music therapist in Austin, Texas.

Classical

Bach–"Air for the G-String"; "Jesu, Joy of Man's Desiring"
Beethoven–"Moonlight Sonata"; "Pastoral Symphony"; "Sonata Pathétique"
Brahms–"Lullaby"
Chopin–"Nocturne in G"
Debussy–"Clair de Lune"
Handel–"Water Music"
Liszt–"Liebenstraum"
Mozart–"Laudate Dominum" from *Solemn Vespers*
Pachelbel–"Canon in D"
Saint-Saëns–"The Swan"
Schubert–"Ave Maria"
Vivaldi–"The Four Seasons"

chronic pain. At the University of Nebraska Medical Center College of Nursing in Omaha, Lani Zimmerman, R.N., Ph.D., associate professor of nursing, gave 40 people with chronic pain a collection of ten music audiotapes. She asked each patient to select one tape that was most relaxing. The patients reported significantly less pain while listening to their tapes. Other studies have shown that music can reduce a hospital patient's need for pain medication by as much as 30 percent.

Music has also been proven beneficial in management of depression. In one study, people with serious depression were separated into three groups. One group received weekly visits from music therapists, who played music and offered instruction in stress management techniques. Another group received weekly phone calls from music therapists and taped music to play independently. The third group received no treatment. All of the patients who listened to music—whether with a therapist or alone—showed significant improvement in mood, compared with the patients who didn't listen to music.

Symphonic
Kitaro–"Silk Road Suite"

Piano
George Winston–"Autumn"; "December"; "Winter into Spring"
Roger Williams–"Nadia's Theme"

Guitar
Will Ackerman–"Childhood and Memories"; "Passages"
Alex de Grassi–"Slow Circle"; "Southern Exposure"

Country
Willie Nelson–"Star Dust"; "Sweet Memories"

Soundtracks
"Born Free"
"Chariots of Fire"
"The Sound of Music"

Music to Your Ears

Studies of music therapy have shown that, in general, soothing, slow-tempo tunes work best for relaxation, stress management, and recovery from illness. But if you're looking to boost your energy level and productivity, or if you want a soundtrack for your workout, choose music that has an upbeat tempo but isn't bombastic.

Most people get the greatest benefit from music that they've selected on their own—no matter what it is, notes music therapist Clare O'Callaghan of the University of Melbourne in Australia. That's because people choose what they like, which helps motivate them and gives them a sense of personal empowerment. If you'd like to give a family member or friend a calming audiotape or CD but you don't know the person's tastes, stick with songs that were popular when he was young. This is the time of life when a person's musical preferences are formed.

Chapter 15

Relationships:
The Bonds That Buoy
Body and Mind

A t Carnegie Mellon University in Pittsburgh, psychologist Sheldon Cohen, Ph.D., devised an interesting experiment to answer a puzzling question: Are people with many social ties more likely or less likely to get sick?

Dr. Cohen polled 276 people between ages 18 and 55 about their social ties. Those ties included their connections to family, friends, coworkers, and neighbors as well as their involvement in social, civic, hobby, and religious organizations.

Once Dr. Cohen had a profile of the volunteers, he gave all of them an equal dose of nose drops containing a live cold virus. After the volunteers were quarantined in hospital rooms for 5 days, Dr. Cohen recorded who had developed colds. He discovered that those with the fewest social ties were the most likely to have become infected. As the number of social ties increased, the rate of infection decreased substantially.

This is just one of a growing number of studies to show that—to paraphrase a popular song—people who need people are the healthiest people in the world. "From the day we are born, social support is essential to our survival," says David Spiegel, M.D., professor of psychiatry and behavioral sciences and director of the Psychosocial Treatment Laboratory at Stanford University School of Medicine. "Humans have a more prolonged period of helplessness and dependency than any other mammal. For years, we rely fully on our parents' physical and social skills."

Social support has guaranteed our survival not only as individuals but also as a species. Thousands of years ago, our ancestors realized that they could better protect themselves against predators—human and animal—by organizing themselves into clans, tribes, villages, cities, and nations. They developed a system of language and symbols that enabled them to communicate with one another and advance the common good. Over time, humans have populated the entire habitable earth—a feat no other species has duplicated.

Even modern-day clichés resonate with the human need and desire to connect with others: "There's strength in numbers." "Two heads are better than one." "One for all, all for one."

Socializing Boosts Disease Defenses

Despite humans' inherently social nature, the health advantages of interpersonal relationships remained virtually unknown until the 1940s. That's when researchers first documented the "marriage bonus": People who are married live longer and have fewer health problems than people who are single, divorced, or widowed. At the time, scientists speculated that spouses might encourage one another to eat better, to break bad health habits (especially smoking and excessive drinking), and to get more timely medical care.

All of these reasons make sense. But another reason for the marriage bonus emerged in the late 1970s, with the advent of psychoneuroimmunology—the study of how emotions influence the immune and nervous systems. Specialists in this field concluded that close social ties enhance the immune system. Just as exercise conditions muscles to handle heavier loads, social interactions condition the immune system to help defend us against illness and to spur healing.

More recent studies have shown that social isolation triggers the release of stress hormones, which not only impede immune function but also raise heart rate, interfere with sugar metabolism, and stimulate feelings of depression and anxiety. "Stress hormones normally ebb and flow," Dr. Spiegel explains. "But when stress becomes chronic, the hormones remain at consistently high levels, impairing the body's ability to heal and stay well."

Having well-developed social bonds helps dam the flood of stress hormones, allowing the body to cope more effectively and heal more efficiently. This helps explain why in Dr. Cohen's study the people with the most social ties were least likely to develop colds.

Everybody Needs Somebody to Lean On

Among the studies substantiating the health value of social bonds, one is considered landmark. In 1974, Leonard Syme, Ph.D., then a professor of epidemiology at the University of California, Berkeley, School of Public Health, and graduate student Lisa Berkman (now a Ph.D. and professor of epidemiology at Yale) unearthed a survey of 6,928 residents of Alameda County, California. The 1965 survey contained detailed information about social ties: marital status, contacts with family and friends, and membership in social, civic, and religious organizations. Dr. Syme and Berkman used the Alameda County death registry to identify who among those polled had died during the intervening 9 years.

Their findings were striking: The more social ties the survey respondents reported, the less likely they were to have died during that 9-year period. The people with the most social ties had one-half the death rate of the people with the fewest social ties.

Since Dr. Syme and Berkman released their findings, dozens of other studies have confirmed that forging and maintaining connections with others provides significant health benefits. Those studies have shown that these benefits include increased longevity and less risk of chronic illness. Survivors of heart attack and people who are recovering from stroke also benefit from more social ties.

Support Groups: A United Front against Illness

Dr. Spiegel once scoffed at the notion that social ties could have health benefits. Then his own research of support groups changed his mind.

Dr. Spiegel theorized that support groups might help people cope with the stress of terminal illness. He invited 86 women with advanced breast cancer to participate in a study. Some of the women met for 90 minutes each week in a support group led by Dr. Spiegel. The rest of the women received standard medical care.

Dr. Spiegel predicted that attending the support group would improve the women's coping abilities, and it did. But it had another effect that he never expected: It extended the women's lives. After 10 years, 83 of the 86 women had died. But those in the support group had survived twice as long—an average of 37 months, compared with an average of 19 months for those receiving standard care.

Support groups number in the millions, according to Edward Madara, director of the American Self-Help Clearinghouse in Denville, New Jersey. They run the gamut from tiny groups that unite people with rare medical problems to the tens of thousands of Alcoholics Anonymous fellowships that hold meetings in virtually every community around the country.

"Support groups reduce isolation," Madara explains. "They're empowering and comforting. They teach practical coping skills. Sometimes they change laws and public perceptions. And usually, they're free."

Support groups turn life wonderfully upside down. They take an illness or another trying experience that usually leaves people feeling isolated and turn it into the sole criterion for membership.

The support that comes from the group goes beyond professional care. "Doctors and psychologists can't be all things to all people," Madara says. "When you sit down with those who have shared your experience—no matter whether it's multiple sclerosis, divorce, or a recent cancer diagnosis—you feel a sense of comfort and closeness that no professional relationship can match." Support groups also encourage participants to help each other, which in turn makes them feel more competent and effective in their daily living.

Anyone in the United States can contact the American Self-Help Clearing-house for referrals to support groups (see How to Find What You Need on page 668 for more information). And if no group exists for the problem that you're dealing with, the Clearinghouse can help you start one.

"We help people launch groups all the time," Madara explains. "Not too long ago, a woman with serious postpartum depression called looking for a support group, but there weren't any. We helped her start one and got her a little publicity in her local newspaper. Now Depression after Delivery has 70 chapters nationwide."

Pets: More Than Just Lap Warmers

More than 100 years ago, pioneering nurse Florence Nightingale said, "A small pet animal is often an excellent companion for the sick." Her words were largely forgotten until 1980, when Erika Friedmann, Ph.D., of the University of Pennsylvania in Philadelphia made an unexpected but important finding: Independent of all other medical and lifestyle factors, men who had experienced heart attacks were more likely to survive if they had pets. In fact, having a pet was a better predictor of heart attack survival than having a supportive family or even having a spouse.

Since Dr. Friedmann's research, many studies have shown that human-pet interactions—playing with a dog, holding a purring cat, even gazing at a fish tank—can be profoundly relaxing and reduce blood pressure as much as some medications. When Warwick Anderson, M.D., of the Baker Medical Research Institute in Prahan, Australia, compared the blood pressure and cholesterol levels of 784 pet owners and 4,957 non–pet owners, he found that the pet owners' readings were significantly lower. And a yearlong study by Judith Siegel, Ph.D., of the University of California, Los Angeles, School of Public Health revealed that pet owners visit their physicians less often than non–pet owners.

Why pets have such profoundly positive effects on their human companions remains something of a mystery. Perhaps pets keep their owners active—after all, dogs must be walked regularly. But cats, birds, fish, and iguanas don't need walking, yet their owners experience the same health benefits as dog owners. So there has to be more to the "pet advantage" than just exercise. Increasingly, researchers believe that pet companionship provides the same immune-enhancing benefits as human companionship.

Of course, some people dislike animals, and some have allergies or other medical conditions that prevent them from keeping animals in their homes. But if you enjoy pets, your relationships with them can be just as health-enhancing as your relationships with other humans. Pets are especially therapeutic for the elderly, who become socially isolated as family members and friends pass away.

Faith: Believing Heals

Another effective antidote to social isolation is religious faith, which often deepens as people grow older and lose other social support. Thomas Oxman, M.D., a psychiatrist at Dartmouth Medical School in Hanover, New Hampshire, polled 232 elderly people—all of whom were scheduled for open-heart surgery—about their lifestyles, including their religious beliefs and activities.

Within 6 months of their surgery, 21 of the patients originally interviewed by Dr. Oxman had died. But many of the patients who survived had something significant in common: They were 3 times more likely to have said that they derived comfort from religious faith. Similarly, survivors were 3 times more likely to have said that although they had little religious faith, they regularly participated in religious social activities such as church suppers and outings and charity work. Those who both had religious faith and participated in religious social activities were 10 times more likely to survive.

In light of the health-promoting effects of companionship, the fact that participating in religious social activities aided survival comes as no surprise. But why did religious faith confer the same benefits?

Faith is a connection to the world—indeed, to the universe—outside ourselves, says David S. Sobel, M.D., director of patient education and health promotion for Kaiser Permanente Northern California, a health maintenance organization. Faith gives meaning to life-threatening events, which is both psychologically and physically calming. Lack of faith makes the same events more stressful—and more likely to cause harm.

Chapter 16

Herbs:
Plants with the
Power to Heal

M ost Americans think that medicinal herbs are a thing of the past. Nothing could be further from the truth.

An estimated 80 percent of the world's population still relies on herbs for treating and preventing disease. In Europe, where physicians have access to the same high-tech treatments that are available in the United States, patients routinely receive "prescriptions" for herbs instead of, or in addition to, pharmaceuticals. And in the United States, an estimated 25 percent of pharmaceuticals continue to be derived from plant sources.

Scientists around the world depend on herbs in developing new, more potent medications. Not long ago, experiments with the Pacific yew tree yielded an extract called taxol, which showed remarkable effectiveness against advanced breast and ovarian cancers—diseases that didn't respond to standard chemotherapy drugs. Today, yew-derived drugs (sold under the brand names Paclitaxel and Taxotere) have become standard treatments for breast and ovarian cancers.

Old Medicine in the New World

Herbs are the common thread that weave through and unite various alternative disciplines. Chinese medicine, Ayurveda (India's traditional healing system), homeopathy, and naturopathy all share a profound commitment to herbal medicine, even though they differ from one another in principle and practice.

The first American settlers brought from the Old World their knowledge of medicine, which at that time still relied on therapeutic herbs. They also learned a good deal about therapeutic herbs from Native Americans.

An Herb Buyers' Guide

Medicinal herbs come in so many different forms that deciding which one to buy can be confusing. Here's a quick summary of the most common forms, so you know what to look for.

Bulk. Bulk herb is raw, dried plant material. It's usually kept in jars or bins in health food stores, and it's sold by the ounce. Bulk herb can be powdered to make capsules or tablets, steeped as teas, or moistened and placed under bandages as poultices. (You can even soak bulk herbs in vodka to make tinctures, but you'll need instructions from an herbal guidebook or herbalist.)

Capsules and tablets. Both contain powdered herb. They store easily and travel well.

Oils. Often called essential oils, these superconcentrated herbal essences are used in aromatherapy. They are intended for external use only and should never be ingested. As little as 1 to 2 teaspoons of some herbal oils can be fatal. For an aromatherapy massage, mix a few drops of oil into an unscented massage lotion.

Teas. Technically hot-water herbal extracts, teas take three forms: beverage teas, infusions, and decoctions. Beverage teas typically steep for a minute or two. Infusions are prepared like teas but steep longer (until the boiling water cools) to draw out more of the plant's healing constituents. Decoctions require simmering the plant material in boiling water for 10 to 20 minutes or soaking it in cold water overnight. Drink infusions and decoctions cool, or reheat them.

Tinctures. These alcohol extracts are highly concentrated. They're packaged in small bottles with eyedropper lids. A few drops of tincture can contain as much healing power as a cup of infusion. Most tinctures go down easier when added to juice or a beverage tea. Tinctures remain potent longer than bulk herbs or tea bags. And their concentration makes them compact—good for traveling or conserving shelf space in medicine cabinets.

15 Herbs to Keep on Hand

In part 3 of this book, you'll find dozens of expert-recommended herbal remedies for an array of common ailments. But the following herbs and herb-containing products make a great starter kit for your home. Most of these preparations are sold in health food stores and some drugstores.

1. Aloe vera to heal minor burns
2. Chamomile to ease indigestion
3. Citronella to repel insects
4. Dill seed to ease indigestion
5. Echinacea to fight infections
6. Feverfew to prevent migraines
7. Garlic as an antibiotic
8. Ginger to prevent motion sickness
9. Goldenseal to fight infections
10. Mint to ease indigestion
11. St. John's wort to beat depression
12. Saw palmetto to combat prostate enlargement
13. Valerian to cure insomnia
14. Willow bark to relieve pain and inflammation
15. Witch hazel to soothe hemorrhoids

Herbs remained a fixture in American medicine until after the Civil War. That's when the medical community experienced a philosophical split between the "regulars"—the forerunners of today's M.D.'s—and the "eclectics," who combined herbal medicine with nutrition (a high-fiber vegetarian diet) and the water-cure movement pioneered in European health spas. Eclectic medicine eventually gave birth to the health food and supplement industries as well as to chiropractic and naturopathy.

Today, the clinic at Bastyr University, the naturopathic medical school in Kenmore, Washington, sees about 25,000 patients a year. But its large pharmacy contains only a handful of pharmaceuticals. Most of its shelves are stocked with Western and Chinese herbal medicines, homeopathic medicines (many of which contain microdoses of medicinal herbs), and nutritional supplements.

Natural Disease-Fighters

Herbs, like all plants, spend their lives anchored to one spot. They can't run away from the insects, fungi, viruses, and bacteria that want to make a meal out of them. So they contain special chemical compounds to keep away the bad guys. Those same compounds give herbs their potent therapeutic powers—and help us humans fight disease.

The scientific literature is filled with studies demonstrating the value of medicinal herbs. But even though many herbs have been proven effective, skeptics may question the reliability of herb dosages. With pharmaceuticals, the argument goes, you know exactly how much of an active ingredient you're getting. With herbs, it's a hit-or-miss proposition, as the amount of active ingredient can vary from one manufacturer to another. Well, yes and no.

Increasingly, medicinal herbs come as standardized extracts. This means that the plant has been painstakingly bred to contain a specific amount of its therapeutic constituents—no more, no less. When the herb is dried or processed into a tincture or tablet, it contains a medicinal dose that can be calculated almost as precisely as those in pharmaceuticals.

Even when herbs are not available as standardized extracts, dose is not as much of an issue as with pharmaceuticals. Pharmaceuticals tend to have a narrow therapeutic range, meaning that if you'd take only a little more than the recommended dose, you'd wind up with enough of an overdose to develop symptoms of toxicity. Commonly used medicinal herbs, on the other hand, have a broad therapeutic range. You usually have to take a good deal more than what's recommended before you'd experience problems.

Of course, there are some potentially hazardous herbs that have narrow therapeutic ranges. But all of the herbs presented in this book are generally regarded as safe when used in the recommended doses.

Chapter 17

Chiropractic: Keeping Your Spine in Line

O f the various alternative healing systems available in the United States, chiropractic is by far the most popular. The more than 50,000 licensed doctors of chiropractic (D.C.'s) make up the nation's third largest medical profession, after M.D.'s and dentists. And they're licensed to practice in every state.

According to a landmark Harvard Medical School survey assessing Americans' use of alternative therapies, 10 percent of the population visits chiropractors at least once a year. People rate chiropractic as their first choice for treating back problems. Overall, it is the second most popular professionally provided alternative therapy—second only to relaxation therapies.

A handful of chiropractors present themselves as primary-care physicians capable of treating the same broad range of conditions as family practice M.D.'s. But the vast majority of chiropractors deal almost exclusively with back problems, joint problems, and muscle aches and pains—what doctors batch together as "musculoskeletal complaints." As many as 90 percent of people who consult chiropractors do so for back pain, neck pain, and headaches (which are often related to muscle tension).

The word *chiropractic* comes from the Greek *cheir*, meaning "hand," and *praxis*, meaning "practice." As a system of treatment, chiropractic is the best example of the mainstreaming of alternative therapies. Chiropractors now serve on the staffs of many hospitals around the country. They've become a fixture in sports medicine—in fact, the U.S. Olympic team has its own chiropractor.

Many M.D.'s are quite familiar with the benefits of chiropractic and willingly refer patients to chiropractors when it seems appropriate. In a study by

Osteopathy: The First Blended Medicine

Osteopathy is a hybrid of mainstream and alternative medicine that has gradually won acceptance from mainstream M.D.'s. Like M.D.'s, doctors of osteopathy (D.O.'s) can prescribe drugs and are eligible to join the American Medical Association. Like chiropractors, some—but not all—osteopaths include manipulation therapies in their practices.

The United States has almost as many licensed osteopaths as licensed chiropractors—about 50,000 of each. An estimated 20 million people consult osteopaths each year. Still, osteopathy remains a mystery to most Americans.

Osteopathy was the brainchild of Andrew Taylor Still, an itinerant country doctor who roamed the Midwest in the years after the Civil War, practicing an eclectic blend of mainstream medicine, folk herbalism, and laying on of hands. Like Palmer, Still viewed spinal manipulation as a complete substitute for drugs. His position earned the wrath of the American Medical Association (AMA). In Still's time, osteopaths were flatly denounced as degenerates. But in addition to riling the AMA, Still managed to stir up antagonism among other osteopaths. A number of them—advocating methods that differed from Still's—opened competing schools that combined training in spinal manipulation with training in other forms of manipulative massage and instruction in conventional medicines.

By 1929, osteopathy had evolved into its present form: a variation of mainstream medicine that includes spinal manipulation. As mentioned earlier, not all osteopaths use spinal manipulation to treat patients. But with the insurgence of alternative therapies—particularly the many styles of bodywork—more osteopaths are using a hands-on approach in their practices.

Daniel L. Blumberg, M.D., of the department of psychiatry at the State University of New York Health Science Center at Syracuse, the majority of primary-care M.D.'s recognized chiropractic as an effective therapy for back pain and said that they would feel comfortable sending patients with back pain to chiropractors for treatment.

From Obscurity to Controversy

Spinal manipulation, which is at the heart of chiropractic, has been an integral part of massage-type therapies since ancient times. The ancient Chinese practiced it. The Greek physician Hippocrates recommended it. And the Greco-Roman physician Galen reported curing hand weakness and numbness by manipulating the seventh cervical vertebra, which is located at the base of the neck.

But the specific type of spinal manipulation used in chiropractic was accidentally discovered in 1895 by Daniel David (D. D.) Palmer of Davenport, Iowa. Palmer ran a fish store, but he practiced laying on of hands—a combination of massage and hypnotherapy—on the side.

In 1899, Palmer opened a chiropractic school in Davenport. (It's still the largest and best-known chiropractic training program in the United States.) He enrolled only a handful of students in the first few years—one of whom was his own son, Bartlett Joshua, better known as B. J.

B. J. Palmer became the chief promoter of chiropractic and an outspoken critic of mainstream medicine. His flamboyance attracted scores more students to his father's school. But his M.D.-bashing rankled the medical establishment. Davenport's mainstream doctors persuaded local authorities to arrest both Palmers. The charge: practicing medicine without a license.

During the 1920s, many chiropractors spent time in jail on similar charges. But prosecutors couldn't find people to testify that they had been harmed by chiropractic. Eventually, the arrests ceased. By the 1930s, states began licensing chiropractors. By 1974, chiropractic was legal in all 50 states, and about 23,000 licensed chiropractors were treating about eight million Americans.

An Unbeatable Treatment for Back Pain

Chiropractic survived decades of hostility from the medical establishment because it had such strong word-of-mouth support as a treatment for back problems. Four of every five Americans experience significant back pain sometime in life. Several studies—some by chiropractors, some by nonchiropractors—have shown that spinal manipulation resolves back pain more quickly, less expensively, and more permanently than conventional therapies.

For instance, British researchers randomly assigned 741 people with back pain to receive either chiropractic care or conventional medical treatment. The participants completed questionnaires about their back pain after 6 weeks, 6 months, and 1, 2, and 3 years. At each interval, those receiving chiropractic care reported greater improvement. Overall, 80 percent of those receiving chiropractic

Safety First

Chiropractic has an excellent safety record. Tens of millions of Americans have undergone chiropractic manipulation, yet only a tiny percentage have experienced serious injuries as a result of the therapy.

Nonetheless, reports have surfaced of people experiencing strokes shortly after receiving chiropractic neck adjustment. The main risk factors for stroke are high blood pressure and a history of ministrokes, which doctors refer to as transient ischemic attacks, or TIAs. Before you receive any treatment from a chiropractor, get yourself checked for high blood pressure. And be sure to tell your chiropractor if you have a history of TIAs, which are characterized by numbness or weakness on one side of the body, slurred speech, difficulty thinking, and sometimes vision disturbances.

If you have any other preexisting medical condition, be sure to inform your doctor that you're considering chiropractic. Also, discuss your condition with your chiropractor before beginning treatment.

care said that it was helpful, compared with 63 percent of those receiving conventional treatment.

Impressed by such studies, in 1994, the federal Agency for Health Care Policy and Research assembled a panel of experts to review research on back care. The panel's report, *Guidelines for Acute Lower-Back Pain*, includes a glowing endorsement of chiropractic care.

Some evidence suggests that chiropractic can successfully treat conditions other than back pain and musculoskeletal problems. These conditions include high blood pressure, migraines, and menstrual cramps. Some researchers have even found that chiropractic adjustment boosts immune function. Almost all of the research has been conducted by chiropractors and published in chiropractic journals, so skeptics may dismiss it as biased. Nonetheless, the results are intriguing.

The "New" Chiropractic

A cornerstone of mainstream medicine's criticism of chiropractic has been that the spinal misalignment that D. D. Palmer postulated (called subluxations) can't been seen on x-rays. Many chiropractors have questioned the concept of subluxations as well. "Positive health changes have never been convincingly correlated with vertebral alignment," notes Daniel Redwood, D.C., a chiropractic physician at Atlantic Chiropractic in Virginia Beach, Virginia. "After an adjustment resulting in dramatic relief from back or headache pain, x-rays rarely show any discernible change in spinal alignment." In addition, a landmark 1994 study found that many people who don't have back pain do have significant spinal misalignment.

According to the current theory, chiropractic works not by realigning vertebrae but by normalizing the motion of the vertebrae as they move against one another. Very subtle changes in the motion of the vertebrae can have a profound impact on the nerves that run through them. One study showed that even the very smallest amount of pressure on the nerve root can decrease electrical transmission through the nerve by as much as 50 percent. These findings make chiropractic seem more like acupuncture. Both therapies seek to free blocked energy within the body, though by different means. And both therapies stimulate the production of endorphins, the body's natural pain relievers.

As acupuncture and other alternative therapies have grown in popularity, most chiropractors have expanded their practices. These days, only 15 percent of chiropractors—the "straights"—limit themselves to spinal manipulation. The remaining 85 percent—the "mixers"—may blend spinal manipulation with Western medicine or with other alternative disciplines such as Chinese herbal medicine, relaxation therapies, and nutritional therapies.

Chapter 18

Homeopathy: Cures Shrouded in Controversy

H omeopathy has the dubious distinction of being the most controversial of the alternative healing systems. It defies the known laws of chemistry, physics, and pharmacology. How and why it works cannot be explained by homeopaths, who swear by it, or mainstream doctors, who mostly swear *at* it.

Although homeopathy is more than 200 years old, only recently have its medicines been subjected to rigorous scientific evaluation. Some studies have shown no effect whatsoever—making them perfect fodder for skeptics. But the naysayers usually fail to mention that many others have shown significant benefits. What's more, homeopathic medicines rarely cause side effects, and they're almost always less expensive than pharmaceuticals.

Despite the mystery surrounding it, homeopathy is definitely worth a closer look. In fact, for several conditions, it may be among your best choices in healing.

Born from a Backlash against Heroic Medicine

Homeopathy developed during the late eighteenth century, a time when little was known about the causes and cures of disease. Physicians treated most conditions with bleeding, powerful laxatives (called cathartics), drugs that caused vomiting (emetics), and mercury, which had evolved from a remedy for syphilis into a veritable cure-all. These therapies were called heroic measures—but the heroism was entirely on the part of the patients, many of whom suffered more from the treatment than from the illness.

Over time, many physicians realized that heroic measures did more harm than good. Among them was a German doctor named Samuel Hahnemann. He became so disgusted with heroic medicine that he closed his practice and worked as a medical translator to better acquaint himself with healing arts from around the world.

Hahnemann was fascinated by some of the treatments that he encountered. In 1790, he began experimenting with cinchona bark, which was the first effective remedy for malaria and, later, the source of the antimalarial drug quinine. He ingested a therapeutic dose of cinchona bark and quickly became cold, achy, anxious, and thirsty—the very symptoms of malaria.

That experience led Hahnemann to develop his Law of Similars. Substances that produce symptoms in healthy people, he proposed, can effectively treat those same symptoms in sick people. In fact, the term *homeopathy* is derived from the Greek for "treatment by similars."

Throughout the rest of his life, Hahnemann tested hundreds of substances, such as salt, copper, onions, and calendula flowers, on himself and cataloged the symptoms they produced. Eventually, he reopened his medical practice and began prescribing homeopathic remedies to his patients. He enjoyed considerable success in Germany and attracted a large following among patients and physicians who, like him, had become fed up with heroic medicine.

Flouting the Medical Establishment

Homeopathy arrived in the United States in the 1830s and quickly won many supporters, including statesman Daniel Webster, oil magnate John D. Rockefeller, psychologist William James, and writer Mark Twain. In an 1890 issue of *Harper's Magazine*, Twain wrote that homeopathy "forced the old school doctor to stir around and learn something of a rational nature about his business."

Despite the glowing endorsements from some of America's most prominent figures, homeopathy stirred controversy from the start. It challenged mainstream medicine's conviction that most diseases are caused by microorganisms, a theory advanced by French chemist Louis Pasteur. Instead, homeopathy suggested that illness is more spiritual in nature, much as Chinese medicine and India's Ayurvedic medicine espoused the idea that illness results from an imbalance of some intangible "life force" within the body.

But what galled mainstream physicians most was Hahnemann's Law of Potentization—the notion that homeopathic substances, when mixed with water and shaken in a certain way, grow stronger as they become more dilute. This flew in the face of a fundamental principle of pharmacology called the dose-response relationship, which says the larger the dose, the greater the effect. Many of the remedies that homeopaths consider "extremely powerful" are actually so dilute that the formulas given to patients actually contain none of the active ingredient. Homeopaths themselves cannot explain how the Law of Potentization works, except to surmise that the water somehow "remembers" the active ingredient and retains that ingredient's healing powers.

Largely because of the Law of Potentization, most of the mainstream medical establishment dismissed homeopathy as nonsense.

But during the past 25 years, homeopathy has enjoyed a modest renaissance. Today, about 9 percent of doctors—some 5,000 M.D.'s—incorporate homeopathy into their practices. Several thousand other health professionals, including dentists, podiatrists, chiropractors, and even veterinarians, use homeopathic medicines as well.

Proof That Homeopathy Works

In the early 1990s, a team of Dutch doctors selected 21 scientifically rigorous studies of homeopathy and analyzed their findings. Fifteen of the studies showed that homeopathic medicines bestow significant health benefits. While the researchers still had questions about how homeopathy works, they concluded that "the evidence presented . . . would probably be sufficient for establishing homeopathy as a regular treatment for certain conditions."

Still, as long as its "mechanics" can't be explained by objective science, homeopathy will likely remain suspect in the eyes of most of mainstream medicine. Over the years, scientific investigation of homeopathy has been scarce. Only since the mid-1980s has mainstream medical literature been publishing a steady trickle of independent studies in support of homeopathy. Research has shown that homeopathic remedies may help a wide variety of health conditions, including hay fever, asthma, flu, and rheumatoid arthritis.

Buying and Using Homeopathic Medicines

Most homeopathic remedies come from the same plants used in traditional herbal medicine. A few are derived from animal sources or from naturally occurring chemical compounds.

Some of the substances used in homeopathic remedies, such as mercury and belladonna, would be poisonous if taken straight, especially in large doses. But when superdiluted, as they are in homeopathy, they're very safe. In fact,

Common Names of Homeopathic Medicines

The tongue-twisting monikers given to homeopathic remedies belie the fact that many of the remedies come from quite ordinary substances—plant parts, animal parts, and naturally occurring chemical compounds. The remedy called Allium cepa, for instance, is really just onion. Bellis perennis is another name for daisy. And Ferrum phosphoricum, or Ferrum phos, is iron phosphate. Each remedy is identified by the Latin name or Latin abbreviation for its active ingredient.

homeopathic remedies rank among the safest treatments around. There have been very few reports of adverse reactions.

In the United States, all homeopathic remedies are sold over the counter. Part 3 of this book will tell you which remedies work for which conditions. For now, here's some basic information that should come in handy when buying and using homeopathic products.

Naming. Homeopathic remedies go by the Latin names or Latin abbreviations of their active ingredients. For example, the remedy Urtica urens comes from the herb stinging nettle, and Chamomilla is derived from chamomile.

Diluting. Homeopaths use two abbreviations to describe a remedy's potency: the decimal, or X, system and the centesimal, or C, system. The X system is more popular in the United States, while the C system is more common in Europe. In both systems, potency is expressed as a number followed by an X or a C—for example, 6X or 12C.

A potency of 1X indicates a 1:10 dilution of the original substance—that is, 1 part of the active ingredient mixed with 10 parts of distilled water. Put another way, the active ingredient is diluted to the point where it retains only $\frac{1}{10}$ of its original strength.

On the label of a homeopathic medicine, the number preceding the X indicates the potency. The higher the number, the greater the level of dilution. A potency of 6X, for example, indicates a 1:1,000,000 dilution of the original substance. (Note that the number preceding the X matches the number of zeros in the dilution.) In the United States, most homeopathic remedies sold for home use have potencies ranging from 3X to 30X.

The C system works in much the same way, except that the number preceding the C equals *half* the number of zeros in the dilution. So a potency of 1C indicates a 1:100 dilution of the original substance, while a potency of 3C indicates a 1:1,000,000 dilution.

Shaking. Homeopathic medicines are not just diluted. They're also shaken vigorously, or "potentized." Homeopaths believe that shaking transfers the essence of a substance to the water in which it's diluted. Homeopathic medicines of 24X (or 12C) potency may not contain even a single molecule of the original substance.

Handling. After a homeopathic medicine is diluted and shaken, a standardized amount of the medicine is placed on a small sugar pellet. A homeopath will instruct you to take a certain number of pellets every so many hours—for example, three pellets every 2 hours.

To work properly, homeopathic remedies should be handled with care. Homeopath Dana Ullman offers this advice.

◆ Keep bottles tightly capped. Store them at room temperature, away from direct sunlight.

◆ Keep bottles away from perfumes, household cleaners, and other strong-smelling chemicals.

◆ Wash your hands before handling homeopathic medicines.

◆ Handle homeopathic medicines as little as possible. Instead of holding the pellets in your hand, shake the recommended number into the bottle cap, then pour them from the bottle cap into your mouth.

◆ Do not leave bottles open. Remove just the number of pellets that you need, then put the cap back on.

◆ When in doubt about dosage, always follow the package directions.

Chapter 19

Chinese Medicine: A Whole New World of Healing

Mention Chinese medicine, and most people think acupuncture. Indeed, if you were to consult a Chinese medical practitioner about a particular health problem, he may suggest acupuncture, which involves the strategic placement of needles at specific points on the body. Acupuncture has been perfected over thousands of years of practice. By itself, it has proved highly effective in the treatment of pain and related conditions.

But Chinese medicine is more than just acupuncture. Oriental medicine doctors usually combine acupuncture with nutritional strategies and a unique kind of herbal medicine. Together, these therapies lay the groundwork for a complex but fascinating healing system that's as different from mainstream medicine as Chinese is from English.

Chinese medicine has attracted a small but ever-growing following in the United States. It provides an alternative for people who want to try a completely different approach to health care. When an oriental medicine doctor treats you, he will follow some generally accepted procedures in the tradition of Chinese medicine. But his diagnosis will take into consideration much more than just your physical symptoms. And his "prescription" will be tailored to you as an individual.

There are two basic assumptions that underlie Chinese medicine's approach to health and healing. First, all things in the universe—living organisms and inanimate objects—are connected to one another. And second, all living organisms are inhabited and animated by an invisible force called *qi* (pronounced "chee").

Advocates of Chinese medicine note that this healing system has endured for thousands of years, holding its own during the rise of Western medicine. In China, most of the country's billion-plus population still depends on Chinese medicine, even as Western medicine becomes more available. In the United States, devotees credit Chinese medicine and, in particular, acupuncture with relieving and even curing all sorts of health problems from asthma and back pain to depression and insomnia. Many of these "success stories" come from people who first tried Western medicine but then turned to Chinese medicine—and got the results they needed.

China's Gift to the Healing Arts

To find the roots of Chinese medicine, you'd have to dig back some 4,500 years. That's when the Fire Emperor Shen Nong first experimented with medicinal herbs. The herbs that he identified were later recorded in the *Shen Nong Ben Cao Jing* (*The Classic Materia Medica of Shen Nong*), which dates from around 200 B.C., according to Kevin V. Ergil, Ph.D., dean of the Pacific Institute of Oriental Medicine in New York City.

Also around 200 B.C., the Yellow Emperor Huang Di wrote the *Nei Jing* (*Yellow Emperor's Inner Classic*). Considered by many Chinese physicians to be required reading, the *Nei Jing* establishes the framework for what would become Chinese medicine.

To understand Chinese medicine, you need to suspend—at least momentarily—your knowledge of the Western definitions of health and disease. Chinese medicine teaches that life is in perpetual flux. "Health," then, refers to an ability to adapt to this state of flux and to the physical and emotional changes that it engenders. "Disease," on the other hand, describes an inability to cope with change, a disruption of resilience.

This philosophy stems from Chinese medicine's fundamental belief in *Tao*, which means "the whole"—the seamless fabric of matter and energy that connects all things in the universe. Tao teaches that all things in the universe depend on one another and influence one another. It views humans as an integral part of nature, and vice versa.

The Chinese believe that Tao consists of two opposite yet complementary phenomena called yin and yang. Within the body, yin and yang manifest as three distinct forces: qi, Blood, and Moisture. (In writings about Chinese medicine, terms such as Blood and Moisture are capitalized to denote their nontraditional usage.) Qi is life energy. Blood is more than the red stuff that flows through your veins and arteries. It regulates all of the body's tissues as well as metabolism, or

Comparing Yin and Yang

Even folks unfamiliar with the principles and practices of Chinese medicine have likely heard of yin and yang. They're the core of Chinese medical philosophy—inseparable but complementary, always keeping each other in balance.

Yin and yang are literally universal. They can be seen in everything that you perceive in the universe, from the planets to the seasons to the various parts of the human body. They're present in tangible qualities like "hard" and "soft" as well as in abstract qualities like "hidden" and "revealed."

The following list highlights yin and yang's respective attributes.

Yin	Yang
UNIVERSAL MACROCOSM	
Moon	Sun
Midnight	Midday
Winter	Summer
Cold	Hot
Wet	Dry
Hidden	Revealed
Hard	Soft
HUMAN MICROCOSM	
Blood	Qi
Feelings, thoughts	Action, expression
Inner body	Body surface
Buildup of tissue	Breakdown of tissue
Weakness	Strength
Emptying	Filling
Decline, death	Growth, birth
Liver, Heart, Spleen	Gallbladder, Small Intestine, Stomach
Lung, Kidney	Large Intestine, Bladder

One Condition, Two Approaches

The following case study helps demonstrate how Western and Chinese medicine follow different paths in the diagnosis and treatment of disease.

Maria developed red welts on her skin. Her M.D. diagnosed her with hives, which mainstream medicine considers an allergic reaction triggered by the release of an excessive amount of a chemical called histamine. The doctor prescribed an antihistamine to suppress the offending chemical's activity.

The antihistamine helped, but it did not cure Maria's hives. It also made her sleepy. Her doctor switched to a nonsedating antihistamine, but it, too, provided only partial relief. Frustrated, Maria decided to try Chinese medicine.

She consulted Harriet Beinfield, L.Ac., a licensed acupuncturist in San Francisco. In response to Beinfield's questions, Maria mentioned that she often felt warm, dry, and thirsty and that she had been plagued for years by frequent bladder infections and canker sores. During the physical exam, Beinfield noticed that Maria had a soft, weak, rapid pulse and a red tongue.

the burning of calories for energy. And Moisture isn't just water and other fluids. Rather, it controls the body's internal environment.

When making diagnoses and crafting treatment regimens, a Chinese medical practitioner considers the status of qi, Blood, and Moisture in the body. He is also alert to other forces that influence qi, Blood, and Moisture. These include the five fundamental elements (Wood, Fire, Earth, Metal, and Water); the five seasons (Spring, Summer, Late Summer, Autumn, and Winter); and the five climates (Wind, Heat, Dampness, Dryness, and Cold).

All three sets of forces also influence the 10 organ networks. In Chinese medicine, the organ networks are not distinct anatomical structures but rather constellations of physical and psychological functions.

Patient-Tailored Treatment

Beyond their different perspectives of health and disease, Chinese medicine and Western medicine espouse different philosophies of diagnosis and

"In Chinese terms," Beinfield explains, "Maria had a Fire imbalance. Her Heart, a Fire organ, was overactive, and its Heat was trying to escape through her skin, causing her welts. Her red tongue, canker sores, thirst, and feeling of warmth provided additional evidence that her Fire qi was out of balance—too much Heat and not enough Moisture."

A Fire imbalance also explained Maria's history of bladder infections: "Fire from the Heart typically descends to the lower body, notably the Kidney," Beinfield says. "An excess of Heat in the Kidney can cause bladder infections."

Beinfield treated Maria with acupuncture along her Heart meridian to cool her Heart Fire and along her Large Intestine meridian to relieve her itching and redirect her Heart Fire out through the digestive tract. Beinfield also prescribed an herbal formula and cooling foods: juicy fruits and vegetables, legumes, and root vegetables with a minimum of hot spices.

Maria took the herbal formula and began eating the cooling foods recommended by Beinfield. This regimen, combined with twice-weekly acupuncture sessions, produced results within 6 weeks. At that point, Maria was nearly free of the hives.

treatment. "Western physicians target germs, but Chinese physicians target forces that are out of balance within the body," explains Efrem Korngold, O.M.D., L.Ac. "Western physicians kill germs, but Chinese physicians reharmonize the currents of qi."

Western and Chinese medicine share two diagnostic tools: the medical history and the physical exam. But Western physicians also utilize an array of high-tech diagnostic equipment. In contrast, Chinese physicians use only their senses—what they see, hear, smell, and feel.

Consider pulse examination, a mainstay of Chinese medical diagnosis. In Western medicine, pulse is the number of times that the heart beats per minute. In Chinese medicine, pulse is a window into the organ networks.

Chinese medicine physicians check the pulse by placing three fingers on a patient's inner wrist. The forefinger feels the pulse closest to the thumb, which corresponds to the Heart and Lung. The middle finger gleans information about the Stomach, Spleen, Gallbladder, and Liver. The ring finger monitors the

How to Use Chinese Herbs

Unlike Western herbs, most of which are readily available in health food stores, Chinese herbs and herbal formulas can be very hard to find. Most of them can be obtained only from Chinese physicians. Actually, that's a good thing, for two reasons. First, you really should see a practitioner anyway so that he can recommend just the right combination of herbs for your symptoms. Second, the few Chinese herbal products that are sold over the counter aren't standardized, so you can't be sure just how potent a product you're getting. Nor can you tell if there are other, possibly toxic ingredients in these products. Contaminants, including lead, have been found in Asian traditional or folk medicines.

If a Chinese physician hands you a prescription for an herb or herbal formula, he'll also likely give you detailed instructions on how to use the formula. For best results, you need to follow those instructions to the letter, just as you would an M.D.'s prescription.

But if the physician provides no special instructions and simply advises you to "make a tea" from the dried herbs, you can use the following recipe: Begin by adding the specified amount of herb to 4 to 6 cups of boiling water. Cover the brew and allow it to simmer for 30 to 60 minutes, or until 1 cup of liquid remains after straining. Then repeat the process, this time using the same amount of herb with 1 less cup of water. Combine the liquids from both simmerings. You should end up with 2 cups of tea.

Unless you're instructed otherwise, that amount of prepared tea can last up to 4 days if divided into ½-cup servings. Just warm up as much as you need to drink and refrigerate the rest.

Kidney, Bladder, and Large and Small Intestines. Experienced Chinese physicians can distinguish up to 32 different pulse patterns.

What's more, where Western medicine treats patients with the same diagnosis similarly, Chinese medicine treats patients individually. "Illnesses may be identical, but the persons suffering them are different," noted eighteenth-century Chinese physician Hsu Ta-ch'un. "Their emotions and stresses are not the same.

If one treats all those who appear to suffer one identical illness with the same therapy, one misses the influences of each individual's qi. Physicians must, therefore, take into account the differences among people and treat each individual's constitution."

Herbs: Healing Essentials

The healing prescriptions that Chinese physicians create for their patients rely heavily on herbal formulas. But these herbs aren't categorized according to their medicinal benefits. Rather, they're classified based on five distinct qualities: Color; Nature (warming, cooling, neutral); Taste (sour, bitter, sweet, bland, spicy, salty); Configuration (shape, texture, moisture); and Property (dispersing, consolidating, purging, tonifying).

Some herbs used in Chinese medicine are also common in traditional Western herbal medicine. Many others are uniquely Chinese and have no English names. These must be identified by their Chinese or Latin names.

While classic Chinese medicine favors individualized herbal formulas, modern Chinese physicians have developed combination formulas that they prescribe for some common ailments. Here are two examples.

Yin Chiao Chieh Tu Pien. This cold remedy (pronounced "yin chow chee dew peein") contains licorice, which soothes a sore throat, and honeysuckle and forsythia, which act as anti-inflammatories.

Yunnan Bai Yao. This formula (pronounced "you-nan bye yow") is often prescribed after an injury or surgery. "I've recommended it to several people who've undergone surgical procedures," Dr. Korngold says. "The surgeons were surprised at how little incisional bruising and swelling the patients experienced."

Acupuncture: An Accidental Discovery

According to legend, an ancient Chinese soldier developed an illness that his physicians could not cure. The soldier was later struck with an arrow in battle, receiving a superficial wound. The wound healed, and oddly, so did his illness.

Intrigued, Chinese medicine doctors began recording the places where stabbing wounds produced improbable healing. Their observations became the basis of acupuncture and its offshoots: acupressure, which uses finger pressure instead of needles; shiatsu, a Japanese massage therapy; and reflexology, acupressure massage of the feet or hands.

Not surprisingly, qi is central to acupuncture. It circulates around the body

Let Your Fingers Do the Working

Have you ever rubbed your temples to relieve a headache? Or gripped your stomach to quiet indigestion? You may not have realized it, but you were practicing a form of the ancient Chinese healing art known as acupressure.

Like acupuncture, acupressure involves the stimulation of specific points around the body. Only instead of needles, practitioners use their fingers and hands. That's what makes acupressure ideal for self-care.

Acupressure and acupuncture use the same points. The points themselves are named for the meridians on which they're located. For instance, Stomach 36 is situated on the Stomach meridian, while Lung 5 appears on the Lung meridian. Most of the points occur in symmetrical pairs. So there's a Stomach 36 on the outside of each leg, and a Lung 5 on the inside of each elbow.

Many of the conditions covered in part 3 of this book recommend acupressure treatment. While the points to be stimulated vary from one condition to another, the general technique remains the same: Apply steady, penetrating pressure with your thumb, finger, or knuckle, depending on where the point is located. In most cases, the middle finger works best since it's longest and strongest. For those points that occur in pairs, you want to press both—one for 3 minutes, then the other for 3 minutes.

How hard should you press? According to acupressure experts, hard enough that it "hurts good." In other words, you should definitely feel pressure, even slight discomfort, but you should stop short of outright pain.

If you try one of the acupressure remedies in part 3 but don't get relief from your symptoms, consider consulting an acupuncturist instead. Often professional needle stimulation works when finger pressure doesn't.

along meandering pathways called meridians, each linked to a particular organ network. Like qi itself, the meridians are invisible and cannot be found by dissection.

Oriental medicine doctors recognize 12 meridians that pass close to the surface of the skin at tender spots called *men*, meaning "gates" but translated as "points." At these spots, insertion of needles strengthens deficient qi or disperses congested qi.

Depending which acupuncture "school" you ascribe to, the number of acupuncture points around the body can range from 360 to 2,000. In practice, most acupuncturists use less than 150. Many of the points have poetic names such as Elegant Mansion or Sea of Tranquillity.

Acupuncture points are plentiful in the ears, hands, and feet, where meridians converge. Some practitioners specialize in performing acupuncture on one specific body part. For example, those who engage in ear acupuncture are called auriculotherapists, while those who focus on the feet or hands are called reflexologists.

Traditional Chinese acupuncturists supplement needling with a heat treatment called moxibustion, which involves burning the medicinal herb moxa (Chinese mugwort). Powdered mugwort is shaped into small cones similar to incense. It may be burned directly on the skin over acupuncture points, on a thin layer of soybean paste on the point, on a slice of gingerroot, or on acupuncture needles themselves.

"Moxibustion is invigorating," Dr. Korngold explains. "It's used to treat conditions involving Cold or deficiency of qi." Some acupuncturists have replaced moxibustion with low-voltage electric current, especially for the treatment of pain.

An enormous number of studies have proven acupuncture to be a remarkably effective alternative therapy for an array of conditions, including osteoarthritis, migraine, nausea, menstrual cramps, and depression. Acupuncture has even been used effectively for the treatment of alcoholism.

What to Expect

A good acupuncturist generally gets results in 6 to 12 sessions. Depending on the severity of the problem, treatment might begin as frequently as once or twice a day. Continued treatment typically takes place once or twice a week, then once or twice a month, with periodic "tune-ups" after that.

Does acupuncture hurt? "Rarely," says acupuncture researcher George A. Ulett, M.D., Ph.D., clinical professor of psychiatry at the University of Missouri School of Medicine. The needles are very fine, and insertion typically feels no worse than a little pinch followed by numbness, warmth, tingling, heaviness, or a dull ache.

Many people who've undergone acupuncture say they experience relaxation, mood elevation, and a dreamy sense of well-being during their treatment sessions. Afterward, some people feel energized, while others feel drowsy. Still others report a transient increase in symptoms. This, Chinese physicians say, is a sign that the body is marshaling its energy to overcome the problem.

Is acupuncture safe? "Very," Dr. Ulett says, "assuming that the practitioner uses sterile needles." His opinion was recently corroborated by Arne Johan Norheim, an acupuncturist at the University of Tromso Medical School in Norway, who searched the world medical literature for reports of harm from acupuncture. The results: 193 mishaps—remarkably few considering the millions of acupuncture treatments each year. The most common adverse effect was infection caused by the use of nonsterile needles. Make sure that your acupuncturist uses sterilized or disposable needles.

Chapter 20

Ayurvedic Medicine: Treating a Person, Not a Disease

In mainstream medicine, doctors often focus on patients' symptoms. Symptoms point to a diagnosis, which in turn dictates a treatment plan.

"Ayurvedic medicine is fundamentally different," explains Deepak Chopra, M.D., creative director and cofounder of the Chopra Center for Well-Being in La Jolla, California, and author of several books that helped introduce Ayurveda in the United States. "Ayurvedic physicians don't just ask, 'What symptoms do you have?' They also delve into who you are." And who you are involves more than your name, age, and occupation. It refers to your constitution, which Ayurvedic physicians believe is a fundamental factor in health and disease.

While Ayurveda has become more popular in the United States, it still isn't widely used. Only a few hundred Ayurvedic physicians have practices in this country. But that may change as interest in Ayurvedic medicine grows and more training programs are established.

A Healing System Steeped in Tradition

The term *Ayurveda* is a combination of two Sanskrit words: *ayus*, meaning "life," and *vid*, meaning "knowledge." According to Scott Gerson, M.D., founder of Ayurvedic Medicine of New York, this alternative healing system dates back some 4,000 years to the Indus River valley in what is now Pakistan.

Ayurvedic medicine has much in common with Chinese medicine. For example, the two share a belief in life energy—called *prana* in the Ayurvedic system, *qi* in the Chinese system. "Life energy" is more than a spark that animates living creatures. It's an overarching cosmic consciousness that connects everything in the universe.

According to Ayurvedic teachings, prana is embodied in earth, water, fire, air, and space (ether)—the five elements that make up all things, including the human body. In Ayurvedic medicine, each of the elements governs specific body parts and functions, with the body itself viewed as a microcosm of the universe, explains Kenneth G. Zysk, Ph.D., assistant professor in the Asian studies department of New York University in New York City.

The element earth influences the body's solid components—bone, skin, nails, and hair. Water controls blood, digestive enzymes, and other bodily fluids. Fire fuels digestion and thinking as well as a number of other bodily processes. Air regulates breathing, the nervous system, and all movement. And space, the most abstract element, governs the cavities within the body—mouth, nose, and respiratory tract.

Each of the five elements also corresponds to one of the five senses. Earth is linked to smell and the nose; water, to taste and the tongue; fire, to sight and the eyes; air, to touch and the skin; and space, to hearing and the ear.

The five elements are constantly interacting with one another and with the "outside" world. Together, they form the three fundamental units of the human body: the seven tissues (dhatus), the three waste products (malas), and the three constitutions (doshas).

◆ The seven dhatus are blood, flesh, fat, bone, marrow, the reproductive organs (sukra), and digested food (rasa).
◆ The three malas are urine, feces, and sweat.
◆ The three doshas are Vata, Pitta, and Kapha.

When the five elements—manifested as the seven tissues, three waste products, and three doshas—are in balance, the body is healthy. When they are out of balance, the body is vulnerable to disease.

Ayurvedic physicians believe that most disease arises from what they call ama, a liquid sludge created by a combination of improperly digested food and imbalance among the digestive enzymes. Ama travels around the body, gravitating toward weak areas as determined by a person's constitution. Ama's effects can be neutralized through dietary changes, which is why Ayurvedic prescriptions often contain detailed instructions about which foods to eat and which to avoid.

Spotlight on Ayurvedic Herbs

Beyond dietary changes, Ayurveda embraces an array of alternative therapies: exercise, especially yoga; stress-management techniques, including meditation and massage; and herbal medicine. Each of these therapies has been the subject of a battery of scientific studies. Perhaps the most intriguing research relevant to Ayurvedic medicine centers on herbal medicine—specifically, on two related Ayurvedic herbal formulas.

Both formulas are called Maharishi Amrit Kalash, or MAK for short. To distinguish them from one another, they have been assigned numbers. MAK-4 contains raw sugar, ghee (clarified butter, a staple in many Ayurvedic remedies), Indian gallnut, Indian gooseberry, Indian pennywort, honey, nutgrass, white sandalwood, butterfly pea, shoeflower, aloewood, licorice, cardamom, cinnamon, cyperus, and turmeric. MAK-5 is made from black musale, heart-leaved moonseed, butterfly pea, licorice, elephant creeper, Indian wild pepper, and three herbs with no English common names (*Gymnema aurentiacum*, *Sphaerantus indicus*, and *Vanda spatulatum*).

MAK-4 and MAK-5 have undergone laboratory testing at the hands of several scientists. These researchers have uncovered evidence that both MAK formulas may provide a number of health benefits. Studies have shown that these formulas—taken separately or together—may help relieve angina, allergies, and the side effects of chemotherapy. And animal studies suggest that MAK-4 might help shrink breast tumors. The MAK formulas have also helped some people improve their eyesight.

As scientists uncover more information about the therapeutic properties of MAK-4 and MAK-5, both formulas may become more widely available. For now, though, they must be obtained from an Ayurvedic practitioner.

Diagnoses and Therapies

In the United States, some Ayurvedic physicians adhere to very traditional Ayurvedic philosophy and practices. Others practice Maharishi Ayurveda, an Americanized discipline created in the 1980s by Maharishi Mahesh Yogi. Traditional and Maharishi Ayurveda are quite similar, with the latter relying a bit more heavily on transcendental meditation.

Regardless of which school they espouse, all Ayurvedic physicians follow pretty much the same protocol for diagnosing disease. They shun most mainstream diagnostic tools in favor of alternative evaluation procedures, such as the following:

Questionnaire. An Ayurvedic physician has each patient complete a simple questionnaire. By evaluating the patient's responses, the physician can determine that person's dominant dosha, or constitution (Vata, Pitta, or Kapha).

What's Your Dosha?

In Ayurvedic medicine, determining a person's constitution, or dosha, is essential to the diagnosis and treatment of disease. There are three doshas: Vata, Pitta, and Kapha. Each of them corresponds to a specific body type and personality, explains Kenneth G. Zysk, Ph.D., assistant professor in the Asian studies department of New York University in New York City. What's more, each dosha has inherent strengths and weaknesses that make a person more susceptible or less susceptible to certain ailments.

If you visit an Ayurvedic physician, you'll be asked to complete a questionnaire that helps identify your dosha. But you may be able to figure out your dosha just by reading the list below. Keep in mind that while some people have characteristics that clearly fit in one dosha, others have traits from two or even all three doshas.

Vata	Pitta	Kapha
PHYSICAL ATTRIBUTES		
Thin	Medium build	Heavyset
Coarse, dry hair	Fine, soft hair	Oily, thick hair
Cool, dry skin	Warm, ruddy skin that perspires easily	Cool, pale, oily skin

Physical examination. Both mainstream and Ayurvedic physicians rely on the physical exam as a diagnostic tool. But an Ayurvedic physician pays particular attention to a patient's skin, nails, tongue, and other physical features. In these features, the practitioner can detect patterns that reveal the influence of each of the three doshas.

Pulse examination. Pulse examination is a subtle art that takes years to master. The physician usually monitors the pulse at the radial artery, located on the inner wrist at the base of the thumb. Certain patterns in the pulse indicate specific imbalances among the doshas. A pulse that resembles the movement of a snake, for example, suggests excessive Vata dosha.

Urine examination. First, the physician examines the color of the urine sample. Pale yellow urine signifies excessive Vata; bright yellow urine, exces-

| Very active | Orderly, efficient | Slow, graceful |
| Eat and sleep at all hours | Don't miss a meal | Eat slowly |

EMOTIONAL ATTRIBUTES

Moody	Intense	Relaxed
Vivacious	Short-tempered	Slow to anger
Imaginative	Intelligent	Affectionate
Enthusiastic	Warm, loving	Forgiving, tolerant
Intuitive	Articulate	Compassionate
Anxious	Perfectionistic	Prone to procrastinate

DOMINANT ELEMENTS

| Air, space | Fire, water | Earth, water |

COMMON HEALTH PROBLEMS

Nervous disorders	Digestive disorders	Obesity
Constipation	Hemorrhoids	Allergies
Cramps	Acne	High cholesterol

sive Pitta; and foamy white urine, excessive Kapha. Next, the physician adds a few drops of sesame oil to the sample and examines it in sunlight, monitoring the dispersal and movement of the oil through the urine. Based on his observations, the physician can detect imbalances among the doshas.

Once they've made a diagnosis, Ayurvedic physicians combine a number of different therapies in a comprehensive treatment program. Those therapies include diet, exercise, meditation, massage, and herbal medicine. In addition, the Ayurvedic physician may recommend various amounts of sun exposure, depending on their patients' dosha profiles.

Chapter 21

Naturopathy: Alternative Medicine's Melting Pot

Mainstream medicine has its drugs and surgery; Chinese medicine, its herbs and acupuncture; Ayurveda, its nutrition and meditation. Each of these healing systems is a collection of individual therapies united by a well-defined philosophy of healing.

But naturopathy is different. "It's more than just a healing system," explains Joseph Pizzorno Jr., N.D., one of America's preeminent naturopaths. "It's a way of life."

Naturopathy espouses a wide-ranging combination of nutrition and supplementation, exercise, stress management, herbal medicine, acupuncture, homeopathy, manipulative therapies, and hot and cold baths. Since so many nondrug therapies fit under the naturopathy umbrella, you're getting a good taste of blended medicine when you visit a naturopath and follow his advice. But the naturopathic approach to healing is so broad and all-encompassing that some critics consider it an alternative smorgasbord with no individual identity.

In fact, naturopathy has a very distinct identity. Its use of multiple alternative therapies serves a single noble goal: to stimulate what the Greek physician Hippocrates, the father of medicine, called *Vis Medicatrix Naturae*—the healing power of nature.

Uncommon Therapies, One Common Goal

The term *naturopathy* was first coined by John Scheel, a New York City physician, in 1895. He later sold the term to Benedict Lust, who applied it to his own unique blend of nondrug therapies. Lust would go on to become the seminal figure in naturopathy.

Around 1895, Lust opened the Health Food Store in New York City, where he sold vegetables, herbs, and homeopathic medicines. (The store's name is the first documented use of the phrase "health food.") The following year, he enrolled in New York's Universal Osteopathic Medical College, and in 1898, he became a licensed osteopath. Lust went on to earn degrees in chiropractic and homeopathy as well as in a discipline then known as eclectic medicine (which was essentially a form of scientifically applied herbalism). In 1919, he founded the American Naturopathic Association to promote his vision of a unified, drug-free approach to healing. Naturopathy espoused the following principles.

◆ Nature is the one and only true healing force. It endows the human body with an inherent restorative power to self-heal.

◆ The physician's job is to teach people that they are their own best healers and to prescribe therapies that strengthen their self-healing powers.

◆ The physician should support people in the elimination of bad habits such as overeating; drinking alcohol, coffee, and tea; staying up late; and "sexual excesses."

◆ The physician should help people develop good habits, which Lust defined as a whole-foods vegetarian diet, regular exercise, adequate rest, a positive mental attitude, and moderation in pursuit of health and wealth.

◆ The physician should encourage his patients to use natural therapies—herbal medicine, homeopathy, osteopathy, chiropractic, massage, and hydrotherapy—to treat and cure illness.

Hydrotherapy: Support for the Water Cure

Many of the alternative disciplines that make up naturopathy have been discussed in previous chapters. While drawing on all of these therapies for healing, a naturopathic doctor may recommend one other as well: hydrotherapy, the water cure advocated a century ago by Benedict Lust.

Anyone who has ever enjoyed an extended soak in the tub knows that a hot bath can be quite relaxing. In fact, hot baths—as well as alternating hot and cold baths—are therapeutic fixtures at hundreds of health spas, where people have retreated for centuries to "take the waters." But hydrotherapy can do more than help you relax.

For centuries, Finnish physicians have prescribed saunas to treat infectious diseases. Native Americans used sweat lodges for the same purpose. And as research shows, such a practice makes sense. Raising the body's temperature in a hot bath or sauna stimulates the immune system and helps discourage disease-causing microorganisms from reproducing. Naturopaths often prescribe hot baths to treat certain types of infections.

In addition, several studies have shown that sweating increases the secretion of certain addictive drugs as well as some toxic metals and chemicals.

Better Health, Naturally

Naturopathy is a good choice for anyone who wants more than mainstream medicine but who feels uncomfortable with the foreignness of alternative therapies. Most naturopathic offices could easily pass for mainstream medical offices. And naturopaths use many of the same tests and diagnostic procedures as M.D.'s. The difference is that when a naturopath hands you a prescription, it's for an herbal formula, a homeopathic remedy, nutritional supplements, a course of acupuncture, or a session of hydrotherapy. It's seldom for any sort of pharmaceutical.

"I'm not opposed to using pharmaceuticals in cases of life-threatening infection or other medical emergencies," Dr. Pizzorno says. "But mainstream medicine uses drugs and surgery as first-line treatments and natural therapies as last resorts. That's backward. For the vast majority of ailments, natural therapies should be the first-line treatments and drugs and surgery the last resorts."

Currently, naturopaths can be licensed to practice in 11 states (Alaska, Arizona, Connecticut, Hawaii, Maine, Montana, New Hampshire, Oregon, Utah, Vermont, and Washington) and four Canadian provinces (British Columbia, Manitoba, Ontario, and Saskatchewan). Criteria for licensure vary from one place to another, but a growing number of states and provinces are adopting a standard test called the Naturopathic Physician Licensing Exam (NPLEX).

Elsewhere, naturopaths practice under other professional credentials—most often as acupuncturists, chiropractors, or clinical nutritionists. As yet, no nationwide certification program exists, but membership in the American Association of Naturopathic Physicians (AANP) comes close. It's open to naturopaths who have completed training at any of the four schools in the United States. (To contact the AANP, see How to Find What You Need on page 668.)

"Keep in mind that different naturopaths have different therapeutic approaches," explains Dr. Pizzorno. "But they're all trained to use the least invasive intervention to achieve the restoration of normal body function."

Chapter 22

Home Remedies: For Minor Ills, You're the Doctor

Home remedies are the treatment of choice for the vast majority of Americans. In a poll of people in the waiting rooms of family practitioners and general internists across the United States, 9 of every 10 said that they had tried to treat their ailments with home care first. They had scheduled appointments with their doctors only when they couldn't get sufficient relief from their symptoms.

A similar survey conducted in England produced nearly identical results: 88 percent of the respondents reported that they had practiced home care before seeing their doctors. In many cases, they had asked relatives or friends what to do for their health problems. And 16 percent said that they had consulted some sort of home medical guide for advice.

Medicine with a Personal Touch

At first, the notion of health-care professionals as last resorts may seem odd. After all, aren't family doctors, chiropractors, naturopaths, and their colleagues the first people we turn to when we need health care? They may be the first *professionals* whom we consult. But before calling them, the vast majority of us try to heal ourselves. And quite often we're successful, using some combination of home remedies. These remedies run the gamut from rest, ice packs, and heating pads to "kitchen cures" such as baking soda and vinegar to lifestyle changes such as quitting smoking and limiting alcohol consumption.

In the broadest sense, *home remedies* are any treatments that you can use on your own, without professional intervention. Many of the therapies presented in this book—including nutrition, supplements, herbs, and exercise—qualify.

But often people think of home remedies as folk remedies, those often quirky treatments that wouldn't seem to have medicinal value but do.

Some of these remedies have been around for centuries. For instance, the idea of eating chicken soup for a cold is attributed to the Egyptian physician Moses Maimonides, who lived some 800 years ago. Others seem to have backed into home remedy status after first being proven scientifically. Probably no one took vitamin C for a cold before Linus Pauling, Ph.D., recommended it in his 1970 book *Vitamin C and the Common Cold*. Now it's among the nation's most popular cold treatments. Millions of people take vitamin C supplements and drink C-rich orange juice at the first sign of a sore throat.

But the vast majority of home remedies have untraceable histories. Often they've been handed down by moms, who learned them from their moms or grandmothers. And they work, though scientists can't always explain why.

Be Your Own Best "Doctor"

While much about their origin and evolution remains unknown, home remedies were long used not by choice but by necessity. For centuries, physicians served only royalty and the very rich. Common people didn't have access to professional care. They were forced to rely almost exclusively on home care.

Today, the trend toward home care is likely to continue, and perhaps even accelerate, as health information becomes more widely available. These days, many people search the Internet to find out what they can do to treat various ills. But long before anyone ever heard of the World Wide Web, books as well as newspapers, magazines, and television were educating the public about health-care issues and breakthroughs. And people used what they learned to take charge of their health and to expand their home-care options.

Another likely reason for the continued popularity of home care is the rise of managed care. To control costs, managed-care programs usually restrict access to specialists as well as to certain treatment and diagnostic procedures. They do this by requiring that all aspects of a patient's treatment be overseen and approved by a primary-care practitioner. Rather than go through that hassle, many people try to treat themselves first.

The line between home care and professional care isn't as clear as it once was. If you read in a magazine that garlic helps control cholesterol, that probably qualifies as a home remedy. But if your doctor suggests that you take garlic, what is it? A prescription or a home remedy?

Actually, it's a little of both. In its own way, it's blended medicine.

Chapter 23

Over-the-Counter Drugs:
Medicines for the Masses

W hat a day you've had. Your head is pounding harder than a bass drummer playing a John Philip Sousa march. So you head for your medicine chest, which you've stocked with an array of pain relievers. You grab a bottle, tap a couple of pills into the palm of your hand, and wash them down with a cup of water. Within a half-hour or so, your headache is history.

Scenes like this one take place in hundreds of thousands of homes across the United States every day. For Americans, over-the-counter (OTC) drugs—that is, drugs available without a prescription—are not just another treatment option. They're a way of life.

Of the approximately 3.5 billion health problems reported by Americans every year, about 2 billion are treated with OTC preparations. These products are often our first choice for conditions ranging from headaches to constipation to athlete's foot.

OTCs are popular, for sure—and many of them work very well. In one survey, researchers asked people to name the last OTC product they had used and to rate its effectiveness. More than 90 percent of the respondents said that they were satisfied enough to use the product again.

According to the American Pharmaceutical Association, OTC sales in the United States have reached $30 billion a year, which works out to more than $100 a year for every man, woman, and child. And these figures will undoubtedly go higher as this country's population gets older. Age brings more aches and pains—and a greater need for OTC pain relievers and other products. Americans over age 65 comprise around 15 percent of the population, but they buy about 33 percent of all OTCs.

Medicinal Herbs: Slipping through the Regulatory Cracks

Overall, federal regulation of drugs—both prescription and over-the-counter (OTC)—has been good for public health. But the regulatory process has been disastrous for medicinal herbs, according to Mark Blumenthal, founder and executive director of the American Botanical Council, an herbal education research organization based in Austin, Texas.

Back in the 1960s, when the Food and Drug Administration (FDA) "grandfathered" approval for OTCs in wide use, herbs had reached a historical low point in American medical history. As a result, very few herbs were grandfathered.

Since then, herbal medicine has become much more popular. But now, under current regulations, a company seeking approval of an herb as an OTC product has to file a "new drug application" with the FDA. Then the company must prove the herb safe and effective through extensive sci-

Less-Than-Noble Beginnings

Until the twentieth century, OTCs were known as patent medicines. The name originated in pre-Colonial England, where pharmacists, or apothecaries, made drugs to order. They did this by using a mortar and pestle to grind herbs into powder form.

In the 1800s, patent medicines were popular throughout the United States, but many of those medicines had a high alcohol content. And some of them also contained opium or morphine, both addictive narcotics. Opium addiction, in particular, was as much of a social problem back then as heroin addiction is today.

By the 1890s, several states had passed laws regulating the narcotic content of patent medicines. But these states had jurisdiction only over products made and consumed within their own borders, a restriction that rendered the laws useless. And in 1905, *Collier's*—the leading magazine of the day—published a series of articles called "The Great American Fraud," written by muckraking journalist Samuel Hopkins Adams. The series was a stinging indictment of the patent medicine industry.

The public fallout from this exposé prompted Congress to pass the Pure

entific study and testing, which can cost tens of millions of dollars.

This process works for prescription drugs because once a drug is approved, the manufacturer gets a patent granting exclusive rights to make and market the drug for many years. In this way, the manufacturer can recoup its initial development and testing costs. "But who would spend millions of dollars to prove that garlic reduces cholesterol or that St. John's wort treats depression?" asks James A. Duke, Ph.D. "Many studies have shown these claims to be true, that these herbs are safe and effective. But no one can own a patent on garlic or St. John's wort. So there's no way to recoup the money invested in the approval process."

Currently, medicinal herbs sold in the United States are classified as food supplements rather than OTCs. In a way, that's a benefit to you, the consumer. It means that you have access to many kinds of herbs. You can consult with an herbalist, naturopath, or other practitioner of alternative medicine, or you can read up on herbs and find out which ones you want to take.

Food and Drug Act of 1906, the federal government's first attempt to regulate the quality of food and drugs. Subsequent amendments to the act created the existing two-tiered drug system, which consists of controlled drugs that require a doctor's prescription and OTCs that anyone can buy.

Once a prescription drug is approved, an OTC version may become available sometime later on. Since 1991, more than 50 prescription drugs—including ibuprofen, naproxen (Aleve), and miconazole (Monistat)—have been reclassified as OTCs. The OTC versions usually aren't as strong as their prescription counterparts, but they work in the same way.

Blended Medicine in a Bottle

Many of the chapters in part 3 of this book recommend taking OTC drugs—and for good reason. These products are safe and effective, in accordance with Food and Drug Administration (FDA) standards. They're convenient to use. They're usually reasonably priced. And they can be used without consulting a health professional.

In their own way, OTCs are a form of blended medicine. Even though these drugs are a cornerstone of mainstream medical treatment, many of them have natural roots. For example, aspirin is derived from the herb willow bark. The decongestant Sudafed takes its name from pseudoephedrine, one of the medicinal compounds in the herb ephedra. Listerine contains thymol, which comes from thyme oil, a traditional infection fighter. And the "pectate" in the diarrhea medicine Kaopectate is pectin, a fiber found in apples.

But don't let an OTC's natural origins—or its widespread availability—trick you into thinking that the drug is absolutely harmless. Every year, hundreds of thousands of Americans use OTCs carelessly and wind up regretting it. According to the American Association of Poison Control Centers in Washington, D.C., pain relievers are the OTC drugs most likely to cause problems if taken improperly. Cough and cold formulas rank second.

Fortunately, the FDA has recognized that not everyone uses drugs as directed. The agency requires drug manufacturers to build a margin of safety into their dosage recommendations. Still, rather than risk any negative effects, you're better off taking an OTC exactly as directed. So carefully read the instructions on the label.

If you're taking prescription drugs or have any known allergies to medications, it's important to look at the OTC drug label in some detail—even if it means reading the fine print. Aspirin, for instance, is contained in many different pain-relief products, and some people are allergic to aspirin. So if you know you're allergic, it's essential to read the label for contents as well as instructions. If you're still in doubt, ask the pharmacist or give your doctor a call.

You can also check with your pharmacist if you're unsure about the appropriate dosage for you. And if the product doesn't seem to work—if your symptoms continue or get worse—consult your physician. You may need a prescription-strength medicine instead.

Chapter 24

Which Therapy Works Best for What?

The new integrated approach to medicine—combining alternative and conventional treatments for the most effective health care—can feel liberating. But it can also be confusing. Which therapy should you choose? How long should you stick with one therapy before moving on to another? Should you try one therapy at a time or several at once?

These questions are moot if you patronize one of the growing number of blended-medicine clinics, which house mainstream doctors and alternative practitioners under one roof. Unfortunately, these medical "department stores" are not yet accessible to all Americans, although more of them are springing up all around the nation.

Most folks must settle for medical "boutiques," in which the professional staff favors one discipline to the exclusion of all others. So patients looking for a solution that lies outside the medical mainstream may find themselves moving from one practitioner to another until they find a therapy that works.

Tips for Finding Your Best Choice in Healing

Choosing from among the many alternative and conventional healing options now available can be difficult. There is no single right way to proceed. But these guidelines can help you find your way through the health-care maze.

Stay well. All of the approaches to self-care described in previous chapters support good health. But the most effective way to stay well is to embrace the health-promoting quartet: Practice good nutrition, get regular moderate exercise, manage stress, and develop your connectedness to others and to the natural world. "These four elements keep your immune system in top condition, so you resist most illnesses and recover quickly from the ones you can't avoid," says Michael Lerner, Ph.D., cofounder of the Commonweal Cancer Help Program, an organization in Bolinas, California, that assists cancer patients.

Practice home care. If you do get sick, proper home care can go a long way toward getting you back on your feet. Most minor ailments respond well to some combination of rest, over-the-counter medications, and self-administered alternative remedies such as herbs, acupressure, and yoga. But use common sense: If your condition does not improve despite a week of home care, or if any symptom worsens, consult a physician promptly.

Call a mainstream M.D. If professional care seems justified, or if your health problem doesn't respond to home care within a week, consult a mainstream physician—ideally one who is open to blending conventional and alternative treatments.

Why a mainstream physician? "Because the first question you want answered is 'Do I have something really serious?'" says Richard Jenkins, M.D., a physician and homeopath in San Francisco. "Mainstream medicine is very good at detecting and treating potentially life-threatening conditions. Starting there is prudent."

What's more, if you have a serious health problem, you'll want to get an accurate diagnosis and start treatment as quickly as possible. A mainstream doctor has the tools to stabilize your condition right away. Later, you can add alternative therapies to speed your recovery and enhance your well-being. Relaxation therapies such as meditation and visualization can be especially helpful since serious illness often causes a lot of stress.

Identify an open-minded doc. To find a mainstream M.D. who's receptive to alternative therapies, start by asking around. You may get helpful leads from family members and friends—or you might make connections through self-help groups or people who share a religious affiliation. Also, many alternative health organizations offer referrals. (You'll find addresses for some of these organizations beginning on page 668.)

Briefly interview prospective doctors over the phone. Mention that you prefer combining mainstream approaches with alternative therapies and see how they react.

Discuss benefits and side effects. If you have a less serious health problem or a health problem that seems to defy diagnosis, you may want to venture outside the medical mainstream and explore other avenues of healing. Before you do, ask your M.D. about the benefits and possible side effects of any mainstream options that he suggests. In addition, ask which alternative therapies might help. Then think about how you would like to proceed.

Once you've decided what to do, explain your plan to your M.D. He should be aware of any other therapies that you're trying, especially if you're taking pharmaceuticals. Besides, you don't gain anything by keeping your doctor in the dark. In fact, many mainstream physicians are curious about the outcomes of alternative therapies.

Keep asking. Sometimes a doctor will say, "There's nothing wrong with you." Many people find this infuriating: "What do you mean there's nothing wrong with me? I'm not imagining my symptoms!"

In most cases, what the doctor actually means is that mainstream diagnostic tests can't find any abnormalities that send up a red flag. Though this is frustrating, it's also good news. It means that standard medical tests aren't showing any life-threatening conditions.

So if your doctor says that there's nothing wrong with you, try not to feel as though you've been dismissed or your sanity has been called into question. Instead, feel free to look elsewhere for answers. Alternative practitioners may not make a conclusive diagnosis either. But they can still offer you options for pain relief, recovery, and healing.

Consult an alternative practitioner. "Mainstream medicine is least effective at treating chronic conditions and vague discomforts that don't fit its criteria of disease," says Deepak Chopra, M.D., creative director and cofounder of the Chopra Center for Well-Being in La Jolla, California. If your health problem fits into the "chronic or vague" category, you can opt to combine mainstream and alternative treatments or to go completely alternative.

Which alternative therapy should you start with? If a mainstream M.D. hasn't given you a diagnosis, you might want to begin by consulting a practitioner of homeopathy, Chinese medicine, Ayurveda, or naturopathy. Because these alternative healing systems have different philosophies of health and disease, one of them may be able to provide a satisfactory diagnosis when mainstream medicine cannot.

Give a treatment a chance to work. How long should you continue with one treatment before you move on to another one? That depends on how long you've had your condition and how much discomfort it's causing. "If you're in severe pain and mainstream medicine doesn't help within a day or two, then by all means try something else," advises Alan P. Brauer, M.D. "But if you have a chronic condition that's persisted for several years, you can give a therapy a few months to work before moving on to something else."

Keep everyone informed. If you change practitioners, be sure to tell your new practitioner about the M.D.'s or practitioners you've already consulted. Also, discuss how well or how poorly each previous therapy worked.

Some people are reluctant to tell their M.D.'s that they've been to alternative practitioners. But Dr. Jenkins urges folks to speak up. "To be effective, your practitioner needs to see the big picture—what's going on with you and everything you've tried," he explains.

Create a health-care team. You're the manager of your health-care team—and every practitioner that you see automatically becomes a member. Check back regularly with those you like, even if they didn't cure you. They may have valuable insights as you pursue other therapies. If you get the best relief from a combination of therapies, urge their respective practitioners to discuss your situation with one another.

Persevere. "No single therapeutic approach provides all of the answers for everyone," says Anne Simons, M.D. "But most therapies have some good answers for some people."

Yes, moving from one practitioner to another can be frustrating. But it's far better than giving up. Because by every measure, your health suffers when you give up: Stress increases and your immune system becomes impaired. So keep trying. Ultimately, your best choice in healing is the approach or combination of approaches that works for you.

PART THREE

Simple Solutions for
Treating
Conditions
from Acne to Yeast Infection

Acne

If you think you're alone in your struggle against adult acne, you may be surprised to learn that some 10 percent of Americans between ages 25 and 44 have the same problem. Most are women, though some men get acne, too.

While acne can be embarrassing, it's seldom serious. The majority of cases respond well to self-care. Combining over-the-counter acne treatments with proven alternative remedies may be your ticket to clear, problem-free skin.

Acne begins in hair follicles that are connected to the sebaceous glands. These glands produce oil, or sebum, which helps keep the skin from drying out. Normally, the oil flows out of the hair follicles and travels through the pores to the surface of the skin. Along the way, it picks up dead skin cells that are constantly sloughing off inside the hair follicles.

This process is disrupted during puberty, when the body's level of male sex hormones called androgens surges higher. Androgens enlarge the sebaceous glands, boosts oil production, makes the walls of hair follicles less flexible, and causes shedding skin cells to clump together. Combine these changes with the bacteria that live inside hair follicles, and conditions are ripe for plugs to form. These plugs, called comedones, block pores and lead to acne.

SIMPLE SOLUTIONS
1. Nutrition
2. Supplements
3. Herbal Medicine
4. Home Remedies
5. Over-the-Counter Drugs
6. Homeopathy
7. Chinese Medicine
8. Ayurvedic Medicine
9. Naturopathy
10. Medical Measures

Once a plug forms, it may get pushed to the surface of the skin, where it protrudes slightly. This is what's known as a blackhead. The dark color of a blackhead comes not from dirt but rather from skin pigment that gets mixed into the plug as it travels to the surface. Usually, a blackhead does not become a full-fledged pimple.

If a plug doesn't move to the surface of the skin but instead continues to grow inside a hair follicle, it can rupture the follicle wall. Then the oil, dead skin cells, and bacteria that made up the plug spill into the tissue around the follicle, causing a minor infection. In response, infection-fighting white blood cells rush to the scene. Their battle against the invading bacteria produces a pimple.

Pimples take three basic forms: Pustules are the classic whiteheads. Papules are red bumps that remain bumps—they don't turn into whiteheads. Nodules are cysts that form on the surface of the skin. These can cause scarring.

Pimples and blackheads seem to prefer facial skin, which has the most sebaceous glands. But they can also appear on the chest and back, where the skin has quite a few of those oil-producing glands, says Nicholas J. Lowe, M.D., clinical professor of dermatology at the University of California, Los Angeles, School of Medicine.

Some 85 percent of young people between ages 12 and 25 experience acne. Most outgrow the condition over time, as their bodies adjust to the higher levels of androgens. But if your acne has lingered well into adulthood, it doesn't mean that you have even more androgens than everyone else. Rather, you may be extrasensitive to these hormones.

There's also the possibility that some other factor is putting you at risk. In women, the hormonal fluctuations that occur during the menstrual cycle and pregnancy can trigger breakouts. So can taking oral contraceptives or postmenopausal hormone-replacement therapy. Other contributing factors include stress, sunlight, cosmetics, and some medications. Facial irritation can also be a problem—for instance, from holding the phone next to your face all day.

No matter what the cause of acne, the treatment remains pretty much the same. Mainstream medicine offers an array of over-the-counter and prescription medicines that do a good job of clearing skin quickly. But if you want to enhance the effectiveness of whatever medication you're using, or if you've tried a number of medications without success, consider adding a blend of natural and alternative remedies to your skin-care regimen.

BEST CHOICES

Nutrition

Partake of more fiber. Several population studies suggest that eating more fiber and less meat and processed foods can help keep your complexion clear.

There's no guarantee that eating more fiber will improve your complexion. But you have plenty of other health reasons to increase your fiber intake. So start replacing animal-derived and processed foods with plenty of whole grains, legumes, fruits, and vegetables. If this dietary change also helps control acne, so much the better.

Keep an eye on iodine. Large doses of iodine can aggravate acne, according to Joseph Pizzorno Jr., N.D. We Americans get most of our iodine from iodized salt. Cutting back on salt-laden foods—especially snack foods like potato chips, crackers, and pretzels—may help control breakouts. Other high-iodine foods include beef liver, turkey, asparagus, broccoli, and white onions.

Supplements

Zap breakouts with zinc. About a dozen studies have analyzed zinc supplementation as an acne treatment. Most suggest that zinc has significant benefit. In one study, people who took 135 milligrams of zinc every day for 12 weeks saw 85 percent of their blemishes disappear.

Zinc works by reducing blood levels of the male sex hormone dihydrotestosterone (DHT). DHT is believed to trigger even more breakouts than other androgens. Dr. Pizzorno suggests taking 50 milligrams of zinc a day until your blemishes clear up. But check with your doctor first since zinc dosages over 30 milligrams should only be taken under medical supervision.

Chocolate Gets the All Clear

Chocolate has ong been blamed for acne. "The chocolate myth has been very persistent," says Alan P. Brauer, M.D. "After all these years, I still hear it."

In fact, the chocolate myth was debunked about a half-century ago. Back then, Albert M. Kligman, M.D., professor of dermatology at the University of Pennsylvania in Philadelphia, gave a group of teens either real chocolate bars or "placebo" bars that only tasted like chocolate. Later, Dr. Kligman photographed the teens' faces and counted the blemishes that had developed. The teens who had eaten the placebo bars got virtually the same number of blemishes as the teens who had eaten the real chocolate.

Herbal Medicine

Become acne-free with tea tree. When the British explorer James Cook first arrived in Australia in 1777, he found the native aborigines treating skin infections with the crushed leaves of the tea tree. As modern science has discovered, the oil released by crushing tea tree leaves is a powerful antiseptic that can help battle acne.

Tea tree oil is available in most health food stores and some drugstores. Read labels and choose a product that contains 100 percent pure oil, advises Andrew T. Weil, M.D., director of the program in integrative medicine at the University of Arizona College of Medicine in Tucson.

Tea tree oil is intended for topical use only. It should never be ingested. And if it irritates your skin, stop using it.

Home Remedies

Poke prudently. Generally, dermatologists discourage squeezing blackheads and popping whiteheads. These practices have long been suspected of aggravating acne and increasing the likelihood of scarring. "But everyone squeezes their pimples," says Alan P. Brauer, M.D. "Saying 'don't do it' is ridiculous. Just do it gently. Wash your hands first, and maybe dab the blemish with rubbing alcohol before and after to keep it disinfected."

Wash gently. Excessive scrubbing with harsh cleansers does little to clear up acne. Worse, it may dry, chap, and irritate your skin, leaving your skin more vulnerable to the side effects of topical acne treatments.

Instead, wash your face twice daily with a mild soap such as Ivory, advises Anne Simons, M.D. Choose a bar that doesn't contain moisturizing oils, which can clog your pores. There's no need to spend money on expensive acne soaps. These aren't particularly effective anyway because you wash off the medication as soon as you rinse your skin.

Use minimal makeup. Many cosmetics manufacturers have developed products that they say won't contribute to acne. Even so, women with especially sensitive skin may get blemishes when using certain cosmetics. If you're a woman who's prone to breakouts, your best bet is to wear as little makeup as possible. Read labels and choose products that are water-based rather than oil-based. You may have to experiment with different brands until you find some that don't provoke pimples.

Learn not to lean. Avoid resting your cheek or chin on your hand, which can irritate your skin enough to trigger a breakout. For the same reason, try not to cradle your telephone receiver between your head and shoulder.

Over-the-Counter Drugs

Pick the best product for you. No less than 50 over-the-counter acne treatments are currently on the market. If you were to compare their labels, you'd notice that all of these products have one of four active ingredients: benzoyl peroxide, salicylic acid, sulfur, or sulfur-resorcinol. Benzoyl peroxide works by opening pores and killing the bacteria that contribute to acne. The other three ingredients break down the plugs that lead to blackheads and pimples.

As of now, all four active ingredients have been deemed safe by the Food and Drug Administration (FDA). But reports that benzoyl peroxide might promote tumor growth have prompted the FDA to investigate the chemical compound further.

No one acne treatment works the same for everyone. For this reason, the American Pharmaceutical Association suggests that you try several different products and see which one gives you the best results. Always follow the package directions for proper use. If you develop redness, irritation, or a rash from a particular product, stop using it immediately.

OTHER GOOD CHOICES

Homeopathy

Fight pimples from the inside out. Several different homeopathic medicines have proved effective in clearing up acne, according to homeopath Dana Ullman. He recommends Silicea for whiteheads, Hepar sulfuris for pimples that are painful to touch, Kali muriaticum for pimples that produce thick white pus, and Graphites for pimples that produce yellowish pus. To find out which of these medicines would work best for you, consult a homeopath.

Chinese Medicine

Cool off, dry out. Chinese medicine attributes acne to excess Heat, which contributes to skin inflammation and infection, and excess Dampness, which produces the pus inside pimples. Acne and other skin problems also are closely linked to the Lung and Large Intestine organ networks, according to Efrem Korngold, O.M.D., L.Ac.

The typical Chinese recommendation for acne involves cooling Heat, drying Dampness, and supporting the Lung and Large Intestine. Dr. Korngold recommends eating more cooling foods such as raw fruits and vegetables and avoiding heat-generating foods such as spices, meats, and anything fatty or greasy. He also prescribes herbs that cool Heat and dry Dampness. These include sarsaparilla, honeysuckle, forsythia, rhubarb, and sophora. To find out which of these herbs would help you most, consult an oriental medicine doctor.

Target the large intestine. The United Nations World Health Organization endorses acupuncture as a treatment for acne. If you're interested in acupuncture, you need to consult an acupuncturist. But for a self-care alternative, try acupressure. Simply apply steady, penetrating finger pressure to each of the following points for 3 minutes.

◆ Large Intestine 11, located at the outer end of your elbow crease on the thumb side

◆ Large Intestine 4, located on the back of your hand where the bones of your thumb and index finger meet

Ayurvedic Medicine

Gravitate toward gugulipid. An extract of the Indian mukul myrrh tree, gugulipid—sometimes called guggul—appears to heal acne. In one study, Indian researchers gave 30 people with moderate to severe acne gugulipid three times a day for 6 weeks. Three-quarters of the study participants got either "good" or "excellent" results from the herb. If you want to try gugulipid for yourself, you'll need to consult an Ayurvedic physician.

Naturopathy

Apply heat to unplug pores. Warm water can help open your pores, allowing oil and dead skin cells to flow out more freely. Dr. Weil suggests applying a comfortably hot compress to the affected skin three or so times a day. Be aware, though, that high humidity can actually aggravate acne in some people. If your blemishes seem to be getting worse instead of better, stop using the compresses.

MEDICAL MEASURES

For an especially severe or stubborn case of acne, you may need a prescription acne treatment to clear up your skin. Dermatologists may recommend benzoyl peroxide gels or topical retinoids such as tretinoin (Retin-A) and adapalene (Differin). Other prescription drugs include isotretinoin (Accutane), antibiotics, alpha hydroxy acids, azelaic acid (Azelex), and triphasic oral contraceptives.

RED FLAGS

If you experience a sudden eruption of severe acne, consult a doctor promptly. It may signal a potentially serious medical condition that has affected your body's hormone production.

Also, see your doctor if your blemishes look like welts and the surrounding skin appears red and feels hot to the touch. This form of acne, called cystic acne, requires professional treatment.

Asthma

For some people, asthma symptoms are unmistakable—like trying to suck air through a straw, they say. But not everyone experiences the severe wheezing that's considered the hallmark of the disease. In fact, one of the most common symptoms is persistent coughing at night.

Despite the misconceptions, folks seem to recognize the seriousness of asthma. And that's important, because more and more Americans are being diagnosed with the condition. In 1982, 3.5 percent of the population had asthma. Today, the figure stands at 5.6 percent.

For years, doctors attributed asthma to the sudden narrowing of the bronchial tubes, the airways that lead into the lungs. This phenomenon, called bronchoconstriction, hampers your ability to move air into and out of your lungs.

SIMPLE SOLUTIONS
1. Supplements
2. Exercise
3. Yoga
4. Visualization
5. Chinese Medicine
6. Home Remedies
7. Qigong
8. Bodywork
9. Homeopathy
10. Medical Measures

Why the bronchial tubes narrow remained something of a mystery until the mid-1980s. That's when scientists realized that the airways of people with asthma become inflamed. The inflammation leads to bronchoconstriction, which in turn triggers asthma symptoms.

Based on this new information, scientists turned their attention to figuring out what causes the airways to become inflamed. They have already identified a number of factors—and the list may get longer. Among the most common culprits are inhalant allergies—caused by airborne substances such as pollens, molds, and pet dander—and occupational exposures to certain chemicals. Other potential irritants are cigarette smoke, air pollution, cold weather, strenuous exercise, and sensitivities to chemicals such as food preservatives and aspirin and medications. Colds, flu, and sinus infections can aggravate asthma—and some women are more prone to asthma during their menstrual cycles.

Because menstruation is a fact of life for women, little can be done to prevent menstruation-related asthma attacks. But many other triggers can be avoided. That's what doctors recommend to reduce the frequency of asthma flare-ups.

Mainstream M.D.'s also prescribe anti-inflammatories and bronchodilators—drugs that open narrowed bronchial tubes—to help control asthma symptoms. "In my experience, these medications help, but they're not *the* answer," says Richard Firshein, D.O., assistant professor of family medicine at the New York College of Osteopathic Medicine. "In managing my own asthma, I've had tremendous success with a comprehensive program that includes drugs as well as alternative approaches. The same goes for my patients. Within 6 weeks of beginning treatment, 95 percent of them are able to cut back on their medications. About 60 percent reduce their dosages by half."

Of course, you should never stop taking any asthma medication or change your dosage without your doctor's okay. That said, the following remedies may help reduce the frequency and severity of your asthma attacks.

BEST CHOICES

Supplements

Breathe easier with C. When Leonard Bielory, M.D., an immunologist at the UMDNJ—New Jersey Medical School in Newark, reviewed dozens of studies of asthma and vitamin C, he confirmed what advocates of nutritional medicine have said for years. His conclusion: The lower your vitamin C level, the more likely you are to experience asthma and other respiratory problems. But as your vitamin C intake increases, asthma subsides.

In testing the vitamin and mineral status of his asthma patients, Dr. Firshein has found that quite a few are deficient in vitamin C as well as the other antioxidant nutrients. He suggests that adults with asthma take 1,000 milligrams of vitamin C every day, along with 400 international units (IU) of vitamin E and 10,000 IU of beta-carotene.

Add magnesium to the mix. At Nottingham City Hospital in England, John Britton, M.D., performed lung function tests on 2,633 adults. The participants also completed a questionnaire about their eating habits, which Dr. Britton used to evaluate their magnesium intakes. Based on the results of the lung function tests and the dietary surveys, he concluded that the people with the lowest magnesium intakes were most likely to have asthma.

Taking his findings one step further, Dr. Britton instructed those volunteers with low magnesium intakes to eat more magnesium-rich foods—primarily whole grains, nuts, seafood, soy products, and low-fat dairy products. Over time, the group showed improvement in their lung function.

Dr. Firshein has also found that many of his asthma patients run low on magnesium. He suggests taking 500 milligrams of the mineral a day, in addition to eating more magnesium-rich foods.

Exercise

Give yourself a break—or two. Dr. Firshein advises everyone with asthma to engage in regular moderate exercise. "It strengthens the lungs, which helps prevent asthma symptoms," he explains. He prefers what he calls pulsed exercise—brief workouts with rest periods in between. The breaks help prevent exercise-induced asthma attacks. Dr. Firshein's exercise of choice is tennis, but he also swims and takes aerobics classes.

Be the early bird. The concentration of air pollutants tends to rise from morning to early evening, then falls at night. So if you exercise outdoors, try to schedule your workouts for the A.M. Choose routes far away from traffic and automobile exhaust. If that isn't possible, consider joining a health club, so you can exercise indoors.

Yoga

Bend to break away from symptoms. The combination of deep, rhythmic breathing and slow, gentle stretching makes yoga an ideal activity for people with asthma. Indeed, many studies have proven yoga to be an effective asthma therapy.

In one such study involving 106 adults with asthma, half of the participants received standard treatment, while the rest received 2 weeks of yoga training. Afterward, they were encouraged to continue practicing on their own. Four years later, the people who had engaged in regular yoga sessions reported improved lung function, fewer asthma attacks, and milder symptoms than the people who hadn't learned yoga. They had also reduced their reliance on asthma medications.

Visualization

Envision your airways opening. "Visualization is a powerful asthma therapy," affirms psychologist David Bresler, Ph.D., L.Ac., associate clinical professor of anesthesiology and licensed acupuncturist at the University of California, Los Angeles, School of Medicine. "It can help many people, especially children, reduce or eliminate their need for asthma drugs."

If you want to use visualization as part of your asthma-management program, Gerald N. Epstein, M.D., director of the Academy of Integrative Medicine and Mental Imagery in New York City, suggests practicing the following exercise: Close your eyes. Take three slow, deep breaths. Envision yourself in a pine forest. Stand next to a pine tree and inhale its aromatic fragrance. As you exhale, sense your breath traveling down through your body and exiting through the soles of your feet. See your breath as gray smoke that becomes buried deep in the earth. Open your eyes.

Chinese Medicine

Get to the points. "In Chinese medicine, asthma represents the stagnation of qi, or life energy, in the lungs," says Efrem Korngold, O.M.D., L.Ac. "Treatment involves dispersing qi to eliminate stagnation." One way to do this is with acupuncture. In fact, acupuncture works so well as an asthma therapy that even the United Nations World Health Organization recommends it.

During a treatment session, an acupuncturist inserts needles at several specific locations around the body. If you prefer, you can try stimulating these points yourself with acupressure. Simply apply steady, penetrating finger pressure to each of the following points for 3 minutes.

◆ Lung 7, located on the thumb side of your inner forearm, two thumb-widths from the wrist crease

◆ Pericardium 6, located on the midline of your inner arm, two thumb-widths above the wrist crease

◆ Stomach 36, located four finger-widths below your kneecap and one finger-width toward the outside of your shinbone

◆ Liver 3, situated on top of your foot in the webbing between your big toe and second toe

The Dos and Don'ts of a Lung-Friendly Diet

Could the foods you eat aggravate your asthma? Absolutely, says Richard Firshein, D.O., assistant professor of family medicine at the New York College of Osteopathic Medicine. And he speaks from first-hand experience.

Because Dr. Firshein has asthma himself, he wanted to find out whether dietary changes could help him manage his condition. So he followed a very rigorous elimination diet to identify the foods to which he was sensitive. Dr. Firshein was able to control the frequency and severity of his asthma attacks.

Dr. Firshein has compiled the following list of dietary do's and don'ts for people with asthma.

◆ Do eat fruits and vegetables. Most contain the antioxidants vitamin C and beta-carotene, which help control asthma as well as allergies.

◆ Do eat foods rich in magnesium. Good sources include whole grains, seafood, and low-fat dairy products.

◆ Do eat foods high in vitamin E: olive oil, wheat germ, sunflower seeds, and soybeans.

Home Remedies

Go with the flow. The phrase *peak flow* refers to the total volume of air that you're able to exhale in one breath. Peak flow decreases shortly before an asthma attack. So by regularly monitoring your peak flow, you know in advance when symptoms are going to strike—and you have time to take steps to prevent them.

A peak flow monitor is easy to operate. It has two basic components: a tube similar to the one at the center of a roll of paper towels and a gauge. You blow into one end of the tube, and the gauge measures the force of your exhalation.

Peak flow monitors are available from asthma specialists as well as from medical supply houses and catalogs. If you have questions about the monitor's operation, ask your doctor.

Breathe from your belly. If you have trouble getting air into your lungs,

◆ Do eat fish, especially oily cold-water species such as salmon, tuna, and mackerel. Studies have shown that fish oils can help reduce airway inflammation.

◆ Do eat whole grains.

◆ Do bake, broil, steam, and sauté foods.

◆ Do experiment with exotic grains such as millet, kasha (buckwheat), quinoa, and amaranth. Try hot cereals made with whole-grain brown rice, whole buckwheat, or whole oats.

◆ Don't eat junk foods. Research has shown that children with asthma who eat the most sugary junk foods have the most asthma attacks.

◆ Don't eat a diet heavy in saturated fats and trans fatty acids. Minimize your consumption of meats, whole-milk dairy products, margarine, fried foods, commercial popcorn, and most commercial baked goods.

◆ Don't eat foods made with unsaturated vegetable oils such as corn and safflower.

◆ Don't eat smoked, cured, barbecued, and grilled foods.

you understandably feel anxious. But this anxiety contributes to rapid, shallow breathing, which can lead to an asthma attack. It's a vicious circle.

To break the circle, Dr. Firshein recommends regular practice of a technique called belly breathing. "Most people think that breathing is automatic," he notes. "Few know that there's a right and wrong way to do it. Belly breathing helps condition the lungs and diaphragm to prevent asthma attacks."

To try belly breathing, lie on your back and place a book on your abdomen. As you inhale and exhale, your abdomen should expand and contract enough to move the book up and down several inches. Practice this exercise for 5 minutes three or four times a day.

Decorate with potted plants. While studying how to freshen the air inside spaceships, NASA scientists discovered that ferns clear out formaldehyde and other airborne pollutants. So fill your home and office with ferns and other environmentally friendly plants, including areca palm, weeping fig, peace lily, corn plant, and philodendron.

Learn to spurn heartburn. To prevent nighttime heartburn and the asthma symptoms that it triggers, avoid eating or drinking anything within 3 hours of bedtime. Also, sleep with your head elevated, suggests Anne Simons, M.D. You can do this by using extra pillows or by propping up your headboard on bricks or wood blocks.

Kick-start with caffeine. According to pharmacists Joe Graedon and Teresa Graedon, Ph.D., coauthors of *The People's Pharmacy* books, coffee can serve as a bronchodilator in a pinch. The caffeine in coffee is chemically related to the bronchodilator theophylline, once a mainstay of asthma therapy. If you're not a fan of coffee, you can get a shot of caffeine by sipping black tea or most any cola.

OTHER GOOD CHOICES

Qigong

Turn away from symptoms. At Life College in Marietta, Georgia, sports medicine researchers measured the respiratory efficiency of 10 people before the group learned a 20-minute qigong routine. After performing the routine, the participants had their respiratory efficiency measured again. It improved by an average of 20 percent, suggesting that qigong may help prevent asthma attacks.

Bodywork

Consult a Trager work practitioner. For one study, physical therapists enrolled people with asthma in a 2-week course on Trager psychophysical integration, a gentle movement-based form of bodywork. Before-and-after tests showed that Trager work significantly improved the participants' lung functions.

Homeopathy

Give triggers a taste of their own medicine. Researchers in Glasgow, Scotland, recruited 28 volunteers with asthma—most of whom also had allergies to dust mites. Some of the volunteers received homeopathic medicines specific to their individual symptoms, while the rest received a placebo (a fake pill).

Everyone continued their usual treatment programs. Within a week, the group given homeopathic preparations reported significantly greater relief from their asthma symptoms.

According to homeopath Dana Ullman, a number of homeopathic medicines help reduce the frequency and severity of asthma attacks. He often prescribes Aconitum, Arsenicum album, Ipecacuanha, Natrum sulfuricum, Pulsatilla, or Spongia to his asthma patients. To find out which of these medicines would work best for you, consult a homeopath.

MEDICAL MEASURES

Pharmaceutical companies have developed a dizzying array of asthma medications. Most of these drugs fall into one of three categories: bronchodilators, anti-inflammatories, or leukotriene modifiers.

These drugs can be taken either orally or as puffs of aerosol spray from an inhaler. Most physicians prefer inhalers because they deliver the medication directly to the respiratory tract, which minimizes side effects. "The problem is that too many doctors simply hand out inhalers without explaining how to use them," Dr. Firshein says. "About half the people who come to me for treatment aren't using their inhalers properly."

Perhaps the most common mistake is putting the inhaler inside the mouth. It should be held an inch away from the lips to give the particles of medication room to separate. Then the particles can travel deep into the lungs. If you use an inhaler, Dr. Firshein recommends having it fitted with a spacer. The spacer is a small tube that attaches to the mouthpiece of the inhaler. The spray hangs like a cloud inside the spacer, giving you more time to inhale and absorb the vapor—and increasing the effectiveness of the medication.

Back Pain

After colds and flu, back pain ranks as the leading reason for days lost from work and school. Between medical care and lost productivity, back pain costs the nation about $24 billion a year.

But that figure may soon start to decline, as more and more people discover that a blended approach to treatment can heal their backs faster and often less expensively than the drugs-or-surgery route advocated by mainstream medicine.

The trouble starts in your spine, which consists of 33 doughnut-shaped bones called vertebrae that are stacked on top of each other to form the subtle S-curve of your spine. Sandwiched between most of the vertebrae are flexible cartilage disks, which provide cushioning.

The alternating bone-cartilage construction gives your spine remarkable flexibility. But unfortunately, that construction also invites injury. The most vulnerable area is your lower back.

SIMPLE SOLUTIONS
1. Exercise
2. Tai Chi
3. Yoga
4. Relaxation Therapies
5. Herbal Medicine
6. Chiropractic
7. Home Remedies
8. OTC Drugs
9. Homeopathy
10. Chinese Medicine
11. Medical Measures

Since most of your body weight lies in front of your spine, your vertebrae are constantly being pulled forward and out of alignment. Other factors can contribute to vertebral strain, including overweight, injury, and everyday wear and tear.

Vertebral misalignment is just one of several structural problems that may contribute to back pain. Structural problems are quite common, primarily because of the spine's complex construction. With so many different parts, a lot can go wrong with the disks, muscles, and nerves.

Until recently, experts believed that structural problems were the source of all back pain. Now they know that's not the case. In fact, a landmark 1994 study found that many people have significant vertebral misalignment, bulging disks, even ruptured disks—yet never experience back pain. Conversely, you may sud-

Sciatica: A Real Pain in the You-Know-Where

As its name suggests, sciatica occurs because of a problem with the sciatic nerve. This nerve is the largest of six that emerge from the spine in your lower back. From there, it branches off down either leg.

If the sciatic nerve becomes pinched or pressed in any way, it causes back or leg pain. The pressure may result from vertebral misalignment or a bulging disk. Or it may occur for no apparent reason.

Sciatic pain usually affects only one side of your body. It may start in your buttock, then run through your hip and leg all the way down to your foot.

Men seem more prone to sciatica than women, possibly because men usually carry their wallets in their hip pockets. Sitting on your wallet can put pressure on your sciatic nerve, causing pain. Steven Subotnick, D.P.M., a sports-medicine specialist in San Leandro, California, and author of *Sports and Exercise Injuries* has seen men "cure" their sciatic pain just by emptying their wallets a bit or moving their wallets from a hip pocket to a front pocket.

Generally, sciatica responds to the same course of treatment prescribed for back pain: a day or two of bed rest followed by regular moderate exercise, plus over-the-counter pain relievers and possibly heat or cold treatments. Chiropractic and acupuncture can also help. The goal is to get you back on your feet and into your regular routine as quickly as possible.

If your sciatic pain lasts for more than 2 weeks, despite home care, consult your doctor. Also seek medical attention if you notice any weakness in your leg or foot, if your bladder or bowel function becomes impaired, or if you experience any other significant symptoms.

denly develop back pain for no apparent reason, and your doctor may be unable to determine what's behind it.

Among mainstream M.D.'s, there has been ongoing debate about the best ways to treat back pain. Until the 1990s, people with back pain routinely received "prescriptions" for extended bed rest and pain-relieving drugs—and quite often surgery. But research has shown that extended bed rest often makes back pain worse and that surgery is rarely necessary. Now most mainstream M.D.'s suggest a day or two of pain relievers and no more than 2 days of bed rest, followed by fairly speedy return to a normal level of activity.

With a conservative approach to treatment, about 90 percent of people with back pain feel significantly better within a few months, says former back-pain sufferer Louis Kuritzky, M.D., assistant professor of family medicine at the University of Florida in Gainesville. For the vast majority of people with back problems, once the pain is gone, it doesn't come back. About 15 percent of people develop chronic pain that persists or recurs for years.

This chapter offers an array of treatment options for an aching back—some that you can use on your own, others that require professional care.

BEST CHOICES

Exercise

Get up and at 'em. British researchers analyzed the results of 10 studies in which a total of 3,222 people with back pain were advised to either get bed rest or stay active. None of the studies found any benefit in bed rest. In fact, the people who stayed in bed recovered more slowly than those who didn't. After a back injury, your best bet is to return to your normal routine as soon as you can, says Wilbert E. Fordyce, Ph.D., professor emeritus at the University of Washington School of Medicine in Seattle.

Be gentle to your back. Most experts recommend resuming exercise within 2 to 3 days of the onset of pain.

For his patients with back problems, Brian Shiple, D.O., director of primary-care sports medicine for Crozer-Keystone Health System in Springfield, Pennsylvania, prescribes a combination of gentle stretching and walking, swimming, or cycling. He recommends working out for about ½ hour, 3 to 5 days a week.

"Just make sure that your exercise program is moderate and doesn't reinjure your back," says physical therapist Eileen Vollowitz, founder of Back Designs, a store in Berkeley, California, that specializes in back-care products. "Anything that pounds, jars, or suddenly twists your back isn't appropriate. So forget high-impact aerobics, racquet sports, and most team sports."

Tai Chi

Enroll in a tai chi class. If you're looking for a no-impact, no-sweat way to work out while your back gets better, try tai chi. In one study, researchers instructed 51 people with chronic lower-back pain to either practice tai chi or continue their usual back-care programs. After 6 weeks, the people doing tai chi reported significant reductions in pain.

Yoga

Strike a pose against pain. When Nashville pathologist Mary Pullig Schatz, M.D., developed chronic lower-back pain, she tried almost everything for relief. Nothing helped. Then just as she was about to agree to surgery, she decided to give yoga a shot. She felt better, so she kept it up. The more yoga classes she took, the less pain she had.

Dr. Schatz was so pleased with the results of her yoga therapy that she eventually became a certified Iyengar yoga instructor. She also wrote *Back Care Basics*, a yoga-based guide to back self-care. "Yoga cured my bad back," she says. "It's a gentle activity that builds strength and promotes flexibility."

Among the various yoga styles, Iyengar yoga is the best choice for back pain. Certified Iyengar instructors learn how to adapt yoga postures to provide maximum benefit and minimum harm to people with lower-back problems.

Relaxation Therapies

Keep yourself calm. Stress and the negative emotions associated with it can contribute to back pain, according to John Sarno, M.D., professor of rehabilitative medicine at the New York University School of Medicine in New York City. In particular, stress triggers the fight-or-flight response, a series of physical changes that prime your body for self-defense. Among these changes is the redirection of oxygen- and nutrient-rich blood to your arms and legs and away from your back. So if stress becomes chronic, the muscles and disks of your back can become malnourished.

At the TotalCare Medical Center in Palo Alto, California, patients with back problems learn biofeedback to manage their stress and control their pain. "We see benefit in about half of the people who try biofeedback," says Alan P. Brauer, M.D., founder of the center.

If biofeedback doesn't interest you, any relaxation technique will do. Try meditation, visualization, self-massage, or music therapy.

Herbal Medicine

Bark up the right tree. Willow bark is the original herbal pain reliever, thanks to several aspirin-like compounds it contains.

To make willow bark tea, add 2 teaspoons of powdered willow bark to 1 cup of boiling water. Simmer for 20 minutes, then strain, says Varro Tyler, Ph.D., Sc.D., distinguished professor emeritus of pharmacognosy (natural pharmacy) at Purdue University in West Lafayette, Indiana. You can drink up to three cupfuls a day.

Thank heaven for devil's claw. An extract of the herb devil's claw root is a traditional folk remedy for the pain associated with musculoskeletal problems, including a bad back.

You can buy devil's claw root in health food stores as an extract, powder, or tincture. Use the extract according to package directions. Or take 1 teaspoon of dried powdered root or tincture three times a day, advises Joseph Pizzorno Jr., N.D.

Chiropractic

Consult a chiropractor. Studies conducted in the United States and around the world have shown that chiropractic is often an effective treatment for back pain. For example, at the Medical College of St. Bartholemew's Hospital in London, researchers randomly assigned 741 people with back pain to receive either chiropractic or standard medical treatment. The participants completed questionnaires about their pain after 6 weeks, 6 months, and 1, 2, and 3 years. At every interval, those receiving chiropractic care reported greater improvement than those receiving standard care.

The evidence in favor of chiropractic is so persuasive that the therapy even won a ringing endorsement from an expert panel appointed by the federal Agency for Health Care Policy and Research. The panel, consisting of 21 M.D.'s and two chiropractors, made the recommendation in its 1994 report *Guidelines for Acute Lower-Back Pain*. These treatment guidelines remain in effect today.

Home Remedies

Apply ice as necessary. In one study, two-thirds of people with back pain reported significant relief after using an ice pack. "Wrap some ice cubes or an ice pack in a towel and lay it over the sore area for 20 minutes," advises Anne Simons, M.D. "Remove the ice for 10 minutes, then repeat." Continue until your pain subsides.

Take a stand against sitting. Sitting puts pressure on the shock-absorbing disks in the spine. That's why truck drivers, office workers, and other people whose jobs require sitting for extended periods are at highest risk for lower-back pain. "The human back isn't designed for 6-hour stints in a chair," says James Zucherman, M.D., medical director of St. Mary's Spine Center in San Francisco. "A sedentary job is a setup for back trouble."

His advice: Sit less and stand more. Take frequent breaks. Get up and walk around at least once an hour. When you do sit, fidget in your chair. Cross and uncross your legs, or twist this way and that. It changes the stress load on your lower back.

Check out your chair. A good desk chair should provide comfortable lower-back support. If yours doesn't, use a curved pillow (called a lumbar pillow) to get the support you need. Also, the chair back should lean backward slightly. Hold your back against it rather than leaning forward. Keep your feet flat on the floor.

If you work at a computer, adjust your chair and keyboard height so that your arms and thighs are parallel to the floor and your eyes are level with the top of your monitor. This helps ensure proper posture.

Redesign your car seat. Many newer-model cars have seats with built-in adjustable lumbar supports for the lower back. If your car doesn't have this feature, consider using a lumbar pillow when you drive, says Steven Subotnick, D.P.M., a sports-medicine specialist in San Leandro, California, and author of *Sports and Exercise Injuries*. As an alternative, try positioning a rolled-up towel between your lower back and the car seat.

Practice perfect posture. When you stand, keep your weight evenly distributed between both legs, Dr. Simons says. Your knees should be slightly bent, your shoulders down and back, and your buttocks tucked in. Never slouch.

Lift like a pro. It doesn't matter how heavy—or light—an object is. Always lift with your legs, making your thigh muscles do the work. Rise straight up, holding the object as close to your body as possible. Don't twist as you lift. Be sure of your footing. And when you set the object down, lower it with your legs.

Make your bed better. Your mattress should be neither too firm nor too soft, Dr. Subotnick says. To make your mattress firmer, place a sheet of plywood underneath it. You might also consider investing in a waterbed, which can provide just the right support for a bad back.

Buy a new bra. Wearing the wrong-size bra can aggravate back pain, Dr. Simons says. If you're a woman who has never been measured for a bra, or if your bra size has recently changed, call your local department stores to find out whether they offer professional fittings. Also, look for bras that have wider back and shoulder straps. This design is more back-sparing because it distributes breast weight over a larger area.

Ditch the high heels. High-heeled shoes were first conceived as a way to accentuate a woman's breasts and buttocks, making her more attractive to men. Thankfully, more sensible styles have become fashionable. Wearing high heels places tremendous strain on the lower back.

Maintain a healthy weight. Even if you're only a few pounds overweight, shedding that extra baggage can bring dramatic relief from back pain.

Over-the-Counter Drugs

Pick a painkiller. At the first twinge of back pain, start taking an over-the-counter pain reliever, Dr. Simons advises. Aspirin, ibuprofen, acetaminophen, and naproxen (Aleve) work equally well. But acetaminophen is least likely to cause stomach upset. Whichever pain reliever you choose, follow the package directions for proper dosage.

OTHER GOOD CHOICES

Homeopathy

Arm yourself with Arnica. For people who've experienced back injuries, Arnica is among the most effective homeopathic medicines, says homeopath Dana Ullman. He suggests using Arnica orally and topically, in pellet and ointment forms, according to the package directions. He may also recommend oral doses of Hypericum, Rhus toxicodendron, or Bryonia, depending on a person's individual symptoms. To find out which homeopathic medicines will work best for you, consult a homeopath.

Chinese Medicine

Zero in on the source. Practitioners of Chinese medicine attribute back pain to one of three causes: overuse; invasion of Wind, Cold, or Damp; or weakness in the Kidney organ network, which governs the bones. For overuse, Efrem Korngold, O.M.D., L.Ac., prescribes strengthening herbs such as astragalus. To expel Wind, Cold, or Damp, he recommends Chinese herbs such as *Angelica pu-*

bescens, clematis root, gentian root, chaenomeles fruit, and cinnamon twig. To support the Kidneys, he suggests the herbs dry ginger, eucommia, dipsacus, and drynaria.

Let your fingers do the working. So many studies have proved acupuncture to be an effective treatment for lower-back pain that it has won the endorsement of both the World Health Organization and the National Institutes of Health. Of course, acupuncture must be administered by a professional. If you prefer a self-care approach, try acupressure. Apply steady, penetrating finger pressure to each of the following points for 3 minutes.

◆ Kidney 7, located on your inner leg, two thumb-widths above your anklebone

◆ Bladder 40, located at the back of your knee, in the hollow of your knee crease

◆ Bladder 60, located on the outside of your leg, in the hollow between your anklebone and Achilles tendon

MEDICAL MEASURES

Only 1 percent of people who have back pain require surgery, Dr. Shiple says. If your doctor recommends surgery, don't rush into it. Get opinions from several back-care specialists before making your decision. Back surgery is traumatic and requires an extended recovery period. It works best for people who have clear symptoms of nerve damage—primarily numbness, tingling, or weakness on one side of the body. It doesn't do much for anyone else.

RED FLAGS

Consult your doctor if you experience persistent pain or pain that becomes more severe over the course of a week or two, despite home care. You may have an underlying health problem that's making your back hurt.

The following also warrant immediate medical attention.

◆ Back pain that's accompanied by fever, leg weakness, bladder or bowel problems, abdominal pain, or unexplained weight loss

◆ Back pain that develops after abdominal surgery

◆ Unrelenting back pain that interferes with sleep

Bad Breath

Y ou wonder about it. You worry that you have it but that no one is telling you
about it. So you discreetly cup your hand over your mouth, exhale, and take
a quick whiff. Hmmm . . . smells okay. But still
you wonder: "Do I have bad breath?"

This fear of foulness may help explain
why Americans spend $1 billion a year on
mouthwashes and other breath-freshening
products.

SIMPLE SOLUTIONS
1. Nutrition
2. Herbal Medicine
3. Home Remedies
4. Chinese Medicine
5. Ayurvedic Medicine
6. Naturopathy
7. Medical Measures

Most cases of bad breath result from
bacteria that live in the mouth, according to
William Replogle, Ph.D., professor of family
medicine at the University of Mississippi Medical Center in Jackson. As these microbes feed
on food residues, they produce foul-smelling
compounds that make your breath offensive. They also produce irritating
toxins that cause your gums to pull away from your teeth, forming pockets
that harbor even more bacteria. And the more bacteria that live in your mouth,
the worse your breath becomes.

In cases of chronic halitosis, the tongue may be an unwitting co-conspir-
ator in this bacterial bacchanalia, according to research conducted by Walter
Loesche, D.D.S., professor of dentistry and microbiology at the University of
Michigan in Ann Arbor. He and his colleague Erika De Boever, D.D.S., found
that the backs of some people's tongues have deep crevices where odor-producing bacteria thrive.

Bad breath tends to become more common with age. As you get older, you
produce less saliva, which normally helps keep bacteria in check. For the same
reason, you're more prone to bad breath if you take drugs that dry your mouth,
such as antihistamines, decongestants, and pain relievers.

Even morning mouth—the first-thing-in-the-morning kind of bad
breath—results from lack of saliva. When you sleep, you stop salivating, which
allows bacteria to build up.

Ironically, most people who worry about bad breath don't have it, according to Dr. Loesche. But how do you know if you do? Apparently, people will try just about anything to avoid the potential embarrassment of having to ask someone else. Unfortunately, the only surefire way to find out is to ask your spouse or a trustworthy friend to tell you the truth.

If you do have bad breath, you'll need to figure out how to bully those odor-producing bacteria into submission. That means good oral hygiene. Brush your teeth at least twice a day and floss at least once, advises Anne Simons, M.D. "Don't just wave the brush around your mouth," she says. "Brush thoroughly, especially around your gum lines. Floss thoroughly as well."

The following strategies can also help keep bad breath at bay.

BEST CHOICES

Nutrition

Give your jaw a workout. When you eat, chew your food thoroughly, Dr. Replogle advises. Chewing stimulates saliva flow.

Choose your foods carefully. Certain foods are notorious for causing bad breath, such as coffee, alcohol, certain cheeses, and garlic and its close relatives (onions, chives, leeks, and shallots). When you consume these foods, the offensive odor emanates not only from your mouth but also from your lungs, Dr. Replogle explains. The foods contain malodorous sulfur compounds, which enter the bloodstream during digestion, travel to the lungs, and then get exhaled.

Even exemplary oral hygiene can't prevent bad breath that originates in the lungs. So if you're worried about your breath, you're better off avoiding problem foods altogether.

Consider meatless meals. Meat eaters are more likely to have halitosis than vegetarians, according to Dr. Replogle. Meats—especially pastrami, salami, and pepperoni—contain sulfur and other compounds that find their way into the lungs and get exhaled.

Fill up on fluids. Drink plenty of water throughout the day, advises Alan P. Brauer, M.D. Water keeps your mouth tissues hydrated and washes away food residues. Citrus juices are great, too. They have the same benefits as water, plus they stimulate saliva flow.

Herbal Medicine

Try the chlorophyll cure. Ever wonder why chefs garnish entrées with a sprig of parsley? They're perpetuating the ancient Roman practice of chewing parsley after meals. Parsley is rich in chlorophyll, a potent breath-freshener. So are basil and cilantro.

"Refrigerate sprigs of fresh parsley, basil, and cilantro in a glass of water," advises James A. Duke, Ph.D. "Then nibble them throughout the day."

Capitalize on cineole. Cineole is a powerful antibacterial antiseptic found in several medicinal herbs. "The richest source is cardamom," Dr. Duke says. "But spearmint, peppermint, ginger, eucalyptus, rosemary, and sweet annie are also good sources." He suggests munching on a few fresh leaves of spearmint or peppermint or making a tea from any of the other herbs. For ginger, use grated fresh root; for the others, dried leaves will do. Add 1 to 2 teaspoons of the herb to 1 cup of boiled water, then allow to steep to taste before drinking.

Make time for thyme. Thyme is another herb with antibacterial properties, thanks to a compound called thymol in its oil. Simply chew some fresh leaves or make a tea from the herb, following the directions in the previous tip.

Be sanguine about your breath. Dr. Brauer recommends rinsing your mouth with Viadent, an over-the-counter mouthwash that contains an extract of the medicinal herb sanguinaria (bloodroot). "Sanguinaria is a powerful antiseptic," he explains. "It kills bacteria in the mouth and under the gums that contribute to bad breath."

Home Remedies

Target your tongue. Tongue scraping isn't all that common in Western oral hygiene. But Ayurvedic physicians have been recommending it for centuries. "It's very helpful, but few people do it," Dr. Brauer says.

Tongue scrapers are hard to come by. If you don't have a tongue scraper, Dr. Brauer recommends using your toothbrush. You have to brush the very back of your tongue, which may cause gagging. "But with a little practice, you can overcome your gag reflex," he says.

Disinfect dentures. If you wear removable dentures or any other dental appliance, clean it daily and soak it in a commercial denture cleanser overnight.

Chew gum. Chewing gum gets your saliva flowing, which helps eliminate bad breath. Any ordinary gum will do—it needn't have special breath-freshening ingredients, Dr. Simons says.

Banish those butts. If you need another reason to give up smoking, here it is: Tobacco causes bad breath.

OTHER GOOD CHOICES

Chinese Medicine

Turn down the Heat. In Chinese medicine, bad breath results from excessive Heat in the Stomach. For treatment, Efrem Korngold, O.M.D., L.Ac., recommends consuming "cooling" foods such as cucumber, peppermint tea, and tomatoes. He also suggests avoiding "hot" foods such as coffee, alcohol, and spicy dishes.

Ayurvedic Medicine

Nibble on fennel. Instead of mints, many Indian restaurants keep a bowl of fennel seeds by the door. Ayurvedic physicians often recommend chewing a pinch of fennel seeds after eating to freshen the breath.

Naturopathy

Discover the digestion connection. Naturopaths such as Joseph Pizzorno Jr., N.D., believe that poor digestion contributes to bad breath. Dr. Pizzorno's advice: Keep your digestive system functioning smoothly by eating a low-fat, high-fiber diet with plenty of grains, fruits, and vegetables.

MEDICAL MEASURES

For bad breath, the most effective mouthwash is a prescription product called Peridex, which contains the antibacterial antiseptic chlorhexidine. In one study, 6 months of regular rinsing with Peridex reduced oral bacteria by more than 50 percent. Dr. Replogle recommends rinsing for 30 seconds twice a day after brushing.

Some people get stains on their teeth when using chlorhexidine, but any stains can be removed by professional cleaning. Also, chlorhexidine may impair the sense of taste. If this happens to you, consult your dentist. He may suggest that you use the mouthwash a few times a week rather than daily.

RED FLAGS

If you suddenly develop persistent bad breath and it doesn't clear up after a few weeks of aggressive home treatment and professional teeth cleaning, consult a physician. A number of potentially serious conditions have bad breath as a symptom, including diabetes, kidney failure, lupus, liver and gallbladder disorders, and certain cancers.

Bronchitis

Acute bronchitis usually develops on the heels of a cold or the flu. Your body's battle to defeat these infections leaves your bronchial tubes sensitive, irritated, and inflamed, explains Alan P. Brauer, M.D. This impairs the ability of the tiny hairs that line the bronchial tubes, called the cilia, to sweep mucus and other debris out of your respiratory tract. With your bronchial tubes inflamed and your cilia impaired, your body resorts to its coughing mechanism to keep those bronchi clear.

Sometimes acute bronchitis causes a dry, hacking cough, says Anne Simons, M.D. Other times the cough is productive, meaning that it brings up mucus.

A case of acute bronchitis usually lasts for a week or two. To make the coughing and hacking disappear more quickly, try these blended-medicine solutions.

SIMPLE SOLUTIONS
1. Supplements
2. Herbal Medicine
3. Homeopathy
4. Chinese Medicine
5. Home Remedies
6. Over-the-Counter Drugs
7. Visualization
8. Aromatherapy
9. Naturopathy
10. Medical Measures

BEST CHOICES

Supplements

"C" your way to relief. Vitamin C has been proven effective as a treatment for allergies and asthma as well as for the common cold. Naturopath Joseph Pizzorno Jr., N.D., believes that C can help clear up bronchitis, too. He recommends taking 500 milligrams of the vitamin every 2 waking hours until your symptoms subside.

Resort to zinc. Several studies have shown that zinc gluconate lozenges help treat the common cold. Dr. Pizzorno also recommends them for bronchitis.

Chronic Bronchitis: Where There's Smoke . . .

Do you smoke? If so, then you're a prime candidate for smoker's cough, or what doctors call chronic bronchitis.

About half of all smokers in the United States—some 14 million Americans—have chronic bronchitis, according to the National Center for Health Statistics. Smoking is almost always the underlying cause of the condition, though exposure to dust, chemical vapors, and other respiratory irritants can aggravate it, notes Kenneth R. Bertka, M.D., clinical associate professor of family medicine at the Medical College of Ohio in Toledo.

Chronic bronchitis starts out just like the acute variety, but the symptoms never completely go away. Over time, the cough becomes deeper and more productive. The worst coughing usually occurs first thing in the morning. Unlike acute bronchitis, which sometimes produces a dry, hacking cough, chronic bronchitis almost always involves bringing up thick, wet mucus.

Call your doctor if your cough suddenly worsens and you feel short of breath, if you develop a fever, if you feel pain when breathing, or if you're bringing up unusually dark or bloody mucus. You may have pneumonia and will need prompt professional treatment.

His prescription: Suck on one lozenge containing 23 milligrams of zinc every 2 waking hours for 1 week. Don't use the lozenges any longer than that, he cautions. Over time, zinc can suppress the immune system.

Bank on an immune booster. An amino acid called N-acetylcysteine not only helps thin mucus but also fortifies your body's defenses, Dr. Brauer explains. You can buy N-acetylcysteine in most health food stores. Take the supplement according to the directions on the label.

Herbal Medicine

Enlist the dynamic duo. Two immune-enhancing herbs, echinacea and goldenseal, can help your body fight off the virus that's causing your symptoms. Dr. Pizzorno recommends taking either herb in tincture form—1 teaspoon three times a day, mixed into juice or tea. Continue taking this tincture formulation for up to 8 weeks. The tinctures are sold in most health food stores.

Give symptoms the slip. Slippery elm bark can work wonders for a dry, hacking cough, says Varro E. Tyler, Ph.D., Sc.D., distinguished professor emeritus of pharmacognosy (natural pharmacy) at Purdue University in West Lafayette, Indiana. The herb is rich in mucilage, a soluble fiber that soothes the respiratory tract and suppresses coughing. Look for slippery elm bark lozenges in health food stores. Use the lozenges as directed on the package.

Loosen the mucus. If you have a productive cough, you don't want to suppress it. Instead, you want to loosen the bronchial mucus so that it's easier to eliminate. The herbal expectorants licorice, horehound, and wild cherry bark can help. Dr. Pizzorno recommends taking any one of these herbs as a tea or tincture. To make a tea, add 1 to 2 teaspoons of dried herb to 1 cup of boiling water. Steep for 10 minutes, then strain. Drink up to three cupfuls a day. To use the tincture, take 1 teaspoon up to three times a day, mixed into juice or tea.

Homeopathy

Attack the hack. For a dry, hacking cough, Aconitum is among the best homeopathic medicines, according to homeopath Dana Ullman. Others that work well include Antimonium tartaricum, Bryonia, Drosera, Phosphorus, and Spongia. Which of these medicines a homeopath prescribes depends on your unique symptoms.

Chinese Medicine

Silence the Wind. Chinese medicine views bronchitis as an invasion of Wind, according to Efrem Korngold, O.M.D., L.Ac. Sometimes the condition is brought on by Wind Cold, which produces a dry cough and whitish mucus. For this type of bronchitis, Dr. Korngold might prescribe ginger. Then there's Wind Heat bronchitis, which is characterized by a thick yellow-green mucus. This type responds well to prescription herbal formulas containing fritillaria bulb and tricosanthis fruit, he says.

Consult an acupuncturist. The United Nations World Health Organization includes bronchitis in its list of conditions treatable with acupuncture. When treating bronchitis, acupuncturists use Lung 5, which is located inside your elbow, on the upper part of the crease. They also use Lung 6, which is high on the thickest part of the forearm. You can try stimulating these points yourself with acupressure. Using your fingertips, apply steady, penetrating pressure to each point for 3 minutes.

Home Remedies

Stay hydrated. Drink plenty of fluids—six to eight 8-ounce glasses a day, Dr. Pizzorno advises. Fluids help liquefy bronchial secretions, making them easier to cough up. Most people with bronchitis find warm fluids more soothing than cold.

If it's dry, humidify. Dry air is irritating and can trigger coughing fits. "At night, run a vaporizer while you sleep," Dr. Simons suggests. During the day, take hot, steamy showers.

Suck on candy. Hard candies help soothe your throat, which in turn helps relieve bronchial irritation, Dr. Brauer says. Use sugarless candies to avoid tooth decay.

Protect your airways. Avoid cigarette smoke, dust, chemical vapors, and other respiratory irritants, Dr. Brauer says.

Over-the-Counter Drugs

Choose a cough medicine. For a dry cough, try an over-the-counter cough suppressant that contains dextromethorphan, Dr. Simons suggests. Both Triaminic DM and Dimetapp DM have dextromethorphan as their active ingredient. But don't use these products if you're bringing up mucus. In that case, you should use an expectorant made with guaifenesin, such as Congestac.

OTHER GOOD CHOICES

Visualization

Breathe in, breathe out. Coughing that you're unable to control makes you anxious. This leads to shallow breathing, which in turn triggers even more coughing.

The following visualization exercise, recommended by Gerald N. Epstein, M.D., director of the Academy of Integrative Medicine and Mental Imagery in New York City, relieves anxiety and restores normal breathing. Practice it for a minute or two every few hours.

1. Close your eyes and focus on your breathing, telling yourself that you can get rid of anything that interferes with your normal breathing. Then open your eyes.

2. Close your eyes again and take three breaths. If you cough, just accept it and keep breathing. Open your eyes.

3. Close your eyes again and take three breaths. Focus on how your breathing is changing, deepening. Open your eyes.

4. Repeat the above steps, this time focusing on breathing from your diaphragm rather than from your upper chest.

Aromatherapy

Get a whiff of relief. Herbalist/aromatherapist Kathy Keville, coauthor of *Aromatherapy: A Complete Guide to the Healing Art*, recommends the following essential oils for bronchitis: clove bud, fir (including balsam and pine), ravensara, and sweet inula. Add 3 to 5 drops of the essential oil of your choice to a bowl of hot water and inhale deeply. Or add 3 to 15 drops to a comfortably hot bath and step in for a soothing soak. Avoid using clove in the bath, as it may irritate your skin.

Naturopathy

Make your own cough syrup. Place six chopped white onions in a double boiler. Add ½ cup of honey. Slowly simmer this mixture for 2 hours to draw out the onion juice, then strain out the remaining onion material. Take 1 to 2 warm tablespoonfuls of the honey–onion juice mixture every hour or two, Dr. Pizzorno says.

Get plastered. Did your grandmother believe in mustard plasters? Naturopaths still do. Here's Dr. Pizzorno's recipe: Mix 2 tablespoons of dry black or brown mustard with 6 tablespoons of flour. Add enough water to make a paste. Spread the paste on a cloth, then lay the cloth over your chest. Inhale the vapors for no more than 20 minutes. After that, be sure to remove the plaster. If you leave it on your chest too long, you could develop blisters.

MEDICAL MEASURES

A study conducted by Ralph Gonzalez, M.D., of the University of Colorado Health Sciences Center in Denver, found that doctors prescribe antibiotics to two-thirds of the people whom they treat for bronchitis. But more than 90 percent of all cases of bronchitis result from viral infections, and antibiotics can't kill viruses. These drugs are effective only against bacteria, which cause comparatively few cases of bronchitis.

"Before prescribing antibiotics, your doctor should take a sputum culture to make sure that you really have a bacterial infection," Dr. Brauer says. If the test comes out positive—that is, you do have bronchitis-causing bacteria in your system—then antibiotics are appropriate.

In that case, there's something that you can do to increase the effectiveness of any antibiotics you're given: Pair them with bromelain, says Alan Gaby, M.D. An enzyme found in pineapple, bromelain helps antibiotics get into your cells. He suggests either eating more pineapple or taking a 250-milligram bromelain supplement with your antibiotics.

RED FLAGS

Consult your doctor immediately if you have bronchitis and you develop a fever or you start coughing up bloody, brown, or greenish yellow phlegm. You may have pneumonia, which requires prompt professional treatment.

Cancer

Cancer is our nation's most feared diagnosis. It's also the second leading cause of death (after heart disease), claiming more than 550,000 lives a year.

Cancer is not one disease. Rather, it's one name for more than 200 diseases, all of which develop similarly. Initially, something goes wrong with cell reproduction. Instead of dividing normally, cells that become cancerous reproduce wildly, producing abnormal growths—what we call tumors. Tumor cells spread (metastasize) around the body, forming more tumors. If tumor growth can't be stopped, it interferes with vital body processes.

Often, cancer can be detected early, when tumors are tiny and have not spread. Doctors agree that early diagnosis is best because small, local tumors tend to be most treatable. But no matter how early it's caught, no one wants to hear a doctor say, "I'm sorry, it's cancer."

Because cancer is not one disease but many, survival depends to a great extent on the type of cancer you have. When diagnosed early, cervical cancer, testicular cancer, skin cancers, and most childhood cancers are very treatable—in fact, curable. But other cancers—including those of the pancreas, liver, and lungs—usually don't respond as well to treatment.

"A cancer diagnosis is like being pushed

SIMPLE SOLUTIONS
1. Decide for Yourself
2. Organize Your Social Support
3. Consider a Support Group
4. Get the Pathology Report in Writing
5. Gather Information
6. Understand Survival Statistics
7. Take Time to Make Decisions
8. Consult an Oncologist
9. Organize Your Doctors
10. Get Several Opinions
11. Use Mainstream Treatments
12. Try a Clinical Trial
13. Use Healthy Strategies
14. Consider Herbs and Acupuncture
15. Use Pain Control
16. Promote Your Own "Healing"

out of a helicopter into a jungle war with no training, no maps, and no idea how to survive," says Michael Lerner, Ph.D., cofounder of the Commonweal Cancer Help Program, an organization based in Bolinas, California, which hosts week-long educational retreats for people with cancer.

In 1981, Dr. Lerner, a former Yale professor, learned that his father, Max Lerner, had been diagnosed with non-Hodgkin's lymphoma, the same cancer that killed Jacqueline Kennedy Onassis. Though the doctors predicted that Max Lerner had only a short time to live, the prediction was in error. Using only mainstream chemotherapy, Dr. Lerner's father survived for 11 years.

During his father's illness, the younger Lerner became fascinated by the then-acrimonious war of words between mainstream oncology and the alternative cancer therapies. He used the money from a MacArthur Foundation genius grant to travel around the world exploring alternative cancer centers. He became convinced that both conventional and alternative approaches have value. The best results, he concluded, usually emerge from a blending of conventional and alternative medicine.

As a result of his research, Dr. Lerner helped launch the Commonweal Cancer Help Program, which teaches people with cancer how to deal with the disease.

In the Cancer Help Program, training includes a vegetarian diet, daily exercise, daily meetings with a support group, and massage and other relaxation therapies. For more information, contact the Commonweal Cancer Help Program. P. O. Box 316, Bolinas, CA 94924.

Treating cancer also involves a big dose of hope. Expectations for long-term cancer survival have increased dramatically in recent decades. Before World War II, surviving with cancer 5 years after diagnosis was considered the exception. Today, it's the rule. About 60 percent of people who have been diagnosed with cancer survive at least 5 years, and many live much longer.

About 40 percent of Americans are diagnosed with cancer at some point in their lives, but only about 20 percent die from it. In fact, some 8.2 million living Americans are cancer survivors. If you walk into a room of 33 people, chances are that one of them is a cancer survivor.

"After decades of frustration, we've finally turned the corner," says James Dougherty, M.D., deputy physician in chief for clinical affairs at Memorial Sloan-Kettering Cancer Center in New York City.

What has turned things around? "Not a miracle cure—at least not yet," Dr. Dougherty says. "But little by little, we've made incremental progress against the disease. We've learned more about how it works, and we've gotten better at preventing it, detecting it early, and treating it. We still have a long way to go, of course. But the death rate is falling, which is very good news."

Since 1990, hundreds of studies have been published supporting the value of alternative therapies for cancer treatment. The evidence clearly shows that the best results—longer cancer-free survival and improved quality of life—come from blending mainstream oncology and alternative therapies. As a result, blended cancer therapy is on the rise. By some estimates, up to 64 percent of cancer patients try at least one alternative approach.

No matter what kind of cancer you have, the experts agree that a step-by-step approach is the way to go. Every step of this process is really a best choice.

BEST CHOICES

1. Decide for Yourself

Some people delegate their cancer care entirely to their family doctors or to an oncologist and prefer not to learn much about their cancer. Others delegate their care but ask their doctors to keep them informed. Still others form a partnership with their doctors and other practitioners and are deeply involved in decision making about their care.

"Everyone deals with cancer their own way," Dr. Lerner says. "If you get cancer and want to join a support group, take herbs, or go for long walks on the beach, fine, do it. But when people you care about get cancer, they need to make the decisions. You can offer suggestions, but if they choose paths different from the one you would choose, it's usually best to support their decisions."

2. Organize Your Social Support

When you're diagnosed with cancer, you typically feel swept up in an emotional whirlwind. The same thing happens, to a lesser extent, to your family and friends.

When you decide what you want to do and how you want to spend your time, ask a few people close to you to handle the other chores, advises Anne Simons, M.D.

"The period right after diagnosis is emotionally the hardest," says Mary Jane

Massie, M.D., a psychiatrist at Memorial Sloan-Kettering Cancer Center in New York City. "For those who have always been self-reliant, it can be difficult to ask for help or accept it. I tell people: 'It's okay to be a little selfish and ask for what you need.'"

3. Consider a Support Group

Beyond support from those you know, joining a support group can provide tremendous comfort—and might even extend your survival. In the late 1970s, Stanford psychiatrist David Spiegel, M.D., now a professor of psychiatry and behavioral sciences and director of the Psychosocial Treatment Laboratory, theorized that support groups might help people cope with the stress of having a life-threatening illness.

In his research with breast-cancer patients, Dr. Spiegel discovered that the women who joined a support group lived almost twice as long as those who didn't.

To find a support group near you, ask your family doctor or oncologist for referrals to the cancer resource organizations in your community.

4. Get the Pathology Report in Writing

When a doctor suspects cancer, the lump or some cells in the affected area are removed. This surgical procedure is known as a biopsy. The suspect tissue is placed on slides, and the cells are examined under a microscope by a pathologist. If the cells are cancerous, the pathologist writes a report that specifies which type of tumor you have.

From the biopsy, the pathologist can also ascertain what stage the tumor is at and how aggressive, or fast-growing, it is. If the tumor is early-stage, the cancer is confined to one area. *Moderately metastatic* means that it has spread somewhat. *Advanced* means that it has spread to distant parts of the body. The lab report may reveal other tumor characteristics as well.

"All treatment decisions follow from the pathology report," says Thomas Grogan, M.D., professor of pathology at the University of Arizona Cancer Center in Tucson. "You need to be very clear about it. Get your pathology report in writing, and make sure that you understand what it says. Ask your doctor. If you still have questions, ask the pathologist."

Because all treatment decisions are based upon the pathology report, it's crucial that it's correct. The best way to be sure is to request a second opinion on your slides. This implies no mistrust of your pathologist, just a need to be sure that the report is correct.

An Experienced Resource

For reliable cancer information, you can count on the Health Resource. Its founder, Janice Guthrie, is a cancer survivor who discovered first-hand that information can be a lifesaver.

The Health Resource publishes reports on all types of cancers for $95 to $375. For more information and the current price of its reports, you can write to the Health Resource at 933 Faulkner Street, Conway, AR 72032.

5. Gather Information

Once you're certain which specific type of cancer you have, it's time to research it. A great deal of information is only a few phone calls away.

Contact your local office of the American Cancer Society. This private, nonprofit education and research organization can provide you with general information about your cancer. The ACS can also refer you to cancer resources and support groups in your area. In addition, the ACS Reach to Recovery program can put you in touch with survivors of your specific cancer, who can share their experiences of treatment and recovery.

Contact the Cancer Information Service. A program of the National Cancer Institute (NCI) in Bethesda, Maryland, the Cancer Information Service (CIS) provides current information about all cancers—for free. Two types of information packets are available: one for patients that contains basic background information and another for physicians that contains state-of-the-art treatment recommendations.

Investigate on the Internet. If you have a computer and modem, the Internet contains a wealth of information about cancer. "Using any search engine, just type in your specific type of cancer, and you're likely to get hundreds of listings," says Tom Ferguson, M.D., adjunct associate professor of human consumer health informatics at the University of Texas Health Science Center at Houston.

6. Understand Survival Statistics

Survival statistics provide a "big picture" look at your cancer, the odds that someone with your disease will live at least 5 years. But overall survival statistics are misleading because they are averages that include cancers diag-

Honor the Herbals

Many Western herbs have antitumor effects. Among the most widely used American herbal cancer therapies is the Hoxsey program, which Harry Hoxsey, a former coal miner with no medical training, began promoting in the 1930s as his family's secret herbal cancer cure.

The Hoxsey formula contains 10 herbs: burdock, red clover, licorice root, poke root, bloodroot, barberry root, buckthorn, prickly ash, and stillingia root. National Cancer Institute studies have shown that 9 of these 10 herbs exhibit antitumor activity in laboratory tests, and there are anecdotal reports of the Hoxsey formula producing dramatic cancer remissions. The Hoxsey formula, however, remains extremely controversial and largely unresearched.

nosed at every stage of development, from very early to far advanced. As you might expect, the odds of survival are reduced if cancer is diagnosed at a late stage. For example, if malignant melanoma has metastasized by the time it's diagnosed, 5-year survival is only 12 percent. But if it's caught early, the survival rate is 96 percent. Because other cancers also follow this pattern, the ACS and NCI promote frequent cancer screening for early detection.

7. Take Time to Make Decisions

After being diagnosed with cancer, many people are very impatient to begin treatment. They are filled with anxiety, and they don't want to waste a moment for fear that their cancer will spread.

This feeling is understandable—but uninformed, Dr. Dougherty explains. "By the time cancer gets diagnosed, it's usually been growing for several years. Except for a very small number of extremely aggressive cancers, waiting a few weeks has no effect on survival. In fact, you should take some time to research your options and get a few opinions on treatment. You don't want to dawdle, but I encourage patients to take up to a few weeks to consult experts and plan their treatment."

8. Consult an Oncologist

According to NCI estimates, only about one-third of cancer patients ever consult oncologists. Some don't want to offend their family physicians by consulting other doctors. Others simply don't know about specialists in nearby clinics or hospitals.

No good family doctor gets offended when people who have been diagnosed with cancer ask for referrals to oncologists, Dr. Simons says. "I'm a family doctor. I refer patients to specialists all the time," she points out.

If your doctor balks at referring you to an oncologist, Dr. Grogan says, "You've got the wrong doctor."

As for access to cancer specialists, there are oncologists and hospital cancer programs from coast to coast. This is where the ACS Reach to Recovery program can help. Ask other people who have survived your cancer to tell you who they consulted. Pay special attention to any oncologist who's affiliated with a comprehensive cancer center or an oncologist who trained at one.

9. Organize Your Doctors

Before you decide on a treatment program, you may need to consult quite a few doctors: your family physician, a medical oncologist, a radiation oncologist, a pathologist, and a surgeon.

It's best to think of your treatment plan as a team effort. You—or the key support person you designate—are captain of your team. Dr. Simons offers these suggestions for coordinating your team effort.

Don't abandon your family doctor. The oncologists you consult may know more about treating cancer, but they don't know you and your family as well as your family doctor does.

Jot down what every specialist recommends. Or tape-record their recommendations. You need to know not only what kind of surgery, radiation, or chemotherapy they recommend but also the order in which these treatments should be administered.

Ask the specialists to talk with each other. If disagreements arise, urge your oncologists to work them out. They may not talk to each other if you don't insist.

10. Get Several Opinions

You need to feel comfortable with the treatment program you choose. Cancer experts agree that before deciding on treatment, it's best to consult several surgeons, radiation oncologists, and medical oncologists.

But what if you don't have the energy to call oncologists all over the country? You might ask a support person to do this for you. Or you might simply

One Study to the Rescue

Megadose antioxidants help prevent bladder cancer recurrences—and those who helped make that discovery were also the beneficiaries of the early research.

In a 5-year study, urologist Donald Lamm, M.D., and colleagues at West Virginia University in Morgantown gave 65 bladder cancer survivors either the Recommended Dietary Allowance (RDA) of vitamins A, C, D, E, the B vitamins, and zinc or very high daily doses of vitamin A, vitamin B_6, vitamin C, vitamin E, and zinc. After 4 years, the group of those who were taking the very high doses of supplements developed only half as many recurrences of bladder cancer as the group on normal daily doses.

consult one of the nation's approximately 100 Multidisciplinary Second Opinion Panels. Today, every major metropolitan area has at least one of these panels.

You send your medical records to the panel coordinator, who forwards them to local cancer specialists. These specialists have volunteered to serve on the panel. You attend a meeting with all of the experts, bringing along anyone you want. The experts discuss your case and develop a consensus set of treatment recommendations.

To find the panel nearest you, contact the R. A. Bloch Cancer Foundation, The Cancer Hotline, 4410 Main Street, Kansas City, MO 64111.

11. Use Mainstream Treatments

Conventional oncology has a great deal to offer. "When it comes to curing cancer, mainstream oncology has a better track record than anything else," Dr. Lerner says. "Every cancer patient should work with an oncologist." He feels so strongly about this that no one is admitted to his Cancer Help Program unless they are under an oncologist's care.

12. Try a Clinical Trial

After promising new cancer treatments have been thoroughly tested in animals, they must be tested on human cancer patients before they can be approved for general use. Of the more than 1 million Americans diagnosed with cancer each year, only 20,000 to 30,000 enroll in these tests of the latest treatments.

Clinical trials were once conducted only at the nation's regional cancer centers. But to open them up to all Americans, the NCI now encourages participation by oncologists everywhere. Even family doctors are informed about trial programs. "No one is excluded simply because they live in a rural area," says Jeffrey Abrams, M.D., a research scientist in the NCI's Cancer Therapy Evaluation Program.

To obtain descriptions and eligibility criteria for the approximately 1,500

Keys to Cancer Prevention

To reduce your risk of cancer, the American Cancer Society recommends the following diet and lifestyle strategies.

Don't smoke. Eighty-seven percent of lung cancer deaths, and about one-third of all cancer deaths, are caused by smoking. In addition to lung cancer, smoking increases risk of cancers of the mouth, throat, esophagus, pancreas, uterus, bladder, cervix, and kidneys.

Eat more fruits and vegetables and less meat. Approximately one-third of cancers are caused by the typical American diet—lots of meat and other high-fat items, and few fruits and vegetables. High-fat foods, particularly animal products, introduce cancer-causing free radicals into the bloodstream. Meanwhile, fruits and vegetables are rich in antioxidant nutrients that prevent free-radical damage.

Limit consumption of alcohol. Alcohol raises the risk of cancers of the mouth, esophagus, and breasts.

Get regular moderate exercise. Exercise helps maintain healthy weight. It helps prevent obesity, which is associated with cancers of the colon, rectum, prostate, uterus, breasts, and kidneys.

Wear protective clothing when you're in the sun. This helps prevent all forms of skin cancer.

Avoid exposure to environmental carcinogens. Many industrial chemicals, toxic wastes, drugs, and pesticides increase cancer risk. Radiation from nuclear weapons and nuclear power plants can also contribute to cancer.

Turn to Nutrition

A nutritional approach called Gerson diet therapy appears to extend survival in people with malignant melanoma. Max Gerson, M.D., whom Albert Schweitzer called "one of the geniuses in medical history," prescribed a nutritional approach to cancer treatment in the 1940s and 1950s.

The Gerson diet is very low in fat and salt. It's a lactovegetarian diet, which means people can eat low-fat dairy items in addition to plant foods. In addition, people on the Gerson diet take supplemental nutrients by drinking large quantities of fruit and vegetable juices.

The Gerson program also involves hormonal thyroid stimulation and coffee enemas. Gerson believed that these procedures could detoxify the liver, removing potential body poisons from that organ.

Over the years, several intriguing studies have hinted that Gerson therapy helps treat some people with a variety of cancers. One report comes from a team of researchers at the University of California, San Diego, Cancer Prevention and Control Program, who studied 82 Gerson patients with malignant melanoma and compared their survival with survival rates reported by conventional oncologists in the medical literature. For localized, early-stage melanoma, 100 percent of the Gerson patients survived 5 years, compared with 79 percent survival among those who used conventional oncology. For moderately metastasized melanoma, 75 percent of the Gerson group lived 5 years, compared with 40 percent of those treated conventionally. For widely metastasized melanoma, the figures were 39 percent for Gerson, 6 percent for conventional oncology.

clinical trials now in progress, ask your oncologist or contact the Cancer Information Service.

13. Use Healthy Strategies

For cancer therapy, the same approaches that help improve your overall health can also help slow the advance of cancer. These include nutritional enhancement and supplementation, exercise, psychological support, and stress management through deep relaxation.

Dr. Lerner wholeheartedly endorses the health-promoting alternative approaches. "If you're eating well, getting regular moderate exercise, enjoying psychological support, and working to manage your stress, you become a healthier cancer patient," he says. "Healthier cancer patients often respond better to conventional care and have better treatment outcomes—better quality of life and longer, healthier, disease-free survival."

14. Consider Herbs and Acupuncture

A growing number of studies suggest that combining mainstream oncology with herbal medicine or Chinese medicine makes sense. Here's what researchers have found so far.

At the Chinese Academy of Medical Sciences in Beijing, researchers treated 188 throat cancer patients with either standard radiation therapy or radiation plus a Chinese herb formula. After 5 years, survival in the radiation-only group was 37 percent. But among those receiving both radiation and Chinese herbs, the figure was 53 percent, a significant difference. Efrem Korngold, O.M.D., L.Ac., says that the herbs most widely used in cancer treatment are considered strengthening ("tonifying") in Chinese medicine. In Western terms, that's the equivalent of immune-enhancing. Chinese herbs used to treat cancer include astragalus, ginseng, Chinese angelica (dang gui), and rehmannia.

Shiitake mushroom extract has also been studied. Long considered a health-promoting delicacy in Asian cuisines, shiitake mushrooms contain the compound lentinan, which stimulates the immune system against infections and cancer. Lentinan injections are increasingly used to complement chemotherapy in Japan—and with good reason. In one study, 275 people with advanced stomach cancer were given chemotherapy with or without lentinan injections beforehand. The lentinan group showed greater immune system activity and survived significantly longer. Maitake mushrooms have similar benefits, thanks to the immune-stimulating beta-glucan they contain.

In Chinese medicine, acupuncture has also proved helpful for some people. Several studies show that acupuncture reduces chemotherapy-related nausea and vomiting. At the University of California, Los Angeles, researchers gave 30 women undergoing chemotherapy for breast cancer either real acupuncture at points used to relieve nausea or acupuncture at placebo points. The real-acupuncture group reported only half as many episodes of nausea and vomiting.

Acupressure can also be beneficial. Researchers at the Queen's University in Belfast, Northern Ireland, came up with the same findings using acupressure in a study of 100 people who vomited as a result of chemotherapy. The patients

Screening: A Must for Early Detection

Fear of cancer is tragic," says Harmon Eyre, M.D., chief medical officer for the American Cancer Society (ACS) in Atlanta. "It prevents many people from taking the quick, easy, inexpensive steps that can detect it early, when it's most treatable."

Tumors detected early are often localized, which means that they haven't spread (metastasized). In the vast majority of cases, the more localized the cancer, the easier it is to treat, and the better the odds of long-term survival.

Here are the ACS cancer screening guidelines.

General cancer exam. Have a cancer-related checkup every 3 years if you're between ages 20 and 40. After age 40, get the checkup every year.

Colon and rectal cancer. These diseases, which usually develop after age 50, are the leading cancer killers in nonsmokers. If you're over 50, do one of the following:

◆ Have a stool test and rectal exam annually, along with a sigmoidoscopy—an internal exam with a flexible viewing instrument that allows your doctor to see trouble spots in the lower colon and rectum—every 5 years.

◆ Have a colonoscopy and internal exam of your entire colon every 5 to 10 years.

◆ Have a double-contrast barium enema x-ray exam of your colon every 5 to 10 years.

were fitted with Sea Bands, elastic bands with buttons that press on Pericardium 6, a point used to treat nausea. More than 75 percent of the patients enjoyed significant relief from nausea. Pericardium 6 is located on the inside of your upper arm two thumb widths above the wrist crease.

15. Use Pain Control

Cancer patients often fear that they will have to endure terrible pain and suffering. But a great deal of cancer pain can be well-controlled with medication.

Tragically, some oncologists undermedicate cancer patients in the belief

A digital rectal exam should accompany the sigmoidoscopy, colonoscopy, or double-contrast barium enema x-ray. If you are at moderate or high risk for colorectal cancer, discuss a different testing schedule with your physician.

Breast cancer. From ages 20 to 39, women should perform monthly breast self-exams and have a professional breast exam every 3 years. Women ages 40 and older should perform monthly breast self-exams and have an annual mammogram. If you're in this age group, you should also see your gynecologist at least once a year for a professional exam.

Prostate cancer. Men over age 50 should have a rectal exam once a year. They should also get blood tests annually for prostate-specific antigen (PSA). When cancer is present, it might be revealed by a significant rise in PSA in the blood. Men with a family history of prostate cancer, as well as all African-American men, should be screened earlier—for example, beginning at age 40. Check with your physician to find out when you should start getting annual checkups.

Uterine cancer. Discuss your risk with your doctor. If you're at high risk, have an endometrial biopsy at menopause. Then consult your doctor about getting regular exams.

Cervical cancer. All women who have been sexually active or who are age 18 or older should have an annual Pap test and pelvic exam.

that they will become addicted. But pain specialists say that the risk of addiction is tiny. They view undermedication of cancer pain as unconscionable and criticize oncologists for being slow to increase dosages. Most puzzling of all, some oncologists are reluctant to embrace nondrug approaches with clearly demonstrated pain-relieving benefits, such as acupuncture, hypnosis, visualization, and TENS machines. (The "TENS" are small devices that deliver mild electrical current into the skin to relieve pain.) "Clinics that specialize in chronic pain management use all these approaches routinely," Dr. Lerner says. "Yet many cancer patients still suffer because of inadequate pain control. It's a terrible shame."

Fish Oil Extends Life

Greek researchers gave 60 people with a variety of advanced, metastatic cancers 18 grams a day of either a placebo or fish oil. Fish oil is a good source of omega-3 fatty acids, anti-inflammatory, immune-boosting compounds that help treat many conditions.

The immune systems of those in the placebo group went downhill. But researchers found that the immune response rallied among those who were taking fish oil. People in the fish oil group also lived significantly longer.

Even massage can help. At the University of South Carolina in Columbia, researchers gave 28 hospitalized cancer patients either a 10-minute visit or a 10-minute massage. Pain levels were assessed using standard psychological tests. After just one 10-minute massage, pain levels decreased significantly. Other studies have shown that longer massages lead to extended pain relief. People with cancer report up to 60 percent less pain with a 30-minute massage.

16. Promote Your Own "Healing"

"Curing is what physicians do. They strive to eliminate disease and allow recovery," Dr. Lerner explains. "Healing is what patients bring to the experience. Healing is a deeply personal process of becoming whole again." If healing is neglected, people who have cancer may feel emotionally shortchanged even if they are cured.

Healing involves coming to terms with your life and working to live it to the fullest, even if cancer cuts it short. The tools of healing involve the complementary therapies: good nutrition, moderate exercise, social support, stress management, and a sense of connection to the natural world around you. They all improve quality of life.

"Even when a cure is impossible, healing need not stop," Dr. Lerner says. "People can continue to grow even in the face of life-threatening illness. All the great religions teach that life involves suffering. Suffering can lead to bitterness and defeatism or to growth and wisdom. When you have a serious illness, you make that choice for yourself."

Carpal Tunnel Syndrome

Experts call carpal tunnel syndrome (CTS) the leading occupational hazard of the computer age. But you don't have to spend your days pounding on a keyboard to develop this condition.

When you repeatedly move your fingers in the same pattern for hours on end, the tendons that connect your finger muscles to your wrist bones get irritated and inflamed. In turn, the ligaments that connect your wrist bones swell. The swollen tissues make for very tight accommodations inside the carpal tunnel, the channel deep inside your wrist where your finger tendons and wrist ligaments come together.

SIMPLE SOLUTIONS
1. Supplements
2. Exercise
3. Herbal Medicine
4. Chinese Medicine
5. Home Remedies
6. Over-the-Counter Drugs
7. Massage
8. Homeopathy
9. Naturopathy
10. Medical Measures

Within the narrow confines of that channel, the tissues press on an important and highly sensitive set of nerve fibers called the median nerve. The median nerve controls sensation and movement in your hand. When the nerve is under pressure, you experience tingling, burning, or numbness in your hand—the classic symptoms of CTS.

Though computers are rightly blamed for the majority of CTS cases, the condition can result from any activity that involves constant, repetitive motion. Even if you're not married to a keyboard all day, you might begin to experience CTS symptoms if you do things like knitting, hammering, playing tennis or racquetball, or playing a musical instrument. CTS is also associated with tasks that deliver a steady vibration to the wrist, such as operating a jackhammer or other power tools. Another cause not commonly known is the repeated flexing of the wrist during sleep.

Try This at Home

Only a doctor can tell for certain whether or not you have carpal tunnel syndrome (CTS). But if you've been experiencing CTS-like symptoms and haven't yet been to your doctor, try the following exercise to find out if your own diagnosis is correct.

Position your arms so that your hands are in front of your chest and your elbows are pointing out to the sides, as shown. Bend your wrists so that your hands point straight down. Press the backs of your hands together. If you experience tingling, burning, or numbness within 1 minute, chances are that you have carpal tunnel syndrome.

CTS can be aggravated by health problems that have nothing whatever to do with repetitive motion. For example, people with diabetes, rheumatoid arthritis, and thyroid problems sometimes develop classic CTS symptoms. Gender plays a role, too: You have a greater risk of developing CTS if you're a woman, because the condition is three times more common among women than among men. Female hormonal fluctuations during the menstrual cycle, pregnancy, and menopause make tissues inside the wrist swell more than usual, putting pressure on the median nerve. If pregnancy is behind the swelling, however, CTS symptoms may vanish after delivery, when hormone levels return to normal.

At first, CTS may affect only the thumb and first three fingers of the hand. (The pinkie is spared because it isn't controlled by the median nerve.) And sometimes it affects only the dominant hand, although more than half of all CTS cases involve both hands.

If you ignore the initial symptoms and continue engaging in a repetitive task, you can end up with constant pain in your hand and arm. In the most severe cases, CTS can permanently damage the hands, making repetitive tasks like keyboarding impossible.

Fortunately, CTS never has to progress to such an advanced stage. With prompt intervention on your part—and a few of the remedies listed below—you can quickly get the upper hand on CTS symptoms.

BEST CHOICES

Supplements

Increase your B$_6$ intake. While researching CTS in 1976, John Ellis, M.D., of Mount Pleasant, Texas, made an intriguing discovery: He noticed that the condition was more common in people who were deficient in vitamin B$_6$. When he gave B$_6$ supplements to patients with CTS, many of them saw their symptoms disappear completely.

Since then, several other studies have confirmed the benefits of vitamin B$_6$ in treating CTS. If you want to try B$_6$, take 100 milligrams a day. But keep in mind that B$_6$ therapy doesn't work overnight, Dr. Ellis cautions. You may have to wait up to 12 weeks before you notice improvement.

Exercise

Twist those wrists. At the Hand Institute and Orthopedic and Reconstructive Center in Oklahoma City, Houshang Seradge, M.D., taught people with CTS simple wrist exercises. The participants stood with their arms outstretched in front of them and gently flexed their wrists up and down and rotated their wrists in circles for a total of 5 minutes. Then Dr. Seradge measured the pressure on the participants' median nerves. The pressure had dropped to near-normal levels and remained low for more than 20 minutes after the participants had completed their exercises.

Dr. Seradge recommends wrist flexes and wrist rotations for everyone with

CTS. "Do them first thing in the morning and hourly during the workday," Dr. Seradge advises. "If you wear a wrist splint, remove it, do the exercises, then put it back on."

Herbal Medicine

Get to know willow. James A. Duke, Ph.D., recommends the herb willow bark for CTS. "Willow bark is an anti-inflammatory," he explains. "It was the original plant source of aspirin." To make an herbal tea, add 1 to 2 teaspoons of powdered willow bark to 1 cup of boiling water. Simmer for 10 minutes, strain out the herb, and drink. Dr. Duke suggests drinking two to three cupfuls a day. You can buy powdered willow bark in health food stores.

Turn to turmeric. "Turmeric has been used for centuries to treat inflammation," says Joseph Pizzorno Jr., N.D. "Scientific research has shown that the herb has anti-inflammatory activity comparable to pharmaceutical hydrocortisone." He recommends taking 250 to 500 milligrams of turmeric extract ($\frac{1}{4}$ to $\frac{1}{2}$ teaspoon) three times a day, before meals.

Be aware that turmeric and nonsteroidal anti-inflammatory drugs don't mix. So if you're taking aspirin or ibuprofen, don't use turmeric, and vice versa.

Bank on bromelain. Bromelain is an enzyme found in pineapple. Several studies have shown that it decreases pain and swelling. You can buy bromelain supplements in most health food stores. Dr. Pizzorno recommends taking 250 to 500 milligrams three times a day, before meals. "Or simply eat more pineapple," Dr. Duke adds.

Chinese Medicine

Press the right point. Periodically pressing the point Pericardium 6 may relieve CTS pain. The point is located in the middle of your inner wrist, $2\frac{1}{2}$ finger-widths above the wrist crease. Apply steady, penetrating finger pressure for 3 minutes every hour or two.

Consider acupuncture. If acupressure doesn't help, you may want to consult an acupuncturist, since acupuncture is a bit more potent. In one study, needle stimulation of the point Pericardium 6 brought relief to 35 of 36 people with CTS—including 14 who had unsuccessful surgery to alleviate their symptoms.

Home Remedies

Go for the cold. Applying cold packs can help control swelling in the wrists, says Susan Isernhagen, a physical therapist in Duluth, Minnesota. You can buy cold packs in drugstores, or you can make your own by putting a few ice cubes in a plastic bag. Wrap the pack in a cloth and apply it to your wrists for 15 minutes, then remove it for 15 minutes. Continue the 15-minutes-on, 15-minutes-off cycle for as long as necessary.

Slip on gloves. Cold hands mean constricted blood vessels. And constricted blood vessels mean less blood—and nourishment—to overworked hand and wrist tissues. Wearing gloves can help keep your hands warm and increase blood flow. What if you're keyboarding? Just cut off the fingertips of each glove, and you can type with ease.

Invest in a splint. Wearing a splint can prevent you from bending your wrist in ways that aggravate CTS symptoms. In one study of 331 people with CTS, 66 percent got relief with a combination of splinting and taking anti-inflammatory drugs.

A splint consists of a cloth-covered metal brace to support your wrist and Velcro straps for fastening. When you're wearing one, your wrist should be almost straight, in about the same position as when you're holding a pen. This position keeps the carpal tunnel as open as possible.

Splinting works best for people who are under age 50 *and* who have had CTS for less than 10 months, with only intermittent symptoms. A splint can be worn at night, during the day, or all the time—whenever your pain is worst. You can buy splints in medical supply stores and many drugstores. But check with your doctor to make sure your splint fits properly.

Cut out caffeine. Steer clear of caffeinated foods and beverages such as chocolate, cola, tea, and coffee. Caffeine constricts blood vessels, which reduces blood flow to the hands and aggravates CTS.

Get off your butts. Like caffeine, smoking constricts blood vessels, which impedes blood flow to the hands. And that worsens CTS symptoms.

Over-the-Counter Drugs

Choose an anti-inflammatory. Aspirin, ibuprofen, and naproxen (Aleve) all reduce pain and inflammation. If aspirin upsets your stomach, try the enteric-coated kind. It dissolves in the intestines rather than in the stomach.

Create a Wrist-Friendly Work Environment

If you spend a lot of time working on a computer, you're a prime candidate for carpal tunnel syndrome (CTS). You can minimize the strain of repeated keystroking by following this advice.

Add a pad. A foam keyboard pad positions your wrists above your fingers, which minimizes strain on your wrists and fingers.

Straighten out. When keyboarding, hold your wrists as straight as possible. Avoid resting them against your keyboard or on your desk in such a way that your fingers are higher than your wrists. This position aggravates CTS symptoms.

Be a softie. Type with a soft touch. Pounding the keys worsens CTS symptoms.

Rest regularly. Take frequent breaks to get your hands off your keyboard. If your job allows, try alternating computer work with other tasks.

What about acetaminophen? It's a pain reliever but not an anti-inflammatory. So it isn't especially effective against inflammatory conditions like CTS.

OTHER GOOD CHOICES

Massage

Let yourself be manipulated. Some people with CTS swear by deep-tissue bodywork targeting their arms, wrists, and hands.

Homeopathy

Try different remedies. According to homeopath Dana Ullman, wrist problems often respond well to microdoses of certain homeopathic medicines. The most effective preparations include Bryonia, Hypericum, Rhus toxicodendron, and Ruta graveolens. Which one will work best for you depends on your individual symptoms, so check with a homeopath.

Naturopathy

Take the plunge. Contrast hydrotherapy, which involves alternately dipping your hands and wrists in hot and cold water, is a favorite treatment among naturopaths. "It's a simple, efficient way to increase circulation to your wrists," says Douglas C. Lewis, N.D., a faculty member at Bastyr University in Kenmore, Washington. "It improves nutrition, eliminates wastes, and helps decrease pain."

Dr. Lewis recommends immersing your hands and wrists in tolerably hot water for 3 minutes, then in cold water for 30 seconds. Repeat three to five times, once or twice a day.

MEDICAL MEASURES

For especially severe CTS symptoms, some mainstream doctors administer injections of powerful anti-inflammatories called corticosteroids. Unfortunately, this approach doesn't always work. In one study, 78 percent of people with CTS saw their symptoms return within 18 months of receiving corticosteroid injections. What's more, long-term use of corticosteroids can cause serious side effects such as high blood pressure, osteoporosis, and adrenal gland damage.

Surgery is considered a last-resort treatment for CTS. During the procedure, the surgeon removes a portion of the ligament that forms one side of the carpal tunnel. This usually relieves pressure on the median nerve—although in 15 percent of cases, CTS symptoms persist. After surgery, you must wear a splint for 2 to 3 weeks. You may experience swelling at the base of your thumb for up to 4 months. Up to 6 months may pass before your hand strength and endurance return to normal.

Cataracts

More than four million Americans have vision-impairing cataracts, and some 500,000 Americans undergo corrective surgery every year. But even though the techniques for repair are very advanced, scientists still don't know how to stop cataracts before they start.

A cataract is a cloudy spot on the normally clear lens, a structure that sits just behind the pupil of your eye. Light has a tough time passing through the cloudy area, so visual images appear as though they're shrouded in fog. And in low-light conditions such as nighttime driving, incoming bright light gets scattered by the cataract, creating a potentially blinding glare.

SIMPLE SOLUTIONS
1. Nutrition
2. Supplements
3. Herbal Medicine
4. Chinese Medicine
5. Home Remedies
6. Homeopathy
7. Medical Measures

Cataracts can develop in conjunction with certain diseases (notably diabetes) or from long-term use of certain drugs (such as corticosteroids). They are also associated with prolonged exposure to ultraviolet radiation, the same kind of sunlight that causes sunburn.

For years, the mainstream medicine establishment maintained the position that cataracts are an inevitable and irreversible consequence of aging. But the latest evidence suggests otherwise. A number of studies published in mainstream medical journals have shown that "age-related" cataracts actually result from oxidative damage.

Oxidative damage occurs when highly unstable oxygen molecules, called free radicals, circulate through the blood and creep into every tissue, including the lenses of the eyes. The free radicals sabotage perfectly healthy molecules, which become free radicals themselves. This molecular chain reaction leaves behind a trail of cellular damage that over time can instigate an array of ailments, including cataracts.

Some free radicals occur naturally, as by-products of various bodily processes. But external factors play a role, too. For instance, eating lots of high-fat foods and smoking cigarettes increase free-radical formation. On the other hand, eating lots of fruits and vegetables reduces free-radical damage. That's because fruits and vegetables supply antioxidants, nutrients that are able to neutralize free radicals.

The oxidative damage theory puts a whole new spin on cataract treatment and prevention. It opens the possibility that you have some control over cataract development. By making certain lifestyle changes, you may even be able to delay or avoid surgery.

If you've already been diagnosed with cataracts, consider trying the following treatment options from the world of blended medicine.

BEST CHOICES

Nutrition

Trim the fat from your plate. Fatty foods increase free-radical activity throughout your body, including in the lenses of your eyes, says Alan P. Brauer, M.D. Meats and whole-milk dairy products are among the prime offenders. Limit your intake of these foods as much as possible.

Feast on antioxidant-rich foods. Four antioxidant nutrients—vitamins C and E, beta-carotene, and the mineral selenium—have been clearly linked to cataract prevention, says Joseph Pizzorno Jr., N.D. Many studies have shown that as consumption of these nutrients goes up, the risk of cataracts plummets. All four nutrients are plentiful in plant-derived foods, especially fruits and vegetables.

The selenium content of foods varies depending on the soil in which they're grown, according to clinical nutritionist Shari Lieberman, Ph.D. But generally, whole grains and most shellfish are good sources of the mineral as are some nuts like cashews and walnuts.

Supplements

Take a daily multivitamin. Taking a daily multivitamin/mineral supplement may be enough to lower cataract risk. Consider the ongoing Physicians' Health Study, a landmark investigation in which Harvard researchers are tracking the lifestyle habits and health status of 17,700 middle-age doctors. Over a 5-year period, the researchers found that the doctors who took daily multivitamins were 27 percent less likely to develop cataracts than the doctors who weren't supplementing.

Add antioxidant supplements. Studies dating back to the 1930s have found that antioxidant supplements—vitamins C and E, beta-carotene, and the mineral selenium—improve vision in people with early-stage cataracts. Dr. Pizzorno recommends taking 1,000 milligrams of vitamin C three times a day, 600 to 800 international units of vitamin E a day, 15 milligrams of beta-carotene a day, and 400 micrograms of selenium a day. If your multivitamin/mineral supplement doesn't supply these nutrients in their respective amounts, consider taking an antioxidant supplement, too. But check with your doctor first, since selenium dosages over 200 micrograms should only be taken under medical supervision.

Herbal Medicine

Be big on bilberry. During World War I, British fliers munched bilberries (also known as European blueberries) before bombing missions to sharpen their vision. Now we know why. According to Dr. Pizzorno, bilberries contain high levels of compounds called anthocyanosides, potent antioxidants that have an unusual affinity for the eyes.

European herbalists have developed a standardized bilberry extract that contains 25 percent anthocyanosides. Dr. Pizzorno suggests taking 80 to 160 milligrams of the extract three times a day. It's available in many health food stores and from most naturopaths.

Have herbal teas. Herbs rich in antioxidants include rosemary, the mints, ginger, and turmeric. All of these can be used in cooking, plus rosemary, the mints, and ginger can be taken as teas. For rosemary or mint tea, use 1 to 2 teaspoons of crushed dried leaves per 1 cup of boiled water; for ginger tea, use 1 to 2 teaspoons of grated fresh gingerroot per 1 cup of boiled water, says James A. Duke, Ph.D.

Try a Japanese remedy. Japanese physicians prescribe an herbal formula called hachimijogan to sharpen cloudy vision. In the early stages of cataract development, the formula's benefits are quite impressive, Dr. Pizzorno says. That may be because the eight herbs that make up the formula are high in antioxidants. Japanese researchers found that when a group of people with early-stage cataracts used hachimijogan, 60 percent showed improved vision. The standard dose is 150 to 300 milligrams a day, according to Dr. Pizzorno. But you must get hachimijogan from a naturopath.

Chinese Medicine

Check out a Chinese herbal blend. Practitioners of Chinese medicine consider cataracts and glaucoma to be two forms of the same problem, says Efrem Korngold, O.M.D., L.Ac.

For people in the early stages of cataract development, Dr. Korngold often prescribes a Chinese herbal formula called Huang Lian Yang Gan Wan. The formula contains many herbs, including bupleurum, coptis, gentian, philodendron, and skullcap.

Chinese physicians also recommend that people with cataracts drink chrysanthemum tea and eat lycii berries. Both chrysanthemum and lycii berries are sold in Asian markets.

Consult an acupuncturist. The United Nations World Health Organization recommends acupuncture for vision problems. Dr. Korngold agrees, noting that acupuncture has proved effective in the early stages of cataract development. If you prefer acupressure, you can stimulate the following points, using your fingertips to apply steady, penetrating pressure to each point for 3 minutes.

◆ Kidney 3, located in the hollow between your Achilles tendon and the inside of your anklebone

◆ Liver 3, situated on top of your foot in the webbing between your big toe and second toe

◆ Gallbladder 14, located just above your eyebrow in line with the pupil of your eye

Home Remedies

Snuff out cigarettes. "Smokers are at high risk for cataracts," says Dr. Duke. "I saw one study that compared the risk of cataracts among nonsmoking women and women who smoked 30 cigarettes a day. The smokers were 60 percent more likely to have cataracts than nonsmokers." That's because smoking boosts free-radical activity, which contributes to cataract formation.

Watch your weight. The Harvard researchers who are conducting the ongoing Physicians' Health Study have determined that obesity is a risk factor for cataracts. In the study, the doctors who weighed the most were more than twice as likely to have cataracts than the doctors who weighed the least.

OTHER GOOD CHOICES

Homeopathy

Get help from a homeopathic medicine. Edward Kondrot, M.D., an ophthalmologist and practicing homeopath in Pittsburgh, has had some success in treating early-stage cataracts with homeopathic medicine. Among the preparations he prescribes to his patients are Causticum, Calcarea phosphorica, Calcarea carbonica, Sepia, and Phosphoricum. Check with a homeopath to find out which medicine will work best for you.

Home Remedies

Let there be lights. If you have cataracts, brighter lightbulbs can help bring objects into focus. Also, position chairs and lamps in such a way that glare is minimized.

Shield your eyes. When you're out in the sun, wear sunglasses that screen out the sun's ultraviolet rays, as well as a hat with a broad, eye-protecting brim. And if your job or a hobby exposes you to very bright light (such as welding), be sure to wear protective goggles, says Anne Simons, M.D.

MEDICAL MEASURES

When cataracts become so bad that they interfere with your daily routine, most doctors recommend corrective surgery. During the procedure, the surgeon makes a small slit in the cornea and removes the lens, replacing it with a clear plastic lens. Then he sews shut the incision with fine thread (sutures) that the body absorbs over time.

The operation lasts about an hour and is performed under low-risk local anesthetic. In 90 percent of cases, it restores clear vision.

For people whose vision becomes permanently impaired as the result of cataracts, a nonprofit organization called Lighthouse International provides an array of support services. You can write to the organization at 111 East 59th Street, 12th Floor, New York, NY 10022-1202.

RED FLAGS

Always consult your doctor when you notice changes in your vision. Be sure to schedule follow-ups if your doctor thinks it's necessary.

Colds

The joke goes like this: "Ignore a cold, and it goes away in a week. Treat a cold, and it goes away in just 7 days."

Still, with blended medicine, you have at your disposal a number of effective strategies that increase your odds of vanquishing a cold virus or two. But you need to know what you're up against.

A cold can be caused by any one of about 200 viruses, according to Anne Simons, M.D. Viruses are living microorganisms, but they don't breathe, digest food, or eliminate wastes. Their main function is reproduction, which they do with a vengeance once they infect the cells located where the back of your nose meets your throat.

Technically, each virus causes a different type of cold. But all colds produce pretty much the same set of symptoms: sore throat,

SIMPLE SOLUTIONS
1. Supplements
2. Herbal Medicine
3. Home Remedies
4. Nutrition
5. Homeopathy
6. Chinese Medicine
7. Ayurvedic Medicine
8. Naturopathy
9. Medical Measures

coughing, sneezing, congestion, and runny nose. These symptoms result not from the virus itself but from your body's immune response to the virus. "You feel fine as you become infected," explains Stephen Rennard, M.D., a pulmonologist at the University of Nebraska Medical Center in Omaha. "You feel ill as your body fights to get well."

Before infected throat cells die, they release special chemicals—notably interferon and immunoglobulin A (IgA). These chemicals signal your immune system to prepare for a "cold war." As your immune system swings into action, the tiny blood vessels in your throat expand, allowing more blood to get to the site of the infection. The extra blood transports a whole army of immune warriors—white blood cells, antibodies, and the compounds histamine and bradykinin. Eventually, the swollen blood vessels trigger local pain nerves. That's when you notice the first signs of a sore throat. "But by the time you actually feel that sore throat, you've already been infected for about 24 hours," Dr. Simons points out.

Beware the Common Cold Myth

Bundle up, or you'll catch a cold!"
Contrary to what your mother may have told you, and what you may have told your own kids, chilliness and dampness have nothing to do with susceptibility to the common cold. Scientists have known this for quite some time.

So why has this common cold myth persisted? Because folks who live or work in environments with central heating and cooling often blame their colds on frigid room temperatures. The problem, however, is not low temperature but low relative humidity. Air can become so dry that it dehydrates the protective mucus in the nose and throat, allowing cold viruses to do their worst.

Extra fluid flows into your throat to help fight the infection. As the fluid accumulates in the sinus cavities surrounding your nose, it makes you feel congested. Some of the fluid may leak out through your nose, giving you the sniffles and triggering sneezes. Meanwhile, the airways that lead to your lungs, called the bronchial tubes, become irritated. This leaves you with a dry, hacking cough.

Once a cold has run its course, you remain immune to that particular virus and its close relatives for 3 to 5 years, according to Elliot Dick, Ph.D., retired chief of the respiratory viruses research laboratory at the University of Wisconsin–Madison.

Of course, that bit of information may be of little consolation when your nose is more stuffed than a Thanksgiving turkey and your throat feels like it's lined with steel wool. Fortunately, you can do a lot to make your cold less miserable. Start with these expert-recommended strategies.

BEST CHOICES

Supplements

Shore up your defenses with vitamin C. Ever since renowned American chemist Linus Pauling published *Vitamin C and the Common Cold* in 1970,

Give Colds the Slip

You hear a coworker sniffling and sneezing, and you assume the worst. A cold virus has entered the building, and it's only a matter of time before that nasty bug finds you.

A cold virus spreads one of two ways: through aerosol exposure or by direct contact. "Aerosol" means that the virus is floating through the air. "Direct contact" means that the virus is transmitted through touch—from infected noses to hands to uninfected noses.

The key to cold prevention, then, is to put some distance between you and cold viruses. Try following precautionary measures.

Wash your hands again and again. "Frequent hand washing is one of your best defenses against colds," says cold researcher Jack M. Gwaltney Jr., M.D., professor in the department of internal medicine at the University of Virginia Health Sciences Center in Charlottesville. "It removes the virus from your hands."

Hands off! If you must rub your nose or eyes, use a knuckle, which is less likely to be contaminated with a cold virus than your fingertips.

Retire cloth handkerchiefs. A cold virus can survive for several hours on cloth handkerchiefs, says Elliot Dick, Ph.D., retired chief of the respiratory viruses research laboratory at the University of Wisconsin–Madison. Switch to disposable facial tissues. Use them once and discard them.

Disinfect hard surfaces. In one study, Dr. Gwaltney contaminated a countertop with cold virus, then sprayed the area with disinfectant. He found that disinfecting greatly reduced the amount of cold virus.

Allow air to circulate. Ventilation disperses cold viruses through the air, so fewer viral particles get into your nose and throat. "You may not want to open windows in winter, but do what you can to keep the air moving," Dr. Dick says.

controversy has surrounded vitamin C's use as a cold remedy. Some studies have shown that the nutrient helps.

Other studies have suggested that vitamin C doesn't help fight colds at all. But many of those studies were flawed because the researchers used too little vitamin C for too short a time, according to Alan P. Brauer, M.D. "In the studies that showed benefits, the participants took at least 2,000 milligrams of vitamin C a day from the first throat tickle until the cold completely cleared up," he observes.

But that doesn't apply to everyone. Dr. Brauer routinely prescribes vitamin C in doses of 5,000 milligrams or more a day. To avoid diarrhea, which is sometimes a side effect, he suggests trying calcium ascorbate powder. "Calcium ascorbate is the form of vitamin C that's least irritating to the digestive tract and least likely to cause diarrhea," he explains. He recommends taking 1 teaspoon, mixed in juice, four times a day.

Suck on lozenges made with zinc. The effectiveness of zinc against cold symptoms was discovered quite by accident, with a little help from 3-year-old Karen Eby of Austin, Texas. Karen's doctor had given her zinc tablets to stimulate her immune system, which had been weakened by leukemia. Karen usually swallowed the tablets whole. But when a cold made swallowing too difficult, she sucked on the tablets instead. Her cold quickly disappeared.

Intrigued, Karen's father, George Eby, persuaded a group of researchers to test zinc as a cold remedy. In their study, the researchers found that cold-infected volunteers who sucked on a 23-milligram zinc gluconate lozenge every 2 hours had significantly shorter colds than cold-infected volunteers who sucked on a placebo (a fake pill). Research has since indicated that lozenges made only with either zinc gluconate-glycine or zinc acetate shorten the duration of cold symptoms.

Zinc works best if you start sucking on lozenges at the first sign of a tickle in your throat, says William Halcomb, D.O., of Mesa, Arizona, coauthor of the zinc study orchestrated by George Eby. Take one lozenge every 2 hours until your symptoms subside, unless the lozenges give you an upset stomach. In that case, use them as often as you comfortably can. (Eating something beforehand may help you avoid an upset stomach in the first place.) Also, don't use the lozenges any longer than one week. Over time, zinc can suppress the immune system.

Herbal Medicine

Embrace echinacea. "Echinacea is my favorite herbal immune stimulant," says James A. Duke, Ph.D. "I take it whenever I have a cold or any viral infection. Many studies have shown that it's beneficial." You can buy echinacea tincture in most health food stores. Follow package directions for proper dosage.

Grate some ginger. Dr. Duke also recommends sipping ginger tea when you have a cold. "Ginger contains a dozen antiviral compounds," he says. "And unlike many other medicinal herbs, it tastes good." To make a tea, add 1 heaping teaspoon of grated fresh gingerroot to 1 cup of boiled water. Allow to steep for 10 minutes. Drink up to three cupfuls a day until your cold gets better.

Home Remedies

Rest as much as you can. Your immune system works hard to vanquish a cold virus. You can support your body's defenses by resting. "That doesn't mean you have to lie in bed until your cold subsides," Dr. Simons says. "Just slow your pace and take it easy for a few days."

Drink lots of hot fluids. Flourishing when the temperature hovers around 90°F, cold viruses are far less comfortable—and less likely to replicate so quickly—when their environment heats up. Drink some hot fluids, and you'll warm your throat, which helps impair viral replication, says David S. Sobel, M.D., director of patient education and health promotion for Kaiser Permanente Northern California, a health maintenance organization. As a bonus, hot fluids have a mild decongestant effect, which helps relieve nasal stuffiness.

Slurp soup. Chicken soup has been a mainstay of folk medicine for 800 years, ever since the Egyptian physician Moses Maimonides recommended it as a cold remedy. And it really works, as many modern studies have shown. Researchers suspect that the soup's cold-fighting powers come not from the chicken but from the vegetables that are usually part of the stock.

OTHER GOOD CHOICES

Nutrition

Eat more mushrooms. Oriental mushrooms such as shiitake, maitake, and reishi contain compounds that bolster your immune system. So by eating these types of mushrooms, you're better able to fight off a cold, says Mindy Green, an herbalist in Boulder, Colorado, and coauthor of *Aromatherapy: A Complete Guide to the Healing Art*. These days, you can buy oriental mushrooms in many supermarkets. Try slicing the mushrooms on salads and into soups.

Steer clear of dairy. Many alternative practitioners recommend avoiding dairy products for the duration of a cold. At least one study has shown that a compound in milk triggers the release of histamine, a chemical that contributes to runny nose and nasal congestion.

Shun sweets. Neutrophils are a special type of white blood cell that engulf and destroy cold viruses and other foreign invaders. When a cold virus is on the march, you want your neutrophils to be as lively as possible. That's a good reason to stay away from sweets until your cold has run its course.

According to Joseph Pizzorno Jr., N.D., neutrophils become lethargic when you eat sweets. In one study, researchers had volunteers consume 100 grams of sugar, the equivalent of two cans of soda. Then the researchers took blood samples from the volunteers. When the researchers analyzed the samples, they found that neutrophil activity in the volunteers had plummeted by 50 percent. Five hours later, neutrophil activity remained substantially below normal.

Anything that contains any form of sugar—including sucrose, fructose, corn syrup, and honey—can impair neutrophil activity. The worst offenders are candy and sweets, which are almost pure sugar and have virtually no nutritional value. Fruits also contain sugar. But because they're rich in vitamins and minerals that support the immune system, their nutritional value more than compensates for their sugar content.

Homeopathy

Make the most of microdoses. For the common cold, homeopaths usually prescribe the medicines Allium cepa, Euphrasia, and Natrum muriaticum, says homeopath Dana Ullman. Depending on a person's symptoms, homeopaths may also recommend Aconitum, Bryonia, Belladonna, and Phosphorus.

These days, you don't have to consult a homeopath to use homeopathic cold remedies. Several homeopathic cold formulas are available in health food stores and some drugstores. Each formula contains some combination of the most common homeopathic medicines, according to Ullman. To use these products, follow package directions.

Chinese Medicine

Calm the Wind. Chinese medicine views the common cold as an invasion of Wind. "There are two basic types of colds—one caused by Wind Heat, the other by Wind Cold," says Efrem Korngold, O.M.D., L.Ac. "Heat colds are flulike; they produce fever. Cold colds produce chills and sensitivity to cold and drafts."

For Heat colds, Dr. Korngold typically prescribes herbal formulas containing chrysanthemum flowers, mulberry leaf, mint, peppermint, honeysuckle, forsythia buds, burdock seed, and licorice. For Cold colds, he recommends formulas made with cinnamon twig, gingerroot, asarum (which is similar to ginger), kudzu root, and licorice.

Like American pharmaceutical companies, Chinese physicians have developed their own cold formulas. Among the most popular is Yin Chiao Chieh Tu Pien, which contains honeysuckle and forsythia, among other herbs. Yin Chiao expels Wind from the respiratory tract, explains Harriet Beinfield, L.Ac., a licensed acupuncturist in San Francisco. She recommends taking six tablets of Yin Chiao every 3 hours at the first sign of a sore throat or runny nose. Dosing in this way can actually prevent symptoms from escalating to a full-blown cold. You can buy Yin Chiao from oriental medicine doctors and some acupuncturists.

Consider acupuncture. According to the United Nations World Health Organization, acupuncture is an effective treatment for colds. Acupressure can help, too, says Michael Reed Gach, founder and director of the Acupressure Institute. For self-treatment, Gach recommends applying steady, penetrating finger pressure to each of the following points for 3 minutes.

◆ Bladder 2, which relieves congestion and itchy eyes. It's located on either side of your nose, where the bridge of your nose meets the ridge of your eyebrows.

◆ Stomach 3, which also relieves congestion and itchy eyes. It's located at the bottom of either cheekbone, directly below your pupil.

◆ Large Intestine 20, which relieves nasal symptoms. It's located on either cheek in the groove beside each nostril.

Ayurvedic Medicine

Correct Kapha. Ayurvedic medicine teaches that the common cold results from an imbalance of the Kapha dosha. Several herbs can restore balance to Kapha—especially ginger but also cinnamon, licorice, basil, and cloves. Try taking 1 to 4 grams of any of these herbs in powdered form, suggests David Frawley, O.M.D. (Four grams equals about 2 to 3 teaspoons.) Add the herb to 1 cup of boiled water, stir, and let it cool before you drink it. Or, add herbs to foods of your liking.

Adjust your eating habits. Ayurvedic medicine also advocates dietary changes to treat colds. Consume more whole grains and steamed vegetables and fewer meats, dairy products, oily foods, nuts, pastries, and sweet fruit juices until your symptoms subside.

Naturopathy

Attack your cold from all angles. Dr. Pizzorno offers the following naturopathic prescription.

◆ Take 500 to 1,000 milligrams of vitamin C every 2 waking hours.

◆ Suck on one zinc gluconate-glycine or zinc acetate lozenge every 2 hours. If they give you an upset stomach, take as often as you can tolerate.

◆ Take the herbs echinacea, goldenseal, and astragalus—either 1 to 1½ teaspoons of tincture three times a day or 250 to 500 milligrams of powdered herb three times a day.

MEDICAL MEASURES

Hundreds of over-the-counter cold formulas claim to relieve every major cold symptom. Do they work?

After analyzing the findings of 51 studies published between 1950 and 1991, researchers determined that over-the-counter cold remedies have no effect on cold viruses or the immune system. What they do is suppress symptoms, providing some degree of relief from nasal congestion, runny nose, and cough.

Most doctors discourage the use of "shotgun" cold formulas that take aim at every major cold symptom. "Why pay for a cough suppressant when you have a stuffed-up nose?" Dr. Sobel asks. "Why risk side effects from medicines that you may not need—jitters and insomnia from decongestants, or drowsiness from antihistamines?"

If you prefer taking an over-the-counter cold remedy, Dr. Sobel suggests selecting a product that targets only the symptom you have. Use anesthetic lozenges for sore throat, a decongestant for congestion, an antihistamine with chlorpheniramine for runny nose, and a cough suppressant with dextromethorphan for a hacking cough.

RED FLAGS

Be sure to see your doctor if you experience shortness of breath or chest pain. You should also talk to your physician if you get a headache accompanied by a stiff neck or if you find that your eyes are sensitive to light.

Cold Sores

Uh-oh. You've had this tingly, pins-and-needles sensation at the corner of your mouth too many times before. Now it's back. And it can mean only one thing: In a day or two, you'll be sporting a cold sore.

Most cold sores are caused by a virus called herpes simplex type 1. Usually, you pick up the virus through direct, skin-to-skin contact with someone who either has a visible sore or is on the verge of getting one.

Because the virus can survive for a few hours outside the body, you could conceivably become infected in another way—say, by using someone else's towel or lip balm. But the virus needs warmth and moisture to thrive, and most environments outside the body don't provide that.

Not everyone who has herpes simplex type 1 develops cold sores, notes Joseph Pizzorno Jr., N.D. Some people have immune systems that are robust enough to keep the virus in check. These fortunate few can go for years without getting sores—without even knowing that they're infected.

SIMPLE SOLUTIONS
1. Nutrition
2. Supplements
3. Relaxation Therapies
4. Herbal Medicine
5. Home Remedies
6. Homeopathy
7. Chinese Medicine
8. Medical Measures

For the rest of us, what happens after infection with herpes simplex type 1 is pretty much the same. Within a few days to 2 weeks, you may feel tingling or itching in the area where the cold sore is about to erupt—usually at the corner of the mouth but sometimes inside the mouth or on the nose. This warning signal is called the prodrome. A day or two later, the prodrome gives way to a red, inflamed blisterlike lesion.

The first time you get a cold sore, you may also experience fever, swollen glands, and an allover ill feeling. The sore, and the symptoms, should clear up within 7 to 10 days—even without treatment.

But that doesn't mean the virus is gone. In fact, once you're infected with herpes simplex type 1, it stays with you for life. That means you may get more cold sores in the future.

Once a cold sore erupts, it can cause considerable pain. It can also be embarrassing, emblazoning your face for all the world to see. So you have every reason to want to make the sore heal quickly—and to protect yourself against future eruptions. With blended medicine, you stand your best chance of clearing up cold sores for good.

BEST CHOICES

Nutrition

Keep your eye on arginine. Protein contains various combinations of approximately two dozen amino acids. A few preliminary laboratory studies have shown that one of these amino acids, arginine, stimulates the herpes virus to multiply. So there is speculation that eliminating arginine-rich foods from your diet may help prevent cold sores. Among the foods you might want to consider avoiding are nuts, seeds, grains, raisins, cocoa, chocolate, carob, and gelatin.

Supplements

Learn the benefits of lysine. Some research suggests that pairing the elimination of arginine-rich foods with supplementation of lysine, also an amino acid, may help prevent the eruption of cold sores. How much lysine you should take depends on which expert you ask.

To be on the safe side, stick with the lowest effective dose, advises Melvyn R. Werbach, M.D., assistant clinical professor at the University of California, Los Angeles, School of Medicine. Because certain doses may raise your cholesterol level, you should check with your doctor before taking lysine. You can buy lysine supplements in health food stores.

Try a trio of healers. At least one study has shown that the combination of vitamin C, zinc, and nutrient compounds called flavonoids can boost your immune system enough to speed the healing of cold sores and prevent recurrences, Dr. Pizzorno says. He suggests taking 2,000 milligrams of vitamin C, 25 milligrams of zinc, and 1,000 milligrams of flavonoids every day from the moment you feel a sore coming on until the sore has healed.

Relaxation Therapies

Seek ways to short-circuit stress. The book *Mind-Body Medicine* describes a study in which researchers assessed the health status and psychological stress levels of a large number of nursing students. Those students under the most stress also had the most frequent recurrences of cold sores.

Not surprisingly, a regular stress-management program can have a major impact on cold sores. "You may be able to prevent outbreaks," says Martin L. Rossman, M.D. "If not, at least you'll recognize the stressors that trigger sores, and you'll be able to take precautions against spreading the infection."

A number of relaxation therapies can help you defuse stress, including tai chi, yoga, meditation, biofeedback, music therapy, and visualization. Dr. Rossman has produced many relaxation tapes that offer a step-by-step program with visualization exercises.

Herbal Medicine

Squeeze lemon from a tube. In 1978, researchers discovered that the herb lemon balm has impressive antiviral properties, thanks to compounds called polyphenols. Subsequent studies have shown that lemon balm ointment speeds the healing of cold sores. In one study, 87 percent of people who used the ointment saw their lesions completely heal within 6 days.

Lemon balm ointment is sold in many health food stores. Apply it two to four times a day for 5 to 10 days from the moment you feel a cold sore coming on, advises Christiane Northrup, M.D., founder of the Women to Women health center in Yarmouth, Maine, and past president of the American Holistic Medical Association.

Get acquainted with the mint family. Lemon balm isn't the only herb with antiviral properties. Its relatives in the mint family are almost as effective, according to James A. Duke, Ph.D. He suggests brewing a strong tea from a blend of sage, oregano, rosemary, thyme, and hyssop and applying it to the sore.

To make the tea, add a total of 2 to 3 teaspoons of any combination of these herbs to ½ cup of boiled water and steep for 10 minutes. Use a cotton ball or cotton swab to dab the tea onto your cold sore every few hours, starting when you feel the sore coming on and continuing until it heals.

Make echinacea your ally. Echinacea is well-known as an immune-stimulating herb. But as Dr. Duke points out, echinacea also has antiviral properties that make it a natural for treating cold sores. He suggests buying an echinacea tincture in a health food store. Follow the package directions for proper dosage.

Some tinctures combine echinacea with goldenseal, another immune-boosting, antiviral herb. Taking both herbs together may help your cold sore heal faster. Again, use the tincture according to package directions.

Swallow a lot of garlic. Dr. Northrup recommends taking 12 capsules of deodorized garlic the moment you feel a cold sore coming on. Then take 3 capsules every 4 waking hours over the next 3 days. Garlic has antiviral properties and can help stop recurrent sores, she says.

Home Remedies

Put your sore on ice. Applying an ice pack directly to your cold sore can help minimize pain, says Andrew T. Weil, M.D., director of the program in integrative medicine at the University of Arizona College of Medicine in Tucson.

Wrap the ice pack in a towel and lay it over your sore for 15 minutes, then remove it for 15 minutes. Continue this 15-minutes-on, 15-minutes-off cycle until you feel relief.

Leave it alone. It may be tempting to pick and poke at your cold sore. But if you get the virus on your fingers, you can easily spread it to another part of your body—or to another person. So keep your fingers away.

Let it breathe. Forget about coating your cold sore with petroleum jelly or an antibiotic or hydrocortisone cream. Generally, the sores heal best when left open to the air to dry out, says Stephen Sacks, M.D., associate professor of medicine at the University of British Columbia in Vancouver.

OTHER GOOD CHOICES

Homeopathy

Go short- or long-term. Homeopathic care for cold sores takes two different forms: acute treatment and constitutional therapy. Acute treatment speeds the healing of sores, explains homeopath Dana Ullman. Constitutional therapy boosts your immune system to prevent recurrences.

For both acute treatment and constitutional therapy, you need to see a homeopath, who can fully evaluate your symptoms and prescribe the appropriate medicines. Ullman usually prescribes one of the following: Rhus toxicodendron, Natrum muriaticum, Hepar sulfuris, Borax, Sepia (usually for women), or Sulfur (usually for men).

Chinese Medicine

Balance the elements. Practitioners of Chinese medicine attribute cold sores to excess Heat, Dampness, and Wind, says Efrem Korngold, O.M.D., L.Ac.

Dr. Korngold recommends eating more cooling foods, such as raw fruits and vegetables, while avoiding Heat-generating foods and beverages, such as spices, meats, sugar, alcohol, and anything fatty or greasy. He also often prescribes herbs that cool Heat and dry Dampness, including coptis, chrysanthemum, scutellaria, rhubarb, and forsythia.

Stimulate the right spot. To help heal a cold sore, try pressing the point Large Intestine 11. It's located at the outer end of your elbow crease on the thumb side. Apply steady, penetrating finger pressure to the point for 3 minutes, then switch arms.

MEDICAL MEASURES

No drug, prescription or over-the-counter, can kill the virus that causes cold sores, but some drugs can help sores heal faster. These include the prescription drugs acyclovir (Zovirax) and its close chemical relatives valacyclovir (Valtrex) and famciclovir (Famvir).

A relatively new prescription antiviral, penciclovir (Denavir), also appears to speed the healing process. Researchers at the University of Utah and several other medical centers around the United States and in England gave either penciclovir or a placebo (a fake pill) to 1,573 people with first-time cold-sore eruptions. Those taking the drug saw their sores clear up a half-day faster than those taking the placebo.

Congestive Heart Failure

Congestive heart failure, or CHF, is a sign that your heart has been working much too hard for too many years. It continues pumping blood, but not nearly as well as it should. As a result, your blood flow slows down.

Blood is responsible for delivering oxygen throughout your body. So when your blood flow becomes impaired, your tissues don't get the oxygen they need. Your body tries to compensate for the shortfall by increasing your breathing rate to get more oxygen into your blood. This is one reason for shortness of breath, a common CHF symptom. But breathing harder doesn't help because your heart can't move blood around your body very well.

That brings up another problem associated with CHF. When your heart pumps ineffi-

SIMPLE SOLUTIONS
1. Nutrition
2. Supplements
3. Exercise
4. Biofeedback
5. Herbal Medicine
6. Social Support
7. Home Remedies
8. Chinese Medicine
9. Ayurvedic Medicine
10. Medical Measures

ciently, it can't pump well enough to power your blood's return trip from your tissues. Instead, blood backs up in your veins and collects in your tissues, a process known as congestion. (This is the "congestive" in *congestive heart failure*.) Blood collects in your lungs, further aggravating shortness of breath and possibly causing a persistent cough. Fluid also pools in areas farthest from your heart, especially in your ankles and feet. This is why swollen ankles are a common CHF symptom.

Impaired blood flow also affects your kidneys. As circulation becomes sluggish, your kidneys can't eliminate excess fluid as they should. The built-up fluid increases congestion and aggravates swelling.

In addition to shortness of breath, fluid retention, and swelling, CHF can cause an irregular heartbeat by interfering with your heart's electrical circuitry. An irregular heartbeat, or arrhythmia, can be serious and should be monitored by a doctor.

Despite its severity, CHF isn't all that well-known. It certainly hasn't gotten the same publicity as coronary heart disease. Yet this condition is surprisingly common. By one estimate, it affects some five million Americans. Most of these people are over age 75, the population for which CHF risk is highest. The condition is almost unheard of in people under age 45.

CHF most often occurs because of damaged heart valves. Normally, a valve momentarily closes between pumps in order to prevent the blood from flowing backward. When the valve is damaged, it doesn't close properly, and the blood doesn't circulate through the heart efficiently. This leads to congestion. Other common reasons for the development of CHF are functional flaws within the heart caused by previous heart attacks, birth defects, or infections. Atherosclerosis, a condition characterized by the hardening and narrowing of the arteries, can play a central role in worsening any of these conditions and can cause CHF.

Atherosclerosis also elevates blood pressure. And high blood pressure contributes to CHF by making the heart work harder than normal. In fact, about three-quarters of people who develop CHF have high blood pres-sure.

Other factors can raise your risk of developing CHF. These include a high salt intake, certain nutritional deficiencies, kidney or liver disease, and emotional stress.

Treatment for CHF depends on the seriousness of the condition. If you have only mild to moderate symptoms, you may be able to manage them with home care under an M.D.'s supervision. But for more severe CHF, there is no substitute for aggressive treatment with mainstream medications, says naturopath Donald Brown, N.D., professor of herbal medicine at Bastyr University in Kenmore, Washington. If you've been diagnosed with congestive heart failure, you should definitely be under an M.D.'s care. And you should stick with any treatment program that your doctor prescribes.

That said, certain natural and alternative remedies may enhance the effectiveness of any therapies your doctor recommends. Here's what the experts say can help.

BEST CHOICES

Nutrition

Shake the salt habit. Sodium, a component of salt, causes fluid retention. And fluid retention raises blood pressure, which aggravates CHF. Reducing your salt intake may help alleviate fluid retention and the ankle swelling that accompanies it.

For people with CHF, Joseph Pizzorno Jr., N.D., recommends consuming no more than 1,800 milligrams of sodium a day. The average American consumes at least twice that much. Most of that amount—a full 75 percent—comes from salty processed foods: fast foods, canned soups and sauces, lunchmeats, frozen dinners, and snack foods.

If you're accustomed to salting everything, your food may seem too bland when you begin cutting back. You can make your own seasoning blend by combining a small amount of salt with herbs and spices.

Get more magnesium. If you have CHF, chances are that you have low blood levels of magnesium. The disease itself depletes the mineral, as do diuretic medications, the kind that help control blood pressure and relieve swelling. A magnesium deficiency can actually aggravate CHF symptoms, according to a study conducted at Mount Sinai School of Medicine of the City University of New York in New York City. To increase your magnesium intake, clinical nutritionist Shari Lieberman, Ph.D., suggests eating more magnesium-rich foods. These include wheat germ, soybeans, oatmeal, nuts, seeds, low-fat dairy items, and seafood.

Pick up more potassium. Like magnesium, potassium can be depleted by CHF as well as by diuretic medications. And when you have low potassium, your blood pressure can go up, which spells trouble for anyone with CHF. To get more potassium in your diet, Dr. Lieberman suggests eating lots of fruits, vegetables, beans, whole grains, low-fat dairy items, and fish.

Emphasize thiamin. Low levels of thiamin, a B vitamin, contribute to sodium retention and heart failure. Older people are at greatest risk for thiamin deficiency. They also have the highest rate of CHF. When researchers at the University of South Florida in Tampa examined 30 healthy older people, half of the group had thiamin levels low enough to aggravate CHF.

An easy way to increase your thiamin intake is to eat more thiamin-rich foods. Good sources of the vitamin include beans, peas, peanuts, whole grains, eggs, fish, and poultry.

Sip, don't guzzle. If you have CHF, you don't want to drink too much, because your body is retaining fluid. But restricting your fluid intake can be tricky. Cutting back too much can lead to dehydration, which causes problems of its own—especially among older people.

Ileana L. Pina, M.D., director of cardiomyopathy and cardiac rehabilitation at Temple University School of Medicine in Philadelphia, urges people with CHF to limit their fluid consumption to 2 quarts a day. When you feel thirsty, don't pour yourself a tall glass of water. Instead, suck on an ice pop or a few ice chips, Dr. Pina suggests. Or suck on hard candies or chew gum to stimulate salivation.

Supplements

Make up for shortfalls. If you think you're not getting enough magnesium or thiamin in your diet, you can take supplements to help raise your levels of these nutrients. For magnesium, Dr. Pizzorno recommends taking 200 to 400 milligrams three times a day. If you're concerned about thiamin, Dr. Pizzorno suggests taking 200 to 500 milligrams a day.

Cash in on carnitine. Chemically, carnitine—also known as L-carnitine—is an amino acid. But it functions like a B vitamin in your body. "About 60 percent of the energy that powers your heart comes from fatty acids. Carnitine helps move fatty acids into muscle tissues, including your heart," Dr. Lieberman explains. "Carnitine deficiency has been linked to heart failure, while carnitine supplementation helps treat CHF and prevent arrhythmias."

If you have CHF, taking supplemental carnitine is a good idea, says Alan Gaby, M.D. You can buy the supplements in health food stores and some drugstores. Take 1 gram of carnitine twice a day. Though carnitine is available over the counter, you should use it only under the supervision of your doctor since its safety isn't well-established.

Count on Q_{10}. A good deal of research has shown that people with CHF can benefit from supplements of a nutrient called coenzyme Q_{10}.

"Coenzyme Q_{10} is a very good treatment for CHF," says Alan P. Brauer, M.D. "The research is convincing." He recommends taking 150 to 200 milligrams a day. You can buy coenzyme Q_{10} supplements in health food stores and some drugstores.

Foxglove: The Original "Cure"

Some 225 years ago, congestive heart failure (CHF) played a pivotal role in demonstrating to mainstream doctors that folk herbalists had more up their sleeves than old wives' tales. Back then, CHF was called dropsy. Doctors had no way of treating the condition or the shortness of breath and swelling that it caused.

In 1775, the fiancée of English physician William Withering mentioned that she knew someone who could treat dropsy. The couple paid a visit to a folk herbalist, or wisewoman, who showed Withering the tea that she gave to people with dropsy. The tea's main ingredient was the herb foxglove.

Withering tested foxglove on patients with dropsy, with considerable success. He reported his findings in one of the prominent medical journals of the day. In doing so, he introduced his colleagues to foxglove and convinced them of the herb's merits.

Subsequently, drugs derived from foxglove—notably digoxin—were prescribed by mainstream doctors for CHF treatment.

Exercise

Ease into an active lifestyle. For years, doctors recommended rest for people with CHF. Not anymore. "We strongly recommend exercise," Dr. Pina says. "It increases your stamina and improves your heart function. It also makes you feel better."

Of course, when you have a fatigued heart, you have to be careful about physical activity. But your physician can test you to determine how much exercise you can safely tolerate. Chances are that you can walk, swim, cycle, golf, garden, or do similar activities that aren't too strenuous. Just check with your doctor before starting a new exercise program.

Biofeedback

Make blood flow better. To treat CHF, mainstream M.D.'s often prescribe medicines that expand blood vessels. Called vasodilators, these drugs lower blood pressure and allow blood to circulate more easily. But they may produce side effects. Biofeedback can provide similar benefits without side effects, as demonstrated in a study led by Debra K. Moser, R.N., D.N.Sc., assistant professor at Ohio State University in Columbus.

Dr. Moser and her colleagues taught 20 people with CHF to use biofeedback to open their blood vessels, with the goal of improving circulatory efficiency. Another 20 people continued receiving standard treatment. Those who practiced biofeedback showed significant increases in blood vessel diameter, which means their circulation improved. Their hearts were pumping more blood, too.

Herbal Medicine

Try a heart-friendly herb. The leaves and flowers of the herb hawthorn contain abundant supplies of compounds called flavonoids. Flavonoids improve the heart's pumping ability and the flow of blood through the circulatory system. "Hawthorn is very useful in treating CHF, especially in the early stages," Dr. Pizzorno says.

Since hawthorn is such a potent herb, check with your doctor before you begin taking it. It may interfere with some high blood pressure medications and could be dangerous to those with low blood pressure.

Feel better with willow bark. The herb willow bark contains a compound, salicin, that's the chemical forerunner of aspirin. Like aspirin, willow bark can help prevent the blood clotting that leads to heart attack and stroke. If the latest research is any indication, the herb may also benefit people with CHF.

If you'd like to try willow bark, take it as a tea, suggests James A. Duke, Ph.D. Simmer 1 teaspoon of the powdered herb in 1 cup of boiling water for 10 minutes, then strain. Drink two to three cupfuls daily.

Social Support

Find someone to lean on. People with CHF who get emotional support from others are much more likely to manage their symptoms effectively. Harland Krumholz, M.D., associate professor of medicine at Yale University School of Medicine, analyzed the medical records of 292 elderly women who had developed heart failure. He found that compared with those who received the most emotional support, the women who felt socially isolated were eight times more likely to complain of CHF symptoms.

To find a CHF support group in your area, ask your doctor or contact your local office of the American Heart Association.

Home Remedies

Lose those extra pounds. Being overweight raises your blood pressure and makes your heart work harder to move blood through all the extra tissue. Losing weight, on the other hand, lowers your blood pressure and gives your tired heart a break.

Research shows that the combination of weight control and sodium restriction can make an even bigger difference in your blood pressure and, therefore, in CHF symptoms.

OTHER GOOD CHOICES

Chinese Medicine

Rejuvenate qi. Practitioners of Chinese medicine believe that heart failure results from chronic fatigue of qi. "As qi weakens, the heart pumps less efficiently, blood doesn't move as it should, and fluids accumulate around the body," explains Efrem Korngold, O.M.D., L.Ac. In the Chinese view, fluids are Moisture, and they're regulated by the Kidneys. To treat CHF, he prescribes herbal formulas that usually contain herbs such as ginseng root, astragalus root, salvia root, angelica root, cinnamon bark, and licorice root.

Aid your heart with acupressure. People with CHF can also benefit from professional acupuncture treatment, Dr. Korngold says. If you prefer a self-care alternative, consider acupressure. Apply steady, penetrating finger pressure to each of the following points for 3 minutes.

◆ Pericardium 6, located in the middle of your inner wrist, 2½ finger-widths above the wrist crease

◆ Heart 7, located on the pinkie side of the wrist crease that's closest to your palm

◆ Kidney 7, located on your inner leg, two thumb-widths above your anklebone

◆ Stomach 36, located four finger-widths below your kneecap and one finger-width toward the outside of your shinbone

⚖ Ayurvedic Medicine

Ask about arjuna. Among Ayurvedic practitioners, arjuna bark is the herb of choice for treating heart failure. Research has shown that it significantly improves heart functions. If you'd like to try arjuna bark, consult an Ayurvedic practitioner for a prescription and dosage information.

MEDICAL MEASURES

For 200 years, the drugs digitalis and digoxin—both derived from the herb foxglove—were the first-line mainstream medical treatments for CHF. But then reports that these drugs might cause heart rhythm disturbances, or arrhythmias, began cropping up.

Today, digoxin is still prescribed for CHF, but it is no longer a first-line treatment. Most doctors now prescribe either diuretics, which help eliminate fluid, or vasodilators, which lower blood pressure and allow blood to circulate more easily. If your doctor recommends a diuretic or vasodilator, be sure to ask about potential side effects. Take the pills on the prescribed schedule. And if you notice any side effects, discuss them with your doctor.

Your doctor might also prescribe low-dose aspirin. In a study conducted at Tufts University School of Medicine in Boston, researchers spent 5 years tracking the health status of 6,800 people with CHF. Some of the people took aspirin, while others did not. In the course of the study, 41 percent of the nonaspirin takers were hospitalized or died because of CHF. Among the aspirin takers, that figure was just 26 percent.

Another option in CHF treatment is enrollment in a cardiac rehabilitation program. These programs are usually recommended for people who have had heart attacks and for people with angina.

For more information about cardiac rehabilitation programs, talk to your doctor.

Constipation

Some people go three times a day. Others, three times a week.
Fine. But what if the person who goes three times a day suddenly can't go even *once* a day?

Now that's what you call constipation.

In other words, whether or not you're constipated depends on how often you *normally* move your bowels. True, 83 percent of Americans go at least once a day, according to one survey. But that doesn't mean the remaining 17 percent are constipated.

"There's nothing sacred about the daily bowel movement," according to pharmacists Joe Graedon and Teresa Graedon, Ph.D., coauthors of *The People's Pharmacy* books. "Everyone is different. Anything in the range of three a day to three a week is perfectly normal."

Everyone has an occasional bout of "irregularity." But for some four million unlucky Americans, constipation is a chronic problem.

SIMPLE SOLUTIONS
1. Nutrition
2. Supplements
3. Exercise
4. Biofeedback
5. Herbal Medicine
6. Home Remedies
7. Homeopathy
8. Chinese Medicine
9. Ayurvedic Medicine
10. Over-the-Counter Drugs
11. Medical Measures

Most cases of constipation result from a combination of too little exercise, too little dietary fiber, and not enough fluids, says Anne Simons, M.D. Exercise stimulates peristalsis, the natural wavelike contractions in the lower colon that give you the urge to void. Fiber adds bulk to stool, which also prompts peristalsis. And fluids keep stool soft, so it passes comfortably.

Other factors can also raise your risk of constipation, says Alan P. Brauer, M.D. Just getting older makes you more prone to irregularity. Roughly 10 percent of American adults over age 60 have chronic constipation, compared with only 4 percent of younger adults.

Why the higher rate of constipation among older folks? One reason is that peristalsis naturally loses some of its oomph over time, Dr. Simons explains.

Another reason is that the body's production of stomach acid and pancreatic enzymes slows down. This makes for less efficient digestion and waste elimination, says Joseph Pizzorno Jr., N.D.

Besides age, certain medical conditions can contribute to constipation as can certain medications and iron supplements. Travel is another common culprit because it alters your eating and exercise habits as well as your bathroom "routine." If you're a woman, pregnancy can make you more prone to constipation, as your expanding uterus puts pressure on your colon and decreases peristalsis.

Of course, if you're like most people, you're probably less concerned about what has made you constipated than about how to get things moving again. Here's what you can do.

BEST CHOICES

Nutrition

Emphasize fiber. "You don't see much constipation in countries with high-fiber diets," observes Marion Nestle, Ph.D., chairperson of nutrition and food studies at New York University in New York City. "You see it in countries like the United States, where many people eat a low-fiber diet."

To increase your fiber intake, Dr. Nestle recommends eating whole grains, beans, fruits, or vegetables at every meal and as snacks. Wheat bran, the leading constipation preventive, is an ingredient in dozens of breakfast cereals such as All-Bran and Bran Buds. Popcorn makes a satisfying high-fiber snack. Enjoy bean soups and bean burritos, or munch on low-fat tortilla chips with bean dip. Prunes, raisins, broccoli, carrots, figs, and dried apricots also contain generous amounts of fiber.

Banish the binders. Some foods are binding, meaning that they contribute to constipation, Dr. Simons says. Limiting your consumption of bananas, cheeses, white rice, applesauce, and foods made with white flour can help keep you regular.

Quaff coffee. Many people have noticed that coffee has a laxative effect on them. The caffeine in coffee helps relieve constipation by stimulating peristalsis. If you're not a coffee drinker, tea, cocoa, and cola may also supply enough caffeine to get your bowels moving.

Supplements

Cure constipation with C. "High doses of vitamin C cause loose stools," Dr. Brauer says. "While that can be a problem for people who are prone to diarrhea, it can help those who are constipated." He recommends taking 1,000 milligrams of vitamin C every 2 waking hours until you're able to go to the bathroom.

Find relief in folic acid. One study found that women who experienced problems with constipation had low levels of the B vitamin folic acid in their blood. When the women began taking folic acid supplements, all of their symptoms subsided. Try taking up to 5,000 micrograms a day until the condition subsides, advises clinical nutritionist Shari Lieberman, Ph.D. But check with your doctor first, since dosages of folic acid over 1,000 micrograms should only be taken under medical supervision.

Receive a push from pantothenic acid. A few studies have suggested that taking supplements of the B vitamin pantothenic acid may help relieve constipation. Melvyn R. Werbach, M.D., assistant clinical professor at the University of California, Los Angeles, School of Medicine, recommends getting 250 milligrams of pantothenic acid a day.

Support the digestive process. Naturopaths often prescribe supplemental stomach acid and digestive enzymes for older people with constipation. Dr. Pizzorno suggests trying one of the following: bromelain, an enzyme in pineapple (250 to 500 milligrams with meals); papain, an enzyme in papaya (500 to 1,000 milligrams with meals); or pancreatin, an enzyme secreted by the pancreas (two to four tablets of 4X potency or one to two tablets of 8X potency). Supplements of all three enzymes are available in most health food stores.

Iron out the problem. The mineral iron can contribute to constipation in some people. If you take a multivitamin/mineral supplement that contains iron, switch to one without it and see if that helps.

Exercise

Get moving to get things moving. Exercise stimulates peristalsis. There's no need to run a marathon, Dr. Pizzorno says. A brisk walk for ½ hour each day usually does the trick.

Biofeedback

Relax to release. At the University of Amsterdam in the Netherlands, researchers taught biofeedback to 29 children who had trouble with chronic constipation because they couldn't relax their anal sphincters. After an average of five biofeedback sessions, 90 percent of the children had learned how to relax their sphincters, and their constipation was considered cured.

Herbal Medicine

Let psyllium be your salvation. The best herbal treatment for constipation is psyllium seed, says James A. Duke, Ph.D. It contains mucilage, a soluble fiber that expands when it absorbs water. In this way, it adds bulk to stools. Bulkier stools press against the colon wall and stimulate peristalsis.

A number of over-the-counter products—including Metamucil and Fiberall—have psyllium as their active ingredient. They usually work within 12 to 72 hours. But as Dr. Duke notes, they must be taken with 8 to 10 ounces of water or juice in order to be effective.

Home Remedies

Use honey as a natural laxative. Some 800 years ago, the Egyptian physician Maimonides prescribed honey mixed with warm water—taken every morning for 3 or 4 days—as a treatment for constipation. More recently, Greek researchers discovered that people have faster bowel movements when they take a high-fructose drink. And fructose is the substance that gives honey its sweetness.

Check your oil. In the Mediterranean region, people have long relied on olive oil as a cure for constipation. They take a tablespoon of the oil every few hours until things get moving again. Olive oil—or any vegetable oil, for that matter—acts as a lubricant, Dr. Simons explains. It coats the stool, promoting easier passage.

Adopt bowel-friendly habits. According to Dr. Pizzorno, constipation often results from bad toilet habits. You can retrain your bowels to move regularly with the following tips.

◆ Eat at roughly the same times every day, without rushing. This helps train the body for regular bowel movements.

◆ Never ignore the urge to go to the bathroom.

◆ Sit, but don't strain. Straining contributes to hemorrhoids.

Give yourself some leverage. While sitting on the toilet, try placing your feet on a small footstool. "It puts you in more of a squatting position, which helps some people go," Dr. Simons explains.

OTHER GOOD CHOICES

Homeopathy

Seek a homeopath's advice. "Used in conjunction with diet and lifestyle changes, homeopathic medicines provide an extra little push in relieving constipation," says homeopath Dana Ullman. Among the medicines he prescribes are Bryonia, as a stool softener; Calcarea carbonica, for those who don't feel the urge to go; and Nux vomica, for those who feel the urge but don't pass anything. Which medicine will work best for you depends on your individual symptoms.

Chinese Medicine

Stick to spicy stimulators. Among practicioners of Chinese medicine, it is thought that constipation develops when there is an imbalance in the Large Intestine and Stomach organ systems, according to Efrem Korngold, O.M.D., L.Ac.

When treating patients who have constipation, practitioners of Chinese medicine often prescribe spicy foods to stimulate peristalsis. These foods include ginger, radishes, orange peel, persimmons, and rhubarb. In cases of mild constipation associated with indigestion or a cold, practitioners may also prescribe Curing Pills, which contain 15 different herbs.

Point a finger at the problem. Acupressure has proved effective in stimulating a balky bowel. Michael Reed Gach, founder and director of the Acupressure Institute, recommends applying steady, penetrating finger pressure to each of the following points for 3 minutes.

◆ Large Intestine 11, located at the outer end of your elbow crease on the thumb side

◆ Large Intestine 4, located on the back of your hand where the bones of your thumb and index finger meet

◆ Conception Vessel 6, located three finger-widths directly below your navel

◆ Stomach 25, located four finger-widths to either side of your navel

◆ Stomach 36, located four finger-widths below your kneecap and one finger-width toward the outside of your shinbone

If acupressure doesn't provide relief from constipation, consult an acupuncturist instead. Frequently, needle stimulation by a professional works when finger pressure doesn't.

Ayurvedic Medicine

Go naturally. Generally, Ayurvedic remedies are very similar to what's prescribed in other healing systems. But Ayurvedic practitioners also prescribe herbal laxatives such as senna, rhubarb, aloe, and cascara sagrada. These herbs are potent chemical stimulants, and they must be used carefully, Dr. Pizzorno says. Otherwise, they may cause cramping, diarrhea, and bloody stools. So check with a knowledgeable Ayurvedic practitioner for the proper herb and dosage.

Over-the-Counter Drugs

Head for the drugstore. If none of the above approaches relieves your constipation within a few days, consider taking an over-the-counter laxative. In addition to the bulk formers described earlier, you can choose from lubricants, saline laxatives, and stool softeners. All of these products are gentle and safe, but be sure to use them only as directed.

Lubricants contain mineral oil, a petroleum product. Like olive oil, mineral oil coats stool to promote easier passage. Lubricants usually work within 6 to 8 hours.

Saline laxatives change the salt balance in your digestive tract. They draw water into stool, which adds bulk and stimulates peristalsis. Milk of magnesia is the best-known saline laxative. It produces results within 1 to 6 hours.

Stool softeners draw more water into stool, making it softer and easier to pass. These products usually work within 12 to 72 hours. For best results, Dr. Simons says, they should be taken with plenty of nonalcoholic fluids.

MEDICAL MEASURES

Among over-the-counter laxatives, those classified as chemical stimulants should be considered last resorts and only taken for a short period of time. Among the active ingredients listed on the back of the package, you're likely to find chemicals such as bisacodyl, senna, and cascara sagrada.

The gentlest stimulant laxatives contain the medicinal herb cascara sagrada

(Nature's Resource). Other, more powerful laxatives have bisacodyl (Dulcolax), buckthorn (Herbal Laxative Tablets), or senna (Senokot). Most have side effects. If you find that you need to use stimulant laxatives, it's best to consult your physician first.

In addition to their possible side effects, stimulant laxatives can actually cause a form of constipation known as lazy bowel syndrome. In this condition, bowel movements no longer occur without chemical stimulation. Lazy bowel syndrome is one reason why physicians discourage using stimulant laxatives more than once or twice a month.

Besides laxatives, some people rely on enemas to relieve constipation. Enemas irrigate the bowel and act as lubricants and stimulants. But frequent enemas can damage the colon and disrupt the balance of key minerals called electrolytes. For these reasons, the American Pharmaceutical Association advises against using enemas as a treatment for constipation.

RED FLAGS

While constipation is bothersome, it's usually not a cause for concern. But it can be a symptom of other, potentially serious conditions such as diabetes, thyroid problems, uterine fibroids, and certain types of cancer. So if your constipation does not clear up after a week of self-care using the approaches described in this chapter, or if it is associated with vomiting, abdominal pain, or fever, consult your physician.

Depression

Everyone gets the blues from time to time. They're a normal part of life. But when those feelings of sadness and despair linger, when nothing seems to lift your spirits, you may have slipped into serious depression, which doctors call either major or clinical depression. *Major* means that your depression is considerably more serious than everyday blues. *Clinical* means that you need professional help. But only a minority of people who are clinically depressed require hospitalization. Most get better with regular visits to a mental health professional and with drug and nondrug treatments.

According to the National Institute of Mental Health, depression is America's leading mental health problem. It's so widespread that it has been likened to the common cold. In any year, more than 15 million Americans experience episodes of clinical depression. Worldwide, the incidence of the condition has increased with each successive generation since 1915.

SIMPLE SOLUTIONS

1. Supplements
2. Exercise
3. Relaxation Therapies
4. Massage
5. Music Therapy
6. Social Support
7. Herbal Medicine
8. Home Remedies
9. Aromatherapy
10. Homeopathy
11. Chinese Medicine
12. Ayurvedic Medicine
13. Medical Measures

According to the American Psychiatric Association, depression can take a number of different forms, ranging from normal grief and "adjustment phases" to major depression, when a person feels overwhelmed with despair and hopelessness. Major depression may also cause anxiety, agitation, irritability, chronic indecisiveness, weight loss or gain, and sleep disturbances.

Despite their differences, the various forms of depression don't have clear boundaries, says Alan P. Brauer, M.D. Only a trained professional can tell when symptoms of normal grief cross the line to more serious depression.

The different forms of depression also share the same biochemical roots, Dr. Brauer says. In blood tests, people with depression invariably show unusu-

Are You Depressed?

If you answer yes to more than two of the following questions, you may have clinical depression. Consult your doctor or a mental health professional.

1. Much of the time, do you feel sad, lethargic, pessimistic, hopeless, worthless, or helpless?

2. Much of the time, do you have difficulty making decisions, have trouble concentrating, or have memory problems?

3. Lately, have you lost interest in things that used to give you pleasure, had problems at work or in school, had problems with your family or friends, or isolated or wanted to isolate yourself from others?

4. Lately, have you felt low in energy; felt restless and irritable; had trouble falling asleep, staying asleep, or getting up in the morning; lost your appetite or gained weight; or been bothered by persistent headaches, stomachaches, backaches, or muscle or joint pain?

5. Lately, have you been drinking more alcohol than you used to; taking more mood-altering drugs than you used to; engaging in risky behavior, such as not wearing a seat belt or crossing streets without looking?

If you have thoughts of hurting or killing yourself, you may well be seriously depressed. You should call a mental health professional or suicide prevention hotline immediately.

ally high levels of a hormone called cortisol. They also show variations in several brain chemicals, including serotonin, dopamine, and norepinephrine.

Scientists have yet to figure out exactly how or why this biochemical imbalance occurs, says Stuart Yudofsky, M.D., of the psychiatry department at Baylor College of Medicine in Houston. But several factors appear to be involved, including the following:

Previous depression. If you have one episode of major depression, you're likely to develop another one.

Family history. The chemical imbalance that characterizes depression can be inherited, which is one reason that the condition tends to run in families. An estimated 20 percent of people who develop depression have close relatives who are affected by the condition.

Gender. According to most surveys, women develop depression twice as often as men, recover from it more slowly, and are more likely to experience re-currences.

Age. An estimated 15 percent of people over age 65 experience depression at some point during their later years. Instead of the classic symptoms, these people may complain of persistent fatigue, appetite loss, weight loss, and difficulty concentrating.

Chronic illness. Depression is one of the most common—and potentially dangerous—complications of chronic illness. Many surveys have demonstrated that living with a chronic illness takes a tremendous emotional toll.

Severely stressful events. For people who are predisposed to depression because of genetics or upbringing, severe stress may be enough to trigger an episode. It doesn't necessarily develop immediately, however. It may take 6 months to a year.

Medications. Several pharmaceuticals can cause or aggravate depression. The primary offenders include diazepam (Valium) and other tranquilizers, oral contraceptives, the flu medicine amantadine (Symmetrel), steroids (prednisone and cortisone), and some cancer chemotherapy drugs.

No matter what causes it, depression is treatable. Unfortunately, some people don't know this—or try to ignore the symptoms. One-third of people who have depression never seek treatment.

Even when people go to their doctors for help, they often fail to mention their depression-related symptoms. As a result, many doctors have difficulty diagnosing the condition.

If you even suspect that you have depression, see your doctor to get an official diagnosis and to discuss your treatment options. Depending on the type of depression, you may benefit most from a combination of antidepressant drugs and alternative therapies. With the array of treatments now available, approximately 85 percent of people with major depression recover, says John McIntyre, M.D., past president of the American Psychiatric Association.

BEST CHOICES

Supplements

Build your supply of Bs. Even marginal deficiencies of the B vitamins—thiamin, riboflavin, B_6, B_{12}, and folic acid—can cause or aggravate depression, says Melvyn R. Werbach, M.D., assistant clinical professor at the University of California, Los Angeles, School of Medicine. And many Americans don't get enough of the Bs in their diets. That's because we tend to eat refined grains rather than whole grains—and refined grains have all of their B vitamins removed during milling. Certain vitamins and minerals have been added to enriched bread, but the B vitamins aren't among them.

If you think that you're coming up short on the B vitamins, take a 50- to 300-milligram B-complex supplement every day, suggests clinical nutritionist Shari Lieberman, Ph.D. Make sure that the supplement contains 25 to 300 micrograms each of B_{12} and folic acid.

Look into L-tryptophan. Some medications treat depression by tinkering with levels of a brain chemical called serotonin. You can achieve roughly the same effect by taking L-tryptophan, an amino acid that boosts the production of serotonin.

"Several studies have shown that L-tryptophan helps relieve depression," says Alan Gaby, M.D. "The typical dose is 1 to 2 grams three times a day with meals." You could buy L-tryptophan over the counter until 1989, when a contaminated batch persuaded the Food and Drug Administration to order the supplement taken off the shelves. Now it's available only by prescription. Ask your doctor about it.

Exercise

Don't fret, sweat. According to Dr. Yudofsky, exercise helps treat depression in four ways. It triggers the release of endorphins, your body's natural mood-elevating, pain-relieving compounds. It reduces your blood levels of the stress-depression hormone cortisol. It helps you put your life in perspective. And it gives you a sense of accomplishment, which enhances your self-esteem.

Which kind of exercise is best? "Whatever you like," says Anne Simons, M.D. "Ideally, it should be something you can do for at least a half-hour a day or at least three times a week." Ride a bike, swim, play volleyball, garden, go bowling, play golf, or take a walk—whatever your choice, it's the right one.

Relaxation Therapies

Wind down, cheer up. People who practice relaxation therapies often report feelings of enhanced well-being. "Many studies have shown mood elevation in people with depression who regularly elicit the relaxation response," notes Herbert Benson, M.D., the Harvard researcher who popularized the relaxation response and introduced meditation into American mainstream medicine.

Incorporate deep relaxation into your life and practice it regularly. Choose from meditation, visualization, biofeedback, and self-hypnosis, among other techniques.

Massage

Rub in relaxation. If you've ever gotten a massage, you know how relaxing and refreshing it feels. Studies have shown massage to be a powerful mood-enhancer. At the Touch Research Institute of the University of Miami Medical School, psychologist Tiffany Field, Ph.D., professor of psychology, pediatrics, and psychiatry at the University of Miami School of Medicine, had massage therapists give twice-a-week 20-minute Swedish massages to women hospitalized for serious postpartum depression. The women experienced decreases in their blood levels of stress hormones, and they reported improvements in mood.

Music Therapy

Sample Saul's salvation. In the biblical Book of Samuel, King Saul exhibited the classic symptoms of depression: persistent sadness, listlessness, and irritability. To ease the monarch's melancholy, David, the future king, played music for him.

David had the right idea. Modern research suggests that music can help ease depression. In one study, two groups of people with serious depression regularly listened to music. A third group didn't listen to music at all. Compared with the people who didn't listen to music, those who did showed significant improvements in mood.

Music therapists say that whatever people like works best. So listen to what you like. If your depression makes you think that you don't like any music, play what you recall having enjoyed in the past.

Social Support

Meet people like you. Since the 1970s, many studies have shown that social isolation releases a flood of stress hormones that can trigger or aggravate depression. "But well-developed social networks reduce blood levels of these hormones," says David Spiegel, M.D., professor of psychiatry and behavioral sciences and director of the Psychosocial Treatment Laboratory at Stanford Uni-

Postpartum Depression: The Birth of the Blues

After childbirth, some two-thirds of new mothers experience "baby blues"—feelings of disappointment, sadness, and anxiety. These feelings usually go away within a week or two, according to Jane Honikman, executive director of Postpartum Support International in Santa Barbara, California.

Another 10 to 15 percent of new moms experience the more severe postpartum depression, according to Barbara Parry, M.D., associate professor of psychiatry at the University of California, San Diego, School of Medicine. Symptoms of postpartum depression typically appear within a few months of delivery. They include deep sadness, frequent crying, insomnia, lethargy, and irritability.

Any woman can develop postpartum depression, says Donna Stewart, M.D., professor of psychiatry at the University of Toronto.

The treatments are the same as those recommended for major depression, Dr. Stewart says. But if you're breastfeeding and your doctor prescribes an antidepressant, make sure that it's one that won't enter your breast milk. Some antidepressants do, but others don't.

In addition, Postpartum Support International provides free crisis counseling and other assistance for women with postpartum depression. You can write to the organization at 927 North Kellogg Avenue, Santa Barbara, CA 93211. The phone number is available through directory assistance.

versity School of Medicine. "We humans are social animals. People help people cope with stress and depression."

To find a support group near you, contact the National Foundation for Depressive Illness. You can obtain the organization's toll-free number by calling toll-free directory assistance.

Seek spirituality. Through faith in a higher power, many people find the inner strength to overcome crises and recover from depression. That's what Duke University researchers discovered when they analyzed the "intrinsic religiosity" of 87 people with depression. Intrinsic religiosity is a measure of inner religious feelings—that is, feelings of spiritual connection to the universe beyond your-self, whether or not you're a member of a religious institution. The researchers found that the greater people's intrinsic religiosity, the faster their recovery from depression.

Embrace family and friends. One of the hallmarks of depression is so-cial withdrawal. This was demonstrated in a study of 506 people hospitalized for heart disease, a condition that often triggers or aggravates depression. A team led by Duke University psychologist Beverly Brummett, Ph.D., evaluated the level of support that each patient received from family and friends. The more support the patients had, the less likely they were to become depressed.

Be your own best friend. "People are generally much harder on them-selves than they are on others," notes Allen Elkin, Ph.D., director of the Stress Management and Counseling Center in New York City. "Look at your problem through a friend's eyes. Tell yourself what a friend would tell you." Suppose, for example, that you get lost on the way to a meeting. Instead of calling your-self an idiot, consider what a friend would say: "So you took a wrong turn. So what? Everyone makes mistakes. Just turn around and get back on track. No big deal."

Herbal Medicine

Praise St. John's wort. Some years ago, German scientists discovered that St. John's wort has effects on brain chemistry similar to certain prescription antidepressants. "I'm very impressed with St. John's wort as a treatment for de-pression," Dr. Gaby says.

Dr. Lieberman suggests taking 300 milligrams three times a day. Make sure that the preparation you choose contains standardized levels of hypericin, the herb's active compound.

If you're already taking a prescription antidepressant, don't take St. John's wort without consulting your doctor first, Dr. Lieberman advises.

Get a lift from ginkgo. Ginkgo improves blood flow through the brain, which is why it's used in the treatment of stroke and Alzheimer's disease. But the herb also normalizes levels of certain brain chemicals and, as a result, can help treat depression.

You can take up to 240 milligrams a day without side effects. Look for a ginkgo product whose label says "24/6," which means the product has been con-centrated and contains 24 percent glycosides and 6 percent terpenes—the most effective compounds.

Seasonal Affective Disorder: Balking in a Winter Wonderland

Everyone recognizes spring fever, that feeling of exhilaration that develops when the longer, sunnier days of spring begin to replace the short, dark days of winter. It's a far cry from the winter blues, which scientists have linked to the shortage of sunlight between November and March. There are three types of winter blues.

Winter blahs. You may know the winter blahs as cabin fever, says Michael Terman, Ph.D., director of the Winter Depression Program at Columbia-Presbyterian Medical Center in New York City. You function normally throughout winter. But by February, you feel vaguely out of sorts, and you can't wait for spring.

Winter doldrums. When you have the winter doldrums, you function normally throughout winter, but not without a struggle. You may also gain a few pounds, need more sleep, and have difficulty getting out of bed in the morning.

Seasonal affective disorder (SAD). This is severe winter depres-

Home Remedies

Quaff coffee. In addition to jump-starting millions of people every morning, coffee has a mild but noticeable antidepressant effect, thanks to the caffeine it contains.

But if you use caffeine to improve your mood, don't exceed your individual tolerance level. Otherwise, you may experience insomnia, agitation, restlessness, and irritability.

Back off the bottle. A central nervous system depressant, alcohol aggravates depression—especially in men. "Alcohol is a powerful depressant," Dr. Gaby notes. "If you're depressed, you shouldn't drink it."

Light up your mood. Bright-light therapy is best known as a treatment for seasonal affective disorder, which is just one type of depression. But at least one pilot study suggests that it also helps major depression.

You can buy appliances that are specially designed for bright-light therapy. Look for light boxes in health-care catalogs or from Web sites or organizations

sion. Your mood goes into a tailspin each autumn, and you can't function normally until spring. SAD usually causes lethargy, joylessness, hopelessness, anxiety, and social withdrawal. In addition, you may experience daytime drowsiness, crave sleep, crave sweets, and gain a good deal of weight.

An estimated 25 percent of the American population experiences some form of the winter blues. The farther north you live, the greater your risk. Studies show that about 1 percent of Floridians develop SAD. Among Alaskans, the rate rises to 10 percent.

For years, scientists thought humans didn't have seasonal rhythms as many animals do. Now they know differently. In fact, they say that the weight gain and cravings for sleep typical of SAD look a lot like hibernation.

No matter which variety of winter blues you have, the basic prescription is the same: Maximize your exposure to bright indoor lights or natural sunlight. This tricks your pineal gland, which controls your body's sleep/wake cycle, into releasing less of the sleep-inducing hormone melatonin.

offering help with seasonal affective disorder. Dr. Brauer offers a less expensive option: Step outdoors and enjoy the sunlight whenever possible.

OTHER GOOD CHOICES

Aromatherapy

Favor a fragrant fix. At Mie University in Tsu, Japan, psychiatrists studied 12 men who had been hospitalized for serious depression and were taking antidepressants. The researchers exposed them to a strong citrus fragrance in addition to their antidepressants. After 11 weeks, all of the men were able to reduce their dosages of medication. Some stopped taking the drugs completely.

You can buy citrus oil where aromatherapy fragrances are sold. Place several drops in a small capped vial and inhale the aroma once every waking hour.

Homeopathy

Take a matching medicine. At Duke University Medical Center in Durham, North Carolina, researchers gave 12 people with major depression, phobias, or panic disorders homeopathic medicines matched to their individual symptoms. The people took the medicines for anywhere from 7 to 80 weeks. When they were evaluated with standard psychological tests, 58 percent showed improvement in their symptoms.

Miranda Castro, who teaches homeopathy at Bastyr University in Kenmore, Washington, recommends consulting a professional homeopath to find out which medicine best suits you. When treating depression, she most often prescribes Aurum metallicum, Causticum, Gelsemium, Ignatia, Kali phosphoricum, Lachesis, Natrum muriaticum, Pulsatilla, Sepia, and Zincum metallicum.

Chinese Medicine

Arouse your qi. Practitioners of Chinese medicine attribute depression to the suppression of qi, says Efrem Korngold, O.M.D., L.Ac.

For depression associated with despair, Dr. Korngold prescribes herbal formulas containing rehmannia root, dioscorea root, cornus fruit, and poria fungus. For depression dominated by lethargy, he recommends schisandra fruit, ziziphus seed, and Chinese angelica (dang gui). And for depression with hostility and irritability, he suggests formulas containing bupleurum root, peony root, Chinese angelica, ginger, and licorice root.

Rise above anguish with acupressure. At the University of Arizona, researchers found that women who were given acupuncture at the correct points showed significantly greater improvements in mood than the women who didn't get these treatments.

For a self-care alternative to acupuncture treatment, consider acupressure. Apply steady, penetrating finger pressure at each of the following points for 3 minutes.

◆ Extra Point Yin Tang, located just above your nose, exactly between your eyebrows

◆ Liver 3, situated on top of your foot in the webbing between your big toe and second toe

◆ Large Intestine 4, located on the back of your hand where the bones of your thumb and index finger meet

◆ Kidney 7, located on your inner leg, two thumb-widths above your anklebone

◆ Stomach 36, located four finger-widths below your kneecap and one finger-width toward the outside of your shinbone

Ayurvedic Medicine

Sip brahmi tea. For all three doshas—Vata, Pitta, and Kapha—the prescription usually involves some combination of herbs, diet, exercise, and meditation, says Alakananda Devi, M.B., of Boulder, Colorado.

In particular, Ayurvedic physicians often prescribe an herbal treatment called brahmi. Brahmi contains B vitamins, and, like several pharmaceutical antidepressants, it appears to help regulate the brain chemical serotonin. Consult an Ayurvedic physician if you are interested in trying brahmi.

MEDICAL MEASURES

While a growing number of mainstream M.D.'s encourage the use of nondrug therapies, they view antidepressants as the first-choice treatment for depression—a position that Dr. Brauer strongly endorses. "When people are seriously depressed, they want relief as quickly as possible," he explains. "Antidepressants usually work faster than St. John's wort and other nondrug therapies. After people come up from the depths of depression using antidepressants, then I start recommending the other approaches."

Antidepressants work by normalizing levels of the brain chemicals associated with depression. These drugs successfully elevate mood in about 75 percent of people who use them as directed for several months. Treatment typically lasts 6 to 12 months, though you should see improvement in your symptoms within 4 to 6 weeks—possibly sooner.

Doctors can prescribe a wide range of antidepressants, and each one has different side effects. Also, each kind of antidepressant affects each person a little differently. If the first drug you try doesn't provide sufficient relief, another probably will. You may have to try several different medications before you find one that works well for you.

If you receive a prescription for one of these drugs, make sure that you understand all of its potential side effects before you start taking it. Some side effects—dry mouth, for example—subside within a few weeks. Others, especially sexual problems, may persist.

In cases of severe depression where antidepressants prove ineffective, doctors may recommend electroconvulsive therapy (ECT), once known as shock therapy. "When used properly, ECT is safe and effective," Dr. Yudofsky says. "Unfortunately, because of the inaccurate ways ECT has been portrayed in movies and on television, many people who could benefit from it don't consider it." Dr. Yudofsky says they should: ECT helps 80 to 90 percent of people with severe depression who try it.

Another mainstream treatment option is psychotherapy. A study by the National Institute of Mental Health showed that after 16 weeks of psychotherapy, 55 percent of people with mild to moderate depression reported significant improvements in their mood. Today, few therapists go in for long-term Freudian psychoanalysis. "For most major depressive episodes, 6 months of therapy is usually about right," Dr. Brauer says.

To find a good psychotherapist, rely on word-of-mouth referrals. Ask your doctor, family members, and friends if they can recommend anyone.

RED FLAGS

If you experience a sudden onset of depression that seems unrelated to any event in your life, consult your doctor. Sometimes depression signals an underlying health problem such as a thyroid problem, lupus, rheumatoid arthritis, multiple sclerosis, or a hormonal imbalance. Treating the underlying condition usually resolves the depression.

Diabetes

More than 2,000 years ago, physicians noticed that some people produced copious amounts of strangely sweet-smelling urine. They named the condition *diabetes mellitus*, from the Greek for "fountain" and the Latin for "honey." Today, doctors continue to call the condition diabetes mellitus. But in common parlance, it's just diabetes.

Diabetes develops when your body either stops producing the pancreatic hormone insulin or can't use the insulin you produce. Without insulin, blood sugar (your body's primary fuel) cannot enter your cells. It builds up in your bloodstream and eventually gets excreted in your urine.

As your blood sugar rises, all sorts of things can go wrong with your body. But many of these complications take years to develop. High blood sugar makes your blood sticky, and this stickiness can trigger many biochemical changes. Most notably, it increases the number of free radicals, unstable oxygen molecules that

SIMPLE SOLUTIONS
1. Nutrition
2. Supplements
3. Exercise
4. Yoga
5. Relaxation Therapies
6. Visualization
7. Biofeedback
8. Herbal Medicine
9. Home Remedies
10. Over-the-Counter Drugs
11. Chinese Medicine
12. Ayurvedic Medicine
13. Medical Measures

damage your blood vessels and clog them with cholesterol-rich deposits. This process, called atherosclerosis, sets the stage for heart disease, kidney failure, eye problems, and a nervous-system condition called diabetic neuropathy.

Diabetes takes two forms. In type 1, your pancreas stops producing insulin. You need injections of the hormone to survive. In type 2, your pancreas continues producing insulin, but your cells have trouble using it.

Most people are familiar with type 1 diabetes, which affects about 1.5 million Americans. Scientists aren't sure what causes type 1 but suspect that it's an autoimmune disease. In other words, something makes the immune system go haywire and destroy the pancreatic cells that produce insulin. Type 1 diabetes develops fairly quickly, with the classic symptoms—thirst, excessive urination, and sweet-smelling urine.

While type 2 diabetes is less well-known than type 1, it's far more common. Some 14.5 million Americans have type 2, accounting for more than 90 percent of all diabetes cases. Type 2 diabetes is strongly associated with a lack of exercise and a poor diet—one that's low in fiber and high in sugar, fat, and animal products. It develops slowly, usually over several years, and rarely produces dramatic symptoms. For this reason, many people with type 2 diabetes have no idea that they are sick. In fact, the American Diabetes Association (ADA) estimates that only half of Americans with type 2 diabetes have been diagnosed.

To control type 1 diabetes, you need to inject insulin regularly—up to eight times a day. You must also test your blood sugar frequently, using a home blood-sugar monitor. You use that information, in consultation with your doctor, to regulate your insulin dosage, diet, and exercise.

Treatment of type 2 diabetes also starts with home blood-sugar testing. But only a fraction of people with type 2 need insulin injections. Most can control their blood sugar with dietary changes, regular exercise, and oral medication. In fact, with proper diet and exercise, many people with type 2 diabetes are able to get off their medication, says Julian Whitaker, M.D., founder and director of the Whitaker Wellness Institute in Newport Beach, California.

If you have been diagnosed with type 1 or type 2 diabetes, you should definitely be under a doctor's care. And you should never stop using your medication or injections, or alter your dosage, without your doctor's approval.

That said, you have the power to keep yourself healthy and free from many potentially serious complications of diabetes. In most cases, all you need are lifestyle adjustments inspired by blended medicine. Most of the measures that follow are tailored to type 2 diabetes, because it's so much more prevalent and because it responds so well to blended medicine.

BEST CHOICES

Nutrition

Trim dietary fat and cholesterol. In 1927, Harvard Medical School professor Elliott P. Joslin, M.D., wrote, "With an excess of fat, diabetes begins,

Diabetes: A Disease of "Convenience" Culture

Perhaps more than any other disease, diabetes is strongly associated with modern Western culture and diet," says Joseph Pizzorno Jr., N.D. This was demonstrated in a study by researchers from the National Institute of Diabetes and Digestive and Kidney Diseases, who examined communities of Pima Indians living in southern Arizona and northern Mexico.

Arizona Pimas have a very high rate of type 2 diabetes. They eat a high-fat diet, which is heavy on convenience foods and low in plant foods. They also lead generally sedentary lives, thanks to the many labor-saving devices they use.

In contrast, Mexican Pimas eat a traditional diet of rice, beans, tortillas, fruits, and vegetables. They also do a great deal of physical labor—for example, they till their fields by hand or using ox-drawn plows. Their diabetes rate is a whopping 84 percent lower than the diabetes rate among the Arizona Pimas.

and from an excess of fat, diabetics die." His words still resonate among his contemporaries.

"Dietary recommendations for control of type 2 diabetes are simple," says Joseph Pizzorno Jr., N.D. "Eat less saturated fat and cholesterol by reducing or eliminating animal products. Eat more fiber-rich plant foods—whole grains, beans, fruits, and vegetables."

Fill up on antioxidant-rich foods. Plant-derived foods are rich in the antioxidant nutrients, including beta-carotene and vitamins C and E. Antioxidants neutralize free radicals, preventing these unstable oxygen molecules from damaging healthy cells. Free radicals not only lay the groundwork for the most serious complications of diabetes, they also raise your blood sugar level. Not surprisingly, several studies have shown that as blood levels of antioxidants rise, diabetes risk drops, and vice versa.

Don't forget fiber. Another good reason to eat plant-derived foods is that they are rich in fiber. "Fiber is essential for good blood-sugar control," Dr. Whitaker explains. "It seems to hold nutrients in the digestive tract longer, allowing a slower absorption rate and reducing blood sugar ups and downs."

Savor soy. Among plant-derived foods, tofu and other soy products can be especially beneficial for people with diabetes. Soy is a good source of fiber, which helps treat and prevent diabetes. Soy also contains two amino acids, glycine and arginine, that help block the body's synthesis of cholesterol.

Make room for magnesium. In one study, researchers tested the blood levels of various nutrients in 12,398 middle-age Americans who did not have diabetes. Six years later, 807 of them had developed the disease. Those diagnosed with diabetes had blood levels of magnesium that were significantly below normal. Good food sources of magnesium include whole grains, nuts, and leafy green vegetables.

Supplements

Avoid complications with E. Research has demonstrated that vitamin E helps treat diabetes and prevent its complications. Clinical nutritionist Shari Lieberman, Ph.D., recommends taking 600 to 800 international units (IU) a day. But daily dosages over 400 IU must be taken under medical supervision.

Increase your supply of zinc. Several studies have shown that animals deprived of zinc develop high blood sugar. Other studies have determined that diabetes increases the excretion of zinc in urine, reducing the amount of the mineral in your blood. Dr. Lieberman suggests taking 30 to 50 milligrams of zinc a day. But check with your doctor first, since zinc dosages over 30 milligrams should only be taken under medical supervision.

Count on chromium. The mineral chromium plays a key role in the manufacture of insulin and in the maintenance of blood sugar within a normal range. "I prescribe chromium for all my patients with diabetes," says Alan P. Brauer, M.D.

Richard Anderson, Ph.D., of the USDA Human Nutrition Research Center in Beltsville, Maryland, advises people with diabetes to take 400 to 600 micrograms of chromium a day. It's best, however, to take doses over 200 micrograms per day only under your doctor's supervision.

Take extra magnesium. Brazilian researchers gave various doses of magnesium to 127 people with type 2 diabetes—some who were taking diabetes medication, some who were not. As the magnesium dose increased, so did the participants' ability to maintain near-normal blood sugar levels. Dr. Lieberman suggests taking 20 to 30 milligrams a day.

Strike oil. Both borage oil and evening primrose oil contain gamma-linolenic acid, which improves blood circulation through your small blood vessels. These are the ones that get clogged up when you have chronically high blood sugar from diabetes. "I've seen good results with gamma-linolenic acid supplements," Dr. Brauer says.

Dr. Lieberman suggests taking one standard capsule of borage oil or two to six capsules of evening primrose oil every day.

Exercise

Start a walking program. "Every person with diabetes, regardless of age, should have a regular exercise program," Dr. Whitaker says. Exercise helps you lose weight, feel less stressed, and reduce your risk of heart disease. In addition, it substantially reduces insulin resistance. (Insulin resistance refers to the inability of insulin to enter cells.)

Most studies examining the relationship between exercise and diabetes have used walking as the activity of choice. In one study, Japanese researchers instructed 24 people with type 2 diabetes to make certain dietary changes. In addition, 10 of the participants were told to walk 4 to 5 miles a day. Compared with those who didn't exercise, those who did walk saw their blood sugar and insulin resistance plummet. Dr. Whitaker recommends taking a 30- to 40-minute walk every day. But before you begin a new exercise program, you should first check with your doctor.

Lift weights, too. Walking isn't the only form of exercise that helps control diabetes. Weight training helps, too. In one study, Australian researchers enrolled 15 people with type 2 diabetes in a weight-training program. Another 12 people with type 2 diabetes remained sedentary. After 8 weeks, those who were weight training had significantly lower blood sugar and less insulin resistance.

Yoga

Discover the healing power of postures. Yoga is surprisingly beneficial for people with type 2 diabetes. In one study, Indian researchers enrolled 149 people with type 2 diabetes in a yoga class. Forty days later, 104 of them had significantly lower blood sugar levels and were able to reduce their medication.

Relaxation Therapies

Mellow out to lower blood sugar. Stress triggers your body's fight-or-flight response, a complicated series of biochemical changes that prepares you to defend yourself or flee from danger. One component of the fight-or-flight response is the release of large amounts of blood sugar. In people who don't have diabetes, this extra blood sugar flows into cells throughout the body to provide energy. But

Simple Tips for Safe Exercise

Exercise is key to treating and preventing diabetes. But if you have the disease, you must work out prudently. Otherwise, you can increase your risk of foot problems, eye problems, and other complications. Here's what the American Diabetes Association recommends.

First, see your doctor. Anyone can exercise. But your physical condition, your complications, and your ability to manage your blood sugar may determine the type of physical activity that is safe for you.

Check your feet frequently. Before you begin your workout, inspect your feet for any sign of irritation and carefully treat any cuts or blisters. After your workout, check your feet again. If any wounds seem slow to heal, call your doctor.

Test your blood sugar before, during, and after. Strenuous exercise stimulates your liver to release glycogen into your blood as glucose, or blood sugar. If your blood sugar level is already high, exercise might push it into the danger zone. That's why it's so important to test before, during, and after exercise until you're confident you know how

in people who have diabetes, the blood sugar can't get into cells. Instead, it remains in the bloodstream, where it raises blood sugar levels.

Richard S. Surwit, Ph.D., professor of medical psychology at Duke University Medical Center and research director of the Duke Neurobehavioral Diabetes Program, both in Durham, North Carolina, has found that deep relaxation can help lower blood sugar levels in people with diabetes who are chronically anxious or upset. Dr. Surwit studied biofeedback, but meditation, visualization, and other stress-management techniques probably work just as well.

Visualization

See yourself with less stress. You can achieve deep relaxation with this visualization exercise suggested by Martin L. Rossman, M.D. Begin by closing your eyes and breathing deeply. Mentally remove yourself from all of your daily hassles by envisioning a stress-free hideaway. Visualize someplace beautiful—a warm, sunny beach, a meadow filled with wildflowers, a mountaintop with a sweeping

your blood sugar level responds. Ask your doctor about your safe blood sugar range and levels that are too high or low for exercise.

Plan to exercise after eating. It's best to work out 1 to 3 hours after a meal. That way, the food can supply the glucose you need to exercise and to replenish glycogen stores in your liver and muscles.

Start slowly and carefully. If you've been out of shape for a long time, start with something nonstrenuous, such as leisurely walking.

Focus on regularity, not intensity. Exercise regularly—ideally, daily. You can set aside 20 minutes a day for a walk.

To avoid injury, warm up and cool down. Stretch or stroll for 5 to 10 minutes before exercising. Then when you're done exercising, stretch or stroll for another 5 to 10 minutes.

Drink lots of water. Drink 1 to 2 cups of water 15 minutes before exercise, take frequent water breaks during workouts, and drink more water afterward.

Watch the temperature. In general, don't exercise outdoors if the temperature is above 80°F or below 15°F. Instead, find a place to exercise indoors.

view. Look around your hideaway, taking in its sights, sounds, smells, and other details. Practice this exercise for 5 to 15 minutes a day.

Biofeedback

Boost blood flow with biofeedback. Because people with diabetes have reduced blood flow through their feet, they often have problems with foot sores that don't heal. With biofeedback, you can learn to increase blood flow to your extremities and speed the healing process. You attach sensitive thermometers to your fingers and toes. Then as blood flow increases, the thermometers register an increase in temperature.

Herbal Medicine

Flavor soup with fenugreek. Like psyllium, fenugreek seeds are rich in soluble fiber. At the Medical College in Agra, India, researchers measured the cholesterol and blood sugar levels of 60 people with type 2 diabetes. Then the volunteers were instructed to maintain their usual lifestyles, with one change: They were to eat a bowl of soup containing almost an ounce of ground fenugreek seed before each meal. After 24 weeks, their cholesterol and blood sugar levels fell significantly.

Adapt to ginseng's benefits. Research has shown that ginseng contains compounds called ginsenosides that are classified as adaptogens. In other words, they help your body resist damage from illness and stress. Alan Gaby, M.D., recommends taking 100 milligrams—about a teaspoon—of a standardized ginseng extract (containing 4 to 7 percent ginsenosides) twice a day.

Eat odoriferous herbs. Garlic and onions are best known for reducing cholesterol—and with it, the risk of heart disease. But there's another reason that these herbs are so important for people with diabetes. Garlic and onions reduce blood sugar levels, according to two Indian studies. Use more of these herbs in cooking or take deodorized garlic capsules, following the package directions.

Protect your eyes with bilberries. Also known as European blueberries, bilberries contain high levels of compounds called anthocyanosides. These potent antioxidants have an unusual affinity for the eye. They help treat diabetic retinopathy, a condition in which the blood vessels in the eyes begin to narrow, sometimes leading to blindness.

European herbalists have developed a standardized bilberry extract that contains 25 percent anthocyanosides. Dr. Pizzorno suggests taking 80 to 160 milligrams of the extract three times a day. If you can't find it in a health food store, ask a naturopath.

You can also get anthocyanosides by eating abundant amounts of blueberries, cranberries, and huckleberries. All of these fruits are close relatives of bilberries.

Drink tea. Studies by Indian researchers show that black tea (such as Lipton and Earl Grey) helps lower blood sugar. "If I had diabetes, I'd drink lots of tea," says James A. Duke, Ph.D.

Home Remedies

Maintain a healthy weight. Being overweight is a primary risk factor for type 2 diabetes. In general, if you exceed the weight recommended for your height and build by 10 percent or more, you're at risk for type 2. For most people, losing just 10 pounds lowers risk significantly.

Drink less alcohol. Alcohol tends to aggravate diabetes. It also contains lots of calories—almost 200 per ounce. The ADA notes that blood sugar levels are not usually problematic if alcohol is consumed in moderation (nursing one or two drinks all evening) and with food by people whose diabetes is well-controlled. They recommend sticking with drinks that have a low alcohol content (light beers and wines), never drinking on an empty stomach, and nibbling on snacks that are high in carbohydrates but not sugar (fruits, vegetables, breads). Check with your doctor before consuming any alcohol if you're currently taking medication for your diabetes, because alcohol may interfere with its action.

Over-the-Counter Drugs
Treat diabetic neuropathy with capsaicin cream. Red peppers get their fiery flavor from a compound called capsaicin. Capsaicin is also a potent pain reliever. When rubbed into your skin, a commercial capsaicin cream (containing 0.025 to 0.075 percent capsaicin) interferes with substance P, a chemical involved in the transmission of pain signals through the nervous system. Several studies have shown that capsaicin cream helps relieve diabetic neuropathy, a condition characterized by tingling, numbness, and persistent pain in the hands and feet. Capsaicin creams are sold in drugstores. Use according to the package directions.

OTHER GOOD CHOICES

Chinese Medicine
Balance yin and yang. Practitioners of Chinese medicine attribute diabetes to the depletion of yin. "Your yin and yang are out of balance," explains Efrem Korngold, O.M.D., L.Ac. This imbalance causes Heat to dry up bodily fluids, leading to the thirst and excess urination associated with diabetes.

To treat diabetes, Dr. Korngold prescribes a low-fat diet. "Fat creates Heat," he explains. He also recommends increasing fluid intake and eliminating sugar, salt, spicy foods, coffee, and alcohol.

In addition, certain Chinese herbs can help treat diabetes, Dr. Korngold says. He prescribes rehmannia root, pueraria root, tricosanthis root, licorice root, and schisandra fruit.

Press the proper points. Acupuncture is another effective treatment for diabetes, Dr. Korngold says. If you want to try acupuncture, you need to consult a professional acupuncturist. For a self-care approach, try acupressure instead.

Simply apply steady, penetrating finger pressure to each of the following points for 3 minutes.

◆ Kidney 3, located in the hollow between your Achilles tendon and the inside of your anklebone

◆ Stomach 44, located on your foot in the webbing your second and third toes

◆ Spleen 6, located four finger-widths above your inner anklebone on the back inner border of your shinbone

Ayurvedic Medicine

Cool Kapha. Ayurvedic practitioners consider diabetes, or *prahema*, a disorder of urine caused by an excess of Kapha dosha, which disrupts metabolism. Ayurvedic treatment of diabetes depends on your own dosha, or constitutional type. But generally, practitioners prescribe a combination of dietary restrictions (less fat, fewer sweets), herbs (including fenugreek and turmeric), daily exercise (including yoga), and Ayurvedic massage therapy (panchakarma).

MEDICAL MEASURES

Whether you have type 1 or type 2 diabetes, your treatment program must be managed by a health-care team that ideally consists of your family doctor, an endocrinologist who specializes in diabetes, a certified diabetes educator, and perhaps a clinical nutritionist. Work closely with your health-care team to manage your condition and reduce your odds of complications.

If you have type 2 diabetes, your doctor may prescribe one of several oral diabetes medications. These medications work in various ways. The sulfonylureas, such as glyburide (Micronase), spur the release of more insulin. Metformin (Glucophage) slows your liver's release of stored sugar. Acarbose (Precose) slows the digestion of carbohydrates. And troglitazone (Rezulin) increases cellular insulin sensitivity.

Unfortunately, none of these drugs is very effective over the long term. During the first year of treatment, they improve blood-sugar control in about 90 percent of people who take them. But as the years pass, they stop working for about half of those who take them. If that happens, you have to use insulin injections instead.

The American Diabetes Association provides information and support services to people with diabetes. To join the organization, contact your local chapter.

RED FLAGS

Very high or very low blood sugar or a diabetes-related buildup of acid in your blood can lead to confusion, lethargy, and—if not treated—coma. If these symptoms develop, call your doctor or emergency medical number without delay. Likewise, if you experience any symptoms of diabetes complications—vision problems or numbness in your feet, for example—consult your doctor promptly.

Diarrhea

Most of the time, you can blame it on something you ate. Like those questionable oysters served up at Sonny's House o' Seafood. Or the strange-smelling leftovers that you just couldn't bear to throw away.

Whether or not you know the cause, there's one thing that you do know: Until diarrhea has run its course, you feel downright miserable. Food is among the most common culprits behind diarrhea. Other possible causes include supplements, medications, and infections.

Diarrhea can also occur in conjunction with dozens of health problems, including chronic anxiety and stress, inflammatory bowel disease, irritable bowel syndrome, and diabetes. Sometimes it serves as an early warning sign for more serious conditions, including AIDS and certain cancers.

SIMPLE SOLUTIONS
1. Nutrition
2. Supplements
3. Herbal Medicine
4. Homeopathy
5. Home Remedies
6. Over-the-Counter Drugs
7. Elimination Diet
8. Chinese Medicine
9. Ayurvedic Medicine

Finally, there's the possibility that you have a condition that's been called leaky gut syndrome. Researchers speculate that if your small intestine gets damaged—by food intolerances, infections, or drugs (including alcohol and cigarettes)—other matter can leach into the bloodstream. This includes incompletely digested fats, proteins, and carbohydrates as well as potentially harmful substances that under normal conditions would be eliminated in solid waste. Leaky gut syndrome has been implicated in chronic diarrhea as well as in inflammatory bowel disease and chronic fatigue syndrome.

Though diarrhea has many different causes, the treatment is generally the same. Part of the recovery process involves getting more fluids into your system. That's because diarrhea, especially a prolonged bout, puts you at increased risk for dehydration.

Both alternative and mainstream medicine offer a range of remedies for recovering from a bout of diarrhea and its sidekick, dehydration. Here's what practitioners recommend.

Nutrition

Be a BRATT. The acronym BRATT stands for bananas, rice, applesauce, tea, and toast. All of these foods are binding, which means they add bulk to loose stools, explains Anne Simons, M.D. Bananas are also rich in potassium, one of the electrolytes that's depleted as diarrhea robs the body of water.

Bring back good bacteria. Diarrhea wreaks havoc on the helpful "probiotic" bacteria that normally live in your intestines and support the digestive process. Naturopaths have long recommended restoring these beneficial bugs by eating yogurt that contains live *Lactobacillus acidophilus* or *L. bulgaricus* cultures. Now mainstream M.D.'s are buying into the yogurt remedy, too.

If you have chronic diarrhea, try eating 4 ounces of yogurt every day, advises Jose Saavedra, M.D., director of pediatric nutrition at Johns Hopkins Children's Center in Baltimore. Just make sure that the yogurt contains live bacterial cultures. The label should say so.

If you don't like the taste of yogurt, you can buy *L. acidophilus* capsules in most health food stores and some drugstores. Take one capsule three times a day.

Gradually rebuild your diet. As your symptoms subside, slowly reintroduce other foods to your diet. Stick with bland items such as crackers, soups, cooked vegetables, skinless chicken, and fish. Steer clear of high-fat items—pizza, burgers, french fries, and ice cream—until the diarrhea is gone for good.

For the time being, avoid certain foods. As long as your bout of diarrhea lingers, stay away from dairy products, fruit juices, and spicy, fried, and junk foods. These items usually aggravate diarrhea instead of making it go away. Also refrain from drinking alcohol, which is dehydrating.

Supplements

Add a multi to the menu. You may need supplements when your body is depleted of vitamins and minerals. Deficiencies of the mineral zinc, for example, have been linked to diarrhea. So if you've been taking a daily multivi-

A Guide to Gut-Friendly Travel

Doctors call it turista. It's the notorious health hazard that haunts travelers who dare drink the water when they're away from home. The condition is characterized by several days of diarrhea, abdominal cramps, fatigue, and loss of appetite, followed by a week or so of general abdominal distress.

Turista is usually associated with travel in countries where standards for water are much lower than in the United States. But you don't have to cross U.S. borders to encounter tainted water. In this country, even the most pristine-looking stream miles from the nearest paved road can be inhabited by diarrhea-causing microorganisms.

To avoid turista and other water- and food-borne illnesses, Karl Neumann, M.D., editor of the *Traveling Healthy* newsletter, offers these travel-tested guidelines.

◆ As much as possible, drink only mineral water, juices, and soft drinks from containers that you open yourself.

◆ Avoid adding ice to beverages.

◆ Eat only thoroughly cooked foods that are served hot.

tamin/mineral supplement, you definitely don't want to skip a pill during a diarrhea episode, says Melvyn R. Werbach, M.D., assistant clinical professor at the University of California, Los Angeles, School of Medicine.

Check your C level. Have you been taking more than 1,000 milligrams of vitamin C on a daily basis? If so, cutting back your dosage may well help get rid of diarrhea, says Joseph Pizzorno Jr., N.D.

Befriend fiber. A certain type of fiber, called soluble fiber, can help solidify your stools and bring an end to diarrhea. James A. Duke, Ph.D., suggests adding a few teaspoons of psyllium seed, which supplies soluble fiber, to water or juice. Psyllium seed is sold in most health food stores.

Herbal Medicine

Temper symptoms with tannins. Tannins are compounds that give many herbs their lip-puckering astringent properties. "Tannins also help relieve

◆ Avoid buying foods from sidewalk vendors even if those foods are served hot.

◆ Stay away from raw fish (sometimes called ceviche).

◆ Steer clear of unpasteurized milk and any dairy products made from it. If you have a sensitive stomach, bypass dairy products altogether.

◆ Peel all fruits before eating them. Just washing the fruit isn't enough.

◆ Skip salads no matter how delectable the fresh vegetables look.

◆ Always wash your hands with soap and water before eating.

It's a good idea to carry with you some Imodium A-D, just in case. The antidiarrheal medication is available in liquid and tablet form. Start taking it according to the label directions at the first sign of diarrhea.

If you prefer a natural remedy, James A. Duke, Ph.D., suggests taking along tincture of the herb goldenseal. You can use it as a treatment or a preventive. Take 1 to 2 teaspoons three times a day, mixed in mineral water or juice.

intestinal inflammation, which is why tannic herbs have been recommended for diarrhea for centuries," says Dr. Duke. One of his favorite tannic herbs is tea, or *Camellia sinensis*. "It's one of the most astringent herbs around, which is why it's widely recommended for diarrhea," he explains.

Probably the easiest way to prepare tea is by using tea bags. Any black or green tea will do. Allow the tea to steep until it's the desired strength, then remove the tea bag and drink up.

Cure the runs with carob. Carob is a fiber-rich herb with a long folk history as a diarrhea remedy. Dr. Duke relied on carob while on a trip through the Panamanian rain forest. His successful experience with the herb has since been confirmed by scientific research.

A 150-pound adult can safely take about 4 ounces of carob a day. But even in such a large amount, the herb is considered safe. Use carob powder, either mixed into hot water as a beverage or added to foods.

Get better with goldenseal. Goldenseal contains an important antibiotic compound called berberine. Several studies have shown that goldenseal is an effective treatment for infectious diarrhea caused by *Escherichia coli*, shigella, and salmonella bacteria as well as by intestinal parasites. Dr. Pizzorno suggests taking 1 to 2 teaspoons of goldenseal tincture three times a day until your diarrhea goes away. You can buy the tincture in health food stores.

Homeopathy

Choose the right microdose medicines. Several homeopathic preparations have proved effective as treatments for diarrhea, according to homeopath Dana Ullman. Generally, he recommends Arsenicum album for diarrhea caused by food poisoning or by eating too much fruit; Chamomilla for diarrhea accompanied by irritability; Mercurius for diarrhea that produces bloody stools; and Podophyllum or Sulfur for diarrhea that's urgent or forceful. Though these medicines are available over the counter, it's best to see your homeopathic physician for a proper diagnosis.

Home Remedies

Keep the fluids flowing. When every ounce of liquid seems to make a beeline for a single exit, you might think the best way to halt diarrhea is to stop taking in fluids. In fact, you ought to drink as much as you can for as long as your diarrhea lasts, Dr. Simons says. She recommends bouillon, Gatorade, and other fluids that contain sodium and potassium. Water is okay, except that it doesn't replace those lost electrolytes.

Dr. Pizzorno offers an old naturopathic remedy for rehydration: Mix equal parts tomato juice and sauerkraut juice, then drink up. "This concoction is high in electrolytes," he explains. "And some naturopathic studies suggest that sauerkraut juice helps heal intestinal problems."

Curb the coffee. The one fluid that you should avoid during a bout of diarrhea is coffee, Dr. Werbach says. It has a laxative effect, which is why many folks use it as a remedy for minor constipation. In addition, there's some evidence that the caffeine in coffee increases the secretion of fluids into the intestines—something that you don't want when you have the runs.

Shun sorbitol. Foods that contain the artificial sweetener sorbitol can cause or aggravate diarrhea in some people. So look for sorbitol in the ingredients lists on food labels. It's most common in sugar-free and low-sugar candies and sweets.

Over-the-Counter Drugs

Run for Imodium A-D. "Imodium works by slowing down intestinal contractions and decreasing fluid loss," says Joe Graedon, coauthor of *The People's Pharmacy* books. Follow package directions for proper dosage.

Pop the pink stuff. Pepto-Bismol, that is. Whether you prefer the liquid or chewable tablets, follow the package directions for proper dosage.

If you're sensitive to aspirin or you're already taking aspirin, Pepto-Bismol isn't for you. Like aspirin, it contains salicylate. And too much salicylate can impair blood clotting and cause other problems.

OTHER GOOD CHOICES

Elimination Diet

Find the offending foods. If you suspect that your diarrhea might be related to a food intolerance, Dr. Pizzorno suggests trying an elimination diet to identify the problem foods. (Consult with a doctor or practitioner for guidance.) Or you can switch to a rotation diet: Don't eat any one food more than once every 4 days. Even if you have a low-level food intolerance, you'll be reducing your exposure to the problem foods. For some people, that's enough to prevent diarrhea.

Chinese Medicine

Strengthen your Spleen. Chinese medicine views diarrhea as a weakness of the Spleen that's often caused by toxins. As the body tries to eliminate the toxins, diarrhea occurs, explains Efrem Korngold, O.M.D., L.Ac.

For patients with diarrhea, Dr. Korngold often prescribes Curing Pills. This formula contains 15 herbs—among them medicated leven, a combination of fermented barley, wheat, and rice sprouts that's rich in the same digestion-enhancing bacteria found in yogurt. "Curing Pills normalize the gut," he says. "I've had very good experience with them, especially for traveler's diarrhea. I give them to many people who are traveling to exotic destinations, and most, if not all, return home saying that they didn't get sick."

Press here, then there. Acupressure can speed relief from diarrhea symptoms, says Michael Reed Gach, founder and director of the Acupressure Institute. He suggests applying steady, firm finger pressure to each of the following points for 3 minutes.

♦ Spleen 4, located on the arch of your foot, one thumb-width behind the ball of your foot

♦ Spleen 16, located at the bottom of your rib cage, about ½ inch in from either nipple toward your breastbone

♦ Stomach 36, located four finger-widths below your kneecap and one finger-width toward the outside of your shinbone

♦ Conception Vessel 6, located three finger-widths below your navel

If your symptoms persist, consider consulting a licensed acupuncturist. Needle stimulation may help when finger pressure doesn't.

Ayurvedic Medicine

Sip an exotic beverage. Ayurvedic practitioners believe that diarrhea is a Pitta condition, caused by excessive dampness in the colon. To treat it, Vasant Lad, B.A.M.S., M.A.Sc., director of the Ayurvedic Institute in Albuquerque, New Mexico, recommends drinking pomegranate juice with a pinch each of ground nutmeg and ginger. Pomegranate juice contains tannins, astringent compounds that help relieve intestinal inflammation.

Both nutmeg and ginger have antibacterial properties and help improve fluid absorption in the colon, according to David Frawley, O.M.D. You can buy pomegranate juice in many health food stores.

RED FLAGS

Before visiting a foreign country, consult a travel medicine specialist or the Centers for Disease Control and Prevention. They can advise you about diseases that may cause diarrhea and about appropriate precautions you should take.

If you experience any of the following, see your doctor right away.

♦ Diarrhea that does not respond to home treatment within 5 days

♦ Diarrhea that's accompanied by fever, vomiting, abdominal pain, bloating, or loss of appetite

♦ Stools that appear black or red, which suggests bleeding

♦ Stools that appear bulky but greasy, which suggests nutrient malabsorption

Eczema

What's making you itch? You may never know. Eczema is like that. While it sometimes has an identifiable cause, like exposure to an irritating or allergy-triggering substance, eczema often shows up for no apparent reason. It doesn't even look all that unusual—just patches of dry, red, slightly thickened skin. If not for the itching, you may not have noticed that anything was wrong.

Also known as atopic dermatitis, eczema takes many forms. But all of them produce the same primary symptom: areas of inflamed, irritated, itchy skin, sometimes accompanied by small, fluid-filled blisters or coin-size wheals. Eczema can erupt just about anywhere on the body, but it most frequently occurs on the neck, elbows, hands, abdomen, knees, shins, and feet.

By one estimate, eczema affects 4 percent of the U.S. population, or about 10 million Americans. It's especially prevalent among people who have asthma or hay fever. For these folks, eczema flare-ups usually start in infancy and continue into adulthood. The familiar rash appears because of an allergic reaction—often to a food, sometimes to another substance.

SIMPLE SOLUTIONS
1. Nutrition
2. Supplements
3. Elimination Diet
4. Visualization
5. Herbal Medicine
6. Naturopathy
7. Home Remedies
8. Over-the-Counter Drugs
9. Homeopathy
10. Chinese Medicine
11. Ayurvedic Medicine
12. Medical Measures

This type of eczema, called allergic eczema, has a strong genetic component. If one of your parents has the condition, you have about a one-in-four chance of getting it, too. If both of your parents have allergic eczema, your risk climbs to one in two.

Eczema can also result from contact with irritants. For example, if your job or a hobby requires you to handle certain chemicals, you may develop a rash on your hands and arms—especially if you're wearing a ring or a watch, which can trap the offending substance against your skin. Exposure to soaps, detergents, clothing fibers, and environmental pollutants can also cause your skin to become itchy and inflamed.

You needn't have direct contact with an irritant to get eczema, however. Stress, profuse sweating, a dry environment, and exposure to extreme hot or cold temperatures can trigger flare-ups.

Even knowing all of these potential causes, you may never pinpoint exactly what brought on your eczema. Your skin may start to itch for no obvious reason. And the itching makes you scratch, which can create problems of its own. As your nails scrape away the outer layer of skin, the bacteria that normally stay on the surface seize the opportunity to invade deeper tissues. This can lead to a bacterial skin infection.

Thankfully, your eczema never has to progress so far. The key is to stop the itch, so you no longer have the urge to scratch. Over-the-counter hydrocortisone creams and antihistamines certainly help. But many alternative remedies work just as well. By taking a blended approach, you'll eradicate the itchiness and inflammation, heal your skin, and prevent future eczema flare-ups.

BEST CHOICES

Nutrition

Reel in relief. The inflammation associated with eczema occurs because your body produces unusually high levels of compounds called prostaglandins. Essential fatty acids, notably the omega-3's found in fish oil, decrease the production of inflammatory prostaglandins, explains Joseph Pizzorno Jr., N.D. Cold-water fish such as salmon, mackerel, and herring supply generous amounts of omega-3's. Eating more of these fish can help relieve eczema, he says.

Supplements

Opt for fish-oil capsules. If you're not a fan of fish, you can get omega-3 fatty acids from fish-oil supplements. Fish oil is sold in capsule form in health food stores. Take 3 to 4 grams a day for a month, then cut back to 1 gram a day, suggests Alan Gaby, M.D.

Take evening primrose oil. When British researchers analyzed the results of nine separate studies, they concluded that evening primrose oil provides significant relief from eczema. Evening primrose oil is rich in omega-6 fatty acids, especially gamma-linolenic acid. The omega-6's are close chemical relatives of the omega-3's and have similar anti-inflammatory properties.

Clinical nutritionist Shari Lieberman, Ph.D., recommends taking 70 to 240 milligrams of gamma-linolenic acid a day. That's the equivalent of two to six standard capsules of evening primrose oil. Don't take more than that, she cautions, or you may upset your body's fatty-acid balance. You can buy evening primrose oil capsules in health food stores.

Shore up your zinc supply. Dr. Pizzorno and other nutrition-minded practitioners have found that zinc supplements can help ease eczema. He recommends starting with 50 milligrams of zinc a day, then cutting your dosage as your symptoms improve. But be patient, Dr. Pizzorno advises: Zinc takes time to work. A few months may pass before you notice a difference. Check with your doctor first, however, since doses of zinc above 30 milligrams should only be taken under medical supervision.

Elimination Diet

Give up offending foods. Scientific studies from around the world have linked eczema, especially in children, to food intolerances. In one study conducted at the University of Arkansas for Medical Sciences in Little Rock, researchers used standard skin tests to identify food intolerances in 165 children, teens, and young adults with eczema. Sixty percent of the study participants had at least one food sensitivity.

If you suspect that a food intolerance is triggering your eczema, you have several options. You can try eliminating those foods that most often trigger reactions: shellfish, eggs, wheat, milk, soy, peanuts, cashews, oranges, pineapple, chocolate, and soft drinks. Or, with the guidance of a doctor, you can follow a full-fledged elimination diet to identify the specific foods that cause problems. Or you can consult an allergist/immunologist, who will administer skin tests to determine if you have food intolerances.

Visualization

See yourself with healthy skin. Research conducted by Iona H. Ginsburg, M.D., a dermatologist in New York City, suggests that anxiety contributes to eczema flare-ups. In her study, Dr. Ginsburg gave standard psychological tests to 34 adults with eczema and 32 without. She found that the people with eczema were significantly more anxious.

Visualization can help alleviate anxiety and prevent eczema flare-ups. For patients with eczema, Gerald N. Epstein, M.D., director of the Academy of Integrative Medicine and Mental Imagery in New York City, prescribes an exercise that he calls Palm Fingers. You can practice Palm Fingers for a few minutes whenever you feel itchy.

To begin the exercise, close your eyes and take three deep breaths. Imagine your fingers becoming palm leaves. Gently place your palm leaves on the areas with eczema. Imagine that your palm leaves are filled with honey that flows over your itchy skin, healing it. Envision your skin clear and healthy. Open your eyes.

Herbal Medicine

Apply a chamomile compress. For centuries, Europeans have been adding chamomile flowers to baths as a treatment for skin problems. As it turns out, chamomile oil has significant anti-inflammatory properties, says Michael T. Murray, N.D., a naturopath in Seattle. In fact, it works so well that Commission E, the German panel that evaluates the safety and effectiveness of medicinal herbs, recommends chamomile compresses for eczema and other inflammatory skin conditions.

To make a compress, add 1 to 2 heaping teaspoons of dried chamomile flowers to 1 cup of boiled water. Steep until cool, then dip a clean cloth into the tea. Apply the cloth to the affected skin.

Bring hazel home. Witch hazel is a clear liquid extract that has potent astringent properties that help treat skin problems. When German researchers had 36 people with allergic eczema apply either witch hazel or a nonmedicinal liquid (a placebo) to their eczema rashes, the witch hazel provided substantially greater relief.

Naturopathy

Wash away the itch. In Japan, people often treat their eczema flare-ups by bathing in hot mineral springs. Soaking in a tub filled with comfortably hot water can work just as well, says Anne Simons, M.D. To make your bath even more therapeutic, she suggests adding one of the following to the water: ½ to 1 cup of baking soda; 1 to 2 cups of Aveeno, a colloidal oatmeal product sold in drugstores; or 1 to 2 cups of finely ground oatmeal. Buy regular oatmeal in the grocery store, then run it through a coffee grinder to get the appropriate consistency.

Be aware that hot baths can aggravate eczema in some people. If this happens to you, discontinue the baths and try another remedy.

Home Remedies

Add bottled moisture. While moisturizers don't cure eczema, they may help break the itch-scratch cycle that can lead to a skin infection. Apply a moisturizing cream, oil, or gel immediately after showering, suggests Charles Camisa, M.D., head of clinical dermatology at the Cleveland Clinic Foundation in Ohio. Reapply as necessary, whenever you feel itchy.

Steer clear of irritants. As much as possible, avoid contact with irritating substances such as soaps, detergents, fragrances, solvents, paints, and tobacco smoke. If you must handle an irritant, Dr. Simons recommends wearing plastic gloves, ideally with cotton gloves underneath. By themselves, plastic gloves can make your hands sweat profusely, which can aggravate eczema.

Change your clothes. If fabrics such as wool and polyester make you itch, build your wardrobe around garments made from cotton and cotton blends.

Switch from baths to showers. For some people, soap and water dries the skin and aggravates eczema. If this happens to you, Dr. Camisa suggests taking quick showers—no more than 5 minutes long—instead of extended baths. Use warm water rather than hot, and experiment with different soaps.

Increase the humidity. If the air in your home or workplace is exceptionally dry, it may trigger eczema flare-ups. Install a humidifier and see if it helps, Dr. Simons recommends.

Go alcohol-free. Many toiletries and personal-care products contain alcohol, which dries your skin, Dr. Camisa notes. Read labels and choose products that are alcohol-free.

Over-the-Counter Drugs

Pop an antihistamine. Over-the-counter antihistamines can relieve the itching associated with eczema, Dr. Camisa says. These medicines tend to cause drowsiness, but this side effect should subside after a few days of regular use. Be sure to follow the package instructions.

Squeeze on hydrocortisone. According to Dr. Simons, another approach to relieving the inflammation associated with eczema is to apply a 0.5 percent over-the-counter hydrocortisone cream. Follow package directions.

OTHER GOOD CHOICES

Homeopathy

Rub on Calendula. Many people with eczema respond well to a homeopathic ointment containing Calendula, says homeopath Dana Ullman. Oral homeopathic medicines—including Kali sulfuricum, Pulsatilla, and Sulfur—can be equally effective. Which medicine will work best for you depends on your individual symptoms. For a recommendation, consult a homeopath.

Chinese Medicine

Fix itching with an herbal formula. While working at a hospital in London, Mary Sheehan, M.D., now chief of pediatric dermatology at Mercy Hospital in Pittsburgh, tested a Chinese medicine and a placebo on 40 adults with eczema. The medicine contained several different herbs, including licorice root, peony root, rehmannia root, and clematis root. While taking the medicine, the participants reported significantly less redness and itching. Their sleep also improved because they didn't feel itchy. To find out whether such an herbal formula would help heal your eczema, consult a practitioner of Chinese medicine.

Point to a cure. The United Nations World Health Organization endorses acupuncture as a treatment for eczema.

If you prefer a do-it-yourself acupressure approach, simply apply steady, penetrating finger pressure for 3 minutes to each point listed below.

◆ Large Intestine 11, located at the outer end of your elbow crease on the thumb side

◆ Spleen 10, located on your inner thigh, four finger-widths above your kneecap and just under your thighbone

Ayurvedic Medicine

Minimize Pitta. Ayurvedic physicians attribute most inflammatory skin conditions to an excess of Pitta dosha. Pitta overheats your blood, which turns your skin red and itchy, explains David Frawley, O.M.D. Vata dosha can also play a role, making your skin dry.

The course of treatment recommended by Ayurvedic physicians depends on your specific dosha, or constitutional type. A typical Ayurvedic prescription includes applications of sesame oil, aloe vera gel, and compresses made from licorice and marshmallow teas.

MEDICAL MEASURES

If your eczema hasn't cleared up after 2 weeks of home care, your doctor may put you on prescription-strength antihistamines or hydrocortisone creams. Generally, prescription antihistamines tend to cause less initial drowsiness than over-the-counter antihistamines.

RED FLAGS

Eczema doesn't affect every person in the same way. What you think is eczema may be another condition requiring a different course of treatment. So when in doubt about any persistent skin problem, consult your doctor.

Emphysema

Inside your lungs are 300 million tiny air sacs called alveoli, where oxygen enters the blood and carbon dioxide leaves it. The alveoli are naturally elastic. When healthy, they expand each time you inhale and contract every time you exhale.

But if you have emphysema, the alveoli lose their elasticity and become permanently stretched. Often, the sacs rupture. As a result, they no longer move oxygen and carbon dioxide into and out of the blood as they are supposed to. The entire body literally becomes starved for oxygen, and you end up gasping for breath.

Some two million Americans have emphysema. The disease claims about 106,000 lives every year. But it's highly preventable and sometimes treatable.

In the vast majority of emphysema cases, damage to the alveoli results from

SIMPLE SOLUTIONS
1. Nutrition
2. Supplements
3. Exercise
4. Qigong
5. Visualization
6. Chinese Medicine
7. Home Remedies
8. Meditation
9. Social Support
10. Herbal Medicine
11. Homeopathy

decades of smoking cigarettes. Long-term exposure to dust, chemical vapors, and other air pollutants can do their share of harm. And some people have a hereditary deficiency of the enzyme responsible for maintaining the alveoli's elasticity.

The main symptom of emphysema is shortness of breath, which often grows worse over time. The chest gradually becomes enlarged and barrel-shaped, a by-product of the constant struggle for air.

If you're a smoker and you already show some signs of emphysema, you can stop the disease from getting worse just by giving up cigarettes. That won't reverse the damage that has already occurred, says Anne Simons, M.D. But it could save your life. If you need help kicking the habit, talk to your doctor or contact the nearest branch of the American Lung Association.

Also, your physician may prescribe a bronchodilator, just like those used to treat asthma. A bronchodilator can help you breathe easier, at least temporarily. To enhance its effectiveness, try pairing it with any—or all—of the remedies that follow.

BEST CHOICES

Nutrition

Reduce your fat intake. Emphysema makes exercising difficult, which in turn makes controlling your weight difficult. But even if you can't engage in strenuous aerobic workouts, you must do something to maintain a healthy weight. Otherwise, carrying extra pounds strains your breathing capacity. To maintain a healthy weight, switch to a low-fat, high-fiber diet. (For nutritional guidelines, see chapter 3.)

Consume C-rich foods. British researchers monitored the eating habits, lifestyles, and health status of 2,633 adult volunteers, about one-quarter of whom were smokers. The researchers concluded that the more vitamin C–rich foods people consumed, the better their lung function. Even the smokers with the highest vitamin C intakes had better lung function than the smokers with the lowest intakes. Among the top sources of vitamin C are guava, red bell peppers, papaya, strawberries, kiwifruit, and, of course, oranges.

Earn an A for good nutrition. Researchers at Georgetown University School of Medicine in Washington, D.C., injected laboratory mice with retinoic acid, an antioxidant in the vitamin A family. Over time, the mice grew healthy new alveoli. Only time and more research will tell whether retinoic acid has the same benefits for humans. In the meantime, eating more vitamin A–rich foods certainly can't hurt. Fill your plate with yellow-orange fruits and vegetables such as apricots, cantaloupe, carrots, and squash.

Make fish your dish. Researchers at the University of Minnesota studied the relationship between fish consumption and lung function in a group of long-time smokers. People who ate fish two or more times a week had significantly better lung function than people who ate fish less than twice a week. "Fish are rich in omega-3 fatty acids," says Alan Gaby, M.D. "Omega-3's have anti-inflammatory properties, which help reduce the lung damage caused by smoking." For the most omega-3's per 3-ounce serving, choose Atlantic herring, canned salmon, whitefish, or fresh tuna.

Chronic Obstructive Pulmonary Disease: Double the Breathing Trouble

By themselves, emphysema and chronic bronchitis are serious enough. Combine the two, and you get an especially menacing malady called chronic obstructive pulmonary disease (COPD).

People with COPD have the damaged air sacs characteristic of emphysema and the mucus-laden cough typical of bronchitis. More often than not, the disease is a product of a lifetime of smoking.

If you have COPD, the following remedies can help minimize its symptoms.

Quit smoking now. Quitting is the best treatment for COPD, says Kenneth R. Bertka, M.D., clinical associate professor of family medicine at the Medical College of Ohio in Toledo. Work with your doctor to develop a smoking-cessation program that you're comfortable with.

Supplements

Strike oil. If you don't like fish, or if you want to get more omega-3 fatty acids into your diet, Dr. Gaby suggests taking fish-oil supplements. They are available in health food stores and some drugstores; follow the package directions for proper dosage.

Exercise

Get active every day. Emphysema limits the amount of exercise that you can tolerate. Still, every little bit helps you control your weight and keeps you strong and limber. The American Lung Association recommends gentle, nonstrenuous activities such as walking or swimming at a leisurely pace.

Qigong

Master qigong's gentle moves. Researchers at Life College in Marietta, Georgia, measured the respiratory efficiency of 10 volunteers, then taught the group a 20-minute qigong routine. After performing the routine, the volunteers showed a 20 percent increase in respiratory efficiency. This finding suggests that

Get your body worked. Trager work is a form of bodywork that combines massagelike manipulation with gentle nonaerobic movements. In one study, researchers found that just 2 weeks of Trager work sessions significantly improved lung function in people with COPD.

Pinpoint the problem. Stimulating certain acupuncture points can make breathing easier, according to Efrem Korngold, O.M.D., L.Ac. He says that a professional acupuncturist would likely include the following points when treating emphysema.

◆ Lung 9, located on the thumb side of your inner forearm between your wrist bone and your wrist crease

◆ Spleen 6, located four finger-widths above your inner anklebone on the back inner border of your shinbone

If you prefer, you can try stimulating these points yourself with acupressure. Apply steady, penetrating finger or thumb pressure to each point for 3 minutes.

qigong may help treat a variety of respiratory problems, including emphysema. Qigong is an ideal activity for people with emphysema because it's so gentle and nonstrenuous.

Visualization

See yourself breathing easily. The feeling of suffocation that characterizes emphysema can contribute to anxiety. Visualization helps alleviate anxiety and stabilize breathing, says Gerald N. Epstein, M.D., director of the Academy of Integrative Medicine and Mental Imagery in New York City. He suggests practicing the following exercise for a minute or two every few hours.

1. Close your eyes and focus on your breathing. Tell yourself that you can get rid of anything that interferes with normal breathing. Open your eyes.

2. Close your eyes again and take three breaths. If you cough, accept it and continue breathing. Open your eyes.

3. Close your eyes again and take three breaths. Focus on how your breathing is changing, deepening. Open your eyes.

4. Repeat the exercise, focusing on breathing from your diaphragm rather than your upper chest.

Chinese Medicine

Fortify the Lung and Spleen. Chinese medicine attributes emphysema to weakness and deficiency in the Lung and Spleen organ systems, according to Efrem Korngold, O.M.D., L.Ac. For patients with emphysema, he prescribes formulas made with strengthening herbs such as ginseng, schisandra, perilla seed, aster root, and orange peel.

Home Remedies

Give your lungs a workout. Slow, deep diaphragmatic breathing—sometimes called belly breathing—can counteract shortness of breath and the anxiety that often accompanies it. To experience what belly breathing feels like, lie on your back and place a book on your abdomen. Inhale and exhale so that the book moves up and down several inches, says Richard Firshein, D.O., assistant professor of family medicine at the New York College of Osteopathic Medicine in New York City. Practice this exercise for 5 minutes three or four times a day.

Change your style. The American Lung Association suggests that people with emphysema practice breathing through pursed lips. This technique deepens respiration and helps prevent gasping and the anxiety that often accompanies it. Keep your lips shut tight, except for a tiny opening in the middle. Slowly inhale and exhale, blowing hard when you exhale so that you make a *sssss* sound. Make each exhalation last twice as long as each inhalation. Practice this technique as often as possible. Try to make it your normal way of breathing.

OTHER GOOD CHOICES

Meditation

Mind what you're doing. At the University of Massachusetts Medical Center in Worcester, Jon Kabat-Zinn, Ph.D., director of the stress reduction clinic, has been experimenting with mindfulness meditation as a treatment for emphysema. Mindfulness involves focusing intently on an aspect of daily living—sometimes an object, but in this case, breathing. Dr. Kabat-Zinn's preliminary findings suggest that mindfulness helps people with emphysema breathe more efficiently. It also reduces the number of respiratory crises that require emergency room visits.

Social Support

Seek out support. There is some evidence that participating in a support group decreases the risk of a respiratory crisis that requires hospitalization. The local chapter of the American Lung Association may be able to refer you to a group in your area.

Herbal Medicine

Make friends with mullein. "If I had emphysema, I'd drink mullein tea," says James A. Duke, Ph.D. "Mullein is rich in mucilage, a soluble fiber that soothes the respiratory tract. Many herbalists that I respect recommend mullein for emphysema." To make a tea from the herb, add 1 to 2 teaspoons of dried, crushed mullein leaves or flowers to 1 cup of boiled water. Steep for 10 minutes, then strain before drinking. Help yourself to as many as three cupfuls of mullein tea a day. You can buy the herb in health food stores.

Homeopathy

Get help from Hepar. The homeopathic medicine Hepar sulfuris may benefit people with emphysema, says homeopath Dana Ullman. Whether the preparation is right for you depends on your unique symptoms, so check with a homeopath.

RED FLAGS

If breathing becomes noticeably more difficult, be sure to consult your doctor. And call 911 or your local ambulance service if you experience a sudden breathing emergency.

Endometriosis

Thirty years ago, endometriosis was known as the career woman's disease. It seemed more prevalent among working women who didn't have children than among stay-at-home moms. That notion has since faded, but much else about endometriosis remains a mystery.

Endometriosis arises from the unpredictable behavior of cells in the uterine lining, or endometrium. These cells are supposed to stay inside the uterus or exit the body during menstruation. But in women with endometriosis, they make their way to other parts of the body and attach themselves to other organs. They may be found on the ovaries, fallopian tubes, bladder, digestive organs, or even the lungs or brain.

Trouble is, even though these endometrial cells have relocated, they continue to act as though they were comfortably ensconced in your uterus. They grow and multiply every month in response to your hormonal cycle. And when you have your period, they bleed. But blood from these runaway endometrial cells can't exit your body. So your body reacts with inflammation, pain, and scarring.

What makes endometrial cells wander outside the uterus is anyone's guess. But whatever the cause, researchers generally agree that immune deficiency appears to play a role in the disease. In studies of laboratory animals, exposure to radiation and other factors that impair immune function appear to raise endometriosis risk. Diminished immunity may explain why women with endometriosis are also prone to yeast infections.

Researchers have also noticed that women with allergies are somewhat more likely to develop endometriosis. And the disease does seem to run in families.

SIMPLE SOLUTIONS
1. Nutrition
2. Supplements
3. Exercise
4. Visualization
5. Social Support
6. Over-the-Counter Drugs
7. Homeopathy
8. Chinese Medicine
9. Ayurvedic Medicine
10. Medical Measures

Women who have endometriosis typically report severe menstrual cramps, persistent pelvic pain, and pain during intercourse. Other possible symptoms include lower-back pain, breast tenderness, nausea, vomiting, headaches, fatigue, and hot and cold flashes. Infertility is common, too: Some 30 to 50 percent of women who are unable to conceive have endometriosis.

If you have endometriosis, your gynecologist may recommend either prescription drugs to suppress cell overgrowth or surgery to remove errant cell deposits (called implants). But advocates of natural and alternative healing are likely to recommend that you try other remedies before turning to prescription drugs, much less surgery. Just give these other treatments time to work, urges Tori Hudson, N.D., professor of gynecology at the National College of Naturopathic Medicine in Portland, Oregon. Within 3 to 6 months, you may experience a dramatic change in your symptoms.

BEST CHOICES

Nutrition

Savor soy. The higher your blood level of the hormone estrogen, the more severe your endometriosis symptoms are likely to be. Soy can help lower your level of estrogen, says James A. Duke, Ph.D. Tofu and other soy foods are rich in two plant estrogens called genistein and daidzein. These plant estrogens, or phytoestrogens, occupy spaces on the endometrial cells where estrogen normally attaches. In effect, the phytoestrogens prevent your body's own estrogen from reaching the endometrial cells.

Love those legumes. If you're not a fan of soy foods, you can still get phytoestrogens from soy's relatives in the legume family. For example, pinto beans supply almost as much genistein and daidzein as soybeans, Dr. Duke says. Other legumes rich in phytoestrogens include kidney beans, black beans, split peas, mung beans, lima beans, fava beans, and peanuts.

Top salads with sprouts. Dr. Duke suggests adding generous portions of bean sprouts to salads and other dishes. "As beans germinate, their total phytoestrogen content increases," he explains.

Feast on other fiber-rich foods, too. Eating lots of plant-derived foods—not only legumes but also grains, fruits, and vegetables—increases your intake of fiber. Fiber binds with estrogen in your digestive tract and escorts the hormone out of your body, says Susan M. Lark, M.D., director of the PMS and Menopause Self-Help Center in Los Altos, California.

Don't forget fish. Cold-water species such as salmon, tuna, and mackerel are rich in fish oil. Fish oil has anti-inflammatory properties that may help relieve endometriosis symptoms, according to Dr. Hudson.

Supplements

Take a daily multivitamin. In a British study, women with endometriosis reported that their symptoms subsided after they began taking multivitamin/mineral supplements. The supplements used in the study contained 100 milligrams each of thiamin, riboflavin, and pyridoxine, plus 300 milligrams of magnesium and 20 milligrams of zinc. While you won't find a multivitamin containing all of these nutrients in the specified amounts, you can try taking individual supplements.

Add the antioxidants. If you opt not to take a multivitamin, Dr. Hudson recommends at least daily supplements of the antioxidant nutrients. She suggests taking 6,000 milligrams of vitamin C, 400 to 800 international units (IU) of vitamin E, 25,000 IU of beta-carotene (which your body converts to vitamin A), and 400 micrograms of selenium. But note that you need to check with your doctor first before trying this combination because most of these doses are much higher than standard recommendations.

Exercise

Get moving. Regular, moderate physical activity is a good idea for everyone. But it offers extra benefits for women with endometriosis, says Anne Simons, M.D. Exercise triggers the release of brain chemicals called endorphins, which elevate mood and relieve pain. Plus, it reduces estrogen levels.

Visualization

Imagine erasing your pain. According to Dr. Lark, the stress of endometriosis disrupts your body's delicate balance of hormones. This may encourage the overgrowth of endometrial cells. To defuse stress, Dr. Lark recommends daily practice of the following visualization exercise: Sit comfortably and breathe deeply with your eyes closed. Imagine looking deep inside your reproductive tract. Picture a giant blackboard eraser wiping away any areas of cell overgrowth. As the eraser eliminates the wayward cells, it also eliminates your pain. Look around inside your clean, pink abdomen. Enjoy the sense of peace and well-being that you feel. Open your eyes.

Social Support

Know that you're not alone. Endometriosis can make you feel isolated and alone—like no one else could understand what you're going through. Meeting other women like yourself provides invaluable emotional support. It also expands your knowledge of endometriosis, as you share with each other what you've learned about the disease. The Endometriosis Association sponsors 150 support groups around the country. For more information, write to the association at 8585 North 76th Place, Milwaukee, WI 53223-2600.

Over-the-Counter Drugs

Pop a pain reliever. For mild endometrial pain, Dr. Simons suggests taking aspirin, ibuprofen, or naproxen (Aleve). Any one of these medicines may provide relief, she says. But they're not appropriate if you have a history of ulcers or another gastrointestinal disease. In that case, stick with acetaminophen. It eases pain but doesn't reduce inflammation, as the others do.

Rub on progesterone cream. Another way to reduce levels of estrogen is to raise levels of the hormone progesterone. You can do that by using a progesterone cream, says Christiane Northrup, M.D., founder of the Women to Women health center in Yarmouth, Maine, and past president of the American Holistic Medical Association. She has seen good results in patients who use 2 percent natural progesterone creams. You can buy these creams in some health food stores. She suggests rubbing ½ teaspoon of cream on your neck, inner arm, or abdomen twice a day from the 10th through 28th days of your menstrual cycle.

OTHER GOOD CHOICES

Homeopathy

Seek help from a homeopath. Homeopaths usually treat endometriosis with a constitutional medicine, a tonic that benefits the entire body. "Which medicine we prescribe depends on your individual endometriosis symptoms as well as any other symptoms you may be experiencing," says homeopath Dana Ullman.

Chinese Medicine

Stimulate the flow of Blood. Practitioners of Chinese medicine believe that endometriosis results from an accumulation of Blood in the uterus. This buildup is caused by the stagnation of Blood and qi, says Efrem Korngold, O.M.D., L.Ac.

Dr. Korngold uses several herbal formulas to treat endometriosis, depending on a woman's individual symptoms. Among the formulas he prescribes: Fu Ke Zhong Zi Wan, which contains Chinese angelica (dang gui), bupleurum root, peony root, and several other herbs; and Wu Jin Wan, which consists of Chinese angelica, peony root, nut grass, and other fruits, roots, and pollens.

Get relief on the spot. Acupressure has proved effective in relieving endometrial pain, says Michael Reed Gach, founder and director of the Acupressure Institute. He suggests stimulating each of the following points for 3 minutes, using your fingertips or thumb to apply steady, penetrating pressure.

◆ Liver 3, situated on top of your foot in the webbing between your big toe and second toe

◆ Conception Vessel 4, located on the midline of your abdomen, four thumb-widths below your navel

◆ Gallbladder 41, located on top of your foot in the hollow where the bones of your fourth and fifth toes meet

Repeat the treatment every hour or two until your pain subsides. If your pain persists, you may want to consult an acupuncturist. Professional needle stimulation of the points often works when finger pressure doesn't.

Ayurvedic Medicine

Quiet your Kapha. According to Ayurvedic medical philosophy, the uterus is governed by the Kapha dosha. So any treatment for endometriosis must focus on rebalancing Kapha, according to Scott Gerson, M.D., founder of Ayurvedic Medicine of New York. His prescriptions for women with endometriosis often include massage (panchakarma) every day for 7 to 10 days as well as daily doses of several medicinal herbs.

Among the herbs Dr. Gerson recommends are ashoka, whose bark contains compounds that act on the uterus, and japa, whose flowers lower estrogen levels. To make ashoka tea, gently boil 1 cup of chopped bark in 4 cups of water until only 1 cup of liquid remains. Strain. He suggests drinking 2 cups of the tea each day. As for japa, Dr. Gerson advises taking 500 milligrams of powdered petals three times a day. You need to obtain both herbs from Ayurvedic physicians.

MEDICAL MEASURES

If your endometriosis doesn't respond to less aggressive treatment, your gynecologist may recommend surgery or prescription drugs. Surgery is usually the first step because it can be performed in conjunction with a routine laparoscopic exam. In a laparoscopy, your doctor uses a long, slender optical instrument to locate places where cell overgrowth has occurred and to guide the removal of the errant cells.

Surgery helps many—but not all—women with endometriosis. It can be especially beneficial if you want to have children. In a study at Laval University in Quebec, 341 women with mild endometriosis underwent laparoscopic procedures. Half of the women received only diagnostic exams, while the rest had areas of cell overgrowth removed right away. Within 9 months, 31 percent of the women who had overgrowths removed became pregnant, compared with just 18 percent of the women who received only diagnostic exams.

Drug treatment for endometriosis involves suppressing the production of estrogen, which shuts down menstruation.

The newest treatment for endometriosis is immune therapy, which is typically administered as an adjunct to surgery. First, you're given skin tests for allergies to several hormones involved in the menstrual cycle. If the tests show any allergic reaction, it's treated through controlled exposure to increasing amounts of the offending substances, a process called desensitization.

To date, no rigorous scientific studies have examined immune therapy and its effects on endometriosis. But many women who've undergone the treatment report improvement in their endometriosis symptoms.

Fibroids

Mere mention of the word *tumor* is enough to send a chill down anyone's spine. But as tumors go, fibroids are a rather docile bunch. That's welcome news for the women who are diagnosed with them.

Actually, the very word *fibroid* is a misnomer, according to Susan M. Lark, M.D., director of the PMS and Menopause Self-Help Center in Los Altos, California. It implies that the tumor consists of fibrous tissue. In fact, the tumor grows from the myometrium, which is the smooth muscle layer of the uterus. So the correct medical name for a fibroid is *myoma* or *leiomyoma*.

SIMPLE SOLUTIONS
1. Nutrition
2. Exercise
3. Visualization
4. Home Remedies
5. Chinese Medicine
6. Ayurvedic Medicine
7. Medical Measures

Fibroids remain something of a medical mystery. No one knows what causes them, although exposure to the hormone estrogen makes them grow faster, Dr. Lark says. Sudden increases in estrogen in the years preceding menopause may explain why fibroids are most common among women who are in their forties.

During this stage of life, called perimenopause, a woman's level of estrogen spikes upward, theorizes Gerson Weiss, M.D., professor and chairperson of obstetrics and gynecology at the UMDNJ—New Jersey Medical School in Newark. Meanwhile, the levels of other hormones that normally counterbalance estrogen stay the same. For fibroids, all that extra estrogen is the hormonal equivalent of fertilizer. The growths balloon—only to shrink during and after menopause, when estrogen production declines.

For much the same reason, fibroids often become larger during pregnancy, when a woman's estrogen level rises considerably. If the growths get too large, they can contribute to miscarriage.

About one-quarter of women over age 35 have fibroids. For reasons that scientists can't yet explain, the growths are three times more likely to affect African-American women than white women. Fibroids also tend to run in families.

In most cases, fibroids produce no symptoms. The growths are detected during a routine gynecological exam. Sometimes they occur alone; other times they form clusters. Each fibroid may range in size from as small as a pea to as big as an orange. Often the growths cause the uterus to enlarge, as it does during pregnancy. Even this doesn't necessarily produce noticeable physical changes, other than some vague discomfort.

Among women who experience problems with their fibroids, the most common complaint is unusually heavy menstrual flow. Scientists suspect that the growths interfere with contraction of the uterine muscles, which help regulate menstrual bleeding. If bleeding remains heavy enough for long enough, it can drain the body's iron supply, setting the stage for iron-deficiency anemia.

Fibroids can also contribute to spotting between periods and dull pain or feelings of fullness or pressure in the lower abdomen or back. If the growths press on your bladder or rectum, you might experience urinary incontinence or constipation. If they occur near your cervix, you might feel discomfort during intercourse. Fibroids have also been implicated as a cause of infertility.

If you have fibroids, you may want to try certain blended-medicine strategies to ease any discomfort that you're experiencing. Here's what experts say can help.

BEST CHOICES

Nutrition

Adjust your eating habits. Building your meals around low-fat plant-derived foods can help reduce your estrogen level. The fiber in whole grains, legumes, fruits, and vegetables binds with estrogen in your digestive tract, speeding the hormone's elimination, Dr. Lark explains. On the other hand, if you eat a high-fat diet, featuring lots of meat and whole-milk dairy products, estrogen goes back into the bloodstream, where it can spur the growth of fibroids.

Introduce yourself to soy. Among plant-derived foods, soybeans stand out for their ability to lower estrogen. They contain ample supplies of two compounds called genistein and daidzein. These plant estrogens, or phytoestrogens, fill spaces on cells where estrogen usually attaches. In other words, the phytoestrogens prevent your body's own estrogen from reaching cells.

Menorrhagia: Strategies to Stem the Flow

If your periods last more than 7 days, you should definitely consult your gynecologist—especially if you're passing large clots or changing your pad or tampon more than once every 2 hours. Such heavy bleeding, called menorrhagia, may be a sign of an underlying health problem such as fibroids, uterine polyps, endometriosis, tubal pregnancy, a thyroid or bleeding disorder, anemia, or infection.

If your gynecologist rules out all of these possible causes, then you have what's known as functional menorrhagia. In other words, you have heavy periods for no apparent reason. Functional menorrhagia usually responds well to a combination of supplements, herbs, and nutritional strategies, says Joseph Pizzorno Jr., N.D. Here's what he and other practitioners recommend.

Take iron supplements. Dr. Pizzorno recommends taking 100 milligrams of iron every day. But check with your doctor first, since dosages over 25 milligrams should only be taken under medical supervision.

Up the ante with antioxidants. Dr. Pizzorno recommends taking 15 milligrams of beta-carotene, 1,000 milligrams of vitamin C, and 200 international units (IU) of vitamin E every day. He also suggests a daily 250-milligram dose of bioflavonoids, nutrients that boost the effectiveness of vitamin C.

Put your money in this purse. The medicinal herb shepherd's purse is a well-established folk remedy for irregular menstrual bleeding. James A. Duke, Ph.D., recommends taking 1 to 2 teaspoons of shep-

In addition to soybeans, you can get genistein and daidzein from soy products such as tofu, tempeh, and soy milk.

Be generous with beans. As soybeans have gained fame for their phytoestrogen content, other members of the legume family have been largely ignored. But many kinds of legumes act as fibroid fighters. Pinto beans, for instance, have almost as much of the phytoestrogens genistein and daidzein as soybeans, according to James A. Duke, Ph.D. Other legumes rich in phytoestrogens include kidney beans, black beans, mung beans, lima beans, fava beans, and split peas.

herd's purse tincture once or twice a day. You can buy the tincture in most health food stores.

Spike beverages with cinnamon. In the same ways as shepherd's purse, cinnamon can help stanch heavy menstrual bleeding, says Jill Stansbury, N.D., chairperson of the botanical medicine department at the National College of Naturopathic Medicine in Portland. Dr. Stansbury recommends adding cinnamon tincture to juice or tea. The tincture is sold in health food stores.

Change your meat-eating ways. Animal-derived foods raise your blood level of arachidonic acid, a compound that concentrates in your uterine lining and stimulates the production of hormones called prostaglandins. Prostaglandins increase menstrual flow, Dr. Pizzorno says. He suggests cutting back on meats and dairy products in favor of vegetarian meals, which help lower your level of arachidonic acid and restore normal menstrual flow.

Opt for over-the-counter aid. Two nonprescription pain relievers, ibuprofen and naproxen (Aleve), work by suppressing prostaglandin production. In this way, they can help regulate heavy menstrual bleeding, says Christiane Northrup, M.D., founder of the Women to Women health center in Yarmouth, Maine, and past president of the American Holistic Medical Association.

Save surgery as a last resort. For heavy menstrual bleeding that doesn't respond to any of the remedies above, surgery may be the only option. The most conservative procedure is endometrial ablation, in which the surgeon cauterizes the uterine lining. While endometrial ablation doesn't work for all women, Dr. Northrup says that you have about an 85 percent chance of benefiting from it.

Sprinkle with sprouts. Bean sprouts are also good sources of phytoestrogens. "As beans germinate, their total phytoestrogen content increases," Dr. Duke explains. He suggests adding generous amounts of sprouts to salads and other dishes.

Eat fish often. Among animal-derived foods, fish may have some value in fighting fibroids. The fish oil in cold-water species such as salmon, tuna, and mackerel has anti-inflammatory properties, which may help relieve fibroid symptoms.

Ovarian Cysts: Growing, Growing . . . Gone

A cyst is a fluid-filled sac that can develop in a variety of places around the body. In women, cysts often appear on the ovaries. Most of these growths are functional, meaning that they don't indicate an underlying illness.

One of the most common types of ovarian cysts, called a follicular cyst, occurs when a follicle within the ovary grows in response to a woman's hormonal cycle but doesn't release its egg. Instead, the follicle keeps on growing beyond the time at which ovulation should have occurred.

Most ovarian cysts cause no symptoms and disappear by themselves over a few menstrual cycles. But some may cause abdominal discomfort, spotting between periods, or—if they press against the bladder—a feeling of urinary urgency, of needing to go *right now*. In rare cases, a cyst becomes twisted, causing severe lower-abdominal pain and possibly bleeding. If you experience any unusual pelvic symptoms, consult your doctor promptly.

In treating ovarian cysts, mainstream physicians typically take a wait-and-see approach. The growth will be monitored for a few months to see if it goes away on its own. If it doesn't, your doctor may recommend high-dose oral contraceptives to stop ovulation and allow the cyst to shrink. If that doesn't work, your doctor may suggest surgical removal of the growth.

But Jackie Germain, N.D., a naturopath in Middletown, Connecticut, suggests an alternative treatment: a vegetarian diet. Whole grains, beans, fruits, and vegetables—the building blocks of a vegetarian diet—are high in fiber. Fiber increases the elimination of the hormone estrogen from your body. As your estrogen level falls, your ovarian cysts may shrink. To lower your estrogen level even more, Dr. Germain recommends avoiding alcohol, fatty foods, and sugar.

Exercise

Stay active. Regular, moderate exercise is a good idea for everyone. But it can be especially beneficial for women with fibroids, says Anne Simons, M.D.

First, exercise reduces your estrogen level, which may help shrink fibroids.

Second, it stimulates the release of your body's own pain-relieving, mood-elevating compounds, called endorphins. Third, it helps you maintain a healthy weight. Compared with slim women, women who are overweight have a higher risk of developing fibroids, because body fat raises estrogen levels, explains naturopath Jackie Germain, N.D., of Middletown, Connecticut.

Visualization

See your fibroids disappear. Knowing that you have fibroids can make you feel anxious. In turn, anxiety can disrupt your body's delicate hormonal balance, causing fibroids to grow faster.

To reduce anxiety, Dr. Lark recommends daily practice of the following visualization exercise: Sit comfortably with your eyes closed. Breathe deeply. Imagine looking deep inside your reproductive tract. See a giant blackboard eraser wiping away your fibroids. Watch as your uterus shrinks to its normal size and shape. Notice how wonderful you feel. Enjoy the sense of peace and well-being. Open your eyes.

Home Remedies

Watch what you're drinking. Both alcohol and caffeine are processed by your liver, which also regulates the amount of estrogen in your blood. So stressing your liver with booze or caffeine-containing beverages, especially coffee, may allow estrogen to accumulate in your blood and stimulate the growth of fibroids.

Since caffeine and alcohol may not affect everyone in the same way, try giving up one of the substances for 6 to 8 weeks and see if you experience a reduction in pain and bleeding. If your symptoms improve, then you may have found the culprit. If not, try eliminating the other substance and see if this has an effect on your symptoms. If this elimination approach has no impact, then you can safely assume that caffeine and alcohol aren't your triggers.

OTHER GOOD CHOICES

Chinese Medicine

Make Blood flow freely. Practitioners of Chinese medicine attribute fibroids to an overaccumulation of Blood in the uterus, brought on by the stagnation of Blood and qi. The excess Blood solidifies and turns into tumors, explains Efrem Korngold, O.M.D., L.Ac.

For his patients with fibroids, Dr. Korngold may prescribe one of several different herbal formulas. One that's especially effective is Fu Ke Zhong Zi Wan, a combination of Chinese angelica (dang gui), bupleurum root, peony root, and other herbs. If Cold contributes to a patient's fibroids, Dr. Korngold will augment the herbal formula with warming herbs such as ginger, cinnamon, and cardamom.

Make your point against pain. Acupuncture has proved to be an effective treatment for fibroids, according to Dr. Korngold. For a do-it-yourself approach, you can stimulate the same points with acupressure. Apply steady, penetrating finger pressure to each point for 3 minutes.

◆ Liver 3, situated on top of your foot in the webbing between your big toe and second toe

◆ Spleen 6, located four finger-widths above your inner anklebone on the back inner border of your shinbone

◆ Conception Vessel 3, located on the midline of your abdomen, five finger-widths below your navel and one thumb-width above your pubic bone

Ayurvedic Medicine

Cleanse your blood. Ayurvedic medicine views fibroids as *raktaja gulma*—that is, tumors resulting from the impurity of your blood. How your fibroids are treated depends on your constitutional type, or dosha, explains Alakananda Devi, M.B., of Boulder, Colorado. In general, Dr. Devi advises patients with fibroids to exercise more and to reduce their intakes of dietary fat and alcohol. Dr. Devi also prescribes several Ayurvedic herbs, including chitrak and ashoka. Chitrak helps eliminate tumors, while ashoka relaxes the uterus, reduces menstrual flow, and shrinks fibroids.

MEDICAL MEASURES

"In general, if your fibroids are not causing much discomfort, you might decide to just live with them until menopause shrinks them naturally," Dr. Simons says. "If you have heavy periods, you can take iron supplements to reduce your risk of iron-deficiency anemia."

For more troublesome fibroids, mainstream medicine offers two treatment options: drugs and surgery. Drug therapy aims to suppress estrogen, which makes fibroids grow. Two of the most commonly prescribed pharmaceuticals are leuprolide (Lupron) and nafarelin (Synarel). Both reduce estrogen by stimulating the secretion of gonadotropin-releasing hormone, or GnRH.

Surgery is usually reserved for the most severe fibroids. The most conservative procedure, called myomectomy, removes just the fibroids and leaves your uterus intact. But myomectomy may not be possible if you have lots of fibroids or if they're hard to reach.

The other, more radical surgical procedure is hysterectomy. Fibroids are the reason for about one-third of the 550,000 hysterectomies performed in the United States each year.

With a hysterectomy, there's no chance of fibroids coming back, because your uterus is gone. If your ovaries are also removed, you may notice a drop in your sex drive afterward. That's because the ovaries manufacture androgens, the hormones that fuel a woman's libido. Taking supplemental androgens can correct this problem.

Hysterectomy is major surgery and should only be considered as a last resort. Before agreeing to it, you need to carefully weigh its benefits and risks in consultation with your doctor. Consider all of your treatment options and get several opinions, so you can make an informed decision.

RED FLAGS

Both oral contraceptives and hormone-replacement therapy (HRT), which some mainstream M.D.'s prescribe for women in or past menopause, contain estrogen. The amount of the hormone is low enough that it shouldn't stimulate the growth of fibroids. Still, you'd be wise to discuss the issue with your doctor before starting a prescription for oral contraceptives or HRT.

If you've already been diagnosed with fibroids and you experience sudden sharp pelvic pain, call your doctor right away. This may be a sign that one of your fibroids has become twisted, cutting off its own blood supply. A strangled fibroid is serious and potentially life-threatening. You may need immediate surgery to remove it.

Fibromyalgia

At first you thought you were coming down with the flu. You had that same vague, allover achiness. But you never got any other symptoms—and the muscle aches never went away. You noticed something else, too: When you pressed on certain spots around your body, you felt sharp pain.

This is the hallmark of fibromyalgia, a condition that affects an estimated four million Americans—mostly adult women. Its name describes its chief symptom: pain (*-algia*) in fibrous and muscle tissues (*fibromy-*).

According to diagnostic criteria established by the American College of Rheumatology, fibromyalgia is characterized by at least 3 months of general flulike muscle aches plus sharp pain affecting at least 11 of 18 specific points around the body. These symptoms may be aggravated by activity, stress, or weather conditions. And they may be accompanied by any or all of the following: sleep problems, fatigue, chronic headaches, numbness or tingling, irritable bowel syndrome, and mental fuzziness.

SIMPLE SOLUTIONS
1. Elimination Diet
2. Supplements
3. Exercise
4. Meditation
5. Biofeedback
6. Social Support
7. Over-the-Counter Drugs
8. Home Remedies
9. Homeopathy
10. Chinese Medicine
11. Medical Measures

No one knows what causes fibromyalgia. Rheumatologist Stuart Silverman, M.D., medical director of the fibromyalgia rehabilitation program at Cedars-Sinai Medical Center in Los Angeles, speculates that the condition develops in response to a physical stress—an injury, an infection, or exposure to certain chemicals in the environment. The episode somehow alters your brain chemistry in ways that amplify your perception of pain. Once these changes have occurred, your muscles don't make energy in the same painless, efficient way that they used to. And sleep may be disrupted, too.

Other experts theorize that fibromyalgia is closely related to two other health problems—namely, chronic fatigue syndrome (CFS) and multiple chemical sensitivities. In a study at Harborview Medical Center in Seattle, researchers determined that all three conditions produce remarkably similar symptoms. Some experts have even suggested that fibromyalgia and CFS are the same illness but with different dominant symptoms—pain in fibromyalgia, fatigue in CFS.

Like CFS, fibromyalgia is a chronic condition. But while the pain is persistent, it usually doesn't get worse over time. That's good news for people with fibromyalgia, many of whom manage their symptoms so well that they continue to work full-time and lead quite normal lives.

If you suspect that you have fibromyalgia but you haven't yet seen your doctor, schedule an appointment as soon as possible. You need a professional diagnosis, especially since fibromyalgia can easily be mistaken for so many other conditions. It shares a number of symptoms with osteoarthritis, rheumatoid arthritis, lupus, Lyme disease, and hypothyroidism (an underactive thyroid gland). Each of these conditions requires a different course of treatment.

For fibromyalgia, treatment focuses on renormalizing your brain chemistry to reduce your sensitivity to pain. Here's what top mainstream physicians and alternative practitioners have found to be most effective.

BEST CHOICES

Elimination Diet

I.D. the offenders. Like fibromyalgia, food intolerances can cause achiness and lethargy. Because of this similarity between the two conditions, Russell Jaffe, M.D., Ph.D., director of Serammune Physician's Laboratory in Sterling, Virginia, wondered whether fibromyalgia might respond to the same type of elimination diet used to treat food intolerances.

Dr. Jaffe recruited 32 people with fibromyalgia and asked some of them to undergo testing for sensitivity to foods, food additives, and certain drugs. He then instructed these volunteers to avoid those items that provoked their symptoms. Meanwhile, the rest of the study participants maintained their usual lifestyles.

Compared with the people who changed nothing, the people who followed an elimination program experienced rapid improvement in their fibromyalgia symptoms. After 6 months on the program, they reported 50 percent less pain, 30 percent less stiffness, 50 percent more energy, and 40 percent less depression.

To find out whether food intolerances are contributing to your fibromyalgia symptoms, you can try an elimination diet with the guidance of your doctor. Another option is to undergo food sensitivity testing, according to Alan P. Brauer, M.D. "It costs more than a do-it-yourself elimination diet, but it produces results faster," he says.

Supplements

Pop M&Ms. No, not the candy, but magnesium and malic acid. These nutrients appear to deliver a potent one-two punch against fibromyalgia symptoms.

If you want to try magnesium and malic acid to see whether or not they help, take 150 milligrams of magnesium and 600 milligrams of malic acid twice a day for 4 weeks. This should be done in consultation with a nutrition-minded doctor. You can buy malic acid supplements in health food stores.

Exercise

Outpace pain. When you're hurting, you may not feel like going for a walk, riding a bike, playing tennis, or taking an aerobics class. But you should, because physical activity can help relieve pain and stiffness. In fact, Theodore Pincus, M.D., professor of medicine at Vanderbilt University School of Medicine in Nashville, has deemed regular exercise "the most helpful therapy for fibromyalgia." Regular means at least an hour 3 days a week, and preferably an hour every day.

Meditation

Relax your body and mind. Researchers at the Arthritis-Fibromyalgia Center and Newton-Wellesley Hospital near Boston assessed the symptoms of 77 people with fibromyalgia. Then over the next 10 weeks, the group participated in meditation classes. Everyone in the group reported improvement in their symptoms, with half describing the improvement as significant.

Biofeedback

Control stress to control pain. Fibromyalgia can trap you in a vicious circle. Stress aggravates your pain, which in turn contributes to stress. Biofeedback can break the circle. "Biofeedback teaches people how to achieve a state of deep relaxation quickly and easily," says Jeanne Melvin, program director of the pain and fibromyalgia rehabilitation program at Cedars-Sinai Medical Center in Los Angeles. "It helps relieve fibromyalgia pain and improves sleep."

Social Support

Meet others like you. Fibromyalgia can be a life-altering experience. There's nothing as comforting as talking with people who know exactly what you're going through. That's why support groups are so popular and powerful. To find a group in your area, contact one of the following organizations.

◆ Fibromyalgia Alliance of America, P. O. Box 21990, Columbus, OH 43221-0990

◆ The Fibromyalgia Network, P. O. Box 31750, Tucson, AZ 85751-1750

◆ The National Chronic Fatigue Syndrome and Fibromyalgia Association, P. O. Box 18426, Kansas City, MO 64133-8426

Over-the-Counter Drugs

Make capsaicin your companion. Ground red pepper gets its spicy heat from a compound called capsaicin. As researchers have discovered, capsaicin is a powerful pain reliever.

Several over-the-counter products have capsaicin as their active ingredient. Ask your pharmacist to recommend one. Follow the package directions for proper use.

Home Remedies

Make yourself comfortable. Experiment with changes in your home and workplace that can help you function more efficiently and minimize your pain, suggests Anne Simons, M.D. For example, try performing at least some tasks—like paying bills and talking on the phone—while standing up rather than sitting down.

Support your neck. Dr. Simons recommends investing in a horseshoe-collar pillow to cushion your neck when you're sitting in high-backed chairs and car and airplane seats. These pillows are sold in medical supply stores as well as some drugstores and department stores.

Slow your pace. You don't want fibromyalgia to crimp your lifestyle. That's understandable. Still, you must learn to treat yourself kindly. Avoid over-exerting yourself. Take breaks when you feel you need to.

Find Relief Where You'd Least Expect It

More than 30 years ago, R. Paul St. Amand, M.D., assistant clinical professor of medicine at the University of California, Los Angeles, accidentally discovered that gout medication seems to improve fibromyalgia symptoms. Over the years, he stopped using prescription gout medicines and switched to a drug called guaifenesin. He had realized that guaifenesin provides the same benefits as gout medications, but with fewer side effects.

As it turns out, guaifenesin is the active ingredient in many over-the-counter cough and cold formulas. In these products, it works as an expectorant, meaning that it loosens mucus in the respiratory tract. According to Dr. St. Amand, about 70 percent of the fibromyalgia patients whom he has treated with guaifenesin report significant improvement in their symptoms.

If you want to try guaifenesin, mention this research to your doctor and discuss the best way for you to use the drug. Dr. St. Amand usually recommends taking either 300 or 600 milligrams of guaifenesin twice a day. At these dosages, it seldom causes side effects, though nausea, heartburn, itching, and rashes are possible. In addition, guaifenesin should not be taken in conjunction with aspirin or products that contain aspirin-like salicylates, Dr. St. Amand says. These substances render guaifenesin ineffective.

OTHER GOOD CHOICES

Homeopathy

Rely on Rhus toxicodendron. At St. Bartholomew's Hospital in London, researchers gave 23 people with fibromyalgia the homeopathic medicine Rhus toxicodendron in addition to standard treatment. Another 23 people with fibromyalgia received a placebo plus standard treatment. The researchers found that the group taking the homeopathic medicine experienced significantly greater pain relief than the group taking the placebo.

If you want to try Rhus toxicodendron, consult a homeopath. He can determine whether the medicine is appropriate for your unique symptoms.

Chinese Medicine

Defend against invading forces. According to Chinese medical doctrine, fibromyalgia occurs because a person's life energy (qi) is too weak to defend against the forces of Wind, Damp, and Cold. "To use a military metaphor, as the Chinese often do, there's no guard at the gate," says Efrem Korngold, O.M.D., L.Ac.

To treat fibromyalgia, Chinese medical practitioners prescribe herbs to strengthen qi and expel Wind, Damp, and Cold. Which herbs a practitioner prescribes depends on what is causing your symptoms. According to Dr. Korngold, the herb astralagus fortifies qi. Herbs that drive out Wind and Damp include clematis root, gentian root, and chaenomeles fruit. And herbs that eliminate Wind and Cold include cinnamon twig and dried ginger.

Get stimulated. At University Hospital in Geneva, Switzerland, 75 percent of the people given acupuncture experienced significant improvement in their fibromyalgia. Of these, 25 percent reported complete relief from their symptoms.

According to Dr. Korngold, acupuncture treatment from a licensed acupuncturist for fibromyalgia usually involves stimulating the following points.

◆ Spleen 9, located one thumb-width below the knee crease in the hollow to the inside of your shinbone

◆ Liver 3, situated on top of your foot in the webbing between your big toe and second toe

◆ Large Intestine 4, located on the back of your hand where the bones of your thumb and index finger meet

If you prefer, you can stimulate these points yourself using acupressure. Apply steady, penetrating finger pressure to each point for 3 minutes.

MEDICAL MEASURES

Certain prescription medications—including pain relievers, muscle relaxants, sleeping pills, and antidepressants—can help manage fibromyalgia symptoms. Of these, pain relievers can be problematic. Antidepressants, however, have shown considerable benefit.

Before You Reach for a Pain Reliever . . .

According to one survey, 91 percent of people with fibromyalgia regularly take pain relievers to alleviate their symptoms. Their pills of choice appear to be nonsteroidal anti-inflammatory drugs (NSAIDs), a category that includes the popular over-the-counter medicines aspirin, ibuprofen, and naproxen (Aleve). Yet research has shown that NSAIDs do little, if anything, to reduce fibromyalgia pain.

"There's no point in taking anti-inflammatories, because fibromyalgia does not cause inflammation," says Jeanne Melvin, program director of the pain and fibromyalgia rehabilitation program at Cedars-Sinai Medical Center in Los Angeles. "With regular use of NSAIDs, a person runs about a 25 percent risk of developing stomach ulcers. For most people with fibromyalgia, that risk outweighs the benefits."

Some people get relief with acetaminophen, which does not have anti-inflammatory properties. But in a study conducted by Russell Jaffe, M.D., Ph.D., director of Serammune Physician's Laboratory in Sterling, Virginia, about 20 percent of people with fibromyalgia were found to have sensitivities to acetaminophen. In other words, acetaminophen caused symptoms rather than curing them.

About one-third of people with fibromyalgia rely on prescription narcotics to manage their pain, but the Cedars-Sinai program discourages this practice as well. "In our experience, narcotics interfere with the approaches that provide real control over fibromyalgia: good nutrition, regular exercise, stress management, and sleep retraining," Melvin says.

At Newton-Wellesley Hospital, researchers divided 19 people with fibromyalgia into four groups. The first group took the antidepressant fluoxetine (Prozac). The second group was given the antidepressant amitriptyline (Elavil). The third group received both drugs; the fourth group received a placebo. The researchers found that both antidepressants produced significant relief from fibromyalgia pain and tenderness. What's more, the two antidepressants worked better together than by themselves. The antidepressant therapy also improved sleep.

Medications alone rarely "cure" fibromyalgia, however. To help you manage and minimize your symptoms, your doctor may refer you to a pain clinic that combines drug treatment with the therapies discussed in this chapter.

Flatulence

Go on, admit it: When you hear someone else pass gas, only your sense of decorum keeps you from laughing out loud. But flatulence isn't nearly as funny when it emanates from you, especially in social situations.

Though sometimes unpredictable, flatulence is an inevitable by-product of the digestive process.

Every day, 1 to 5 ounces of undigested carbohydrates pass into your small intestine in little lumps. The lumps slowly make their way into your colon, where they're broken down by bacteria. This process, called fermentation, produces a biochemical soup composed of hydrogen and methane as well as several foul-smelling trace gases. Collectively, these compounds are known as flatus. The flatus travels out of the colon toward the nearest exit, where it's expelled (much to your chagrin).

SIMPLE SOLUTIONS
1. Nutrition
2. Supplements
3. Visualization
4. Herbal Medicine
5. Home Remedies
6. Homeopathy
7. Chinese Medicine
8. Ayurvedic Medicine

A number of factors can influence the frequency and severity of flatulence, including a high-carbohydrate diet. Beans and other legumes, which contain specific kinds of carbohydrates called oligosaccharides, are the most notorious gas-producers. Some people get gassy as well when they eat broccoli, brussels sprouts, cauliflower, onions, radishes, fruits, bagels, pretzels, or anything made with fruit sugar (fructose) or the artificial sweetener sorbitol.

Flatulence may also be related to lactose intolerance, certain medications, or a number of digestive problems. In addition, you may have more flatulence just because you're eating more healthfully. A diet that favors fiber-rich grains, beans, fruits, and vegetables over meats and other fatty foods is naturally gas-producing. "The health experts all agree: Eat less fat and more fiber," say pharmacists Joe Graedon and Teresa Graedon, Ph.D., coauthors of The People's Pharmacy. "They're right, but your digestive tract pays a penalty. Plain and simple, fiber makes you fart."

Of course, knowing that everyone gets flatulence now and then is of little consolation when you're the one tooting the old horn. Fortunately, you can take steps to minimize the number of gaseous episodes that you experience. Here's what the experts recommend.

BEST CHOICES

🍽 Nutrition

Soak beans before cooking. Yes, beans cause flatulence. But they're also inexpensive sources of high-quality protein, fiber, and other nutrients. So instead of avoiding them, soak them in water before cooking them, suggests Anne Simons, M.D. Soaking removes some of those gas-causing oligosaccharides.

Put the beans in a pot of water and allow them to sit overnight. Then drain off the soaking water and replace it with fresh water. Cook the beans thoroughly before serving.

Savor every morsel. When you eat fast, you swallow your food in large lumps. These lumps are more likely to enter your small intestine undigested, increasing the odds of flatulence. So eat slowly and chew every bite thoroughly.

Disregard dairy. Try eliminating milk and other dairy products for a week, advises Alan P. Brauer, M.D. If you notice any improvement in your symptoms, you may well be lactose-intolerant. In that case, you need to see your doctor for proper diagnosis.

Take copious notes. If you're particularly prone to gassiness, keep a food diary in which you write down what you eat and when you experience symptoms. Review your notes to identify the foods that you think may be causing problems. Then give up those foods for a week and notice whether your symptoms improve. If they do, you can make better-informed decisions about what *not* to eat when.

🥫 Supplements

Befriend the good bugs. To prevent gaseous episodes, try daily supplementation with acidophilus bacteria, suggests Andrew T. Weil, M.D., director of the program in integrative medicine at the University of Arizona College of Medicine in Tucson. Acidophilus bacteria are friendly microorganisms that re-

Bloating: Best Buddies with Gas

Do you ever feel uncomfortably full, like someone has inflated a balloon in your abdomen? That's bloating, and it ranks right behind abdominal pain as the most common gastrointestinal symptom, according to Satish Rao, M.D., Ph.D., director of neurogastroenterology at the University of Iowa College of Medicine in Iowa City.

Bloating and gas often go hand-in-hand. The two conditions respond to the same treatments. In addition, many women experience bloating right before their menstrual cycles, usually as the result of water retention.

Some experts suspect that bloating may have a mind-body element, too. In one study, researchers measured the amount of gas in the abdomens of 18 people who complained of chronic bloating and 10 people who said they never experienced it. Surprisingly, the people who felt bloated actually produced less gas than the people who didn't—176 milliliters compared with 199 milliliters.

So what's going on? There are two possibilities, Dr. Rao says: Either those who feel bloated experience more severe intestinal spasms or they're more sensitive to discomfort from the gas they produce. To reduce intestinal spasms, Dr. Rao recommends peppermint tea. One caution, however: Don't take peppermint too close to bedtime, as it can cause heartburn in some people.

To treat abdominal sensitivity, Dr. Rao suggests relaxation techniques such as meditation, visualization, tai chi, yoga, and massage.

side in your intestines and support good digestion. Look for yogurt containing live culture bacteria (the label will tell you). Or buy acidophilus powder—it's sold in health food stores—and follow the package directions for proper dosage.

Visualization

See what's going on in your gut. Research by Michael D. Gershon, M.D., professor and chairperson in the department of anatomy and cell biology at Columbia-Presbyterian Medical Center in New York City, has shown that the digestive tract is lined with an enormous number of nerve cells. These cells are responsible for the "butterflies" that you feel when you're anxious. They also cause abdominal spasms that contribute to the explosive release of gas.

You can reduce abdominal spasms—and control the noisiness of flatulence—by practicing relaxation techniques, says Martin L. Rossman, M.D.

He has produced visualization audiotapes that might help soothe your abdominal spasms. Whether you choose visualization or another relaxation technique, Dr. Rossman adds, regular practice is key to controlling flatulence. "Make deep relaxation part of your daily life," he says.

Herbal Medicine

Pass the peppermint. "Peppermint is a very specific remedy for relief of flatulence," notes Stephen Holt, M.D., professor of medicine at Seton Hall University in South Orange, New Jersey. Studies dating back as far as the 1920s have shown that peppermint helps soothe gastrointestinal spasms, which contribute to explosive flatulence. The herb also has anti-foaming properties: It breaks down large gas bubbles into smaller ones, which pass more easily and cause less abdominal distress.

Peppermint is most effective when taken in tincture form. James A. Duke, Ph.D., suggests adding 1 to 2 teaspoons of tincture to 1 cup of boiled water. Allow to steep for 10 minutes, then drink up. You can buy peppermint tincture in health food stores.

Toot less with an herbal tea. In addition to peppermint, Dr. Duke recommends allspice, caraway, chamomile, cloves, dill, fennel, ginger, sage, and thyme. All of these herbs contain compounds that relax the smooth muscle of the digestive tract. In this way, they discourage spasms that contribute to explosive flatulence.

To make a tea from any of these herbs, add 1 to 2 teaspoons of dried herb to 1 cup of boiled water. Allow to steep for 10 minutes, then strain out the herb and drink.

Home Remedies

Make a beeline for Beano. Beano supplies alpha-galactosidase, the enzyme that your stomach needs to digest the carbohydrates in beans and other legumes. With this over-the-counter product, you can enjoy bean-laden dishes without fear of repercussions. Follow the directions on the bottle.

OTHER GOOD CHOICES

Homeopathy

Try a microdose medicine. A number of homeopathic medicines effectively relieve flatulence, according to homeopath Dana Ullman. Which remedy he prescribes depends on a client's individual symptoms. But he most often recommends Bryonia, Carbo vegetabilis, Nux vomica, or Pulsatilla.

Chinese Medicine

Free your qi. Practitioners of Chinese medicine view flatulence as a stagnation of qi brought on by Heat in the intestines, says Efrem Korngold, O.M.D., L.Ac. To stimulate the flow of qi, Dr. Korngold often recommends gentle, mildly spicy foods and herbs such as radishes, citrus fruits and peels, cardamom, and licorice. He may also prescribe Curing Pills, an over-the-counter Chinese medicine made from 15 different herbs.

Apply pressure to ease pressure. Acupressure can help quiet flatulence, according to Michael Reed Gach, founder and director of the Acupressure Institute. He suggests using your fingertips to apply steady, penetrating pressure to each of the following points for 3 minutes.

◆ Conception Vessel 6, located three finger-widths directly below your navel

◆ Conception Vessel 12, located halfway between the end of your breastbone and your navel on the midline of your abdomen (do not stimulate this point if you've just eaten or if you're a woman who's pregnant)

◆ Large Intestine 11, located at the outer end of your elbow crease on the thumb side

If flatulence persists, consider consulting an acupuncturist. Needle stimulation of these points often helps when finger pressure doesn't.

Ayurvedic Medicine

Go gaga for ginger. Ayurvedic physicians rely on ginger to treat an array of digestive problems, including flatulence. Vasant Lad, B.A.M.S., M.A.Sc., director of the Ayurvedic Institute in Albuquerque, New Mexico, recommends taking 1 teaspoon of freshly grated gingerroot in 1 teaspoon of lime juice after every meal.

RED FLAGS

If your flatulence is accompanied by bloating, diarrhea, and abdominal cramps, think back over the past 6 months. Did you do any traveling in that time period, especially to a foreign country or a remote American locale? If so, you may have picked up intestinal parasites, Dr. Brauer says. Ask your doctor to test you for them.

Flu

Like the common cold, the flu is a viral infection that targets the upper respiratory tract. But of the two conditions, the flu—short for influenza—is much more severe.

In the United States, the worst flu outbreaks usually occur in the winter months, from December to early March. The entire flu season stretches from Thanksgiving to Easter. In that time, flu viruses fell some 40 million Americans, knocking them off their feet for a week to 10 days.

There are three types of flu viruses, designated as A, B, or C. Type A flu produces the worst symptoms and the most complications, says Nancy Arden, R.N., research associate in the department of microbiology and immunology at Baylor College of Medicine in Houston. By comparison, Type B flu tends to have less serious symptoms and doesn't last as long. And the symptoms of Type C flu are so

SIMPLE SOLUTIONS
1. Nutrition
2. Herbal Medicine
3. Homeopathy
4. Home Remedies
5. Chinese Medicine
6. Medical Measures

mild that it barely qualifies as an illness. When public health officials talk about the flu, they're referring to either Type A or Type B strains. New strains of each flu virus emerge every year, which explains how they manage to stay one step ahead of your immune system.

Flu viruses are easily transmitted through the air. You just have to inhale to get infected. Cold viruses spread in the same way, but for some reason, they're not as potent as flu viruses. "If you put a person with a cold in a room full of healthy people, several of them will get sick," Arden says. "But if you put a person with the flu in that same room, most of those people will get sick within 1 to 3 days."

There's another crucial difference between a cold and the flu. At its worst, a cold might lead to bronchitis or a sinus infection—both unpleasant but curable. But the flu can be fatal if it progresses to an infectious condition called bacterial pneumonia.

Pneumonia: Flu's Fiendish Accomplice

The most serious flu-related lung infection is bacterial pneumonia. Of all the varieties of pneumonia, it's by far the most serious. It causes more deaths than any other infectious disease.

The first signs of bacterial pneumonia usually show up just as you feel as though you're recovering from the flu. Your fever returns, and you develop one or more of the following symptoms: chest pain, rapid pulse, difficult or rapid shallow breathing, persistent chills, and a severe cough with brown or bloody mucus.

If your fever comes back just as your flu seems to be subsiding, see your doctor right away. People who are diagnosed with bacterial pneumonia usually must be treated with intravenous antibiotics, which requires hospitalization, says Steven Mostow, M.D., associate dean for outreach and professor of medicine at the University of Colorado Health Sciences Center and University Hospital in Denver. Recovery typically takes a few weeks for young adults, longer for older adults and people with chronic illnesses.

"Most people still consider the flu no big deal. That's a big mistake," says flu specialist Steven Mostow, M.D., associate dean for outreach and professor of medicine at the University of Colorado Health Sciences Center and University Hospital in Denver. "Even if you're healthy and in the prime of life, the flu can knock you flat on your back for a week." The infection is even harder on people who are up in years or who have chronic respiratory problems.

Fortunately, there's a lot that you can do to take some of the misery out of the flu. For starters, take your pick of the following remedies.

BEST CHOICES

Nutrition

Slurp your meals. For a day or two, consume only liquids—water, juices, teas, and soups. "Digesting liquids requires a lot less energy than digesting foods," says Alan P. Brauer, M.D. "This means that your body has more energy to fight the flu."

Add mushrooms to your soup. If you eat soup while you're sick, make it mushroom. But not just any old mushroom, says Mindy Green, an herbalist in Boulder, Colorado, and coauthor of *Aromatherapy: A Complete Guide to the Healing Art*. You want shiitake, maitake, and reishi mushrooms, which have been shown in studies to boost the body's immune response.

Herbal Medicine

Ease symptoms with echinacea. In a German study, people with flu symptoms took 900 milligrams of echinacea extract, 450 milligrams of the extract, or a placebo (a fake pill) every day. Those on the 900-milligram regimen developed much milder symptoms than those on either the 450-milligram regimen or the placebo.

Most herbalists recommend using liquid echinacea extracts, which are sold in vials in health food stores. The dose in the German study, 900 milligrams, equals about 1 tablespoon of extract.

"You can also buy echinacea tincture premixed with goldenseal, which has some antiviral action," says Alan Gaby, M.D. "These herbs make a good combination for treating flu." Follow the package directions for proper dosage.

Get some ginger aid. "Ginger contains a dozen antiviral compounds," says James A. Duke, Ph.D. "And unlike many medicinal herbs, it tastes good." To make a tea, add 1 heaping teaspoon of grated fresh gingerroot to 1 cup of boiled water. Let steep for 10 minutes, then strain. Drink up to four cupfuls a day.

Test Sambucol. An herbal flu medicine, Sambucol is made from sweet black elderberries. Elderberries have a long folk history as a treatment for flu as well as for colds and fever. Sambucol is available in many health food stores and some drugstores. An Israeli study shows that it helps.

Homeopathy

Buy Oscillococcinum. The most effective homeopathic flu preparation has a tongue twister of a name: Oscillococcinum (pronounced "AH-sill-oh-cock-SINE-um"). In a French study, doctors gave either Oscillococcinum or a placebo to 487 people with flu symptoms. The study participants were asked to record their temperatures and other symptoms twice a day. Compared with the people taking the placebo, those taking the homeopathic medicine were almost twice as likely to report significant relief from their symptoms after 48 hours.

You can buy Oscillococcinum in most health food stores. Follow package directions for dosage. "The key to using Oscillococcinum is to start taking it during the first 48 hours that you have symptoms," says homeopath Dana Ullman. "If you wait longer, the remedy doesn't work as well."

Home Remedies

Drink plenty of fluids. A survey asked a large number of family doctors which home remedies they considered most important in treating flu. Seventy-nine percent of the physicians rated fluids "very important." Why? Because fever is dehydrating, and even minor dehydration aggravates flu symptoms. In addition, drinking warm fluids can help relieve sore throat, coughing, and nasal congestion. So consume as much water, juice, or tea as you can. Sip steadily throughout the day rather than guzzling a few big glasses.

Give your bod a break. When you're stricken with the flu, you have little desire to do anything but curl up in bed. That's a good thing. By resting, you conserve energy, explains Anne Simons, M.D. Your body can invest that energy in making you well.

OTHER GOOD CHOICES

Chinese Medicine

Calm the Wind, cool the Heat. According to Chinese medical philosophy, the flu results from an invasion of Wind that's aggravated by Heat from fever. "The flu is basically a Heat cold," says Efrem Korngold, O.M.D., L.Ac. For people with flu symptoms, he typically prescribes herbal formulas that contain some combination of chrysanthemum flowers, mulberry leaf, mint, peppermint, honeysuckle, forsythia buds, burdock seed, and licorice.

Press the right spots. About a dozen different acupressure points provide relief from flu symptoms. The following three points are recommended by Michael Reed Gach, founder and director of the Acupressure Institute. Using your fingertips, apply steady penetrating pressure to each point for 3 minutes.

◆ Bladder 2, located on either side of your nose, where the bridge of your nose meets the ridge of your eyebrows. This point relieves congestion and itchy eyes.

A Shot at Flu Prevention

Because flu viruses are airborne, the only surefire way to avoid them is to stop breathing—which, of course, has undesirable consequences of its own. The next best thing is a flu shot.

Do flu shots work? Yes—though better for some folks than for others. Research has shown that for people under age 65, the flu shot is 70 percent effective in preventing flu. For people 65 and over, it doesn't work quite as well. People in this age group have less robust immune systems, so the vaccine doesn't stimulate as powerful an immune response.

But even if flu shots don't always prevent flu, they at least reduce its severity. "Its symptoms will be milder, no matter what your age," says Nancy Arden, R.N., research associate in the department of microbiology and immunology at Baylor College of Medicine in Houston.

Almost anyone can get a flu shot, including women who are pregnant. The only people who should not receive shots are those with serious allergies to eggs, which are used to manufacture the vaccine.

The Centers for Disease Control and Prevention (CDC) recommends getting immunized in October or November, before the start of flu season. It takes a week or two for the shot to produce effective immunity, Arden says.

Because new strains of flu develop every year, you must get reimmunized every year. The CDC constantly tracks flu outbreaks around the world. Each spring, it directs pharmaceutical companies to produce vaccines that will protect against the Type A and Type B strains expected to strike in the United States the following winter.

Many public health departments and some pharmacy chains offer free or low-cost flu shots every fall. Watch your local newspaper for announcements. If you don't see anything by October, you might want to call your doctor's office and schedule an appointment for a shot.

◆ Stomach 3, located at the bottom of either cheekbone, directly below your pupil. This point also relieves congestion and itchy eyes.

◆ Large Intestine 20, located on either cheek, in the groove beside each nostril. This point relieves nasal symptoms.

MEDICAL MEASURES

To treat the flu, mainstream doctors typically prescribe one of two pharmaceuticals: amantadine (Symmetrel) or rimantadine (Flumadine). Either medicine can significantly reduce your symptoms, provided you start taking it within 48 hours of getting sick and continue for 3 to 5 days.

Both amantadine and rimantadine may cause side effects such as nervousness, anxiety, light-headedness, and difficulty concentrating. In one study, 14 percent of amantadine users reported at least one side effect, compared with 6 percent of rimantadine users and 4 percent of people taking a placebo.

RED FLAGS

Anyone over age 65 or with a chronic illness should see a doctor at the first sign of flu. The same applies to women who are pregnant.

In addition, doctors advise you to see your physician right away if you experience any of the following:

◆ Fever higher than 100°F that lasts longer than 5 days

◆ Fever higher than 103°F

◆ Fever accompanied by sore throat, swollen glands under the jaw, and possibly a red, sandpaper-like rash

◆ Fever accompanied by a rash, stiff neck, severe headache, and marked irritability or confusion

◆ Difficulty breathing

◆ Nasal congestion that lasts longer than 7 days or causes ear pain, hearing loss, or headache with pain in the nose, cheeks, or upper teeth

◆ Coughing that lasts longer than 7 days or produces chest pain, wheezing, shortness of breath, or bloody, brown, or greenish mucus

Fungal Skin Infections

You may not notice anything special about your bathroom. But for certain types of fungi, it's a little corner of paradise.

These microorganisms thrive in the warm, moist environments of bathtubs and showers. That's where they find their way onto you. And once they get under your skin, you're in for some combination of itching, burning, and oozing—the unpleasant symptoms of a fungal skin infection.

Fungal skin infections are sometimes called tinea, or ringworm. But don't let the word *ringworm* scare you: The infections have nothing whatsoever to do with worms. Rather, ringworm describes the telltale ring-shaped rash that the invading fungi often cause.

Perhaps the best-known fungal skin infections are athlete's foot and jock itch. Athlete's

SIMPLE SOLUTIONS
1. Herbal Medicine
2. Home Remedies
3. Over-the-Counter Drugs
4. Medical Measures

foot (or tinea pedis) produces mild to severe itching and burning on your feet, especially between your toes. The affected skin becomes soft and painful. It may also crack, allowing fluid to ooze out. Athlete's foot is more common among men than women, but anyone can get it. In fact, an estimated 70 percent of Americans have a bout of athlete's foot at least once in their lives.

While athlete's foot targets the feet, jock itch (tinea cruris) invades the groin area. It produces persistent itching, along with redness and thickening of the skin. Jock itch is often thought of as a man's disease, as wearing an athletic supporter creates the warm, moist environment that fungi love. But women can get fungal infections in the groin area, too—especially if they wear tight leotards to exercise.

Fungal skin infections can also occur on the scalp (tinea capitis) and trunk (tinea corporis). When the infection develops on the scalp, especially in young children, the fungi can trigger hair loss that leaves behind patchy bald spots. On the trunk, the infection spreads outward in its characteristic ring pattern.

Toenails are vulnerable to fungal infections, too. The affected nails thicken and become discolored and perhaps deformed, a condition known as ony-chomycosis.

While fungal infections are uncomfortable and unpleasant, they are seldom serious. Still, once you've experienced one, you probably don't want another. Avoiding the offending fungi can be a challenge, since they hang out just about anyplace warm and moist. That includes not only in bathtubs and showers but also in locker rooms, around hot tubs, and even in sweat-drenched socks and poorly ventilated shoes.

Compounding the problem is the fact that the fungi are so contagious. For example, if you develop a case of athlete's foot, you can pass the infection to other family members simply by walking barefoot on your bathroom floor.

There are things that you can do to create a less hospitable environment for invading fungi and to reduce your exposure to them. But, if you pick up a fungal infection anyway, take your pick of the remedies that follow. Your skin should be in the pink in no time.

BEST CHOICES

Herbal Medicine

Try a different kind of tea. When the British explorer James Cook first arrived in Australia in 1777, he found the native aborigines treating skin infections with the crushed leaves of the tea tree. Almost two centuries later, scientists discovered that the oil released by crushing the leaves has powerful antifungal and antiseptic properties. It's even effective against the most stubborn fungal infection, the kind that thickens and discolors toenails.

To heal any kind of fungal infection, apply 100 percent tea tree oil twice a day to the affected skin, advises Andrew T. Weil, M.D., director of the program in integrative medicine at the University of Arizona College of Medicine in Tucson. You can buy tea tree oil in most health food stores. But never ingest the oil: Swallowing as little as a few teaspoons can prove fatal.

Chase the fungi with garlic. According to James A. Duke, Ph.D., garlic is packed with antifungal compounds. Many studies have demonstrated that the herb can fight athlete's foot and other fungal infections. In one study, Indian researchers found garlic to be as effective as a pharmaceutical product called ketoconazole in killing the fungi that cause athlete's foot.

To treat athlete's foot, Dr. Duke recommends making a garlic footbath by crushing several cloves and stirring them into warm water with a little rubbing alcohol. Or if you have more time, add the crushed cloves to a bottle of olive oil and allow the mixture to steep for a few days. Then use a cotton ball to dab the oil onto your feet and between your toes, once or twice a day.

Be forewarned: Both of these remedies can leave your feet smelling garlicky. "Try these treatments when you're at home and not expecting company," Dr. Duke advises. Also, keep in mind that you may have to wait 3 to 6 months before seeing any improvement in your symptoms.

Get chummy with ginger. While ginger has been touted for an array of ailments, its antifungal properties have gotten little notice. Yet a chemical analysis by Dr. Duke found that the herb contains 23 different antifungal compounds. Among these is caprylic acid, which is exceptionally potent.

To use ginger as a treatment for fungal skin infections, Dr. Duke suggests adding 1 ounce of chopped gingerroot to 1 cup of boiled water. After the water has cooled a bit, dip a cotton ball or clean cloth into the liquid and dab the affected skin.

Beat the infection with licorice. Practitioners of Chinese medicine routinely prescribe licorice for fungal skin infections. As it turns out, licorice has quite a few compounds with antifungal properties.

Dr. Duke suggests placing 6 heaping teaspoons of powdered dried licorice root in 1 cup of boiled water. Let steep for 20 minutes, then strain out the herb and let the liquid cool. Dampen a cotton ball or clean cloth with the liquid and apply it to your skin.

Home Remedies

Limit your exposure. The best way to prevent a fungal skin infection is to avoid direct contact with anyone who has one.

Wear sandals or flip-flops when walking around bathrooms, locker rooms, and spas, advises Alan Gaby, M.D. Even in your own bathroom, you're less likely to get athlete's foot—or to transfer the fungus to another member of the family—if you avoid walking barefoot.

To prevent the spread of other kinds of fungal infections, never share towels, clothing, or hairbrushes and combs with another person. That includes your spouse and other family members.

Minimize moisture. Keep infection-prone areas of skin as dry as possible, says Anne Simons, M.D. After bathing, use a blow-dryer on a low setting to dry the skin in your groin area and between your toes. Dust these areas with cornstarch or powder made from cornstarch to absorb excess moisture. Choose underwear made from cotton rather than synthetics, which tend to trap heat. And dress in loose-fitting clothes whenever possible.

Give your feet some elbow room. To avoid athlete's foot, wear socks made from a moisture-wicking fabric such as acrylic, nylon, CoolMax, or Polartec. You'll find them in sporting goods stores. For best results, change your socks often. Also wear well-ventilated shoes—ideally, sandals or open-toe styles.

Maintain a healthy weight. People who are overweight tend to be more susceptible to fungal skin infections. Those excess pounds create folds of skin that provide a warm, moist environment in which fungi thrive.

Over-the-Counter Drugs

Soothe your skin with an antifungal cream. Wander down the aisles of almost any drugstore, and you're bound to encounter an impressive array of antifungal creams. These products have a number of different active ingredients, including clotrimazole, miconazole nitrate, terbinafine, tolnaftate, undecylenic acid, or zinc undecylenate. All of these ingredients have been proven effective. But for you, one may work better than another.

Dr. Simons's advice: Experiment. "If one cream doesn't provide sufficient relief, try another," she says. "Or try rotating or combining them." In general, the instructions for these products suggest application once or twice daily over the course of 4 weeks. Continue applying the cream for the recommended duration, even if your symptoms begin to clear up sooner (as they usually do). Extended treatment helps prevent a recurrence of the infection.

If you're treating athlete's foot, be sure to apply the cream all over your feet. Even though certain parts of your feet don't itch or burn, they may still be infected.

MEDICAL MEASURES

Some fungal skin infections are so stubborn that even over-the-counter antifungal creams can't make them go away. If your symptoms persist for more than a month despite home treatment, your doctor may recommend a prescription-strength antifungal cream. Some of these, however, have potentially serious side effects.

Gallstones

About 20 million Americans have gallstones. Yet many of them don't even know it. That's because they have tiny stones that don't produce symptoms. Only when stones get wedged in tiny places do they make their presence known. Then they feel as though they are the size of the Rock of Gibraltar.

Gallstones form in the gallbladder, a small pear-shaped organ that sits to the right of the breastbone, directly below the liver. The gallbladder stores bile, a yellowish green fluid that aids in the digestion of fats. As food leaves your stomach, your gallbladder contracts, squirting bile into your small intestine.

Bile is a mixture of many things, notably bile acids and cholesterol. Cholesterol is the troublemaker. It accounts for only 5 percent of bile but about 80 percent of gallstones.

SIMPLE SOLUTIONS
1. Nutrition
2. Supplements
3. Herbal Medicine
4. Homeopathy
5. Chinese Medicine
6. Ayurvedic Medicine
7. Medical Measures

Normally, the proportions of cholesterol and bile acids in bile keep the cholesterol dissolved. But if the cholesterol level rises too high or the bile acid level falls too low, the cholesterol can't stay dissolved. Instead, it forms solid granules that grow over time, like pearls.

Sometimes a granule becomes large enough to block one of the bile ducts, the tiny tubes that link the gallbladder to the liver and the small intestine. The obstruction is what produces gallstone symptoms. Scientists estimate that it takes about 8 years for a granule of cholesterol to grow large enough to cause gallstone attacks.

Most people notice gallstone symptoms shortly after eating. The pain starts in the upper right abdomen and radiates around to the shoulder blades. It usually builds to an intense peak, then subsides over the course of an hour or so as the stone either falls back into the gallbladder or gets pushed into the small intestine. The pain may be accompanied by indigestion, bloating, an unusual feeling of fullness in the upper abdomen, vomiting, or fever. Once you have an episode involving gallstones, it's likely that you'll have trouble again in the future.

Whether you want to avoid getting a gallstone or you want to treat one that you already have, blended medicine offers several effective strategies. Here's what the experts recommend.

BEST CHOICES

Nutrition

Steer clear of stone formers. For both prevention and treatment of gallstones, Joseph Pizzorno Jr., N.D., says that an elimination diet can help. He suggests avoiding all of the foods that have been linked to stone formation: pork, poultry, eggs, milk, onions, citrus, corn, legumes, and nuts.

Eat mostly vegetarian meals. British researchers compared gallstone risk in two groups of healthy women: one vegetarian and the other nonvegetarian. The vegetarians were significantly less likely to develop stones. That's because they ate lots of fiber from whole grains, fruits, and vegetables but little fat from meats and dairy products. "A vegetarian diet devoid of animal fat and cholesterol and high in fiber should be recommended to anyone concerned about gallstones," says Melvyn R. Werbach, M.D., assistant clinical professor at the University of California, Los Angeles, School of Medicine.

Serve up fish on occasion. When Spanish researchers compared the diets of 54 people with gallstones and 46 people without, they noticed that the people without gallstones ate more fish. Fish contains an oil that other studies have shown can reduce gallstone risk. Among the species with the most fish oil are salmon and mackerel.

Have a cuppa java. Animal studies suggest that coffee—even the decaffeinated variety—can inhibit the formation of gallstones. Coffee strengthens gallbladder contractions, which helps keep stones from getting caught in your bile ducts.

Sip plain old H$_2$O, too. Drink at least eight 8-ounce glasses of water a day, suggests Dr. Pizzorno. This keeps the water content of bile within a healthy range, he says.

Supplements

Add extra C and E. Because low levels of vitamins C and E have been linked to gallstones, Dr. Pizzorno recommends taking supplements of both nutrients. He suggests daily doses of 2,000 milligrams of vitamin C and 300 international units (IU) of vitamin E.

Check your calcium intake. Running low on calcium can also raise your risk of gallstones. You should be getting at least 1,000 milligrams a day, the Daily Value. If you don't eat a lot of calcium-rich foods, especially dairy products, consider taking a supplement.

Get fish oil without the fish. In a study conducted at Johns Hopkins University in Baltimore, researchers fed 16 prairie dogs a diet designed to induce gallstone formation. Half of the animals also received supplemental fish oil. After 2 weeks, the group that had been given fish oil had developed fewer stones than the group that hadn't been given it.

The dosage of fish oil used in the study was 200 milligrams per kilogram of body weight per day. For a 150-pound human, that translates to 14 grams— or roughly ½ ounce—a day. You can buy fish oil in health food stores and some drugstores.

Don't overlook lecithin. A fatty acid, lecithin can be beneficial as part of a comprehensive gallstone treatment plan. It helps keep cholesterol dissolved in bile. Dr. Pizzorno suggests taking 500 milligrams a day. Lecithin supplements are available in health food stores.

Herbal Medicine

Crush stones with mint. Herbs in the mint family, particularly peppermint and spearmint, have traditionally been used to treat gallstones. "The British even have an over-the-counter gallstone remedy called Rowachol," says James A. Duke, Ph.D. "It contains several mint compounds, notably menthol from peppermint oil."

In one study, 31 people with gallstones took either Rowachol alone or the herbal formula plus a stone-dissolving prescription drug. After 4 years, 42 percent of the Rowachol-only group no longer had gallstones. The results were even more impressive in the herb-plus-drug group: 73 percent saw their gallstones disappear.

Rowachol is hard to find in the United States. But Dr. Werbach says that enteric-coated peppermint oil has similar benefits. He suggests taking one or two capsules three times a day with meals. One capsule contains 1.2 milliliters of oil. You can buy enteric-coated peppermint oil in most health food stores.

Tap into turmeric. Turmeric, a tasty spice that's a key ingredient in Indian cuisine, contains a compound called curcumin. According to Commission E, the German panel that evaluates the safety and effectiveness of herbal medicines, curcumin can help prevent and treat gallstones. It works by keeping the cholesterol in bile dissolved.

You'd have to use a lot of turmeric in your cooking in order to get a therapeutic dose of curcumin. Instead, take curcumin in tablet form—300 to 600 milligrams three times a day.

Make use of milk thistle. Silymarin, a mixture of the medicinal compounds in milk thistle, helps reduce the concentration of cholesterol in bile. In one study, 19 people with gallstones took either 420 milligrams of silymarin or a placebo (a fake pill) every day. After 30 days, the silymarin group showed significant reductions in their concentrations of cholesterol.

If you're interested in trying silymarin, make an appointment with your doctor. You may need liver function tests while taking this herbal supplement.

OTHER GOOD CHOICES

Homeopathy

Ask a homeopath for advice. A number of homeopathic medicines have proved effective in the treatment of gallstones, according to homeopath Dana Ullman. Which medicine you're given depends on your individual symptoms. But your homeopath may recommend one of the following: Aconitum napellus, Belladonna, Berberis, Chelidonium, Magnesia phosphorica, Nux vomica, or Podophyllum.

Chinese Medicine

Free qi. In Chinese medicine, gallstones result from a stagnation of qi and Blood under the influence of Heat. "First comes an accumulation of phlegm," explains Efrem Korngold, O.M.D., L.Ac. "Then Heat turns the phlegm into stones."

For people with gallstones, Dr. Korngold often prescribes a low-fat diet and the Chinese herbal formula Li Dan Pian. The formula contains a dozen different herbs, including lysimachia, skullcap root, honeysuckle, bupleurum, rhubarb, and artemesia. He also recommends peony and licorice to relax spasms in the gallbladder.

Stimulate just the right spots. Dr. Korngold also uses acupuncture to treat gallstones. If you'd rather not go to an acupuncturist, you can stimulate the appropriate points yourself with acupressure. Apply steady, penetrating pressure to each of the following points for 3 minutes.

◆ Large Intestine 11, located at the outer end of your elbow on the thumb side

◆ Stomach 36, located four finger-widths below your kneecap and one finger-width toward the outside of your shinbone

◆ Gallbladder 34, located on the outside of your leg, below and in front of the head of your shinbone

Ayurvedic Medicine

Placate Pitta. Ayurvedic practitioners view gallstones as an inflammatory condition caused by excess Pitta, according to David Frawley, O.M.D. When treating gallstones, he starts with aloe, rhubarb root, senna, and cascara sagrada—all liver-cleansing herbs that also act as powerful laxatives. He follows up with stone-eliminating Ayurvedic herbs such as pashana bheda, gokshura, and katuka.

MEDICAL MEASURES

M.D.'s usually treat gallstones in one of two ways: Either they prescribe stone-dissolving drugs or they recommend surgery.

Stone-dissolving drugs—primarily ursodeoxycholic acid (Actigall)—make bile more acidic. The increased acidity slowly dissolves cholesterol gallstones.

If you're looking for a more permanent fix, or if you frequently have severe gallstone pain, you may want to consider surgery. Surgical treatment of gallstones involves removal of the gallbladder. In the past, many surgeons used a procedure called a cholecystectomy. But this procedure left a huge scar—and left some people out of commission for weeks afterward.

In a newer procedure, called a laparoscopic cholecystectomy, the surgeon makes several small incisions rather than one big one. The gallbladder is removed with instruments that can be inserted through the small incisions. With this procedure, there's less postoperative pain and a shorter recovery time.

Unfortunately, gallbladder surgery doesn't guarantee that you'll be stone-free for the rest of your life. At least 15 percent of people who undergo surgery continue having gallstone attacks. Even though the gallbladder is gone, the liver continues to produce bile, making it susceptible to stone formation.

RED FLAGS

Consult a physician promptly anytime you experience intense pain in your upper right abdomen, especially if it's accompanied by fever, nausea, or vomiting. It might be appendicitis.

Also, if you are a woman at or past menopause and you or someone in your immediate family has had gallstones, be sure to tell your doctor. Some M.D.'s recommend hormone-replacement therapy (HRT) to ease menopausal discomforts and prescribe it to their patients at high risk for osteoporosis. But because it contains estrogen, which increases the concentration of cholesterol in bile, HRT can also make you more susceptible to gallstones. You and your doctor must weigh the benefits and risks of HRT before deciding whether it's right for you.

Glaucoma

Inside each of your eyes is a gelatinous transparent fluid called the aqueous humor. Normally, this fluid circulates around the eye, then flows through a tiny structure called the drainage angle into a little tube. The tube directs the fluid into your bloodstream.

In glaucoma, something stops the aqueous humor from draining, explains Anne Simons, M.D. With no place to go, the fluid builds up. This creates pressure that gradually destroys the optic nerve, which sends visual messages from the eye to the brain. As a result, your field of vision shrinks.

Some three million Americans have glaucoma, but about half of them don't even realize it. That's why getting your eyes checked is so important. If you catch the disease early, you can usually save your eyesight.

SIMPLE SOLUTIONS
1. Supplements
2. Chinese Medicine
3. Ayurvedic Medicine
4. Home Remedies
5. Nutrition
6. Herbal Medicine
7. Homeopathy
8. Medical Measures

There are two types of glaucoma: open-angle and closed-angle. In open-angle glaucoma, the drainage angle functions properly, but the tube attached to it becomes blocked. Fluid backs up into the eye, and pressure inside the eye slowly rises. This produces subtle changes in your peripheral vision—that is, your ability to see things to either side of you. Open-angle glaucoma accounts for 90 percent of all glaucoma cases.

The other 10 percent of cases involve closed-angle glaucoma. In this condition, the drainage angle becomes blocked. The affected eye becomes red, your vision turns blurry, and you see halos around lights. Closed-angle glaucoma is a medical emergency that requires immediate treatment to prevent permanent vision loss.

Glaucoma is most common among people over age 60, which means your risk rises as you get older. But there are other risk factors as well. These include smoking, long-term use of steroid medications, and family history of the disease. African-Americans are three times more likely than Whites to develop glaucoma.

Because glaucoma can lead to blindness, the Glaucoma Research Foundation urges everyone to get periodic screenings—at age 35, at age 40, every 2 to 3 years between ages 41 and 60, and every 1 to 2 years after age 60. If you have any risk factors for glaucoma, your doctor or ophthalmologist may want you to get tested more often. The screenings themselves are quick and painless.

While you can't reverse any vision loss caused by glaucoma, you can stop it from getting worse. That's where the following strategies, paired with your doctor's treatments, can help.

BEST CHOICES

Supplements

Take C to see. The tubes that drain fluid from your eyes are rich in a protein called collagen. Vitamin C plays a key role in maintaining the integrity of collagen, says Joseph Pizzorno Jr., N.D. In addition, several studies have shown that vitamin C supplementation lowers fluid pressure in the eye. Dr. Pizzorno recommends taking 2,000 milligrams of vitamin C a day.

Focus on chromium. The trace mineral chromium helps your eye muscles focus on close objects, explains Richard Barrett, N.D., associate professor of medicine at the National College of Naturopathic Medicine in Portland, Oregon. If your chromium level is low, your body compensates by increasing pressure inside your eyes. Dr. Barrett suggests taking 200 micrograms of chromium a day.

Chinese Medicine

Try an herbal formula. In the early stages of the disease, a Chinese herbal formula called Huang Lian Yang Gan Wan can help, says Efrem Korngold, O.M.D., L.Ac. It contains a number of herbs, including the root of coptis, gentian, philodendron, skullcap, and bupleurum. All of the herbs work together to reduce fluid pressure in the eye.

In addition, oriental medicine doctors may recommend drinking chrysanthemum tea and eating lycii berries. "Chrysanthemum clears Heat and soothes the eyes," Dr. Korngold explains. "Lycii berries are like bilberries. They contain compounds called anthocyanosides." Anthocyanosides prevent the breakdown of vitamin C and protect the collagen in your eyes' drainage tubes.

Both lycii berries and chrysanthemum tea can be purchased in Asian groceries. Eat lycii berries as you would any other berries. To make chrysanthemum tea, put a tea ball containing 1 to 2 teaspoons of bulk herb or a tea bag in 1 cup of boiled water. Steep to taste, strain, and drink.

Reduce pressure with an herbal formula. To drain excess fluid from the eyes, oriental medicine doctors often prescribe Wu Ling San, an herbal formula made from hoelen, polyporus, atractylodes, cinnamon, and alisma. When researchers gave daily doses of this formula to 55 people with glaucoma, 64 percent of the participants experienced significant decreases in fluid pressure within 1 month.

Let salvia be your salvation. The Chinese herb *Salvia miltiorrhiza* has shown promise as a treatment for eye diseases. One study suggests that the herb may be an effective long-term treatment for glaucoma.

Visit an acupuncturist. According to Dr. Korngold, acupuncture treatments can help in the early stages of glaucoma by reducing fluid pressure in the eyes. The treatments would likely focus on points around the eyes. In addition, the acupuncturist may stimulate points located just below the base of your skull and on the top of either foot.

Ayurvedic Medicine

Praise potato power. According to Ayurvedic medical doctrine, glaucoma results from an excess of Kapha dosha. To balance Kapha, Ayurvedic physicians prescribe drying herbs, says Karta P. S. Khalsa, C. D. N., an Ayurvedic physician in Seattle. Among the herbs that are prescribed is the kaffir potato, whose root contains a compound called forskolin. Forskolin reduces fluid pressure in the eyes.

"In the studies I've seen, forskolin eyedrops can keep fluid pressure low for about 5 hours," reports James A. Duke, Ph.D. If you'd like to try forskolin, consult an Ayurvedic physician, a naturopath, or an herbalist.

Home Remedies

Be cautious with caffeine. Caffeine is known to raise blood pressure. For this reason, researchers suspect that it may increase fluid pressure in the eyes. So far, they haven't reached a definitive conclusion, Dr. Barrett says. Some studies have found that as little as one cup of espresso significantly raises fluid pressure. Other studies have shown that as much as four cups of coffee doesn't affect fluid pressure at all. Still others suggest that caffeine elevates fluid pressure, but only very briefly.

Until researchers know for certain what effect caffeine has on fluid pressure in the eyes, Dr. Barrett suggests that anyone with glaucoma steer clear of the substance. That means cutting back on coffee, tea, and cola and avoiding over-the-counter drugs that contain caffeine. (The label will tell you.)

Snuff out those butts. People who smoke have a higher risk of developing glaucoma. That's something to keep in mind if you're a smoker who is trying to quit.

OTHER GOOD CHOICES

Nutrition

Eat less protein and margarine. Researchers polled 52 people with glaucoma and 348 people with other eye conditions about their eating habits. Upon analyzing the survey results, the researchers determined that the people with glaucoma consumed significantly more proteins—specifically, meats and dairy products—than everyone else. They also consumed more trans fatty acids, the fats found in margarine. This study adds to evidence that eating less meat, whole-milk dairy products, and margarine is a good idea.

Herbal Medicine

Make berries your buddies. Bilberries—also known as European blueberries—have a centuries-old reputation for improving vision, Dr. Duke says. During World War I, British fliers munched bilberries to sharpen their eyesight for bombing missions. By all accounts, the berries helped. That's because they contain high levels of eye-friendly anthocyanosides.

European herbalists have developed a standardized bilberry extract that contains 25 percent anthocyanosides. Dr. Pizzorno suggests taking 80 to 160 milligrams of the extract three times a day. It's available in many health food stores and from most naturopaths.

Drop in a remedy with natural roots. Mainstream physicians may treat glaucoma with eyedrops containing the active ingredient pilocarpine. Originally an extract of the South American jaborandi tree, the drug is synthesized in laboratories and prescribed by doctors. Ask your doctor about this "herbal" remedy that's gone mainstream.

Homeopathy

Consult a homeopath. When treating glaucoma, a homeopath selects the medicine that best suits a person's symptoms, explains Edward Kondrot, M.D., an ophthalmologist and practicing homeopath in Pittsburgh. The most commonly prescribed remedies include Aconitum, Belladonna, Bryonia, and Nux vomica.

MEDICAL MEASURES

Since glaucoma is not a disease that you should try to manage by yourself, it's important to seek the help of an ophthalmologist. To manage the disease, you need to consistently maintain low eye pressure. Your ophthalmologist will help you do this—so be sure to keep your scheduled appointments and sustain the recommended treatments.

Always tell your doctor about any alternative therapies that you're using. It's possible that some alternative treatments may conflict with your conventional treatments.

Mainstream physicians treat glaucoma with drugs that reduce fluid pressure in the eyes. These medicines—most often from a class of pharmaceuticals called beta-blockers—come in eyedrop form. You administer the drops yourself, a few times each day. If they don't help, your doctor may recommend laser surgery to open blocked drainage tubes.

A nonprofit organization called Lighthouse International provides an array of support services for people who experience any degree of vision impairment as a result of glaucoma. You can write to the organization at 111 East 59th Street, 12th Floor, New York, NY 10022-1202.

RED FLAGS

Closed-angle glaucoma is an urgent medical problem characterized by the sudden onset of pain, redness, and blurred vision in the affected eye. The pain may be severe, and it may be accompanied by nausea or vomiting. Some people report seeing halos around light sources. These symptoms may occur as occasional, momentary episodes for weeks or months before a major attack.

If you experience any combination of these symptoms, contact your family doctor or ophthalmologist immediately, or have someone take you to a hospital emergency room. You must get treatment within 12 hours of the attack. Otherwise, you may experience permanent vision loss within 3 to 5 days.

Treatment for closed-angle glaucoma usually involves a surgical procedure called an iridotomy. The surgeon uses a laser to create a new opening for fluid to drain from the eye. This technique is much faster and safer than traditional scalpel surgery.

Hay Fever

Have you ever known a child to scream bloody murder after just barely bumping his knee? If you have hay fever, your immune system overreacts in much the same way.

Your immune system is responsible for identifying and destroying any disease-causing microorganisms that invade your body. But sometimes it mistakes perfectly harmless substances for germs. In response, it releases certain compounds—in particular, immuno-globulin E (IgE) and histamine—to obliterate the "enemy." IgE and histamine are what cause hay fever symptoms.

Hay fever is an inhalant allergy. In other words, you breathe in the offending substances, which then stimulate your body's immune re-sponse. Traditionally, *hay fever* has been defined as an allergic reaction to pollen. But now the term is used more broadly to describe reactions to other airborne triggers such as mold, dust, animal dander, and dust mites. These substances are referred to as allergens because they provoke allergy symptoms.

SIMPLE SOLUTIONS
1. Supplements
2. Herbal Medicine
3. Homeopathy
4. Chinese Medicine
5. Home Remedies
6. Nutrition
7. Ayurvedic Medicine
8. Over-the-Counter Drugs
9. Medical Measures

Of the 26 million Americans who have inhalant allergies, most experience their first symptoms before age 20, notes allergist/immunologist Peter Boggs, M.D., author of *Sneezing Your Head Off?* But you can get allergies at any age.

If you suspect that you have hay fever, you should consult an allergist or immunologist to find out exactly what substances trigger your symptoms. Var-ious tests are available, but the scratch test is most widely used. The doctor uses a needle to scratch your skin in several places—it sounds painful, but it isn't—then rubs a different allergen into each scratch. If the scratch becomes inflamed, then you're allergic to that substance.

The best way to avoid hay fever symptoms is to minimize your exposure to trigger substances. But when that's not possible, you can count on blended medicine to defuse your reaction and alleviate your discomfort.

BEST CHOICES

Supplements

Take a natural antihistamine. Research has shown that vitamin C can reduce blood levels of histamine, one of the compounds that cause hay fever symptoms. In one study, a group of volunteers took 1,000 milligrams of vitamin C every day for 3 days. Blood tests before and after supplement therapy showed impressive reductions in levels of histamine. You can try vitamin C for yourself, in the same dosage used in the study, to see whether it makes a difference in your symptoms.

Benefit from a little-known B vitamin. "I often get good results by treating hay fever with supplements of pantothenic acid," says Alan Gaby, M.D. He suggests taking 100 to 1,000 milligrams every day.

Herbal Medicine

Take advantage of nettle. The medicinal herb stinging nettle has a long history as a treatment for respiratory problems. "It's my first choice," says Andrew T. Weil, M.D., director of the program in integrative medicine at the University of Arizona College of Medicine in Tucson. "I use stinging nettle myself during the spring ragweed season in southern Arizona."

Many health food stores sell capsules of freeze-dried nettle. Take 600 milligrams a day. Some people report that their hay fever gets worse when they start using stinging nettle. If this happens to you, stop taking the herb and try another remedy.

Sit in your tea. To calm an overactive immune system, soak in an herbal bath, recommends Lisa Meserole, R.D., N.D., chairperson of the department of botanical medicine at Bastyr University in Kenmore, Washington. For optimum benefit, prepare the herbal mixture the day before you plan to use it.

First, choose two or three of the following herbs: calendula flowers, lavender flowers, eyebright flowers, or German chamomile. (You'll find all of these in health food stores.) Blend together roughly equal amounts of the herbs so that you end up with ¼ cup. Add the herb mixture to 4 cups of cool water and allow to steep overnight. The next day, bring the tea to a boil, then remove the pot from the stove and cover it with a lid. Allow the tea to steep for 15 minutes before straining. Pour the liquid into your bathwater, then soak.

Homeopathy

Get relief from grass. Researchers at the University of Glasgow in Scotland gave 140 people with pollen allergies either a homeopathic preparation of mixed grass pollens or a placebo. Compared with the people taking the placebo, those taking the homeopathic preparation showed significant improvement in their symptoms. In fact, they were able to reduce their use of antihistamines by 50 percent.

Other homeopathic medicines do an equally impressive job of alleviating hay fever symptoms, says homeopath Dana Ullman. Among the medicines he often prescribes are Allium cepa, Arsenicum album, Arum triphyllum, Euphrasia, Histaminum, Kali bichromicum, Natrum muriaticum, Nux vomica, Pulsatilla, Sabadilla, and Wyethia helenioides. To find out which of these will work best for you, consult a homeopath.

Chinese Medicine

Calm the Wind. Chinese medicine views hay fever as an invasion of Wind. "Itching is a typical symptom of Wind, and itchy eyes are a hallmark of hay fever," observes Efrem Korngold, O.M.D., L.Ac. He treats hay fever with herbal formulas that contain magnolia flowers, mulberry bark, honeysuckle flowers, licorice root, asarum, and black cohosh root.

Select the right spot. To relieve hay fever symptoms, Dr. Korngold suggests stimulating the point Large Intestine 4. It's located in the fleshy webbing between the thumb and index finger of either hand. Stimulate the point for 3 minutes, using steady, penetrating finger pressure. Then switch hands. (Women who are pregnant should not use this remedy, as it may trigger uterine contractions.)

Home Remedies

In a pinch, drink coffee. The caffeine in coffee is a potent decongestant. In one study, people with hay fever received either 400 milligrams of caffeine—the equivalent of about 18 ounces of coffee—or a placebo. The placebo

Coming Soon to a Nose Near You

Summer is the season for blockbuster movies. It's also the season for a little-known allergic phenomenon. Call it post-matinee nasal syndrome. You may have experienced it yourself: You step out of a dark theater into the bright afternoon sunlight, and suddenly you're sneezing and dabbing at a runny nose.

So are you allergic to sun? To popcorn? To something else in the theater? Probably not, says Peter Boggs, M.D., author of *Sneezing Your Head Off?* Rather, he explains, what you're experiencing is a reflex response.

While you're inside the theater, your eyes get used to the low-light conditions. Then when you step out into the sunshine, the bright light strikes a nerve at the back of the eye. This causes certain glands inside your nose to produce fluid and stimulate sneezing—just like allergy symptoms.

Incidentally, post-matinee nasal syndrome isn't unique to people with allergies. It can affect just about anyone.

takers reported a 19 percent improvement in their symptoms. Among the caffeine takers, that figure rose to 51 percent.

Invest in a new stove. At St. Thomas' Hospital in London, Deborah Jarvis, M.D., polled 1,000 British adults about their health and lifestyles. Dr. Jarvis found that compared with people who cooked on electric stoves, those who used gas stoves were 20 percent more likely to have hay fever. Apparently, the substances released when natural gas burns cause respiratory irritation in some people. And that irritation can lead to hay fever.

Be picky about lodgings. When you're planning your vacation, look for hotels that have no-smoking rooms, no-pet policies, and daily linen changes. Ask whether there are any rooms without carpeting. Also ask about the air-conditioning system: Has it recently been inspected for mold? Does it have a filter capable of removing airborne allergens such as pollens, mold spores, and animal dander? If not, consider taking a portable HEPA filter with you. This may seem like a lot of hassle, but if you're staying in one place for your vacation, it can make the difference between a magnificent time and a miserable one.

OTHER GOOD CHOICES

Nutrition

Revise your diet. According to Dr. Weil, meats and dairy products tend to promote allergic reactions, while fruits and vegetables tend to deter them. "Dietary changes aren't likely to offer immediate relief, but they may help over time," he says.

Supplements

Control symptoms with quercetin. A member of the bioflavonoid family, quercetin (pronounced "KWER-seh-tin") helps block the immune response that produces hay fever symptoms, Dr. Weil says. He takes 400 milligrams twice a day, between meals, from 2 weeks before the expected start of ragweed season until the season ends. You can buy quercetin in tablet and capsule form in most health food stores.

Ayurvedic Medicine

Try an Ayurvedic formula. Researchers at Maharishi University in Fairfield, Iowa, divided 46 people with active hay fever symptoms into two groups. One group received an Ayurvedic antioxidant formula called MAK-5, while the other received a placebo. After a month, the people taking MAK-5 reported significantly less severe symptoms. If you'd like to try MAK-5, consult an Ayurvedic practitioner.

Over-the-Counter Drugs

Try antihistamines. If alternative therapies don't provide sufficient relief from hay fever symptoms, pharmacists Joe Graedon and Teresa Graedon, Ph.D., coauthors of *The People's Pharmacy* books, suggest trying an over-the-counter antihistamine such as chlorpheniramine (Chlor-Trimeton) or diphenhydramine (Benadryl). These drugs can cause drowsiness, so they aren't appropriate for people who must operate machinery or drive. Nonsedating antihistamines are available, but they must be prescribed by a physician.

Consider sprays. Over-the-counter nasal spray decongestants can relieve the stuffiness associated with hay fever. These products, however, shouldn't be used for more than 3 days in a row, says Anne Simons, M.D. Prolonged use often leads to "rebound congestion," which makes you feel even worse.

As an alternative to nasal sprays, you may want to try an over-the-counter oral decongestant such as pseudoephedrine (Sudafed). But be aware that these drugs can raise blood pressure and contribute to insomnia and nervousness.

MEDICAL MEASURES

If you have trouble avoiding your hay fever triggers, consider getting allergy shots. This treatment involves injections of tiny amounts of the substances to which you're sensitive. Over time, you become desensitized. In other words, the stuff that made you sniffle and sneeze won't bother you as much.

"Unfortunately, allergy shots don't work well for everyone," Dr. Simons says. "And at first, you have to get frequent injections, which can be a hassle. But if you respond to the treatment, you'll feel a lot better the next time hay fever season rolls around."

Headache

Headache pain is one of the leading reasons why people see doctors, accounting for some 10 million office visits a year. But that's probably just the tip of the headache iceberg.

According to the International Headache Society, there are 129 distinct types of headache. The three most common are tension headache, which is caused by stress; migraine, which results from the expansion and contraction of blood vessels in the head; and sinus headache, which stems from sinus infections or hay fever–type allergies. Many headaches are not strictly one type but rather a combination of two or more.

This chapter deals with tension headaches. (For more information about migraines, see page 473; for headaches from sinus infections; see page 572.) You know what a tension headache feels like: a steady, aching pain that wraps around your entire head. It's this pattern of pain that earned tension headaches the nickname "hatband headaches."

(For more information about migraines, see page 473; for headaches from sinus infections; see page 572.)

SIMPLE SOLUTIONS
1. Visualization
2. Biofeedback
3. Massage
4. Aromatherapy
5. Herbal Medicine
6. Chinese Medicine
7. Home Remedies
8. Over-the-Counter Drugs
9. Nutrition
10. Supplements
11. Homeopathy
12. Ayurvedic Medicine
13. Medical Measures

Like most other types of headaches, tension headaches have nothing to do with your brain. Rather, they originate in the muscles that run through your scalp and neck. Tension headaches are usually associated with stress, hence their name.

A tension headache can strike at any time, though it's most likely to occur toward the end of a long, hard day. The pain can last from as little as ½ hour to as long as several days.

Only the most severe or persistent tension headaches require a doctor's attention. For more run-of-the-mill pain, you can usually get relief through self-care, using any of several effective mainstream and alternative remedies. The next time you feel a tension headache creeping up on you, try one of the following measures to keep the pain at bay.

BEST CHOICES

Visualization

Picture pain vanishing. As an alternative to over-the-counter medicines, visualization exercises provide prompt relief from headache pain. They are an especially valuable treatment option for moms-to-be, who are advised not to take medication during their pregnancies.

Of course, you needn't be a mom-to-be to practice visualization. When you feel a tension headache coming on, try this exercise recommended by Gerald N. Epstein, M.D., director of the Academy of Integrative Medicine and Mental Imagery in New York City. Begin by closing your eyes and taking three slow, deep breaths. Imagine that you're looking down at the top of your head. Lift off the top of your skull as if you were removing the top of the shell of a soft-boiled egg. Look inside. Imagine that your brain is a lake and that your nerve fibers are underwater plants gently waving in the current. Now imagine that the lake is being drained, and with it, all of your tension. Once drained, your brain fills with new, clear water, as fresh blood circulates all around your head, your neck, and the rest of your body. Imagine replacing the top of your skull. Take a final deep breath and open your eyes.

Biofeedback

Learn how to relax. Biofeedback typically relieves headache pain in 70 percent of people who try it, says Mark Schwartz, Ph.D., a staff psychologist at the Mayo Clinic in Jacksonville, Florida. Many studies back up his claim.

In one study, researchers at the Medical College of Georgia in Augusta asked 26 people with chronic tension headaches to record the frequency, intensity, and duration of their pain. Then the participants received training in either progressive muscle relaxation or biofeedback, which focused on relaxing their neck muscles. After 3 months, the people who practiced progressive muscle relaxation showed only 34 percent improvement in their pain. By comparison, the people who learned biofeedback reported 74 percent improvement.

Massage

Rub the right place. When headaches strike, many people rub their temples. Right approach, but maybe the wrong location. Studies by neurosurgeon Walker L. Robinson, M.D., at the University of Maryland Medical Center in Baltimore have shown that tension headaches often originate in the muscles at the back of the neck. Dr. Robinson suggests massaging those muscles for relief.

Aromatherapy

Be partial to peppermint. Researchers at the neurology clinic of the University of Kiel in Germany instructed 32 people with headaches to treat their pain with self-massage of their heads and necks. Each person also used one of four aromatherapy preparations.

The two preparations that contained large amounts of peppermint oil proved most effective in relieving headache pain. You can buy peppermint oil in most health food stores and bath and beauty shops. Add a few drops of the oil to unscented skin or massage lotion and rub it in.

Another good remedy is Tiger Balm, the popular Asian pain reliever that has been a health-food-store fixture for decades. It contains no tiger parts, but it boasts a generous helping of menthol, a major component of peppermint oil.

To purchase Tiger Balm, check your local health food store. Make sure that you follow package directions when using the ointment because it is very strong.

Herbal Medicine

Let willow whip your pain. Willow bark contains salicin, the natural precursor of the active ingredient in aspirin. "Any mild pain problem that you might treat with aspirin you can also treat with willow bark tea," says James A. Duke, Ph.D. To make the tea, add 1 to 1½ teaspoons of powdered white willow bark to 1 cup of boiled water, simmer for 10 minutes, then strain.

Two other herbs, wintergreen and meadowsweet, also contain salicin. To make a tea from either herb, add 1 to 1½ teaspoons to 1 cup of boiling water. Simmer for 10 minutes, then strain.

Chinese Medicine

Revive your qi. Practitioners of Chinese medicine attribute pain to stagnation of qi, Blood, or Moisture, says Efrem Korngold, O.M.D., L.Ac. Many headaches involve some degree of stagnation of all three elements, he says.

The classic Chinese herbal formula for headache is called Chuan Xiong Cha Piao. It contains quite a few herbs, including ligusticum, angelica, asarum, and peppermint. "It breaks up stagnation," Dr. Korngold explains. If you want to try this herbal formula, you need to consult an oriental medicine practitioner.

For relief, press on. When staff members from the National Institutes of Health reviewed research involving acupuncture as a headache treatment, they found that in eight of nine studies, acupuncture relieved headache pain significantly better than a placebo treatment. In light of such research, both the National Institutes of Health and the United Nations World Health Organization endorse acupuncture for headaches.

Of course, acupuncture must be administered by a trained professional. If you prefer a self-care approach, try acupressure instead. Apply steady, penetrating finger pressure to each of the following points for 3 minutes, says Michael Reed Gach, founder and director of the Acupressure Institute.

◆ Large Intestine 4, located on the back of your hand where the bones of your thumb and index finger meet

◆ Governing Vessel 24.5, located between your eyebrows where the bridge of your nose meets your forehead

◆ Governing Vessel 16, located in the center of the back of your head, in the hollow at the base of your skull

◆ Bladder 2, located on either side of your nose, where the bridge of your nose meets the ridge of your eyebrows

◆ Stomach 3, located at the base of the cheekbone, directly below your pupil

◆ Liver 3, situated on top of your foot in the webbing between your big toe and second toe

For chronic headaches, however, Dr. Korngold recommends professional acupuncture treatments. Acupuncture generally provides greater pain relief than acupressure.

Home Remedies

Give pain the cold shoulder. Two-thirds of people with tension headaches experience at least some relief when they use cold treatments, says David Trachtenbarg, M.D., clinical assistant professor at the University of Illinois College of Medicine in Peoria. Here are two ways in which you can use cold treatments.

◆ Place a wet towel in your freezer until it's cold but not frozen. Drape it over your forehead or wrap it around your head or neck. Leave the towel in place for 10 to 15 minutes.

◆ Put a few ice cubes in a plastic bag, then wrap the bag in a clean cloth. Apply the ice pack across your forehead for 20 minutes, then remove it for 10 minutes before reapplying. "Just don't apply ice directly to your skin, or you may give yourself frostbite," says Anne Simons, M.D.

Wash down your aspirin with coffee. Studies dating back about 20 years show that 65 milligrams of caffeine—roughly the amount in a cup of instant coffee or ½ cup of brewed—boosts the effectiveness of aspirin and other over-the-counter pain relievers by about 40 percent. Scientists believe caffeine helps because moderate, occasional consumption constricts the blood vessels in your head. It's the sudden opening, or dilation, of these vessels that causes headaches.

Some over-the-counter pain relievers, including Excedrin, Midol, and Vanquish Caplets, already contain caffeine. Or you can simply wash down your pills with a cup or two of coffee.

Keep a headache diary. Many tension headaches have triggers: emotional upsets, sleep disturbances, artificial sweeteners, certain foods, or drugs or alcohol (especially red wine). So if you're prone to tension headaches, Dr. Simons suggests keeping a headache diary. "Every time you get a headache, write down the date and time as well as any psychological, physical, or environmental factors that might have contributed to it," she says. "Also list all of the foods and beverages that you consumed within the previous 12 hours. You may see a pattern that you can change."

Over-the-Counter Drugs

Head for the drugstore. Most everyday tension headaches respond well to aspirin, acetaminophen, ibuprofen, or naproxen (Aleve), says Robert Smith, M.D., professor and director emeritus of the department of family medicine and founder of the Headache Center, both at the University of Cincinnati. Which of these pain relievers works best? Despite what the television commercials say, they all work about the same when taken in their recommended dosages. Which you choose depends on your individual preferences. Of the four drugs, aspirin is the most likely to cause stomach distress.

When taking a pain reliever, don't exceed the dosage indicated on the label. Overdosing is rare, but it can happen. According to the American Association of Poison Control Centers, acetaminophen accounts for 66 percent of overdoses involving over-the-counter pain relievers, with ibuprofen causing 19 percent, and aspirin, 15 percent. Overdoses of all three drugs can cause nausea and vomiting. Aspirin overdose also produces ringing in the ears and, ironically, headache. At very high doses—10 to 15 grams—these drugs may cause liver damage.

OTHER GOOD CHOICES

Nutrition

Cutting back on caffeine? Proceed with caution. If you're a java junkie, beware: Caffeine is addictive. If you drink coffee regularly and then stop suddenly, you're in for a rough ride in the form of a caffeine withdrawal headache that can last for several days. To avoid this type of headache, taper off regular coffee slowly, over several weeks.

Eat ice cream wisely. While a cold pack can help relieve a headache, a cold food—especially ice cream—can actually cause one. Neurologist Joseph Hulihan, M.D., of Temple University School of Medicine in Philadelphia, calls ice cream "the most common cause of food-induced headaches." At least 30 percent of people develop head pain within moments of scooping a spoonful of ice cream into their mouths, he says.

One veteran of ice cream headaches is Dr. Smith. Intrigued by the phenomenon, he tried applying crushed ice to different parts of his mouth. He discovered that the ice produced a headache only when it touched the back of his palate. His advice: Eat your ice cream slowly, in small bites or licks. Let it melt in your mouth. That way, it's less likely to touch the back of your palate and trigger a headache.

Supplements

Increase your magnesium intake. Magnesium deficiency has been linked to both tension headache and migraine, says Alan Gaby, M.D. He advises people who experience chronic or fairly frequent headaches to take 200 milligrams of magnesium three times a day.

Homeopathy

Discover a healing quartet. According to homeopath Dana Ullman, homeopaths typically rely on four medicines to treat tension headaches. They are Belladonna, Bryonia, Gelsemium, and Nux vomica. "But for chronic headaches, you might be better off with a constitutional remedy," he says. A constitutional remedy treats the whole body rather than specific conditions. See a homeopath to find the treatment that is best for you.

Ayurvedic Medicine

Blame your bowels. Ayurveda attributes tension headaches to problems in the colon, primarily constipation, says David Frawley, O.M.D. When treating people with tension headaches, Ayurvedic physicians often prescribe laxative herbs—notably, aloe powder and rhubarb—along with other herbs, including ginger, calamus, bayberry, and wintergreen. In addition, they suggest massaging the head, neck, and shoulders with sesame oil.

MEDICAL MEASURES

Doctors treat especially severe or persistent tension headaches with an array of medications, including prescription-strength nonsteroidal anti-inflammatory drugs (NSAIDs), combinations of pain relievers and narcotics, and even antidepressants. Often these pharmaceuticals help. But NSAIDs may cause abdominal distress and ulcers, while narcotics are associated with drowsiness and confusion. And antidepressants cause a variety of side effects, including dry mouth.

Because headaches are so common—and because they're often chronic and complicated—special clinics that focus exclusively on treating them have sprung up around the country. To find a headache clinic near you, contact either of the following organizations.

◆ American Association for the Study of Headache, 19 Mantua Road, Mount Royal, NJ 08061-1006

◆ National Headache Foundation, 428 West Saint James Place, Second Floor, Chicago, IL 60614-2750

RED FLAGS

A headache can be a symptom of an enormous number of conditions. So if you have a headache that doesn't respond to home treatment within 3 days, you should see your doctor to rule out an underlying medical problem, Dr. Simons advises.

In addition, see your doctor right away if you experience any of the following:

- ◆ An unusually severe headache
- ◆ A headache accompanied by a fever of 102°F or higher or a stiff neck
- ◆ Head pain that gets worse when you bend your chin to your chest
- ◆ A headache accompanied by slurred speech, blurred vision, or numbness or weakness in the arms or legs
- ◆ A headache following a head injury
- ◆ Headaches that recur with increasing frequency or get worse over time

Heartburn

The sign on the buffet said, "All You Can Eat." So you ate all you could . . . and then some. After all, you wanted to get your money's worth. But now you're paying the price: You have a four-alarm fire beneath your breastbone.

That's heartburn, a condition often associated with gustatory excesses.

Heartburn is a gastrointestinal condition that generally develops for one of two reasons. Either the muscle between your stomach and esophagus isn't doing its job or your stomach is under too much pressure.

The potentially problematic muscle, called the lower esophageal sphincter, forms a ring around the bottom end of your esophagus. Whenever you swallow, this sphincter opens to allow food to enter your stomach. Then it closes so that your stomach's caustic acid can't slosh back up into your esophagus. But if the sphincter becomes weakened, it can no longer close properly. As a result, stomach acid can splash into your esophagus, literally burning it.

SIMPLE SOLUTIONS
1. Nutrition
2. Visualization
3. Herbal Medicine
4. Home Remedies
5. Homeopathy
6. Chinese Medicine
7. Ayurvedic Medicine
8. Over-the-Counter Drugs

Even the strongest, most resilient sphincter can have a hard time withstanding the pressure exerted by an overstuffed stomach. If your stomach expands after a big meal, the sphincter may not close properly. Stomach acid can seep through the opening, like air leaking from an overinflated balloon.

You may also get heartburn if you eat too fast or if you decide to stretch out for a catnap after your meal. If you gobble your food without chewing it thoroughly, your stomach has to produce more acid to break down the food particles. And lying down too soon after a meal can create pressure in the stomach, forcing acid up past the sphincter and into the esophagus.

There may be other factors, too, including smoking, unmanaged stress, obesity, and pregnancy. Even wearing clothing that's too tight over the abdomen can trigger a flare-up by placing extra pressure on your stomach.

Is It a Heart Attack or Heartburn?

Each year, some six million frightened Americans show up in emergency rooms with chest pain, key symptom of a heart attack. About 15 percent of these people find out that what they're experiencing is not a heart attack but heartburn.

The confusion is understandable. Both conditions produce pain in the general area of the heart. Some people get heartburn so severe that it feels just like a heart attack. Others, unfortunately, dismiss heart attacks as "just heartburn."

In general, heartburn develops shortly after eating, says Anne Simons, M.D. It causes a burning sensation in your chest, possibly accompanied by hoarseness, a sore throat, and a foul acidic taste in the back of your mouth.

A heart attack, on the other hand, can occur at any time—including after a meal. It produces squeezing or crushing chest pain, with no burning sensation. The pain often radiates up into the jaw or out along an arm. It can be accompanied by sweating, nausea, dizziness, or shortness of breath.

Of course, you should *never* attempt to self-diagnose chest pain. If you think you're experiencing a heart attack, call your local medical emergency number or have someone take you to the nearest emergency room without delay. Let a doctor determine the cause of your pain.

Of course, you can change your wardrobe. You can quit smoking. You can do a better job of managing your stress. But if you really want to avoid heartburn, you *must* adjust your eating habits.

BEST CHOICES

Nutrition
Unwind to dine. "Mealtime should be a time of relaxation, not stress," says Alan P. Brauer, M.D. His advice: Always sit down to eat. Play soothing back-

ground music. Proceed through your meal at a slow pace, chewing each bite thoroughly. Never wolf down your food.

Graze instead of gorging. Consider forgoing the standard three square meals a day in favor of five small, snacklike meals, recommends Anne Simons, M.D. The less food you consume in one sitting, the less acid your stomach will produce.

Beware the burners. Limit or, even better, eliminate those foods that can trigger heartburn flare-ups. Among the primary heartburn offenders are citrus fruits, garlic, chocolate, milk, carbonated beverages, tea, coffee, and alcohol. Also steer clear of anything that's fatty, greasy, or spicy. Tomato-based foods can also cause problems.

Avoid nocturnal noshing. At the Veterans Affairs Hospital in Hines, Illinois, staff physician Stephen Sontag, M.D., recruited 24 people who said they had never been bothered by heartburn. Dr. Sontag had the volunteers eat a big breakfast, then lie down while technicians measured the amount of acid that sloshed from the stomach into the esophagus. All of the study participants showed unusually high levels of what's called acid reflux. Based on these results, Dr. Sontag concluded that lying down shortly after eating is a one-way ticket to heartburn.

If you tend to experience heartburn while you sleep, it may be because you're lying down too soon after a meal or snack. Refrain from eating anything within a few hours of your bedtime and see if it helps.

Take notes. If you have frequent episodes of heartburn, Dr. Simons suggests keeping a food diary. Write down everything that you eat and drink as well as when you experience symptoms. Then review your diary to find out whether you tend to develop heartburn within a few hours of consuming certain foods or beverages. If you identify any possible offenders, eliminate them from your diet.

Drown discomfort with carrot juice. Carrots and their relatives—herbs and vegetables such as angelica, celery, fennel, and parsley—have long been used as folk remedies for upset stomach. James A. Duke, Ph.D., also endorses them for heartburn. He suggests making a juice as follows: In a juicer or blender, combine one or two carrots, several angelica stalks, a few celery stalks, a fennel bulb, and a handful of parsley. "If you don't have some of these ingredients, feel free to leave them out," he says. "Just go with what you have." Use whatever quantities suit your tastebuds, and add water to make the juice even more palatable. Drink a cup before every meal.

Visualization

Envision tranquillity. For one study, volunteers were hooked up to monitors that measured their stomach acid secretions. When the volunteers were asked to visualize eating their favorite foods, their stomach acidity soared by 89 percent. But when they envisioned a beach scene or a sunset, their stomach acidity dropped by 39 percent. "This research demonstrates the value of making mealtimes as calm and relaxed as possible," says Martin L. Rossman, M.D.

Virtually any relaxation therapy can relieve or prevent heartburn, adds William E. Whitehead, Ph.D., professor of medical psychology at Johns Hopkins University School of Medicine in Baltimore. He suggests trying deep breathing, meditation, massage, or aromatherapy.

Herbal Medicine

Cool the burn with chamomile. "Chamomile is my first-choice herb for treating heartburn," Dr. Duke says. "Many studies have shown that chamomile soothes the digestive tract." To make an herbal tea, add 2 to 3 teaspoons of dried chamomile flowers to 1 cup of boiled water. Steep for 10 minutes, then strain before drinking. You can buy dried chamomile flowers in health food stores.

If you prefer, you can use ready-made chamomile tea bags, which are sold in supermarkets as well as health food stores. Prepare according to the package directions.

Treat your symptoms "ginger-ly." Ginger is among the most venerated digestive herbs. In scientific research, it has been proven to be an effective treatment for the nausea associated with motion sickness and morning sickness. Many herbalists, including Dr. Duke, recommend ginger for heartburn as well. To make an herbal tea, add 1 teaspoon of freshly grated gingerroot to 1 cup of boiled water. Steep for 10 minutes, then strain and drink. Fresh gingerroot is sold in health food stores and most supermarkets.

Take another look at licorice. In three separate studies, people who took a licorice extract plus an antacid for their heartburn reported significantly greater and longer-lasting relief than people who took the antacid alone.

The herb's active ingredient comes in the form of an extract called deglycyrrhizinated licorice (DGL). You can buy chewable wafers of DGL in many health food stores. Take two to four 380-milligram wafers about 20 minutes be-

Hiatal Hernia: The Sign of a Wandering Stomach

Like heartburn, a hiatal hernia can cause a burning sensation in your chest. The condition occurs because of a weakness in the diaphragm, the sheath of muscle that spans the base of the rib cage and plays a key role in breathing.

Within the diaphragm is an opening called the hiatus. Through this opening, the esophagus connects to the stomach. But sometimes the hiatus loses its shape and tautness. When this happens, the stomach can push up through the opening, forming a bell-shaped pocket at the base of the esophagus. Stomach acid splashes into the pocket, causing a burning sensation and sometimes nausea.

Hiatal hernias are quite common, especially among people who smoke or who are overweight. In some cases, the hernias produce little or no discomfort. In other cases, episodes of heartburn can be quite frequent and severe.

The same treatments that relieve heartburn can ease the symptoms associated with hiatal hernia, says Anne Simons, M.D. Deep breathing exercises can also alleviate symptoms.

If you're bothered by a hiatal hernia, Richard Firshein, D.O., assistant professor of family medicine at the New York College of Osteopathic Medicine in New York City, suggests practicing what he calls belly breathing. Lie on your back and place a book on your abdomen. As you inhale and exhale, the book should move up and down several inches. Continue this deep-breathing exercise for several minutes or until you feel some relief. This exercise helps strengthen the diaphragm and reinforce the hiatal opening. But don't do it right after eating: Lying down after a meal can encourage acid reflux and aggravate hiatal hernia pain.

fore a meal, advises Seattle naturopath Michael T. Murray, N.D. Don't take DGL more than three times a week since repeated use can cause toxicity.

Brew your own herbal blend. According to Dr. Duke, a tea made from anise, caraway, dill, or fennel seed can diminish the heat of heartburn. Add 1 to

2 teaspoons of any combination of herbs to 1 cup of boiled water, then steep for 10 minutes and strain before drinking.

Don't pooh-pooh peppermint. In the 1950s and 1960s, a few studies identified peppermint as a cause of heartburn because the herb can relax the lower esophageal sphincter. Yet for centuries, herbalists have been prescribing peppermint and other mints as a *treatment* for heartburn—with excellent results. So who's right?

The most recent research suggests that peppermint is more likely to relieve heartburn than to aggravate it. In addition to peppermint oil's soothing effects on the entire digestive tract, its mild anesthetic properties can help soothe heartburn pain, according to Stephen Holt, M.D., professor of medicine at Seton Hall University in South Orange, New Jersey.

To make peppermint tea, add 1 to 2 teaspoons of chopped fresh peppermint leaves to 1 cup of boiled water. Steep for 10 minutes, then strain out the leaves and drink. If you want, you can save the leaves and munch on them separately.

Of course, if peppermint seems to aggravate your heartburn, by all means don't use it. The herb's effects on the sphincter are generally mild and should pass within 5 minutes.

Home Remedies

Elevate your bed. If you're bothered by heartburn at night, try raising the head of your bed. The best way is to put some bricks or wood blocks under the legs of the headboard to raise it a few inches off the floor. That creates just enough tilt for gravity to help keep stomach acid in your stomach, where it belongs.

You might think that you would get similar results just by using a few extra pillows or a foam wedge to raise your upper body. But that's not as effective. Raising your upper body forces you to bend at the waist. That extra "kink" actually increases pressure in your stomach.

Monitor postmeal activities. Lying down too soon after eating isn't the only express route to heartburn. If you bend over or do any lifting after a meal, you'll put extra pressure on your stomach.

Don't just sit there. If you can't lie down or bend over without getting heartburn, what can you do? Try taking a walk, suggest Joe Graedon and Teresa Graedon, Ph.D., coauthors of *The People's Pharmacy* books. Because walking keeps you upright, it helps gravity do its job—and keeps stomach acid in your stomach, where it belongs.

Chew gum. At the University of Alabama, researchers divided 78 pregnant women into two groups. One group chewed gum for 30 minutes after eating, while the other did not. The gum chewers reported significantly less heartburn than those who did not chew gum.

How does chewing help? It boosts your production of saliva, which helps wash acid back into your stomach and soothe an irritated esophagus.

Banish those butts. If you need another reason to give up smoking, maybe heartburn can persuade you. The nicotine in cigarettes not only relaxes the lower esophageal sphincter but also increases the secretion of stomach acid.

Maintain a healthy weight. If you're carrying extra pounds, you're putting more pressure on your stomach. That's a surefire setup for heartburn.

Hang loose. Avoid wearing garments that fit snugly around your abdomen. They increase pressure on your stomach, too.

OTHER GOOD CHOICES

Homeopathy

Fight fire with fire. Calcarea carbonica and Nux vomica are just two of several homeopathic medicines that have been proven effective in relieving heartburn, according to homeopath Dana Ullman. To find out which medicine best matches your symptoms, consult a homeopath.

Chinese Medicine

Temper the temperature. Practitioners of Chinese medicine attribute heartburn to excess Heat rising up through a weak Stomach, explains Efrem Korngold, O.M.D., L.Ac. For patients bothered by heartburn, he usually recommends foods and herbs that cool and balance qi. These include radishes, radish seed, citrus fruit peels, and cardamom.

Press a point to short-circuit symptoms. Stimulating a point called Conception Vessel 12 can actually prevent heartburn, according to Michael Reed Gach, founder and director of the Acupressure Institute. Conception Vessel 12 is located on the midline of your body, three finger-widths from the end of your breastbone. Press this point for up to 3 minutes before eating, he says. Do not use this remedy if you've just eaten or if you're a woman who's pregnant.

If acupressure doesn't help control your heartburn, acupuncture still might. Consult an acupuncturist.

Ayurvedic Medicine

Sip a soothing tea. Ayurvedic practitioners recommend stomach-soothing herbs to treat heartburn, according to David Frawley, O.M.D. Among the more familiar of these herbs are cinnamon and cardamom as well as ginger and licorice. Any one of these makes a tasty tea. Simply add 1 teaspoon of crushed or powdered herb to 1 cup of boiled water, steep for 10 minutes, and strain before drinking.

Other, lesser-known stomach-soothing herbs include amalaki, shatavari, trikatu, triphala, vidanga, and trivrit. If you want to try any of these, consult an Ayurvedic practitioner.

Over-the-Counter Drugs

Take away the sting. As their name suggests, antacids alleviate heartburn by reducing the acidity of stomach acid, a process called neutralization. When neutralized acid splashes into the esophagus, it doesn't burn.

You may have to try several different antacids before you find one that works well for you. No matter which product you choose, follow the package directions for proper dosage. Within 15 minutes, you should notice some improvement in your symptoms. The effects usually last about an hour or two.

Stem acid at its source. H_2 blockers are relatively new heartburn medications. These products—which include Pepcid AC, Tagamet HB, and Zantac 75—used to be available only by prescription and only for the treatment of ulcers. But in the past few years, they've gone over the counter for the treatment of heartburn and indigestion.

If you decide to try an H_2 blocker, follow the package directions for proper dosage. With these products, serious side effects are rare, though some people have reported headaches, drowsiness, dizziness, confusion, and dry mouth.

RED FLAGS

If you experience heartburn two or more times a week and you find yourself taking lots of antacids or H_2 blockers, you need to see your doctor. You may have chronic heartburn, also known as gastroesophageal reflux disease (GERD). Left untreated, GERD can seriously damage your esophagus.

Heart Disease

You never thought much about your heart before. You never had to. After all, it has always done its job without any assistance from you.

But now your doctor is telling you that your heart might be in trouble. You're hearing words like "coronary arteries," "blockages," and "heart attack." Words that scare you.

Heart disease is scary—partly because it's the nation's leading cause of death, partly because it seems to come on so suddenly. You never would have suspected anything was wrong if your doctor hadn't picked up on it.

In fact, by the time heart disease is diagnosed, it has already been years in the making. It usually results from a combination of a high-fat, low-fiber diet, lack of exercise, and uncontrolled stress, among other factors.

A heart attack is the culmination of a process that starts in childhood. It begins when something injures the lining of the arteries that supply blood to your heart, called the coronary arteries. That "something" usually is highly unstable oxygen molecules, free radicals, that cause oxidative damage. Your immune system

SIMPLE SOLUTIONS
1. Nutrition
2. Supplements
3. Exercise
4. Relaxation Therapies
5. Music Therapy
6. Social Support
7. Herbal Medicine
8. Home Remedies
9. Over-the-Counter Drugs
10. Chinese Medicine
11. Ayurvedic Medicine
12. Medical Measures

sends white blood cells to repair the damage. But in doing so, they cause inflammation and create scar tissue that attracts circulating cholesterol.

Cholesterol is a waxy substance with a fearsome reputation. When cholesterol collects at the site of scar tissue within the arteries, it leads to the formation of deposits called plaques. Over several decades, the plaques grow and slowly narrow your arteries, a process called atherosclerosis.

Plaques are like acne pimples. If one pops, its contents spill into your bloodstream and may completely plug a section of coronary artery that's already severely narrowed by other plaques. Once blocked, that artery cannot deliver food and oxygen to part of your heart, and cells in the affected area die. That's a heart attack.

A number of risk factors have been linked to heart disease. Your risk is elevated if heart disease runs in your family. Older people are at greater risk than young ones, and at any age, men are more vulnerable than women. Other risk factors include smoking, a high-fat diet, high cholesterol, high triglycerides (blood fats), and high homocysteine levels. (Homocysteine is an amino acid derived from methionine, another amino acid that's found in abundance in animal foods.) People who have high blood pressure, are overweight, or have diabetes also have elevated risk. And you may be putting your heart health in jeopardy if you don't exercise very much, if you're under a lot of emotional stress, or if you're socially isolated.

Some risk factors can't be changed. "We're all stuck with our age, gender, and heredity," explains Martha Hill, R.N., Ph.D., professor at Johns Hopkins University School of Nursing and past president of the American Heart Association. "But it's never too late to work on risk factors that can be changed. Even if you've already had a heart attack, risk-factor reduction can prevent another one." And reducing your risk factors with a comprehensive program of alternative therapies—like those that follow—can actually reverse heart disease.

BEST CHOICES

Nutrition

Score a victory through vegetarianism. There's a good reason why a low-fat vegetarian diet is the cornerstone of Dr. Dean Ornish's famed program for reversing heart disease. It works. "No question about it," says Tim Byers, M.D., professor of preventive medicine at the University of Colorado Health Sciences Center in Denver. "A plant-based diet with plenty of fruits and vegetables reduces risk of heart disease."

How does a vegetarian or near-vegetarian diet help? "By preventing and repairing a lot of the damage caused by free radicals," says Alan Gaby, M.D. "Plant foods are high in the antioxidant nutrients—vitamins C and E, beta-carotene, and selenium. The more plant foods you eat, the less likely you are to develop high blood pressure, high cholesterol, obesity, diabetes, and high homocysteine and high triglyceride levels."

A vegetarian diet can also boost the effectiveness of mainstream heart disease medication, studies show.

Journey to the Mediterranean. The Mediterranean diet first attracted scientific attention in the 1960s, when researchers noticed that people in Greece, Italy, Spain, and southern France eat fairly high-fat diets but have much lower rates of heart disease than Americans. As it turns out, people in the Mediterranean region eat little saturated fat and margarine but liberal amounts of mono- and polyunsaturated oils—mostly olive oil.

For several years now, many nutrition experts have been touting the Mediterranean diet as a tasty, heart-healthy way to eat. The Mediterranean diet consists mostly of fruits, vegetables, beans, nuts, and grains, with some cheese, fish, and poultry and very little red meat.

If you've survived a heart attack, a Mediterranean diet can go a long way in protecting you from another. That's what French researchers discovered in the Lyon Diet Heart Trial. They instructed 605 heart attack survivors to eat either a modestly low-fat diet (with meats, saturated fat, and margarine allowed) or a Mediterranean diet. Over the next 5 years, the people following the Mediterranean diet had 72 percent fewer second heart attacks.

Go fishing. Whether you have heart disease or want to prevent it, make fish your dish. Certain cold-water species, including salmon, mackerel, herring, and halibut, are rich in omega-3 fatty acids. Omega-3's are a special type of fat that's actually good for your heart. They help prevent and treat heart disease in several ways, according to the American Heart Association.

"Hundreds of studies have shown that cold-water fish lower cholesterol and triglycerides and help prevent and treat heart disease," says Joseph Pizzorno Jr., N.D.

Make like Bugs Bunny. The cartoon rabbit loves carrots. And carrots and other orange and yellow vegetables as well as dark leafy greens are rich in carotenoids. These antioxidant nutrients, members of the vitamin A family, can help reduce your risk of heart disease.

Throw a tea party. You may not think of tea as being good for heart health, but it is. A study conducted by researchers at the University of Kansas found that some of the flavonoids in tea are considerably more potent antioxidants than either vitamin C or vitamin E.

Be a bean counter. Beans, especially soybeans, are good for your heart, but not for the reason touted in that old playground ditty. Several studies have shown that beans help lower cholesterol.

Supplements

Fight disease with E. In 1993, two landmark Harvard studies—one of men, the other of women—showed that supplemental vitamin E makes a major dent in heart disease. Compared with men who did not take the vitamin, those who did experienced 37 percent fewer heart attacks. And women who took vitamin E supplements for more than 2 years saw their heart disease risk drop 41 percent.

Alan P. Brauer, M.D., recommends taking 400 to 800 international units (IU) a day. But if you are considering taking amounts above 400 IU, talk to your doctor first.

"C" your heart heal. In Britain, 30 percent more people die of heart attacks during winter than during summer. A Cambridge University study offers an explanation for this phenomenon: The British consume nearly 50 percent more vitamin C in summer—90 milligrams a day, compared with 65 milligrams in winter.

Vitamin C appears to be especially beneficial to people with heart disease who smoke. If you want to try taking C, clinical nutritionist Shari Lieberman, Ph.D., recommends 500 to 4,000 milligrams a day.

Bank on the Bs. The recent discovery that a high homocysteine level boosts heart disease risk has focused new attention on the B vitamins, which reduce homocysteine.

According to Eric Rimm, Sc.D., assistant professor of epidemiology and nutrition at the Harvard School of Public Health, the heart-healthiest daily doses are 3 milligrams of B_6 and 400 micrograms of folic acid. Many supplements supply these higher levels.

Mind your magnesium intake. In a study of Seventh-Day Adventists—most of whom are vegetarian or near-vegetarian—those who ate the most whole-grain breads and nuts (walnuts, peanuts, and almonds) had the lowest rates of heart disease. Part of the reason appears to be that these foods are good sources of magnesium.

Magnesium helps reduce high blood pressure. According to several studies, it also reduces deaths from heart attacks when administered intravenously in emergency rooms. In a study of 930 people treated at Middlesex Hospital in London, researchers gave some patients standard care and the rest standard care plus intravenous magnesium. Among the people who received magnesium, there were 54 percent fewer deaths.

Of course, you can't give yourself intravenous magnesium. But oral supplements also help. Dr. Lieberman recommends taking 500 to 1,000 milligrams a day.

Oil your arteries. Fish-oil supplements help keep your arteries open and working properly after angioplasty and bypass surgery. James P. Gapinski, M.D., of the Clement J. Zablocki Veterans Affairs Medical Center in Milwaukee, analyzed seven studies of fish-oil supplementation after angioplasty. He found that taking 3,000 to 6,400 milligrams a day significantly reduced re-narrowing of the arteries.

Befriend coenzyme Q_{10}. Several studies have shown that supplementation with coenzyme Q_{10} helps treat the chest pain of angina as well as symptoms of congestive heart failure. The latest research suggests that supplementation also reduces your risk of developing arterial blood clots, which can lead to heart attack. Dr. Lieberman recommends taking 50 to 300 milligrams of coenzyme Q_{10} a day.

Exercise

Get physical. "If you're physically active, you're far less likely to die of a heart attack than people who are sedentary," says William L. Haskell, Ph.D., professor of cardiovascular medicine and deputy director of the Center for Research on Disease Prevention at Stanford University School of Medicine. "Exercise helps in many ways. It makes your arteries healthier, helps control your weight, lowers your stress and blood pressure, and increases your levels of 'good' high-density lipoprotein (HDL) cholesterol."

Most experts recommend being physically active for at least 30 minutes a day. Your workout doesn't need to be aerobic to help your heart. Even brisk walking helps. You should always check with your doctor before starting any new exercise program.

Do it your way. Any regular, moderate exercise helps treat and prevent heart disease, says Dr. Ornish, who is president of the Preventive Medicine Research Institute in Sausalito, California. His program emphasizes walking and yoga. But any physical activity—including gardening, cycling, dancing, tai chi, and swimming—is beneficial.

Which should you do? "Do what you enjoy," says Joan Price, a Sebastopol, California, exercise instructor, trainer, speaker, and author of *Joan Price Says, Yes, You Can Get in Shape!* "Don't think of it as exercise. Think of it as fun. If you can't think of any physical activity you enjoy, think back to what you liked as a kid. Chances are, you'll still like it."

Work out for recovery. If you've already had a heart attack, exercise can help you recover. "About 3 weeks after a heart attack, your heart has probably healed enough to allow you to exercise again," says Robert F. DeBusk, M.D., director of the cardiac rehabilitation program at Stanford University. "When you do, you get the same benefits that healthy people get: healthier arteries, weight loss, more HDL, less stress, and lower blood pressure."

Of course, you should return to physical activity under a physician's supervision, ideally through a medically supervised cardiac rehabilitation program.

Just don't overdo it. Every winter, there are news reports of people dropping dead from heart attacks while shoveling snow. Researchers in one study concluded that about 5 percent of heart attacks may be triggered by intense exertion. The bottom line: If you're out of shape and are concerned about how much physical activity of any kind you can safely handle, talk to your doctor.

Relaxation Therapies

Change your type A ways. At the University of California, San Francisco/Mount Zion Medical Center, cardiologist Meyer Friedman, M.D., director of the Meyer Friedman Institute, divided 1,013 extreme type A heart attack survivors into two groups. The people in one group received standard care. Those in the other group agreed to quit smoking. They also had to enroll either in a healthy-eating class or in the healthy-eating class plus a counseling program to change their type A behavior.

In true type A style, most of the participants in the counseling program initially dismissed suggestions to mellow out as stupid or ridiculous. But those who stuck with it quickly began to report positive changes in their lives. They felt happier. Their families and colleagues were happier with them. They enjoyed life more and liked taking some time to "smell the roses."

Three years later, the former type A's who had become more type B's could enjoy something else: Compared with the other people in the study, they had just half the risk of second heart attacks.

Discover the magic of mantras. At the State University of New York at Buffalo, John Zamarra, M.D., and colleagues tested the exercise ability of 21 people with heart disease. Then the participants learned transcendental meditation to practice for 20 minutes twice a day at home. Eight months later, they could exercise 15 percent more strenuously before experiencing chest pain.

Enhance recovery with self-hypnosis. Forget the nightclub hypnotists and their big gold watches. Self-hypnosis—which involves meditative deep breathing, muscle relaxation, and visualization of relaxing scenes—has become well-accepted in mainstream medicine, especially as preparation for surgery.

"The evidence is very strong that relaxation therapies help prevent heart attack and aid recovery from them," says stress-management specialist Martin L. Rossman, M.D. He has produced many relaxation tapes that combine music and visualization exercises. For a catalog, write the Academy for Guided Imagery at P. O. Box 2070, Mill Valley, CA 94942-2070.

Music Therapy

Tune in, tune out. Few medical crises are as stress-provoking as heart attacks. Music reduces levels of stress hormones, says David S. Sobel, M.D., director of patient education and health promotion for Kaiser Permanente Northern California, a health maintenance organization.

To examine whether music therapy could support the heart attack recovery process, Cathie Guzzetta, R.N., Ph.D., professor of nursing at the Catholic University School of Nursing in Washington, D.C., worked with 80 people who were newly admitted to coronary-care units at three hospitals. The study showed that those who practiced the relaxation response or listened to music had significantly lower heart rates and stress hormone levels. Those who listened to music were the least stressed, suggesting that music can be even more relaxing than meditation.

Social Support

Reach out and touch someone. Like Dr. Friedman's you-can-get-mellow class and counseling, the Ornish program includes a similar message as part of a weekly support group. In addition to helping participants evolve away from type A patterns, the support group also helps minimize the social isolation that raises risk of heart attack.

Your local chapter of the American Heart Association might be able to refer you to a support group. Or simply spend more time with family, friends, and others whose company you enjoy.

Make a pet part of your family. More than a century ago, pioneering nurse Florence Nightingale said, "A small pet animal is often an excellent companion for the sick." Her words were largely forgotten until 1980, when Erika Friedmann, Ph.D., of the University of Pennsylvania in Philadelphia, stumbled upon an unexpected correlation: Men who'd had heart attacks were more likely to survive if they had pets.

Go from A to B

We owe our current understanding of the relationship between stress and heart disease not to age-old wisdom but rather to a half-dozen chairs. Back in the 1950s, San Francisco cardiologist Meyer Friedman, M.D., noticed that the chairs in his waiting room needed re-covering. The upholsterer idly remarked how odd it was that only the fronts were worn: "Your patients sit on the edge of their seats."

Dr. Friedman thought nothing of the observation until years later, when he and fellow cardiologist Ray Rosenman, M.D., began studying stress as a possible risk factor for heart disease. In interviews with dozens of men who'd had heart attacks, they were struck by how many seemed unusually competitive, belligerent, hostile, and time-pressured. "They could hardly sit still," recalls Dr. Friedman, now director of the Meyer Friedman Institute at the University of California, San Francisco/Mount Zion Medical Center. "They were like runners straining at the starting blocks." That's when he remembered the upholsterer's comment. If life were an endless race, and the men were always at the starting blocks, how would they sit? On the edge of their seats.

Drs. Friedman and Rosenman coined the term *type A* to describe people who seemed perpetually hostile, anxious, time-pressured, and driven to accomplish more and more in less and less time. They and other researchers have shown that type A behavior approximately triples risk of heart attack in men and quadruples it in women. *Type A* became a house-hold word. By some estimates, 40 percent of the U.S. population is type A.

Are you among them?

If you have classic type A behavior patterns, you probably try to do many things at once, become impatient if you have to wait for people, and express your anger or impatience in a wide variety of ways. But even if you are type A, you can change. You can evolve your behavior toward

In the years since Dr. Friedmann's discovery, many studies have shown that human-pet interactions—playing with a dog, having a cat curled up in your lap, or gazing at fish in a tank—can be profoundly relaxing and reduce blood pressure as much as some medications.

more mellow type B, which could reduce your risk of heart attack. Among the strategies:

◆ Listen to your spouse and friends. When they recommend that you slow down and relax, it's time to listen.

◆ Can you stop trying to do many things at once? Perhaps it will help if you keep in mind that life is a work in progress, and no one can finish everything he sets out to do.

◆ You may be able to clear your calendar if you try to look ahead about 5 years. Ask yourself which events on your calendar you will truly care about 5 years from now. If you see events that don't pass that test, try to cancel them.

◆ The next time you see someone working too slowly for your taste, don't interfere. Let that person finish the task at his own pace.

◆ When people criticize you, find something in their comments that you agree with. Discuss the points of agreement before you defend yourself.

◆ When people do things that injure you, assume that they've made a mistake—and they're not attacking you maliciously. Forgive the mistake.

◆ Read a long novel that has nothing to do with your occupation.

◆ Drive in the right lane and stay there, no matter how many cars pass you. If you find that you're getting impatient, enjoy some music on the radio or reflect on some pleasant memories.

◆ Write a letter to an old friend without saying anything about your job.

◆ Laugh at yourself at least once a day.

Have faith in healing. People who observe a religion typically have close social ties to others in their houses of worship. They also feel that their beliefs bring them into a close relationship with their vision of God.

At Dartmouth Medical School, psychiatrist Thomas Oxman, M.D., studied

232 people who had open-heart surgery. Six months after surgery, compared with those who described themselves as "not religious," those who professed deep religious convictions were 3 times more likely to have survived. The religious people who also had other close social ties were 10 times more likely to have survived.

Herbal Medicine

Gobble garlic. Some mainstream drugs lower cholesterol and triglycerides. Others reduce blood pressure. And some help prevent the internal blood clots that cause heart attack. But garlic does all of these things. "If I wanted to prevent or treat heart disease, I'd use more garlic in cooking and consider taking it in capsule form as well," says James A. Duke, Ph.D.

To make the most of garlic, you have to eat a fair amount of it—on the order of one to four cloves a day, Dr. Gaby says. If you'd rather not do that, you can opt for the odor-free garlic supplements sold in health food stores.

Odor-free garlic provides all the benefits of fresh garlic, but it's more socially acceptable, Dr. Pizzorno says. Commission E, the German expert panel that evaluates the safety and effectiveness of herbal medicines, recommends an odor-free preparation that contains the equivalent of 4,000 milligrams of fresh garlic—10 milligrams of alliin or 4,000 micrograms of allicin.

Say hello to willow bark. A great deal of research shows that low-dose aspirin—one-half to one standard tablet a day—reduces heart attack risk substantially and aids recovery from mainstream heart surgery. A half-teaspoon of willow bark contains about 100 milligrams of salicin, the herbal precursor of the familiar white pills, Dr. Duke says. "That should be enough to provide aspirin's heart-protective benefits."

You can take willow bark as a tea. Add ½ teaspoon of the herb to 1 cup of boiling water. Simmer for 10 minutes, then strain. Drink a cupful of tea a day.

Try hawthorn, the herbal heart tonic. The leaves and flowers of hawthorn are rich in antioxidants, including flavonoids, explains naturopath Donald Brown, N.D., professor of herbal medicine at Bastyr University in Kenmore, Washington. Naturopaths most often prescribe hawthorn to treat congestive heart failure because it strengthens your heart. In addition, the herb improves blood flow through your heart, pumps antioxidants into your blood, and lowers your blood pressure a little. As a result, it helps treat angina and can support recovery from heart attack. Dr. Brown recommends taking 80 milligrams of a standardized hawthorn extract twice a day.

HEART DISEASE

343

Angina: Gripped by Chest Pain

You can walk with no problem. But if you run, climb stairs, or play tennis, you experience chest pain. That's angina, technically, "angina pectoris"—chest pain during exertion. Like heart attack, angina is caused by atherosclerosis.

When you have atherosclerosis, the arteries that nourish your heart become substantially narrowed by plaques, fatty deposits on your inner artery walls. You might not see any evidence of the problem as long as you're at rest. That's because when you don't exert yourself, your heart gets enough blood—and gets enough of the food and oxygen your blood carries. But when you're active, your heart essentially becomes blood-starved, a condition called ischemia. The result is chest pain.

Some 4 million American men and 3 million women have angina. Many cope with the condition by carrying around nitroglycerine, the medication often prescribed by mainstream doctors. Chemically, the medication is exactly the same as the nitroglycerine used to make explosives. But its effect on the body is completely benign. Nitroglycerine relaxes your coronary arteries, allowing more blood flow through them, so you don't develop chest pain so quickly.

But nitroglycerine isn't the only substance that can come to the rescue. Other approaches have also proved effective and are recommended by alternative practitioners. Among the supplements that look promising in studies are vitamin E, coenzyme Q_{10}, and L-carnitine. In Ayurvedic medicine, practitioners recommend two kinds of substances, labeled MAK-4 and MAK-5. Both have been tested in India and were shown to reduce angina in some people.

Home Remedies

Quit smoking cigarettes. Regardless of how long you've smoked, your risk of heart attack declines rapidly once you quit. Three years after quitting a pack-a-day habit, you have about the same heart attack risk as lifelong non-smokers, according to the American Heart Association.

Imbibe wisely. Dozens of studies have suggested that a little alcohol—

no more than two drinks a day—can reduce your risk of heart disease. "It raises HDL cholesterol, the kind that reduces heart attack risk," Dr. Brauer says.

Researchers with the Pawtucket (Rhode Island) Heart Health Program have estimated that one drink a day—the equivalent of 12 ounces of beer, 5 ounces of wine, or a cocktail made with 1½ ounces of 80-proof distilled spirits—raises HDL levels by about 6 percent in men and 10 percent in women. For every 1 percent that your HDL rises, your risk of heart attack drops about 3 percent.

Should you drink a little to prevent heart disease? That depends on your personal health history, say Columbia University epidemiologists Thomas A. Pearson, M.D., Ph.D., and Paul Terry. You shouldn't drink for good health if you have a drinking problem, if alcoholism runs in your family, or if you have a medical condition that can be aggravated by alcohol, such as liver disease or heart failure.

If none of these applies to you, you may drink, but limit yourself to about two drinks a day. That is equivalent to two 12-ounce beers, two 5-ounce glasses of wine, or two cocktails made with 1½ ounces of 80-proof liquor. And never have more than three drinks in one sitting, they advise.

But if you don't drink, don't start just for the sake of protecting your heart. You can get a good deal of alcohol's benefits without drinking a drop of booze. Just drink red or purple grape juice. It has all the phenols and flavonoids found in red wine, which means that it's high in antioxidants and helps prevent the blood clots that trigger heart attack.

Over-the-Counter Drugs

Make the most of low-dose aspirin. "Aspirin helps prevent the internal blood clots that cause heart attacks," says Charles Hennekens, M.D., retired professor of medicine at Harvard Medical School. It also helps dissolve clots in people who are having heart attacks.

Many studies have shown that taking one standard aspirin tablet a day or every other day reduces heart attack risk by about 40 percent.

Low-dose aspirin is unlikely to upset your stomach. If it does, you can switch to an enteric-coated brand. These pills dissolve in your intestine rather than your stomach, so they shouldn't cause problems.

OTHER GOOD CHOICES

Chinese Medicine

Move your Blood. Chinese medicine attributes heart disease to a chronic weakness of qi that eventually leads to the blocked flow of Blood through your heart.

"In the Chinese view, the heart not only circulates Blood, it also sustains consciousness," says Efrem Korngold, O.M.D., L.Ac. "Good circulation promotes tranquillity, and any disturbance of tranquillity—for example, stress—can cause heart disease. In other words, the Chinese view of heart disease dovetails with the Western concept of type A behavior."

To treat heart disease, Dr. Korngold prescribes herbs that open the blood vessels and promote the flow of blood. These include tea, hawthorn, salvia, frankincense, myrrh, santalum wood, aristolochia root, and borneol crystals.

Stimulate heart health. Stimulating certain points around your body with acupressure can help treat heart disease, Dr. Korngold says. The following two points are especially beneficial. Just apply steady, penetrating finger pressure to each point for 3 minutes.

◆ Pericardium 6, located in the middle of your inner wrist, 2½ finger-widths above the wrist crease

◆ Heart 8, located on the palm of your hand, between the bones of the ring finger and pinkie

Ayurvedic Medicine

Make arjuna your ally. Ayurvedic physicians believe that heart disease can develop from imbalances in any of the three doshas, according to David Frawley, O.M.D. Your treatment depends on your specific symptoms and constitutional type. But, in general, Dr. Frawley recommends stress management through meditation and anger control and regular moderate exercise in the form of yoga. Along with that, he advocates nutritional approaches that are similar to those now espoused by Western medicine: Eat more fish and less red meat and salt, and drink modest amounts of red wine.

Peripheral Artery Disease: Give Leg Pain the Boot

When atherosclerosis affects your legs, there's a buildup of artery-narrowing plaque that reduces blood flow. The result is peripheral artery disease (PAD). It resembles angina—but instead of getting the pain in your chest, it hits your legs. When you exert yourself, you may experience leg pain, aching, or cramping. These are the telltale symptoms of intermittent claudication.

Because PAD is caused by atherosclerosis, you'll help prevent it—along with the pain of intermittent claudication—if you can prevent heart disease. In fact, all the approaches to preventing and treating heart disease also work for PAD.

Treatments for intermittent claudication are different from those for angina. The mainstream drug of choice for intermittent claudication is pentoxifylline (Trental). But there are alternative substances that may also work—specifically ginkgo and L-carnitine.

"Ginkgo is the premier herbal medicine for intermittent claudication," says James A. Duke, Ph.D. "It improves blood flow through your legs. Nine excellent studies that I've reviewed show that ginkgo extract provides better relief than Trental." He recommends 40 milligrams two or three times a day.

L-carnitine is the substance resembling an amino acid that's sometimes recommended for angina. A few studies have also shown that taking 2 grams of L-carnitine a day helps people with intermittent claudication walk farther without developing leg pain. But don't take L-carnitine or any amino acid without a doctor's guidance. The use of individual amino acids in large doses is considered experimental, and the long-term effects on health are unknown.

Dr. Frawley also prescribes medicinal herbs such as garlic, hawthorn, ginger, guggul, and arjuna, which he calls "Ayurveda's heart medicine par excellence." Arjuna strengthens your heart's pumping ability. Dr. Frawley says it also stimulates blood circulation and promotes healing after a heart attack. If you want to try arjuna, consult an Ayurvedic practitioner.

MEDICAL MEASURES

To treat and prevent heart disease, a growing number of mainstream doctors are recommending a combination of low-fat eating, supplements, regular moderate exercise, and stress-management techniques.

In addition, they perform 420,000 angioplasties, 570,000 bypasses, and 2,300 heart transplants every year. None of these procedures is curative. As Dr. Ornish observes, they're simply very expensive and traumatic "bandages."

Recently, some doctors have been using a new treatment for heart disease: antibiotics. Certain chronic infections increase risk of heart attack, so it didn't take long for doctors to try antibiotics in people recovering from heart attacks. A few pilot studies suggest that antibiotics help prevent second heart attacks.

RED FLAGS

Heart attacks are so common that everyone should recognize their symptoms and know how to respond to them.

◆ Pain, squeezing, pressure, or fullness in your chest that lasts more than a few minutes, or comes and goes

◆ Pain that spreads up to your neck or out to a shoulder or arm

◆ Sweating, light-headedness, shortness of breath, or nausea

Few heart attacks produce all these symptoms. The most frequent is persistent chest pain.

If you think you—or anyone—might be having a heart attack, get emergency medical help immediately. Call 911 and say, "Suspected heart attack." Give your name, address, and phone number, and then follow the operator's instructions.

If the person with the suspected heart attack can swallow without difficulty, give him an aspirin, says cardiologist Carl Pepine, M.D., professor in the College of Medicine at the University of Florida in Gainesville.

Hemorrhoids

In 1815, Napoleon's troops were trounced by the British and Prussians at Waterloo. How could a brilliant strategist like Napoleon go down to such stunning defeat? History is mum, but legend suggests that the one-time French emperor may have had something other than warfare on his mind. As the story goes, he was suffering from a particularly painful—and clearly ill-timed—bout of hemorrhoids.

Hemorrhoids are varicose veins that develop around or inside the anus. Three veins are responsible for draining blood away from the anal area, explains Anne Simons, M.D. Normally, these veins expand during bowel movements, then shrink afterward. But if you repeatedly strain while defecating, the veins become permanently swollen.

As the swelling triggers pain nerves in the anal area, you start hurting. The swelling also weakens blood vessels in the anal area, making

SIMPLE SOLUTIONS
1. Nutrition
2. Herbal Medicine
3. Home Remedies
4. Visualization
5. Homeopathy
6. Chinese Medicine
7. Ayurvedic Medicine
8. Naturopathy
9. Over-the-Counter Drugs
10. Medical Measures

them more likely to rupture when you move your bowels. You may notice faint pink streaks of blood when you wipe—or bright red blood in the toilet or on your underwear.

Having hemorrhoids makes you a member of an enormous, uncomfortable club. An estimated one-third of American adults—some 80 million people—develop hemorrhoids and the rectal pain and bleeding that go with them. For about 9 million Americans, hemorrhoids become a chronic problem, creating discomfort during ordinary activities such as sitting and walking. In fact, anything that causes tightening of the muscles in the anal area—even sneezing and laughing—can aggravate symptoms.

Most people who develop hemorrhoids also have another common ailment: constipation. "Constipation is the underlying cause of hemorrhoids," says Alan Gaby, M.D. "The low-fiber diet that so many Americans eat produces smaller, denser, harder stools, which are difficult to pass. You have to strain to pass them, and when you do, you get hemorrhoids."

As the risk of constipation increases with age, so does the risk of hemorrhoids. But diet isn't solely to blame. "Compared with younger adults, older adults tend to get less exercise and drink less fluid, both of which contribute to constipation," Dr. Simons explains. "What's more, older people generally lose rectal muscle tone over time. They have to strain more to move their bowels, which makes them more likely to develop hemorrhoids."

For especially severe hemorrhoids, mainstream M.D.'s may recommend surgery. Milder cases usually respond well to a combination of alternative therapies, home remedies, and over-the-counter drugs. You have plenty of treatment options from which to choose.

BEST CHOICES

Nutrition

Treat your veins berry well. Blueberries, blackberries, and cherries are rich in compounds that strengthen the walls of veins, including those in the anal area, says Joseph Pizzorno Jr., N.D. The stronger the veins become, the less likely they are to turn varicose. As a bonus, berries are high in fiber, which helps prevent constipation. Enjoy these fruits fresh, frozen, or canned.

Herbal Medicine

Wipe with witch hazel. According to James A. Duke, Ph.D., witch hazel is a soothing, cooling astringent that helps relieve hemorrhoid pain. In fact, it's the active ingredient in several over-the-counter hemorrhoid products, including Rantex Medicated Personal Cloth Wipes and Tucks Hemorrhoidal Pads. "But you don't have to spend extra for a brand-name product to benefit from witch hazel," he says. "Just buy witch hazel water in a drugstore and apply it to your hemorrhoids with a small cloth or cotton balls."

Allay pain with aloe. The gel inside the fleshy leaves of the aloe plant has astringent properties that help ease hemorrhoid pain, Dr. Duke says. In fact, the gel is such a versatile healer that you may want to consider keeping an aloe plant in your home. Then when you're bothered by hemorrhoids, just snip off a leaf, slit it open, and scoop out the gel. Apply it directly to the affected area.

If you don't have an aloe plant handy, you can use one of the commercial aloe gels that are sold in drugstores. Make sure that the label says "100 percent aloe gel" or something similar.

Buy a new broom. The root of butcher's broom, an herb native to the Mediterranean region, has a long history as a treatment for hemorrhoids. It remains a popular remedy in Europe, and with good reason. Butcher's broom contains compounds called ruscogenins, which reduce inflammation and help constrict distended veins.

Dr. Pizzorno suggests taking 100 milligrams of butcher's broom extract three times a day. Look for an extract that supplies 9 to 11 percent ruscogenins. If you can't find one in a health food store, check with a naturopath.

Sip kola. A medicinal herb that's native to India, gotu kola is a well-established hemorrhoid remedy. Dr. Pizzorno recommends taking 30 milligrams of gotu kola extract three times a day. Make sure that the extract you use contains 70 percent triterpenic acid, the compound that gives gotu kola its therapeutic powers. If you can't find such an extract in a health food store, you may be able to get one from a naturopath.

Get serious about psyllium. "Several studies have shown that bulk-forming fibers such as psyllium significantly reduce hemorrhoid pain, itching, and bleeding," Dr. Pizzorno says.

Psyllium is the active ingredient in many commercial laxatives, including Fiberall and Metamucil. You can use one of these products, following the package directions, or you can buy psyllium seed in a health food store. Dr. Duke suggests taking the herb three times a day, adding 3 to 5 teaspoons to water or juice. Whenever you take a dose of psyllium, be sure to drink at least one 8-ounce glass of water, too.

Home Remedies

Put your hemorrhoids on ice. Dr. Simons recommends treating swollen, inflamed hemorrhoids with an ice pack. The ice helps shrink swollen tissue, and the cold is soothing. To make your own ice pack, put some ice in a plastic bag and wrap the bag in a thin cloth. Apply the pack to the affected area for 20 minutes, then remove for 10 minutes before repeating. Continue this 20-minutes-on, 10-minutes-off cycle for as long as necessary.

Never put ice directly on your skin or leave it on for more than 20 minutes, Dr. Simons cautions. You could give yourself frostbite.

Control constipation. Because constipation is the leading cause of hemorrhoids, just taking steps to get things moving can keep you hemorrhoid-free. Above all else, eat a high-fiber diet featuring primarily whole grains, legumes, fruits, and vegetables.

Take care of business. The longer you sit on the toilet, the more stress you put on your anal veins—even if you're not straining to move your bowels. So enter the bathroom with a singular objective: to heed nature's call. Leave the newspaper and other reading materials outside.

Act natural. When you're on the toilet, try to relax and let things happen. Avoid straining or bearing down, advises Alan P. Brauer, M.D. Straining places considerable pressure on tender anal veins.

Squat when you sit. If you have trouble moving your bowels, try putting your feet on a small footstool when you sit on the toilet. You're in more of a squatting position, which helps many people go, Dr. Simons says.

Pick the right paper. Toilet paper often contains perfumes and dyes, which can irritate hemorrhoids. Stock unscented white paper in your own bathroom, and carry unscented white facial tissues to use when you're away from home. Also, always wipe with restraint.

Stretch your legs. Hemorrhoids are an occupational hazard of people whose jobs require them to sit for long periods. If you work sitting down, get up and walk around every hour or as often as you can, Dr. Gaby says.

Park your duff on a doughnut. For greater comfort while you're sitting, outfit your chair with an inflatable doughnut-shaped cushion.

OTHER GOOD CHOICES

Visualization

See 'em shrivel. For people with hemorrhoids, psychiatrist Gerald N. Epstein, M.D., director of the Academy of Integrative Medicine and Mental Imagery in New York City, recommends the following visualization exercise: Close your eyes and breathe deeply three times. While continuing to breathe deeply, see your hemorrhoids slowly shriveling up and disappearing. Picture your anal wall becoming smooth and healthy. Open your eyes. Practice this visualization for a minute or two every waking hour until your hemorrhoids heal.

Homeopathy

Attack from the inside or outside. A number of homeopathic medicines are effective treatments for hemorrhoids, says homeopath Dana Ullman. These include Aesculus, Hamamelis, Nux vomica, and Sulfur. Aesculus Hamamelis Collinsonia (AHC) is available as a topical ointment. Which of these will work best for you depends on your symptoms. Consult a homeopath.

Chinese Medicine

Cool off. Chinese medicine teaches that too much food in the gut causes an overaccumulation of Heat. When your Blood gets too hot, your anal veins swell and bleed to release the excess Heat.

Practitioners of Chinese medicine treat hemorrhoids with cooling foods, especially raw fruits and vegetables. In addition, they may prescribe cooling herbs such as rhubarb, skullcap root, coptis root, gardenia buds, and philodendron rhizome. Cooling beverages such as water, peppermint tea, and licorice tea can also help, says Efrem Korngold, O.M.D., L.Ac. To make the tea, add 1 to 2 teaspoons of dried peppermint or licorice leaves to 1 cup of boiled water. Steep for 10 minutes, then strain and drink.

Recharge your qi. For acupressure treatment, simply apply steady, penetrating finger pressure at each of the following points for 3 minutes.

◆ Governing Vessel 20, located on top of your head, where a line drawn from ear to ear would intersect with the midline of your body

◆ Stomach 36, located four finger-widths below your kneecap and one finger-width toward the outside of your shinbone

◆ Bladder 57, located in the middle of your calf, halfway between your knee crease and heel

◆ Large Intestine 11, located at the outer end of your elbow crease on the thumb side

If your hemorrhoids don't improve with acupressure treatment, consider consulting an acupuncturist instead. Professional needle stimulation of the same points may help when finger stimulation doesn't.

Ayurvedic Medicine

Defer to your dosha. In Ayurveda, the course of treatment for hemorrhoids is determined by your constitutional type, or dosha, explains David Frawley, O.M.D. For people with Vata doshas, he prescribes buttermilk, cumin, ginger, turmeric, and warm sesame oil. People with Pitta doshas often benefit from turmeric, barberry, and neem, but they should avoid members of the nightshade family, including tomatoes, potatoes, eggplant, and peppers. For people with Kapha doshas, treatment centers on ginger, bayberry, calamus, and pepper.

Swallow an unusual juice. Ayurvedic physicians recommend aloe juice as a stool-softening laxative. You can buy the juice in most health food stores. Follow the package directions for proper use. But experts caution against trying to make your own aloe juice. The leaves contain powerful compounds that can cause severe abdominal cramps.

Naturopathy

Spend some time submerged. Sitz baths, in which you immerse your posterior region in tolerably hot water, can relieve the discomfort of hemorrhoids and speed the healing process, Dr. Pizzorno says. He recommends taking 20-minute sitz baths a few times a day.

Over-the-Counter Drugs

Butter your butt. Cocoa butter soothes irritated hemorrhoids. It's an ingredient in several over-the-counter hemorrhoid products, including Anusol and Preparation H.

Numb the discomfort. Many over-the-counter hemorrhoid products—including Hemorid and Lanacane Creme—contain anesthetics. The problem with anesthetics is that some people are sensitive to them.

If you try a hemorrhoid product that's made with anesthetics and your itching or burning gets worse, stop using the product and try another remedy.

MEDICAL MEASURES

For severe hemorrhoids, surgical removal may be the only way to get relief. If you have only a few hemorrhoids and they're easily accessible, a procedure called rubber band ligation may work. The surgeon wraps special elastic bands around

Anal Itching: No Need to Scratch Surreptitiously

If you're bothered by anal itching, you undoubtedly have the urge to scratch. That's one of the worst things you can do, says Anne Simons, M.D. Scratching injures delicate anal skin, making matters worse. Instead, Dr. Simons suggests trying the following anti-itch strategies.

Keep clean. Wipe thoroughly, but no more than three times per bowel movement. Use white unscented toilet paper without perfumes or dyes. Moisten the paper with a little vegetable oil or mineral oil.

Skip scrubbing. In an effort to be squeaky clean, some people scrub the anal area with harsh soaps and rough washcloths. This actually contributes to irritation and itching. Wash your anal area gently.

Wear cotton undergarments. Cotton allows moisture to escape. If you're a woman who wears panty hose, choose a style with a cotton crotch panel.

Be alert to allergies. Many over-the-counter hemorrhoid products contain anesthetics, which trigger allergic reactions in some people. Stop using the product for a few weeks and see if the itching subsides.

Pamper with powder. Cornstarch can help keep your anal area dry and itch-free.

Resort to zinc oxide. Like cornstarch, zinc oxide may help keep your anal area dry. It also prevents chafing. Look for zinc oxide ointments in drugstores.

At bedtime, take an antihistamine. Anal itching is often worst at night. Over-the-counter antihistamines can help minimize nighttime itching and may help you sleep soundly.

If relief is elusive, see an M.D. Using some or all of the above measures, you should be able to clear up anal itching within a week or two. If not, give your doctor a call. The itching may be a symptom of some other medical problem such as psoriasis, a yeast infection, or anal fissures.

the hemorrhoids, which cuts off their blood supply. Eventually, they fall off. But they may come back if you continue to strain at stool because of constipation.

RED FLAGS

Consult your doctor immediately if you have hemorrhoids and you experience any of the following:

◆ Significant anal bleeding

◆ Dark blood in your stools

◆ Significant, persistent fecal incontinence, indicated by brown spots on your underwear

◆ Increased pain

Hepatitis

Literally translated, the word *hepatitis* means "liver inflammation." The disease itself takes several forms, some more serious than others. Left untreated, the most severe forms can progress to cirrhosis or liver cancer. That's why catching the disease early is so critical.

Your liver is your largest internal organ, and one of the most complex. It regulates the amount of fat, sugar, and protein that circulates in your blood. It also manufactures cholesterol, vitamin A, blood-clotting compounds, and bile, a fluid that helps digest fat. Finally, it detoxifies your blood, removing potentially harmful substances so that they can be eliminated from your body.

One substance synthesized by your liver is bilirubin, a compound formed during the breakdown of old red blood cells. In a healthy liver, bilirubin gets mixed with bile and passes into the small intestine on its way out of the body.

SIMPLE SOLUTIONS
1. Supplements
2. Herbal Medicine
3. Chinese Medicine
4. Ayurvedic Medicine
5. Home Remedies
6. Nutrition
7. Homeopathy
8. Medical Measures

A damaged liver can't filter out bilirubin as it should. As a result, the compound builds up in the blood and eventually gets deposited on the skin and eyes, turning them yellow. That's jaundice, a classic sign of liver disease.

Hepatitis can damage the liver and impede its ability to process bilirubin. While the disease is often associated with alcohol or drug abuse, it can also result from an immune system malfunction or even a viral infection.

The three most common forms of viral hepatitis are denoted by the letters A, B, and C. Here's how they differ from one another.

Hepatitis A. The most common viral liver disease in the United States, hepatitis A spreads through contaminated food or water. It often makes the rounds of day-care centers, where the virus is easily transmitted among children and staff through the handling of food and dirty diapers. The virus is also prevalent in areas with poor sanitation, posing a risk for international travelers who visit nonindustrialized locales.

Two to 3 weeks after getting infected with hepatitis A, you develop flulike symptoms as well as jaundice. Plus, your urine turns dark as it mixes with bile. If you take care of yourself by getting adequate rest and avoiding alcohol, your symptoms may completely disappear within 2 months. Hepatitis A does not cause cirrhosis, nor does it become chronic.

Hepatitis B. Like hepatitis A, hepatitis B produces flulike symptoms, jaundice, and dark urine. But the symptoms last longer and can damage the liver in ways that sometimes lead to cirrhosis or liver cancer.

Hepatitis B doesn't always produce recognizable symptoms. But even people who are infected but don't develop symptoms can pass the virus to others via blood-to-blood or sexual contact.

Because of blood-to-blood transmission, hepatitis B is a major occupational hazard among nurses and other health-care workers, who could accidentally get stuck by needles containing contaminated blood. And pregnant women who have hepatitis B can pass the infection to their babies.

Hepatitis C. Like hepatitis B, hepatitis C spreads via blood-to-blood and sexual contact. It may not cause symptoms for years after infection, maybe just a vague under-the-weather feeling. But within 10 years of infection, about 25 percent of people with hepatitis C develop cirrhosis, and 10 percent develop liver cancer.

All forms of viral hepatitis are to some degree preventable. For example, if you're traveling to a part of the world that has a high rate of hepatitis A or B, you can get immunized to protect yourself against the disease. You should also consider getting immunized against hepatitis B if you're at higher-than-normal risk for exposure to the virus. Among the highest-risk groups are health-care workers, people on kidney dialysis, people with infected sex partners, male homosexuals, and intravenous drug users.

If you've already been diagnosed with hepatitis, you should be under an M.D.'s care. And be sure to keep your doctor informed of any nonmainstream therapies that you decide to try. That said, don't overlook alternative medicine, which has its own sound strategies for hepatitis treatment. For hepatitis, as for so many conditions, a blended approach appears to work best.

BEST CHOICES

Supplements

Get enough selenium. In China, researchers distributed selenium-fortified table salt among the 21,000 residents of a town in Jiangsu, a province with a high rate of hepatitis B infection. By the second year of follow-up, the researchers recorded a 59 percent reduction in the rate of infection among the people who had been given selenium-fortified salt.

You won't find this special salt in the United States. But you can get all the selenium you need just by taking a supplement, according to Joseph Pizzorno Jr., N.D. Take a total of 200 micrograms of selenium a day.

Add extra E. Italian researchers have found that vitamin E may help resist hepatitis B infection. For that dose, take a vitamin E supplement. You can take up to 400 international units (IU) per day in supplement form.

Raise your C level. Large doses of vitamin C appear to alleviate the symptoms of viral hepatitis. Dr. Pizzorno suggests taking 10,000 milligrams a day until your symptoms subside.

Be gung-ho for glutathione. A powerful antioxidant protein, glutathione helps maintain a healthy liver. "In my experience, it's a good treatment for hepatitis," says Alan P. Brauer, M.D. Talk to your doctor about the appropriate dosage. You can buy glutathione supplements in health food stores.

Herbal Medicine

Give a thumbs-up to milk thistle. In 1968, German researchers identified three compounds that give milk thistle its liver-protecting powers. Collectively, the compounds are known as silymarin.

When German researchers gave people with viral hepatitis either silymarin or a placebo for 3 weeks, those taking the herb were more likely to show improved liver function. Other European studies have produced similar results.

If you want to try silymarin, check with your doctor first. You may need liver function tests while taking this herbal supplement.

Catch up on catechin. A compound isolated from the Asian herb pale catechu, catechin is a potent antioxidant that helps stimulate the immune system. "In several studies, catechin has been shown to decrease levels of bilirubin in people with all types of hepatitis," Dr. Pizzorno says. "It also speeds relief of hepatitis symptoms."

You won't find catechin in your health food store, so ask a naturopath for assistance and dosage information.

Ask a naturopath about licorice. According to Dr. Pizzorno, licorice root has both antiviral and anti-inflammatory properties. Several studies have shown that the herb helps treat hepatitis when given by injection.

Because the licorice must be administered intravenously by a health professional, it's not appropriate for home care. Consult a naturopath instead.

Chinese Medicine

Fill your diet with bitter greens. For people with hepatitis, Efrem Korngold, O.M.D., L.Ac., recommends eliminating all fats in favor of bitter greens such as spinach, chard, chicory, and beet greens. He also suggests eating Chinese lycii berries, which you can buy in Asian groceries. Eat them as you would any other berries.

Dr. Korngold also prescribes Xiao Chai Hu Tang, an herbal formula that's revered in China as a powerful liver medicine. It contains seven different herbs, all of which have anti-inflammatory and antiviral properties.

Stimulate healing. As part of hepatitis treatment, Dr. Korngold recommends acupuncture. If you prefer a self-care approach, you can stimulate the following points yourself using acupressure. Apply steady, penetrating finger pressure to each point for 3 minutes.

◆ Liver 3, situated on top of your foot in the webbing between your big toe and second toe

◆ Gallbladder 34, located below the knee on the outside of your leg, below the "bump" that's at the very top of your shinbone

◆ Stomach 36, located four finger-widths below your kneecap and one finger-width toward the outside of your shinbone

◆ Conception Vessel 12, located halfway between the end of your breastbone and your navel on the midline of your abdomen

Ayurvedic Medicine

Experiment with an Indian herb. The traditional Ayurvedic prescription for hepatitis is the herb bhumyamalaki (*Phyllanthus niruri*) or a close relative of this herb, *Phyllanthus amarus*. If you want to try *P. niruri* or *P. amarus* for yourself, consult an Ayurvedic practitioner or a naturopath.

Cirrhosis: Help for an Imperiled Liver

Normally, when liver cells die, the body replaces them. But once a liver becomes permanently damaged, its cells eventually stop regenerating. Instead, scar tissue and fatty deposits form and spread. That's cirrhosis.

Mainstream medicine has yet to develop a fully effective treatment for cirrhosis. So M.D.'s sometimes have to focus on managing the symptoms rather than curing the disease. On the other hand, alternative medicine offers several remedies that may slow or even stop the progression of cirrhosis. Here's what some alternative practitioners recommend in conjunction with standard medical care.

Make milk thistle your first choice. Several studies have shown that the herb milk thistle, which contains a mixture of medicinal compounds known as silymarin, can normalize liver function in people with cirrhosis.

If you want to try silymarin, check with your doctor first. You may need liver function tests while taking this herbal supplement.

Get a helping hand from Siberian ginseng. For people with drinking problems, giving up booze is a difficult but essential component of cirrhosis treatment. According to naturopath Donald Brown, N.D., professor of herbal medicine at Bastyr University in Kenmore, Washington, Siberian ginseng can help wean people off alcohol and help them stay "dry." He recommends taking 300 to 400 milligrams of a standardized Siberian ginseng root extract every day.

Stock up on nutrients. People with drinking problems usually develop nutritional deficiencies. Dr. Brown suggests taking a daily multivitamin/mineral supplement, along with 400 to 800 international units (IU) of vitamin E and 200 micrograms of chromium. But do not take more than 400 IU of vitamin E per day without a doctor's supervision.

Trim saturated fat. "A diet high in saturated fat aggravates alcohol-induced liver disease," says Joseph Pizzorno Jr., N.D. He suggests cutting back on meats and whole-milk dairy products, the main sources of saturated fat.

Home Remedies

Limit your liquor. Alcohol abuse is a leading cause of hepatitis. If you imbibe, do so only in moderation, limiting yourself to no more than one or two drinks a day, advises Thelma King Thiel, R.N., former president of the American Liver Foundation in Cedar Grove, New Jersey. A drink is defined as 12 ounces of beer, 5 ounces of wine, or a cocktail made with 1½ ounces of 80-proof distilled spirits.

Check your meds. Many medicines stress the liver. Among the primary offenders are antibiotics, steroids, supplemental estrogen, diabetes medications, anti-inflammatories, and acetaminophen in large doses. Of course, if you've been prescribed one of these drugs, you can't just stop taking it. Instead, talk to your doctor about pairing it with milk thistle to help protect your liver against medicine-induced damage.

OTHER GOOD CHOICES

Nutrition

See a weed in a whole new light. Research has proved that dandelion can help treat hepatitis. The plant has more vitamin A, a liver-protecting nutrient, than carrots. One hundred grams of dandelion greens or flowers supplies 14,000 IU of vitamin A. By comparison, 100 grams—about 4 ounces—of carrots provides just 11,000 IU.

"Dandelion greens taste bitter," acknowledges James A. Duke, Ph.D. "You can add them to salads if you like. But I prefer to steam the greens and flowers like spinach. Steamed dandelion isn't as bitter—in fact, I think it's delicious."

Homeopathy

Try a customized treatment. Homeopaths rely on a number of different medicines to treat hepatitis, says homeopath Dana Ullman. Among the most prescribed medicines are Aconitum, Belladonna, Chelidonium, Lycopodium, Mercurius, and Nux vomica. To find out which of these best suits your symptoms, consult a homeopath.

MEDICAL MEASURES

For a long time, mainstream M.D.'s didn't have much to offer people with hepatitis. The usual "prescription" was to get plenty of rest and avoid drugs and alcohol. But now physicians have another weapon in their anti-hepatitis arsenal—a prescription pharmaceutical called interferon (Infergen). So far, about half of the people who've tried interferon have gotten good results.

According to researchers at Pennsylvania State University in University Park, people with hepatitis C who don't respond to interferon may benefit from the antiviral drug amantadine (Symmetrel). Amantadine has traditionally been prescribed as a treatment for flu. Doctors hope that new antiviral drugs being developed to combat AIDS may also help treat hepatitis.

For the worst cases of hepatitis, the treatment of last resort is a liver transplant.

High Blood Pressure

About one in four Americans has high blood pressure, or hypertension. But only two-thirds of these people actually know about it, and only half are taking steps to control it. The main reason people ignore high blood pressure is that it causes no symptoms—until they collapse from a stroke or find out they have heart disease. No wonder that it's called a silent killer.

To understand how blood pressure works, imagine that your blood vessels are a closed system of interlocking garden hoses. The water flowing through the hoses is your blood, and it's circulated by a pump, your heart. Just as water pushes against the inside of a hose, your blood pushes against the inside of your blood vessels, exerting pressure.

Every time your heart beats, blood exerts extra pressure on your blood vessels. That's systolic pressure, the first, or top, number in a blood pressure reading. When your heart rests between beats, there's residual pressure inside your vessels. That's diastolic pressure, the second, or bottom, number in a blood pressure reading. These numbers are expressed as millimeters of mercury (mm Hg).

"Normal" blood pressure is 120/80. But that's misleading, says Anne Simons, M.D. Your blood pressure varies over the course of the day. When you wake up in the morning, it's on the low side. Then it rises as the day goes on. And if you exert yourself—say, running to catch an elevator or a bus—it spikes sharply.

Because blood pressure varies so much, the term *high blood pressure* refers to persistently high readings. One high reading is meaningless, especially if it

SIMPLE SOLUTIONS
1. Nutrition
2. Supplements
3. Exercise
4. Tai Chi and Qigong
5. Yoga
6. Meditation
7. Visualization
8. Biofeedback
9. Music Therapy
10. Social Support
11. Herbal Medicine
12. Chiropractic
13. Home Remedies
14. Chinese Medicine
15. Ayurvedic Medicine
16. Medical Measures

shows up during a doctor visit. (Doctor visits make many people anxious and can raise their blood pressures significantly.)

Until recently, physicians diagnosed blood pressure as high if it remained above 140/90 for a month or two. Now researchers have discovered that even readings in the high-normal range—from 130/85 to 139/89—can cause problems.

If you have high blood pressure but don't treat it for many years, it can contribute to a number of serious conditions, including atherosclerosis (hardening of the arteries), stroke, congestive heart failure, and kidney disease.

Anyone can develop high blood pressure, but some people are more susceptible to the condition than others. Men are more likely than women to develop high blood pressure, and a higher percentage of African-Americans than Whites have this problem.

You've probably heard that consuming too much sodium can raise your blood pressure. But you may not realize that consuming too little vitamin C, potassium, magnesium, or calcium can have the same effect.

"High blood pressure is one of the many diseases associated with our Western diet," says Joseph Pizzorno Jr., N.D. "The condition exists almost exclusively in developed countries. People living in remote areas of China, New Guinea, Brazil, and Africa show virtually no evidence of high blood pressure, nor do they experience a rise in blood pressure as they age. What's more, when members of these societies emigrate to less remote areas and adopt more 'civilized' diets, their risk of high blood pressure rises dramatically."

Researchers note that you have a higher risk if your family has a history of stroke or high blood pressure. You also have elevated risk if you are obese, if you drink excessively, or if you smoke.

To treat high blood pressure, mainstream doctors tend to rely on prescription medications. But many studies have shown that in cases where blood pressure is only mildly elevated (140/90 or lower), nondrug therapies work just as well.

"Few patients with (mild) high blood pressure require drug treatment," writes Edward D. Freis, M.D., of the Hypertension Clinic at the Veterans Administration Medical Center in Washington, D.C., in the *American Journal of Cardiology*. "There is little evidence that they will achieve enough benefit to justify the costs and adverse effects of drug treatment."

If you're diagnosed with high blood pressure and your doctor advises drug therapy, ask whether you could first try a nondrug approach combining dietary changes, exercise, and alternative remedies like those recommended below.

BEST CHOICES

Nutrition

DASH to a healthy diet. Throughout the 1980s and early 1990s, several studies found that vegetarians have lower blood pressure than meat eaters. Such research prompted Thomas Moore, M.D., associate clinical professor of medicine at Brigham and Women's Hospital in Boston, to launch a study called DASH, Dietary Approaches to Stop Hypertension.

Dr. Moore and other researchers around the country instructed 459 people with mildly high pressure to follow one of three diets. None of those eating high-fat diets showed decreases in their readings. But the people who followed near-vegetarian diets saw their systolic pressures drop by an average of six points, and their diastolic pressures by three points.

The results produced by the DASH diet rival those produced by any blood pressure medication. And there's a lot to be said for this near-vegetarian low-fat diet: In addition to lowering blood pressure, it can reduce your risk of heart disease, diabetes, osteoporosis, and several cancers.

Skimp on salt. Salt is sodium chloride. The more salt—actually, the more sodium—you consume, the more water your body retains, and the more fluid circulates in your blood vessels. This extra fluid raises your blood pressure.

Based on many studies, the National High Blood Pressure Education Program, an organization of researchers, recommends that Americans limit their sodium intakes to control their blood pressures. Your body needs no more than 2,000 milligrams of sodium a day. But most Americans consume twice that much.

In addition, some people with high blood pressure are salt-sensitive. This means that their blood pressure rises considerably when they consume even a small amount of sodium. These people should limit their sodium intakes to even less than 2,000 milligrams a day. Your doctor can help determine whether or not you're salt-sensitive.

To reduce your intake, read nutrition labels and steer clear of processed foods that are often high in sodium—especially canned soups, frozen dinners,

Check Your Pressure at Home

If your blood pressure tends to shoot up when you get to the doctor's office—the phenomenon known as white-coat hypertension—you're likely to get truer readings if you take your blood pressure yourself at home. In fact, home monitoring is a good idea for anyone with high blood pressure. If you take your blood pressure regularly at home, you can quickly detect elevated pressure and fine-tune your treatment program.

With home monitoring, your doctor may be able to reduce your dose of blood pressure medication. That's what happened in a European study that involved 419 people on blood pressure medications. Some of these people had their blood pressures monitored by doctors. The rest used home monitoring. After 6 months, 26 percent of the people who monitored their own blood pressures were able to stop taking their medications, compared with just 7 percent of the people whose pressures were monitored by doctors.

There are a host of electronic devices that are accurate and easy to use. You can buy home blood pressure devices in drugstores and medical supply houses as well as from mail-order catalogs. Ask your doctor to recommend a brand. Also, have your doctor check the calibration of the cuff annually.

and snack foods. And taste your food *before* you reach for the saltshaker. Your meal may not need as much salt as you think.

Pick foods with a proper sodium-potassium ratio. Sodium is only one of several minerals that affect your blood pressure. Another biggie is potassium, primarily because your body's sodium-potassium balance is crucial to blood pressure control. According to Michael T. Murray, N.D., a naturopath in Seattle, you should consume five times as much potassium as sodium to maintain normal blood pressure. Unfortunately, the typical American has that ratio reversed, consuming twice as much sodium as potassium.

Among the foods with the best potassium-to-sodium ratios are bananas (440:1), oranges (260:1), potatoes (110:1), apples (90:1), and carrots (75:1). If you want to control your blood pressure, eat more of these foods—and other fruits and vegetables as well.

"C" the difference. Another reason fruits and vegetables help reduce blood pressure is that they're high in vitamin C. To ensure that you're getting enough vitamin C, clinical nutritionist Shari Lieberman, Ph.D., recommends eating more C-rich foods: broccoli, bell peppers, cabbage, cauliflower, spinach, strawberries, and citrus fruits.

Go on a calcium kick. Calcium has complicated effects on your hormones, nervous system, and blood vessels, according to blood pressure specialists D. C. Hatton and D. A. McCarron of Oregon Health Sciences University in Portland. If you get enough of the mineral, your blood pressure stays low. If you don't, you risk developing high blood pressure.

To get more calcium in your diet, feast on low-fat and nonfat dairy products, salmon, sardines, shrimp, green leafy vegetables, and tofu.

Mind your magnesium intake. Magnesium plays a key role in the muscle tone of your blood vessels. If you get enough of the mineral, your blood vessels relax, which helps reduce your blood pressure, Dr. Lieberman explains. If your intake is low, your blood vessels can constrict or even go into spasm, which raises your blood pressure. Good food sources of magnesium include nuts, seeds, wheat germ, soybeans, seafood, dairy foods, and whole grains.

Make salmon your favorite fish. In addition to being a good source of calcium, salmon is rich in omega-3 fatty acids. Omega-3's may be known for cutting cholesterol, but they also help lower blood pressure, according to a review of more than 20 studies by Howard R. Knapp, M.D., Ph.D., assistant professor of medicine at Vanderbilt University in Nashville.

Dr. Simons suggests eating salmon or other cold-water fish such as mackerel or herring once or twice a week.

Crunch bunches of celery. Celery contains a compound called 3-n-butyl phthalide, which can lower blood pressure considerably. A very small amount does the trick in laboratory animals, reducing blood pressure by about 12 percent (and lowering cholesterol a bit as well). "I'm not surprised," says James A. Duke, Ph.D. "You can get the equivalent amount of the compound by munching about four average celery stalks."

Skimp on sugar. Several studies have shown that table sugar, or sucrose, raises blood pressure. If you have high blood pressure, avoid sugar as much as possible, recommends naturopath Enrico Liva, N.D., director of the Connecticut Center for Health in Middletown. Instead, satisfy your sweet tooth with fruit, which contains a different type of sugar called fructose.

Supplements

Take potassium in pills. Potassium supplementation is especially important if you're on diuretic blood pressure medications, because these drugs deplete your potassium supply. Because of potential side effects, speak with your doctor to see if potassium supplementation is necessary for your condition.

Add magnesium to the mix. At Erasmus University in Rotterdam, Netherlands, researchers gave 91 women with high blood pressure either a magnesium supplement or a placebo (a fake pill) for 6 months. Compared with the placebo takers, the magnesium takers' blood pressure readings fell by an average of three points systolic and three points diastolic. Dr. Lieberman recommends taking between 500 and 750 milligrams of magnesium a day.

Include calcium, too. In studies, calcium helped to reduce the systolic reading by 10 points and the diastolic reading by 25 points. Dr. Pizzorno recommends taking up to 1,500 milligrams of calcium a day.

Don't forget fish oil. If you don't care for salmon or other cold-water fish, you can get your omega-3 fatty acids by taking fish oil. Dr. Murray suggests taking one tablespoon (about 4 grams) of fish oil a day.

Exercise

Get fit to defeat high blood pressure. According to Stephen Fortmann, M.D., deputy director of the Center for Research in Disease Prevention at Stanford University, exercise can help lower your blood pressure mainly by helping you slim down. But even if you don't lose weight, exercise can lower your blood pressure. That's what investigators at the Cooper Institute for Aerobics Research in Dallas discovered when they studied 56 sedentary people with mild high blood pressure. Twelve of these people remained sedentary, while the rest began walking for an hour three times a week. After 16 weeks, the nonexercisers showed no change in their blood pressure readings. But the exercisers' average reading dropped from 146/94 to 134/87, even though they didn't lose weight.

Exercise also helps reduce stress, which often contributes to high blood pressure. By engaging in regular physical activity, such as brisk walking, you stimulate the release of your body's natural tranquilizers, called endorphins. That's why exercise feels calming. And if you're already taking blood pressure medication, exercise can help you reduce your dosage—and maybe even help you get off the drugs completely.

If you have high blood pressure, do at least a daily half-hour of endurance-building exercise at least three times a week, recommends Alfred Bove, M.D., chief of cardiology at Temple University School of Medicine in Philadelphia.

Tai Chi and Qigong

Try tai chi. At Johns Hopkins School of Medicine in Baltimore, Deborah Young, Ph.D., assistant professor of internal medicine, enrolled 62 older people with high blood pressure in either a brisk walking program or a less strenuous tai chi class.

Tai chi lowered blood pressure almost as much as brisk walking, even though tai chi feels like less of a workout.

Consider qigong. Chinese researchers taught a qigong routine to 244 people with very high blood pressure—average reading, 175/108 mm Hg. Some of the people made qigong practice a regular ritual. Some practiced the exercises only from time to time. And some gave up qigong completely.

Twenty years later, the researchers counted how many of the study participants had died from stroke, whose major risk factor is high blood pressure. Among the qigong dropouts, 42 percent had died of stroke. Among those who practiced qigong occasionally, 29 percent had died of stroke. But among people who practiced qigong regularly, only 11 percent had died of stroke.

Yoga

Strike a pose for low pressure. Indian researchers taught a yoga routine to 25 people with high blood pressure. The participants were encouraged to practice the routine two or three times a day. After 6 months, their average blood pressure fell from 153/103 mm Hg to 139/90 mm Hg.

Meditation

Before you medicate, meditate. Stress constricts your blood vessels and simultaneously makes your heart beat harder. This sends your blood pressure soaring. But relaxation dilates your blood vessels, calms your heart, and decreases your levels of stress hormones. In this way, it helps bring your blood pressure back to normal.

In the late 1960s, Harvard cardiologist Herbert Benson, M.D., was intrigued when people who practiced transcendental meditation (TM) claimed they could lower their blood pressures at will by meditating. In a series of studies, Dr. Benson proved the claims to be true.

His research eventually led him to develop a version of meditation called the relaxation response. This relaxation technique involves 20 minutes of deep breathing, during which you close your eyes, empty your mind, and focus on a single word or phrase (what practitioners of classic Indian meditation and TM call a mantra). Dr. Benson has found that when people with stress-induced high blood pressure practice the relaxation response, they can lower their blood pressures significantly.

Visualization

See your blood pressure falling. Visualization exercises are another relaxation technique that can lower your blood pressure. Gerald N. Epstein, M.D., director of the Academy of Integrative Medicine and Mental Imagery in New York City, suggests this exercise: Close your eyes and breathe deeply. Imagine opening your freezer and removing several ice cubes. Imagine slowly rubbing your head, face, and neck with the ice. Feel the coolness seeping through your skin and into your bloodstream. Envision an icy feeling tumbling from your head to your toes. Open your eyes. Practice this exercise two or three times a day.

Biofeedback

Dial down your pressure. Biofeedback can teach you to lower your blood pressure quickly and easily in just a few months. The biofeedback trainer attaches electrodes to various parts of your body and hooks them up to a visual meter. As you tense your muscles, the meter dial moves in one direction; as you relax your muscles, the dial moves the other way. You breathe deeply and focus on moving the needle into the deep relaxation zone.

Music Therapy

Mellow out with music. As long ago as 1929, when radio and phonographs were still novelties, two researchers showed that listening to music could help reduce blood pressure. In a more recent study, researchers found that those who listened to music were less stressed than those who practiced the relaxation response, suggesting that music may be even more relaxing than meditation.

What sort of music should you listen to? Whatever you like that's light, soft, and not too rhythmic, according to Andrew T. Weil, M.D., director of the program in integrative medicine at the University of Arizona College of Medicine in Tucson.

Social Support

Talk to the animals. Many studies have shown that human-pet interactions—playing with a dog, holding a cat, gazing at fish in a tank—can have a profoundly positive effect on blood pressure.

Of course, some people don't care for dogs or are allergic to them. But if a dog or another animal holds a special place in your heart, your pet may be helping you in ways you may not have imagined.

Herbal Medicine

Root for garlic. You may already know about garlic's cholesterol-lowering properties. As it turns out, this odoriferous bulb can also lower blood pressure. Dr. Duke recommends consuming the equivalent of one clove of garlic a day. "If you cook with garlic, getting that much should be a snap," he says. Garlic's close botanical relatives—onions, scallions, leeks, chives, and shallots—can also lower blood pressure. They don't pack garlic's punch, but they help.

Seek help from hawthorn. Hawthorn helps reduce blood pressure by dilating the coronary arteries, the ones that feed your heart. Dr. Liva recommends taking 100 to 240 milligrams of a standardized hawthorn extract three times a day.

If you are currently on medication for high blood pressure, check with your doctor before taking hawthorn. You may need your medication dosage adjusted.

Chiropractic

Adjust to lower blood pressure. At the Canadian Memorial Chiropractic College in Toronto, R. G. Yates, D.C., and colleagues divided 21 people with high blood pressure into three groups. One group received chiropractic adjustment. Another group received treatment that mimicked chiropractic adjustment but wasn't the real thing. The third group received no treatment at all. Among those who got sham treatment or no treatment, blood pressure did not change. But among those who got chiropractic, blood pressure decreased significantly.

Home Remedies

Maintain a healthy weight. Studies have shown that to reduce blood pressure quickly without drugs, nothing beats weight loss. In these studies, the people who lost 10 pounds saw their diastolic pressures drop as much as three points. No wonder the National High Blood Pressure Education Program urges people with high blood pressure to lose weight by eating a low-fat diet and engaging in regular moderate exercise.

Snuff out the butts. The nicotine in cigarettes constricts your blood vessels, which in turn elevates your blood pressure. So if you smoke, quit.

Drink in moderation. Research has shown that a little alcohol—up to two drinks a day for men and one for women—can reduce heart attack risk by raising levels of high-density lipoproteins (HDL), the "good" cholesterol. But if you drink more than that, you're more likely to develop high blood pressure and, eventually, heart disease. The National High Blood Pressure Education Program recommends limiting alcohol consumption to no more than one drink a day. A drink equals 12 ounces of beer, 5 ounces of wine, or a cocktail made with 1½ ounces of 80-proof distilled spirits.

Go easy on caffeine. As every java junkie knows, caffeine is a powerful stimulant. Shortly after drinking a cup or two, your blood pressure rises. But there's conflicting evidence on the long-term effects of regular coffee consumption. Most studies show that if you habitually drink up to a few cups of coffee a day, you become tolerant of the caffeine, and your blood pressure returns to normal.

But many people with high blood pressure seem particularly sensitive to the pressure-raising effects of caffeine. If you have high blood pressure, many alternative practitioners, including Dr. Liva, recommend reducing your intake of caffeine by minimizing your consumption of coffee, tea, cola, cocoa, and chocolate.

OTHER GOOD CHOICES

Chinese Medicine

Nourish your yin. Efrem Korngold, O.M.D., L.Ac., treats high blood pressure with formulas that contain yin-nourishing, Liver-regulating herbs. These include gastrodia rhizome, polygonum, and leonurus leaf.

Direct pressure downward. You can also lower your blood pressure with acupressure. Simply apply steady, penetrating finger pressure to each of the following points for 3 minutes.

◆ Liver 3, situated on top of your foot in the webbing between your big toe and second toe

◆ Governing Vessel 20, located on top of your head, where a line drawn from ear to ear would intersect with the midline of your body

◆ Spleen 6, located four finger-widths above your inner anklebone on the back inner border of your shinbone

Ayurvedic Medicine

Rebalance your Vata. Ayurvedic practitioners view high blood pressure as primarily a Vata disorder, according to Virender Sodhi, M.D. (Ayurveda), N.D., professor at Bastyr University in Kenmore, Washington.

To treat high blood pressure, Dr. Sodhi recommends daily meditation. He also advocates dietary changes that include eating more fruits and vegetables, especially garlic and onions, and less salt and saturated fat. And he prescribes an array of Ayurvedic herbs, such as sarpagandha, arjuna, and ashwagandha.

MEDICAL MEASURES

If nondrug approaches don't reduce your blood pressure sufficiently, your doctor may prescribe blood pressure medication. There are many different kinds of antihypertensive drugs. They all lower blood pressure, but they also cause side effects—and you may have to take them for life. The most widely prescribed blood pressure medications are diuretics, beta-blockers, calcium channel blockers, and ACE inhibitors.

Diuretics. These drugs work by speeding the elimination of water from your body. Less water means less fluid in your blood vessels, which lowers your blood pressure. Diuretics also promote the elimination of salt in your urine.

Beta-blockers. These medications slow your heart so that it beats less forcefully. Less force means lower blood pressure.

Calcium channel blockers. By stopping calcium from entering your cells, these drugs open your blood vessels and reduce the force of your heart's contractions.

ACE inhibitors. These medications keep your body from making angiotensin, a compound that increases the fluid volume of your blood and constricts your blood vessels. ACE inhibitors reduce your blood volume and dilate your blood vessels.

All of these drugs may produce side effects, though calcium channel blockers and ACE inhibitors cause fewer side effects than diuretics or beta-blockers.

Keep in mind that while medications can control high blood pressure, they don't cure it. Whichever drug you're prescribed, you may have to take it for life. If you stop taking it, your blood pressure may soar.

"Even if you must take blood pressure medication, don't stop using the nondrug approaches," urges Alan Gaby, M.D. "Drugs are no substitute for the diet and lifestyle therapies that control blood pressure."

High Cholesterol

Cholesterol has a nasty reputation as a major risk factor for heart disease. But wait a minute: It's not all bad. In fact, the waxy substance is vital to your life and health. Without it, your body can't make sex hormones or the bile acids that help you digest fats. Cholesterol is also a major component of your cell membranes.

The bad part is *overdosing* on that waxy stuff. It takes only a little cholesterol—very little—to meet all of your body's needs. And your liver makes just enough. As soon as you start eating foods that contain cholesterol, you're at risk for having too much.

All that extra cholesterol gets processed by your liver and sent out into your bloodstream attached to low-density lipoprotein (LDL) molecules. That's why LDLs are called bad cholesterol. When your LDLs are high, you have lots of cholesterol floating around in your blood.

SIMPLE SOLUTIONS
1. Nutrition
2. Supplements
3. Exercise
4. Relaxation Therapies
5. Herbal Medicine
6. Home Remedies
7. Chinese Medicine
8. Ayurvedic Medicine
9. Medical Measures

High-density lipoprotein (HDL) molecules, on the other hand, pluck cholesterol out of your blood and return it to your liver for elimination. That's why HDLs are called good cholesterol. The higher your HDLs, the more excess cholesterol gets swept out of your blood.

As LDLs—and their relatives, the very low density lipoproteins (VLDLs)—circulate in your blood, much of their cholesterol load gets incorporated into pimplelike deposits that develop along the walls of your arteries. These deposits, or plaques, narrow your arteries and impair blood flow. Once your arteries become significantly narrowed, you're at risk for serious health problems: heart attack, stroke, congestive heart failure, angina, high blood pressure, impotence, and intermittent claudication (impaired blood flow in the legs).

According to the American Heart Association, almost half of American adults have cholesterol levels higher than 200 mg/dl (milligrams per deciliter of blood), the top end of the official desirable range. About 18 percent have cholesterol levels higher than 240, which make them candidates for heart attack.

Lowering your cholesterol can have a big impact on your risk of heart attack and other cholesterol-related conditions. For every 1 percent drop in your total cholesterol, your chances of having a heart attack fall by 2 to 3 percent. And for every 1 percent increase in your HDLs, your risk drops by about 3 percent.

There are two basic approaches to cutting cholesterol: lifestyle modifications and drugs. A combination of the two may provide the fastest results. "Aggressive treatment of elevated cholesterol prevents heart attacks, slows atherosclerosis, and saves lives," says James Cleeman, M.D., coordinator of the National Cholesterol Education Program, a project of the National Heart, Lung, and Blood Institute of the National Institutes of Health in Bethesda, Maryland.

BEST CHOICES

Nutrition

Minimize animal products. Oxford University epidemiologist Robert Clarke, M.D., analyzed 395 studies of the relationship between diet and blood cholesterol. His conclusion: If you replace 60 percent of saturated fat with polyunsaturated fat and eliminate 60 percent of dietary cholesterol, your total cholesterol would fall by 10 to 15 percent. The chief dietary sources of saturated fat and cholesterol are meats and whole-milk dairy products.

Avoid margarine. Many Americans believe that margarine is healthier than butter. In fact, the opposite is true. To make margarine, manufacturers add hydrogen to vegetable oils, a process that creates trans fatty acids. Research has shown that trans fatty acids raise LDLs and lower HDLs.

"Butter is better than margarine, but both should be restricted," says Joseph E. Pizzorno Jr., N.D. As an alternative, he recommends using canola, safflower, or olive oil.

Enjoy fish twice a week. The American Heart Association recommends fish as an excellent source of lean protein and omega-3 fatty acids, which can help lower your cholesterol. For cholesterol control and general heart health, make fish your main dish twice a week, advises William Connor, M.D., professor of medicine at the Oregon Health Sciences University in Portland. Cold-water species such as salmon, mackerel, and halibut are the best sources of omega-3's. But make sure that it's broiled, baked, or steamed—not fried or drowned in butter.

Look beyond oat bran. In the late 1980s, a highly publicized study showed that eating oat bran—a soluble fiber found in oatmeal—can lower cholesterol by spurring its elimination from the body in bile. "But any and probably all plant fibers lower cholesterol," says James A. Duke, Ph.D. He recommends eating plenty of fiber-rich whole grains, beans, fruits, and vegetables.

Eat an apple a day. Apple pulp is rich in pectin, a soluble plant fiber. One apple a day can cut your total cholesterol by around 5 percent, Dr. Pizzorno says. Other good sources of pectin include carrots, pears, oranges, and grapefruit.

Cut cholesterol with carotenoids. Red, orange, and yellow fruits and vegetables get their vibrant colors from carotenoids, compounds in the vitamin A family. Carotenoids are potent antioxidants that help protect your heart. "Many studies show that as fruit and vegetable consumption increases, risk of heart attack and stroke decreases," Dr. Pizzorno says.

Experiment with soy. "Soy foods definitely help lower cholesterol," says Alan P. Brauer, M.D. "But you have to eat at least an ounce a day." That's not difficult: Just add cubed or shredded tofu to the dishes you ordinarily make.

Eat a heart-healthy breakfast. According to the second National Health and Nutrition Examination Study (NHANES-II), skipping breakfast is associated with high cholesterol levels. Of course, a breakfast of bacon and eggs can also boost your cholesterol into the danger zone. "But for most people, breakfast is the meal that's easiest to transform into a cholesterol-lowering experience," says Anne Simons, M.D. "Just eat a whole-grain cereal or bread with some fruit."

Supplements

Oil your arteries. If you're not fond of fish, you can get omega-3 fatty acids from fish oil or flaxseed oil. According to Seattle naturopath Michael T. Murray, N.D., flaxseed oil is a better choice because the effective, cholesterol-lowering dose is just 1 tablespoon a day. With fish oil, you need a great deal more.

Benefit from niacin. One of the B vitamins, niacin lowers cholesterol by reducing the liver's production of VLDLs, the chemical building blocks of LDLs. "Niacin is especially useful for people like me, who have a stubborn hereditary predisposition to high cholesterol," says clinical nutritionist Shari Lieberman, Ph.D. "Using diet and exercise only, I was able to lower my cholesterol from 270 to 245. Now that I've added extra niacin to my program, my cholesterol stays at or below 200."

The effective dose of niacin ranges from 250 to 1,800 milligrams a day, well above the Daily Value of 20 milligrams. In such high doses, the vitamin causes flushing, a sudden, uncomfortable feeling of heat and discomfort similar to a menopausal hot flash. So you need to check with your doctor before supplementing with doses above 35 milligrams.

Pop pills of pantethine. Pantethine is the most active form of pantothenic acid, a B vitamin that helps your body digest fats and interferes with your liver's production of cholesterol. Dr. Lieberman recommends taking 300 milligrams of pantethine three times a day.

Raise your C level. Vitamin C helps increase your supply of HDLs, which lower your risk of heart attack, says Melvyn R. Werbach, M.D., assistant clinical professor at the University of California, Los Angeles, School of Medicine. For the most benefit, you need to take 2,000 milligrams of vitamin C a day. You may want to combine your supplements with a soluble fiber source, such as oat bran or pectin, to help your HDLs eliminate cholesterol.

For extra protection, add E. According to Alan Gaby, M.D., vitamin E

Therapies on Double Duty

Low-density lipoproteins (LDLs) carry cholesterol out of your liver and into your bloodstream, where it contributes to the narrowing of your arteries. High-density lipoproteins (HDLs) return cholesterol to your liver, where it gets incorporated into bile and leaves the body.

You might think that if LDLs go down (less cholesterol going out), HDLs should go down as well (less cholesterol out there to come back). But James Cleeman, M.D., coordinator of the National Cholesterol Education Program, a project of the National Heart, Lung, and Blood Institute of the National Institutes of Health in Bethesda, Maryland, explains that the relationship between LDLs and HDLs is not so simple. In addition to transporting cholesterol, HDLs have other functions. Your HDL level is independent of your LDL level. Therapies that simultaneously lower LDLs and raise HDLs do so by affecting the various biochemical processes that lead to the synthesis of both of them. They shift the balance of lipoprotein production away from LDLs and toward HDLs, so you wind up with less bad cholesterol and more good.

Should You Lower Your Cholesterol?

Unfortunately, there is no simple way to determine if your cholesterol levels are too high. The National Cholesterol Education Program, part of the National Institutes of Health, determines dangerously high cholesterol levels and treatment recommendations based not only on your cholesterol reading but also on heart disease risk factors and history of cardiovascular disease. Take a look below to see if you fall into one of the categories.

You are at high risk for a heart attack or stroke if your level of low-density lipoprotein (LDL) cholesterol is:

◆ 130 or greater and you have been diagnosed with cardiovascular disease

◆ 160 or greater and you presently have two or more heart disease risk factors, such as high blood pressure, diabetes, family history, smoking, obesity, or sedentary lifestyle

◆ 190 or higher

If you fall into the high-risk category, ask your doctor about cholesterol-lowering drugs as well as a diet and exercise regimen that's best suited for you.

You are borderline high risk if your level of LDL cholesterol is:

◆ 100 or higher and you've been diagnosed with cardiovascular disease

◆ 130 or higher and you have two or more of the heart disease risk factors mentioned above

◆ 160 or higher

If you fall into this borderline high-risk category, your doctor will probably forgo the drugs and place you on a strict diet and exercise regimen.

may offer the greatest protection against high cholesterol because it speeds the breakdown of LDLs while simultaneously increasing HDLs. "Several large studies have demonstrated that blood vitamin E levels may be better predictors of future heart attack than total cholesterol levels," he says.

Exercise

Stay one step ahead of high cholesterol. Any type of exercise improves your cholesterol profile, according to William L. Haskell, Ph.D., professor of cardiovascular medicine and deputy director of the Center for Research on Disease Prevention at Stanford University School of Medicine. It's especially good for shifting your LDL/HDL balance by lowering levels of LDLs and raising levels of HDLs.

Relaxation Therapies

Aim for less stress. Stress is a well-documented risk factor for heart attack. It doesn't raise cholesterol directly. "But when some people are under stress, they console themselves by eating fatty foods, cutting back on exercise, and generally veering away from a healthy lifestyle to a lifestyle that raises cholesterol," Dr. Cleeman says.

Martin L. Rossman, M.D., urges everyone to adopt a daily stress-management routine. Practice whatever relaxation technique appeals to you—meditation, visualization, music therapy, massage, tai chi, or yoga.

Herbal Medicine

Be generous with garlic. Dozens of studies have demonstrated that garlic lowers cholesterol. How much of the herb do you need? The studies used anywhere from 1 to 10 cloves a day. Commission E, the German expert panel that evaluates the safety and effectiveness of herbal medicines, recommends 4 grams of fresh garlic a day—that's 2 to 4 average-size cloves.

For an odorless alternative, try garlic supplements. In one study, 23 men with heart disease who took 300 milligrams of a popular deodorized supplement every day had significantly lower cholesterol within 3 weeks.

Salute psyllium. Rich in soluble fiber, psyllium is the main ingredient in the bulk-forming laxative Metamucil. It also helps lower cholesterol. Dr. Simons recommends taking 1 tablespoon of Metamucil three times a day, at mealtimes. Be sure to drink at least 8 ounces of water along with it.

Get acquainted with gugulipid. An extract of the Indian mukul myrrh tree, gugulipid contains a compound called guggulsterone that lowers cholesterol by stimulating the liver to break down LDLs. A few studies suggest that after 3 months or so, gugulipid can cut total cholesterol by about 20 percent, reduce LDLs by 30 percent, and raise HDLs by about 18 percent. Look for gugulipid

Keeping Tabs on Cholesterol

In general, the same foods that are high in dietary fat are also high in dietary cholesterol. That makes eating a low-fat, low-cholesterol diet a little bit easier. The following chart compares the cholesterol contents of various foods, based on 100-gram (3½-ounce) servings.

Food	Cholesterol (mg)
Liver	354
Butter	219
Cream cheese	110
Lard	95
Beef	70
Lamb	70
Pork	63
Chicken	60
Eggs	59
Ice cream	45
Fruits	0
Grains	0
Legumes	0
Nuts	0
Seeds	0
Vegetable oils	0
Vegetables	0

supplements that contain 25 milligrams of guggulsterone per pill, Dr. Pizzorno says. Take 500 milligrams three times a day.

Find fenugreek. Rich in soluble fiber, fenugreek seeds are widely used as a condiment in India. The seeds taste like an odd combination of bitter celery and maple syrup. If you like their flavor, try adding them to soups, salads, and sauces.

Home Remedies

Lift a glass to lower cholesterol. Several studies have shown that moderate alcohol consumption can raise HDL levels by 7 to 10 percent. Even a modest increase in HDLs means major protection against heart attack, the nation's leading killer.

Of course, alcohol has its downside, too. It can be addictive, and excessive consumption can raise your risk of liver disease and several types of cancer. Many experts agree: If you don't drink, don't start. If you do drink, do so in moderation. That means one drink a day for women, two for men. A drink is defined as 12 ounces of beer, 5 ounces of wine, or a cocktail made with 1½ ounces of 80-proof distilled spirits.

Drink filtered coffee. Unfiltered coffee contains large amounts of cafestol and kahweol, both of which raise cholesterol. By using paper filters, you remove most of these compounds. Both the Nurses' Health Study and the Health Professionals' Follow-Up Study, which together involve more than 100,000 people, have found no evidence that drinking as many as five cups of filtered coffee a day significantly raises cholesterol. And don't worry about instant coffee: Its processing removes cafestol and kahweol.

Kick the cigarette habit. Smoking lowers HDLs and is considered a major risk factor for heart disease. So if you smoke, make every effort to quit.

OTHER GOOD CHOICES

Chinese Medicine

Prevent phlegm. Practitioners of Chinese medicine attribute high cholesterol to excess mucus brought on by a diet too rich in fatty, greasy foods. "Greasy foods generate Heat," explains Efrem Korngold, O.M.D., L.Ac. "Heat dries Moisture in your body and increases phlegm to the point where it congeals as deposits on your arteries."

To lower cholesterol, Dr. Korngold prescribes herbs that prevent deposits, improve circulation, and clear Heat. The herb of choice is pseudoginseng root, but sage root, borneol crystals, and tea also help. "The Chinese always drink lots of tea when they eat fried foods because it promotes circulation and helps clear Heat, which keeps the blood vessels healthy," he says.

Nudge your cholesterol with needles. Acupuncture can also help lower cholesterol, Dr. Korngold says. But it must be administered by a professional acupuncturist. If you prefer a self-care approach, try acupressure instead. Apply steady, penetrating finger pressure for 3 minutes to each of the following points.

◆ Stomach 36, located four finger-widths below your kneecap and one finger-width toward the outside of your shinbone

◆ Large Intestine 11, located at the outer end of your elbow crease on the thumb side

◆ Gallbladder 34, located on the outside of your leg, below and in front of the head of your shinbone

◆ Liver 3, situated on top of your foot in the webbing between your big toe and second toe

Ayurvedic Medicine

Try Ayurvedic herbs. To treat high cholesterol, Ayurvedic physicians prescribe a high-fiber diet and a number of herbs, including garlic, fenugreek, and gugulipid. Vasant Lad, B.A.M.S., M.A.Sc., director of the Ayurvedic Institute in Albuquerque, New Mexico, also recommends cinnamon and trikatu (a mixture of ginger and two kinds of peppers). If you want to try trikatu, talk to an Ayurvedic practitioner.

MEDICAL MEASURES

Today, an estimated 5 percent of American adults take cholesterol-lowering medication. There are three major types of cholesterol-lowering drugs. Each has advantages and disadvantages, and each is appropriate for some people but not others.

Statins, the most popular class of drugs, interfere with the action of an enzyme involved in cholesterol synthesis in the liver. Bile acid sequestrants act in the digestive tract to prevent the release of cholesterol into the bloodstream. Gemfibrozil (Lopid) is usually prescribed only when triglycerides are very high. All of these have side effects.

Cholesterol-lowering drugs may be prescribed individually or in combination. Some physicians combine them with niacin. They also work much better if you eat a low-fat, low-cholesterol diet and exercise regularly.

Hyperthyroidism

In 1991, when First Lady Barbara Bush began looking slimmer, the gossip columnists speculated that she had adopted some miracle diet or had begun working out with a personal trainer or both. The White House promptly issued curt denials.

Then Mrs. Bush's face began looking different . . . something about her eyes. They seemed larger and the skin around them looked puffy.

Concerned, Mrs. Bush paid a visit to the White House doctor. He diagnosed Grave's disease, an autoimmune disorder that's the most common cause of an overactive thyroid gland, or hyperthyroidism.

Your thyroid is a butterfly-shaped gland whose "wings" nestle on either side of your windpipe, just below your Adam's apple. The thyroid plucks iodine from your blood and uses it to make two hormones, called triiodothyronine (T_3) and thyroxine (T_4). These hormones regulate an enormous number of body processes, including your metabolism—that is, the rate at which your body uses food to produce energy.

SIMPLE SOLUTIONS
1. Visualization
2. Home Remedies
3. Nutrition
4. Herbal Medicine
5. Homeopathy
6. Chinese Medicine
7. Naturopathy
8. Medical Measures

In hyperthyroidism, the pituitary gland in your brain spurs your thyroid to make more of its hormones, which in turn speeds up your metabolism. You feel hungrier than usual, but oddly, you lose weight. Your heart races. You feel warm, and you sweat more. You're nervous, and your hands may shake. You have more frequent bowel movements, along with possible diarrhea, fatigue, and muscle weakness. And if you have Grave's disease, which causes about 85 percent of all cases of hyperthyroidism, you're more likely to have teary eyes. Your eyeballs are also likely to protrude and may redden easily.

Some women who have hyperthyroidism notice that their menstrual periods are lighter and less frequent.

Usually, hyperthyroidism affects adults in their twenties or older, says

Lawrence C. Wood, M.D., president and medical director of the Thyroid Foundation of America in Boston. While anyone can develop the condition, it's 5 to 10 times more common in women than in men, according to endocrinologist Laird D. Madison, M.D., Ph.D., of the Center for Endocrinology, Diabetes, and Molecular Medicine at Northwestern University in Chicago. The American College of Physicians urges doctors to test every woman over age 50 for hyperthyroidism every 5 years.

Scientists have identified several risk factors for hyperthyroidism. You may be at greater risk of hyperthyroidism if you're a smoker or if you've recently had stressful experiences. Your family history may also be a factor. If you had head or neck x-rays during childhood or if you have an autoimmune disorder such as rheumatoid arthritis, you may be at higher risk for hyperthyroidism.

Also, new mothers should be on the lookout for possible thyroid problems. Giving birth sometimes alters levels of thyroid hormones.

If you're at risk for hyperthyroidism, or if you're displaying any symptoms of the condition, your doctor may recommend diagnostic tests.

If you've been diagnosed with hyperthyroidism, your doctor has probably put you on a prescription medication. Pharmaceuticals are the first line of treatment, and they do an excellent job of controlling thyroid problems. While alternative therapies usually cannot reverse hyperthyroidism by themselves, they may help when combined with mainstream therapies, says Joseph Pizzorno Jr., N.D.

BEST CHOICES

Visualization

Calm your spirit. According to Dr. Pizzorno, stress control is the single most important thing you can do on your own to normalize your thyroid function.

The following visualization technique is recommended by Gerald N. Epstein, M.D., director of the Academy of Integrative Medicine and Mental Imagery in New York City.

Close your eyes and take three breaths. See yourself becoming very tall, with your long arms reaching up to the sun. Take a piece of sun in your hands and place it on your lower throat. Visualize golden rays of light streaming around your body. See red and blue beams of light crisscrossing in your thyroid, helping it function normally. Sense a channel of red light guiding hormone flow from your pituitary gland to your thyroid. When the red and blue lights move evenly and smoothly between your pituitary gland and thyroid, feel your thyroid functioning well. Exhale and open your eyes.

Home Remedies

Toss tobacco. Smoking raises your risk of hyperthyroidism. So if you smoke, quit.

Cut your caffeine intake. When you feel overstimulated by an overactive thyroid, the last thing you need is a caffeine buzz. Dr. Pizzorno recommends avoiding caffeine-containing foods and beverages such as coffee, tea, cola, cocoa, and chocolate.

Also steer clear of over-the-counter drugs that supply caffeine. If you're not sure, ask your pharmacist.

Get your Zzzs. Sleep is a marvelous stress reducer, says Scott Luper, N.D., an instructor at the National College of Naturopathic Medicine in Portland, Oregon. By controlling your stress, you minimize your thyroid symptoms. He urges you to get a full night's sleep—and to squeeze in a daily postlunch nap when you can.

OTHER GOOD CHOICES

Nutrition

Whip up some coleslaw. Cabbage, turnips, rutabagas, peanuts, pine nuts, and millet all contain compounds that may help regulate an overactive thyroid.

Because the compounds are inactivated when cooked, these foods should be eaten raw. So make yourself some coleslaw from cabbage or munch on handfuls of peanuts or pine nuts.

Keep in mind that these foods have only modest effect on your thyroid. Still, including them in your diet can't hurt and might help, Dr. Pizzorno says.

Herbal Medicine

Trumpet bugleweed. "Bugleweed has a long folk history as a treatment for hyperthyroidism," says James Duke, Ph.D., "It's widely used in Europe to treat early-stage Grave's disease."

Quit using kelp. Commission E, the German panel that evaluates the safety and effectiveness of herbal medicines, advises people with hyperthyroidism not to take kelp supplements. A type of seaweed, kelp is high in iodine. And too much iodine can aggravate hyperthyroidism.

Homeopathy

Consider your constitution. According to Dr. Luper, homeopaths usually prescribe a constitutional medicine for hyperthyroidism. *Constitutional* means that the medicine treats your whole body, not just a particular symptom. Natrum muriaticum and Iodium are two such medicines. To find out which one best suits your individual symptoms, consult a homeopath.

Chinese Medicine

Douse the flames. "Hyperthyroidism is difficult to treat with Chinese medicine," says Efrem Korngold, O.M.D., L.Ac. "But in mild cases, Chinese medicine may help." For treatment, Dr. Korngold prescribes herbs such as gentian root, bupleurum root, gardenia fruit, and Chinese angelica (dang gui). He also prescribes mother-of-pearl shell, a mineral.

Target your thyroid. You may get relief by applying steady, penetrating finger pressure to each of the following points for 3 minutes.

◆ Pericardium 6, located in the middle of your inner wrist, 2½ fingerwidths above the wrist crease

◆ Kidney 3, located on your inner ankle in the hollow between your anklebone and Achilles tendon

◆ Extra Point Yin Tang, located just above the bridge of your nose, exactly between your eyebrows

Naturopathy

Get goose bumps. Applying a cold compress may help. It's an old naturopathic remedy for an overactive thyroid. Hold the compress to your throat for 15 minutes a day, Dr. Pizzorno suggests.

MEDICAL MEASURES

There are three mainstream treatments for hyperthyroidism: radioactive iodine (^{131}I), antithyroid drugs, and surgery. Most physicians recommend radioactive iodine because it's quick and simple. Just one capsule or cup of liquid usually does the job within 2 months, though sometimes you need a second dose.

The downside of all three treatments is that in the long run, they often cause *hypo*thyroidism—that is, an underactive thyroid. If this happens, you must take a supplemental hormone called thyroxine every day for the rest of your life.

Hypothyroidism

At first you thought you were getting the flu. After all, you had two classic flu symptoms: muscle aches and fatigue. Then weeks went by, and your symptoms lingered.

You noticed other changes, too. You couldn't concentrate, and your memory seemed fuzzy. You barely had enough energy to get through the day, so exercising was out of the question. Worst of all, you began gaining weight.

You paid a visit to your doctor, who sent you for a blood test after hearing your symptoms. The diagnosis: hypothyroidism, or an underactive thyroid.

The most common thyroid problem in the United States, hypothyroidism affects some seven million Americans, according to Lawrence C. Wood, M.D., president and medical director of the Thyroid Foundation of America in Boston. As with hyperthyroidism (see the previous chapter), the problem arises in the thyroid—that gland just below your Adam's apple.

SIMPLE SOLUTIONS
1. Nutrition
2. Supplements
3. Exercise
4. Yoga
5. Chinese Medicine
6. Medical Measures

If you have hypothyroidism, your thyroid doesn't produce enough thyroxine. As levels of this hormone fall, your metabolism slows down. As a result, you may experience a host of persistent symptoms. These include fatigue, mental dullness, depression, muscle aches, a slowed heart rate, loss of sexual desire, constipation, dry skin, dry hair or hair loss, excessive sleepiness, and intolerance of cold.

You may also notice that these symptoms are accompanied by weight gain, usually in the range of 5 to 10 pounds. Your cholesterol level may rise. If you're a woman, your periods may become heavier and longer than usual.

Ironically, some people get hypothyroidism after a bout of *hyper*thyroidism. That's because the primary treatments for an overactive thyroid can leave it underactive.

More than 6 percent of women over age 60 have significantly underactive thyroids. Another 20 percent have mild hypothyroidism that produces some but not all of the classic symptoms. For this reason, the American College of Physicians advises doctors to test women over age 50 for thyroid problems every 5 years.

There are a number of reasons why people develop hypothyroidism. The most common risk factors include a family history of hypothyroidism; head or neck x-rays during childhood; autoimmune disorders, such as rheumatoid arthritis; and pregnancy.

To diagnose hypothyroidism, doctors use a simple blood test that measures your level of the hormone thyroxine, or T_4.

The treatment of choice for hypothyroidism is mainstream medication. But when combined with mainstream pharmaceuticals, alternative therapies may help. "I have patients who've been able to reduce their doses of replacement thyroid hormone by using natural approaches," says Andrew T. Weil, M.D., director of the program in integrative medicine at the University of Arizona College of Medicine in Tucson.

OTHER GOOD CHOICES

Nutrition

Bypass the iodine blockers. Several foods can interfere with your thyroid's ability to use iodine, thus raising your risk of a thyroid condition called goiter. If you have an underactive thyroid, Joseph Pizzorno Jr., N.D., recommends limiting your consumption of the offending raw foods: cabbage, turnips, rutabagas, peanuts, pine nuts, and millet. Cooking, however, inactivates the compounds that prevent your thyroid from absorbing iodine.

Pass up some protein. According to Dr. Weil, certain autoimmune disorders, including hypothyroidism, often improve on a low-protein diet. He recommends reducing your consumption of meats and dairy products. Replace these animal-derived foods with whole grains, vegetables, and fruits.

Supplements

Take extra zinc. Your body needs zinc to produce thyroid hormones. "Low levels of zinc are common in the elderly. So is hypothyroidism," Dr. Pizzorno says. "There may be a connection between the two." He recommends taking 30 milligrams of zinc every day.

Get help from kelp. A form of seaweed, kelp is rich in iodine. Dr. Weil suggests taking up to 12 tablets of Norwegian kelp every day. You can buy these supplements in health food stores. Give them a try for 6 to 12 weeks, and then reevaluate your condition to see if you've noticed any improvement in your symptoms.

Exercise

Focus on fitness. "Exercise stimulates your thyroid to secrete hormones and increases your body's ability to respond to those hormones," Dr. Pizzorno says. "Personally, I believe that many of the health benefits of exercise are rooted in improved thyroid function." He recommends a daily 15- to 20-minute session of aerobic exercise, the kind that gets your heart pumping. A brisk walk should do the trick.

Yoga

Take a (shoulder) stand against symptoms. As part of a hypothyroidism treatment program, Dr. Weil recommends daily practice of a yoga posture called shoulder stand. "I have found it to be of great benefit," he says. "It's even more effective when combined with visualization." Here's how to do it.

1. Lie on your back with your arms at your sides, palms down.
2. Raise your legs at your hips so that they are perpendicular to the floor.
3. Raise your hips so that your chin rests against your chest. Support your hips with your hands—thumbs in front, fingers in back. Keep your neck and shoulders on the floor while stretching your legs and torso as perpendicular to the floor as possible. Breathe normally.
4. Hold the pose as long as you can, working up to 20 minutes a day.
5. Come down slowly, lowering your knees toward your head, then lowering your legs to the floor.

Chinese Medicine

Strengthen your Kidney and Spleen. Efrem Korngold, O.M.D., L.Ac., prescribes a number of herbs that strengthen the Kidney, including lotus seed, astragalus seed, rehmannia root, dioscorea root, and cornus fruit. He also prescribes herbs that strengthen the Spleen, such as gingerroot, licorice root, codonopsis root, and atractylodes root.

For relief, get to the point. In a small study conducted by Andreas Bayer,

M.D., of the department of internal medicine at Stockerau General Hospital in Austria, six patients with hypothyroidism were treated by combining acupuncture and an unusually low dose of replacement thyroid hormone. According to Dr. Bayer, the patients showed "a marked decrease in symptoms and an improved well-being."

If you prefer a self-care approach, consider trying acupressure on each of the following points for 3 minutes.

◆ Kidney 7, located on your inner leg, two thumb-widths above your anklebone

◆ Stomach 36, located four finger-widths below your kneecap and one finger-width toward the outside of your shinbone

◆ Conception Vessel 4, located on the midline of your abdomen, four thumb-widths below your navel

◆ Liver 3, situated on top of your foot in the webbing between your big toe and second toe

MEDICAL MEASURES

Doctors treat hypothyroidism with levothyroxine, a thyroxine-replacement drug that you take every day for the rest of your life. Once you start taking this replacement thyroxine, your doctor must closely monitor your treatment. Too high a dose of the hormone can accelerate bone loss and lead to osteoporosis.

Immune Impairment

You can remember a time when you hardly ever got sick. Now, it seems, you pick up every bug that goes around. And you don't bounce back from illness as quickly as you used to.

Even when you aren't sick, you don't feel truly well. You've thought about going to your doctor, but you're not sure how you'd explain how you feel. The only word that comes to mind is *blah*.

Your doctor has probably heard that word before. It tends to come up in conversations with people whose immune systems are functioning below par. When your immune system isn't healthy, it has a hard time protecting your body from disease-causing invaders. It can't keep you optimally well.

Mainstream medicine has traditionally focused on the end result of impaired immunity: treating disease. Alternative medicine, on the other hand, offers numerous effective approaches for strengthening the immune system. And a strong immune system can prevent you from getting sick in the first place.

SIMPLE SOLUTIONS
1. Nutrition
2. Supplements
3. Exercise
4. Tai Chi and Qigong
5. Visualization
6. Massage
7. Music Therapy
8. Social Support
9. Herbal Medicine
10. Chiropractic
11. Chinese Medicine
12. Home Remedies
13. Homeopathy

Your immune system has two main functions, according to Ronald Glaser, Ph.D., vice president for health sciences research at Ohio State University in Columbus. First, it monitors your body for invading microorganisms, which it is able to distinguish from your body's own tissues. Second, when it identifies anything as threatening, it attempts to destroy the offenders—and usually succeeds.

In the battle for your health, your frontline defenders are your white blood cells. Actually, you have several different kinds of white blood cells: neutrophils, granulocytes, monocytes, and lymphocytes. All of them engulf and devour foreign invaders.

How do they know when to jump into action? They are alerted to the presence of invading microorganisms by chemical messengers called interferons, interleukins, and immunoglobulins. These compounds are released when other cells in your body come under attack—a sort of chemical SOS.

With so many components carrying out so many different tasks, your immune system is a marvel of coordination and efficiency. But it's also quite fragile. If any one component fails to do its job properly, the entire system is weakened. That's when germs get the upper hand.

Many things can impair your immune system. People over 65 generally have reduced immunity responsiveness, and the same goes for people under a lot of stress. Your immune system can also be affected by depression, social isolation, nutritional deficiencies, dieting, lack of exercise, or sleep deprivation.

While many factors can weaken your immune system, you have control over most of them. You can take steps to boost your body's disease defenses so that you stay healthy—even when those around you get sick.

BEST CHOICES

Nutrition

Prevent disease with produce. "Eat your fruits and vegetables," says Marion Nestle, Ph.D., chairperson of nutrition and food studies at New York University in New York City. "About one-third of cancers are caused by poor diet—too much fat and too little of the nutrients found mostly in fruits and vegetables that equip the immune system to prevent cancer."

Master the language of mushrooms. Forget those bland, almost tasteless specimens that you find in the typical mushroom omelet. Your immune system craves exotic mushrooms, notably shiitake, maitake, and reishi. "Shiitake and maitake mushrooms strengthen the immune system," notes Santa Cruz, California, herbalist Christopher Hobbs, L.Ac., the author of several authoritative herb guides. "Reishi mushrooms build up bone marrow, where white blood cells are made."

Shiitake, maitake, and reishi mushrooms can be found in most health food stores as well as in a growing number of supermarkets. Use them as you would any mushrooms.

Say yes to yogurt. In Eastern Europe, where yogurt originated, it is revered as health-enhancing. Now research suggests that it may indeed have immune-enhancing benefits.

At the University of California, Davis, School of Medicine, George Halpern, M.D., of the department of internal medicine, and his colleagues used blood tests to analyze the immune activity of 68 adults between ages 20 and 40. They found that those who ate live-culture yogurt experienced what Dr. Halpern describes as a striking fourfold increase in immunity-enhancing chemicals.

Not all yogurt contains live cultures. To find one that does, read the product labels.

Supplements

Develop a multi personality. Take a daily multivitamin rather than single-nutrient supplements, recommends immune system researcher and two-time Nobel Prize nominee Ranjit Chandra, M.D., head of the immunology and allergy departments at Janeway Child Health Center in St. John's, Newfoundland, in Canada. "If you take certain vitamins and minerals by themselves, levels of others go down," he explains. "It's best to get some of everything from a multivitamin/mineral formula." He adds that multivitamins containing modest amounts of nutrients—up to twice the Daily Values—appear safe even when taken for a long time.

Boost immunity with melatonin. "I've been impressed by Italian studies suggesting that the hormone melatonin has immune-enhancing properties," says Alan P. Brauer, M.D. He recommends taking 3 to 9 milligrams of melatonin before going to bed.

Exercise

Work out regularly. A great deal of research has shown that as sedentary people become physically active, their immune systems become invigorated. In one study, one group of women took brisk walks for 45 minutes a day, while another did not. After 15 weeks, the exercisers experienced cold symptoms on half as many days.

Exercise also revs up your immune system against some cancers, notably breast and colon cancers. In one large-scale study, Harvard University researchers monitored the health of 47,000 male health professionals for 5 years. Compared with men who were inactive, those who worked out for at least 2 hours a week were 30 percent less likely to develop colon cancer.

How much exercise do you need? Most experts recommend being physically active for at least 30 minutes every day. But talk to your doctor before starting any new exercise program.

Tai Chi and Qigong

Move your whole body. Many studies have shown that tai chi's graceful, dancelike movements increase vitality, diminish anxiety, elevate mood, burn fat, exercise the heart, increase respiratory efficiency, and promote longevity. All of these benefits add up to improved immune function.

Keep qi in balance. In Asia, qigong—the forerunner of tai chi—has a well-deserved reputation for preventing disease. To test its effectiveness as an immune enhancer, Korean researchers taught qigong exercises to a group of volunteers. Another group didn't practice qigong. When all of the participants had their immune function evaluated, those who had learned qigong showed greater vitality.

Visualization

Use your mind to boost your defenses. At Washington State University in Pullman, a team of psychologists showed a video describing the immune system to 65 college students. Then the students were divided into three groups. Those in one group learned to visualize their immune systems growing stronger and then practiced the visualization twice a day. Another group meditated twice a day. The third group did nothing. After a week, the students practicing visualization experienced the greatest increases in white blood cell counts.

Here's a visualization that you can try on your own. Begin by breathing deeply. Close your eyes. Imagine your immune system as a doorman at a nightclub. As people enter, the doorman sizes them up, letting some right in, asking others for identification, and insisting that anyone acting rowdy, obnoxious, or at all violent leave. Watch the doorman size up a dozen imaginary people. Then look around the club, where all is calm and everyone is having a good time. Open your eyes.

Massage

Give your immune system a hand. "We know that massage reduces stress, depression, and social isolation, all of which impair immune response," says psychologist Tiffany Field, Ph.D., professor of psychology, pediatrics, and psychiatry at the University of Miami School of Medicine. "So it should come as no surprise that massage improves immune function."

Music Therapy

Turn on some tunes. Perhaps one of the easiest ways to give your immune system a boost is to listen to music. In one study, Carl J. Charnetski, Ph.D., professor of psychology at Wilkes University in Wilkes-Barre, Pennsylvania, measured students' levels of immunoglobulin A (IgA), a protein that helps defend the body against viral infections, before and after 30 minutes of exposure to various sounds. When the students listened to music, their IgA levels rose 7 to 19 percent. On the other hand, silence actually lowered the students' IgA levels by 1 percent.

Social Support

For stronger immunity, mingle. In the late 1970s, David Spiegel, M.D., professor of psychiatry and behavorial sciences and director of the Psychosocial Treatment Laboratory at Stanford University School of Medicine, organized weekly support meetings for a group of women with advanced breast cancer. Another group of women continued receiving standard care. Over the next 10 years, the women who participated in the support group survived twice as long as those who didn't. "We're still not certain exactly why social support helps," Dr. Spiegel says. "But we know that support reduces stress hormones in the blood, and stress hormones suppress immune function. It looks like support helps free the immune system from the harm inflicted by stress."

In another study of the effect of social support on immune function, Sheldon Cohen, Ph.D., professor of psychology at Carnegie Mellon University in Pittsburgh, asked 276 healthy volunteers to complete surveys about their social ties. Then the volunteers had live cold virus squirted up their noses. Those who were most socially isolated were most likely to develop colds. This finding may come as a surprise, since colds spread from person to person. But as Dr. Cohen notes, the immune boost provided by strong social ties more than compensates for the increased risk of infection created when you're in the company of others who might have colds.

Herbal Medicine

Depend on echinacea. "Several Western herbs improve immune function," says James A. Duke, Ph.D. "My favorite is echinacea. There's a great deal of research showing that echinacea's immune-stimulating effects help the body fight fungal, bacterial, and viral infections."

You can buy echinacea tincture in health food stores. Use it according to the directions on the label. "Take echinacea when you are ill and need a quick immune boost. But don't take it long term," advises Alan Gaby, M.D. "It's not a tonic that has a strengthening effect over time. It's best for treatment, not prevention."

Take garlic. In addition to being a natural antibiotic, garlic helps strengthen your immune system, Dr. Brauer says. He recommends taking 4 to 12 capsules of deodorized garlic a day. You can buy the capsules in health food stores and many drugstores.

Chiropractic

Get adjusted for stronger immunity. At the National College of Chiropractic in Lombard, Illinois, a group of volunteers received either chiropractic spinal manipulation or massagelike soft-tissue manipulation. Blood tests administered before and after treatment showed that both therapies raised the participants' white blood cell counts, an indicator of immune response. But chiropractic spinal manipulation had a significantly greater effect.

Chinese Medicine

Try an herb from the East. "The Chinese herb astragalus deserves special mention as an immune stimulant," says Daniel Mowrey, Ph.D., an herb researcher in Salt Lake City and author of *The Scientific Validation of Herbal Medicine*. "It has been shown to stimulate T-cell activity." T-cells are special types of white blood cells that engulf and destroy invading germs. If you want to try astragalus, consult an oriental medicine doctor.

Home Remedies

Laugh loud, laugh often. At Western New England College in Springfield, Massachusetts, psychologist Kathleen Dillon, Ph.D., noticed that people who seemed cheerful and used humor to deal with adversity had higher IgA levels than those who seemed dour. Dr. Dillon wondered if she could boost IgA levels by encouraging mirth. To find out, she had five students watch the comedy video *Richard Pryor Live*, followed by an education video about the health hazards of anxiety. Another five students watched the same videos, only in the opposite order. After each viewing, the students had their IgA levels tested. IgA rose significantly after the comedy video but dropped after the anxiety video.

Embrace life's highs. Just as minor daily hassles undermine your immune system, everyday pleasures boost immunity. In fact, according to Arthur Stone, Ph.D., a psychologist at the State University of New York at Stony Brook, the positive impact of uplifting events seems to outweigh the negative impact of upsetting events.

In a study of 100 men, Dr. Stone found that on days when the joys outnumbered the stresses, the men's immune function rose and stayed elevated for 2 days afterward. On bad days, the men's IgA levels fell but remained low for only a day.

Watch the alcohol. An occasional beer or glass of wine probably won't increase your risk of catching a cold. But if you drink on a daily basis, your neutrophil activity can become impaired, says Joseph Pizzorno Jr., N.D. That means you're more susceptible to infection.

OTHER GOOD CHOICES

Homeopathy

Take a constitutional medicine. "Homeopaths offer two types of treatment," explains homeopath Dana Ullman. "They can treat specific symptoms, and they can prescribe constitutional medicines, preparations matched to your own unique health characteristics that help keep you healthy. Constitutional medicines are individualized immune boosters." To find out which of these medicines would work best for you, consult a homeopath.

Home Remedies

Get some quality snooze time. Many studies show that lack of sleep impairs immune function. Studies by the National Commission on Sleep Disorders Research show that many, if not most, Americans are at least somewhat sleep-deprived. "If you feel run-down, try getting at least 8 to 9 hours every night for a week," says William Dement, M.D., Ph.D., director of the Stanford University Sleep Disorders Clinic and chairperson of the National Commission on Sleep Disorders Research. "You'll probably feel better."

Incontinence

According to the American Urological Association, an estimated 17 million American adults—primarily women—have some form of incontinence. *Estimated* is the operative word here. No one knows the exact number because so many people with bladder-control problems are too embarrassed to talk about them.

The word *incontinence* refers to loss of bladder or bowel control. (For information on bowel-control problems, or fecal incontinence, see "Fecal Incontinence: A Case of Disobedient Bowels.") Urinary incontinence takes several forms.

Stress incontinence. Certain muscles support your bladder and urine tube (urethra), holding these structures in their proper positions. If these pelvic-floor muscles weaken, anything that puts pressure on your abdomen can cause you to involuntarily release some urine.

Urge incontinence. When you have urge incontinence, something causes your bladder muscles to contract, and you suddenly feel the need to relieve yourself.

> **SIMPLE SOLUTIONS**
> 1. Nutrition
> 2. Exercise
> 3. Biofeedback
> 4. Social Support
> 5. Herbal Medicine
> 6. Home Remedies
> 7. Homeopathy
> 8. Chinese Medicine
> 9. Over-the-Counter Drugs
> 10. Medical Measures

Mixed incontinence. As the name suggests, this is a combination of stress and urge incontinence. You suddenly feel the need to urinate, and your muscles aren't strong enough to prevent it.

Overflow incontinence. This condition usually affects middle-age men with enlarged prostates. Your prostate is pinching your urethra, which makes your bladder feel full and creates a weak urine stream.

Medication-related incontinence. Many blood pressure drugs can impair the function of your bladder and urethral muscles.

In its various forms, urinary incontinence can affect just about anyone of any age, but definitely women more than men. Among men, the leading risk

Fecal Incontinence: A Case of Disobedient Bowels

Fecal incontinence is considerably less common than urinary incontinence. Older people are more likely to have this problem, and it's often related to health conditions that affect the digestive tract. The most common causes include chronic diarrhea, chronic constipation, and weakening of the muscles in the rectum and anus. But neurological problems should also be considered. If you don't sense the urge to go—due to nerve damage—there's no signal telling you it's time to head for the bathroom.

For fecal incontinence caused by diarrhea or constipation, you need to treat the underlying condition. For incontinence caused by weak rectal and anal muscles, you may benefit from biofeedback training. In this therapy, the biofeedback trainer inserts an anal probe that measures the strength of your muscle contractions. Then you practice contracting those muscles, which makes them stronger. Studies have shown that for incontinence associated with muscle weakness, biofeedback helps in up to 75 percent of cases.

factor for loss of bladder control is an enlarged prostate. Women, on the other hand, have a number of risk factors to contend with, including pregnancy and childbirth, overweight, smoking, infections, weakening pelvic-floor muscles due to aging, and any neurological disease that damages the nerves needed for bladder control. Pelvic trauma and radiation therapy can also contribute to incontinence.

If you have urinary incontinence, you should discuss your condition with your doctor. There may be an underlying health problem causing your loss of bladder control. If that's the case, you really need to get a diagnosis and begin treatment.

More than likely, though, your incontinence is not a symptom of another condition. So once your doctor determines what type of incontinence you have, you can use a combination of mainstream and alternative therapies to treat it. Here's what experts say can help.

BEST CHOICES

Nutrition

Avoid the irritators. Steer clear of foods and beverages that can irritate your bladder. They include dairy products, spicy foods, foods containing artificial sweeteners such as aspartame, citrus fruits and juices, alcohol, and caffeinated beverages. "I've cured several cases of stress incontinence just by telling women to stop drinking coffee," says Christiane Northrup, M.D., founder of the Women to Women health center in Yarmouth, Maine, and past president of the American Holistic Medical Association.

Exercise

Flex your PC. Back in 1948, urologist Arnold Kegel, M.D., theorized that strengthening the pelvic-floor muscles might help the urethral sphincter stay closed. He developed a specific set of exercises to condition the pubococcygeus (PC) muscle, which plays an important role in bladder control.

As a treatment for urinary incontinence, Kegel exercises have been shown to significantly improve bladder control in 50 to 90 percent of women.

To do Kegels properly, you must first identify your PC muscle. It's the one you flex to stop urinating in midstream. Try this a few times to make sure you're working the right muscle. But don't get in the habit of interrupting urination. It's not good for your bladder.

Once you've located your PC, practice contracting and releasing it. Hold each contraction for 10 seconds, then relax for 10 seconds. Do 10 repetitions four times a day for 8 weeks. If you don't notice any improvement after 8 weeks, consult your doctor. You may not be working the right muscle.

Biofeedback

Retrain your muscles. If you have urge incontinence, you may benefit from biofeedback training. At the University of Alabama at Birmingham, researchers taught 197 women with urge incontinence to use vaginally inserted biofeedback devices. The devices allowed the women to view graphic displays of their bladder and urethral muscle activity. By the end of the study, 74 percent of the women using biofeedback reported substantial decreases in incontinence. And biofeedback treatment produced no side effects, as incontinence drugs can.

Social Support

Get help from a trusted source. If you're too embarrassed to discuss incontinence with anyone, even your doctor, you may feel isolated and alone. But you can get help discreetly, from the National Association for Continence (NAFC). This organization provides information, advice, and support for people with bladder-control problems. You can contact the NAFC by writing to P. O. Box 8310, Spartanburg, SC 29305-8310.

Herbal Medicine

Fight leakage with phytos. Mainstream doctors often prescribe estrogen replacement for postmenopausal incontinence. The hormone boosts blood flow to your bladder and urethral muscles, which helps strengthen them. You can get similar benefits from naturally occurring compounds called phytoestrogens, supplied by the herb black cohosh. Herbalist Susun Weed, of Woodstock, New York, who specializes in women's health, recommends taking 10 drops of black cohosh tincture once or twice a day in water or juice.

Home Remedies

Plan your toilet time. To treat urge incontinence, some experts recommend that you ignore the impulse to relieve yourself. Instead, try to urinate at about the same time every day. You can start by going to the bathroom every 30 to 60 minutes if necessary—but over the next several months, gradually extend the time between "pit stops." Eventually, you may be able to wait 3 to 4 hours between bathroom visits. According to researchers at the Medical College of Virginia in Richmond, this type of bladder retraining cut accidents in half among 123 women with incontinence.

Take a seat—twice. If you're a man with overflow incontinence, sit down when you urinate. Stay on the toilet until you feel finished, then stand up and sit down again. You may be able to eliminate more urine this way.

Dress loosely. Tight clothes can aggravate stress incontinence by putting pressure on your lower abdomen. Women should avoid wearing girdles, corsets, and tight exercise outfits.

Drink more. When you have incontinence, you may be tempted to avoid fluids for fear that you'll have an accident. In fact, dehydration makes your urine more concentrated, which can irritate your bladder and aggravate your bladder-control problem, says Andrew T. Weil, M.D., director of the program in integrative medicine at the University of Arizona College of Medicine in Tucson.

Keep a diary. For a week or two, write down the number of times each day that you urinate, the number of times you experience leakage or feel a sudden urge to urinate, the approximate amount of urine you leak, and your fluid intake. By tracking these factors, you may notice a pattern in your incontinence. For example, you may realize that you have leakage every time you drink coffee. In that case, cutting back on coffee may help you avoid accidents. Your doctor can also use this information in deciding how best to treat your condition.

OTHER GOOD CHOICES

Homeopathy

Count on Causticum. For stress incontinence, homeopaths often prescribe Causticum, says homeopath Dana Ullman. For overflow incontinence associated with an enlarged prostate, he recommends Sabal serrulata. Consult a homeopath for a dosage that best suits your needs.

Chinese Medicine

Fortify with herbs. To treat incontinence, Efrem Korngold, O.M.D., L.Ac., prescribes a number of strengthening and astringent herbs. These include lotus seed, astragalus seed, rehmannia root, dioscorea root, and cornus fruit.

Press points to prevent it. Stimulating certain points on your arms and legs may help prevent urine leakage. Apply firm, steady finger pressure to each of the following points for 3 minutes.

♦ Lung 9, located on the thumb side of your inner forearm in the hollow between your wrist bone and wrist crease

♦ Kidney 7, located on your inner leg, two thumb-widths above your anklebone

♦ Spleen 6, located four finger-widths above your inner anklebone on the back inner border of your shinbone

Over-the-Counter Drugs

Discover a new use for decongestants. Decongestants may help relieve stress incontinence by increasing urethral constriction, which inhibits urine flow, says Patrick Culligan, M.D., of the Evanston Continence Center in Illinois. For the same reason, these drugs can aggravate overflow incontinence.

If you have stress incontinence, Dr. Culligan suggests taking 30 to 60 milligrams of pseudoephedrine (Sudafed) four times a day. If you are unsure of the equivalent number of tablets or capsules, ask your pharmacist. Avoid using pseudoephedrine after dinner, because it can keep you wide awake if taken too close to bedtime.

MEDICAL MEASURES

Various kinds of urine retention devices have been recommended to patients by many generations of physicians. Before the French Revolution, court ladies at Versailles had porcelain gravy boats attached under their petticoats to catch little dribbles. Today, little cups made from rubber, foam, or plastic serve the same purpose, but far more efficiently. They fit over the urethral opening and physically block leakage. While these retention devices are effective, many women find them uncomfortable.

For stress, urge, or mixed incontinence, mainstream M.D.'s often prescribe supplemental estrogen in pill or cream form or as a ring inserted in the vagina. The hormone strengthens the bladder and urethral muscles by improving blood circulation to them.

For stress incontinence, doctors may opt to prescribe a drug similar to over-the-counter decongestants to increase urethral resistance to urine flow. For urge incontinence, they sometimes prescribe a number of drugs that reduce involuntary bladder muscle contractions, such as oxybutynin (Ditropan) and tolterodine (Detrol). All of these medications are effective but produce many side effects. They may cause dry mouth and eyes, blurred vision, nausea, constipation, drowsiness, and confusion. Some women who can't tolerate the side effects simply stop taking the drugs.

Your doctor might also recommend injections of collagen, a natural protein. As a last resort, you can have surgery to help reinforce your pelvic-floor muscles, providing extra support for your bladder and urethra.

Indigestion

Quick: Where's your stomach?

If you think it's somewhere in the vicinity of your navel, you're a bit too far south. Underneath your navel are your intestines. Your stomach actually sits considerably higher—beneath your rib cage, slightly to the left of your breastbone.

The point of this brief anatomy lesson: What most people call a stomachache has nothing to do with the stomach. It's really abdominal distress, or indigestion.

In and of itself, indigestion is seldom serious. It usually comes on after meals as a sharp or aching pain in the area of your navel. Perhaps you ate something that didn't agree with you. Many people get indigestion after eating dairy products—a tip-off that they may be lactose-intolerant—or after eating greasy, fatty foods. Then again, maybe it's not what you ate but how much or how fast you ate. Overeating and rushing through meals contribute to abdominal distress.

Other factors may raise your risk of developing indigestion, says Alan Gaby, M.D. You're more vulnerable to abdominal distress

SIMPLE SOLUTIONS
1. Nutrition
2. Supplements
3. Relaxation Therapies
4. Yoga
5. Herbal Medicine
6. Home Remedies
7. Over-the-Counter Drugs
8. Aromatherapy
9. Homeopathy
10. Chinese Medicine
11. Ayurvedic Medicine
12. Naturopathy
13. Medical Measures

when you're under emotional stress, taking certain medications (especially non-steroidal anti-inflammatory drugs), drinking, smoking—even wearing too-tight clothes, which increases pressure on your abdomen.

In addition, some people are prone to indigestion because they don't produce enough stomach acid or pancreatic secretions. Antacid commercials imply that excess stomach acid is a major public health problem. "But probably more significant health problems, including indigestion, are caused by a deficiency of stomach acid," says Joseph Pizzorno Jr., N.D. A deficiency of pancreatic enzymes can cause similar problems, he says. As you grow older, your body loses its ability to manufacture these digestive juices—one reason why indigestion tends to increase with age.

No matter what has caused your indigestion, you have plenty of options for relief. Here's what can help.

BEST CHOICES

Nutrition

Enjoy a relaxing repast. "Mealtime should be a time of relaxation, not stress," says Alan P. Brauer, M.D. So sit down while you eat. Play mellowing music if you want. Most important, eat slowly and chew your food thoroughly. Wolfing down your meal is a surefire setup for indigestion.

Graze, don't gorge. Instead of the standard three square meals a day, try eating four or five smaller, snack-size meals, suggests Anne Simons, M.D. By eating less in one sitting, you reduce your odds of developing indigestion.

Phase out high-fat foods. Compared with other foods, those that are high in fat are harder to digest. Switching to a low-fat diet can help prevent indigestion.

Ply yourself with pineapple. Pineapple is rich in bromelain, an enzyme that helps digest proteins. (That's why you can't add pineapple to gelatin. The bromelain breaks down the protein that makes gelatin gel.) "Fresh or canned, pineapple is a sweet dessert that helps digestion," says James A. Duke, Ph.D.

Wash down your meals with water. Sipping water as you eat often helps prevent indigestion, Dr. Brauer says. It lubricates your food's passage through your intestines. And if you take a sip every few bites, it slows your eating.

Supplements

Get bromelain in a bottle. If you're not a fan of pineapple, you can get bromelain in pill form. Naturopaths recommend taking 250 to 500 milligrams of the enzyme with meals.

Relaxation Therapies

Appease your abdomen. Ever feel as though your digestive tract has a mind of its own? In fact, it does.

Research by Michael D. Gershon, M.D., professor and chairperson in the department of anatomy and cell biology at Columbia-Presbyterian Medical Center in New York City, has shown that the human body actually has two brains. You know about the one in your head. The other, called the enteric nervous system, lines your digestive tract. It contains in excess of 100 million nerve cells—more than your spinal cord. "No wonder even minor emotional upsets can trigger abdominal distress," says Martin L. Rossman, M.D.

According to William E. Whitehead, Ph.D., professor of medical psychology at Johns Hopkins University School of Medicine in Baltimore, any relaxation therapy can calm the nervous system tissue in your digestive tract and help relieve indigestion. Practice the ones that appeal to you: deep breathing, meditation, visualization, massage, aromatherapy, exercise, tai chi, or yoga.

Yoga

Squeeze your knees. For indigestion, Stephen Nezezon, M.D., of the Himalayan International Institute of Yoga Science and Philosophy in Honesdale, Pennsylvania, recommends an exercise called the knee squeeze. Lie on your back with your hands at your sides, your legs straight, and your toes slightly pointed. Slowly inhale as you raise your right knee to your chest. Embrace your knee with your hands. Hold this position for a few seconds. Then exhale as you release and straighten your right leg. Repeat the sequence, this time using your left leg. Do the exercise three times per leg.

Herbal Medicine

Pursue relief with peppermint. Studies dating back to the 1920s show that peppermint helps soothe gastrointestinal spasms. Peppermint is best taken in tincture form. Dr. Duke recommends putting 1 to 2 teaspoons in a glass of pineapple juice. That way, you get bromelain as well.

Calm your gut with chamomile. "Many studies show that chamomile soothes the digestive tract," Dr. Duke says. To make chamomile tea, add 2 to 3 heaping teaspoons of dried flowers to 1 cup of boiled water. Steep for 10 minutes, then strain. If you prefer, you can take chamomile in tincture form—1 to 2 teaspoons of tincture in a glass of pineapple juice.

Get better with ginger. Ginger is among the most venerated digestive herbs. Studies show that it helps relieve motion sickness and the nausea of pregnancy. Many herbalists—including Daniel Mowrey, Ph.D., an herb researcher in Salt Lake City and author of *The Scientific Validation of Herbal Medicine*—recommend ginger for indigestion as well. To make ginger tea, add 1 teaspoon of freshly grated gingerroot to 1 cup of boiled water. Steep for 10 minutes, then strain.

Make your own herbal tincture. In medical lingo, indigestion is known as dyspepsia. Dys-Pepsi-Cola is Dr. Duke's tongue-in-cheek name for a tincture that he makes from several herbal stomach-soothers, or carminatives. "My recipe is pretty loose," he says. "I just mix together any carminative herbs that I have on hand—peppermint, chamomile, ginger, anise, caraway seed, catnip, coriander, fennel seed, marjoram, rosemary, and turmeric. Then I steep the herbs overnight in the refrigerator in a mixture of alcohol and water—1 ounce of vodka per 1 cup of water." Take 1 tablespoon of the tincture as needed, either by itself or mixed into tea or pineapple juice.

Home Remedies

Kiss your butts goodbye. If you smoke, here's another good reason to quit. Smoking often contributes to indigestion.

Lose the booze. If you drink, cutting back often helps prevent episodes of indigestion, Dr. Gaby says. But you probably don't have to give up alcoholic beverages entirely.

When indigestion strikes, take notes. If you have frequent bouts of abdominal distress, try keeping an indigestion diary, Dr. Simons suggests. Tracking your pain on paper can help you see whether your indigestion consistently arrives at certain times—after you eat certain foods, for example.

Over-the-Counter Drugs

Try an old standby. Antacids help relieve indigestion by neutralizing stomach acid. Among the available brands are Tums, Rolaids, Di-Gel, Maalox, Mylanta, Alka-Seltzer, and Bromo-Seltzer. Whichever product you choose, take it according to the package directions.

Check out the H_2 blockers. Once available only by prescription, H_2 blockers—sold under the brand names Tagamet, Zantac, and Pepcid AC—are now sold over the counter. They're usually recommended for heartburn, but they sometimes help relieve abdominal distress. They work by reducing stomach acid secretion. If you decide to try an H_2 blocker, take it according to the package directions.

OTHER GOOD CHOICES

Aromatherapy

Inhale soothing scents. The herbs used to treat indigestion are effective because of the aromatic oils they contain. Aromatherapists discard the plant material and work entirely with these oils. For indigestion, Kathy Keville and Mindy Green, coauthors of *Aromatherapy: A Complete Guide to the Healing Art*, recommend caraway, cardamom, celery, chamomile, cinnamon, cumin, fennel, ginger, and peppermint essential oils.

To use an essential oil, place a few chips of rock salt in a small capped vial. Add a drop or two of the essential oil of your choice. The rock salt quickly absorbs the oil, so the oil doesn't spill. Whenever you feel indigestion coming on, uncap the vial and take a whiff.

Homeopathy

Try a different kind of medicine. Homeopaths recommend several highly diluted medicines for indigestion, says homeopath Dana Ullman. They include Calcarea carbonica, Nux vomica, and Pulsatilla. Which of these medicines works best for you depends on your individual symptoms. For a recommendation, consult a homeopath.

Chinese Medicine

Stimulate digestion. Practitioners of Chinese medicine attribute indigestion to stagnation of qi in the Intestine caused by eating too much or too fast, says Efrem Korngold, O.M.D., L.Ac. To treat the condition, Dr. Korngold prescribes fragrant, spicy herbs to stimulate digestion. They include pepper, cardamom, radish, citrus peel, and hawthorn root. "I also recommend licorice root," he says. "Licorice is the great harmonizer. It normalizes digestive function."

Another digestive normalizer that Dr. Korngold prescribes is a Chinese medicine called Curing Pills. The pills contain a combination of 15 herbs, including atractylodes, poria fungus, and medicated leven.

Point the way to relief. As a treatment for indigestion, acupuncture has received the endorsement of the United Nations World Health Organization. Of course, acupuncture should be administered only by a trained acupuncturist.

If you prefer a do-it-yourself approach, Michael Reed Gach, founder and director of the Acupressure Institute, recommends acupressure. Apply steady, penetrating finger pressure to each of the following points for 3 minutes.

◆ Conception Vessel 12, located halfway between the end of your breast-bone and your navel on the midline of your abdomen (do not press this point if you've just eaten or if you're a woman who's pregnant)

◆ Conception Vessel 6, located three finger-widths directly below your navel

◆ Stomach 36, located four finger-widths below your kneecap and one finger-width toward the outside of your shinbone

◆ Pericardium 6, located in the middle of your inner wrist, 2½ finger widths above the wrist crease

◆ Spleen 4, located on the arch of your foot, one thumb-width behind the ball of your foot

Ayurvedic Medicine

Take herbs for ama. If you've ever eaten in an Indian restaurant, you may have noticed a bowl of seeds sitting by the door. They are fennel seeds, the Ayurvedic version of after-dinner mints.

Ayurvedic physicians believe that undigested food, or ama, is the cause of indigestion. To treat the condition, they prescribe an array of stomach-soothing herbs, according to David Frawley, O.M.D. Some of these herbs are no doubt familiar to you: fennel, cinnamon, licorice, and cardamom. You can make a tea by adding 1 teaspoon of crushed or powdered herb (or a blend of herbs) to 1 cup of boiled water. Steep for 10 minutes, then strain.

Certain Ayurvedic herbs also relieve indigestion. These include amalaki, shatavari, trikatu, triphala, vidanga, and trivrit. If you'd like to try one of these herbs, you need to consult an Ayurvedic practitioner.

Peel a banana. Bananas are a favorite Ayurvedic remedy for indigestion. In one study, three-quarters of those treated with dried banana powder reported relief. You may be able to get the same benefit by eating a fresh, ripe banana.

Naturopathy

Take digestive aids. Naturopaths often treat indigestion with supple-mental stomach acid and digestive enzymes. Dr. Pizzorno suggests taking one of the following with meals: 250 to 500 milligrams of bromelain; or two to four tablets of 4X potency or one or two tablets of 8X potency pancreatin, an enzyme secreted by the pancreas. You can buy these supplements in most health food stores.

MEDICAL MEASURES

For particularly persistent indigestion, mainstream M.D.'s usually recommend prescription-strength antacids and H_2 blockers. Keep in mind that some medications—especially aspirin and other nonsteroidal anti-inflammatory drugs—can actually cause indigestion. If you're taking a prescription or over-the-counter medicine and you're bothered by persistent abdominal distress, talk to your doctor or pharmacist. They may be able to recommend another drug that doesn't have indigestion as a side effect.

RED FLAGS

If you experience any of the following, see your doctor immediately.

◆ You have a dull ache in your chest or abdomen that's accompanied by nausea or sweating

◆ Your pain begins as a dull ache around your entire midsection, then localizes in your lower right abdomen within a few hours

◆ Your abdominal pain is accompanied by vomiting; black, blood-tinged, or bloody stools; or fever and vaginal discharge

◆ Your abdominal pain keeps getting worse

◆ Your abdominal pain persists after 2 weeks of self-care

Inflammatory Bowel Disease

Inflammatory bowel disease is an umbrella term that's often used to refer to two distinct but similar conditions: colitis and Crohn's disease. Both affect the lower gastrointestinal tract, producing cramplike abdominal pain and urgent, bloody diarrhea.

Which type of inflammatory bowel disease, or IBD, you have depends on the location and severity of the small sores, or ulcers, that develop. In colitis, the sores dot the lining of the large intestine as well as the lining of the rectum. In Crohn's disease, the sores bore deeper into the wall of the colon and spread into the lower portion of the small intestine, called the ileum.

SIMPLE SOLUTIONS
1. Nutrition
2. Supplements
3. Elimination Diet
4. Visualization
5. Herbal Medicine
6. Chinese Medicine
7. Medical Measures

Both types of IBD have essentially the same symptoms: abdominal pain and diarrhea. IBD may also cause weight loss, fatigue, skin rashes, and joint pain. In addition, Crohn's disease sometimes produces fever.

IBD affects more women than men, although scientists have yet to figure out why. It also starts early in life: Most people with IBD are between ages 15 and 35 when they're diagnosed.

Because both colitis and Crohn's disease often run in families, scientists suspect that IBD may have a genetic component. Compared with the general population, people of Jewish heritage are at higher risk. But even among non-Jews, there are marked differences in risk. Scientists have noticed that IBD is two to five times more common in Whites than in people of African or Asian descent.

Of course, you can't do much about your gender, age, or ethnicity. They're predetermined. On the other hand, you can change your eating habits. And naturopaths maintain that diet outweighs all other risk factors in determining who gets IBD and who doesn't.

Some studies have determined that food sensitivities contribute to IBD and that elimination diets often provide considerable relief from IBD symptoms, says Alan Gaby, M.D. In particular, food sensitivities appear to play a role in Crohn's disease by setting the stage for what alternative practitioners have dubbed leaky gut syndrome.

As these experts theorize, leaky gut syndrome occurs when your small intestine gets damaged, whether by food sensitivities or some other factor. Normally, your small intestine allows only nutrients that your body needs to pass into your bloodstream. But a damaged small intestine leaks, dripping potentially harmful substances into your bloodstream—substances that ought to be eliminated as solid waste.

Depending on the severity of your IBD, you may want to consider alternative therapies before going the drug-and-surgery route advocated by many mainstream M.D.'s. Discuss your treatment options with your doctor. If you decide to try alternative therapies, here's what may help.

BEST CHOICES

Nutrition

Feature fiber on your plate. Mainstream doctors have traditionally recommended a low-fiber diet to people with IBD, thinking that such a diet is easier on the digestive tract. But research now suggests that a high-fiber diet is the way to go.

If you have IBD, Joseph Pizzorno Jr., N.D., recommends that you eat an abundance of fiber-rich fruits and vegetables. He suggests avoiding whole-wheat bread and wheat bran since so many people with IBD are sensitive to wheat.

Reduce your sugar intake. If fiber relieves IBD, would a diet containing lots of low-fiber sugar aggravate the condition? Quite possibly, if the latest research is any indication.

In one study, volunteers who went on a high-sugar diet showed changes linked to Crohn's disease—specifically, high concentrations of bile acids in stools and increased activity of bacteria in the intestines.

The amount of sugar that triggers these digestive changes varies from person to person. But if you have IBD, you'll probably do yourself a favor by eating as little sugar as possible.

Make fish your main dish. IBD is an inflammatory condition. People who have it also have unusually high levels of inflammatory compounds in their small intestines and colons. To fight the inflammation, Andrew T. Weil, M.D., director of the program in integrative medicine at the University of Arizona College of Medicine in Tucson, recommends increasing your intake of omega-3 fatty acids. These "good fats" are found in abundance in salmon and other cold-water fish.

Supplements

Opt for fish oil. Besides eating fish, you can get omega-3 fatty acids by taking fish-oil supplements. At the University of Bologna in Italy, researchers saw benefit when people with Crohn's disease supplemented with 24.3 grams of fish oil per day, taken as nine 2.7-gram enteric-coated capsules. Amounts this high should be taken only with the guidance of a doctor. The supplements sold in health food stores and some drugstores supply much smaller doses of fish oil. But they're still considered beneficial to people with IBD.

If you decide to try fish oil, Dr. Pizzorno says to give it time to work. Four to 6 months may pass before you notice results.

Get necessary nutrients in a multi. For people with IBD, eating often produces intense abdominal pain. No wonder some 70 percent of those who have IBD restrict their food intakes. As a result, they unintentionally shortchange themselves on essential vitamins and minerals.

If you're on prescription medication for IBD, or if you're eating less because of IBD, Dr. Pizzorno suggests that you take a multivitamin/mineral supplement. A multi can help compensate for any nutritional shortfalls.

Elimination Diet

Weed out offending foods. At Addenbrooke Hospital in Cambridge, England, researchers put 93 people with Crohn's disease on an elemental diet, a type of elimination diet that replaces all regular foods with a nutrient-rich formula. After just 2 weeks, 84 percent of the study participants reported substantial improvement in their symptoms. The researchers concluded that "an elemental diet is as effective in producing remission of Crohn's disease as corticosteroids." (Corticosteroids are the anti-inflammatory drugs that are often prescribed for IBD.)

Dr. Pizzorno urges people with both types of IBD to follow an elimination diet. Consult with a practitioner or doctor for guidance.

Visualization

Use your brain to heal your bowel. According to Dr. Weil, IBD seems to have a strong mind-body component. He believes that relaxation therapies, including visualization, can help alleviate IBD symptoms.

If you want to experiment with visualization, here's a brief exercise recommended by Gerald N. Epstein, M.D., director of the Academy of Integrative Medicine and Mental Imagery in New York City: Close your eyes. Slowly inhale and exhale three times. As you continue this slow, relaxed breathing, envision a mermaid with flowing golden hair and a sleek silvery body and tail. See her swimming rhythmically through your digestive tract, which is calm. Sense her there. Direct her to any places that you feel cramping, pain, or any other symptoms. Have her touch those places and gently massage them until they are healed and you no longer feel discomfort. Have her swim through your entire digestive tract, making sure that everything is in order. When she's finished, open your eyes. Do this exercise twice a day, morning and evening.

Herbal Medicine

Deliver an herbal double whammy. In IBD, the mucous lining that serves as a barrier between intestinal cells and digestive wastes becomes damaged. A group of herbs called demulcents have the ability to soothe injured or inflamed mucous membranes. Among the most effective of these herbs are slippery elm and marshmallow. Both are ingredients in Bastyr's Formula, a combination of eight herbs, two digestive enzymes, and niacin developed by the late Seattle naturopath John Bastyr, N.D., as a treatment for IBD. If you want to try Bastyr's Formula, you must see a naturopath.

Be partial to peppermint. Peppermint oil helps relax the digestive tract, says Stephen Holt, M.D., professor of medicine at Seton Hall University in South Orange, New Jersey. This makes the herb an effective treatment for all sorts of digestive problems, including IBD.

You can buy enteric-coated capsules of peppermint oil in most health food stores. Follow the package directions for proper dosage.

Chinese Medicine

Turn down the Heat. "I treat IBD with tonifying, anti-inflammatory, cooling, astringent herbs," says Efrem Korngold, O.M.D., L.Ac. Among the herbs he usually prescribes to his patients are licorice, ginger, skullcap root, peony, lotus, euryales, and atractylodes. Many of these herbs are found in a Chinese herbal formula called Jian Pi Ling, which Dr. Korngold often prescribes.

Point the way to relief. According to Dr. Korngold, stimulating certain spots at various locations around the body can help relieve IBD symptoms. If you'd rather not go to an acupuncturist, you can stimulate the points yourself with acupressure. Simply apply steady, penetrating finger pressure on each of the following points for 3 minutes.

- ◆ Large Intestine 11, located at the outer end of your elbow crease on the thumb side
- ◆ Stomach 36, located four finger-widths below your kneecap and one finger-width toward the outside of your shinbone
- ◆ Spleen 4, located on the arch of your foot, one thumb-width behind the ball of your foot
- ◆ Liver 3, situated on top of your foot in the webbing between your big toe and second toe

MEDICAL MEASURES

Mainstream doctors generally believe that IBD cannot be cured. The goal of treatment, then, is to control IBD symptoms. To do this, M.D.'s rely on a variety of anti-inflammatory drugs. Among these prescription pharmaceuticals are the 5–aminosalicylic acids or 5-ASAs, such as sulfasalazine (Azulfidine), olsalazine sodium (Dipentum), and mesalamine (Rowasa). Other commonly prescribed medications include the corticosteroids (Prednisone), cyclosporine (Sandimmune), and methotrexate (Folex). All of these drugs work reasonably well, but they have many side effects.

If you can't tolerate the side effects of the drugs you're taking, if the drugs fail to control your IBD symptoms, or if you notice bloodier diarrhea, your doctor may recommend surgery. In this procedure, called a colostomy-ileostomy, the surgeon removes the colon, the rectum, and the affected part of the small intestine. Then he creates an opening in the abdominal wall for the elimination of digestive wastes, which collect in a bag attached over the opening.

At one time, these bags had to be worn permanently and changed regularly. Nowadays, they're only temporary. Once your abdomen heals, the surgeon can use your own tissue to fashion a "new" rectum, connecting it to what's left of your small intestine. This allows you to go to the bathroom normally.

RED FLAGS

Contact your doctor immediately if your abdominal pain becomes more severe, if you notice more blood in your stools, or if you experience fever or other unusual symptoms.

Insomnia

According to the Nielsen Media Company, which tracks television viewing habits in the United States, some 20 million Americans are watching TV at 2:00 in the morning. But that's only a fraction of the people who are kept awake by insomnia.

Perhaps you fall asleep easily, but wake up at 3:00 A.M. and can't fall back to sleep. Or maybe you wake up and fall asleep several times each night, but rarely get one lone, uninterrupted stretch of restful, refreshing sleep. All these problems are insomnia.

"People think that insomnia just means trouble falling asleep," says Peter Hauri, Ph.D., director of the Mayo Clinic Insomnia Program in Rochester, Minnesota, and co-author (with Shirley Linde, Ph.D.) of *No More Sleepless Nights.* "Actually, it's any problem with falling or staying asleep."

It is estimated that 30 million to 60 million Americans—mostly women—experience chronic sleeplessness, and 10 million consult doctors for the problem. Half of all American adults have taken sleep medication at some point in their lives, and millions use sleeping pills frequently.

Insomnia's costs extend beyond the bedroom. Compared with normal sleepers, people with insomnia are less productive at work and have twice as many auto accidents. They also report generally poorer health, because sleep is critical to immune function.

"Insomnia is so common that it's accepted—mistakenly—as a normal part of getting older," says William Dement, M.D., Ph.D., director of the Stanford University Sleep Disorders Clinic and chairperson of the National Commission on Sleep Disorders Research.

SIMPLE SOLUTIONS
1. Nutrition
2. Supplements
3. Exercise
4. Relaxation Therapies
5. Visualization
6. Biofeedback
7. Aromatherapy
8. Herbal Medicine
9. Home Remedies
10. Homeopathy
11. Chinese Medicine
12. Over-the-Counter Drugs
13. Medical Measures

Obstructive Sleep Apnea: Some Snoring Can Kill

Many people snore. But one form of snoring, called obstructive sleep apnea, is more than just an annoyance. The word *apnea* means "no breathing."

Ordinary snoring does not affect your breathing, says William Dement, M.D., Ph.D., director of the Stanford University Sleep Disorders Clinic and chairperson of the National Commission on Sleep Disorders Research. But apnea does. If you have it, you periodically suck your airway closed and stop breathing—typically for a few seconds but possibly for up to a minute. When you stop breathing, a choking silence replaces your snoring.

When your airway collapses, the lack of oxygen sets off an internal alarm, and the brain rouses you, which restores your breathing. But every apnea episode—and you may have dozens each night—causes subtle physical harm. Your blood-oxygen level plummets. To compensate, your heart pumps harder, causing a sharp increase in your blood pressure and residual high blood pressure during the day. Over time, this can raise your risk of heart attack and stroke.

Apnea also destroys your sleep. "People don't wake up each time they stop breathing, but they get roused so often that they sleep ter-

But there's hope. Sleep specialists typically help about 80 percent of even chronic insomniacs fairly quickly with a program that combines home remedies, mainstream medicine, and alternative therapies.

BEST CHOICES

Nutrition

Eliminate caffeine. "Caffeine causes more sleep problems than most people realize," says Katherine Albert, M.D., Ph.D., director of the sleep lab-

ribly," Dr. Dement explains. "They are constantly sleepy during the day, have trouble concentrating, and are prone to dozing off when they shouldn't—for example, while driving."

Obstructive sleep apnea is surprisingly common. It affects about 18 million Americans, particularly overweight middle-age men. Apnea affects many women as well. About 90 percent of people with apnea are undiagnosed. "It's tragic," Dr. Dement says. "The National Commission on Sleep Disorders Research estimates that treating sleep apnea could prevent almost 38,000 deaths a year from heart attack and stroke."

Apnea is easy to diagnose. Just listen for a combination of loud snoring and choking silences. It's also easy to treat. All it takes is a continuous positive airway pressure (C-PAP) machine. This machine comes with a mask that fits over your nose. The mask is connected to a small pump that gently pushes extra oxygen into your lungs with each breath. A C-PAP prevents airway collapse and maintains a healthy level of oxygen in the blood. It costs about $1,200 and is available from sleep centers.

For a referral to a sleep center near you, send a stamped, self-addressed envelope to the American Academy of Sleep Medicine, 6391 Bandel Road N.W., Suite 101, Rochester, MN 55901-8758.

oratory at New York Presbyterian Hospital/Cornell Medical Center in New York City. But don't eliminate caffeine cold turkey, or you'll experience withdrawal symptoms—notably, a headache that can last for several days. Instead, taper off over a few weeks by mixing decreasing proportions of regular with increasing proportions of decaf. In addition, sip less regular tea and more herbal teas, and drink fewer caffeinated soft drinks and more that are caffeine-free.

Confirm that it's decaf. If a restaurant server makes a mistake and gives you regular coffee instead of decaf, you could be up all night. When you're served what you think is decaf, make sure. Ask, "This is decaf, isn't it?"

Say no to nightcaps. "Doctors used to tell insomniacs to have a cocktail or glass of wine before bedtime," says Peter Hauri, Ph.D., director of the insomnia program and co-director of the Sleep Disorders Center at the Mayo Clinic in Rochester, Minnesota. "But many people find that drinking late in the evening produces troubled, fragmented sleep." A glass of wine with dinner won't hurt, but don't drink alcohol within a few hours of retiring.

Watch what you eat. The healthier you are, the better you sleep. The healthiest diet is low-fat and near-vegetarian, based on whole grains, beans, fruits, and vegetables. Go easy on fatty, hard-to-digest foods: meats, deep-fried foods, fast foods, and greasy snacks.

Watch *when* you eat. Bedtime snacks are fine, as long as they're small and light. Don't eat a big dinner or anything heavy within an hour or two of bedtime, Dr. Hauri advises. Digestive processes can disturb sleep.

Eat sleep-inducing foods. An amino acid, tryptophan is a component of serotonin, a chemical messenger in the brain that helps induce sleep. In 1996, the Food and Drug Administration made tryptophan a prescription-only item. Ask your doctor for a prescription if you like—or get the amino acids from food sources such as tuna, cottage cheese, rice, oatmeal, eggs, peanut butter, and milk.

Supplements

Mellow with melatonin. This hormone is involved in regulating sleep. Several studies have demonstrated its sedative effect, but melatonin has been used as a sleep aid for only a few years. Its long-term safety is still unknown.

Melatonin is available over the counter in health food stores and most drugstores. Use it according to the package directions. Melatonin is not appropriate for women who are pregnant or breastfeeding or who are considering pregnancy. Nor should it be taken by anyone who is prone to depression; who is taking an antidepressant; or who has diabetes, epilepsy, migraine, or rheumatoid arthritis. Possible side effects include nausea, headache, giddiness, difficulty concentrating, and daytime sleepiness.

Defy deficiencies with a multi. "Deficiencies in the B vitamins, calcium, copper, iron, magnesium, and zinc can contribute to sleep problems," Dr. Hauri says. By eating a healthy, well-balanced diet, you can cover your nutritional bases. As insurance, clinical nutritionist Shari Lieberman, Ph.D., recommends taking a daily multivitamin/mineral supplement that supplies all of these nutrients.

Exercise

Sweat, then sleep. Regular exercise is one of the best things you can do to sleep soundly, Dr. Hauri says. Any activity helps, but he especially recommends walking—ideally, one brisk half-hour walk every day.

"Exercising in the late afternoon releases the day's stress and decreases your appetite for dinner, which helps you stick to the light supper that sleep experts recommend," Dr. Albert says. "Just don't exercise too close to bedtime. That's stimulating and can keep you up."

Relaxation Therapies

Breathe your way to Zzzs. Deep breathing is a fundamental relaxation technique. Five to 20 minutes of sitting quietly and breathing deeply before going to bed might help you fall asleep, Dr. Hauri says.

Focus on a mantra. A panel of experts appointed by the National Institutes of Health (NIH) investigated nondrug approaches to treating insomnia. They concluded that meditation produces "significant improvement in sleep."

Soak before snoozing. Bathing is a traditional relaxing bedtime ritual. Researchers at the University of California, Santa Barbara, put it to the test. Not surprisingly, their study showed that compared with nonbathers, people who took a tolerably hot bath an hour or so before bedtime fell asleep faster.

Boost sleep with the Bootzin Technique. This behavior therapy program was developed in the 1970s by Richard Bootzin, Ph.D., then at Northwestern University in Chicago. It's often quite helpful in inducing sleep. Here's what to do.

1. Go to bed only when you feel sleepy. Ignore the clock. Tune in to how you feel.

2. Use your bed only for sleeping and sex. No eating, reading, watching TV, talking on the phone, or anything else.

3. If you go to bed but can't fall asleep, get up and leave the bedroom. Read, watch TV, listen to music—do something until you feel sleepy again. Then return to bed.

4. Repeat step 3 as often as you need to throughout the night.

Restless Leg Syndrome: Stop the Shaking

You turn out the light, go to bed, snuggle into your pillow, and slowly begin to drift off to sleep. Then you feel this itchy, tingly, fidgety, jerky, creepy-crawly sensation in your legs. It's strange, annoying, and frightening—and you fall can't sleep. Unfortunately, you're one of the estimated 12 million Americans with restless leg syndrome (RLS).

Scientists don't know what causes RLS, though poor circulation through the legs appears to play a role. It can strike at any age but becomes increasingly common as people age. It's not hereditary, but in about one-third of cases, RLS seems to run in families, according to Peter Hauri, Ph.D., director of the insomnia program and co-director of the Sleep Disorders Center at the Mayo Clinic in Rochester, Minnesota.

It also seems to be stress-related. Here are some things that you can do.

Eliminate all stimulants. That means coffee, tea, chocolate, and most cola soft drinks, says Melvyn R. Werbach, M.D., assistant clinical professor at the University of California, Los Angeles, School of Medicine.

Try a sugar-free, high-protein diet. Eating a sugar-free, high-protein diet—lots of chicken, turkey, beans, and lean meats and low-fat dairy products—helped one group of people with restless leg syndrome. Symptoms often returned when they went off the special diet, however.

5. No matter when you go to sleep, set an alarm for the same time every morning.

6. Don't nap during the day.

The first night or two of using the Bootzin Technique, you may repeat step 3 several times. But over a few nights, the repetitions typically diminish and often disappear. If your insomnia recurs after a period of sleeping well, simply return to the six steps.

Get regular exercise. Any exercise helps, but focus on activities that stretch the legs—yoga, walking, gardening, dancing, and biking. Begin and end your day with leg stretches.

Manage your stress. Relaxation therapies can help restless leg syndrome, according to Dian Buchman, Ph.D., author of *The Complete Guide to Natural Sleep.* Try any approach that appeals to you: meditation, visualization, biofeedback, music, massage, aromatherapy, tai chi, qigong, or yoga.

Massage your legs before bed. Elliot Green, past president of the American Massage Therapy Association, suggests long, firm, downward strokes with the palm and heel of the hand, followed by gentle squeezing and kneading of the calf muscles.

Warm your legs. The American Sleep Disorders Association suggests taking a hot bath and using a heating pad before bed. (Don't take a heating pad to bed, however. If you fall asleep, you could get burned.)

Support your legs. Try sleeping on your side with a soft pillow between your knees. Or wear long support socks to bed.

Sleep late. Legs tend to be most restless at night and least restless in the morning, Dr. Buchman says. Try going to bed later and sleeping later in the morning.

If nothing helps, see your doctor. For persistent RLS, your doctor may prescribe medication. The drugs of choice are the same as those used to treat Parkinson's disease, but in lower doses.

Visualization

See yourself in dreamland. "Visualization therapy can be a powerful tool for inducing sleep," says Martin L. Rossman, M.D. The Academy for Guided Imagery in Mill Valley, California, offers a visualization audiocassette called *A Restful Sleep: An Imagery Experience with Getting a Good Night's Sleep.* For ordering information, write to the Academy for Guided Imagery at P. O. Box 2070, Mill Valley, CA 94942-2070.

Biofeedback

Slip into slumber with biofeedback. The NIH panel also gave high marks to biofeedback relaxation training as a sleep aid. It's similar to meditation.

Aromatherapy

Entice the Sandman with the scent of lavender. Lavender is an aromatherapy favorite for relaxation and insomnia. You can buy lavender essential oil in many health food stores and through mail-order catalogs. To use it, place a few chips of rock salt in a small, capped vial, then add a few drops of the oil. The salt absorbs the oil, so it doesn't splash out when you open the vial. Uncap the vial and inhale the scent as needed.

Herbal Medicine

Take tea and sleep. Many medicinal herbs are gentle sedatives. James A. Duke, Ph.D., recommends chamomile, catnip, hops, lavender, lemon balm, passionflower, and valerian. With the exception of valerian, you can enjoy these herbs in teas, either individually or in combination. Add 1 to 2 teaspoons of herb to 1 cup of boiled water, steep for 10 minutes, then strain.

Valerian is very effective, but it has an unpleasant taste. As a tea, the herb is virtually undrinkable. Look for capsules or a tincture in health food stores and drugstores. Use it according to the package directions.

Home Remedies

Try sex. Lovemaking has a well-deserved reputation for improving sleep. But not all sex works. "It depends on how the sex makes you feel," Dr. Hauri explains. "If you feel loved and cared for, sex can help you sleep. But if it's unsatisfying or takes place in a problematic relationship, it might be the prelude to a very poor night's sleep."

Keep a sleep diary. A sleep diary can be quite helpful in overcoming sleep problems, Dr. Albert says. It can reveal sleep-disrupting behavior patterns that might otherwise remain hidden. For 2 weeks, simply jot down what and when you eat, drink, and do everything else during the day. Also note your emotional stressors, any drugs you take, and how long and how well you sleep. Look for connections between nights when you sleep poorly and what's going on in the rest of your life.

Ditch the double bed. If you and your spouse sleep in a double bed, switch to a queen- or king-size bed, Dr. Hauri advises. "Larger beds become especially important as you age," he explains. "After age 40, you sleep less soundly and are more likely to be disturbed by a restless bedmate."

Create comfort. Test different types of mattresses. Splurge on sleepwear that feels just right for you. If you have arthritis or a bad back, try extra pillows or specially shaped therapeutic pillows.

Preserve peace. You can probably sleep through steady noise—for example, the hum of a nearby freeway, Dr. Hauri explains. But you're likely to get rudely awakened by sudden, intermittent noises—cats fighting in a neighbor's yard or a motorcycle roaring up the street. To preserve nighttime quiet, try wearing foam earplugs.

Create a dark environment. For a darker bedroom, Dian Buchman, Ph.D., author of *The Complete Guide to Natural Sleep*, suggests investing in blackout drapes, blinds, or shades. Or wear a sleep mask.

Banish your bedroom clock. "Many insomniacs have big, illuminated digital clocks staring at them all night and making them anxious," Dr. Hauri says. If you use an alarm clock, place it so that you can't see the time while you're in bed.

Sleep separately. What if one of you likes a hard foam mattress but the other prefers a waterbed? Many couples with very different sleep styles feel obligated to share the same bed. Consider twin beds or different bedrooms. "You'll both sleep better and probably feel more loving toward one another, which can lead to better sex," says Louanne Cole-Weston, Ph.D., a sex and marital therapist in Sacramento, California.

Distract yourself. Sleep is like love: It arrives only when you don't try to force it. Think about something else. Years ago, the traditional advice was to count sheep. But a Gallup survey showed that one-third of American adults read themselves to sleep.

Avoid oversleeping. Many people with insomnia stay in bed too long. If you need 7 hours of sleep but are in bed for 9, you'll toss and turn for two. Maybe you just need to go to bed later.

Establish a schedule. Every sleep expert agrees: Go to bed and wake up at the same time every day, even on weekends. "Many people need regular sleep/wake cycles and have trouble sleeping if they don't stick with them," Dr. Hauri says.

Getting regular is particularly important if you suffer from "Sunday night insomnia," the inability to fall asleep on Sunday night. "Maintain your weekday schedule on the weekend, and you may get relief come Sunday," Dr. Hauri says.

Adopt bedtime rituals. Before turning in, most people lock up their homes, change into their pajamas, brush their teeth, and turn out the lights. If you have trouble sleeping, you might add a few more rituals. Drink a cup of herbal tea, chat with your spouse, do some light reading, or take a tolerably hot bath. If you lie awake worrying that you might forget what you have to do the next day, make a "to do" list of everything you need to remember before you retire. Then let go of your list until morning.

Quit smoking. As if you need another reason to quit: Where there's smoking, there's often insomnia. Nicotine is a powerful stimulant, and insomnia is a frequent complaint among smokers.

OTHER GOOD CHOICES

Homeopathy

Buy a homeopathic sleep aid. Depending on your specific insomnia symptoms, a homeopath might prescribe any of a number of medicines. Homeopath Dana Ullman frequently recommends Arsenicum, Coffea, Ignatia, Lycopodium, and Nux vomica.

Many health food stores and some drugstores now carry homeopathic sleep aids. If you try one of these products, take it according to the package directions.

Chinese Medicine

Point the way to sleep. Oriental medicine doctors often use acupuncture to treat insomnia. But you can't very well visit an acupuncturist at 2:00 every morning. Acupressure is an effective do-it-yourself alternative. Apply steady, penetrating finger pressure for 3 minutes to each of the following points.

- ◆ Bladder 62, located in the first indentation directly below your outer anklebone
- ◆ Kidney 6, located in the slight indentation directly below your inner anklebone
- ◆ Governing Vessel 24, located between your eyebrows, where the bridge of your nose meets your forehead
- ◆ Heart 7, located on the pinkie side of the wrist crease that's closest to your palm

Restore tranquillity to your Heart. In Chinese medicine, if insomnia is not caused by some other medical problem, it is brought on by a lack of harmony in the Heart organ network, according to Efrem Korngold, O.M.D., L.Ac. To calm the Heart, Dr. Korngold prescribes pacifying herbs such as ziziphus seed, jujube seed, poria fungus, gardenia fruit, and schisandra fruit.

Home Remedies

Catch 40 winks. "Most insomniacs sleep better when they don't nap," Dr. Hauri says. "But this isn't true for everyone. Napping helps some people sleep better. Experiment and see what works best for you."

Check your medications. Caffeine is an ingredient in a surprisingly large number of drugs, including many pain and weight-loss medications. Ask your pharmacist about the possible stimulant effects of every medication you take.

Be aware of the depression connection. The myth is that people who are depressed sleep most of the day. Some do, but others hardly sleep at all. Ironically, Dr. Albert says, depression-related insomnia often responds to a counterintuitive solution—sleeping less. "Reduce your sleep time by ½ hour every 2 to 3 weeks until you limit your sleep to 5 hours a night. That often helps. You sleep less, but you sleep fairly deeply. Most people call it an improvement."

Unfortunately, if you have depression-related insomnia, the antidepressants your doctor prescribes might make it worse. The most popular family of antidepressants—fluoxetine (Prozac), paroxetine (Paxil), and sertraline (Zoloft)—often disrupts sleep. Ask your doctor about newer drugs that don't have this effect.

Over-the-Counter Drugs

Savor a sedative side effect. Over-the-counter antihistamines are notorious for causing drowsiness. This side effect can be a problem if you need to drive a long distance, but it comes in handy if you have insomnia. Over-the-counter sleep aids—including Alka-Seltzer PM, Compoz, Excedrin PM, Nytol, Sominex, and Unisom—contain the antihistamine diphenhydramine. Follow the directions on the package.

MEDICAL MEASURES

Sleeping pills may knock you out, Dr. Albert explains, but they prevent good, deep, refreshing sleep. They can be helpful when used in the short term for up to a week if you're dealing with a major trauma—for example, the death of a loved one. But after a week, they begin to lose their effectiveness.

Years ago, when doctors prescribed barbiturate sleeping pills, addiction was a real problem. But current sleep aids carry much less risk of dependence. According to Dr. Dement, today's sleeping pills are rarely abused. "In fact, they're underprescribed," he says. "A recent Gallup survey found that only 10 percent of people with serious insomnia get prescriptions and that few of them use sleeping pills for more than 5 nights."

For his patients with severe insomnia, Dr. Dement prescribes the drug zopidem (Ambien). Because of the small but real risk of abuse, he provides only 10 pills at a time while working to find nondrug solutions to the sleep problem. Refills are rarely necessary.

If your doctor gives you sleeping pills for short-term use and you find yourself needing refills of your prescription, ask your doctor for something else—a referral to an accredited sleep clinic. Few people require more than three visits to a sleep clinic. "Clinical sleep work is very gratifying," Dr. Dement explains. "The vast majority of insomniacs can be diagnosed and treated fairly quickly, and then they feel great."

The American Academy of Sleep Medicine makes referrals to the more than 200 accredited sleep centers in the United States. For a list of these centers, send a stamped, self-addressed envelope to the association at 6391 Bandel Road N.W., Suite 101, Rochester, MN 55901-8758.

Irritable Bowel Syndrome

Irritable bowel syndrome isn't a disease. Rather, it's a collection of persistent, distressing gastrointestinal symptoms: abdominal cramps, bloating, flatulence, and diarrhea or constipation.

When you have irritable bowel syndrome (IBS), you feel as though your gastrointestinal tract is out of control, according to Anne Simons, M.D. It's not only uncomfortable but also unnerving because you never know when symptoms are going to strike.

If you have IBS, you probably first experienced symptoms in your late teens or twenties. And you probably are a woman: An estimated two-thirds of people with IBS are female. The condition seems more common among Whites than among non-Whites.

SIMPLE SOLUTIONS
1. Nutrition
2. Elimination Diet
3. Relaxation Therapies
4. Meditation
5. Visualization
6. Herbal Medicine
7. Homeopathy
8. Chinese Medicine
9. Supplements
10. Medical Measures

Doctors describe IBS as a functional problem, a glitch in how your colon works. The muscles that surround your colon contract in waves to move solid wastes into your rectum. These contractions, called peristalsis, are supposed to be gentle and hardly noticeable. But in IBS, they become irregular, poorly coordinated, and at times unusually forceful or lethargic. The result? Pain, cramping, diarrhea, constipation, and other IBS symptoms.

While no one knows exactly what causes IBS, there is evidence that stress aggravates the condition. Your gastrointestinal tract has some 100 million nerve cells—more than even your spinal cord. When you're under stress, these nerve cells become irritated, which can disrupt gastrointestinal function—especially in those with IBS.

For some people, the link between stress and IBS becomes a vicious circle.

"Your IBS symptoms may make you anxious because they're painful and unpredictable," explains Alan P. Brauer, M.D. "But your anxiety only aggravates your symptoms because your gastrointestinal tract is so sensitive to stress." This is why stress management plays such an important role in controlling IBS symptoms.

While IBS is persistent, it doesn't steadily worsen over time, says William E. Whitehead, Ph.D., professor of medical psychology at Johns Hopkins University School of Medicine in Baltimore. Nor does it predispose you to other diseases. In one long-term study of 112 people with IBS, only 10 developed other gastrointestinal conditions over a period of 30 years.

If you've been experiencing persistent gastrointestinal distress, you should see your doctor for a proper diagnosis. If you're told that you have IBS, you can use the following remedies to minimize your symptoms.

BEST CHOICES

Nutrition

Eat smaller meals more often. Instead of the standard three squares a day, try eating four or five smaller, snack-size meals. That way, your digestive system won't have to work so hard to process so much food.

Take your time to dine. Make your mealtimes as relaxed as possible. Eat slowly and chew your food thoroughly. Stay focused on your meal—don't read the newspaper, watch TV, or answer the phone.

Eschew fat. In one study, researchers fed a high-fat meal to 16 people who had IBS and to 8 people who didn't. The fatty food caused colon spasms in those with IBS, especially in those whose primary symptom was diarrhea.

Gradually add fiber. Gastroenterologists agree that eating more fiber can help relieve IBS. But you need to add fiber slowly so that your digestive system has time to adjust. Write down how many servings of high-fiber foods—whole grains, beans, fruits, and vegetables—you eat each day for 1 or 2 weeks. Then add one or two servings a week until you're eating seven to nine servings a day.

Banish bran. One high-fiber food that you may want to avoid is wheat bran. For people with IBS, wheat bran may provide too much of a good thing. Researchers recommend getting fiber from other foods.

Be smart about sugar. At least one study suggests that sugar may raise the risk of IBS symptoms. In the study, researchers had two groups of volunteers follow the same diet for 2 weeks. In addition, one group ate 4 ounces of sugar a day. Among those who ate the sugar, both peristalsis and intestinal gas formation increased significantly.

Avoid other irritants. Anything that irritates your gastrointestinal tract can aggravate your IBS symptoms, says G. Nicholas Verne, M.D., assistant professor of medicine in the division of gastroenterology and hepatology at the Medical University of South Carolina College of Medicine in Charleston. So steer clear of carbonated and caffeinated beverages as well as foods made with the artificial sweetener sorbitol. If you're lactose-intolerant, eliminate milk and other dairy products.

Elimination Diet

Ferret out offending foods. If your IBS symptoms tend to flare up after you eat, they may be triggered by certain foods. To identify the offenders, try following an elimination diet with the guidance of your doctor.

For one study, 113 people with IBS went on a strict elimination diet. Within 3 to 6 weeks, they were able to identify their problem foods. Then they resumed their normal eating habits, minus the foods to which they were sensitive. Over the next year, 88 percent reported less bloating, 85 percent experienced less diarrhea, and 65 percent had less constipation.

Relaxation Therapies

Learn to destress. Researchers at the Center for Stress and Anxiety Disorders at the State University of New York at Albany trained 19 people with IBS in progressive muscle relaxation and biofeedback. The participants also received IBS education. Four years later, 90 percent of those in the program saw more than 50 percent improvement in their symptoms.

According to Dr. Whitehead, any relaxation therapy can calm your gastrointestinal tract and help relieve IBS symptoms. If progressive muscle relaxation and biofeedback don't appeal to you, try deep breathing, massage, aromatherapy, tai chi, or yoga.

Meditation

Use your mind to master your symptoms. At the University Hospital of Wales in Cardiff, researchers divided 35 people with IBS into two groups. One took antispasmodic drugs to control IBS symptoms. The other enrolled in a class that provided IBS education and training in a meditation-based relaxation routine. Among those who took medication, few experienced any improvement in their symptoms. But two-thirds of the meditators reported that their symptoms had gotten better.

Visualization

Envision your abdomen at ease. If you want to try visualization, here's an exercise from Gerald N. Epstein, M.D., director of the Academy of Integrative Medicine and Mental Imagery in New York City: Begin by closing your eyes. Slowly inhale and exhale three times. As you continue this slow, relaxed breathing, imagine a mermaid with flowing golden hair and a sleek, silvery body and tail. She's swimming rhythmically through your digestive tract, which is calm. Sense her there. Have her swim to any places where you feel pain, cramping, or any other symptoms. Have her touch those areas, gently massaging them until they are healed and you no longer feel discomfort. Then have her complete her swim through your gastrointestinal tract to ensure that everything is in order. When your mermaid is finished, open your eyes. Do this exercise twice a day, morning and evening.

Herbal Medicine

Partake of peppermint. The use of peppermint as a digestive soother dates back to ancient times. Modern research has shown that the herb's oil relaxes the smooth muscle tissue throughout the gastrointestinal tract. This reduces colon spasms, a key component of IBS.

Take one or two enteric-coated peppermint-oil capsules after every meal, recommends Joseph Pizzorno Jr., N.D. If you can't find enteric-coated capsules in a health food store, consult a naturopathic physician.

Take fiber by the spoonful. If you have trouble eating enough fiber-rich foods, James A. Duke, Ph.D., suggests using psyllium seed as a fiber supplement. "Psyllium is a great source of fiber that helps treat the diarrhea and constipation of an irritable bowel," he says. You can find psyllium seed in most health food stores. Take up to 3 tablespoons a day, mixing each dose into 8 ounces of water or juice.

Homeopathy

Assuage your symptoms with Asafoetida. German researchers gave people with IBS either a homeopathic preparation of asafoetida, an Ayurvedic herb, or a placebo. Those who took the homeopathic preparation experienced significantly greater relief from their symptoms.

Asafoetida doesn't work for everyone with IBS, says homeopath Dana Ullman. "Because IBS symptoms vary, you need to consult a homeopath to get the right medicine," he explains. Other medicines that may help include Argentum nitricum, Arsenicum album, and Mercurius.

Chinese Medicine

Harmonize your Spleen and Stomach. Practitioners of Chinese medicine attribute IBS to an imbalance in the Spleen and Stomach organ networks. "The first thing to consider is food sensitivities—lactose intolerance or problems digesting wheat or other grains," says Efrem Korngold, O.M.D., L.Ac. "They're best treated by avoidance."

In addition, Dr. Korngold often treats IBS with prescribed Chinese medicines called Curing Pills and Shen Qu Cha. Curing Pills contain a combination of 15 herbs, including atractylodes, poria fungus, and medicated leven (a combination of fermented barley, wheat, and rice sprouts). Shen Qu Cha is a hard square cake that is simmered in hot water and taken as a tea. It consists primarily of medicated leven, with other herbs that help normalize digestion.

Get relief point by point. Dr. Korngold recommends acupuncture as a treatment for IBS. Which points are stimulated depends on your specific symptoms. For treatment, you need to consult a professional acupuncturist.

OTHER GOOD CHOICES

Supplements

Beat IBS with bacteria. Often people with IBS have unusually low levels of beneficial (probiotic) bacteria in their colons, Dr. Pizzorno says. To correct this problem, he recommends taking 1 teaspoon of supplemental *Lactobacillus acidophilus* every day. You can also get *L. acidophilus* by eating yogurt that contains live bacterial cultures (the label should say so). If you have any serious gastrointestinal problems that require medical attention, check with your doctor before taking *L. acidophilus* supplements.

MEDICAL MEASURES

A growing number of mainstream M.D.'s are recommending dietary changes and relaxation therapies as treatments for IBS. They also prescribe various drugs, including antidiarrheals such as loperamide (Imodium), antispasmodics such as dicyclomine (Di-Spaz), and, in severe cases, antidepressants.

RED FLAGS

If you experience any of the following, see your doctor right away.

◆ You pass black or bloody stools.

◆ Your abdominal pain becomes more severe or changes from periodic to constant.

◆ Your abdominal pain is accompanied by fever or vomiting.

◆ Your symptoms don't noticeably improve after 2 weeks of self-care.

Jet Lag

Jet lag is the bane of many an airline passenger. It doesn't do your health any serious harm, but it sure can spoil the better part of a vacation or business trip.

But maybe you can lessen the symptoms of jet lag and start having fun sooner. Create your own travel kit of blended-medicine measures, and you might be able to send jet lag packing.

Jet lag results from a disruption of your body's internal clock, the mechanism that regulates your sleep/wake cycle. Your internal clock is set to the time zone in which you live. If you travel into another time zone, your internal clock has to adjust itself.

SIMPLE SOLUTIONS
1. Nutrition
2. Supplements
3. Exercise
4. Home Remedies
5. Homeopathy
6. Chinese Medicine

Normally, this internal process runs . . . well, like clockwork. But problems can arise when you change time zones rapidly, as you do when you travel by plane.

Your internal clock can't reset itself fast enough. Until it catches up, you feel out of sorts.

That's jet lag.

Most people develop jet lag only when they cross three or more time zones. Virtually everyone feels it after transoceanic flights between the United States and Europe or Asia.

Until your internal clock synchronizes with the new time zone, you're likely to experience fatigue, irritability, and mental fogginess—the classic jet lag symptoms. You may also be bothered by sleep problems, as your body's sleep/wake cycle is temporarily disrupted.

Even if you do nothing to treat these symptoms, jet lag eventually goes away on its own. You'll definitely be better off, however, if you take steps to minimize the effects of "time travel."

Here's what you can do.

BEST CHOICES

Nutrition

Count your liquid assets. Even mild dehydration can make you feel mentally fuzzy and out of sorts, aggravating jet lag. So drink plenty of water and juices while flying, advises William Dement, M.D., Ph.D., director of the Stanford University Sleep Disorders Clinic and chairperson of the National Commission on Sleep Disorders Research.

Eat light for a day or two. Your digestive system is tied to your internal clock. Stick with light meals of easily digestible foods such as fruits, breads, and salads, recommends Stanley Coren, Ph.D., professor of psychology at the University of British Columbia in Vancouver.

Steer clear of spicy cuisine. For a few days after arriving in your destination, avoid eating spicy foods close to bedtime, Dr. Dement says. They disrupt sleep, which will only make you more tired.

Supplements

Minimize discomfort with melatonin. A hormone produced in your brain, melatonin plays a key role in resetting your internal clock. Many studies have shown that melatonin can speed recovery from jet lag.

Melatonin works best when you take it at specific times and coordinate its use with exposure to sunlight, says Alfred Lewy, M.D., Ph.D., professor of psychiatry and director of the sleep laboratory at Oregon Health Sciences University in Portland.

If you're flying west, he suggests taking a 0.5-milligram dose of melatonin the moment you wake up on the day before your departure. Do the same the day you travel and the day after you arrive. On the second and third days after your arrival, take a dose of melatonin an hour after waking up. If you can, set aside time in the afternoons to head outdoors for some sun.

If you're flying east, Dr. Lewy suggests taking a 0.5-milligram dose of melatonin at about 3:00 P.M. on the day before your departure and the day you travel. The day after your arrival, take a dose of melatonin at 3:00 P.M. on the "old time." So if you flew from Los Angeles to Philadelphia, 3:00 old time would be 6:00 new time. On days two and three after your arrival, take a dose of melatonin an hour *earlier* than on day one of your arrival. Try to get some sun during the morning hours.

Exercise

Wake up, work out. Exercise helps reset your internal clock. So try to squeeze in some physical activity on the first morning after you arrive in your destination. "Calisthenics, aerobics, even running in place for 10 minutes can help," Dr. Coren says.

Have fun in the sun. If possible, head outdoors for your workout. "Exposing yourself to sunlight is one of the best ways to reset your internal clock," says Dr. Coren.

Home Remedies

Stock up on Zzzs. Jet lag hits harder if you arrive at the airport tired. "Forget the bon voyage party," Dr. Coren says. "Get a full night's sleep before your trip." For most adults, that means at least 7 hours of shut-eye.

Change your bedtime. Before your departure, when you sleep can be as important as how long you sleep. "Determine the number of time zones that you'll be crossing, then count back an equal number of days from your departure date," advises Anne Simons, M.D. "If you're flying east, go to bed and get up 1 hour earlier every day until you leave. If you're flying west, go to bed and get up 1 hour later every day. This technique presets your internal clock, so when you finally arrive in your destination, your body should already be on destination time."

Pretend you're already there. If you're wearing a watch, reset it to destination time while you're waiting for takeoff. Then during your flight, eat and sleep according to the new time.

Or stay on home time. If you're making a quick trip across time zones, consider staying on your home time, Dr. Simons suggests.

Improve your odds of snoozing. If you plan to sleep while flying, book a window seat, suggests travel medicine specialist Samuel Shelanski, M.D. That way, your row-mates won't disturb you when they get in and out of their seats. Also, pack earplugs and a sleep mask in your carry-on in order to block out noise and light.

Arrive in the late afternoon. For reasons that remain a mystery, your internal clock has less trouble adjusting itself if you schedule your arrival for late afternoon. Seasoned flyers follow this rule of thumb: Travel east, fly early; travel west, fly late.

Skip the in-flight drinks. Alcohol is dehydrating and intoxicating, and it disrupts sleep—which makes jet lag worse.

Be careful with caffeine. On transoceanic flights, go easy on caffeine if you're scheduled to arrive at night, Dr. Simons says. Otherwise, it can keep you awake while you should be sleeping, so your body can't adjust to local time.

OTHER GOOD CHOICES

Homeopathy

Relieve symptoms with Arnica. The primary homeopathic treatment for jet lag is Arnica, says homeopath Dana Ullman. "It's the medicine of choice for shock and traumatic injury," he explains. "Jet lag isn't an injury, but it's a shock to the system."

Other homeopathic medicines can also relieve jet lag. Ullman recommends Gelsemium for jet lag that causes extreme fatigue. For jet lag that causes stomach distress, he suggests Ipecacuanha. If you feel dizzy, you may need Cocculus, he says. A homeopath can analyze your symptoms and prescribe the right medicine for you.

Chinese Medicine

Press away stress. Acupuncture treatment by a professional acupuncturist before departure and after arrival can prevent the stress that leads to jet lag, says Efrem Korngold, O.M.D., L.Ac. If you prefer a self-help approach, try acupressure. Apply steady, penetrating finger pressure to each of the following points for 3 minutes.

◆ Liver 3, situated on top of your foot in the webbing between your big toe and second toe

◆ Large Intestine 4, located on the back of your hand where the bones of your thumb and index finger meet

◆ Extra Point Yin Tang, located just above the bridge of your nose, exactly between your eyebrows

Kidney Stones

Kidney stone pain is so excruciating that women say it's worse than childbirth. In fact, it sends some 325,000 people to the hospital every year, thinking that they're at death's door.

But kidney stones are rarely life-threatening. In fact, they are a little disappointing when you get a glimpse of them. Many are so tiny that they're barely visible to the naked eye.

It's not entirely clear how kidney stones develop. But most scientists agree that the main culprit is oversaturated urine.

Consider this analogy: If you mix a little salt into water, the salt dissolves with no difficulty. But if you keep adding salt, the water eventually becomes saturated—that is, it can't hold any more salt. If you continue adding salt to the already saturated water, the salt remains in solid form. It just can't dissolve, so it becomes crystallized. Kidney stones form by a similar process.

SIMPLE SOLUTIONS
1. Nutrition
2. Supplements
3. Herbal Medicine
4. Over-the-Counter Drugs
5. Chinese Medicine
6. Ayurvedic Medicine
7. Naturopathy
8. Medical Measures

Your kidneys extract a waste product called urea from your blood and combine it with water to make urine. But if the urea content of your urine becomes too high, certain compounds in your urine can solidify into stones.

The vast majority of kidney stones, about 82 percent, form from calcium—usually calcium oxalate but sometimes calcium phosphate. Another 10 percent of stones are made from magnesium ammonium phosphate, also known as struvite. Seven percent of stones consist of uric acid, while 1 percent of stones contain the amino acid cystine. This chapter focuses on calcium stones because they are the most common.

You've probably passed kidney stones before without even knowing it. Most stones are so tiny that they navigate your kidneys with ease, then travel down the ureters—the tubes that connect your kidneys to your bladder—without a hitch. You never see them, and you certainly never feel them.

But a larger stone can get stuck in your kidneys and cause severe pain—renal colic, as doctors call it. The pain usually strikes at waist level on either side of your spine, which is where your kidneys sit. It typically comes and goes in waves, though it may be more constant. You may also feel nauseated.

As the stone slowly inches its way out of your kidney and down the ureter to your bladder, the pain moves from your back to your front and eventually into your groin. It finally goes away once the stone enters your bladder.

The whole process of passing the stone lasts anywhere from a few minutes to 48 hours. Afterward, as urine carries the stone out of your body, you may feel some pain or burning on urination. You may also notice a small amount of blood in your urine, which should clear up within a day or two after you pass the stone.

Only the most stubborn stones require surgical removal. The vast majority vacate the premises on their own. You can take steps to hasten their departure and to discourage them from coming back. Here's what the experts recommend.

BEST CHOICES

Nutrition

Make your stone swim. When you have a kidney stone, drink lots of water—at least one 10-ounce glass every hour. This may be difficult if you feel nauseated, but drink as much as you can. The fluid helps flush the stone out of your system.

Drink a toast to prevention. Some beverages do a better job of preventing stones than others, presumably because they keep stone-forming minerals dissolved in urine. The most protective drink is wine: Eight ounces a day reduces stone risk by 59 percent. By comparison, coffee cut risk by 10 percent; tea, by 8 percent; and water, by just 2 percent.

Of course, if you don't drink, don't start for the sake of preventing kidney stones. But if you do drink, know that one glass of wine a day may be enough to stop stones from forming.

Pour a glass of "lemon-aid." Citric acid, a compound found in lemons, also helps prevent stone formation, says Alan Gaby, M.D. "Some people find that drinking lots of lemonade helps keep stones from recurring," he notes.

Ax the oxalate. Most kidney stones are composed of calcium oxalate. An enormous number of foods contain oxalate, but fortunately, only a small number appear to raise urinary oxalate levels enough to contribute to stone formation. If you've ever had a kidney stone, or if you're at risk, naturopathic doctors Silena Heron, N.D., and Eric Yarnell, N.D., of Sedona, Arizona, advise you to avoid spinach, beet greens, rhubarb, grapefruit, strawberries, wheat bran, nuts, and chocolate.

Ironically, coffee and tea are also high in oxalate. But as researchers found, these beverages actually discourage stone formation. There's a simple explanation, the researchers say: Very little of the oxalate in coffee and tea gets absorbed, so even less ends up in the kidneys.

Consume more calcium. Because most kidney stones are calcium oxalate, you may think that reducing your intake of the mineral would help prevent stone formation. In fact, studies have shown that in people on low-calcium diets, the concentration of oxalate in urine increases substantially. It seems that calcium helps keep oxalate dissolved in urine. So if you reduce your calcium intake, the oxalate in your body is more likely to trigger stones.

To increase your calcium intake, eat more leafy greens, broccoli, and tofu and other soy foods. Don't rely on dairy products, though. Because they're high in protein, they can actually raise your risk of kidney stones. And if you're taking a calcium supplement, save it to take with lunch or dinner.

Supplements

Reap big benefits from potassium and magnesium. At the Kaiser Permanente Medical Care Program in Oakland, California, Bruce Ettinger, M.D., gave 64 people with recurrent kidney stones either a supplement containing potassium and magnesium citrate or a placebo (a fake pill). After 3 years, the supplement takers had 85 percent fewer recurrences than the placebo takers.

For her patients, clinical nutritionist Shari Lieberman, Ph.D., prescribes 200 milligrams of potassium and 500 milligrams of magnesium every day. Because of potential serious risks associated with potassium, take supplements only under your doctor's care.

Make a beeline for B_6. In a study conducted in India, people with recurrent calcium oxalate stones took 10 milligrams of vitamin B_6 every day. After 3 months, their urinary oxalate levels declined significantly, reducing their risk of future stone formation. If you want to try B_6, Joseph Pizzorno Jr., N.D., recommends taking 25 milligrams a day.

Herbal Medicine

Go for the goldenrod. In Europe, goldenrod is widely used to treat and prevent kidney stones, according to Varro E. Tyler, Ph.D., Sc.D., distinguished professor emeritus of pharmacognosy (natural pharmacy) at Purdue University in West Lafayette, Indiana. The herb works so well that it has received the endorsement of Commission E, the German expert panel that evaluates the safety and effectiveness of herbal medicines.

To treat kidney stones, Dr. Tyler recommends adding 2 teaspoons of the dried above-ground parts of the herb to ½ pint of water. Bring the water to a boil, then let it stand for 2 minutes before straining out the plant material. Drink up to two cupfuls of tea a day.

Sample other healing herbs. Naturopaths sometimes prescribe the herb saw palmetto as a treatment for kidney stones. It is believed to help relax the ureter, allowing stones to pass more easily. See your naturopath about dosage information.

Over-the-Counter Drugs

Put out your pain. Any one of the popular over-the-counter pain relievers—aspirin, ibuprofen, or acetaminophen—can help ease your discomfort until your stone passes.

OTHER GOOD CHOICES

Chinese Medicine

Try Chinese herbs. To help kidney stones pass, Efrem Korngold, O.M.D., L.Ac., prescribes a number of herbs, including licorice root, astragalus root, peony root, rehmannia root, and lonicera flowers. To help stones dissolve, he prescribes the herbs lysimachia, ligodium, andrographis, and pseudoginseng, along with powdered amber.

Take a poke at pain. At Yang-Ming Medical College in Taiwan, some people with kidney stones were given pain relievers, while others received acupuncture. Both treatments worked equally well in relieving pain, but acupuncture produced fewer side effects.

If you want to use acupressure instead, apply steady, penetrating finger pressure at each of the following points for 3 minutes during a kidney stone attack.

◆ Gallbladder 25, located on the outer tip of your lowest rib, on the same side as your stone

◆ Spleen 6, located four finger-widths above your inner anklebone on the back inner border of your shinbone

◆ Bladder 60, located on the outside of your leg, in the hollow between your anklebone and Achilles tendon

Ayurvedic Medicine

Let your dosha determine your treatment. An Ayurvedic physician creates a prescription that's tailored to your individual dosha, or constitutional type. Generally, treatment involves eating certain foods (squash, cilantro, honey, cucumber, grapes, watermelon, rice, and coconut milk) while avoiding others (beans, milk, spinach, tomatoes, eggplant, and onions). It also features Ayurvedic herbs and a type of massage known as panchakarma.

Naturopathy

Treat stones with heat. Naturopaths recommend soaking in tolerably hot baths or applying hot compresses to the painful area until your stone passes. The warmth is relaxing, and it helps lessen the anxiety brought on by a kidney stone.

MEDICAL MEASURES

Once your pain subsides, try urinating into a strainer so that you can catch your stone. Then take it to your doctor for analysis. If your pain is due to kidney stones, chances are that a calcium oxalate stone is to blame. But if it's another type of stone, you may need additional professional treatment. Your doctor should also check you for kidney obstructions and urinary tract infections.

If your stone seems to be stuck—that is, if your pain doesn't steadily move south toward your bladder—don't hesitate to head for the nearest hospital emergency room. Assuming your pain is due to kidney stones, emergency treatment usually involves fluids and powerful pain relievers. The doctor will likely wait a while to see if the stone passes on its own. About 85 percent eventually do. The rest must be surgically removed to prevent kidney damage.

These days, invasive surgery has largely given way to lithotripsy, which involves pulverizing kidney stones into powder using ultrasound shock waves.

RED FLAGS

If your kidney stone attack is accompanied by any of the following symptoms, consult your doctor without delay.

◆ Intense back or abdominal pain that doesn't improve after 1 hour
◆ Bleeding on urination
◆ Vomiting
◆ Fever and chills

Lactose Intolerance

"The water of human kindness" might not sound as poetic as "the milk of human kindness." But to anyone with lactose intolerance, there's no kindness at all in milk.

Lactose intolerance is the condition that leaves some people unable to consume dairy products without serious repercussions. The list of symptoms is long and includes such discomforts as bloating, diarrhea, flatulence, and abdominal distress. If you get these symptoms after eating dairy products or drinking milk, you may have already pegged your problem as lactose intolerance. And perhaps you've already cut way back on dairy products, and now you feel better.

SIMPLE SOLUTIONS
1. Nutrition
2. Supplements
3. Homeopathy
4. Chinese Medicine

Well, you may really be lactose-intolerant. Then again, you may have another digestive problem that mimics lactose intolerance, such as irritable bowel syndrome. Or you may be one of many people who simply have nervous stomachs.

Between ages 5 and 14, many of us lose as much as 95 percent of our ability to produce an enzyme called lactase. Without lactase, we can't very well digest lactose in milk and milk products. The result is lactose intolerance, says Michael Levitt, M.D., professor of medicine at the University of Minnesota Medical School in Minneapolis.

The rate of lactose intolerance varies widely among racial and ethnic groups. People of African-American, Asian, Middle Eastern, Mediterranean, or Native American heritage have a four-in-five chance of being lactose-intolerant. But if your ancestors came from Central or Northern Europe, your risk of having lactose intolerance is more like one in five.

To find out for certain whether you're lactose-intolerant, talk to your doctor about getting a breath hydrogen analysis. Prior to the test, you must fast for 8 to 12 hours, then eat a food containing about 1 ounce of lactose. If your stomach doesn't digest the lactose, it passes into your large intestine. There, the sugar ferments, releasing unusually large amounts of hydrogen. You'll begin exhaling this hydrogen starting about an hour after you eat the food and continuing for several more hours.

Even if you are indeed lactose-intolerant, you may not have to give up milk and other dairy products altogether. With a combination of dietary changes, lactose supplements, and perhaps a few other blended-medicine options, you can enjoy dairy while still being kind to your digestive tract.

BEST CHOICES

Nutrition

Spread out your indulgences. If you're lactose-intolerant, you're smart to monitor the amount of milk and milk products that you consume. But more important than cutting back on dairy is making sure that you don't eat a lot of dairy all at once, Dr. Levitt says. In other words, don't invite trouble by having cheese and milk in the same meal. Such a meal can really punish your digestive tract.

Pair dairy and nondairy. Unless you're severely lactose-intolerant, you can probably consume a modest amount of dairy—about 2 cups of milk or its equivalent—every day without problems. Pair a dairy food with nondairy foods, and eat the nondairy foods first. This helps prevent digestive symptoms.

Find foods that don't offend. You may find that certain dairy products don't cause much trouble at all, such as yogurt with live-culture bacteria. That's because the live cultures in the yogurt predigest the lactose, so it doesn't cause problems.

Not all yogurt contains live cultures, however. Make sure that the one you choose says "live active cultures" on the label.

Other dairy products that may go down easy are buttermilk—which is cultured like yogurt—and certain cheeses. Also, look for milk and other dairy products with added lactase.

Keep up your calcium intake. If you're cutting back on your dairy consumption, you may be shortchanging yourself on calcium, a mineral that's absolutely essential for strong bones. So add other calcium-rich foods to your diet. Good sources of the mineral include sardines, mackerel, salmon, sesame seeds, sunflower seeds, almonds, spinach and other leafy greens, tofu, and bean sprouts.

Leave Lactose Behind

In terms of lactose content, not all dairy foods are created equal. So while some may give you no end of trouble, others may pass through your digestive system without a hitch

The following chart compares the lactose content of various dairy foods. The amounts listed in the right-hand column indicate grams of lactose per 100 grams—about 3.6 ounces—of the food. If you can't bear to part with dairy, you may be able to tolerate foods with less lactose, like those toward the end of the chart.

Food	Lactse (g)
Condensed or evaporated milk	11
American cheese	5
Cow's milk (whole, 2%, 1%, and skim)	5
Cream	4
Feta cheese	4
Half-and-half	4
Ice cream	3–6
Cottage cheese	3
Ricotta	3
Sour cream	3
Cream cheese	2
Roquefort	2
Sherbet	2
Swiss	1–2
Butter or margarine	1
Camembert	1
Muenster	1
Mozzarella	0–3
Parmesan	0–3
Blue	0–2
Brie	0–2
Cheddar	0–2
Provolone	0–2

Supplements

Latch on to Lactaid. An over-the-counter lactose supplement, Lactaid is a safe and inexpensive way to make milk tolerable. Just add the recommended number of drops to your milk, then refrigerate for 24 hours.

OTHER GOOD CHOICES

Homeopathy

Look at the big picture. According to homeopath Dana Ullman, the symptoms of lactose intolerance often are just part of a larger symptom picture. To treat such a broad spectrum of symptoms, many homeopaths prescribe constitutional medicines, which heal the whole body. To find out which constitutional medicine would work best for you, consult a homeopath.

Chinese Medicine

Get an expert's opinion. Practitioners of Chinese medicine view lactose intolerance as a weakness within the Spleen and Stomach organ networks, accompanied by stagnation of qi. Because the symptoms of lactose intolerance vary, a practitioner must assess your unique situation before deciding on an appropriate course of treatment.

Use your fingers for relief. Acupressure can help relieve the symptoms of lactose intolerance, according to Michael Reed Gach, founder and director of the Acupressure Institute. Apply steady, penetrating finger pressure at each of the following points for 3 minutes.

◆ Conception Vessel 12, located halfway between the end of your breastbone and your navel on the midline of your abdomen (do not stimulate this point if you've just eaten or if you're a woman who's pregnant)

◆ Conception Vessel 6, located three finger-widths below your navel

◆ Stomach 36, located four finger-widths below your kneecap and one finger-width toward the outside of your shinbone

◆ Pericardium 6, located in the middle of your inner wrist, 2½ finger-widths above the wrist crease

◆ Spleen 4, located on the arch of your foot, one thumb-width behind the ball of your foot

Macular Degeneration

If you have macular degeneration, it may seem as though your eyes are playing tricks on you. Door frames, telephone poles, and the edges of buildings appear bent or wavy. Other objects seem to change in color or size when you look at them with one eye closed, then the other. And you may notice a blurry blank spot in the middle of your field of vision, as though someone erased part of the scenery.

SIMPLE SOLUTIONS
1. Nutrition
2. Supplements
3. Herbal Medicine
4. Home Remedies
5. Homeopathy
6. Chinese Medicine
7. Medical Measures

At the back of each of your eyes is a light-sensitive, nerve-rich area called the retina. The retina translates light into visual images, which then travel to your brain via the optic nerve. At the center of the retina is the macula, a tiny but supersensitive area that enables you to see color and fine detail.

If the macula deteriorates, as it does in macular degeneration, objects at the center of your field of vision appear wavy and change from color to black and white. As the condition advances, you begin viewing the world from the corners of your eyes rather than straight ahead.

What causes the macula to deteriorate? Oxidative damage, the same process that leads to the formation of cataracts. Oxidative damage occurs as highly unstable oxygen ions, called free radicals, circulate in your blood and find their way into every bodily tissue. Just as oxygen rusts iron, the oxygen ions harm healthy cells. When the affected cells are located in the macula, macular degeneration results.

Some free radicals form naturally as a by-product of various bodily functions, explains Alan P. Brauer, M.D. But certain lifestyle factors—especially eating a high-fat diet and smoking—greatly increase the number of free radicals floating around inside your body.

Try This at Home

In its earliest stages, macular degeneration produces no symptoms. But changes in the macula can be detected during an eye exam. That's why everyone over age 50 should schedule a professional exam—especially people who haven't been to an eye doctor for a few years, says Anne Simons, M.D. Most experts recommend an exam every 2 years, more often if a problem is found.

That said, here's a simple self-test that you can use to check yourself for macular degeneration. It's called an Amsler grid. If you wear glasses or contacts, put them on first. Hold the grid at a comfortable reading distance. With one eye covered, look at the dot at the center of the grid. Repeat with your other eye covered. If any of the lines near the dot appear wavy, or if you see any blank spots on the grid, consult your doctor for further testing.

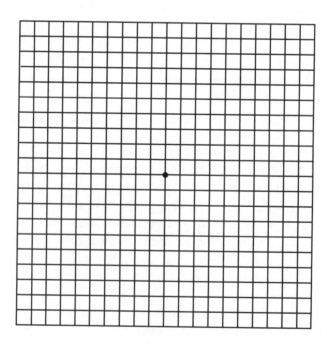

Other factors help decide who gets macular degeneration and who doesn't. Age certainly plays a role. Macular degeneration is rare before age 50 but becomes more common between ages 50 and 65. One in four people between the ages of 65 and 75 has the condition; the figure jumps to one in three people over the age of 75.

Macular degeneration doesn't always develop in the same way. In fact, the condition takes two distinct forms: dry and wet. The dry form is much more common, accounting for 80 to 90 percent of all cases. The wet form is much more severe.

In dry macular degeneration, the macula becomes thin and peppered with yellow spots called drusen. This happens quite slowly and painlessly. But over time, it can seriously affect your central vision.

By comparison, wet macular degeneration can destroy central vision very quickly. This form occurs when abnormal blood vessels grow underneath the retina and displace the macula, much like tree roots buckling a sidewalk. The blood vessels often leak, leading to the formation of scar tissue. The scar tissue is what alters your eyesight.

No matter which type of macular degeneration you have, you need to be under the care of an ophthalmologist. The treatment should focus on preventing the condition from getting worse. For the wet form, this most likely means surgery. For the dry form, alternative therapies show the most promise. Here's what the experts recommend.

BEST CHOICES

Nutrition

Make like Popeye—eat your spinach. Compounds in the vitamin A family of nutrients called lutein and zeaxanthin, as well as the other carotenoids, seem to thwart macular degeneration. They're antioxidants, which means that they have the ability to neutralize harmful free radicals. In this way, antioxidants safeguard the maculae against free-radical damage.

Spinach contains all of these compounds. But if you're not partial to spinach, don't worry. You can also get lutein and zeaxanthin by eating other vegetables.

Foods to Set Your Sights On

Lutein and zeaxanthin belong to the vitamin A family of nutrients, the carotenoids. They are particularly effective at protecting the maculae from free-radical damage. Both compounds discourage the cellular changes that lead to macular degeneration.

To get more lutein and zeaxanthin in your diet, be sure to eat plenty of the following foods. The figures in the right-hand column indicate the total amount of both nutrients per 3½-ounce serving.

Food	Lutein and Zeaxanthin (mcg)
Kale	21,900
Spinach, cooked	12,600
Spinach, raw	10,200
Mustard greens	9,900
Celery	3,600
Broccoli, cooked	1,900
Leaf lettuce	1,800
Peas	1,700

Supplements

Take extra antioxidants. By eating lots of fruits and vegetables, you get healthy doses of carotenoids and other antioxidant nutrients. Supplements can raise your antioxidant intake even higher—and possibly boost your defense against macular degeneration.

For people with macular degeneration, Joseph Pizzorno Jr., N.D., offers the following antioxidant prescription: 1,000 milligrams of vitamin C three times a day, 600 to 800 international units (IU) of vitamin E a day, 400 micrograms of selenium a day, and 45 milligrams of zinc a day. But note that you need to check with your doctor first before trying this prescription because all of these doses are much higher than standard recommendations.

Herbal Medicine

Become acquainted with bilberries. Bilberries, sometimes called European blueberries, have an age-old reputation for improving vision. They contain high levels of potent antioxidant compounds called anthocyanosides, which have a special affinity for the eyes, Dr. Pizzorno explains.

European herbalists have developed a standardized bilberry extract that contains 25 percent anthocyanosides. Dr. Pizzorno suggests taking 80 to 160 milligrams of the extract three times a day. It's available in many health food stores and from most naturopaths.

As an alternative to the extract, James A. Duke, Ph.D., suggests eating blueberries. Like bilberries, blueberries are rich in anthocyanosides. Choose fresh berries when they're in season, frozen or canned berries at other times of the year. You can also get anthocyanosides by eating blackberries, raspberries, red or purple grapes, plums, raisins, and prunes.

Get to know ginkgo, too. Ginkgo is widely used in Europe as a treatment for stroke and Alzheimer's disease because it improves blood flow through the brain. Like bilberry, it also contains antioxidants that have a special affinity for the eyes.

Dr. Pizzorno suggests taking 40 milligrams of a standardized extract containing 24 percent ginkgo heterosides three or four times a day. You can buy this extract in health food stores.

Home Remedies

Kick butts. Smoking is a major cause of the oxidative damage that sets the stage for macular degeneration. Researchers have concluded that people who smoke a pack or more of cigarettes a day are 2.4 times more likely to develop macular degeneration than people who have never smoked. Ex-smokers are twice as likely to develop macular degeneration as lifelong nonsmokers.

Raise a glass to better eyesight. A little red wine—very little, just 2 to 12 glasses a year—can help protect against macular degeneration, judging from a study by Thomas Obisesan, M.D., chief of geriatrics at Howard University School of Medicine in Washington, D.C.

Of course, if you don't drink, don't start. But if you already drink in moderation, you should know that an occasional glass of wine might do your eyesight good.

OTHER GOOD CHOICES

Homeopathy

Consider Secale. Edward Kondrot, M.D., an ophthalmologist and homeopath in Pittsburgh, sometimes prescribes the homeopathic medicine Secale for people in the early stages of macular degeneration. To find out whether Secale might benefit you, consult a homeopath.

Chinese Medicine

Help your eyes with Chinese herbs. For patients with macular degeneration, Efrem Korngold, O.M.D., L.Ac., often prescribes salvia root, lycii berries, and chrysanthemum tea. "Salvia root protects the retina and discourages the growth of new blood vessels there," he notes. "Lycii berries are similar to bilberries in that both contain anthocyanosides. And chrysanthemum tea clears Heat and soothes your eyes."

Stimulate better vision. Dr. Korngold also recommends acupuncture or acupressure as a treatment for macular degeneration. For acupressure, apply steady finger pressure to each of the following points for 3 minutes.

◆ Liver 3, situated on top of your foot in the webbing between your big toe and second toe
◆ Spleen 10, located on your inner thigh, four finger-widths above your kneecap and just under your thighbone

MEDICAL MEASURES

For dry macular degeneration, mainstream medicine has little to offer in the way of effective treatments. But wet macular degeneration may respond to laser surgery, provided it's performed in the early stages of the disease.

If you experience any degree of vision impairment because of macular degeneration, you may want to take advantage of the support services offered by a nonprofit organization called Lighthouse International. You can write to the organization at 111 East 59th Street, 12th Floor, New York, NY 10022-1202.

Menopause

For decades, mainstream medicine viewed menopause as an illness, something that required professional treatment. But over the past 20 years, that perception has gradually changed, as women have learned more about their bodies and their health and have demanded that their physicians do the same. Today, women have reclaimed menopause as an occasion to celebrate, a rite of passage into maturity and wisdom.

SIMPLE SOLUTIONS
1. Nutrition
2. Supplements
3. Exercise
4. Relaxation Therapies
5. Herbal Medicine
6. Home Remedies
7. Homeopathy
8. Chinese Medicine
9. Ayurvedic Medicine
10. Medical Measures

Today, there are an unprecedented number of women at or past menopause. In America, that number is more than 40 million. At the turn of the twentieth century, the average life expectancy for women was just 48 years, so relatively few got to experience life after menopause. Today, the average life expectancy for women is about 80 years. Considering that most women enter menopause around age 50, they are postmenopausal for more than one-third of their lives.

Of course, not every woman experiences menopause in the same way. Some breeze through "the change" with nary a hot flash. For others, the discomforts are so severe that they're intolerable.

Most women realize that they're going through menopause when they stop having their periods or they start experiencing hot flashes and other common discomforts. In fact, menopause is a long, slow process that begins while you're in your late thirties. Even though you're still menstruating, your ovaries are producing less estrogen. In your early forties, you may develop some menstrual irregularities; after age 45, you may experience mild hot flashes and vaginal dryness. These symptoms become more noticeable as you approach age 50.

Between ages 45 and 55, your periods become even more irregular. They may come more frequently, or they may not come at all. They may last longer or be heavier than normal. You may have spotting between periods.

As your menstrual cycles come to an end, ovulation becomes sporadic but may still occur. "If you don't want to get pregnant, you should keep using contraception for several months after your last period," advises Anne Simons, M.D.

Among women who enter menopause naturally, some 20 percent notice no changes other than a gradual cessation of menstruation. About 50 percent experience mild discomforts. For the remaining 30 percent, menopause brings on severe physical and emotional symptoms. The most bothersome symptoms include the following:

Hot flashes. These sudden feelings of warmth come on without warning and last from 30 seconds to 5 minutes. Your face, neck, and chest may become flushed. You may perspire considerably and experience heart palpitations.

Vaginal dryness. As estrogen production declines, the mucous membrane that lines the vagina begins to thin. As a result, there is less vaginal lubrication. This can lead to itching, irritation, and discomfort during intercourse.

Emotional distress. During menopause, some women experience bouts of depression, nervousness, and irritability. These emotional upsets are most common among those who have personal histories of premenstrual syndrome or postpartum depression. All of these conditions are associated with cyclical hormonal changes, says Christiane Northrup, M.D., founder of the Women to Women health center in Yarmouth, Maine, and past president of the American Holistic Medical Association.

To minimize your menopausal symptoms, you have a number of conventional and alternative measures at your disposal. Here's what the experts say can help.

BEST CHOICES

Nutrition

Savor soy foods. In China and Japan, few women experience hot flashes. The reason: Their traditional diet is rich in soy foods, especially tofu. Soy contains plant estrogens, which have properties similar to human estrogen. Several studies have shown that phytoestrogens may help relieve hot flashes, just like hormone-replacement therapy (HRT).

Stephen Holt, M.D., professor of medicine at Seton Hall University in South Orange, New Jersey, suggests consuming 50 to 100 milligrams of soy isoflavones a day. You can get this amount by consuming 2 to 4 ounces of tofu, 1 ounce of soy-based textured vegetable protein, 2 to 4 cups of soy milk, or 6 to 12 tablespoons of roasted soy nuts.

Become partial to plant foods. Women who are vegetarians seem to glide through menopause with little discomfort, observes Andrew T. Weil, M.D., director of the program in integrative medicine at the University of Arizona College of Medicine in Tucson. A vegetarian diet emphasizes plant-derived foods, many of which contain phytoestrogens. Besides soy, good sources of phytoestrogens include apples, carrots, green beans, chickpeas, wheat, oats, corn, peanuts, cashews, and almonds.

Sip your way through the day. By keeping yourself well-hydrated, you help maintain natural vaginal lubrication. So drink plenty of water and juices throughout the day, Dr. Weil advises. "Plenty" means at least eight 8-ounce glasses of fluids.

Supplements

Ease discomfort with E. Studies dating back to the 1940s show that vitamin E helps relieve menopausal symptoms. "I've had excellent results using vitamin E to treat hot flashes," says clinical nutritionist Shari Lieberman, Ph.D. The vitamin also helps prevent vaginal dryness in about half of women who take it, Dr. Weil says. And it may help reduce your risk of heart disease, the leading cause of death among postmenopausal women.

Both Dr. Lieberman and Dr. Weil recommend taking 800 international units (IU) of vitamin E a day. But check with your doctor first since doses over 400 IU a day should only be taken under a doctor's supervision.

Exercise

Stay one step ahead of symptoms. According to Dr. Weil, exercise is beneficial because it builds muscle. Muscle cells contain an enzyme called aromatase that can produce estrogen from other sex hormones. In this way, exercise acts as a natural form of HRT.

Most experts recommend getting at least 30 minutes of physical activity

The Pros and Cons of HRT

Doctors have long recommended the short-term use of hormone replacement therapy (HRT) to prevent hot flashes and other menopausal symptoms. Used for a few months to a few years, HRT can effectively relieve symptoms in women who don't respond to or who aren't interested in trying non-drug alternatives.

In recent years, doctors have also encouraged menopausal women to use HRT on an ongoing basis because of evidence that it might curb the risk of heart disease, osteoporosis and other problems. But the medical profession's confidence in the long-term use of HRT was shaken when researchers recently halted years ahead of schedule a major study of HRT, the Women's Health Initiative (WHI).

After five years of study, WHI researchers found that women who took Prempro, a daily tablet of synthetic estrogen and synthetic progesterone, had a 26% higher rate of breast cancer, a 29% higher rate of heart attack and a 41% higher rate of stroke than those taking a placebo. On the positive side, those taking HRT had a 37% decrease in colorectal cancer and a 34 % fewer hip fractures.

Dr. Christiane Northrup, a holistic physician who generally favors a natural approach to menopause, believes that some perimenopausal and menopausal women need hormones to control symptoms or to feel their best. Northrup recommends that a woman should have her hormone levels checked before HRT is prescribed since some menopausal women's bodies make adequate levels of hormones while others don't.

If hormones are recommended, Northrup believes they should be bio-identical. This means they are chemically identical to the hormones manufactured in a woman's body—not animal versions or synthetic substitutes, which are commonly prescribed. She also suggests the doctor check hormone levels every year, since a woman's body changes.

every day. But you don't have to sweat much to reap the benefits. According to Susan M. Lark, M.D., director of the PMS and Menopause Self-Help Center in Los Altos, California, the gentle stretches and postures of yoga are just as effective as more strenuous workouts.

Relaxation Therapies

Calm down to cool off. Several studies have shown that deep relaxation can take the heat out of hot flashes. No matter which relaxation technique you prefer, you get the best results with daily practice. Thirty minutes a day is ideal, but even 10 minutes a day helps, says Tori Hudson, N.D., professor of gynecology at the National College of Naturopathic Medicine in Portland, Oregon.

Herbal Medicine

Turn to black cohosh. Black cohosh has a long history as a treatment for gynecological complaints. Scientists have determined that the herb works because it contains plant estrogens.

In Germany, women use a black cohosh preparation called Remifemin. Dr. Northrup prefers Remifemin to black cohosh tincture because it's a standardized extract. "Numerous clinical trials have shown that Remifemin compares very favorably with conventional HRT," she says. "Black cohosh decreases hot flashes, vaginal dryness, and depression as effectively as conventional hormones but without the side effects."

In the United States, a growing number of health food stores sell Remifemin. If you're able to find it, use it according to the package directions. Otherwise, look for a standardized black cohosh extract. Take two capsules of the extract a day, advises Christopher Hobbs, L.Ac., an herbalist in Santa Cruz, California, and the author of several herb guides.

Try an herbal trio. For hot flashes and other menopausal symptoms, Dr. Weil recommends a combination of dang gui (Chinese angelica), chasteberry, and damiana. "Dang gui balances female hormones," he says. "Chasteberry helps regulate estrogen and progesterone production. And damiana is a female tonic."

Look for these herbs in tincture form. To use the tinctures, add one dropperful of each to a glass of water or juice. Drink the mixture at midday every day until your symptoms subside, Dr. Weil says. Then gradually taper off the herbs.

Home Remedies

Defeat hot flashes by degrees. If you're bothered by hot flashes, take steps to keep yourself and your environment cool. Dress in layers of loose, lightweight, natural-fabric clothing that you can take off easily, Dr. Simons suggests. Then when a hot flash strikes, remove the outer layer. At night, wear lightweight

Hormone Replacement, Naturally

Most menopausal women who opt for hormone-replacement therapy (HRT) get their estrogen from the prescription drug Premarin. The estrogen in Premarin comes from horses—horse urine, to be exact. In fact, the word *Premarin* is an acronym for "pregnant mares' urine."

"I no longer recommend Premarin," says Christiane Northrup, M.D., founder of Women to Women health center in Yarmouth, Maine, and past president of the American Holistic Medical Association. "Many women simply don't feel good on it, which is the reason so many stop taking it." Why? Because Premarin doesn't contain the mix of estrogens found naturally in your body.

Estrogen is not one hormone but three: estriol, which accounts for 60 to 80 percent of the estrogens in your blood; estrone, 10 to 20 percent; and estradiol, 10 to 20 percent. By comparison, Premarin is 5 percent equilin (horse estriol), 75 to 80 percent estrone, and 5 to 20 percent estradiol.

Conventional HRT also includes the hormone progesterone, to reduce the risk of uterine endometrial cancer. (Estrogen without progesterone can raise the risk of this type of cancer.) But pharmaceutical progesterone is not the same as the human hormone.

What HRT usually doesn't replenish is testosterone and DHEA, two other hormones that are in short supply in postmenopausal women. Few mainstream M.D.'s include testosterone and DHEA in their HRT prescrip-

pajamas and use lightweight blankets and bedspreads. If possible, set the thermostats in your home and office at or below 68°F. Otherwise, run fans.

Watch what you're drinking. According to Dr. Simons, caffeinated and alcoholic beverages seem to trigger hot flashes in some women. In addition, caffeine and alcohol are diuretics. By depleting your body of water, they may contribute to vaginal dryness.

If you smoke, quit. One study showed that compared with women who don't smoke, those who smoke have more frequent and more severe hot flashes.

Enjoy intercourse. One study examined the relationship between women's sexual activity and the thickness of their vaginal mucous mem-

tions, even though the hormones are often beneficial, says Kent, Washington, physician Jonathan Wright, M.D., coauthor of *Natural Hormone Replacement*.

As an alternative to conventional HRT, Drs. Wright and Northrup recommend natural hormone-replacement therapy, or NHRT. Natural hormones are derived from hormonelike compounds in soybeans and yams. The molecular structure of these compounds is modified to exactly match human estrogens, progesterone, and testosterone. (DHEA is available over the counter as a supplement but should only be taken under a doctor's supervision.)

When you begin to notice menstrual changes that may signal the onset of menopause, Dr. Northrup suggests having a saliva test to gauge your levels of estrogen, progesterone, testosterone, and DHEA. Then your physician can prescribe natural hormones at the doses that would work best for you. "In my opinion, individually customized NHRT is far superior to the conventional one-size-fits-all approach," Dr. Northrup says.

Natural hormone replacement can be tricky, Dr. Wright says. To use it safely and effectively, you should work with a physician who knows NHRT. Your best bet is a naturopath, though an increasing number of M.D.'s and D.O.'s have abandoned Premarin in favor of natural alternatives.

For a referral to a physician in your area who practices NHRT, contact the American College for Advancement in Medicine, 23121 Verdugo Drive, Suite 204, Laguna Hills, CA 92653-1339.

branes. The more women had sex, the thicker their membranes became.

How does sex help? "Sensitive lovemaking and regular orgasm improve blood flow to vaginal tissues," Dr. Lark says.

Lubricate before lovemaking. If you're experiencing vaginal dryness, sex may be the last thing on your mind. The lack of lubrication makes intercourse painful. But it doesn't have to be that way, says sex and marital therapist Louanne Cole-Weston, Ph.D., of Sacramento, California. She suggests trying a commercial water-based lubricant or even a little olive oil. Don't use petroleum-based products such as Vaseline, she cautions. They are difficult to wash out of the vagina.

OTHER GOOD CHOICES

Homeopathy

Ask for homeopathic help. Homeopaths prescribe several medicines for menopausal discomforts, says homeopath Dana Ullman. Among the most popular are Lachesis, Natrum muriaticum, and Sepia. Which of these works best for you depends on your individual symptoms. For a recommendation, consult a homeopath.

Chinese Medicine

Strengthen your Kidney. Practitioners of Chinese medicine attribute menopause to a decline in Kidney qi, says Efrem Korngold, O.M.D., L.Ac. "You treat menopause by strengthening the Kidney," he explains.

For this purpose, he prescribes several herbal preparations. One formula, called Zhi Bai Ba Wei Wan, contains rehmannia root, peony root, philodendron bark, and several other herbs. Another formula, called Da Bu Yin Wan, is made with rehmannia root, philodendron bark, and tortoise shell.

Let your fingers provide relief. Acupressure can help ease menopausal symptoms. Michael Reed Gach, founder and director of the Acupressure Institute, suggests applying steady, penetrating finger pressure to each of the following points for 3 minutes.

◆ Heart 7, located on the pinkie side of the wrist crease that's closest to your palm

◆ Kidney 3, located in the hollow between your Achilles tendon and the inside of your anklebone

◆ Spleen 6, located four finger-widths above your inner anklebone on the back inner border of your shinbone

◆ Extra Point Yin Tang, located just above the bridge of your nose, exactly between your eyebrows

If acupressure doesn't seem to improve your symptoms, consider consulting a trained acupuncturist for treatment. Sometimes professional needle stimulation works when finger pressure doesn't.

If you're premature, count on Chinese cures. Women who receive radiation or chemotherapy for cancer often become menopausal prematurely—as early as their late thirties. For women who want children, this poses a big problem. Premature menopause also increases a woman's risk of heart disease and osteoporosis.

If you're to be treated for cancer, you may want to ask your doctor about using Chinese medicine in conjunction with radiation or chemotherapy. "In my experience, a course of acupuncture and Chinese herbs administered at the same time as radiation or chemo can often prevent premature menopause," Dr. Northrup says. "It can also alleviate many side effects of cancer treatment."

Ayurvedic Medicine

See about saffron. Ayurvedic physicians view menopause as primarily a Vata condition, says David Frawley, O.M.D. He prescribes anti-Vata herbs that support the reproductive system, such as saffron, shatavari, kapikacchu, and ashwagandha.

Hot flashes, on the other hand, are more of a Pitta condition. They respond to treatment with saffron and shatavari.

MEDICAL MEASURES

HRT is the most effective treatment for menopausal symptoms such as hot flashes and vaginal dryness. A typical regimen consists of daily doses of estrogen along with extra progesterone. (Taking estrogen without progesterone substantially increases the risk of uterine endometrial cancer.)

HRT is controversial. Whether or not it's appropriate for you depends on your individual medical situation. Discuss the benefits and risks with your doctor. Together, the two of you can decide if HRT is right for you.

Menstrual Cramps

For Christiane Northrup, M.D., menstrual cramps have been a persistent and painful fact of life. "As a teenager, I had such severe cramps that I sometimes was sent home from school," recalls Dr. Northrup, founder of the Women to Women health center in Yarmouth, Maine, and past president of the American Holistic Medical Association. "And during my medical residency, I once had to excuse myself from surgery—that's how miserable I felt."

Such incapacitating pain is the exception rather than the rule. Still, roughly half of all women of reproductive age experience some degree of menstrual cramping every month.

Cramps are actually the result of contractions. Every month, as part of your menstrual cycle, your uterus undergoes certain changes to prepare itself for the arrival of a fertilized egg. If the egg remains unfertilized—that is, if you don't become pregnant—the uterus has no need for the blood-rich lining that would have provided nourishment for a developing fetus.

SIMPLE SOLUTIONS
1. Nutrition
2. Supplements
3. Exercise
4. Aromatherapy
5. Herbal Medicine
6. Chiropractic
7. Chinese Medicine
8. Home Remedies
9. Over-the-Counter Drugs
10. Homeopathy
11. Ayurvedic Medicine
12. Medical Measures

So your uterus expels its lining by contracting. You experience the contractions as cramps.

Cramping causes pain by interfering with blood flow, which temporarily limits the amount of oxygen available to the uterus. The pain is made worse by hormones called prostaglandins, which are released by your uterus and uterine lining during menstruation.

For most women of reproductive age, "menstrual cramps" means 1 to 3 days of mild to moderate abdominal pain around the time of their periods. But an estimated 10 percent of women experience more severe cramping, characterized by stronger, longer-lasting, and more frequent uterine contractions. Such intense cramping may be accompanied by nausea, vomiting, diarrhea, headache, fatigue, dizziness, and nervousness.

A number of factors influence the degree of menstrual cramping that you experience. For example, the more prostaglandins you produce, the more painful your cramps are. Smoking makes cramps worse, too, by constricting blood vessels and impeding blood flow in the uterus.

If you're like most women, you'll notice your menstrual cramps becoming less severe as you get older. And, of course, they'll go away completely once you reach menopause and your periods cease. In the meantime, you can do a lot to control cramping and ease your monthly misery. Here's what the experts recommend.

BEST CHOICES

Nutrition

Frequently feast on fish. Cold-water fish such as salmon and oil-packed sardines are rich in omega-3 fatty acids, Dr. Northrup explains. Omega-3's inhibit uterine production of prostaglandins, the hormones that contribute to menstrual cramps.

Limit fats and sweets. Meats and high-fat sweets such as cakes, cookies, and candy stimulate the production of prostaglandins. Dr. Northrup suggests eating meat no more than twice a week and cutting way back on sugary junk foods.

Ditch dairy foods. According to Dr. Northrup, some of her patients have managed to rein in menstrual cramping by eliminating dairy products from their diets. "This doesn't work for everyone," she says, "but it helps often enough to be worth a try."

Supplements

Favor fish-oil capsules. To reap the benefits of omega-3 fatty acids without eating fish, take fish-oil capsules instead. Research has shown that supplemental fish oil can relieve menstrual cramping. You can buy fish oils in health food stores and some drugstores. Follow the dosage instructions on the label.

Embrace vitamin B$_6$. Many nutrition-minded health practitioners recommend vitamin B_6 as a treatment for premenstrual syndrome. But some also prescribe the vitamin for menstrual cramps. Take 300 milligrams of B_6 every day while you have cramps, advises clinical nutritionist Shari Lieberman, Ph.D. But check with your doctor first, since vitamin B_6 dosages over 100 milligrams should only be taken under medical supervision.

Don't miss out on magnesium. The mineral magnesium helps relax the smooth muscle tissue of the uterus, reducing the severity of uterine contractions. Dr. Northrup suggests taking 100 milligrams of magnesium every 2 hours during your period and two or three times a day during the rest of your menstrual cycle.

Boost your intake of bromelain. An enzyme found in pineapple, bromelain also helps relax the smooth muscle tissue of the uterus, says Joseph Pizzorno Jr., N.D. He suggests taking 250 to 500 milligrams three times a day between meals for the duration of your period.

Exercise

Stay one step ahead of pain. Physical activity of any kind boosts your body's production of natural pain-relieving compounds called endorphins, explains Anne Simons, M.D. The more strenuous your workout, the more endorphins your body churns out.

Aromatherapy

Sniff soothing scents. Inhaling certain essential oils helps relax you, which reduces the intensity of menstrual cramping. Mindy Green, an herbalist in Boulder, Colorado, and coauthor of *Aromatherapy: A Complete Guide to the Healing Art*, offers the following anti-cramping "recipe": Place a few chips of rock salt in a small vial. The salt absorbs the oil, so it doesn't spill. Add the following essential oils to the vial: 4 drops of lavender, 2 drops of marjoram, 2 drops of chamomile, and 3 drops of geranium. Then when you feel cramps coming on, just uncap the vial and inhale deeply.

Herbal Medicine

Have haw. Native American women used the bark of black haw, a woody white-flowered shrub, to treat gynecological complaints. The herbal remedy caught on among colonial women, who dubbed it cramp bark and relied on it to ease menstrual cramps.

You'll find black haw—sometimes called viburnum—sold in several forms in health food stores. If you buy the tincture, take 2 teaspoons three times a day, mixed into juice.

Reach for raspberry. For centuries, herbalists have prescribed raspberry leaf tea as a treatment for menstrual cramps as well as for the uterine irritability associated with pregnancy.

The beneficial compound in raspberry leaf is called oligomeric procyanidin, or OPC, says James A. Duke, Ph.D. You can get OPC in a supplement called pycnogenol, but he says that it's expensive.

Instead, Dr. Duke suggests drinking raspberry leaf tea during your period. To make the tea, add a teaspoon or two of the herb to 1 cup of boiled water. Allow to steep for 10 minutes, then strain and drink.

Feel better with black cohosh. Black cohosh contains plant estrogens, also called phytoestrogens. These suppress the secretion of luteinizing hormone, which plays a role in menstrual cramps. The herb has proved so effective for cramping that it has received the endorsement of Commission E, the German panel that evaluates the safety and effectiveness of herbal medicines.

Choose the tincture form, suggests Christopher Hobbs, L.Ac., an herbalist in Santa Cruz, California, and the author of several authoritative herb guides. Take 2 to 4 dropperful of the tincture two or three times a day for a few days before your period as well as during your period.

Chiropractic

Adjust to life without cramps. At the National College of Chiropractic in Lombard, Illinois, researchers studied 45 women who had long histories of severe menstrual cramping. Half of the women received chiropractic spinal manipulation, while the rest received treatment that mimicked chiropractic but wasn't actually spinal manipulation. Blood tests before and after the treatment sessions showed that the women in both groups experienced decreases in pain-provoking prostaglandins. But only the women who received real spinal manipulation reported less cramping.

Chinese Medicine

Get your Blood going. When treating women with menstrual cramps, Efrem Korngold, O.M.D., L.Ac., often prescribes one of two herbal formulas. One has pseudoginseng root as its active ingredient. The other is a combination of Chinese angelica (dang gui), peony root, turmeric root, and several other herbs.

Count on on-the-spot relief. Both the United Nations World Health Organization and the National Institutes of Health endorse acupuncture as a treatment for menstrual cramping. That's no doubt because of the compelling scientific evidence proving that acupuncture really works.

According to Dr. Korngold, an acupuncture session to relieve menstrual cramps may include stimulation of the following points.

◆ Spleen 6, located four finger-widths above your inner anklebone on the back inner border of your shinbone

◆ Liver 3, situated on top of your foot in the webbing between your big toe and second toe

◆ Large Intestine 4, located on the back of your hand where the bones of your thumb and index finger meet

If you prefer a do-it-yourself approach, you can stimulate each of the above points with acupressure. Apply steady, penetrating finger pressure to each point for 3 minutes, suggests Michael Reed Gach, founder and director of the Acupressure Institute.

Home Remedies

Warm your abdomen. Many women swear by heating pads, hot-water bottles, and hot baths to relieve menstrual cramping—and with good reason, according to Martin L. Rossman, M.D. "Every kind of pain, including cramping, has an anxiety component," he explains. "Heat is relaxing. When you feel relaxed, menstrual cramps don't bother you as much."

Drink plenty of fluids. If you become dehydrated, your brain releases a hormone called vasopressin that instructs your body to conserve water. Unfortunately, vasopressin also increases the intensity of uterine contractions. The best way to derail this process is to drink lots of fluids so that you stay hydrated. "Sipping water, juice, or noncaffeinated tea throughout the day helps some women control their menstrual cramps," Dr. Simons says.

Furlough the tampons. It's possible that wearing tampons can aggravate menstrual cramping in some women. If you use tampons, try switching to sanitary napkins for a while and see if that helps.

Over-the-Counter Drugs

Reach for a prostaglandin inhibitor. According to the American Pharmaceutical Association, nonsteroidal anti-inflammatory drugs (NSAIDs)

do the best job of all the over-the-counter medicines in relieving menstrual cramps. The NSAIDs include aspirin, ibuprofen, naproxen (Aleve), and ketoprofen (Orudis KT). All of them work by decreasing uterine production of pain-provoking prostaglandins. Of the NSAIDs, ibuprofen is your best choice, says W. Y. Chan, Ph.D., a pharmacologist at Cornell University in New York City.

For an NSAID to effectively stop prostaglandin production, you should begin taking it 3 days before the expected start of your period. Continue taking the medication on a round-the-clock schedule according to label directions for the duration of your period. If your cramping has already started, you can still get relief from NSAIDs.

OTHER GOOD CHOICES

Homeopathy

Pick the right remedy. Homeopaths prescribe an array of medicines for women with menstrual cramps. Pulsatilla works well if your cramps are accompanied by occasional nausea, especially if your menstrual flow changes from month to month, says homeopath Dana Ullman. Belladonna is effective for intense cramps that begin suddenly. But Magnesia phosphorica or Colocynthis is a better bet if you get some relief by massaging your abdomen or applying heat.

Because homeopathic prescriptions are based on a wide array of symptoms and personal characteristics, your best bet is to visit an experienced homeopath, who can determine which medicine is best suited to you.

Ayurvedic Medicine

Bring balance to Vata. Ayurvedic practitioners view menstrual cramps as an imbalance of Vata, one of three doshas that make up your constitution, according to Raymond Rosenthal, M.D., a physician in Kona, Hawaii, who practices integrated medicine. He recommends rebalancing your Vata and nurturing your uterus and ovaries by eating more fish, getting sesame oil massages (panchakarma), and taking various medicinal herbs. One especially effective herb is called shatavari, which Dr. Rosenthal suggests using in a dosage of 3 to 6 grams a day. Shatavari is available from Ayurvedic practitioners.

MEDICAL MEASURES

If none of the above therapies provides sufficient relief from menstrual cramps, your doctor may put you on stronger prostaglandin inhibitors. Even though they are sold as Motrin and other familiar brand names, these medications are available by prescription only.

As an alternative to the prostaglandin inhibitors, your doctor may give you the option of going on oral contraceptives. For some women, birth control pills effectively reduce cramping.

RED FLAGS

See your doctor promptly if you experience any of the following:

◆ A sudden increase in the intensity of your menstrual cramps
◆ Menstrual cramps accompanied by fever, vomiting, chills, or any unusual vaginal discharge
◆ A sudden increase in the volume of your menstrual flow
◆ Severe cramping or pain that isn't related to menstruation
◆ Pain radiating into your thigh

Migraine

As headaches go, migraines are in a class by themselves. They don't just hurt. They pound, they throb, they incapacitate. When a migraine comes on, it can knock you off your feet for hours, possibly days.

Some 24 million Americans—about 18 million women and 6 million men—get migraines. They account for 31 percent of all doctors' appointments for headaches, making them the second most common type of headache. (Tension headaches rank number one.)

Scientists still aren't certain what causes migraines. But they have identified one culprit: the blood vessels in your head. These vessels contract and expand in response to foods, drugs, hormones—all sorts of things. If these changes happen to aggravate nearby pain nerves, you may get a migraine.

Also to blame are your platelets, the blood cells involved in forming clots. If you're prone to migraines, your platelets are more likely than normal to clump together—a process that triggers the release of the brain chemical serotonin. And serotonin, in turn, plays a role in triggering migraines.

Migraines often strike in the morning. In about 20 percent of cases, they announce their

SIMPLE SOLUTIONS
1. Nutrition
2. Supplements
3. Elimination Diet
4. Visualization
5. Herbal Medicine
6. Chiropractic
7. Homeopathy
8. Chinese Medicine
9. Home Remedies
10. Over-the-Counter Drugs
11. Ayurvedic Medicine
12. Naturopathy
13. Medical Measures

impending arrival with peculiar smells or visual disturbances—flashing lights, blurred vision, blind spots. These unusual symptoms, called auras, usually begin about 20 minutes to an hour before the onset of a migraine.

Whether or not you experience an aura, the migraine itself is unmistakable. It produces severe pounding, throbbing pain, usually on one side of your head. You may also experience nausea and vomiting. These symptoms can last anywhere from a few hours to a couple of days.

How often migraines occur varies from one person to the next. Most people get between two and five migraines a month. But for some poor souls, migraines occur almost daily.

If you're prone to migraines, you're probably a woman. About 75 percent of all migraine sufferers are female. Some two-thirds of these women get their headaches around the time of their periods, according to endocrinologist Ivy Fettes, M.D., Ph.D., assistant professor of medicine at the Sunnybrook Health Science Center at the University of Toronto.

Why do so many women develop menstrual migraines? As Dr. Fettes explains, the hormone estrogen causes the blood vessels in the head to expand. So when estrogen levels fluctuate over the course of the menstrual cycle, the blood vessels respond by contracting and expanding. This is what triggers migraines.

Gender isn't the only factor that influences your risk of migraines. For instance, family history appears to play a role. While no clear genetic link has been identified, migraines tend to run in families.

Age is another factor. Most people experience their first migraines during their childhood or teenage years, often after years of motion sickness. The headaches typically peak by age 35, then gradually decline—one of the nicer benefits of getting older.

Many mainstream M.D.'s prescribe medications that can not only stop migraine pain but also minimize the frequency and severity of recurrences. But because these medications have side effects, many people prefer to explore other treatment options first. That's where blended medicine can help.

BEST CHOICES

Nutrition

Reduce dietary fat. At least one study suggests that switching to a low-fat diet can reduce the frequency, severity, and duration of migraines. The easiest way to cut your fat intake is to steer clear of meats, dairy products, snacks, and desserts. Replace them with naturally nutritious grains, beans, fruits, and vegetables—except for those that are known migraine triggers. (More on migraine-causing foods in a bit.)

Eat less meat, more fish. Meat is one of the top sources of fat in the typical American diet. Much of that fat is saturated, the kind that makes platelets more likely to clump together and trigger migraines, says Joseph Pizzorno Jr., N.D.

On the other hand, fish—especially salmon and other cold-water species—contain an abundance of essential fatty acids. These "good fats" help keep platelets from clumping.

Get to know tofu. If you're a woman who's prone to menstrual migraines, Susan M. Lark, M.D., director of the PMS and Menopause Self-Help Center in Los Altos, California, suggests eating more tofu. Tofu contains plant estrogens, or phytoestrogens. They're weaker than your own estrogen, but they have similar effects on your body. So by eating tofu, you raise your body's estrogen level naturally. This counteracts the hormonal fluctuations that cause blood vessels in your head to contract and expand, triggering migraines.

Head off pain with garlic and onions. Both garlic and onions as well as their close relatives shallots, chives, and leeks make your platelets less likely to clump. "You don't want to knock out your platelets altogether because then your blood won't clot," says James A. Duke, Ph.D. "But making them a little less active helps prevent migraines, and garlic and onions do that." Increasing your intake of garlic and onions is easy: Use the two as ingredients in your cooking as often as possible.

Supplements

Make magnesium your medicine. According to Alan Gaby, M.D., magnesium has many of the same effects as the drugs mainstream M.D.'s use to treat migraines. It makes platelets less likely to clump together. It helps minimize the contraction and expansion of blood vessels. And it inhibits the release of compounds involved in pain and inflammation. Dr. Gaby recommends taking 200 milligrams of magnesium one to three times a day.

Experiment with riboflavin. One of the B vitamins, riboflavin plays a role in certain cellular processes that don't work quite right in those who are migraine-prone, Dr. Gaby says. To find out whether supplemental riboflavin could help treat migraines, researchers asked 49 people to chart their headaches. Then the participants began taking 400 milligrams of riboflavin every morning at breakfast. After 3 months, the average number of migraines fell 67 percent.

The findings of this study have yet to be confirmed by further research. Still, Dr. Gaby says, riboflavin is a safe and inexpensive supplement. It may be

Cluster Headaches: They Gang Up on You

Some people—overwhelmingly men—experience what are known as cluster headaches. They are very severe migraines in which pain localizes around or behind one eye. The pain lasts about an hour, but it rapidly comes and goes several times over the course of a few days. It may be accompanied by nasal stuffiness, sensitivity to light, agitation, and tearing of the affected eye.

Cluster headaches usually begin between ages 20 and 40. Like migraines, they often have triggers, says neurologist Robert Smith, M.D., professor and director emeritus of the department of family medicine and founder of the Headache Center, both at the University of Cincinnati. The most common triggers include stress, smoking, alcohol, perfume, gasoline, and other chemical fumes.

To treat cluster headaches, mainstream M.D.'s and alternative practitioners usually rely on the same therapies that they use for migraines. These approaches often help. In addition, the following have shown some benefit.

Melatonin. A hormone, melatonin is most commonly used to treat insomnia and jet lag. Research suggests it may help relieve cluster headaches, too. You can buy melatonin supplements in health food stores and many drugstores. Take them according to the label directions.

Oxygen. Inhaling 100 percent oxygen through a face mask can be very helpful, Dr. Smith says. If you want to try this treatment, you need to consult your doctor.

worth a try. Use the same dosage as in the study: 400 milligrams every day at breakfast.

Grow fond of fish oil. If you're not especially fond of fish, you can get those migraine-fighting essential fatty acids from fish-oil supplements, Dr. Gaby says. In one study, 15 migraine-prone people who had not responded to mainstream drugs reported significantly milder migraines while taking fish oil. If you want to try fish oil, take 5 grams three times a day, as done in the study.

Elimination Diet

Get rid of food triggers. "There is little doubt that food intolerances are the major cause of migraines," Dr. Pizzorno says. "Several studies show that eliminating offending foods greatly reduces migraine symptoms." To discover which foods may be triggering your migraines, Dr. Pizzorno recommends an elimination diet. (Consult with a doctor or practitioner for guidance.)

Weed out the primary offenders. If you'd rather not follow a true elimination diet, you can simply cut out the foods with the nastiest reputations for triggering migraines, Dr. Gaby says. The leading offenders include cow's milk, cheese, wheat and bread products, corn, rice, beef, eggs, oranges and other citrus fruits, chocolate, and alcohol (especially red wine). Other possible food triggers include shellfish, tomatoes, bananas, figs, nuts, lunchmeats, fermented or pickled foods, and foods containing artificial sweeteners (such as saccharin or aspartame), monosodium glutamate (MSG), or sulfites.

Turn to a rotation diet. If you give up the common food triggers and still get migraines, you may have low-level sensitivities to other foods. In this case, Dr. Pizzorno suggests trying a 4-day rotation diet. This means that you don't eat any food more than once every 4 days.

Visualization

See yourself migraine-free. Dawn Marcus, M.D., assistant professor of neurology at the University of Pittsburgh School of Medicine, recruited 44 pregnant women with migraines, tension headaches, or both. Thirty of the women enrolled in a class in which they learned a combination of deep breathing, muscle relaxation, and visualization. The rest of the women received no treatment. By the time the class ended, 80 percent of the participants reported less headache pain, compared with just 43 percent of the women who received no treatment.

Martin L. Rossman, M.D., has produced many relaxation tapes that combine music and visualization exercises to help prevent migraines. For a free catalog, write to the Academy for Guided Imagery at P. O. Box 2070, Mill Valley, CA 94942-2070.

Herbal Medicine

Have fewer migraines with feverfew. Israeli researchers gave either feverfew or a placebo to 57 people with migraines, none of whom had ever tried the herb. After 2 months, everyone switched treatments, so those who had been taking feverfew were on the placebo, and vice versa. All of the participants reported significantly fewer headaches while taking the herb.

Feverfew is believed to stop migraines in several ways. It discourages blood vessels from constricting and dilating in response to certain things. It prevents the release of serotonin from platelets. And it reduces the production of prostaglandins, leukotrienes, and thromboxanes, compounds that play roles in your body's pain response. Most studies involving feverfew have used 82 milligrams of dried, powdered leaf, taken once a day.

Try herbal aspirin. The herb willow bark contains salicin, which is the natural precursor to aspirin. "Any pain problem that you treat with aspirin you can also treat with willow bark tea," Dr. Duke says.

Commission E, the German expert panel that evaluates the safety and effectiveness of herbal medicines, also endorses willow bark for headaches, including migraines. The commission recommends taking the herb as a tea. Simmer 1 to 1½ teaspoons of powdered willow bark in 1 cup of boiling water for 10 minutes, then strain. Drink up to three cupfuls of tea a day.

Take ginger. Like garlic and onions, ginger helps prevent platelets from clumping. The herb also relieves nausea, a common symptom of migraine. "There aren't any good studies of ginger as a treatment for migraines," Dr. Gaby says. "But there are good reasons to use ginger. It can't hurt." He suggests taking 500 milligrams of ginger every 4 hours during a migraine episode.

Chiropractic

Manipulate migraine pain. Australian researchers asked chiropractors to perform spinal manipulation on 85 migraine-prone people. Meanwhile, another group received head and back massages from doctors. After 6 months, both groups experienced fewer and briefer migraines. But only the people who received chiropractic manipulation reported less pain.

Homeopathy

Get a personalized prescription. French homeopaths evaluated 60 people with migraines, then recommended homeopathic medicines based on each person's specific symptoms. Half of the participants took the prescribed medicines every 2 weeks for 2 months. The rest took a placebo for the same amount of time. Seventeen percent of the placebo takers reported significant relief from migraine pain. Among those taking homeopathic medicines, that figure rose to 93 percent.

The medicines used in the study were Belladonna, Cyclamen, Gelsemium, Ignatia, Lachesis, Natrum muriaticum, Silicea, and Sulfur. To find out which of these medicines might benefit you, consult a homeopath.

Chinese Medicine

Revive your Blood. The classic Chinese herbal formula for treating headache is called Chuan Xiong Cha Piao. It contains quite a few herbs, including ligusticum, angelica, asarum, and peppermint. It breaks up the stagnation of Blood, which causes the sharp, stabbing, localized pain that characterizes migraine, says Efrem Korngold, O.M.D., L.Ac. If you want to try Chuan Xiong, you need to consult an oriental medicine practitioner.

Take care of your Liver and Gallbladder. The irritability and light sensitivity associated with migraines points to a problem in the Liver and Gallbladder. To prevent migraines, you want to nurture these organ networks by eliminating dietary fat, spicy foods, alcohol, and stimulants (the pharmaceutical variety as well as caffeine) and avoiding strong odors, Dr. Korngold says.

Let your fingers provide relief. A number of studies suggest that acupuncture is an effective treatment for headaches, including migraines. In fact, it works so well that it has won the endorsement of both the United Nations World Health Organization and the National Institutes of Health.

Of course, if you want to try acupuncture, you need to consult a trained acupuncturist. If you prefer a do-it-yourself approach, you can use acupressure instead, says Michael Reed Gach, founder and director of the Acupressure Institute. He suggests applying steady, penetrating finger pressure to each of the following points for 3 minutes.

◆ Large Intestine 4, located on the back of your hand where the bones of your thumb and index finger meet

◆ Governing Vessel 25, located between your eyebrows, where the bridge of your nose meets your forehead

◆ Bladder 2, located on either side of your nose, where the bridge of your nose meets the ridge of your eyebrows

◆ Governing Vessel 16, located in the center of the back of your head, in the hollow at the base of your skull

◆ Stomach 3, located at the base of your cheekbone, directly below your pupil

◆ Liver 3, situated on top of your foot in the webbing between your big toe and second toe

If acupressure doesn't seem to relieve your migraine pain, you may want to consider seeing an acupuncturist. Professional needle stimulation of the points above may help even when finger stimulation doesn't.

Home Remedies

Use caffeine to control your pain. Studies dating back to the 1970s show that 65 milligrams of caffeine—about the amount in a cup of instant coffee or a half-cup of brewed—boosts the effectiveness of aspirin and other over-the-counter pain relievers by about 40 percent. Scientists believe caffeine helps ease migraine pain because moderate, occasional consumption constricts the blood vessels in your head.

Steer clear of offenders. According to Jerome Goldstein, M.D., director of the San Francisco Headache Clinic, certain lifestyle and environmental factors can cause migraine pain. Among the potential triggers: emotional stress, hunger, fatigue, changes in sleep habits, sex, flashing lights, sun glare, loud noises, changes in the weather, and strong smells.

To help you identify what may be behind your migraines, try keeping a migraine diary, advises Anne Simons, M.D. Whenever you have a migraine episode, write down the date and time that it occurs as well as all of the foods and beverages you consumed within the previous 12 hours. Also note any physical, psychological, or environmental factors that may have contributed to your migraine. Over time, you may see a pattern that you can change.

Over-the-Counter Drugs

Take half an aspirin a day. In the late 1980s, a Harvard study involving 22,000 American male doctors made headlines by showing that low-dose aspirin—one standard tablet every other day—cuts heart attack risk by 44 percent. When the researchers examined their data more carefully, they made another startling discovery. Among the doctors who were prone to migraines, taking low-dose aspirin reduced migraine frequency by 20 percent. Aspirin prevents migraines by making platelets less likely to clump together.

If you want to try aspirin, take half a pill every day. This dosage has the same effect as the every-other-day regimen.

Keep Excedrin on hand. The Food and Drug Administration has approved Excedrin as the first over-the-counter drug treatment for mild to moderate migraines. You can take either regular Excedrin or Excedrin Migraine. Both contain a combination of aspirin and caffeine. As mentioned earlier, caffeine boosts the pain-relieving power of aspirin by about 40 percent.

Rely on NSAIDs. According to Dr. Goldstein, mild migraines sometimes go away with help from over-the-counter nonsteroidal anti-inflammatory drugs (NSAIDs). This category of medicines includes aspirin, ibuprofen, and naproxen (Aleve). Whichever one you choose, follow the dosage recommendations on the label.

OTHER GOOD CHOICES

Ayurvedic Medicine

Put your finger in your nose. To treat migraines, John Douillard, D.C., a chiropractor who practices Ayurvedic medicine at the Invincible Life Spa in Boulder, Colorado, recommends an Ayurvedic technique called nasya. Place 2 to 3 drops of sesame oil into your left hand. Mix in a pinch of salt and pepper. Rub your right pinkie in the oil, then insert it into your right nostril as far as you comfortably can. Repeat the procedure, this time putting the oil in your right hand and inserting your left pinkie into your left nostril. Continue alternating sides until you use all of the oil. Then hold each nostril closed in turn and inhale deeply.

Investigate Ayurvedic herbs. Depending on your dosha, or constitutional type, various herbal treatments may help relieve your migraine pain, Dr. Douillard says. For people with Vata doshas, Dr. Douillard prescribes calamus and valerian. For people with Pitta doshas, he recommends peppermint oil and a paste made from sandalwood powder. People with Kapha doshas may benefit from red pepper, clover, and an Ayurvedic formula called trikatu. To find out which of these treatments is most appropriate for you, consult an Ayurvedic practitioner.

Naturopathy

Heat your body, cool your head. At the first sign of migraine pain, soak in a comfortably hot bath while holding a cold compress against the affected side of your head, advises Tori Hudson, N.D., professor of gynecology at the National College of Naturopathic Medicine in Portland, Oregon. For extra benefit, she suggests adding dry mustard to your bathwater. Use approximately 1 teaspoon of dry mustard for every 2 gallons of water. Stay in the water for as long as you wish.

If you can't jump into a bathtub, try alternating hot and cold compresses instead. Hold each compress against your head for about 10 minutes, or as long as it stays hot or cold.

MEDICAL MEASURES

Mainstream M.D.'s treat migraines with some 200 different medications. Some of these drugs help relieve pain. They include prescription-strength NSAIDs, ergot derivatives, lidocaine nosedrops, antinausea drugs, and medications that constrict blood vessels—notably sumatriptan (Imitrex) and zolmitriptan (Zomig). Other drugs help prevent migraine episodes. Among them are beta-blockers, calcium channel blockers, antidepressants, and anticonvulsants.

Depending on your medical situation, you may not be able to use one or more of these medications. Before you start taking any migraine medication, ask your physician or pharmacist to explain all of the possible side effects.

For menstrual migraines, your doctor may prescribe an estrogen gel or patch. You apply the estrogen 2 days before the time in your cycle when you get your migraines, then continue using it for a week. Research has shown that estrogen decreases the frequency and severity of menstrual migraines.

According to Dr. Goldstein, certain prescription drugs can actually cause migraines. If you're taking any drug and you're experiencing migraines, talk to your doctor about switching to another pharmaceutical.

Because migraines and other headaches are so common, special clinics have sprung up around the country that focus exclusively on treating them. To find a practitioner near you, contact one of the following organizations.

◆ The American Council for Headache Education, 19 Mantua Road, Mount Royal, NJ 08061-1006

◆ National Headache Foundation, 428 West Saint James Place, Second Floor, Chicago, IL 60614-2750

RED FLAGS

If you experience any of the following, see your doctor right away.

◆ An unusually severe headache

◆ A headache that lasts longer than 3 days, despite home treatment

◆ Headaches that recur more often or get worse over time

◆ A headache accompanied by a fever of 102°F or higher

◆ Head pain that increases when you bend your chin to your chest

◆ Headache accompanied by slurred speech, blurred vision, or numbness or weakness in the arms or legs

◆ Head pain that results from a head injury

Muscle Soreness

Your muscles are susceptible to three main types of injury: soreness, cramps, and strains and tears. Cramps, strains, and tears cause sudden sharp pain. Soreness—or as doctors call it, delayed-onset muscle soreness—produces dull, aching pain 24 to 48 hours after physical activity.

From a medical perspective, muscle soreness isn't serious. Even without treatment, it goes away within a few days. But with more Americans remaining athletic into middle-age and beyond, muscle soreness and other minor sports injuries are becoming much more common. In the last decade, sales of creams, ointments, and other rub-on products used to treat such injuries have boomed to more than $400 million a year.

SIMPLE SOLUTIONS
1. Supplements
2. Exercise
3. Visualization
4. Massage
5. Herbal Medicine
6. Home Remedies
7. Over-the-Counter Drugs
8. Homeopathy

Well into the 1980s, many scientists attributed muscle soreness to lactic acid, a by-product of your muscles' energy-producing processes. The theory was that as you exercised, excess lactic acid accumulated in your muscles. Then as the lactic acid dispersed, it made you achy and uncomfortable. "Today, we know that lactic acid has nothing to do with postexercise soreness," says Scott Hasson, Ed.D., professor of physical therapy at the University of Connecticut in Storrs. "The acid dissipates within minutes after you finish your workout."

So what really causes muscle soreness? According to Dr. Hasson, microscopic damage to your muscle fibers is to blame. "Any exercise injures some of your muscle cells. Your body usually repairs the cells without you feeling a thing," he explains. "But when you push your muscles beyond their level of conditioning, you get a lot of micro-injury—enough to cause inflammation that you feel as delayed-onset muscle soreness."

There's a lot you can do to speed your recovery process and possibly prevent future episodes of soreness. To start, adopt a blended approach to care.

Muscle Cramps: Untie Those Knots

A muscle cramp occurs when something causes the muscle to suddenly spasm, making it shorten. If you touch or rub the area that's cramping, you may feel the muscle knotting up.

You can develop a muscle cramp at any time. Many people get cramps at night, especially if they sleep on their stomachs or under heavy blankets. Either way, it's likely that they are pointing their toes, which can trigger a muscle spasm.

To relieve a muscle cramp, Anne Simons, M.D., recommends this three-step approach.

1. Stop what you're doing.
2. Massage your cramped muscle with a kneading motion.
3. Gently stretch the muscle.

If you seem particularly prone to cramps, try these preventive measures.

Maximize magnesium in your diet. "Magnesium helps your muscle relax," says clinical nutritionist Shari Lieberman, Ph.D. Eat more whole grains, wheat germ, nuts, seeds, seafood, and low-fat dairy products. Or take 500 milligrams of supplemental magnesium every day, she suggests.

Pick up more potassium. If you have low levels of potassium, you also run an increased risk of muscle cramping. You can take supplements of the mineral, but you probably don't need to, Dr. Lieberman says. Instead, fill your plate with potassium-rich foods such as whole grains, beans, fruits, vegetables, lean meats, fish, poultry, and low-fat dairy products other than cheese.

Become fluent in fluids. According to fitness expert Robert K. Cooper, Ph.D., author of *Health and Fitness Excellence*, you can easily prevent muscle cramps when you exercise by drinking plenty of water, especially in hot weather. "There was a time when athletes and coaches believed that consuming fluids caused cramps," he says. "But now we know better."

Muscle Strains and Tears: A Step Beyond Soreness

M uscle soreness results from microscopic injuries to a muscle's fibers. Similar but more extensive injuries lead to muscle strains—what you may know as pulled muscles. The most serious type of strain is called a muscle tear or rupture.

In most cases, sudden muscle pain results from a strain rather than a tear. You can usually treat a strain at home with RICE: rest, ice, compression, and elevation, says San Leandro, California, sports-medicine specialist Steven Subotnick, D.P.M., author of *Sports and Exercise Injuries*.

◆ Rest: When you get that first stab of pain, stop whatever you're doing.

◆ Ice: Apply an ice pack to the injury site for 20 minutes every few hours. If you don't have a gel pack handy, use ice cubes in a plastic bag or a bag of frozen peas or corn. Wrap the ice pack in a towel before putting it against your skin.

BEST CHOICES

Supplements

Ease aches with E. William J. Evans, Ph.D., professor of nutrition and applied physiology at Pennsylvania State University in University Park, has done research that suggests that vitamin E, an antioxidant, can reduce levels of free radicals and prevent muscle soreness. But the nutrient appears to benefit only older "weekend warriors," not young, conditioned athletes. Clinical nutritionist Shari Lieberman, Ph.D., suggests taking 400 international units (IU) a day.

Curb soreness with carnitine. According to Dr. Lieberman, the nutrient carnitine helps fatty acids get into muscle tissue, where they're burned for energy. Taking carnitine supplements improves muscle efficiency, which may help minimize muscle soreness.

◆ Compression: After you have treated the injury with ice, wrap the area with an elastic bandage. Continue using the bandage for several days.

◆ Elevation: Raise the injury site above the level of your heart to help regulate blood flow to the area. If you have strained a leg muscle, prop up your feet. If you have strained an arm muscle, try wearing a sling.

Once the inflammation has begun to subside, you can switch from cold treatments to heat treatments. Heat stimulates blood flow to the injured area, which speeds healing. You can soak in a tolerably hot bath, or you can apply a heating pad or a heated gel pack. (Most gel packs can be warmed in the microwave.)

To control pain and inflammation until your injury heals, take aspirin, ibuprofen, or naproxen (Aleve). Acetaminophen can also relieve pain, but it's not anti-inflammatory.

If your injury doesn't respond to home treatment within a week or so, or if the area becomes badly swollen or discolored, see your doctor.

Carnitine supplements should be used only under the supervision of a knowledgeable medical professional who's familiar with amino acids.

Exercise

Resist the urge to rest. When muscle soreness strikes, you might be tempted to take a break from physical activity. "Don't veg out," advises certified athletic trainer Michael McCormick, director of Athletico, a Chicago-area sports-medicine and physical therapy clinic. "You want to maintain blood flow, so your muscles are getting the oxygen and nutrients they need to heal. Don't do anything strenuous, but don't just lie around, either. Do some gentle stretches. Take a walk."

Don't overdo. If you've been exercising regularly, you can minimize muscle soreness by restricting any increase in the intensity or duration of your workout to no more than 10 percent a week. Stretching before and after workouts helps, too. When you stretch, move slowly through your full range of motion. Never bounce.

Stretch to Soothe Soreness

To prevent and treat soreness and other muscle injuries, athletic trainers and sports-medicine specialists often recommend stretches like the ones that follow. When you practice these stretches, remember to hold each position rather than bouncing.

For your ankle muscles: Sit on the floor and loop a towel around the ball of your foot, holding the ends of the towel in your hands. Point and flex your toes against the resistance of the towel for about 5 minutes.

For a cramp in your calf muscles: Stand facing a wall, far enough away that you can step forward with one foot. Lean toward the wall, placing your hands and forearms against it. Make sure that both feet point directly toward the wall. Lock the knee of your cramped leg. Step toward the wall with your other leg, bending that knee. Press forward until you feel a moderate stretch along the back of your cramped leg. Hold for 15 seconds. Then bend the knee of your cramped leg until you feel a moderate stretch along the back of it. Hold for 15 seconds. Repeat each stretch five times with each leg.

Visualization

Try mental medicine. When you're hurting, visualization exercises may help relieve your discomfort. Gerald N. Epstein, M.D., director of the Academy of Integrative Medicine and Mental Imagery in New York City, offers this exercise: Close your eyes and take three deep breaths. Imagine your sore muscles encased in ice. Picture the ice melting. As it does, sense your soreness melting away. Practice this visualization for 2 to 3 minutes several times a day until your soreness subsides.

Massage

Rub out pain. At East Carolina University in Greenville, North Carolina, researchers found that people who received massages reported significantly less muscle soreness.

To reap the benefits of massage, you can visit a professional massage ther-

For your hamstring muscles: The hamstrings are the large muscles at the backs of your thighs. To stretch these muscles, sit on a bed or sofa with one leg stretched straight out and the other hanging over the side. Lean forward until you feel a stretch in the back of your thigh. Hold for 15 seconds. Repeat several times with each leg.

For your quadriceps muscles: The quadriceps are located at the fronts of your thighs. To stretch these muscles, stand on one leg and bend the other leg back. Grab your bent leg with your hand and gently pull until your ankle touches your buttocks. Hold for 15 seconds. Repeat several times with each leg.

For your shoulder muscles: Draw one arm across your chest at shoulder height. Then with your other hand, gently pull your arm closer to your chest. Hold for 10 seconds. Repeat six times with each arm.

For your wrist muscles: For this stretch, you need a 3- to 5-pound dumbbell. Grasp the dumbbell in one hand and extend your arm out in front of you, palm up. Bend your wrist up and down several times. Next, move your wrist in circles several times. Repeat with your palm facing down, then repeat the entire sequence with your other arm.

apist, or you can try massaging your own sore muscles. If you opt for the self-care approach, herbalists Kathi Keville and Mindy Green, coauthors of *Aromatherapy: A Complete Guide to the Healing Art*, recommend using a relaxing, pain-relieving aromatherapy massage lotion. To prepare it, add the following essential oils to 1 ounce of olive oil or an unscented lotion: 6 drops of helichrysum, 4 drops of marjoram, 3 drops of chamomile, 3 drops of lavender, 3 drops of ginger, and 2 drops of juniper.

Herbal Medicine

Feel better with willow bark. The herb willow bark contains salicin, which is the chemical forerunner of aspirin. Sipping willow bark tea may help relieve muscle soreness, says James A. Duke, Ph.D. To make the tea, simmer about 2 teaspoons of powdered bark in 1 cup of boiling water for 10 minutes. Then strain, cool, and drink.

Home Remedies

First, apply ice. At the first sign of muscle soreness, apply an ice pack to the sore spot for 20 minutes every few hours. If you don't have one of those gel packs handy, put a few ice cubes in a plastic bag. Even better, use a bag of frozen peas or corn, suggests Jeffrey Housner, M.D., clinical assistant professor at the University of Michigan Medical Center in Ann Arbor. It can be molded to fit the contours of the injury site.

Whatever sort of ice pack you use, be sure to wrap it in a towel before putting it against your skin. Otherwise, you could give yourself frostbite, says Bryant A. Stamford, Ph.D., director of the Health Promotion and Wellness Center at the University of Louisville in Kentucky.

Later, apply heat. You don't want to use heat treatments immediately after muscle soreness sets in, because they can aggravate inflammation and swelling. So wait a day or two, then feel free to soak in a hot tub or to apply a heating pad or heated gel pack. (Most gel packs can be warmed in the microwave.)

Heat not only soothes soreness but also promotes blood flow to your muscles, which speeds healing.

Over-the-Counter Drugs

Opt for the right OTC. Most people rely on over-the-counter painkillers to relieve muscle soreness. All of these drugs provide relief, but according to Dr. Hasson, some work better than others. He recommends taking aspirin or ibuprofen because they treat both pain and inflammation. But do not take ibuprofen or aspirin if you have a history of ulcers or other gastrointestinal problems or if you're a woman who's pregnant.

Counteract discomfort with a counterirritant. Ben-Gay and similar topical preparations also relieve muscle soreness. These products are called counterirritants.

If you use a counterirritant product, follow the package directions. You can cover the treated area with a loose bandage to keep the cream from smearing. But the American Pharmaceutical Association cautions against applying tight bandages or using heating pads in conjunction with counterirritants. These combinations may cause skin irritation or blistering.

OTHER GOOD CHOICES

Homeopathy

Rely on Arnica. Homeopaths usually treat muscle soreness with Arnica ointment, says Steven Subotnick, D.P.M., a sports-medicine specialist in San Leandro, California, and author of *Sports and Exercise Injuries*. You can buy the ointment over the counter in health food stores. Follow the package directions for proper use.

Home Remedies

Drink even if you're not thirsty. Your muscles are 70 percent water. "If you dehydrate a muscle by just 3 percent, it loses 10 percent of its strength," says fitness expert Robert K. Cooper, Ph.D., author of *Health and Fitness Excellence*. Drinking water before you exercise helps keep your muscles hydrated and strong, which in turn helps prevent the micro-injuries that lead to muscle soreness. Aim for at least eight 8-ounce glasses of water a day. "Steady sipping throughout the day is usually easier than guzzling large amounts a few times a day," he says.

Nausea and Vomiting

Think of nausea as the great equalizer. All of us—no matter what our age, gender, race, religion, or economic status—get queasy from time to time. And all of us react in pretty much the same way: We close our eyes, clutch our stomachs, and pray that the feeling passes.

All sorts of things can cause nausea. Perhaps you've eaten too much or drunk too much. Maybe you've seen or smelled something disagreeable. Or perhaps you're prone to motion sickness or migraines.

Certain prescription drugs can make you feel nauseated. So can surgical anesthesia and cancer chemotherapy. If you're a woman who is pregnant, you may have nausea because of morning sickness. Persistent nausea may signal an underlying health problem, such as ulcers, appendicitis, or liver disease.

SIMPLE SOLUTIONS
1. Relaxation Therapies
2. Herbal Medicine
3. Chinese Medicine
4. Home Remedies
5. Aromatherapy
6. Homeopathy
7. Ayurvedic Medicine
8. Over-the-Counter Drugs

When you're nauseated, you feel as though you're going to vomit. Often that's exactly what happens. As bad as vomiting is, it's over and done with quickly. In a way, nausea is worse. It keeps you wondering whether you're going to vomit and when you're going to feel better.

By using a combination of mainstream and alternative remedies at the onset of nausea, you can beat it before it gets the best of you.

BEST CHOICES

Relaxation Therapies

Relax to relieve nausea. In one study, researchers divided 60 people with nausea into three groups. One group learned meditative deep relaxation and visualization. Another group received counseling. The third group received standard care. Compared with the people getting counseling or standard care, those who practiced deep relaxation and visualization reported significantly less nausea.

"Nausea is a mind-body experience, so the fact that mind-body approaches help control it comes as no surprise," says stress-management specialist Martin L. Rossman, M.D.

Herbal Medicine

Keep ginger on hand. Herbal medicine experts are unanimous in their praise of ginger. "Ginger reduces all symptoms of motion sickness—nausea, vomiting, dizziness, and cold sweating," notes Seattle naturopath Michael T. Murray, N.D.

James A. Duke, Ph.D., agrees: "Ginger is my first choice for treating motion sickness and morning sickness."

You can take ginger in several ways. If you're using the herb to prevent motion sickness, then capsules are probably your most convenient choice. Take one 1-gram capsule 30 minutes before your departure. Chewing some candied gingerroot is another option.

Ginger tea may also help. To brew the tea, add 1 tablespoon of freshly grated gingerroot to 1 cup of boiled water. Steep for 10 minutes, then strain.

If you live near an Asian grocery, you can pick up some candied gingerroot. Chew a piece about the size of your thumb to get 1 gram of the herb, says Varro Tyler, Ph.D., recently retired professor of pharmacognosy (the study of medicinal plants) at Purdue University.

Chinese Medicine

Control your qi. To treat nausea and vomiting, Efrem Korngold, O.M.D., L.Ac., recommends spicy foods and herbs that normalize qi. These include radishes, radish seed, ginger, and citrus fruit peel.

Focus on your forearm. For centuries, Chinese physicians have treated nausea by performing acupuncture at the point Pericardium 6. This point is located in the middle of your inner wrist, 2½ finger-widths above the wrist crease. You can stimulate the point by applying firm, steady finger pressure for 3 minutes. Or you can wear an elastic band with a button that stimulates the point for you. Sold under the brand name Sea-Band, these bands are available in drugstores and health food stores.

Morning Sickness: Bane of Moms-to-Be

Talk about misnomers. Morning sickness seldom confines itself to the A.M. hours. True, you may feel nauseated only around breakfast during your first trimester. But you may also feel sick all day long for much of your pregnancy.

About half of pregnant women get nauseated, and approximately one-third of them vomit. No one knows why. Some studies pin the blame on the hormonal changes of pregnancy, while others say s have nothing to do with it.

If you have morning sickness, you may be able to use some of the same remedies recommended for nausea and vomiting. But to be safe, always check with your doctor before trying a new remedy, and never take any anti-nausea medications without your doctor's approval.

Here are some additional measures that may help you keep morning sickness in check.

Choose your foods wisely. Avoid eating fatty foods, which are

Home Remedies

Sip something sugary. Did your mother or grandmother ever give you flat Coca-Cola or 7UP when you felt queasy? That's not a bad idea, according to Robert Warren, Pharm.D., a pharmacist at Valley Children's Hospital in Fresno, California. Concentrated carbohydrates—that is, sugar—often help settle upset stomachs.

Crunch crackers. If you want, you can have some crackers along with your soda. They are another good source of carbohydrates, so they may help to relieve your nausea.

Keep your eyes on the horizon. If you're plagued by motion sickness, you may be able to prevent it by focusing on faraway stationary objects as you travel, advises Anne Simons, M.D. "Looking at something that's not moving can fool your brain's balance center into believing that you're not moving, either," she explains.

Be a middle man. To prevent seasickness, position yourself midway between the bow and stern. The middle of the boat rocks the least.

difficult to digest, advises Alan Gaby, M.D. Instead, build your meals around pastas, breads, vegetables, and fruits.

Eat less more often. Divide your standard three squares into six smaller meals, spaced evenly throughout the day. That way, your stomach doesn't have to work so hard to digest large quantities of food.

Take the anti-vomiting vitamin. Many pregnant women have low blood levels of vitamin B_6, notes Bonnie Worthington-Roberts, Ph.D., retired professor of nutrition at the University of Washington School of Public Health in Seattle. At the very least, supplements can help ensure that you have all the B_6 you need. Be sure to consult with your doctor before you begin supplementation.

Don't rush to brush. Don't brush your teeth until after you've eaten breakfast. Sticking a toothbrush in your mouth before you've put anything in your stomach encourages vomiting, according to Barbara Abrams, Dr.P.H., of the University of California, Berkeley, School of Public Health.

OTHER GOOD CHOICES

Aromatherapy

Inhale soothing scents. Certain essential oils can calm a queasy stomach, according to Kathi Keville and Mindy Green, coauthors of *Aromatherapy: A Complete Guide to the Healing Art*. They suggest placing a piece of rock salt in a small capped vial, then adding a few drops each of basil, ginger, peppermint, rose, rosewood, and sandalwood essential oils. Carry the vial with you, and whenever you feel nauseated, open it and take several deep breaths.

Homeopathy

Say "hooray" for Ipecacuanha. Emergency medicine specialists use syrup of ipecac to induce vomiting in some cases of accidental poisoning. Ipecac comes from the herb ipecacuanha. Homeopaths often prescribe a superdilute homeopathic formulation of Ipecacuanha to treat persistent nausea, says homeopath Dana Ullman.

Other effective homeopathic medicines include the following: Arsenicum album, for nausea caused by food poisoning or the sight or smell of foods; Bryonia, for motion sickness; Nux vomica, for nausea related to hangover, overeating, or food poisoning; Podophyllum peltatum, for nausea and vomiting with diarrhea; and Pulsatilla, for nausea caused by indigestion, with bloating and possibly headache.

To find out which of these medicines best suits your symptoms, make an appointment with a homeopath.

Ayurvedic Medicine

Sip some spices. Practitioners of Ayurvedic medicine attribute vomiting to an upward movement of air from the stomach. It's most common in people with Kapha doshas, according to David Frawley, O.M.D.

Ginger is a key Ayurvedic medicinal herb, and it's one that Dr. Frawley recommends as a treatment for nausea and vomiting.

He also offers this remedy to help quell an upset stomach: Add 1 teaspoon of cardamom and 1 teaspoon of fennel to 1 cup of warm water, mix in a little honey for taste, and take frequent sips.

Over-the-Counter Drugs

Allay symptoms with an antihistamine. Several over-the-counter antihistamines—including Dramamine, Bonine, Marezine, and Benadryl—may help prevent motion sickness. If you choose one of these products, use it according to the package directions. For side effects and drug interactions, be sure to read warnings on the labels.

Partake of the "pink stuff." For nausea caused by indigestion, try Pepto-Bismol. Take it according to the package directions. This product is not appropriate for anyone who is taking aspirin regularly or who is aspirin-sensitive.

Sample a stomach soother. As an alternative to flat Coca-Cola or 7UP, you may want to try Emetrol. This over-the-counter product contains fructose and glucose, both naturally occurring sugars. Use it according to the directions on the package.

Note: You should avoid Emetrol if you have diabetes.

RED FLAGS

Sometimes vomiting is a symptom of a more serious underlying medical condition. Dr. Simons advises you to consult a physician promptly in any of the following situations.

◆ Vomiting persists for more than 24 hours in an adult or more than 12 hours in a child

◆ You're vomiting blood, which may appear either red or black and tarry

◆ Vomiting is accompanied by fever

◆ Vomiting occurs after an injury, particularly a head injury

◆ You're vomiting everything that you ingest, including sips of water

◆ Vomiting occurs in an infant who cries inconsolably

◆ Vomiting plus diarrhea occur in an infant or an elderly person

If vomiting is associated with a suspected poisoning, call your local emergency number without delay. The operator will tell you what to do.

Osteoarthritis

The word *arthritis* means "joint inflammation." Arthritis is not a disease. It's a symptom of more than a dozen conditions, including bursitis, fibromyalgia, and Lyme disease. It's also a potential side effect of many common drugs.

For this reason, if you experience persistent joint pain, you'll need to see your doctor. But chances are, your doctor will tell you that you have osteoarthritis, or degenerative joint disease.

The most common form of arthritis, osteoarthritis usually results from decades of wear and tear on your joints. Your joints are lined with cartilage, the tough, flexible, shock-absorbing material that keeps your bones from grinding into one another. In osteoarthritis, your cartilage breaks down, and your bones develop little outgrowths, or spurs. If you're a woman with osteoarthritis in your fingers, you may also develop bony bulges in the joints nearest your nails. Doctors call these bumps Heberden's nodes.

Most people with osteoarthritis experience their worst stiffness and aching first thing in the morning, with diminishing discomfort as the day progresses. But you might get the most grief when you overuse your affected joints and enjoy some relief when you rest them.

SIMPLE SOLUTIONS
1. Nutrition
2. Supplements
3. Elimination Diet
4. Exercise
5. Tai Chi
6. Yoga
7. Social Support
8. Herbal Medicine
9. Home Remedies
10. Over-the-Counter Drugs
11. Homeopathy
12. Chinese Medicine
13. Ayurvedic Medicine
14. Naturopathy
15. Medical Measures

Many people—including many mainstream M.D.'s—view osteoarthritis and its progression from mild to more severe as inevitable. Joint wear and tear may be a fact of life, but joint pain that interferes with your life is not. There is plenty that you can do to prevent and relieve osteoarthritis.

BEST CHOICES

Nutrition

Prevent damage with antioxidants. Antioxidant nutrients—notably vitamin C, vitamin E, and the vitamin A family of nutrients (including beta-carotene and other carotenoids)—help prevent the cell damage linked to many age-related conditions, including osteoarthritis. Of these nutrients, vitamin C seems to play the greatest role in preventing cartilage loss. Foods rich in vitamin C include broccoli, bell peppers, citrus fruits, cabbage, cauliflower, spinach, and strawberries.

"D-lay" arthritis. In a study at Boston University Medical Center, researchers found that vitamin D significantly reduced the progression of osteoarthritis, presumably because the vitamin plays a role in cartilage repair. Food sources of vitamin D include D-fortified dairy products and fatty saltwater fish such as salmon, halibut, sea bass, tuna, cod, and herring.

Benefit from berries. Cherries, blueberries, raspberries, and blackberries owe their deep, dark color to pigments that are potent antioxidants. These pigments also have some anti-inflammatory action, says Joseph Pizzorno Jr., N.D., and they are remarkable for their ability to stabilize cartilage. He suggests eating more of these berries.

Supplements

Take extra antioxidants. If antioxidants in food help relieve osteoarthritis, do antioxidant supplements do the same? The research is scant, but in one pilot study, 32 people with osteoarthritis were given either 600 international units (IU) of the antioxidant vitamin E or a placebo (a fake pill) every day. Among those taking vitamin E, 52 percent experienced significant relief. If you are thinking about taking amounts above 400 IU, discuss this with your doctor first.

Alan P. Brauer, M.D., says that vitamin C supplements also help: "I'm a big believer in the power of vitamin C. I always suggest it to people with osteoarthritis."

Try GS and CS. GS is glucosamine sulfate, a nutrient popularized in the book *The Arthritis Cure* by Jason Theodosakis, M.D. About one-half to two-thirds of people who try GS experience benefits, according to Marc Hochberg, M.D., chief of rheumatology at the University of Maryland School of Medicine in Baltimore. But a good deal of research shows that in some people, GS supplementation helps repair damaged cartilage and quite often provides considerable pain relief. Dr. Hochberg suggests taking 500 milligrams of GS three times a day for a month. "If you notice improvement, you can keep taking it as long as it seems to work without uncomfortable side effects," he says. "If it doesn't, stop taking it after a month."

The Arthritis Cure also advocates combining GS with chondroitin sulfate (CS), a compound that helps draw fluid into cartilage.

Several of the studies showing benefits from GS and CS supplementation used one brand, called Cosamin. It contains 500 milligrams of GS and 400 milligrams of CS per capsule. New York Times health columnist Jane Brody, who has osteoarthritis, tried Cosamin and reported noticeable joint pain relief.

Bring on the boron. An essential trace mineral, boron helps control inflammation, says New York City clinical nutritionist Shari Lieberman, Ph.D. People with osteoarthritis often have low blood levels of boron. If you want to take a supplement, Dr. Lieberman suggests 3 to 6 milligrams a day.

Elimination Diet

Investigate food sensitivities. According to Dr. Brauer, food sensitivities often play a role in osteoarthritis: "I've seen many people improve when they eliminate foods to which they are sensitive." Consider an elimination diet, in consultation with your physician. If you get relief after eliminating certain foods, stick with the diet.

Exercise

Do it regularly. Years ago, if you had arthritis, your doctor would have advised minimizing physical activity. But that has changed. "Today, we know that one of the best ways to manage osteoarthritis is to be as physically active as your condition allows," says Anne Simons, M.D.

Low-impact exercise that gently moves your joints through their full range of motion minimizes pain, reduces swelling, and helps keep them supple. It promotes nourishing blood flow to your cartilage. It strengthens the muscles around your joints, which helps support them. It releases endorphins, the body's own pain-relieving compounds. And it helps you control your weight.

But you might wonder: Won't exercise wear out your joints? That's possible, but only if you overdo it with high-impact activities—for example, running or contact sports. "Be patient with yourself," Dr. Simons advises. "Over time, your range of motion, strength, and stamina should increase, and your pain, stiffness, and disability should decrease."

In general, good activities include walking, gardening, swimming, cycling, and in-pool calisthenics. The Arthritis Foundation has produced several excellent exercise videos for people with osteoarthritis. Contact your local chapter for information.

Tai Chi

Move through your pain. David B. Lumsden, M.D., a fourth-year resident in the department of orthopedic surgery at Union Memorial Hospital in Baltimore, likens tai chi to swimming without a pool. It's a gentle, low-impact range-of-motion activity that puts very little stress on your joints.

Yoga

Say yes to yoga. Yoga involves the kind of gentle, low-impact movements that experts recommend for osteoarthritis. At the University of Pennsylvania School of Medicine in Philadelphia, researchers assigned people with osteoarthritis in their hands to attend one yoga class a week or to receive standard treatment with drugs. After 8 weeks, the people who practiced yoga reported significantly less pain and greater range of motion in their fingers.

Social Support

Discuss your situation with your loved ones. If you have trouble with some daily tasks, you might hesitate to ask family and friends for help. On the other hand, some well-meaning friends and relatives may get on your nerves by "helping" when you don't need assistance. "The best way to handle this issue is to sit down with your family and friends and tell them gently but firmly that you intend to do as much as you can for yourself," Dr. Simons says. "Training family and friends takes time, but it gets you the help you need while maintaining your dignity and independence."

Take a class. In 1978, Stanford University nurse and health educator Kate Lorig, R.N., launched the Arthritis Self-Help Course. The program consists of six weekly 2-hour sessions, combining osteoarthritis education, relaxation techniques, exercise, problem-solving support from class members, and assertiveness training when dealing with doctors. The goal was to persuade people that they could control their pain and minimize the impact of osteoarthritis on their lives.

Over a 4-year period, Lorig and her colleagues found that class participants reported less pain, significantly less depression, greater self-confidence, fewer doctor visits, and more active, fulfilling lives. "The course's main benefit is that it improves participants' self-confidence about their ability to cope with their condition," says David S. Sobel, M.D., director of patient education and health promotion for Kaiser Permanente Northern California, a health maintenance organization.

The Arthritis Self-Help Course is now sponsored by the Arthritis Foundation and offered in more than 700 locations around the United States. To find a class near you, write to the foundation at 1330 West Peachtree Street, Atlanta, GA 30309-2922.

Herbal Medicine

Welcome willow. "Willow bark tea provides some relief from the pain and inflammation of osteoarthritis," says James A. Duke, Ph.D. "And it's less likely than aspirin to upset your stomach, so a few cups a day might be the better choice for some people."

Treat your joints gingerly. Ginger is an age-old treatment for inflammation, particularly in Ayurvedic medicine. Dr. Duke suggests using more fresh ginger in your cooking.

Temper symptoms with turmeric. A relative of ginger, turmeric is a staple ingredient in Indian cuisine. Its yellow pigment, called curcumin, is also one of nature's most potent anti-inflammatory agents, Dr. Pizzorno says. He recommends taking 400 milligrams of curcumin (available at health food stores) three times a day.

Dr. Duke also suggests preparing more curries and other Indian dishes with lots of turmeric.

Home Remedies

Make adjustments. "Take a close look at your life," Dr. Simons advises. "Try to make your daily tasks easier." Here are some suggestions that she and the Arthritis Foundation endorse.

◆ If your hands are the problem, junk your manual can opener and invest in an electric model. In addition, try not to hold objects in a tight grip for extended periods. When holding anything, such as a telephone or a steering wheel, flex your fingers frequently.

◆ If reaching up hurts your shoulder, place frequently used items on lower shelves.

◆ Use good posture. It places the least stress on your joints.

◆ Try not to stay in one position for a long period of time.

◆ Get up and move around as much as possible.

◆ When standing for long periods, place one foot on a box or stool to take stress off your back.

◆ Try to keep your joints extended rather than bent.

◆ Check consumer product catalogs for items that help relieve arthritis pain.

◆ Use the largest joint possible to accomplish any task. For example, carry a shoulder bag rather than a clutch purse, because your shoulder joint is larger than your finger joints.

◆ Learn your limits and don't push yourself beyond them. If you push yourself to the point of feeling pain, stop what you're doing.

Shed your extra baggage. Being overweight stresses your weight-bearing joints, especially your hips, knees, and ankles. Losing 10 to 15 pounds often provides noticeable relief from osteoarthritis in the knees, Dr. Hochberg says.

Make love. "Sex is great exercise for people with arthritis," says Palo Alto, California, sex and marital therapist Marty Klein, Ph.D. "It provides gentle, low-impact, massagelike exercise. It moves your major joints through their range of motion. It releases pain-relieving endorphins. And the closeness of lovemaking, the feeling of being loved, also helps relieve pain."

Over-the-Counter Drugs

Rub on red pepper. Capsaicin is the compound that gives red pepper its fiery flavor. Capsaicin also has unique pain-relieving properties. When rubbed into your skin, it short-circuits a compound called substance P that's involved in the transmission of pain signals through your nerves. Capsaicin creams are available at drugstores in two strengths: 0.025 percent and 0.075 percent. Experiment to see which strength works best for you.

Should You Try a Copper Bracelet?

For decades, some people with arthritis have sworn that wearing a copper bracelet helps relieve their pain, much to the chagrin of the Arthritis Foundation, which scoffs at copper bracelets and warns against getting hoodwinked by hucksters.

An Australian study also casts doubt on the effectiveness of copper bracelets. Researchers at St. Vincent's Hospital in Darlinghurst, New South Wales, rubbed either a gel containing 1.5 grams of a copper compound or a placebo gel into the forearms of 116 people with osteoarthritis of the hip or knee. The participants reported no significant difference in pain relief.

First choose acetaminophen, then aspirin or ibuprofen. Until recently, most doctors recommended aspirin and ibuprofen as the over-the-counter drugs of choice for osteoarthritis. But researchers at the University of Indiana School of Medicine have found that acetaminophen provides just as much relief. The American College of Rheumatology has recommended acetaminophen as first-line treatment for osteoarthritis.

Some studies suggest taking 2 ounces of stewed stinging nettle leaves along with your pain reliever. The combination appears to provide effective pain relief while allowing a dramatic decrease in the drug's dose and side effects.

OTHER GOOD CHOICES

Homeopathy

Take a little medicine for a lot of relief. Homeopaths recommend more than a dozen medicines for osteoarthritis, depending on a person's individual symptoms. But homeopath Dana Ullman says the two most widely prescribed are Rhus toxicodendron, for joints that are initially stiff but feel better after some activity, and Bryonia, for joints that hurt more with activity. Two other medicines that often help are Apis and Ledum. To find out which of these medicines best suits your symptoms, consult a homeopath.

Chinese Medicine

Chase away Wind, Cold, and Damp. Chinese medicine does not distinguish between rheumatoid arthritis and osteoarthritis. "The Chinese use the general term *arthralgia*, meaning joint pain," says Efrem Korngold, O.M.D., L.Ac. In the Chinese view, joint pain is caused by a combination of inflammation and invasion of Wind, Cold, and Damp that penetrates deep into your joints.

To treat the inflammation, Dr. Korngold prescribes gardenia buds, forsythia, honeysuckle, and sarsaparilla. To expel Wind, Cold, and Damp, he recommends clematis root, gentian root, chaenomeles fruit, and cinnamon twig.

Arthritis may also involve some organ weakness, particularly your Kidney, which governs your bones. To strengthen it, Dr. Korngold prescribes dry ginger, eucommia, dipsacus, and drynaria.

Stimulate joint points. "There is strong evidence that acupuncture relieves osteoarthritis pain," says Gary Kaplan, D.O., who combines mainstream and Chinese medicine in his practice in Arlington, Virginia.

Which points acupuncturists stimulate depends on which joints are affected. They often insert needles in the opposite joint. For example, if your right knee bothers you, your acupuncturist might stimulate points in your left knee. "The idea is to move your qi from the healthy part to the weak part," Dr. Korngold explains.

In addition to acupuncture, some Chinese physicians burn moxa (mugwort) on the affected area to draw out Wind, Cold, and Damp. Others massage the area with herbal oils.

Ayurvedic Medicine

Be generous with guggul. Ayurvedic physicians consider osteoarthritis an imbalance of the Vata dosha caused by toxic air. For external treatment, David Frawley, O.M.D., prescribes frequent massages with warm sesame oil medicated with various Indian herbs, followed by a hot shower.

For internal use, Ayurvedic physicians often prescribe treatment with guggul. Sometimes called Indian frankincense, guggul is the resin of a tree that grows in the dry, hilly areas of India. The resin has a long history of use as a treatment for joint pain.

Ayurvedic physicians sometimes combine guggul with two other Indian herbs: turmeric and ashwagandha. At the Interdisciplinary School of Ayurvedic

(continued on page 508)

Gout: Kicking the Pain

Gout is a form of arthritis that causes inflammation and often intense pain in one or more joints, most commonly the big toe.

About one million Americans have gout. For reasons that remain unclear, the vast majority of these (some 95 percent) are men over the age of 30.

Gout is caused by the buildup of uric acid, a metabolic waste product and major component of urine. Normally, your kidneys filter uric acid out of your blood. But in people with gout, some uric acid forms crystals that get deposited in joints. A gout attack occurs when these crystals irritate the joint lining, causing inflammation and often severe pain.

Although about half of gout attacks affect the big toe, other joints can also be affected—though mercifully, gout usually strikes only one joint at a time.

First gout attacks produce intense pain. They usually occur at night, after eating a high-fat meal and drinking alcohol. Swelling may cause the affected joint to appear red or purple, and it may produce sensitivity to pressure that makes even the weight of a bedsheet intolerable. Initial attacks usually last a few days.

Unlike osteoarthritis, gout is rarely chronic. Some people never have another attack, but many experience recurrences from time to time.

If you've ever experienced gout, you can prevent most attacks by following these suggestions.

Weed out purines. The Arthritis Foundation recommends avoiding meats, organ meats (such as liver, brains, and sweetbreads), dairy foods, shellfish, sardines, herring, mackerel, anchovies, and anything high in protein (such as beans, fish, and poultry). High-protein foods cause a buildup of chemicals called purines in your blood. Purines elevate your uric acid level and increase your risk of a gout attack.

Avoid alcohol. "Alcohol increases uric acid production, which is why gout attacks often follow an evening of drinking alcoholic beverages," explains Joseph Pizzorno Jr., N.D. "For many people who suffer from gout, eliminating alcohol ends their attacks."

Fill up on other fluids. Drink plenty of nonalcoholic fluids—ideally 8 ounces with each meal, and at least 8 ounces between meals and after supper, recommends Anne Simons, M.D. Water, juices, teas, and other nonalcoholic fluids dilute your urine and promote the excretion of uric acid.

Drop your excess baggage. If you're overweight, try to lose those extra pounds, Dr. Simons advises. Weight loss reduces uric acid levels.

Take essential fatty acids. The main ones are gamma-linolenic acid (GLA) and eicosapentaenoic acid (EPA). Both are available in supplement form.

Add vitamin E. "Vitamin E reduces production of the compounds in the body that cause inflammation," Dr. Pizzorno explains. He recommends taking 400 to 800 international units (IU) of vitamin E daily. If you are thinking about taking amounts above 400 IU, discuss this with your doctor first.

Go easy on the vitamin C and niacin. Large doses of vitamin C and niacin can increase uric acid levels, Dr. Pizzorno says. The amounts you get in a typical multivitamin probably won't hurt. But don't take higher doses of vitamin C or niacin.

Munch some cherries. Cherries can be beneficial because they contain compounds that help prevent the type of inflammation that triggers gout attacks.

Chomp on celery. James A. Duke, Ph.D., noticed a study suggesting that celery extract might help eliminate uric acid. "I stopped taking the drug I was on (allopurinol) and began taking four tablets of celery seed extract a day," he says. "One week, I ate four celery stalks instead of taking the extract. My uric acid level has stayed below the level that triggers gout."

Go the drug route. Mainstream physicians treat gout with the dietary changes recommended above and with four types of medication: nonsteroidal anti-inflammatory drugs; colchicine, an anti-inflammatory; uricosuric drugs, which increase uric acid excretion; and allopurinol (Zyloprim), which decreases uric acid production.

Medicine at the University of Poona, India, researchers gave 42 people with osteoarthritis either a combination of guggul, turmeric, ashwagandha, and zinc or a placebo every 8 hours. After 3 months, everyone switched treatments, so the placebo group took the herb-mineral formula, and vice versa. The study participants reported significantly less pain and disability while they were taking the herb-mineral formula.

Naturopathy

Make the most of moist heat. Heat often soothes the joint pain and stiffness of osteoarthritis. Moist heat usually works best, says rheumatologist John Abruzzo, M.D., of Thomas Jefferson University Hospital in Philadelphia. He suggests applying moist heat packs, taking tolerably hot baths or showers, soaking in a hot tub, or swimming in a well-heated pool.

MEDICAL MEASURES

If alternative therapies and over-the-counter pain relievers don't adequately control your pain, your doctor can prescribe prescription nonsteroidal anti-inflammatory drugs (NSAIDs). NSAIDs are effective, but their gastrointestinal side effects can be serious. When people are admitted to hospitals with life-threatening gastrointestinal bleeding, more than half have been taking NSAIDs.

But the NSAID future looks brighter. A new class of NSAIDs, COX-2 inhibitors, promises to provide all the pain and inflammation relief of today's NSAIDs but with very few side effects.

In some cases, your doctor may recommend a splint or some other joint-protection device to reduce joint stress and deformity. Depending on your individual situation, you might need to use your joint-sparing device only a few hours a day, or you might have to wear it much of the time.

Don't hesitate to ask your doctor for a referral to a physical therapist or a physiatrist, a physician who specializes in rehabilitation medicine. In addition, an occupational therapist may be able to suggest helpful assisting devices and less stressful ways to accomplish necessary tasks of daily living.

If severe osteoarthritis of the knee or hip limits your mobility and does not respond well to other treatments, your doctor may recommend surgery—knee or hip joint replacement with an artificial joint.

RED FLAGS

Some joint pain requires immediate professional attention.

◆ A single warm, swollen, painful joint suggests a joint infection.

◆ Persistent joint pain after an injury might signal a fracture.

◆ Joint pain accompanied by other symptoms—fever, loss of appetite, or an ill feeling—might be one of a dozen conditions.

◆ Joint pain with numbness, weakness, burning, or tingling might indicate a problem in your nervous system.

Osteoporosis

Osteoporosis is an age-related condition that causes a loss of bone mass and increased brittleness in the remaining bone tissue. Like heart disease, the bone-thinning of osteoporosis sneaks up on you, says Ethel S. Siris, M.D., director of the Toni Stabile Center for the Prevention and Treatment of Osteoporosis at Columbia-Presbyterian Medical Center in New York City.

Osteoporosis currently affects some 25 million Americans. While both men and women develop the condition, it's about 10 times more common—and much more severe—in women. Postmenopausal women with osteoporosis account for the vast majority of the nation's annual 700,000 spinal fractures, 300,000 hip fractures, and 200,000 wrist fractures.

SIMPLE SOLUTIONS
1. Nutrition
2. Supplements
3. Exercise
4. Herbal Medicine
5. Home Remedies
6. Homeopathy
7. Chinese Medicine
8. Ayurvedic Medicine
9. Medical Measures

Women's bones are strongest around age 30. From then until menopause, you don't lose much bone. But in the 5 to 7 years after menopause, you lose 1 to 5 percent of your bone mass every year, Dr. Siris says. After that, bone loss continues, but slows.

For women, menopause is the turning point in osteoporosis. Your bones' ability to incorporate calcium from your blood depends on the hormone estrogen. As you pass through menopause, you produce less estrogen, and you can't absorb enough calcium to replace the bone you naturally lose.

But menopause isn't the whole story. There are many other risk factors for osteoporosis. For example, excessive alcohol and caffeine consumption can accelerate bone loss. And there are many drugs that rob your bones of calcium, according to the National Osteoporosis Foundation. They include glucocorticoids such as cortisone (Cortone), prednisone (Prednisone Tablets), thyroid hormone such as levothyroxine (Synthroid), anticonvulsants such as phenytoin (Dilantin), and aluminum hydroxide-based antacids (like Maalox).

You can help protect your bones by maintaining a nutritionally well-balanced diet, exercising regularly, and not smoking. The following strategies will also help keep your skeleton strong.

BEST CHOICES

Nutrition

Start with calcium. Most adults should consume 1,500 milligrams of calcium a day, according to the National Institutes of Health. The best way to get your calcium is from food. Calcium-fortified foods, such as breads, cereals, and certain fruit juices, are a good idea, Dr. Siris says. (For other good sources, see "Counting Calcium" on page 513.)

Pair calcium with D. In order to absorb calcium, your body needs vitamin D, which is why milk is fortified with this nutrient. Unfortunately, just as you grow old enough for osteoporosis to become a significant health threat, you also start having trouble getting enough vitamin D.

The best food sources of vitamin D include fortified low-fat or nonfat dairy items and fatty saltwater fish such as sea bass, halibut, tuna, herring, and swordfish.

You can also get vitamin D by stepping outside. It takes only about 15 minutes a day of sun on your face for your body to produce enough vitamin D. But if you live in northern climes, that might be a problem in winter. And if you live in the Sunbelt, chances are you use a lot of sunscreen, which interferes with vitamin D synthesis. That's why it's prudent to eat plenty of D-rich foods.

Get more of the secret bone builders. When it comes to osteoporosis, you don't hear much about magnesium, manganese, vitamin K, and boron. But these nutrients are crucial to the health of your bones.

People with osteoporosis often have low blood levels of magnesium, says Joseph Pizzorno Jr., N.D. When you're deficient in magnesium, your vitamin D isn't as effective in moving calcium into your bones.

Clinical nutritionist Shari Lieberman, Ph.D., recommends getting the mineral from the following food sources: seeds, soybeans, wheat germ, seafood, and dairy items.

If you're low in manganese, your bones can't absorb calcium. Good food sources of manganese include nuts (especially hazelnuts and pecans), avocados, and oatmeal.

Vitamin K activates osteocalcin, a protein that holds calcium in place in the bone matrix. Vitamin K is found in abundance in leafy green vegetables, notably spinach, broccoli, green cabbage, and tomatoes, Dr. Lieberman says.

"Boron seems to activate both estrogen and vitamin D," Dr. Pizzorno says. According to Dr. Lieberman, the best food sources of boron are fruits and vegetables, particularly carrots, applesauce, broccoli, peaches, pears, and cherries.

Discover the phyto factor. There's solid research showing that compounds called phytoestrogens increase bone mineral density. Foods rich in phytoestrogens include tofu and other soy products (except soy sauce) as well as beans.

Build bone with berries. Blueberries, blackberries, raspberries, and cherries get their deep color from compounds called anthocyanins and proanthocyanins. Both are remarkable in their ability to stabilize collagen structures, Dr. Pizzorno says. Since collagen is a major protein structure in bone, eating plenty of these berries may increase your chances of preventing osteoporosis.

Be smart about sugar. Studies involving laboratory animals have shown that a high-sugar diet weakens bone. And one small study involving humans found that a high-sugar diet increases the excretion of calcium in urine. So trim as much sugar as possible from your menu.

Steer clear of salt. For every 500 milligrams of salt you consume, you lose 10 milligrams of calcium, according to Stephanie Atkinson, Ph.D., professor of nutrition at McMaster University in Hamilton, Ontario. Many health experts recommend limiting salt intake to 2,400 milligrams a day.

Embrace vegetarianism. Compared with the general American population, vegetarians have a lower risk of osteoporosis, Dr. Pizzorno says. Vegetarians consume less protein and less phosphorus, a bone-robbing mineral. And their blood is less acidic, so their bodies don't have to tap their bones' calcium stores to keep the acid-base balance of their blood where it should be.

Supplements

Compare carbonate and citrate. There are several different kinds of calcium supplements. Some should be avoided because they may contain the toxic metal lead. These include any supplements made from bonemeal, dolomite, or oyster shells. The two best calcium supplements are calcium carbonate and calcium citrate.

Counting Calcium

Not fond of dairy? There are plenty of foods that offer generous supplies of calcium, as the following chart shows. Values are based on a 1-cup serving, except for sardines and cottage cheese, which are based on a ½-cup serving.

Food	Calcium per Serving (mg)
Sardines	375
Yogurt	350
Calcium-fortified fruit juice	300
Nonfat milk	300
Swiss cheese	270
Spinach	245
Cheddar cheese	205
Chickpeas	200
Baked beans	155
Tofu	150
Broccoli	136
Carrots	100
Cooked beans	100
Almonds	80
Cottage cheese	78

Dr. Siris recommends taking calcium supplements in divided doses throughout the day, but no more than 600 milligrams at a time.

Get the dope on D. Because you may have a hard time getting enough vitamin D from foods alone, especially if you're over age 60, Dr. Lieberman and most other experts recommend supplementing with 400 to 800 international units (IU) a day.

Add more magnesium. Even if you get a good deal of magnesium from

Men Get Osteoporosis, Too

Osteoporosis is more common in women, but it also affects men. In the United States alone, some 1.5 million elderly men have it, and 3.5 million more are at risk. About one-third of hip fractures occur in elderly men.

Half of American men show evidence of significant bone loss by age 75. This is one reason why the National Osteoporosis Foundation recommends bone-density testing for men as well as women who have multiple risk factors for the disease (like advanced age, cigarette smoking, or inadequate exercise).

Although there has not been much research on osteoporosis in men, the same prevention and treatment strategies appear to work in both sexes. One 3-year study by researchers at the Tufts University Calcium and Bone Metabolism Laboratory in Boston showed that daily supplements of calcium (500 milligrams) and vitamin D (700 international units) had the same effect on both elderly women and men. It cut their fracture rates in half.

your diet, "magnesium supplementation is as important as calcium supplementation," Dr. Pizzorno says. He recommends taking 500 milligrams of magnesium citrate a day.

Kick in some K. Dr. Lieberman also recommends taking 80 micrograms of vitamin K a day. But do this only with a doctor's recommendation.

Build your supply of boron. To be sure that you're getting enough boron, Dr. Pizzorno suggests taking 3 milligrams a day.

Exercise

Pick 'em up and lay 'em down. In one study, half of a group of 84 sedentary women over age 60 began taking daily 20- to 50-minute walks. The rest of the women remained inactive. After a year, the sedentary women showed significant bone loss, but the walkers did not.

Once osteoporosis develops, weight-bearing exercise can help slow the rate of bone loss, Dr. Simons says. "But extremely strenuous exercise—for example, training for marathons—is counterproductive," she adds. "In premenopausal women, it can lower your estrogen level to the point where you lose bone. And in postmenopausal women, it increases the risk of fractures."

Pump iron. Resistance training can also help increase bone mass, which is why the American College of Sports Medicine recommends it for prevention of osteoporosis. Even if you can't get out for a walk, a little resistance training, which is easy to do almost anywhere, can help preserve your bone mass.

Herbal Medicine

Get phytoestrogens from herbs. Several medicinal herbs contain phytoestrogens that can help prevent osteoporosis. Among them are Chinese angelica (dang gui), licorice, and black cohosh. Dr. Pizzorno suggests taking 1 teaspoon of each daily in tincture form.

Home Remedies

Quit smoking. Compared with women who don't smoke, those who do typically have 15 to 30 percent less bone mass.

Watch the alcohol. Alcohol has been associated with an increased risk of hip fracture, because drinking to the point of intoxication makes hip-fracturing falls more likely. But a little alcohol does not appear to increase risk of osteoporosis. Alcohol contains phytoestrogens that help prevent osteoporosis.

Can the colas. Two studies show a link between cola soft drinks and osteoporosis. Carbonated beverages other than colas showed only a slight association with fractures. Christiane Northrup, M.D., founder of the Women to Women health center in Yarmouth, Maine, and past president of the American Holistic Medical Association, urges women to avoid colas.

Be careful with caffeine. Caffeine increases calcium excretion. "But any increase in risk from consuming a few cups of coffee a day can be overcome by taking extra calcium," says Alan Gaby, M.D.

OTHER GOOD CHOICES

Homeopathy

Count on Calcarea phos. Homeopaths prescribe several medicines to prevent and treat osteoporosis. But according to homeopath Dana Ullman, the primary medicine is Calcarea phosphorica. He recommends taking it for 3 to 5 days every month, in consultation with a homeopath.

Chinese Medicine

Strengthen your Kidney. Practitioners of Chinese medicine attribute osteoporosis to a decline in Kidney qi, says Efrem Korngold, O.M.D., L.Ac. "Bones are ruled by the Kidney, and when the Kidney declines, the bones weaken. You treat osteoporosis by strengthening the Kidney."

Dr. Korngold prescribes herb formulas that contain drynaria root. The Chinese name for drynaria means "strengthen bone." One of Dr. Korngold's favorite formulas contains a combination of drynaria, Chinese angelica (dang gui), ginseng, astragalus, rehmannia root, poria fungus, and several other herbs.

Stimulate points to stop bone loss. Acupuncture treatment can help treat osteoporosis, Dr. Korngold says. If you're interested in trying acupuncture, you need to consult a professional acupuncturist. If you prefer a self-care approach, try acupressure instead. Apply steady, penetrating finger pressure for 3 minutes to each of the following points.

◆ Kidney 3, located in the hollow between your Achilles tendon and the inside of your anklebone

◆ Spleen 6, located four finger-widths above your inner anklebone on the back inner border of your shinbone

Ayurvedic Medicine

Open up to sesame. Sesame seeds are remarkably high in calcium. One cup contains 900 milligrams of the mineral. Vasant Lad, B.A.M.S., M.A.Sc., director of the Ayurvedic Institute in Albuquerque, New Mexico, suggests eating a handful of sesame seeds each day. The seeds make an excellent garnish for salads and fruit and vegetable dishes.

MEDICAL MEASURES

These days, you don't have to wait until you break a bone or shrink a few inches to find out that you have osteoporosis. Doctors have several noninvasive ways to diagnose the disease. Chief among these diagnostic techniques is dual-energy x-ray absorptiometry (DEXA), an x-ray exam of your spine or hip that allows

Prevent That Fall

Of course, you should do everything you can to prevent bone loss. But Ethel S. Siris, M.D., director of the Toni Stabile Center for the Prevention and Treatment of Osteoporosis at Columbia-Presbyterian Medical Center in New York City, also urges older women to work to prevent the falls that break weakened bones.

Watch where you're going. If your vision is poor, you might not see that step. Install good lighting, and make sure that you have stair rails where you need them.

Avoid slip and trip traps. Secure your rugs to the floor. Use a nonslip bath mat in your shower. Eliminate electrical cords that are tripping hazards.

Work out. You're never too old to start exercising. If you do, your strength, flexibility, balance, and coordination increase, all of which help prevent falls.

Study tai chi. At Emory University in Atlanta, researchers divided 200 men and women—average age 76—into three groups. One attended a class about preventing falls. Another received biofeedback-based balance training. The third attended a tai chi class. Compared with the other two groups, those who took tai chi went 48 percent longer before falling.

Beware of drugs. Sleeping pills, tranquilizers, many antihistamines, and a myriad of other medications cause light-headedness, dizziness, or drowsiness that can make you lose your balance. Ask your doctor or pharmacist about the side effects of your medications.

Pass up the booze. Of all the drugs that interfere with balance, alcohol is probably the major offender. Even moderate drinking can impair balance.

In winter, raise cane. If winter brings icy conditions where you live, consider a cane, walker, rubber-soled boots, or other balance aids.

Get your dizziness treated. Dizziness is a common complaint. If you experience it, don't ignore it. Discuss it with your doctor.

your doctor to calculate your bone mineral density. Other similar exams x-ray your forearm.

There are three drugs approved for prevention of osteoporosis: estrogen (Premarin), alendronate (Fosamax), and raloxifene (Evista). And three are approved to treat it: estrogen, alendronate, and calcitonin (Miacalcin).

If you take estrogen, be sure to keep consuming calcium. In an analysis of 31 studies, Columbia University researchers discovered that compared with women who took estrogen and consumed less than 600 milligrams of calcium a day from food and supplements, those who took the hormone and consumed about 1,200 milligrams of calcium showed almost triple the bone mass.

If you opt for drug treatment, make sure that you understand how to take your medication and all the possible side effects that your treatment may cause.

Overweight

This is it.

This time, you're really going to lose weight.

Sure, maybe you've tried to lose weight before. But almost inevitably, the pounds come back. Why?

The reasons, as you've probably realized, are complicated. And that's why weight loss is never a simple matter.

From a medical perspective, being overweight means that you carry more pounds than recommended for your height and build by experts at places like the Centers for Disease Control and Prevention (CDC). Being obese means that you're over your recommended weight by 20 percent or more, with body fat accounting for 30 percent of your weight if you're a woman, 25 percent if you're a man. (Women naturally carry more fat than men.)

But the experts still don't agree on what the recommended weight ought to be. And weight standards have varied among cultures

SIMPLE SOLUTIONS
1. Nutrition
2. Supplements
3. Exercise
4. Relaxation Therapies
5. Meditation
6. Visualization
7. Aromatherapy
8. Social Support
9. Home Remedies
10. Homeopathy
11. Chinese Medicine
12. Ayurvedic Medicine
13. Medical Measures

throughout history. Until the early twentieth century, Americans viewed being heavy—"portly" or "corpulent" in the lexicon of that bygone era—as a sign of good health. Then actuaries with the life insurance industry realized that compared with people of average weight, the fattest people died younger.

The CDC estimates that 35 percent of American adults, 12 percent of adolescents, and 14 percent of children are overweight.

How heavy do you have to be to experience weight-related health problems? Harvard researcher JoAnn Manson, M.D., investigated that issue using data from the ongoing Nurses' Health Study, which has tracked more than 100,000

Are You an Apple or a Pear?

To assess your risk of weight-related health problems, you need to consider your body-fat distribution. Some people, primarily men, carry their fat abdominally. They're said to have an apple shape. Others, primarily women, carry their fat in their hips and thighs. They're pears. Many studies have shown that being an apple is much worse for your health than being a pear, because your body reacts differently to fat depending on where you store it.

Dutch researchers measured the waist circumference and waist-to-hip ratios of 5,887 men and 7,018 women, ages 20 to 59. Compared with those who were pear-shaped, those who were apple-shaped had significantly more diabetes, lower-back pain, respiratory problems, high cholesterol, and high blood pressure.

You can't change your shape, of course, but a look in the mirror can tell you a lot about risk factors. If you see an apple shape in the mirror, it means weight loss is very important. By losing weight, you may be preventing a host of weight-related health problems.

women nurses for almost 20 years. Her conclusion: Risk begins to increase when you weigh 22 pounds more than you did at age 18.

Actually, most of us don't have to lose many pounds to reduce our risk of weight-related health problems. "Convincing studies have shown that the diseases most commonly associated with obesity—type 2 diabetes, high blood pressure, high cholesterol, and heart disease—can be significantly improved with a loss of just 10 percent of your weight," says Robert Kushner, M.D., medical director of the nutrition and weight-management program at Northwestern Memorial Hospital in Chicago.

The fundamentals of weight loss are simple: You have to burn more calories than you consume. To lose 1 pound a week, you have to burn 500 more calories a day than you consume.

Frankly, that's not easy. Eating 500 fewer calories leaves most people feeling deprived, and burning that many calories in exercise means engaging in strenuous aerobics for 45 minutes or walking briskly for over an hour.

A goal of reducing by 1 pound a week is simply beyond what most people are prepared to maintain for more than a month or two. That's why psychologist Ronnette Kolotkin, Ph.D., of the Diet and Fitness Center at Duke University in Durham, North Carolina, suggests a goal of 1 pound every 2 to 4 weeks, meaning that you lose 12 to 24 pounds in a year.

But even at that pace, weight loss can be difficult. Part of the problem relates to genetics and upbringing. A child with one obese parent has a 40 percent chance of becoming obese. A child with two obese parents has an 80 percent chance. But genetics and upbringing are not destiny.

Most of us Americans are overweight because of our poor eating and exercise habits. On the nutrition side, our rising weight reflects our increased intake of fat. As a nation, we've become so fat-conscious that food manufacturers now make low-fat and nonfat versions of just about everything. But at the same time, our consumption of high-fat fast foods has soared. In 1984, fewer than one-third of Americans ate pizza twice a month. Now half of us do.

"Americans have unprecedented access to a poor diet—to high-calorie foods that are widely available, low in cost, heavily promoted, and good-tasting," says weight-control expert Kelly Brownell, Ph.D., professor of psychology, epidemiology, and public health at Yale University. "We've created a toxic food environment."

As for exercise, the average American gets nowhere near enough. A few generations ago, people had more physical jobs, and they walked a lot more. Today, we drive, take elevators, and use dozens of labor-saving devices. What's more, most of us work in physically undemanding professions, spending most of our workdays sitting at a desk.

A big reason so many Americans are overweight is that many of us equate weight loss with dieting—that is, food restrictions. Dieting American-style is noteworthy for two things: fads and failure. Every few months, it seems, some new fad diet appears, and legions of people try it.

But studies of very low calorie diets by researchers at the University of Pennsylvania School of Medicine in Philadelphia show that after a few months and weight loss of around 30 pounds, the weight comes back with a vengeance. Within a year, most people regain two-thirds of their lost weight, and within 5 years, they're back to their pre-diet weight—or they're heavier.

But if you strip away the hype from fad diets, diet books, and the various commercial and medically supervised weight-loss programs that are generated

The Simple Secrets of Success

No doubt you've heard the grim statistics: Of those who enroll in commercial weight-loss programs, 70 percent don't complete them. Ditto for half of those who are in medically supervised weight-loss programs. And here's the real killer: Nine in 10 dieters who lose weight regain most or all of it within 5 years. It's enough to send you to the freezer case for a pint of Ben and Jerry's.

But take a closer look at that last statistic. If 90 percent of dieters regain their weight, that means that 10 percent actually succeed at permanent weight loss. Sure, the percentage is low, but with millions of Americans trying to lose weight, hundreds of thousands succeed.

Unfortunately, the media have harped on the 90 percent who regain their weight, fueling a myth that permanent weight loss is impossible. But a team of researchers, including nutritionist James Hill, Ph.D., of the University of Colorado Health Sciences Center in Denver, and psychiatrist Rena Wing, M.D., of the University of Pittsburgh Medical Center, decided to focus on the 10 percent who have succeeded to learn how they've done it.

Drs. Hill and Wing established the National Weight Control Reg-

by the diet industry, the experts generally agree that there are four interrelated keys to permanent weight loss.

- ◆ A low-fat, moderate-calorie diet
- ◆ Regular exercise
- ◆ Emotional readiness to commit to weight loss
- ◆ A lifelong commitment to weight control

This strategy has been embraced by the small but significant number of Americans who have successfully, permanently lost a great deal of weight. Very few of those who win at losing rely on fad diets, drugs, or commercially prepackaged diet meals. Instead, they change their lives, and slowly but surely, they shed unwanted pounds. You can do the same just by embracing the strategies that follow.

istry (NWCR), a database of people who have lost at least 30 pounds and kept it off for more than a year. The NWCR now boasts more than 2,000 success stories. Eighty percent of the people in the database are women, and the average age is 45. The average NWCR participant has lost 66 pounds (from 220 down to 154) and kept if off for 5 years.

How did those people succeed with weight loss? Here are the strategies they have in common.

Diet and exercise. Among weight-loss victors, 89 percent changed both how they ate and the amount they exercised.

A low-fat, low-calorie diet. The researchers estimate that the typical participant's diet contains 24 percent of calories from fat and around 1,500 calories a day.

Regular exercise—religiously. Almost all of NWCR participants (96 percent) exercise regularly, burning around 2,800 calories a week in physical activity, the approximate number consumed by walking briskly for around 45 minutes a day.

Realistic goals. Most NWCR enrollees set goals of no more than 10 percent of their body weight. After achieving that, they set new goals, another 5 to 10 percent of their new weight.

BEST CHOICES

Nutrition

Eat! "Perhaps the most important recommendation for people trying to lose weight is to eat more," notes Michael T. Murray, N.D., a naturopath in Seattle. "Starving yourself is a big mistake."

But you have to choose your foods wisely. Fat contains 9 calories per gram, while carbohydrates and protein contain only 4. You can eat twice as much carbohydrate and protein and still consume fewer calories than you would by eating fat.

For weight loss, your best bet is to build your meals and snacks around whole grains, beans, fruits, and vegetables. These foods are high in fiber and complex carbohydrates. Further, they derive no more than 15 to 20 percent of their calories from fat—so they fill you up, not out.

Be big on breakfast. "Eating a high-carbohydrate breakfast—a whole-grain cereal or toast—raises your BMR for several hours," says Anne Simons, M.D. BMR is your basal metabolic rate, the rate at which your body burns calories while resting. "Combine a healthy breakfast with exercise during the day, and your BMR stays high, you burn more calories, and you have an easier time controlling your weight," Dr. Simons explains. "But if you do what many overweight people do—skip breakfast, eat a light lunch, and then have a big dinner and snack until bedtime—your BMR stays low during the day, and you consume most of your calories shortly before it goes even lower during sleep. That's a setup for weight gain."

Know that low-fat doesn't mean low-calorie. The trouble with all of the low-fat and nonfat foods on the market these days is that many people think they can eat as much of these foods as they want. Unfortunately, that's not the case. In fact, low-fat and nonfat foods usually have almost as many calories as their higher-fat counterparts.

The bottom line is that calories still count, says Ron Goor, Ph.D., coauthor of the *Eater's Choice* low-fat cookbooks. If you gorge on low-fat cookies or even fat-free fare such as nonfat pretzels, bagels, or yogurt, you can consume an enormous number of calories and gain weight.

Watch your portion size. Every restaurant and fast-food outlet, it seems, has "super-sized" its menu. Portions are much larger today than they were 20 years ago, Dr. Goor says. From those large-size meals, you're destined to get more calories. When you eat out anywhere, stick to portions that are reasonable and satisfying rather than the giant offerings.

Don't fall for high-protein hype. Every few years, a fad diet comes along that advocates low-carb, high-protein eating. Steer clear of them. They alter your balance of brain chemicals, specifically lowering levels of the important brain chemical serotonin that influences mood and appetite. This can lead to tension, irritability, and depression—and trigger food cravings.

In one study, 40 obese women who had not lost weight on a variety of diets were placed on 1,400-calorie diets that were either low-protein/high-carbohydrate or high-protein/low-carbohydrate. Those following the low-protein/high-carb diet lost significantly more weight and kept it off more successfully.

Feast on fiber. Dietary fiber plays a key role in preventing and treating obesity, says Joseph Pizzorno Jr., N.D. It's bulky, so you feel full more quickly than you would with low-fiber foods. And when you eat lots of fiber, your intestines release hormones that tell your brain that you feel full. Also, since fiber has to be chewed thoroughly, you tend to eat more slowly when you're munching on high-fiber foods. The best dietary sources of fiber are whole grains, beans, fruits, and vegetables.

Snack on fruits and vegetables. Nutritionist Bonnie Liebman of the Center for Science in the Public Interest in Washington, D.C., advises making a habit of snacking on fruits and vegetables—apples, oranges, bananas, carrots, cherry tomatoes, and summer fruits. They fill you up but are low in fat and calories. They are also loaded with vitamins and minerals.

Think before you drink. Soft drinks, fruit drinks, alcoholic beverages, and cappuccino and other fancy coffee drinks can contain up to several hundred calories. Alcohol contains almost 200 calories per ounce. Instead, choose water, sparkling water, coffee, and teas, which are virtually calorie-free, Liebman advises.

Write it down. People who are overweight often underestimate how much they eat. The Diet and Fitness Center at Duke University is just one of many weight-loss programs that ask participants to keep a food diary. That way, you can see exactly what you've been eating and where you can make beneficial changes most easily.

Supplements

Take extra fiber. Like high-fiber foods, fiber supplements appear to enhance weight loss and simultaneously reduce feelings of hunger.

If you'd like a fiber supplement, try psyllium seed, suggests James A. Duke, Ph.D. Psyllium seed is the main ingredient in the bulk-forming laxative Metamucil. He suggests taking 1 teaspoon of psyllium seed, mixed with juice or water, before every meal.

Count on chromium. At least one study suggests that chromium supplements can aid weight loss, provided they're used in conjunction with regular exercise. In this study, researchers at the University of Texas at Austin divided 43 obese women into three groups. One group combined chromium supplementation (400 micrograms a day) with exercise. Another group took the same dosage of chromium but didn't exercise. The third group combined a placebo with exercise. The women who took only chromium gained weight. On the other hand, those who took the supplement and exercised lost significantly more weight than those who took the placebo and exercised.

If you want to try chromium, take 400 micrograms a day, as in the study. And follow the exercise guidelines below. Doses above this amount should only be taken under medical supervision.

Exercise

Get fit to burn fat. When you compare the pound-shedding benefits of diet to the benefits of exercise, the clear winner is exercise. That's what University of Chicago researchers found when they studied 23 obese women who agreed to follow one of three programs: a low-fat diet, a low-carbohydrate diet, or daily aerobic exercise with no diet restrictions. After 12 weeks, the exercisers lost significantly more weight and more fat than those in the other groups.

In addition to burning calories, exercise boosts your BMR, so you keep burning more calories even when you're not exercising. Exercise also spurs weight loss because it elevates mood, reduces stress, and improves self-esteem.

Finally, regular exercise helps keep you on the dietary straight and narrow. That's what University of Chicago researchers discovered in another study: 30 women were enrolled in a 12-week weight-loss program. All were placed on a restricted-calorie diet. In addition, some took a 45-minute aerobics class three times a week. The exercisers were significantly more likely to stay on the diet.

How much exercise do you need to lose weight and keep it off? The experts generally recommend a total of 30 to 60 minutes of physical activity every day.

Take a walk. Among its many benefits, walking helps control weight. "If you've been physically inactive, walking is one of the best ways to start exercising," Dr. Kolotkin says. "There's nothing to learn, no clothes to buy or gym to join, and it's fun, so you keep doing it."

"Walk as little as 1 mile a day (15 to 20 minutes of effort), and in a year, you lose about 10 pounds of fat," says Marcia Stefanick, Ph.D., a senior scientist at the Stanford University Center for Research in Disease Prevention.

Break it up. There's no need to set aside a half-hour to an hour for your workout. Studies show that exercising in chunks—say, 10 minutes here and there over the course of a day—can be just as effective.

Fidget away the weight. Married women often note that their husbands seem to gain less weight even if both spouses are eating the same foods and getting the same amounts of exercise. Why is it that women seem to gain weight so much more easily?

James Levine, M.D., an endocrinologist at the Mayo Clinic in Rochester, Minnesota, may have found the answer: A lot of men can't sit still. They're always shifting and squirming. Actions like climbing stairs, carrying objects, even fidgeting seem to help control weight gain.

Relaxation Therapies

End emotional eating. People who are slim eat when they feel hungry and stop when they're full. But if you're overweight, chances are that you also eat when you feel anxious, sad, afraid, bored, lonely, or upset. The experts call this emotional eating.

At the University of California, San Francisco, Medical Center, dietitian Laurel Mellin, R.D., teaches overweight individuals to identify their emotional triggers for overeating and to fulfill those needs in other ways. For example, if you feel lonely, you might call a friend. Or if you're stressed out from work, you might take a walk or make an appointment for a massage instead of running out for a hot fudge sundae.

Mellin developed her program while working with overweight kids. That program, called Shapedown, is currently used in some 400 hospital-based weight-control programs around the country. Participants ask themselves two questions whenever they feel the urge to eat: "What am I really feeling? What do I need right now?" With practice, the answers help them become more self-aware and help them stay out of the kitchen.

In a pilot study, Mellin found that a similar approach also works for overweight adults. Mellin's adult program is called the Solution. She taught it to 22 adults who lost an average of 17 pounds and kept it off for 2 years.

People in the program also began exercising more. Mellin found that adults who enrolled in the Solution program were likely to exercise 3 hours more each week than they did before joining the program.

Try hypnosis. In one study, psychologists placed 109 overweight individuals on a medically supervised weight-loss program. In addition, some of the participants received regular hypnotherapy. Nine weeks later, both groups had lost the same amount of weight. But at 8-month and 2-year intervals, those who received hypnotherapy had lost additional weight or maintained their weight better than those who didn't get the treatment. Similarly, an analysis of 18 studies found that compared with psychotherapy alone, a combination of psychotherapy and hypnotherapy produces greater, longer-lasting weight loss.

To find a professional hypnotherapist in your area, send a self-addressed, stamped envelope to either of the following organizations.

◆ The American Society of Clinical Hypnosis, 2200 East Devon Avenue, Suite 291, Des Plaines, IL 60018-4534

◆ The Society for Clinical and Experimental Hypnosis, 2201 Haeder Road, Pullman, WA 99163-8619

Meditation

Get to know your emotions. Meditation is a key part of Dr. Dean Ornish's weight-control, heart-disease-reversal program. "I consider it food for the soul," he says. Meditation is relaxing, and it increases self-awareness, so you're less likely to succumb to emotional eating when you're practicing meditation.

Visualization

See a slimmer you. A deeply relaxing visualization comes from Gerald N. Epstein, M.D., director of the Academy of Integrative Medicine and Mental Imagery in New York City. Close your eyes and breathe deeply. Picture yourself standing before a mirror, seeing a noticeably thinner you. Imagine entering the mirror and merging with that image, becoming that slimmer you. Feel your clothes hang more loosely on you. Now separate yourself from the image and step out of the mirror, but keep your eyes on it. Open your eyes.

Each time you sit down to eat, take a minute or two to practice this exercise, Dr. Epstein advises. It can help you eat more sensibly and reinforce your commitment to losing weight.

Aromatherapy

Smell success. At the Diet and Fitness Center at Duke University, psychologist Susan S. Schiffman, Ph.D., combats emotional, anxiety-driven eating with a relaxation program based on aromatherapy. She teaches relaxation techniques to participants, and at the same time, she asks them to inhale whiffs of apricot oil, so they associate the aroma with feeling calm.

During the program, people learn to carry along a vial of the apricot oil wherever they go. Whenever they feel anxious, they can inhale the fragrance, which triggers a relaxation response. In effect, they are substituting apricot's re-

Herbal Weight-Loss Aids

Step into your local health food store, and you're sure to find quite a few herbal weight-loss formulas. Herbal medicines can treat many conditions successfully, as shown throughout this book. But unfortunately, they are of little, if any, value if your goal is permanent weight loss.

Herbal diuretics. For women with premenstrual bloating, herbal diuretics can be useful a few days a month. But the popular diuretic herbs—dandelion, buchu, juniper, and uva-ursi—should not be used more often to lose weight. All you lose is water weight, not fat.

Herbal laxatives. It's never appropriate to use any kind of laxative in an attempt to lose weight. It never works and what's more, it's dangerous. Many herbal weight-loss products contain the potent chemical-stimulant laxatives senna or cascara sagrada. These herbs can be valuable when used occasionally to relieve constipation that's not responsive to gentler methods. But with laxative herbs, the only weight you lose is stored stool, not fat. Chemical-stimulant laxatives should be used only occasionally. Overuse can interfere with your ability to defecate and can cause electrolyte imbalances that lead to potentially serious heart rhythm disturbances.

laxing effect for their former stress-relieving activity, eating. Dr. Schiffman says that her aromatherapy technique has helped control compulsive eating in more than half of those who have adopted the technique.

Social Support

Draw courage from encouragement. Social support is a cornerstone of coping with challenges like weight loss and making significant life changes, which weight loss requires. In a study of three commercial weight-loss programs, British researchers discovered that the most important predictors of success were participation in group meetings and encouragement from the group leader. So it makes sense to join any kind of weight-loss group that offers support.

If you'd like to join a weight-loss support group, try Overeaters Anonymous. This organization is listed in the Yellow Pages of most telephone directories.

Home Remedies

Turn off your TV. Television watching is one of the strongest predictors of future weight problems, Dr. Pizzorno says. In other words, the more you watch the tube, the more likely you are to be overweight. It's possible to exercise while watching TV—but for most people, television time is couch time. In addition, the steady stream of food commercials fuels cravings. And the hypnotic quality of television keeps you from paying attention to how much you eat while watching.

Throw away your scale. "Scales can't distinguish among water loss, muscle loss, and fat loss," Dr. Goor says. "A more accurate way to measure your progress is to check how your clothes fit. When they get loose, you're losing fat—and pounds as well."

OTHER GOOD CHOICES

Homeopathy

Seek a homeopath's help. "Homeopathic medicines can help you lose weight by improving digestion, elimination, and metabolism," says homeopath Dana Ullman. "But the medicines need to be individually prescribed, based on your own unique pattern of symptoms. Be wary of homeopathic products marketed as weight-loss aids."

Chinese Medicine

Break up fat. If you overeat persistently and don't get enough exercise, you accumulate too much fat, which can damage your Liver and Spleen, says Efrem Korngold, O.M.D., L.Ac. To eliminate fat, he suggests drinking several kinds of tea, including black or green tea, chrysanthemum flower tea, and tuo (twa) cha tea. Black and green teas are sold in tea bag form in supermarkets. A Chinese medicine doctor can help you find the others.

Stimulate weight loss with acupressure. Simply apply steady, penetrating finger pressure to each of the following points for 3 minutes.

◆ Stomach 36, located four finger-widths below your kneecap and one finger-width toward the outside of your shinbone

◆ Large Intestine 11, located at the outer end of your elbow crease on the thumb side

Weighing In against Smoking

O ne of the allures of smoking is that it helps control weight. Smoking impairs your tastebuds, so food loses some of its taste appeal. In addition, nicotine is a stimulant that boosts your basal metabolic rate (BMR), the rate at which your body burns calories while resting.

Weight gain is an important factor that keeps many people from quitting smoking. When you quit, your BMR slows a bit, and food tastes much better. As a result, you may put on a few pounds.

In a long-term study, Katherine Flegal, Ph.D., of the National Center for Health Statistics in Hyattsville, Maryland, tracked 5,247 adults for 10 years. She found that men who quit smoking gained an average of 9 pounds, while women gained about 12.

"But that's no reason not to quit," says Anne Simons, M.D. "For most people, the risks of smoking are much greater than the risks of the weight gain associated with quitting."

To keep off the pounds when you quit smoking, redouble your efforts to eat low-fat, low-calorie foods and exercise regularly. Don't be discouraged if you gain a few pounds. As your body recovers from smoking, you may notice that exercise feels increasingly fulfilling. This encourages you to work out more, which in turn helps you control your weight.

◆ Liver 3, situated on top of your foot in the webbing between your big toe and second toe

Ayurvedic Medicine

Take an Ayurvedic approach. Classic Ayurvedic medicine valued heaviness (a trait of the Kapha dosha or constitutional type) over thinness (an attribute of the Vata dosha). Heaviness implied affluence and plenty to eat, explains David Frawley, O.M.D.

But despite this cultural bias in favor of a certain girth, Ayurvedic physicians recognize that too many extra pounds can become a problem. Specifically, being overweight can lead to a buildup of toxins that contribute to heart disease, high blood pressure, diabetes, and arthritis.

To stimulate weight loss, Ayurvedic physicians generally prescribe a light diet, fasting, spicy herbs to stimulate digestion, mild laxatives, and tonic herbs such as guggul. Dr. Frawley suggests taking a teaspoon of guggul two or three times a day, mixed with ginger and honey. You may be able to buy guggul in a health food store. If not, consult an Ayurvedic practitioner.

MEDICAL MEASURES

The vast majority of mainstream physicians urge weight loss by the methods described above—a lifelong commitment to low-fat, low-calorie eating and regular exercise. Remarkably, as little as 5 minutes of counseling from a doctor often inspires people to make these weight-reducing life changes.

Weight-loss specialists offer two other treatments—drugs and surgery—that often produce disappointing results. The history of diet drugs, in particular, is a cautionary tale about quick-and-easy solutions.

In the 1930s, doctors discovered that amphetamines suppress appetite and boost BMR. Amphetamines became the first diet drugs. They worked, but the weight loss they produced was modest and almost always temporary. Meanwhile, amphetamines caused potentially serious side effects including severe insomnia, extreme irritability, and addiction.

In the mid-1990s, doctors began combining two diet drugs—fenfluramine and phentermine—into a treatment that became known as fen-phen. Eventually, more than 18 million Americans used it. Then in 1997, the drug combination was linked to potentially fatal complications, and the maker of the "fen" drug withdrew it at the request of the Food and Drug Administration.

Despite the fen-phen scandal, many doctors maintain that the other, safer weight-loss drugs can help. But they must be used as part of a comprehensive, long-term, physician-supervised program that includes a low-fat diet, regular exercise, and emotional support.

For people who are seriously obese, doctors sometimes recommend surgical procedures to shrink or bypass the stomach. The bypass is the more popular operation, and it's more effective at reducing weight and high blood pressure and controlling diabetes. But many complications are possible, including persistent nausea and nutrient deficiencies. And some people who have a stomach bypass operation eventually regain the weight they have lost.

Premenstrual Syndrome

About 7 percent of American women have such severe premenstrual syndrome (PMS) that it disrupts their lives.

Contrary to popular perception, PMS and menstrual cramps are not one and the same. "Many women with PMS have completely cramp-free periods," notes Christiane Northrup, M.D., founder of Women to Women health center in Yarmouth, Maine, and past president of the American Holistic Medical Association. "And many women with severe cramps have no PMS."

PMS usually flares up a week to 10 days before menstruation. According to researchers at the National Institute of Mental Health, the condition primarily involves mood changes—namely irritability, anxiety, depression, and absentmindedness. Sometimes these symptoms are accompanied by breast tenderness, food cravings, bloating, and weight gain.

Researchers have noticed that women who experience PMS symptoms are unusually sensitive to hormonal fluctuations that occur throughout the menstrual cycle. For example, levels of the hormone estrogen drop prior to menstruation, a change that triggers a decline in levels of a brain chemical called serotonin. Low levels of serotonin have been associated with depression as well as food cravings and insomnia.

In addition, women with severe PMS tend to have unusually low levels of endorphins just before menstruation. Similar to serotonin, endorphins are brain chemicals that help elevate mood.

SIMPLE SOLUTIONS
1. Nutrition
2. Supplements
3. Exercise
4. Meditation
5. Visualization
6. Herbal Medicine
7. Home Remedies
8. Over-the-Counter Drugs
9. Aromatherapy
10. Homeopathy
11. Chinese Medicine
12. Ayurvedic Medicine
13. Medical Measures

Other factors—including diet, exercise, and stress—may influence the severity of PMS symptoms. But the significance of these factors appears to vary from one woman to the next.

Many women have used some combination of nutritional strategies, stress reduction techniques, and other alternative and mainstream therapies to successfully control their PMS. You, too, can create a customized PMS management program using a selection of the remedies presented below. But first, you really need to get a clear understanding of exactly how PMS affects you, says Anne Simons, M.D. "Chart your symptoms daily for three or four cycles," she suggests. "Then you're in a better position to decide how to deal with them."

BEST CHOICES

Nutrition

Cultivate carbs in your cooking. If you have PMS, chances are that you run low on serotonin before your period. Eating carbohydrates can help raise your level of serotonin, Dr. Northrup says. Build your meals around high-carbohydrate foods such as whole grains, legumes, fruits, and vegetables, she advises.

Say "ahoy" to soy. Be sure that your diet includes plenty of soy and soy products such as tofu, tempeh, and soy milk. Soy helps stabilize your estrogen levels by supplying an abundance of plant estrogens, or phytoestrogens. And that, in turn, helps relieve PMS symptoms, according to Susan M. Lark, M.D., director of the PMS and Menopause Self-Help Center in Los Altos, California.

Get enough good fats. Nuts, seeds, and sesame and walnut oils are rich in essential fatty acids. These "good fats" help minimize PMS symptoms as well as menstrual cramps, Dr. Northrup explains.

Skip sugar and salt. Compared with women who don't have PMS, women who do have it tend to consume a lot more sugar and salt. Both sugar and salt contribute to premenstrual water retention, says Melvyn R. Werbach, M.D., assistant clinical professor at the University of California, Los Angeles, School of Medicine. Water retention causes bloating and weight gain, two common premenstrual symptoms.

Snack, don't dine. You can control premenstrual food cravings by changing the way you eat, advises Jean Endicott, Ph.D., director of the Premenstrual Evaluation Unit at Columbia-Presbyterian Medical Center in New York City. Instead of eating the standard three squares a day, divide them into five or six snack-size mini-meals. And never skip meals.

Supplements

Bank on B$_6$. Among vitamin and mineral supplements, vitamin B$_6$ is the most widely recommended for premenstrual symptoms. The proper dosage of vitamin B$_6$ remains somewhat controversial. Pamela D. Parker, M.D., a family practitioner in Moses Lake, Washington, suggests starting with a dose of about 50 milligrams a day. Then if you don't notice any improvement in your symptoms, slowly increase your dose over a few cycles. If you begin feeling numbness or tingling, cut back.

Experiment with E. According to Dr. Lark, vitamin E helped cure her PMS. Her personal experience is supported by several studies demonstrating that the vitamin helps minimize premenstrual mood changes.

"Many of my women patients have shown marked improvement in their symptoms after as little as 2 months of vitamin E supplementation," says clinical nutritionist Shari Lieberman, Ph.D. Take 200 to 400 international units (IU) a day.

Make the most of magnesium. Women with PMS often have abnormally low levels of the mineral magnesium in their red blood cells, says Joseph Pizzorno Jr., N.D. He suggests taking 400 to 800 milligrams of magnesium a day.

Try evening primrose oil. The oil in primrose seeds contains gamma-linolenic acid, a substance that makes women with PMS less sensitive to premenstrual hormonal fluctuations. In some studies, gamma-linolenic acid reduced mood swings, fluid retention, and breast tenderness by as much as 65 percent. Evening primrose oil is available in supplement form, under the brand name Efamol. Follow the package directions.

Add enough oil. Both fish oil and flaxseed oil contain essential fatty acids, the good fats that combat PMS symptoms. Whichever supplement you choose, take 500 milligrams four times a day, preferably with food.

Exercise

Be active at every opportunity. "When I was a teenager, no one told me about exercise as a treatment for PMS," Dr. Lark says. "I didn't discover its value until I was a medical intern. Then I began to swim and bicycle more as my period drew near."

If you can't set aside time for a daily workout, try to incorporate more physical activity in your day-to-day routine.

Meditation

Tap your mind's healing power. "Before you take medication, try meditation," says Martin L. Rossman, M.D. "In my experience, meditation helps relieve the mood swings associated with PMS."

Visualization

See yourself feeling fabulous. Like meditation, visualization can help defuse premenstrual symptoms, according to Gerald N. Epstein, M.D., director of the Academy of Integrative Medicine and Mental Imagery in New York City. He recommends the following exercise: Close your eyes and take three slow, deep breaths. Envision yourself in a desert. Lie down and cover yourself with sand. Feel the hot sun baking the sand into your skin. Feel your irritability and excess fluid getting soaked up by the sand, then evaporated by the sun. Open your eyes.

Herbal Medicine

Chase symptoms with chasteberry. In Europe, where herbal medicine is widely practiced and accepted, chasteberry is a popular PMS treatment. And research has proven that the herb works.

If you'd like to try chasteberry for yourself, Christopher Hobbs, L.Ac., an herbalist in Santa Cruz, California, and the author of several authoritative herb guides, recommends taking 40 drops of the herb in tincture form every day, mixed in juice or water. The tincture is sold in health food stores as either chasteberry or Vitex. Once you start using the herb, be patient: You may need to wait a few months before you see results.

Consider black cohosh. Scientific evidence of this herb's hormone-regulating effects has persuaded Commission E, the German panel that evaluates herbal medicines, to endorse black cohosh as a PMS remedy.

Hobbs recommends taking two or three dropperful of black cohosh tincture two or three times a day. (Tincture bottles come with droppers built into their lids.) The herb should not be used for more than 6 months, according to Commission E. While black cohosh's long-term safety has yet to be studied, any herb that has hormonal effects should be used conservatively. If you stop taking black cohosh after 6 months and your symptoms return, consult your doctor before resuming treatment.

Home Remedies

Kick the caffeine habit. The caffeine in coffee, tea, and caffeinated soft drinks often contributes to PMS-related irritability and anxiety. "Even if you drink only one cup of coffee or one can of cola a day, getting off caffeine can have a dramatic effect," Dr. Northrup says. But reduce your caffeine intake slowly. If you try to quit all at once, you're likely to get a caffeine withdrawal headache, which can be worse than the PMS symptoms that you're trying to control.

Avoid alcohol. While you have PMS-induced moodiness, steering clear of mood-altering substances is a good idea, Dr. Parker advises. That includes alcoholic beverages.

Increase your snooze time. Even a minor sleep deficit can aggravate premenstrual irritability, says Dr. Parker. So get as much extra rest as possible.

Be regular with your Zzzs. Be sure to go to bed and get up at the same time every day, even on weekends, Dr. Parker advises. By establishing a regular sleep pattern, you're more likely to sleep better.

Light up your life. Many symptoms common to PMS—including irritability, depression, food cravings, and weight gain—are also associated with a condition called seasonal affective disorder, or SAD.

Both PMS and SAD are characterized by a low level of the brain chemical serotonin. What's more, many women with PMS respond well to light therapy, the standard treatment for people with SAD.

If you're interested in purchasing your own light-therapy unit, ask your doctor to recommend one and to provide instructions on how to use the device safely. For a less expensive alternative, simply spend as much time as you can outdoors during daylight hours, especially in fall and winter.

Plan accordingly. You can't avoid every stressful situation. But when you have the option, Dr. Endicott says, don't schedule stress-provoking tasks and events for those days when you expect your premenstrual symptoms to be in full swing. Stress only aggravates PMS.

Be open. Because PMS has become something of a social punch line, many people don't realize just how distressing and debilitating the condition can be. Discuss your premenstrual symptoms with those closest to you—family members, friends, even trusted coworkers. They'll become more supportive once they understand what the symptoms are and how they affect you.

Over-the-Counter Drugs

Enter the progesterone zone. Although best known as a sex hormone, progesterone also relaxes the nervous system and promotes tranquillity. According to Dr. Northrup, progesterone creams often produce profound improvement in PMS symptoms.

Dr. Northrup recommends using a 2 percent natural progesterone cream, which you can buy in a health food store. Apply ¼ teaspoon to an area of soft skin such as your neck, inner arm, or abdomen once each morning and again each evening during the second half of your menstrual cycle. Change sites with each application to avoid skin irritation.

OTHER GOOD CHOICES

Aromatherapy

For relief, just inhale. The essential oils lavender, geranium, and rose can alleviate the mood changes associated with PMS, according to Kathy Keville and Mindy Green, coauthors of *Aromatherapy: A Complete Guide to the Healing Art.* They suggest putting a few chips of rock salt in a small vial, then adding 2 or 3 drops of each of the three oils. (The rock salt prevents the oil from splashing out when you open the vial.) For an immediate emotional lift, just uncap the vial and inhale deeply.

Homeopathy

Try a symptom-specific remedy. A number of homeopathic medicines have proved effective as treatments for premenstrual symptoms, according to homeopath Dana Ullman. These medicines include Ignatia, Lachesis, Lycopodium, Nux vomica, Pulsatilla, and Sepia. To find out which one would work best for you, consult a homeopath.

Chinese Medicine

Mellow with an herbal formula. Efrem Korngold, O.M.D., L.Ac., prescribes several different herbal formulas to patients with PMS. One such formula is Xiao Yao Wan, made with Chinese angelica (dang gui), ginger, licorice root, mint leaf, peony root, bupleurum root, and other herbs. There's also Bai Feng

Wan, a blend of several herbs, including Chinese angelica, ginseng, and peony root, in honey.

Pinpoint the problem spots. Dr. Korngold and other practitioners of Chinese medicine also use acupuncture to treat PMS. If you prefer a do-it-yourself approach, try acupressure treatments. Simply apply steady, penetrating finger pressure to each of the following points for 3 minutes.

◆ Spleen 6, located four finger-widths above your inner anklebone on the back inner border of your shinbone

◆ Liver 3, situated on top of your foot in the webbing between your big toe and second toe

◆ Heart 7, located on the pinkie side of the wrist crease that's closest to your palm

Ayurvedic Medicine

Blame your dosha. Ayurvedic practitioners believe that PMS arises from some problem with apana vata, the force that directs life energy into a woman's reproductive organs, explains John Douillard, D.C., a chiropractor who practices Ayurvedic medicine at the Invincible Life Spa in Boulder, Colorado. PMS symptoms vary from woman to woman, depending on constitutional type, or dosha.

If you have a Vata dosha, Dr. Douillard says, you're most likely to experience mood changes and constipation. A Pitta dosha, on the other hand, is associated with irritability, hunger, headache, diarrhea, and acne. And a Kapha dosha elicits primarily physical symptoms—bloating, weight gain, breast tenderness, and acne. For a treatment program tailored to your dosha, consult an Ayurvedic practitioner.

MEDICAL MEASURES

If none of the above remedies provides sufficient relief from your premenstrual symptoms, your doctor may recommend drug therapy. Among the drugs most often prescribed for PMS are the antidepressants known as selective serotonin reuptake inhibitors, including fluoxetine (Prozac), paroxetine (Paxil), and sertraline (Zoloft). While research has shown that these pharmaceuticals are effective, they also have side effects.

Other pharmaceuticals also control premenstrual symptoms, but in different ways. For example, anti-anxiety drugs such as alprazolam (Xanax) help alleviate moodiness. And oral contraceptives alter the way your sex hormones cycle, so hormonal fluctuations are less intense.

RED FLAGS

If your premenstrual symptoms are severe, get a complete physical exam, Dr. Endicott advises. You want to make sure that you don't have another condition that could be misdiagnosed as PMS, such as endometriosis, lupus, or a thyroid disorder.

Also, keep in mind that PMS can be aggravated by allergies, asthma, irritable bowel syndrome, and migraines. If you have any of these conditions, controlling them with appropriate therapeutic measures can help minimize your premenstrual symptoms.

Prostate Enlargement

You used to sleep like a rock every night. Now your slumber is routinely interrupted by trips to the bathroom. You even stopped drinking liquids after dinner so that your bladder would be empty by the time you went to bed. But still you have to get up and go—sometimes two or three times a night.

Frequent nighttime urination is a trademark symptom of an enlarged prostate, says Phillippa Kennealy, M.D., a family practitioner at the University of California, Los Angeles, Medical Center in Santa Monica. "Anyone can feel the urge to urinate at night," she explains. "But many men have no idea that frequent wake-ups mean prostate enlargement."

The prostate is a walnut-size, doughnut-shaped gland that sits directly below a man's bladder. It's responsible for producing most of the fluid in semen. It wraps around a tube called the urethra, which carries urine and semen out of a man's body.

SIMPLE SOLUTIONS
1. Nutrition
2. Supplements
3. Herbal Medicine
4. Home Remedies
5. Homeopathy
6. Chinese Medicine
7. Naturopathy
8. Medical Measures

Unless it gets infected, your prostate maintains such a low profile that you probably don't pay much attention to it. But once you reach age 30, the gland starts growing.

Sometimes this growth signals prostate cancer, a leading cause of cancer deaths among men, according to James Smolev, M.D., assistant professor in the department of urology at Johns Hopkins University School of Medicine in Baltimore. That's why all men over age 45 should have annual prostate exams. But most midlife prostate growth is noncancerous. Doctors call it benign prostatic hypertrophy (BPH)—*benign*, meaning noncancerous, and *hypertrophy*, meaning enlargement.

As BPH progresses, your swelling prostate gland pinches your urethra. At the same time, muscle tissue around your urethra tightens, pinching it even more. This process is painless, but it causes urinary problems: difficulty getting

Do You Have BPH?

Only your doctor can tell you for certain whether or not you have benign prostatic hypertrophy, or BPH. But this simple self-test, created by the American Urological Association, can help you assess your symptoms. Read each question and score it as noted. Then add up your responses and compare the total to the key that follows.

During the Day

Score each question on a scale of 0 to 5.

0 - Not at all
1 - Less than 20 percent of the time
2 - Less than half the time

3 - About half the time
4 - More than half the time
5 - Almost always

During the past month or so, have you:

1. Had a sensation of not emptying your bladder completely after you finished urinating?

2. Had to urinate again less than 2 hours after your last urination?

3. Stopped and started urinating several times during a single voiding?

started, decreased flow, difficulty finishing. You feel the urge to urinate more often, and—most annoying of all—you have to get up at night to go.

Researchers believe that the prostate balloons because of age-related hormonal changes that occur after age 40. Half of all men experience BPH symptoms in their fifties, and the percentage rises with age. BPH usually gets worse over time, but its course is unpredictable, says Richard J. Macchia, M.D., professor and chairperson of the department of urology at the State University of New York Health Science Center at Brooklyn. In some men, symptoms go from mild to severe in a half-dozen years. In others, the process takes 15 years.

If you've been diagnosed with BPH, when should you seek medical treatment? "That's an individual decision," Dr. Smolev says. "When you feel persistently uncomfortable during the day, or when you get tired of waking up at night, then you may want to discuss treatment options with your doctor."

4. Found it difficult to postpone urination?

5. Had a weak urinary stream?

6. Had to push or strain to begin urinating?

At Night

Score the following question on a scale of 0 to 5.

0 - None   **3** - Three times

1 - Once   **4** - Four times

2 - Twice   **5** - Five times or more

7. During the past month or so, how many times have you gotten out of bed at night to urinate? (Do not count your first urination after getting up in the morning.)

SCORING

Add your responses.

0 to 7: You have mild BPH.

8 to 18: Your BPH is moderate.

19 to 35: You have a severe case of BPH.

In the meantime, you may be able to manage your symptoms without drugs or surgery. "BPH often responds to nutritional and herbal approaches," says Joseph Pizzorno Jr., N.D.

──────── **BEST CHOICES** ────────

Nutrition

Squelch symptoms with soy. Compared with American men, Japanese men have far fewer problems with BPH, according to Stephen Holt, M.D., professor of medicine at Seton Hall University in South Orange, New Jersey. Researchers attribute this lower rate of BPH to the Japanese diet, which

Prostatitis: Sometimes an Infection, Sometimes Not

The word *prostatitis* simply means inflammation of the prostate. There are two kinds of prostatitis: acute and chronic.

Acute Prostatitis

Acute prostatitis is an infection that leads to trouble urinating, penile discharge, lower-back pain, and flulike symptoms. The bacteria that cause acute prostatitis are the same ones that cause urinary tract infections—primarily *Escherichia coli*.

An estimated one-third of men experience acute prostatitis at some point in life. Oddly, many of these men show no evidence of bacterial infection. "No one knows why, but with acute prostatitis, we quite often don't find the bug," says James Smolev, M.D., assistant professor in the department of urology at Johns Hopkins University School of Medicine in Baltimore.

Even without evidence of bacteria, mainstream M.D.'s usually treat acute prostatitis with antibiotics, based on a man's symptoms. "If the antibiotic produces substantial relief in a day or so, you know you have acute prostatitis," Dr. Smolev says.

Several medicinal herbs, notably garlic and goldenseal, have antibacterial action that can boost the effectiveness of antibiotics. James A. Duke, Ph.D., suggests using liberal amounts of garlic in cooking and taking 1 to 2 teaspoons of goldenseal tincture, mixed into juice, a few times a day while your symptoms persist.

features an abundance of tofu and other soy foods. Soy is rich in plant estrogens, or phytoestrogens. These compounds can help control BPH.

Supplements

Zap prostate growth with zinc. Dr. Pizzorno describes zinc as "paramount to effective BPH prevention and treatment." He suggests taking 60 milligrams of zinc picolinate every day for up to 6 months. Since this is a high dose,

Chronic Prostatitis

In chronic prostatitis, the main symptom is pain—pain when you urinate and ejaculate, along with lower-back pain and pain between your legs. Your semen may appear pinkish because of blood.

"Chronic prostatitis is much more common than the acute condition," Dr. Smolev says. "You don't get as sick, and the prostate doesn't feel as tender. But the treatment takes much longer—sometimes months."

In some 80 percent of chronic prostatitis cases, there is no bacterial infection. Many urologists refer to nonbacterial chronic prostatitis as prostatodynia—literally, prostate pain. According to Tucson, Arizona, naturopath Francis Brinker, N.D., most prostatodynia results from stress. When you're under stress, you unconsciously tense your pelvic muscles. This prevents you from completely emptying your bladder. As a result, some urine backfires into the prostate gland, causing chemical irritation.

Most urologists treat prostatodynia with muscle relaxants. These drugs help relieve chronic muscle tension, normalize urine flow, and diminish the back pressure that causes prostate irritation.

Dr. Smolev says that drugs are usually not necessary, however. "It is often enough to explain that muscle tension causes the problem and that the man should consciously relax his pelvic-floor muscles every time he urinates," he explains.

Because prostatodynia is a stress-related condition, it often responds to relaxation therapies. Try tolerably hot baths, meditation, visualization, biofeedback, and other relaxation therapies.

you should be under a doctor's supervision while taking it. Your nutrient status should be reviewed and tested by a doctor at the end of 6 months and before you resume any dosages.

Pamper your prostate with primrose. Evening primrose oil is rich in essential fatty acids. Dr. Pizzorno says that supplementation with essential fatty acids has given many men significant relief from BPH symptoms. He recommends taking 1 teaspoon of evening primrose oil a day. If you

Bashful Bladder: Too Shy to Go

Women often envy the convenience of urinals. But few women are aware of the emotional discomfort many men feel about the loss of privacy that urinals impose. For some men, the distress of using a crowded bank of urinals produces a bashful bladder, an inability to relax enough to allow the urine to flow. A man stands there with a full bladder, and nothing happens.

Martin L. Rossman, M.D., suggests a simple relaxation therapy: Close your eyes, breathe deeply, and count backward from 100 (or any large number) by sevens. "Urination happens best when we don't think about it," he explains. "Serial subtraction distracts from the discomfort of semi-public urination and allows your urethral muscles to relax enough to let the urine flow."

can't find evening primrose oil, feel free to substitute sunflower, linseed, or walnut oil.

Herbal Medicine

Try a Native American herbal remedy. "I'm betting my own prostate gland that herbs work better than drugs or surgery in treating BPH," says James A. Duke, Ph.D. High on Dr. Duke's list of effective herbal remedies is saw palmetto, a dwarf palm tree native to the southeastern United States.

At least a dozen studies have shown that saw palmetto can help shrink an enlarged prostate and relieve BPH symptoms. But because saw palmetto's effects are so powerful, you should use it only under a qualified practitioner's guidance.

Get aid from Africa. South African herbalists have long recommended the root of African star grass for prostate enlargement. But consult a qualified practitioner before you begin taking this herb. The recommended dosage is 160 milligrams taken twice a day for 3 to 6 months, at which time your caregiver can assess your progress.

Get more aid from Africa. In Africa's central and southern highlands grows an evergreen called pygeum, or African prune. For centuries, Africans have used a tea made from powdered pygeum bark to treat urinary problems. Dr. Duke recommends taking 50 milligrams of pygeum bark extract twice a day.

Treat your prostate with pollen. In 1959, a Swedish urologist found that rye flower pollen extract helps treat BPH. He developed a product called Cernilton, which became popular in Scandinavia. Cernilton found its way to England, where it was rechristened ProstaBrit. Scientists aren't sure how the remedy works, but several studies show benefit after at least 6 months of treatment.

In the United States, you can buy Cernilton in some health food stores. Follow the instructions on the package for proper dosage. But don't use this product if you have pollen allergies.

Nip nature's call with nettle. Nettle root is an age-old European remedy for urinary problems. Modern research has shown that the herb contains a number of compounds, including phytosterols, that appear to provide some relief from BPH symptoms. According to naturopath Donald Brown, N.D., professor of herbal medicine at Bastyr University in Kenmore, Washington, nettle root works best in combination with saw palmetto. You can buy over-the-counter capsules containing a combination of the two herbs in doses effective enough to treat BPH. But check with your doctor before taking a combination formula, since saw palmetto should be taken only with medical supervision.

Pick a pumpkin prescription. In Turkey, Bulgaria, and the Ukraine, the traditional treatment for BPH is a handful of pumpkin seeds a day. "In my experience, pumpkin seeds don't do much by themselves," says Alan P. Brauer, M.D. "But in combination with saw palmetto and pygeum, they help." You can eat the seeds by the handful.

Home Remedies

Practice patience. As BPH develops, it takes longer to start urinating and even longer to finish, notes Herbert Lepor, M.D., professor of pharmacology at New York University School of Medicine in New York City. His advice: Don't rush. Relax at the beginning, which helps start your stream flowing. And take time at the end, which helps you push out the last few squirts.

Ban beverages before bedtime. To minimize nighttime urination, don't drink fluids after 7:00 P.M., Dr. Lepor suggests.

Cut out caffeine. Caffeine is a urinary irritant. Many men get some relief from their BPH symptoms when they limit their intakes of coffee, tea, colas, and chocolate, Dr. Lepor says.

OTHER GOOD CHOICES

Homeopathy

Defeat BPH with Chimaphilla. In rare cases, BPH results from the formation of an adenoma, a noncancerous mass of tissue, in the prostate gland. In one study, Russian homeopaths used homeopathic medicines to treat 37 men with adenomas. Of the 27 who had experienced weak urine streams and frequent nighttime urination, 23 reported improvement within 6 months.

Homeopath Dana Ullman says that the primary homeopathic treatment for BPH is Chimaphilla. But depending on a man's symptoms, homeopaths may also prescribe Clematis or Selenium. To find out which remedy is appropriate for you, consult a homeopath.

Chinese Medicine

Be kind to your Kidney. Practitioners of Chinese medicine attribute BPH to an excess of damp Heat brought on by too much sex, alcohol, or spicy foods that impair urine flow. "The inflammation causes enlargement, which the Chinese consider Heat," says Efrem Korngold, O.M.D., L.Ac. "The dampness comes from the fact that the prostate both holds fluid and secretes it."

The Kidney organ network is also involved in BPH. In the Chinese view, the Kidney regulates the discharge of reproductive essence and is weakened by the factors that cause BPH, especially sexual excess.

To treat BPH, Dr. Korngold prescribes formulas containing diuretic, anti-inflammatory herbs that strengthen the Kidney. These herbs include dandelion root, astragalus root, and dioscorea root.

Pin hope on acupuncture. Dr. Korngold also prescribes acupuncture to help treat BPH. If you're interested in trying acupuncture, you need to consult a trained acupuncturist. Among the points that an acupuncturist may stimulate is Spleen 6, located four finger-widths above your inner anklebone on the back inner border of your shinbone. You can try stimulating this point yourself, with acupressure. Simply apply steady, penetrating finger pressure to the point for 3 minutes.

Naturopathy

Consider the sitz solution. Naturopaths sometimes recommend hot sitz baths, or shallow baths, to relieve BPH symptoms. "A sitz bath can relax and open the urinary passageway," Dr. Pizzorno explains. He recommends a 3- to 15-minute bath in tolerably hot water.

MEDICAL MEASURES

Until recently, the only mainstream treatment for BPH was a surgical procedure called transurethral resection of the prostate, or TURP. Under general anesthesia, the surgeon threads a flexible tube through the urethra and snips away enough overgrown prostate tissue to relieve urethral pinching. TURP usually provides long-term relief of BPH symptoms, but the operation carries a small risk of infection, incontinence, and erection impairment.

These days, many men are able to avoid or at least postpone TURP, thanks to the prescription drugs terazosin (Hytrin) and finasteride (Proscar). Terazosin relaxes the muscles around the urethra, widening it. Finasteride reverses the overgrowth of prostate tissue.

"Terazosin generally works best for men in their fifties whose prostates have not grown that large," explains William A. Norcross, M.D., professor of clinical family medicine at the University of California, San Diego, School of Medicine. "Finasteride works best for men over age 60, whose prostates are larger."

Several surgical procedures that are less invasive than TURP have begun gaining acceptance. One is transurethral needle ablation, or TUNA. Like TURP, TUNA involves inserting a flexible tube into the urethra. But instead of cutting away excess tissue, TUNA zaps it with radio waves. This eliminates prostate overgrowth without affecting nearby nerves or muscles, meaning fewer side effects.

Keep in mind, too, that certain medications can aggravate BPH symptoms. These include prescription drugs for ulcers, irritable bowel syndrome, high blood pressure, and depression as well as over-the-counter cold formulas. If you have BPH and you're taking one of these medications, ask your doctor whether it may aggravate your symptoms.

Psoriasis

No one knows exactly what psoriasis is. It isn't an infection or an allergic reaction, nor is it contagious. But somehow it disrupts the growth-replacement cycle of skin cells.

Cells develop in the inner layers of skin and migrate to the outer layer, where they flake off. Normally, this entire process lasts about a month. But in psoriasis, it lasts only a few days. The cells can't shed fast enough, so they start to build up on the surface of the skin. Eventually, they form gray, white, or silvery lesions—creating the scaly-looking skin characteristic of psoriasis. The affected skin thickens, and it may turn red and develop cracks.

SIMPLE SOLUTIONS
1. Nutrition
2. Supplements
3. Meditation
4. Social Support
5. Herbal Medicine
6. Home Remedies
7. Over-the-Counter Drugs
8. Homeopathy
9. Chinese Medicine
10. Ayurvedic Medicine
11. Medical Measures

Psoriasis can erupt just about anywhere on the body, but it most often occurs on the scalp, chest, back, elbows, knuckles, and knees. If you have a mild case, the patches may hardly be noticeable. The worst cases produce unsightly patches almost everywhere.

Psoriasis can also affect fingernails and toenails, making them appear pitted and discolored. It can even cause significant joint pain, a condition known as psoratic arthritis.

Most people who develop psoriasis are initially diagnosed in their teens, twenties, or thirties. The disease follows a very unpredictable course. That first flare-up may also be the last. Or it may signal the start of a lifetime of flare-ups that come and go for no apparent reason. Fortunately, when the lesions disappear, they leave no scars.

While the experts continue to debate what triggers psoriasis, you're probably more interested in what gets rid of it. That's understandable, since at its worst, psoriasis can be as embarrassing as it is frustrating. By combining mainstream and alternative therapies in a blended approach to treatment, you stand the best chance of experiencing significant relief.

BEST CHOICES

Nutrition

Send protein packing. Eating fewer protein-rich foods—primarily meats and dairy products—may help alleviate flare-ups, several studies show.

Switching from a high-protein diet to a low-protein, largely vegetarian diet has another advantage. Grains, legumes, fruits, and vegetables are packed with fiber, and fiber escorts psoriasis-triggering chemicals out of the intestines.

Favor fishy fare. If you cut back on meats, don't stop eating fish, specifically cold-water species such as salmon, mackerel, and herring. These contain an abundance of omega-3 fatty acids, whose potent anti-inflammatory properties can help ease a psoriasis flare-up. Joseph Pizzorno Jr., N.D., advises people with psoriasis to eat a serving of cold-water fish every day.

Supplements

Get fish oil in a pill. Researchers around the world have tested fish-oil supplements as a treatment for psoriasis, often with excellent results. Look for fish-oil supplements that supply both eicosapentaenoic acid and docosahexaenoic acid. (On labels, these compounds may be listed as EPA and DHA.) Take four to six capsules every day, advises clinical nutritionist Shari Lieberman, Ph.D.

Heal with beta-carotene. Vitamin A is essential for healthy skin. But in too-large doses, the vitamin can have serious side effects. A safer alternative is beta-carotene, which your body converts to vitamin A. "I've found beta-carotene useful in treating psoriasis," Dr. Lieberman says. Take 25,000 international units (IU) once a day.

Meditation

Stop stress from affecting your skin. "There's no question in my mind that many cases of psoriasis are stress-related," says Alan P. Brauer, M.D. "But it's not as though psoriasis patches show up the day after some stressful event. Rather, they tend to develop after an extended period of stress, which is why people don't necessarily make the connection."

Psoriasis can also *contribute* to stress. If lesions occur in highly visible places, people become concerned about their appearance, which contributes to tension and anxiety.

To short-circuit stress and prevent psoriasis flare-ups, try practicing meditation. In one study conducted at the University of Massachusetts Medical School in Worcester, people with psoriasis who combined meditation and light therapy (discussed a bit later in the chapter) saw their skin heal about twice as fast as people who used light therapy alone.

Many experts have developed audiotapes, which will help guide you through meditation exercises. (For more information on ordering these tapes, refer to How to Find What You Need on page 668.)

Social Support

Seek out others with psoriasis. Discussing your psoriasis experience with people who know exactly what you're going through can help ease the distress and embarrassment associated with the condition. The National Psoriasis Foundation offers support group meetings from coast to coast. To locate the support group nearest you, write to the foundation at 6600 S.W. 92nd Street, Suite 300, Portland, OR 97223-7195.

Herbal Medicine

Eliminate lesions with licorice. Licorice root contains a number of anti-inflammatory compounds. Check at your local health food store for licorice tincture or some other licorice extract. Using a cotton ball or a clean cloth, apply the liquid directly to your psoriasis lesions, suggests James A. Duke, Ph.D.

Soothe sore skin with chamomile. Like licorice, chamomile contains anti-inflammatory compounds that can help relieve psoriasis flare-ups.

To make a chamomile compress, add 1 heaping teaspoon of chamomile flowers (sold in health food stores) to 1 cup of boiled water. Allow to steep for 10 minutes, then strain out the herb. Soak a clean cloth in the liquid, then apply the cloth to the affected skin.

Assuage psoriasis with aloe. In a study, Swedish researchers found that 83 percent of people using aloe cream reported significant relief. Some health food stores carry aloe cream. If you're able to buy the cream over the counter, use it according to package directions. Otherwise, consult an herbalist or naturopath.

Home Remedies

Remember to moisturize. Applying a moisturizing lotion can help relieve a mild case of psoriasis, especially one that's associated with dry skin or low humidity.

Soak up sunshine. Sunbathing has become unfashionable in recent years, largely because people fear developing skin cancer. But for those with psoriasis, exposure to sunlight can have significant therapeutic benefits, says Eugene Farber, M.D., professor of dermatology at Stanford University and president of the Psoriasis Research Institute in Palo Alto, California. Psoriasis patches tend to go away in summer, when the sun's rays are strongest. For treatment indoors, use a sun lamp. Either way, ask your doctor how long you can safely stay in the sun or under a sun lamp unprotected.

Shun spirits. At the National Public Health Institute in Helsinki, Finland, researchers evaluated the drinking habits of 144 men with psoriasis and 285 men without the condition. The researchers determined that the men with psoriasis consumed twice as much alcohol on a daily basis as the men who were psoriasis-free—1.5 ounces compared with 0.75 ounce. Other studies have shown unusually high rates of psoriasis among people who abuse alcohol. So if you have psoriasis, your best bet is to avoid alcoholic beverages, says Melvyn Werback, M.D., assistant clinical professor at the UCLA School of Medicine and author of *Nutritional Influences on Illness.*

Over-the-Counter Drugs

Rub in some heat. Capsaicin, the substance that gives chile peppers their fiery flavor, is the active ingredient in many over-the-counter pain-relieving creams. Now research suggests that these creams may help treat psoriasis as well.

Heal skin with hydrocortisone. If you have a mild case of psoriasis, it may respond to treatment with an over-the-counter 1 percent hydrocortisone cream. "I've found that the cream works even better if the treated skin is covered with plastic wrap overnight," says Anne Simons, M.D. You can wind the plastic wrap around the affected body part, or you can use medical tape to hold the wrap in place—whichever works best.

Maybe You Need a Vacation

Looking for a more exotic psoriasis treatment? Then pack your bags and take a trip to the Middle East. Your destination: the Dead Sea.

Since biblical times, the Dead Sea has been a renowned site of healing. Its mineral-rich waters have proved therapeutic for people with an array of ailments, including psoriasis.

Today, the shores of the Dead Sea are home to Israel's Dead Sea Psoriasis Clinic. The clinic offers a 28-day psoriasis-treatment program that combines hour-long baths in the Dead Sea with applications of skin cream and exposure to intense sunlight for up to 6 hours a day.

How effective is the treatment? To find out, David Abels, M.D., a doctor at the clinic, reviewed the medical records of 1,448 people with psoriasis who participated in the 28-day program. He found that every single person experienced at least some improvement in their psoriasis symptoms. More than half reported complete remission of their skin patches.

OTHER GOOD CHOICES

Homeopathy

Discover Calendula. For psoriasis, Calendula is often the homeopathic medicine of choice, according to homeopath Dana Ullman. But before trying Calendula on your own, consult a homeopath. Another medicine may work better for your individual symptoms.

Chinese Medicine

Let your Blood flow. In Chinese medicine, psoriasis is viewed as a condition brought on by the stagnation of Blood, explains Efrem Korngold, O.M.D., L.Ac. Among the herbs a Chinese medicine doctor may prescribe are zedoria (similar to ginger), turmeric, red peony, dang gui (Chinese angelica), and sarsaparilla. Other herbs—including dittany, sophora, and tribulus—may be prescribed to relieve any psoriasis-related itching.

Needle it. In his practice, Dr. Korngold also uses acupuncture as a psoriasis treatment. If you prefer to use acupressure, apply steady, penetrating pressure to each of the following points for 3 minutes.

◆ Large Intestine 11, located on the outer end of your elbow crease on the thumb side

◆ Large Intestine 4, located on the back of your hand where the bones of your thumb and index finger meet

◆ Spleen 10, located on your inner thigh, four finger-widths above your kneecap and just under your thighbone

◆ Liver 3, situated on top of your foot in the webbing between your big toe and second toe

Ayurvedic Medicine

Put a lid on Pitta. Ayurvedic practitioners believe that most inflammatory skin conditions, including psoriasis, result from excess Pitta dosha, according to David Frawley, O.M.D.

To treat psoriasis, Ayurvedic practitioners often prescribe applying emollients such as sesame oil, aloe vera gel, and an Ayurvedic herb called bakuchi. The herb contains psoralens, the compounds that slow skin cell division and inhibit the scaling characteristic of psoriasis.

MEDICAL MEASURES

Among the most effective prescription psoriasis medications is a topical preparation called anthralin (Anthra-Derm). Using anthralin can be quite an elaborate regimen, but by following this regimen every day for about 3 weeks, your psoriasis may go into remission for up to 6 months.

Coal-tar ointments are an old standby in psoriasis treatment. These ointments are sold over the counter in 1 percent to 5 percent strengths.

Prescription-strength hydrocortisone creams (such as Nutracort) are another option. They're more potent than their over-the-counter relatives and may cause more serious side effects.

Two topical psoriasis preparations seem to have fewer side effects than hydrocortisone creams. One of these preparations, called calcipotriene (Dovonex), is derived from vitamin D. It slows skin-cell turnaround, which prevents the formation of skin patches. The other, called tazarotene (Tazorac), appears to produce prolonged psoriasis remissions. It's especially effective when used in conjunction with moisturizers and ultraviolet light therapy.

Certain oral medications can also help heal psoriasis. Among the most effective are etretinate (Tegison), a vitamin A derivative, and methotrexate (Folex), which is used in cancer chemotherapy. Both drugs can cause significant side effects.

Finally, some doctors advise people with psoriasis to try a combination treatment involving the drug psoralen and ultraviolet light therapy. This treatment, called PUVA, has been known to raise the risk of a certain type of skin cancer if used for several years. But a newer form of light therapy, called 311 nanometer therapy, appears to be just as effective as ultraviolet light therapy but less likely to cause skin cancer. If your doctor recommends PUVA, ask him about the newer form of treatment.

Raynaud's Syndrome

If there's any truth to the old adage "Cold hands, warm heart," then anyone who has Raynaud's syndrome must be burning with passion. Raynaud's makes a person's hands feel so cold that they absolutely ache.

Raynaud's syndrome is named for the French physician Maurice Raynaud, who first documented the condition in the mid-1860s. Since then, scientists have determined that Raynaud's occurs because of spasms in the small arteries that deliver blood to your fingers.

It's normal for these blood vessels to constrict a little when you're exposed to cold or when you're under stress. But if you have Raynaud's, the vessels clamp down big-time, causing pain. Your fingers turn blue or white. In some people, it's more than fingers that are affected. Toes, cheeks, the nose, and ears may chill and change color as the blood vessels constrict in those areas.

SIMPLE SOLUTIONS
1. Nutrition
2. Supplements
3. Exercise
4. Visualization
5. Biofeedback
6. Herbal Medicine
7. Home Remedies
8. Chinese Medicine
9. Ayurvedic Medicine
10. Naturopathy
11. Medical Measures

About 5 percent of Americans have Raynaud's, and at least four out of five of those are women. Most people first notice symptoms sometime between ages 20 and 35.

If you have Raynaud's, you may also be prone to migraines. Similar to Raynaud's, migraines begin when blood vessels in your head constrict. If the vessels in your fingers tend to spasm, there's a good chance that the vessels in your head do the same.

With proper home care, however, you might be able to relieve your frigid digits and possibly help your migraines as well. Here's what the experts recommend.

BEST CHOICES

Nutrition

Sink your teeth into salmon. Salmon and other cold-water fish contain an abundance of omega-3 fatty acids. These "good fats" improve blood flow throughout your body by making your blood-clotting cells, called platelets, less likely to clump together. Besides salmon, enjoy mackerel, herring, and tuna—all excellent sources of omega-3's.

Supplements

Opt for omega-3 capsules. If you're not a fan of fish, you can get your omega-3's by taking fish-oil supplements. At Albany Medical College in New York, researchers saw improvement in 45 percent of a group taking fish-oil capsules.

The fish-oil capsules used in the study contained 330 milligrams of eicosapentaenoic acid (EPA) and 220 milligrams of docosahexaenoic acid (DHA). The study participants took 12 of these capsules a day. You can buy fish-oil capsules in health food stores and some drugstores.

Open blood vessels with niacin. Several studies have shown that taking large doses of a form of niacin called inositol nicotinate reduces spasms in the blood vessels of the fingers. This helps control the frequency and severity of Raynaud's flare-ups.

If you want to try niacin therapy, consult a nutritionist or a nutrition-minded doctor, advises Melvyn R. Werbach, M.D., assistant clinical professor at the University of California, Los Angeles, School of Medicine. It's best to take doses over 35 milligrams per day only under professional supervision.

Warm up to magnesium. Magnesium therapy has been used to treat some conditions that involve blood vessel constriction. One study has shown that those with Raynaud's have significantly lower magnesium levels during the winter months, suggesting that lack of magnesium could be linked to the problem.

"I think magnesium supplementation is worth a try," says Alan Gaby, M.D. He suggests taking 400 milligrams a day.

Exercise

Whirl your arms. To help relieve your Raynaud's symptoms, Seattle naturopath William Mitchell, N.D., cofounder of Bastyr University in Kenmore, Washington, recommends this simple exercise: First, raise your hands over your head. Hold them there for about a minute so that the blood drains from your fingers. Then rapidly whirl your arms in big circles for a minute to send the blood back to your fingers. Repeat the exercise several times a day.

Visualization

Envision relief. Martin L. Rossman, M.D., has had considerable success in treating Raynaud's with visualization therapy. He suggests practicing this visualization when your symptoms flare up: Imagine that you are lying on warm sand in the warm sun. See yourself running your fingers through the sand, absorbing its warmth.

Biofeedback

Train your vessels to relax. Using biofeedback, you can learn how to keep the blood vessels in your fingers open and free from spasms. Certified biofeedback therapist Nancy Schwartz of Orange Park, Florida, has taught biofeedback to many people with Raynaud's. "Most reduce their symptoms by about two-thirds," she says.

Herbal Medicine

Go with ginkgo. "Europeans often recommend ginkgo for Raynaud's," says James A. Duke, Ph.D. "This makes sense to me. If I had Raynaud's, I'd try ginkgo."

If you'd like to try this herb, naturopath Donald Brown, N.D., professor of herbal medicine at Bastyr University in Kenmore, Washington, recommends taking 80 milligrams of a standardized ginkgo extract twice a day. You can buy the extract in health food stores.

Home Remedies

Bundle up your hands. Before retrieving anything from your refrigerator or freezer, slip on a pair of gloves or mittens, advises Anne Simons, M.D. To keep your hands really warm, wear a pair of lightweight glove liners underneath your gloves or mittens.

Give your fingers the military treatment. While stationed in Alaska, some members of the U.S. Armed Forces had problems with Raynaud's. So Army researchers developed the following treatment, which you can try at home during the cold winter months.

In a room at a comfortable indoor temperature, soak your hands in a container of warm, not hot, water for 3 to 5 minutes. Then go outside into the cold and soak your hands in warm water for 10 minutes. Army studies have shown that people who repeat this treatment three to six times every other day for a week usually notice improvement in their Raynaud's symptoms.

Go soak. As an alternative to the Army program, try soaking your hands in warm to hot water for about 10 minutes once or twice a day. You may get some relief from your symptoms.

Cut out caffeine. The caffeine in coffee, tea, colas, and some over-the-counter drugs constricts your blood vessels, which can aggravate your Raynaud's symptoms. "People with Raynaud's often experience noticeable relief when they cut out caffeine," Dr. Gaby says.

Be wise when you imbibe. When you drink, alcohol increases blood flow to the surface of your skin. This produces a sensation of warmth that extends right to the tips of your fingers. But the effect is only temporary, Dr. Gaby says. The heat is soon lost to the air, and your hands end up colder than they were to begin with. So alcohol can actually make your symptoms worse.

Snuff out those cigarettes. If you smoke, the nicotine in your cigarettes may aggravate your Raynaud's. That's because nicotine constricts blood vessels, including those in your fingers.

In fact, even if you don't smoke, you should try to limit your exposure to secondhand smoke. Some people are so sensitive to nicotine that even inhaling someone else's cigarette smoke can cause their blood vessels to spasm.

OTHER GOOD CHOICES

Chinese Medicine
Stimulate your circulation. Raynaud's is often anxiety-related, explains Efrem Korngold, O.M.D., L.Ac. "Anxiety leads to constriction in the

body, including constriction of the blood vessels in the hands and feet."

To treat Raynaud's, Dr. Korngold often prescribes the herbs pseudoginseng root and sage root, and borneol crystals.

Apply pressure to relieve pain. In a study conducted in Germany, acupuncture helped 33 people with severe Raynaud's who received seven acupuncture treatments just as winter arrived.

If you prefer a self-care approach, try acupressure. Apply steady, penetrating finger pressure to each of the following points for 3 minutes.

◆ Pericardium 6, located in the middle of your inner wrist, 2½ finger-widths above the wrist crease (according to Dr. Korngold, this point is especially effective for Raynaud's that affects the hands)

◆ Liver 3, situated on top of your foot in the webbing between your big toe and second toe (this point is beneficial for Raynaud's that affects the feet, Dr. Korngold says)

Ayurvedic Medicine

Rebalance your Vata. Practitioners of Ayurveda believe that Raynaud's is a Vata disorder, says Scott Gerson, M.D., founder of Ayurvedic Medicine of New York. The Vata dosha governs your circulatory system and regulates the constriction and dilation of your blood vessels.

To treat Raynaud's, Dr. Gerson prescribes a daily regimen of walking, hot baths, meditation, and whole-body massages with warm sesame oil (panchakarma). He also advocates a diet that emphasizes certain foods, such as cherries.

Naturopathy

Turn up the heat. Sitting in a sauna or a tolerably hot bath can help ease your Raynaud's symptoms by increasing your blood circulation, Dr. Mitchell says. While you're in the sauna or bath, massage your hands for a few minutes as an additional way to help promote blood circulation.

MEDICAL MEASURES

If your Raynaud's causes such intolerable pain that you consult a doctor, you may receive a prescription for drugs called vasodilators, which can open your blood vessels. About two-thirds of people with Raynaud's who take vasodilators report improvement in their symptoms. Like most pharmaceuticals, however, vasodilators may produce side effects.

RED FLAGS

Many common medications, including over-the-counter decongestants, can constrict your blood vessels. So if you're taking any prescription or over-the-counter medicine, ask your doctor or pharmacist whether it could aggravate your Raynaud's symptoms. If so, ask your doctor whether you could take a different drug that doesn't have this effect.

Rheumatoid Arthritis

What did Thomas Jefferson, Teddy Roosevelt, and painter Pierre Auguste Renoir have in common?

Rheumatoid arthritis, which today affects some 2 million Americans. It's the second most common form of joint pain and inflammation, after osteoarthritis, but it's much more debilitating. It leads to joint deformity and often crippling loss of joint function.

Rheumatoid arthritis typically causes pain, swelling, warmth, and tenderness in the small joints of your hands and feet, although other joints may be affected as well. Sometimes the joints appear purplish. Symptoms tend to come and go—flare-ups followed by periods of remission. The pain is often severe and, unlike osteoarthritis, does not subside with rest. Morning pain and stiffness can last for several hours.

Oddly, flare-ups are usually symmetrical, involving both hands or both feet. You might develop small bumps under your skin, especially near your elbows (rheumatoid nodules).

SIMPLE SOLUTIONS
1. Nutrition
2. Supplements
3. Elimination Diet
4. Exercise
5. Tai Chi
6. Relaxation Therapies
7. Massage
8. Herbal Medicine
9. Home Remedies
10. Homeopathy
11. Chinese Medicine
12. Ayurvedic Medicine
13. Medical Measures

You may also experience flulike symptoms, lethargy, and low-grade fever. In some cases, rheumatoid arthritis affects your heart and lungs as well as your joints, causing difficulty breathing and further loss of energy.

Doctors generally consider rheumatoid arthritis an autoimmune disease. For reasons that remain unclear, your immune system attacks your joint tissue, especially the membrane that lines your joints. This smooth membrane, called the synovium, becomes red, inflamed, and swollen.

Rheumatoid arthritis is not classically hereditary, but it tends to run in families. Diet also plays a role. "Rheumatoid arthritis is not found in cultures where people eat a traditional, healthful diet high in fruits, vegetables, and fiber and low in meat, sugar, and saturated fat," says Joseph Pizzorno Jr., N.D. "But it's common in cultures that eat a diet high in meat, sugar, and saturated fats and low in fruits, vegetables, and fiber."

Some studies have suggested that a bacterial infection may cause rheumatoid arthritis. Researchers have not identified an offending microorganism, so this theory remains controversial. But a few studies have shown that one kind of antibiotic helps relieve symptoms.

Also, a few studies suggest that stress may play a role in rheumatoid arthritis. In one study, University of Rochester researchers interviewed eight pairs of identical twins, one each of whom had rheumatoid arthritis. In the year before they were diagnosed, the twins who developed rheumatoid arthritis had significantly more stressful life events—work pressure, marital conflict, and other family problems.

Doctors once believed that rheumatoid arthritis caused permanent joint damage only when affected joints became deformed. But recent studies have shown that significant joint damage occurs within the first year of this condition. This underscores the need to treat rheumatoid arthritis quickly, aggressively, and comprehensively.

BEST CHOICES

Nutrition

Become a vegetarian. Dr. Pizzorno believes that many mainstream M.D.'s don't appreciate the powerful role that food plays in inflammation. "A compound found almost exclusively in animal fats contributes greatly to the inflammatory process because it's converted into compounds that trigger inflammation," he explains. He advises people with rheumatoid arthritis to switch to a vegetarian diet.

Swim with the fishes. At the Fred Hutchinson Cancer Research Center in Seattle, Jean A. Shapiro, M.D., and colleagues found that the women least likely to develop rheumatoid arthritis ate more than two servings of broiled or baked cold-water fish a week. Cold-water species such as salmon, tuna, mackerel, trout, sardines, and herring contain oils that are rich in omega-3 fatty acids. Omega-3's decrease your body's production of compounds that trigger inflammation.

Supplements

Get fish oil without fish. You can get the benefits of omega-3 fatty acids from anti-inflammatory fish-oil supplements. "In more than a dozen studies conducted in the past decade, rheumatoid arthritis sufferers who took omega-3 capsules had fewer tender, swollen joints and less morning stiffness than those who didn't," says Andrew T. Weil, M.D., director of the program in integrative medicine at the University of Arizona College of Medicine in Tucson. "And they were able to taper their use of anti-inflammatory medication."

Consider plant oils, too. Like fish oil, certain plant oils contain an essential fatty acid. One of the best sources of gamma-linolenic acid (GLA), an omega-6 fatty acid, is borage seed oil. "Personally, I've seen the best results with borage seed oil," says Alan Gaby, M.D.

Clinical nutritionist Shari Lieberman, Ph.D., suggests taking a daily capsule containing 70 to 240 milligrams of the oil.

Make up for nutritional shortfalls. People with rheumatoid arthritis tend to have low blood levels of several nutrients that help reduce the production of compounds that trigger inflammation. Dr. Pizzorno recommends the following daily supplement regimen: 1,000 to 3,000 milligrams of vitamin C, 400 international units (IU) of vitamin E, 2,000 milligrams of pantothenic acid (taken as four 500-milligram doses), 200 micrograms of selenium, and 45 milligrams of zinc. Amounts this high of vitamin E and zinc, however, should only be taken under a qualified practitioner's supervision.

If you'd rather not take so many pills, Dr. Lieberman suggests a daily multivitamin/mineral supplement that contains some of every essential vitamin and mineral. Read labels to be sure.

Elimination Diet

For fast relief, fast. Although the theory remains controversial, some experts attribute rheumatoid arthritis to leaky gut syndrome, in which certain potentially harmful substances pass from your intestines into your bloodstream. "Because a leaky gut can play a role in rheumatoid arthritis, an elimination diet or fasting often relieves symptoms," says New York City internist Leo Galland, M.D., director of the Foundation for Integrated Medicine.

A strict elimination diet may help you identify foods that trigger your symptoms. Depending on your individual sensitivities, almost any food can aggravate rheumatoid arthritis, but the most common offenders are meats, dairy products, and wheat.

If you'd like to try an elimination diet, work with a naturopath or a clinical nutritionist who can help you design your diet and provide support as you implement it. "Fasting should only be done under medical supervision," Dr. Pizzorno says.

Exercise

Don't fear fitness. Want to have significantly less morning stiffness? Then take regular walks and do stretching exercises. That's what Mary J. Bell, M.D., assistant professor of rheumatology and clinical epidemiology at Sunnybrook Health Science Center of the University of Toronto, discovered in a study of 150 people with rheumatoid arthritis. Compared with those who did not exercise regularly, the participants who took brief daily walks and did stretches for a total of just 3 hours over 6 weeks experienced an hour less morning stiffness.

Unfortunately, according to a survey by researchers with the Centers for Disease Control and Prevention, people with arthritis are less likely to exercise than the general population. "Their pain discourages them from physical activity," says Alan P. Brauer, M.D. "Few seem to understand that exercise is key to relieving their pain."

During remissions, get regular exercise, advises Joseph J. Biundo Jr., M.D., professor of medicine and chief of physical medicine and rehabilitation at Louisiana State University Medical Center in New Orleans. He recommends aerobic activities such as walking, swimming, or cycling as well as stretching and strengthening exercises. But during flare-ups, take it easy, or rest your affected joints using a splint. Exercising or stressing your affected joints when you have symptoms aggravates joint damage.

Show up for class. "People with rheumatoid arthritis often become wary of exercise, fearing that it will bring on a flare-up," says Anne Simons, M.D. "I suggest joining a medically supervised class, where you get safe exercise and emotional support." Contact the Arthritis Foundation office nearest you or ask your physician for a referral to a rehabilitation specialist.

Tai Chi

Gently move your joints. Exercise within your limits should not aggravate your symptoms. But if you're concerned that it might, researchers at Charlotte Rehabilitation Hospital in North Carolina have good news for you: Tai chi does not trigger rheumatoid arthritis symptoms. They taught 20 people with rheumatoid arthritis a tai chi routine and supervised two hour-long sessions a week for 10 weeks. None of the participants experienced any aggravation of symptoms.

Relaxation Therapies

For less pain, destress. While stress makes pain worse, relaxation provides relief. Researchers at the Harry Truman V. A. Hospital in Columbia, Missouri, studied 141 people with rheumatoid arthritis. All of the participants received standard care, but some also got training in stress management. Ten weeks later, those who practiced stress management reported significantly less pain, better overall health, and greater ability to cope with their rheumatoid arthritis.

Massage

Experience the healing power of touch. It's hard to relax when you have persistent pain from a chronic condition like rheumatoid arthritis. Massage can help. Tiffany Field, Ph.D., professor of psychology, pediatrics, and psychiatry at the University of Miami School of Medicine, took saliva samples from 20 youngsters with juvenile rheumatoid arthritis and analyzed the samples for levels of the stress hormone cortisol. Then Dr. Field taught the parents to give their children daily 15-minute massages. A month later, she took new saliva samples from the children. The samples contained significantly less cortisol, indicating less stress.

Herbal Medicine

Treat your joints to ginger. Ginger is an age-old treatment for inflammation, particularly in Ayurvedic medicine. James A. Duke, Ph.D., suggests taking 1,000 to 2,000 milligrams a day in capsule form or using more ginger in cooking.

Tame pain with turmeric. A staple ingredient in Indian cuisine, turmeric contains a yellow pigment called curcumin that Dr. Pizzorno describes as one of nature's most potent anti-inflammatory agents. Take 300 milligrams of curcumin three times a day.

As an alternative, you can season your food with turmeric, Dr. Duke says. Experiment with curries and other Indian dishes, which call for lots of the spice.

Banish pain with bromelain. An enzyme in pineapple, bromelain has powerful anti-inflammatory properties. "I think it's a good bet for people with arthritis," Dr. Duke says.

Dr. Pizzorno recommends taking 250 milligrams three times a day, before meals.

Discover a dream cream. While red pepper causes pain on your tongue, it can relieve pain in your joints. The herb gets its heat from a compound called capsaicin. Researchers at Case Western Reserve University asked 31 people with rheumatoid arthritis to apply either a capsaicin cream or a placebo cream to their painful knees four times a day for 4 weeks. Among those using the capsaicin cream, 57 percent reported relief from their symptoms.

You can buy capsaicin cream over the counter. Follow the label instructions, wash your hands thoroughly after application, and keep it away from your eyes and other mucous membranes. It can really burn.

Home Remedies

Make adjustments. "Analyze your daily chores," Dr. Simons advises. "Try to make them as easy as possible. Use your imagination, and give yourself permission to take shortcuts."

Many medical supply stores sell products that take some of the pain out of living with arthritis. Look for items such as reach-and-grab devices and extended shoehorns. Also, avoid overexertion. Don't stop moving, but learn your limits and don't push yourself beyond them. Pain is a signal that means you need to stop what you're doing, especially if you have rheumatoid arthritis, Dr. Simons says.

Go for the gold. Drugs containing gold are a standard treatment for rheumatoid arthritis. British researchers have determined that enough gold can pass from a ring into finger skin to minimize rheumatoid arthritis symptoms. When the researchers compared symptoms in 30 people who wore gold rings and 25 who did not, they found that the ring wearers had significantly less pain and swelling in the finger with the ring than in the same finger of the opposite hand. These people also had fewer symptoms in their ringed fingers than did the non–ring wearers.

Get your Zzzs. If you have rheumatoid arthritis, you need to get enough deep, restorative sleep. Stanford rheumatologist Richard B. Gremillion, M.D., recommends at least 8 hours a night, plus at least one 30-minute rest period each day. If you have trouble sleeping, he recommends asking your physician for a referral to a sleep center.

Choose your temperature. During flare-ups, both heat and cold can provide some pain relief. Which should you use? "It's up to you," Dr. Biundo says. "Whichever feels better." But in his experience, the inflammation of flare-ups responds best to cooling, while heat works best for less severe pain and inflammation and as preparation for stretching exercises.

For heat therapy, Dr. Biundo recommends using a heating pad, hot pack, or hot bath. For cold therapy, he suggests applying ice or a cold pack wrapped in a towel.

OTHER GOOD CHOICES

Homeopathy

Ease symptoms with Aurum. Homeopaths treat rheumatoid arthritis with a variety of medicines, depending on a person's individual symptoms, says homeopath Dana Ullman. But perhaps the most frequently prescribed medicine is Aurum metallicum, a microdose of gold. To find out which medicine best suits your symptoms, consult a homeopath.

Chinese Medicine

Banish Wind, Cold, and Damp. Chinese medicine does not distinguish between rheumatoid arthritis and osteoarthritis. "The Chinese use the general term *arthralgia,* meaning joint pain," says Efrem Korngold, O.M.D., L.Ac. In the Chinese view, joint pain is caused by a combination of inflammation and invasion of Wind, Cold, and Damp that penetrates deep into your joints.

To treat the inflammation, Dr. Korngold gives his patients several herbs including gardenia buds, forsythia, honeysuckle, and sarsaparilla. To expel Wind, Cold, and Damp, he prescribes clematis root, gentian root, chaenomeles fruit, and cinnamon twig.

Arthritis may also involve some organ weakness, particularly in the Kidney, which governs your bones. To strengthen the Kidney, Dr. Korngold prescribes dry ginger, eucommia, dipsacus, and drynaria.

Schedule an acupuncture session. The United Nations World Health

Organization endorses acupuncture as a treatment for arthritis. Which points an acupuncturist uses depends on which joint is affected. For example, if you have pain in your right knee, your acupuncturist may stimulate points in your left knee. "The idea is to move qi from the healthy part to the weak part," Dr. Korngold says.

Ayurvedic Medicine

Be good as guggul. Ayurvedic physicians consider arthritis an imbalance of the Vata dosha caused by toxic air. For external treatment, David Frawley, O.M.D., prescribes frequent massages with warm sesame oil to which various Indian herbs—such as sandalwood, shatavari, and ashwagandha—have been added. Each massage should be followed by a hot shower.

For internal use, Ayurvedic physicians often prescribe ginger, turmeric, and guggul. Sometimes called Indian frankincense, guggul is the resin of a tree that grows in the dry, hilly areas of India. It has a long history of use as a treatment for joint pain.

MEDICAL MEASURES

Until recently, doctors recommended treating rheumatoid arthritis with aspirin or other nonsteroidal anti-inflammatory drugs (NSAIDs). But James O'Dell, M.D., chief of rheumatology at the University of Nebraska Medical Center in Omaha, notes that since the mid-1990s, aspirin and NSAIDs have fallen from favor as treatments for rheumatoid arthritis. They treat only pain and inflammation; they don't help heal affected joints. And they can cause painful abdominal distress, ringing in the ears, and severe—even life-threatening—digestive tract bleeding.

Today's first-line mainstream medical treatments are disease-modifying antirheumatic drugs, or DMARDs. DMARDs not only treat the pain and inflammation of rheumatoid arthritis but also help coax the condition into remission. Methotrexate (Folex) is the most effective and least toxic of the DMARDs, but it doesn't work all that well by itself. Dr. O'Dell says that it's usually prescribed in combination with other DMARDs, among them, gold. To help prevent side effects from methotrexate, you may want to take 400 micrograms of folic acid a day.

Antibiotic treatment has also become popular, thanks to studies suggesting that a bacterial infection might play a role in rheumatoid arthritis. Several studies have shown that minocycline (Dynacin), a drug related to tetracycline, significantly relieves rheumatoid arthritis symptoms and minimizes joint damage.

Your doctor might also prescribe corticosteroids. These drugs act quickly and have potent anti-inflammatory action, but they cause a large number of potentially severe side effects.

Narcotics do a good job of relieving severe pain, but doctors are reluctant to prescribe them for rheumatoid arthritis because of the risk of tolerance (meaning that you need a higher dose over time) and addiction.

In the future, doctors may prescribe a new type of NSAID, called COX-2 inhibitors, to treat rheumatoid arthritis. Some studies have shown that these drugs relieve pain and inflammation as well as traditional NSAIDs, but with minimal side effects.

Sinus Infection

Comparing a sinus infection to a runny nose is like comparing the Atlantic Ocean to a puddle. At its worst, a runny nose is inconvenient and maybe a little annoying. But a sinus infection can really knock you for a loop.

It usually comes on just as you're getting over a cold. You begin to feel pain in the area right around your eyes, from your forehead to your cheekbones. The pain can become intense. Meanwhile, your nose continues to run—only the discharge changes from clear and watery to thick and yellow-green.

All this trouble starts in eight hollowed-out structures called nasal sinuses. They may seem pretty useless—after all, they are just empty space. But they provide three important benefits, according to Anne Simons, M.D. First, they decrease the weight of your skull, so your neck muscles don't have to work so hard to support your head. Second, they give reso-nance to your voice, which is why you sound different when they become clogged. And third, they filter and warm the air you breathe.

> ## SIMPLE SOLUTIONS
> 1. Nutrition
> 2. Supplements
> 3. Herbal Medicine
> 4. Home Remedies
> 5. Homeopathy
> 6. Chinese Medicine
> 7. Over-the-Counter Drugs
> 8. Medical Measures

Your sinuses are lined with glands that secrete mucus, which normally drains through narrow tubes into your throat. But sometimes drainage becomes impaired, perhaps because of a cold, allergies, asthma, exposure to irritating chemicals, or a structural abnormality in the nose or facial bones. With no place to go, the mucus accumulates inside your sinuses, creating an environment in which bacteria and other microorganisms thrive.

Clogged sinuses that breed bacteria are responsible for the vast majority of sinus infections. Occasionally, fungi cause problems, too, says Gary S. Rachelefsky, M.D., clinical professor of allergy and immunology at University of California, Los Angeles, School of Medicine. No matter which bug is to blame, the primary symptoms are the same: an intense headache, thick nasal discharge, and possibly fever. These symptoms may be accompanied by wheezing, coughing, sore throat, hoarseness, tooth pain, earache, or a general ill feeling.

If you have a sinus infection, proper home care—using a combination of natural remedies, alternative treatments, and possibly over-the-counter drugs—may be all you need to relieve your symptoms. Here's what the experts have to say.

BEST CHOICES

Nutrition

Eat a sinus-clearing snack. Spread prepared horseradish or wasabi (Japanese horseradish) on some crackers and nibble on them, suggests Andrew T. Weil, M.D., director of the program in integrative medicine at the University of Arizona College of Medicine in Tucson. The heat from these condiments can make your nose run, helping to open up your clogged sinuses. If you're more daring, enjoy an entire meal of hot and spicy foods. Japanese, Mexican, and Indian cuisines are known for their fiery dishes.

Supplements

Let C come to your rescue. Various studies have shown that vitamin C can help treat an array of respiratory ailments, including colds, allergies, and asthma. Joseph Pizzorno Jr., N.D., prescribes vitamin C for sinus infections. He suggests taking 500 milligrams every 2 waking hours until your symptoms subside.

Herbal Medicine

Triple your odds of relief. The bacteria-blasting trio of echinacea, goldenseal, and garlic can help wipe out a sinus infection, says James A. Duke, Ph.D. "Echinacea is an immune stimulant that helps your body fight infection. And goldenseal and garlic have antibiotic properties, as many studies have confirmed."

Most health food stores and some drugstores stock tinctures that are made from a combination of echinacea and goldenseal. Take 1 teaspoon of the tincture two or three times a day, mixed into juice or herbal tea, Dr. Duke suggests.

As for garlic, your best bet is to chew the raw cloves. If you don't like the

Are You Sure It's a Sinus Infection?

Sinus infections share many symptoms with colds and allergies. How can you tell which is which?

The following chart can help you figure out exactly what you have so that you can treat it properly. If it's a cold, it will last from 3 to 10 days. A sinus infection will last longer—10 to 14 days. The duration of allergy sumptoms varies. If still in doubt, see your doctor.

Symptom	Sinus Infection	Cold	Allergy
Nasal discharge	Thick and yellow-green	Thin and watery, or thick and whitish	Clear, thin, and watery
Nasal congestion	Almost always	Almost always	Sometimes
Headache	Almost always	Sometimes	Sometimes
Facial pain or pressure	Almost always	Sometimes	Sometimes
Fever	Possible	Possible, but rare in adults	No
Cough	Almost always	Almost always	Sometimes
Sneezing	Rarely	Almost always	Sometimes
Ear pain	Sometimes	Sometimes	Sometimes
Pain in upper teeth	Sometimes	No	No
Bad breath	Sometimes	No	No

taste or smell, take 500 to 1,000 milligrams of deodorized garlic in capsule form once a day. And use more garlic in cooking.

Make a mint tea. Peppermint does a good job of opening clogged sinuses—such a good job, in fact, that peppermint has been approved by the Food and Drug Administration as a nasal decongestant. To make a tea, add 1 teaspoon of dried herb to 1 cup of boiled water. Steep for 10 minutes, then strain. Drink several cupfuls a day.

Discover a not-so-secret formula. For some 60 years, the people of Germany have been using an herbal formula called Sinupret, which contains a combination of elder flowers, gentian root, cowslip flowers, sour dock flowers (also known as sorrel or sheep sorrel), and vervain (also known as verbena).

Right now, you can't buy Sinupret in the United States. But you can buy all of its ingredient herbs in health food stores. Add 1 to 2 teaspoons of each herb to 5 cups of boiled water, steep for 10 minutes, then strain. Drink several cupfuls a day. Be aware that gentian root may cause nausea and vomiting in large doses. Don't use it if you have high blood pressure, gastric or duodenal ulcers, or gastric irritation and inflammation. If you have a history of kidney stones, do not take sour dock flowers without medical supervision. It contains oxalates and tannins that may adversely affect this condition.

Home Remedies

Sip fluids constantly. While you're sick, try to drink 10 or more 8-ounce glasses of water or juice a day, advises Philip Perlman, M.D., an ear, nose, and throat specialist at North Shore Otolaryngology in Manhassett, New York. "Fluids help liquefy thick mucus, so it can drain from the sinuses."

Apply a hot compress. At the first sign of a sinus infection, soak a towel in comfortably hot water (or in peppermint tea) and place it over your sinuses for 15 minutes. Repeat four times a day. Hot compresses are an excellent home treatment for clearing clogged sinuses, Dr. Weil says.

Rinse your nose with salt water. Another home treatment for a sinus infection is what Dr. Weil calls nasal douching. Mix ¼ teaspoon of salt in 1 cup of water. Draw some of the solution into a rubber bulb syringe. Then tilt your head back and gently squirt the solution into each nostril. "You want to get enough salt water in there that you can spit it out of your mouth," he says. Repeat two or three times a day.

Enjoy a soothing shower. Standing in a hot, steamy shower can help open your clogged sinuses. While you're in the shower, concentrate on inhaling the vapors. Then afterward, gently blow your nose, one nostril at a time. Repeat the treatment twice a day—once in the morning and once at night, advises Richard Lockey, M.D., professor of medicine at the University of South Florida in Tampa.

Put some steam in your dreams. Set a vaporizer in your bedroom, close to your bed. Turn it on at bedtime and let it run overnight. The vapors can help keep your sinuses open while you sleep.

OTHER GOOD CHOICES

Homeopathy

Take a symptom-specific medicine. Homeopaths use a number of different medicines to treat sinus infections, says homeopath Dana Ullman. Among the medicines most often prescribed are Arsenicum album, Belladonna, Hepar sulfuris, Kali bichromicum, Mercurius, and Pulsatilla. To find out which of these best suits your specific symptoms, consult a homeopath.

Chinese Medicine

Quiet the Wind. To treat sinus infections, Efrem Korngold, O.M.D., L.Ac., prescribes herbal formulas that contain the following ingredients: forsythia and honeysuckle, which help heal acute respiratory problems; platycodon, which helps eliminate mucus; and gardenia buds, which treat fever and soothe the eyes.

Target your Large Intestine. Dr. Weil describes acupuncture as a very effective treatment for sinus infections. "It often relieves pain and promotes sinus drainage within minutes," he says. Of course, if you want to try acupuncture, you need to consult a qualified acupuncturist. But if you prefer a do-it-yourself approach, consider acupressure.

According to Michael Reed Gach, founder and director of the Acupressure Institute, one acupressure point that's especially helpful for treating sinus infections is Large Intestine 20. It's located on either cheek in the groove beside each nostril. Gach recommends applying steady, penetrating finger pressure to both points at once for about 3 minutes.

Over-the-Counter Drugs

Defer to a decongestant. You may get relief from a sinus infection by taking an over-the-counter decongestant, Dr. Simons says. These products are sold as pills and nasal sprays. You're better off with one that doesn't con-

Sign Up for Sinus Protection

If you've already had one sinus infection, you can probably tell when you're getting another one. But that also means you can take steps to prevent a recurrence. Here's how.

Butt out. "I see the worst cases of sinusitis in smokers," says Andrew T. Weil, M.D., director of the program in integrative medicine at the University of Arizona College of Medicine. So if you smoke, quit. And even if you're not a smoker, try to limit your exposure to secondhand smoke and other respiratory irritants.

Ditch dairy. Milk and milk products contain a protein called casein, which may stimulate mucous production and increase your risk of sinus infection. "I know a number of people who have experienced dramatic improvement in their sinus conditions after 2 months of eliminating dairy," Dr. Weil says.

Take care of your teeth. About 25 percent of people with chronic sinus problems turn out to have an underlying dental infection, according to Joseph Pizzorno Jr., N.D. So be sure to practice good oral hygiene: Brush after every meal, floss at least once a day, and see your dentist twice a year.

Invest in an air filter. If the air in your home keeps sinus infections coming back again and again, a high-efficiency particulate air (HEPA) filter might help. HEPA filters are effective in clearing the air of respiratory irritants. Air-conditioning works almost as well.

tain antihistamines, which dry up mucus and prevent it from draining out of your sinuses.

If you buy a nasal spray, use it for up to 3 days, then stop. Otherwise, you might develop rebound congestion: Your symptoms return, and they are even worse than the first time around.

You can safely take decongestant pills for up to a week. But don't take them too late in the day since they may cause insomnia. If your sinuses remain clogged after a few days, see your doctor.

MEDICAL MEASURES

For sinus infections, mainstream M.D.'s have usually prescribed a 10- to 21-day course of antibiotics—either amoxicillin (Amoxil) or sulfamethoxazole-trimethoprim (Septra). Unfortunately, overuse of these drugs has led to the development of antibiotic-resistant germs. Dr. Perlman believes that physicians should reserve antibiotic treatment for the most severe infections—specifically, those that produce fever along with a yellow-green nasal discharge.

If your sinus infection is severe enough to require antibiotics, you should also take supplements of bromelain. An enzyme found in pineapple, bromelain helps the medicine get into your cells, explains Alan Gaby, M.D. He suggests taking 250 milligrams with your antibiotic pills. Or you can simply eat more pineapple.

If you have chronic sinus infections brought on by a structural abnormality in your nose or facial bones, your doctor may recommend corrective surgery.

RED FLAGS

See your doctor if your sinus infection does not respond to home treatment within a few days or if you develop a fever that exceeds 100°F.

Sprains

One second you were walking, the next you were sprawled on the ground. At first only your dignity seemed the worse for wear. But as you began to collect yourself, you noticed intense pain gripping your ankle. You could barely stand up, much less walk. Then your ankle began to swell. That's when you realized that you might have a sprain.

People tend to use the term *sprain* to refer to any painful joint injury. But a sprain is actually a torn ligament, says Anne Simons, M.D. Ligaments are fibrous, elastic bands of connective tissue that attach bones to one another.

You can tear a ligament in any number of ways: overturning your ankle as you step off a curb, wrenching your knee during a pickup game of basketball, or twisting your wrist as you try to break a fall.

Some research suggests that sprains may be stress-related. Stress increases muscle tension, and tense muscles don't allow joints to move as they should. Plus, stress can be distracting, so you may not be as careful to avoid situations that can lead to sprains.

SIMPLE SOLUTIONS
1. Supplements
2. Exercise
3. Herbal Medicine
4. Home Remedies
5. Over-the-Counter Drugs
6. Massage
7. Aromatherapy
8. Homeopathy
9. Chinese Medicine
10. Ayurvedic Medicine
11. Medical Measures

Not all sprains are created equal, however. In mild sprains, fewer than 25 percent of the ligament fibers tear. In moderate sprains, 25 to 75 percent of the ligament fibers tear. But if you have a severe sprain, more than three-quarters of the ligament fibers have been torn.

All sprains produce the same telltale symptoms: sudden sharp pain in the affected joint, followed by swelling. While the swelling will usually subside within a week, don't be surprised if the pain lasts a lot longer. And even after the pain goes away, you may feel so stiff that you have to limit your movements until the damaged ligament completely mends.

For a lot of pain and swelling, you will want to see your doctor—particularly if you think there might be a fracture. But if it's a mild to moderate sprain, you can treat it on your own, following a blended approach.

BEST CHOICES

Supplements

Boost healing with bromelain. An enzyme found in pineapple, bromelain has potent anti-inflammatory properties. "There's good evidence that bromelain can help treat sprains and other musculoskeletal injuries," says Alan Gaby, M.D.

Joseph Pizzorno Jr., N.D., recommends taking 450 milligrams three times a day before meals.

Exercise

Build better muscles. "Successful healing of a sprain depends on controlling inflammation plus conditioning the muscles around the injury," says Francis O'Connor, M.D., director of the primary-care sports-medicine fellowship at the Uniformed Services University of the Health Sciences in Bethesda, Maryland. By "conditioning," Dr. O'Connor means exercising your muscles in ways that stretch and strengthen them.

Herbal Medicine

Try bark with a bite. The herb willow bark contains salicin, which is a chemical forerunner of aspirin. To make willow bark tea, add about 2 teaspoons of powdered herb to 1 cup of boiling water. Simmer for 10 minutes, then strain. Allow the tea to cool before drinking it.

Get help from hawthorn. According to Dr. Pizzorno, hawthorn contains compounds that help stabilize collagen, the protein that's responsible for maintaining the integrity of ligaments and tendons. He recommends taking 2 teaspoons of standardized hawthorn tincture three times a day. You can take hawthorn for 3 to 4 weeks.

Home Remedies

At first, rely on RICE. RICE stands for rest, ice, compression, and elevation. It's standard first-aid for sprains, says Steven Subotnick, D.P.M., a sports-medicine specialist in San Leandro, California, and author of *Sports and Exercise Injuries*. Here are the guidelines.

◆ Rest: At the first sign of pain, stop what you're doing. Then for the next few days, use the injured joint as little as possible. As your pain subsides, slowly ease your joint back into action. For example, take slow, short walks to mobilize a sprained ankle or knee.

◆ Ice: Apply an ice pack to the injured joint for 20 minutes every few hours. The cold helps reduce swelling and inflammation.

Never apply ice directly to your skin, cautions Bryant A. Stamford, Ph.D., director of the Health Promotion and Wellness Center at the University of Louisville in Kentucky. It can actually cause frostbite. Instead, wrap the pack in a towel or lay a towel between the pack and your skin.

◆ Compression: When you're not applying an ice pack, wrap the injured joint with an elastic bandage. This reduces swelling and helps minimize your discomfort as your joint heals. Keep using the bandage for several days.

◆ Elevation: To regulate the flow of blood to the site of the sprain, raise the injured joint above the level of your heart.

Later on, switch to heat. Once your swelling has begun to subside, replace the ice packs with heat. You can soak the affected joint in tolerably hot water or apply a heated gel pack.

Over-the-Counter Drugs

Pick the right pills. To relieve the pain and inflammation of a sprain, take aspirin or ibuprofen rather than acetaminophen. Acetaminophen relieves pain, too. But unlike aspirin and ibuprofen, it doesn't have anti-inflammatory action, so it won't reduce swelling.

If aspirin upsets your stomach, choose enteric-coated capsules or tablets. They are gentler on your stomach.

OTHER GOOD CHOICES

Massage

Rub yourself for relief. After the initial pain has subsided, Dr. Subotnick suggests lightly massaging the injured joint for 10 minutes twice a day.

Massage stimulates blood circulation through the affected area, which promotes healing.

Aromatherapy

Apply essential oils. To make your self-massage even more therapeutic, try using healing essential oils. Kathi Keville and Mindy Green, coauthors of *Aromatherapy: A Complete Guide to the Healing Art*, suggest making your own massage lotion or oil with the following: 6 drops of helichrysum, 4 drops of marjoram, 4 drops of birch, 3 drops of chamomile, 3 drops of lavender, 3 drops of ginger, and 2 drops of juniper. Add all of these essential oils to 2 ounces of unscented lotion or vegetable oil. Then rub the lotion or oil into your skin as part of your self-massage.

Homeopathy

Take three steps toward healing. According to Dr. Subotnick, homeopaths follow a three-step approach to treating sprains. They start with medicines that undo the trauma of a sprain. Then they switch to medicines that support the healing process. Next, they prescribe medicines that help prevent reinjury.

During the first 24 hours after a sprain, Dr. Subotnick recommends taking one of the following homeopathic medicines. Choose the one that most closely matches your symptoms.

- Arnica, if ice packs relieve your pain
- Sulfuricum acidum, if Arnica helps only a little
- Bellis, if you can't tolerate ice packs and prefer heat
- Bryonia, if you're having difficulty moving the affected joint
- Ledum, if you often have sprains
- Phytolacca, if rest and elevation help significantly
- Stellaria, if rest and motion cause pain

Take the medicine in the 6th, 12th, 15th, or 30th potency. If you don't notice any improvement in your symptoms within 2 hours, try another medicine. When you find one that helps, take it once or twice a day until your symptoms subside.

At that point, Dr. Subotnick says, you should start taking a medicine that promotes recovery. From the following list, choose the medicine that most closely matches your symptoms.

◆ Rhus toxicodendron, if the injured joint feels stiff in the morning, if massage and warmth help, and if you feel restless

◆ Ruta graveolens, if gentle movement helps, and if you worry about your injury ("Will I ever get better?")

◆ Phytolacca, if rest continues to feel better than motion

◆ Bryonia, if your swelling is slow to subside and it feels better with continued compression

Take the medicine in the 6th, 12th, 30th, or 200th potency once a day for 3 or 4 days. After that, begin taking Calcarea phosphorica in the 12th or 30th potency twice a day for 2 weeks. Calc phosphorica can help protect your joint against reinjury.

Chinese Medicine

Stop Blood from stagnating. "Here's a case where Chinese medicine advises doing the opposite of what Western medicine advocates," says Efrem Korngold, O.M.D., L.Ac. "In Western medicine, you're told to ice the injury. But the Chinese alternate ice and heat—the ice to prevent swelling, the heat to stimulate Blood circulation."

In addition, Chinese physicians prescribe topical application of herbs that expel Cold, Wind, and Damp, such as clematis root, gentian root, chaenomeles fruit, and dried ginger. They may also recommend herbs that can get Blood moving, such as cinnamon twig, peppermint oil, camphor, and red pepper.

Try needle treatment. Acupuncture can stimulate healing of a sprain. Which points the acupuncturist uses depends on which joint you have injured. "If you have a sprained right knee, an acupuncturist would likely insert needles in your left knee, then burn moxa (mugwort) over the affected knee," Dr. Korngold says. This procedure, called moxibustion, is intended to draw out Cold, Wind, and Damp and stimulate circulation.

Consider bleeding and cupping. There are two other procedures that an oriental medicine doctor may use in conjunction with acupuncture to draw out external forces such as Cold, Wind, and Damp. They're called bleeding and cupping. "Chinese bleeding is much different from the bloodletting that Western medicine practiced centuries ago," Dr. Korngold says. "The Chinese use tiny pinpricks, so actual blood loss is negligible."

Cupping involves burning alcohol-soaked cotton in small jars. When the fire dies out, the practitioner places the jar mouth-down over the affected area. The fire reduces the air pressure in the jar, so when the jar is placed against your skin, your skin gets sucked up inside. This is believed to draw out Cold, Wind, and Damp. If performed by a qualified oriental medicine doctor, both bleeding and cupping are considered safe and useful.

Ayurvedic Medicine

Make a turmeric paste. The spice turmeric has potent anti-inflammatory properties. For this reason, it's an effective topical treatment for sprains, says Vasant Lad, B.A.M.S., M.A.Sc., director of the Ayurvedic Institute in Albuquerque, New Mexico.

He suggests combining one part salt and two parts turmeric with enough water to create a paste. Apply the paste to the affected joint and cover with a cloth. Leave on the paste for 20 minutes to an hour, then rinse it off. Repeat once a day until your joint feels better.

Turmeric can stain fabric as well as your skin. During treatment, use an old cloth that you won't mind discarding. To protect your clothing, make sure that the cloth fully covers the paste. But don't worry about the discoloration of your skin. Once you stop the treatment, your skin color should return to normal within 2 weeks, Dr. Lad says.

MEDICAL MEASURES

Until recently, doctors often used splints or casts to immobilize moderate to severe sprains. But studies have shown that muscles around the torn ligament get weakened if the joint is immobilized for a long time.

If your doctor wants you to wear a splint or cast, ask for how long. Ideally, your joint should be immobilized for only a few days, until the pain and swelling begin to subside, says John Connolly, M.D., clinical professor of orthopedic surgery and rehabilitation at the University of Miami School of Medicine. Then you should begin doing gentle exercises, with a goal of getting the joint into better shape within a week or so.

If you have a really bad sprain, your doctor may recommend surgery to repair the torn ligament. Or you may need physical therapy to strengthen the muscles around the ligament.

If you've experienced multiple foot, ankle, or knee sprains in your lifetime, consider consulting a podiatrist. You may have a foot abnormality that can be corrected with custom-made shoe inserts, called orthotics.

RED FLAGS

If your joint pain is accompanied by fever, chills, or night sweats, or if there's a break in your skin near the affected joint, see your doctor right away. You may have an infection. Also see your doctor immediately if you have swelling but don't recall injuring yourself.

Stress

At some point in life, everyone faces a personal crisis that creates over-whelming stress. For a while, you feel as though your world has fallen apart. But eventually, you learn to cope.

But job loss and deaths in the family usually don't happen that frequently. Other stressors can be just as bad. In fact, it's the day-to-day hassles—the flat tires, the bounced checks, the last-minute projects at work—that repeatedly push your body's panic button. The result: chronic stress.

Stress mobilizes your body's fight-or-flight reflex, which prepares you to cope with threatening situations, according to psychologist Georgia Witkin, Ph.D., director of the stress program at Mount Sinai Medical Center in New York City. In emergencies, the fight-or-flight reflex has clear value. It floods your bloodstream with stress hormones that enable you to defend yourself or run from danger. These stress hormones, notably cortisol, increase respiration and heart rate, elevate blood pressure, raise blood sugar level, and slow digestion (because digestion is not a priority in emergencies).

When your body remains in this red-alert stage, which is what happens in chronic stress,

SIMPLE SOLUTIONS
1. Walking
2. Tai Chi and Qigong
3. Yoga
4. Relaxation Therapies
5. Meditation
6. Visualization
7. Massage
8. Aromatherapy
9. Music Therapy
10. Social Support
11. Herbal Medicine
12. Homeopathy
13. Chinese Medicine
14. Naturopathy
15. Home Remedies
16. Nutrition
17. Supplements
18. Medical Measures

it can lead to a host of physical and psychological symptoms: diarrhea, constipation, an irritable bowel, nausea, heartburn, headache, neck and shoulder pain, chronic fatigue, cold hands and feet, irritability, and anxiety attacks. It also contributes to what Dr. Witkin calls the Four Ds: disorganization, decision-making difficulties, depression, and dependency fantasies (wishing to be rescued by someone who makes everything all better).

How can you keep stress from overwhelming you? "It all comes down to regaining control—or at least partial control—over your stressors," says Paul J. Rosch, M.D., president of the American Institute of Stress in Yonkers, New York. "Reasserting some control is the basic key to coping."

Each of us experiences stress individually, so each of us must come up with our own unique coping strategies. The good news is that there are dozens to choose from. And they work.

BEST CHOICES

Walking

Put one foot in front of the other. An Australian study showed that brisk walking relieves stress as well as meditation or tai chi. When you walk, you deepen your breathing, lower your blood pressure, and stretch your arms and legs. No wonder it's the nation's most popular form of exercise.

Tai Chi and Qigong

Meditate while moving. Tai chi reduces levels of the stress hormone cortisol. Except for the fact that you meditate sitting down and do tai chi exercises standing, the two are quite similar, which is why tai chi is often described as a "moving meditation."

Bend your body, boost your mood. Qigong exercises are more subtle than tai chi and involve less motion. But Korean researchers found that qigong significantly increases levels of beta-endorphins, your body's own mood-elevating, stress-relieving compounds.

Yoga

Practice peaceful postures. In an Indian study, 40 physical education teachers, who were already in excellent shape, enrolled in a 3-month yoga class. Afterward, they breathed more deeply, had lower blood pressures, and were less likely to experience jumps in heart rate when exposed to emotional stressors. "Yoga can be a powerful tool for coping with stress," says Mary Pullig Schatz, M.D., author of *Back Care Basics*.

Stretch into relaxation. Yoga postures involve slow, gentle stretching. But even without the discipline of a yoga class, stretching is a quick, easy way to relieve stress. Louanne Cole-Weston, Ph.D., a sex and marital therapist in Sacramento, California, recommends this quick stretch: While standing and breathing deeply, rise to your tiptoes. Reach as high as you can over your head. Slowly move your arms in big circles, lowering your heels to the floor and rising again with each arm circle. Repeat five times.

Relaxation Therapies

Inhale, exhale. Inhale, exhale. Deep breathing is fundamental to meditation, yoga, sleep, sex, aerobic exercise—just about everything that's deeply relaxing, says Robert K. Cooper, Ph.D., author of *Health and Fitness Excellence*. But if you don't have the time to meditate or take a nap, a few deep breaths at the first sign of trouble can help nip your stress in the bud.

When you breathe deeply from your diaphragm, your blood becomes well-oxygenated without straining your heart. Also, your mind and body relax.

Meditation

Mellow out with a mantra. Dozens of studies have shown that meditation—sitting quietly for 20 minutes once or twice a day and repeating a word or phrase, your mantra—helps relieve stress.

Focus on mindfulness. "Mindfulness involves keeping your attention focused on the present moment without judging it as good or bad, happy or sad," says David S. Sobel, M.D., director of patient education and health promotion for Kaiser Permanente Northern California, a health maintenance organization. "You simply observe what's going on around you and strive to experience it deeply and accept it."

Mindfulness offers many of the same benefits as formal meditation. Here's a quick mindfulness exercise: Pick up a pencil. Notice its shape, color, weight, and feel. Experience how it feels to hold the pencil and write with it.

Visualization

Contemplate calmness. When stress gets the best of you, take a minute or two to practice the following visualization exercise, advises Gerald N. Epstein, M.D., director of the Academy of Integrative Medicine and Mental Imagery in New York City. Begin by closing your eyes and breathing deeply. Imagine a relaxing scene: a walk in the woods, a hug from your honey, a walk on the beach with your dog. Focus on the details—the sights, sounds, smells, the wind in your hair.

Say a little prayer. Several studies have shown that compared with those who profess no religious faith, religious people are calmer and healthier. Dr. Sobel explains that praying is a form of visualization, a meditation that can feel quite relaxing.

Massage

Manipulate your muscles. According to studies at the Laboratory of Clinical Neurophysiology at Rogaland Central Hospital in Stavanger, Norway, massage increases blood levels of endorphins, your body's own mood-elevating, stress-relieving compounds. Ask your spouse or a friend for a back or neck rub. Or take off your shoes and rub your feet vigorously on the carpet.

Aromatherapy

Formulate a fragrant fix. To relieve stress, Kathy Keville and Mindy Green, coauthors of *Aromatherapy: A Complete Guide to the Healing Art*, recommend oils of anise, basil, bay, chamomile, eucalyptus, lavender, peppermint, rose, and thyme. Here's a handy way to use them: Place a few pieces of rock salt in a small vial. Add a few drops of the oil of your choice. The salt absorbs the oil, so the oil doesn't splash out when you open the vial. Whenever you feel stressed, uncap the vial and inhale deeply.

Music Therapy

Temper stress with tunes. Keep a radio or tape player in your kitchen or office, Dr. Sobel suggests. Listen to music in your car. Get headphones if you commute by bus or train. Listen to whatever relaxes you. If you need suggestions, try "Air for the G-String" by Bach, "Pastoral Symphony" by Beethoven, "Nocturne in G" by Chopin, "Water Music" by Handel, the soundtrack to "Chariots of Fire," or "Autumn" or "December" by jazz pianist George Winston.

Listen to a relaxation tape. These tapes combine soothing music with stress-relieving visualizations and affirmations. "I've found that combining those elements is especially effective," says Martin L. Rossman, M.D. He has produced many stress-relieving relaxation tapes. For a free catalog, write to the Academy of Guided Imagery at P. O. Box 2070, Mill Valley, CA 94942-2070.

Social Support

Call and connect. Social ties are an excellent way to relieve stress, Dr. Cooper says. "Self-absorption leads to loss of perspective and stress," he notes. "Reaching out to others—spouse, family, friends, pets, plants, anything alive—helps you gain perspective and change how you think about your problems, which helps relieve your stress."

Pen a note to a friend. Writing provides perspective. Writing to a friend combines that with social support, another good stress reliever, Dr. Cooper says.

Love your pet. Psychologist Karen Allen, Ph.D., a research scientist in the department of medicine at the University of Buffalo, studied 100 women who lived alone. Half of the women had dogs, while the rest didn't. Repeated blood pressure tests showed that the pet owners' readings were lower. The findings of this study are consistent with other research showing that pets help reduce stress. Of course, pets aren't for everyone. But if you love animals, a pet can help keep you calm.

Volunteer somewhere. There's nothing like helping the less fortunate to show you very clearly how lucky you are—despite all of the stress in your life. "That's the selfish reason for being altruistic," Dr. Sobel says. "Volunteering helps you count your blessings."

Learn to say no. Although companionship is a powerful stress reliever, problematic relationships can cause tremendous stress. "It's simply not possible to please everyone all the time," Dr. Rosch says. Trying to be perfect is a one-way ticket to serious stress. Be clear on your limits and enforce them. "No one will respect you until you respect your own limits," he adds.

Delegate something. Okay, so your spouse refuses to split the housework 50-50. But he's willing to make the bed in the morning and wash the dishes after dinner. "That's progress," says Allen Elkin, Ph.D., director of the Stress Management and Counseling Center in New York City. "Instead of fretting over all the things he won't do, take heart from what he does."

Herbal Medicine

Calm with chamomile. According to James A. Duke, Ph.D., chamomile tea is a traditional remedy for jangled nerves. To make the tea, add 2 to 3 heaping teaspoons of chamomile flowers to 1 cup of boiled water. Steep until cool, then strain. Drink up to three cupfuls a day.

Adopt the adaptogens. Scientists use the word *adaptogen* to describe what traditional herbalists called tonics, according to Varro Tyler, Ph.D., Sc.D., distinguished professor emeritus of pharmacognosy (natural pharmacy) at Purdue University in West Lafayette, Indiana. Adaptogenic herbs increase your body's resistance to physical and emotional stress.

Dr. Tyler recommends adding ½ teaspoon of ginseng tincture to juice or tea once or twice a day or taking one or two 250-milligram capsules a day.

Don't overlook other calming herbs. For stress and anxiety, Dr. Duke also recommends catnip, passionflower and skullcap. You can make a tea from any of these herbs by adding 1 teaspoon of herb to 1 cup of boiled water. Steep for 10 minutes, strain, and drink, or follow package directions.

Homeopathy

Manage with a microdose. For stress relief, homeopath Dana Ullman recommends Argentum nitricum, Gelsemium, or Lycopodium. To find out which of these medicines best suits your symptoms, consult a homeopath.

Chinese Medicine

Steel your qi. Practitioners of Chinese medicine view stress as a weakness of qi, or life energy, according to Efrem Korngold, O.M.D., L.Ac. They treat stress with many different herbs, depending on a person's particular problem and constitution. Dr. Korngold often prescribes astragalus root, ginseng, gardenia fruit, jujube seed, atractylodes, schisandra fruit, eleutherococcus, poria fungus, and amber.

Relieve stress on the spot. According to Dr. Korngold, acupuncture can strengthen qi and reharmonize the Kidney, Spleen, and Lung. If you'd like to try acupuncture, you need to consult a professional acupuncturist. If you'd prefer a do-it-yourself approach, consider acupressure. Apply steady, penetrating finger pressure for 3 minutes to each of the following points.

◆ Triple Warmer 15, located on your back, ½ inch down from the crest of your shoulder, midway between the base of your neck and your shoulder joint

◆ Bladder 10, located slightly below the base of your skull, ½ inch from your spine

◆ Governing Vessel 24, located between your eyebrows, where the bridge of your nose meets your forehead

Putting Your Problems in Perspective

Stress does its physical and emotional damage only when you begin to feel overwhelmed. How can you keep from losing it? "One quick, effective way is to change the way you think about your stressors," says Allen Elkin, Ph.D., director of the Stress Management and Counseling Center in New York City. It all comes down to gaining perspective. Here's what to do.

Stop thinking that every problem is a disaster. Unless someone dies or your house burns down or you get fired out of the blue, most of life's challenges are not disasters. "But thinking that they are causes stress," says David S. Sobel, M.D., director of patient education and health promotion for Kaiser Permanente Northern California, a health maintenance organization. "By the same token, training yourself to think that stressors are manageable helps make them so."

Use a 1-to-10 scale. If you have trouble thinking that your stressors are manageable, Dr. Elkin suggests rating them on a 1-to-10 scale, with 10 being a true catastrophe and 1 being a minor hassle. "You'll find that most problems fall somewhere in the 2 to 5 range," he says.

◆ Pericardium 3, located on your inner arm, low on the inside of the crease of your elbow joint

Naturopathy

Soak away tension. Since the early nineteenth century, health spas all over the United States and Europe have served as welcome retreats for the weary, depressed, and stressed. "After a long, hard, stressful day, few things are as relaxing as a hot bath or a soak in a hot tub," says Anne Simons, M.D.

Home Remedies

Laugh at your stress. Embrace humor, Dr. Sobel urges. Keep a joke book within arm's reach. When stress strikes, open it to a random page and read.

Try an affirmation. Affirmations are short, clear, positive statements that focus on your coping abilities. "They're a good way to silence the carping self-critical voice we all carry with us that adds to our stress," Dr. Elkin says. The next time stress strikes, repeat the following phrase 10 times: "I feel calm. I can handle this."

Ask yourself a question. The moment you begin to feel stressed, Dr. Elkin suggests asking yourself what's really bothering you. "If you feel stressed and don't know why, you're powerless to change things," he explains. "But once you're clear about the problem, you can assert some control."

Forgive yourself. Most people are much harder on themselves than they are on others. Be your own best friend. Comfort yourself as you would a friend with problems.

Face your foibles. Certain silly little things really irritate each of us: hair on the bathroom soap, lights left on in an empty room, someone bringing you Pepsi when you specifically asked for Diet Coke. Assess your foibles, Dr. Elkin advises. Accept them. Try to laugh at them.

For more ways to incorporate humor into your life, contact the Humor Project, 480 Broadway, Suite 210, Saratoga, NY 12866-2288.

Set aside minor stressors. Some stressors—a ringing smoke alarm or an overflowing toilet—demand immediate attention. But many minor stressors—bills, phone calls, a broken toaster—can be dealt with another time. "File your minor stressors away in a little mental compartment," Dr. Rosch suggests. "Then deal with them when you decide the time is right. Don't let them take control of you."

Look forward to something. When you're in the midst of a stressful situation, think of something pleasurable that lies ahead. "Looking forward to something provides calming perspective," Dr. Elkin says.

Plan something. Of course, in order to look forward to future pleasures, you have to make plans. "Buy concert tickets," Dr. Elkin suggests. "Schedule a weekend getaway. Make a restaurant reservation or an appointment for a massage or hot tub."

Tend a garden. For many people, connections with the natural world are calming. "My 6-acre herb garden is my major stress reliever," Dr. Duke says. But even if you don't have land for a garden, you can reap similar benefits by caring for houseplants. "Take some potted plants to work," he suggests.

OTHER GOOD CHOICES

Nutrition

Crack open some crackers. High-carbohydrate foods—crackers, a bagel, pasta salad—stimulate the release of brain chemicals that promote relaxation, Dr. Cooper says.

Pass the potassium. Chronic stress exhausts—and can actually shrink—the adrenal glands, which help control your mood, blood pressure, anxiety reactions, and cholesterol and blood sugar levels, according to Joseph Pizzorno Jr., N.D. A key nutrient for healthy, resilient adrenal glands is potassium. To help relieve stress, he recommends eating foods rich in this mineral, including avocados, potatoes, lima beans, salmon, chicken, bananas, tomatoes, and dried apricots.

Switch to decaf. If your fuse is short, Dr. Duke suggests replacing regular coffee with decaf. "You'll probably notice that you feel calmer and less stressed," he says. But don't quit caffeinated coffee all at once, he cautions, or you may experience several days of caffeine-withdrawal headache.

Supplements

Manage your mood with a multi. Registered dietitian Elizabeth Somer, R.D., author of *Age-Proof Your Body*, recommends a daily multivitamin/mineral supplement. Make sure that your multi supplies the B vitamins, vitamins C and E, calcium, magnesium, chromium, copper, iron, manganese, molybdenum, selenium, and zinc. "But avoid so-called stress formulas," she cautions. "They often contain large amounts of randomly formulated nutrients."

Home Remedies

Use distractions. Esther M. Orioli, president of Essi Systems, a San Francisco company that organizes stress-management programs for major corporations, does crossword puzzles when she's stuck in traffic. "They focus my mind and take me emotionally away from the stress of gridlock," she says.

Dr. Sobel sometimes makes a paper airplane and sails it across the room or wads up a piece of paper and uses a wastebasket as a basketball hoop.

"Use your imagination," Orioli says. "It's something you control, and feeling in control is the basis of stress management."

MEDICAL MEASURES

For overwhelming or unrelenting stress, many doctors prescribe tranquilizers—notably the benzodiazepines, including diazepam (Valium) and alprazolam (Xanax). These drugs can provide short-term relief until you get back on your feet, but all have side effects.

Stroke

More than 300 years ago, physicians noticed that some people—almost always the elderly—suddenly keeled over dead or paralyzed, often after complaining of headaches, dizziness, or weakness. These attacks seemed to come out of the blue, like a stroke of bad luck. So they named the condition stroke.

Stroke is the nation's third leading cause of death, after heart disease and cancer. About 700,000 Americans suffer strokes each year, and almost 160,000 die from them, according to the American Heart Association.

With statistics like these, you'd think people would be able to recite the warning signs of stroke as easily as the lyrics of "Jingle Bells." But unfortunately, few can. For a leading cause of death, stroke is a tragically well-kept secret. Many people don't even know the six key warning signs: dizziness, numbness, weakness on one side, slurred speech, vision problems, and severe headache.

There are two main types of stroke: is-

SIMPLE SOLUTIONS
1. Nutrition
2. Supplements
3. Exercise
4. Relaxation Therapies
5. Music Therapy
6. Social Support
7. Herbal Medicine
8. Home Remedies
9. Chinese Medicine
10. Medical Measures

chemic, caused by blocked blood flow through part of the brain, and hemorrhagic, caused by a burst blood vessel that bleeds into your brain. Ischemic stroke accounts for 75 percent of all strokes.

Ischemic strokes are virtually identical to heart attacks, except that they happen in your brain instead of your heart. These strokes begin with tiny injuries to brain arteries caused by high blood pressure, smoking, or a high-fat, high-cholesterol diet. Over time, these injured areas get covered with cholesterol-rich deposits called plaques that narrow the injured arteries.

Sometimes a plaque ruptures, causing a blood clot in the artery and cutting off the blood supply to part of your brain. That's an ischemic stroke. In fact, heart attacks and ischemic strokes are so similar that the American Heart Association now calls them brain attacks.

Some time before you have a stroke, you experience one or more mini-strokes (transient ischemic attacks, or TIAs). During a TIA, there's a temporary blockage of blood flow in your brain. But then the blockage dissolves on its own, and blood flow returns to normal. You seem to recover completely. The average TIA lasts about a minute.

Ischemic strokes have many of the same risk factors as heart attacks. Anything you can do to reduce these risk factors is likely to reduce your risk of stroke, too.

BEST CHOICES

Nutrition

Make do without meat. If you eat meat every day, you may double your stroke risk, according to Yale neurologist John Lynch, M.D. For 10 years, Dr. Lynch tracked 6,500 stroke-free men between ages 57 and 67. In that time, 12 percent of the men who ate meat daily had strokes. But among those who ate meat only one to three times a month, just 5.4 percent experienced strokes.

Eat copious quantities of produce. A high-fat, high-cholesterol diet increases stroke risk by contributing to the formation of free radicals. These unstable oxygen molecules damage the arteries in your brain. Fortunately, a great deal of this damage can be prevented by special nutrients called antioxidants, found in abundance in fruits and vegetables. One British study found that those who eat the most fruit experience 32 percent fewer strokes.

A diet high in antioxidants helps prevent hemorrhagic as well as ischemic stroke, according to Alan Gaby, M.D. "Vitamin C and the flavonoids usually found with vitamin C in foods help maintain blood vessel integrity," he explains. "This reduces the likelihood of bleeding in the brain."

Boost your intake of Bs. In addition to being rich in antioxidants, fruits and vegetables contain generous supplies of vitamin B_6 and folic acid. These B vitamins reduce levels of homocysteine, a recently identified risk factor for stroke.

For vitamin B_6, clinical nutritionist Shari Lieberman, Ph.D., recommends spinach, carrots, peas, walnuts, sunflower seeds, wheat germ, fish (especially salmon and herring), chicken, and eggs. Foods rich in folic acid include spinach and other dark green leafy vegetables, broccoli, asparagus, and whole wheat.

Feast on fish. Dutch researchers who have tracked the health, diet, and lifestyles of people in Zutphen, the Netherlands, for many years have found that those who eat fish regularly have a lower rate of stroke than those who don't. Cold-water fish such as salmon, mackerel, and herring are the richest sources of beneficial omega-3 fatty acids, but most other fish and seafood contain some as well.

Munch a few walnuts. Besides being delicious, walnuts contain an oil rich in alpha-linolenic acid, an essential fatty acid similar to the health-enhancing omega-3 fatty acids found in fish. Alpha-linolenic and omega-3 fatty acids help prevent the internal blood clots that trigger stroke. You can also obtain alpha-linolenic acid from canola and soybean oils.

Pounce on potassium. Dietary potassium helps prevent high blood pressure, and researchers have found that it might help prevent stroke. Good food sources of potassium include fruits, vegetables, beans, whole grains, poultry, and fish. "Basically, the higher your blood potassium level, the lower your risk of stroke," Dr. Gaby says.

Supplements

Buy your Bs in a bottle. If you're concerned that your diet might not provide enough vitamin B_6 and folic acid to prevent stroke, Dr. Lieberman suggests taking supplements of both nutrients. Aim for 300 milligrams of B_6 and 800 micrograms of folic acid a day. Vitamin B_6 doses this high, however, should only be taken under medical supervision.

Add E for extra protection. "Several large population studies have demonstrated that blood levels of vitamin E may be better predictors of future stroke than total cholesterol levels," says Joseph Pizzorno Jr., N.D. Vitamin E speeds the breakdown of "bad" low-density lipoprotein (LDL) cholesterol while simultaneously increasing levels of "good" high-density lipoprotein (HDL) cholesterol.

Vitamin E is a potent antioxidant that appears to reduce the likelihood of the internal blood clots that trigger ischemic stroke. Unfortunately, the vitamin may increase your risk of hemorrhagic stroke. If you're thinking about taking supplements, check with your doctor first.

Exercise

To stop strokes, sweat. Chances are, you know that exercise helps prevent heart attack. But you may not realize the value of exercise for stroke prevention. Much research shows that physical activity helps prevent ischemic stroke. In one study, for instance, researchers found that people who engaged in moderate to high levels of exercise had less than half the stroke risk of people who engaged in low levels of exercise. Beneficial physical activities include walking, gardening, dancing, bowling—just about anything that gets your body moving.

Relaxation Therapies

Manage your anger. According to research by Susan A. Everson, Ph.D., of the University of Michigan School of Public Health in Ann Arbor, angry outbursts double your stroke risk. She recommends identifying your anger triggers and working to stay calm so that you don't lose your temper and send your blood pressure soaring. She suggests deep breathing, counting to 10, and walking away from potentially anger-provoking situations.

Music Therapy

Strike up the band. Many stroke survivors become depressed, which makes them less willing to work at rehabilitation. Music improves stroke rehabilitation because it has an antidepressant effect.

At Woodend Hospital in Aberdeen, Scotland, music therapist Heather Purdie divided 40 stroke survivors into two groups. One group received standard care, while the other received 40 minutes of music therapy a day. After 12 weeks, the people in the music-therapy group were less depressed, less anxious, and more motivated to participate in rehabilitation.

Social Support

Recruit a team of cheerleaders. Duke University researchers studied 46 people who had been hospitalized for strokes. Eight had little emotional support, 24 had a moderate amount, and 14 had a great deal. The researchers correlated the stroke survivors' social support with their recovery after 6 months. Those with the most support recovered much more quickly and fully.

Count on your spouse. Close relationships also help reduce risk of stroke. In a risk-factor-reduction program at the London School of Hygiene and Tropical Medicine in London, Stephen D. M. Pyke, M.D., worked with both individuals and couples. The people who participated as couples were significantly more successful at reducing their blood pressures and cholesterol levels and at quitting smoking.

Herbal Medicine

Boost blood flow with ginkgo. European physicians often prescribe an extract of ginkgo leaves for stroke survivors because of studies showing that it improves blood flow through the brain. "I consider ginkgo preventive for stroke," says Alan P. Brauer, M.D. "In addition to its effectiveness, it's nontoxic." He recommends 100 to 200 milligrams a day. If you are regularly taking any type of blood-thinning medication, including aspirin, seek medical advice before taking ginkgo.

Prevent clots with garlic. Garlic helps prevent ischemic stroke in three ways: It reduces blood pressure, it lowers cholesterol levels, and it's an anticoagulant. "If I were at risk for ischemic stroke, I'd increase my use of garlic in cooking," says James A. Duke, Ph.D. "I'd also take garlic capsules." Onions, scallions, leeks, chives, and shallots have similar benefits.

Home Remedies

Know your numbers. Because high blood pressure and high cholesterol greatly increase stroke risk, the National Stroke Association recommends having both checked at least once a year. Lowering your blood pressure to normal reduces your stroke risk about 40 percent, according to Roger E. Kelley, M.D., chairperson of neurology at Louisiana State University School of Medicine in Shreveport.

In addition, cutting your cholesterol by 25 percent lowers your stroke risk by 29 percent, according to an analysis of 16 studies by researchers at Brigham and Women's Hospital in Boston. "If you bring your blood pressure and cholesterol to recommended levels, you greatly reduce your risk of stroke and heart disease," Dr. Pizzorno says.

Get test for atrial fibrillation. This condition—which can be detected during a check-up is treatable with medication. Atrial fibrillation increases your risk of the internal blood clots involved in stroke.

Join the nonsmokers. Researchers at the University of Birmingham in England compared 125 men and women who had just experienced first strokes with 198 similar people who hadn't. The stroke victims were much more likely to smoke (and to be overweight and not exercise).

In the United States, every surgeon general since 1964 has urged Americans to quit smoking. Stroke is one of the many reasons.

OTHER GOOD CHOICES

Chinese Medicine

Let your Blood flow. Practitioners of Chinese medicine attribute stroke to a chronic weakness of qi that eventually blocks the flow of Blood through the brain. "Chinese medicine has equated stroke and heart attack for centuries," says Efrem Korngold, O.M.D., L.Ac. "Western medicine has come to this view only recently."

To treat stroke, Dr. Korngold prescribes herbs that open the blood vessels and promote the flow of Blood. These include hawthorn, frankincense, myrrh, santalum wood, aristolochia root, and borneol crystals.

Make an appointment with an acupuncturist. Both the United Nations World Health Organization and the National Institutes of Health endorse acupuncture as a treatment for stroke-related disabilities. Successful acupuncture studies with stroke patients have been conducted in Norway and Sweden, with promising results. If you're interested in trying acupuncture, consult a professional acupuncturist.

MEDICAL MEASURES

If your doctor recommends taking an anticoagulant to prevent stroke, ask whether you can try aspirin. Constance Johnson, M.D., professor of neurology at Johns Hopkins University School of Medicine, calls aspirin the best-choice anticoagulant. She prefers it over prescription drugs because it's almost as effective, yet it is much cheaper and causes fewer side effects. Many studies have shown that taking regular low-dose aspirin helps prevent stroke.

Instead of aspirin, your doctor might prescribe other anticoagulants such as dipyridamole (Persantine), ticlopidine (Ticlid), or warfarin (Coumadin).

If a doctor administers a clot-dissolving drug within 3 hours of an ischemic stroke, normal blood flow can often be restored, and the risk of death or permanent disability drops by about 30 percent. There are also brain-saving drugs that reduce the number of brain cells killed by the stroke and help minimize disability.

RED FLAGS

To benefit from clot-dissolving and brain-saving drugs, you have to be treated quickly—within a few hours. That's why it's so important to recognize the warning signs of stroke. Here's what the American Heart Association says to watch out for.

◆ Sudden weakness or numbness in the face or in an arm or leg on one side of the body

◆ Sudden dimness or loss of vision, particularly in one eye

◆ Sudden loss of the ability to speak, or slurring of words, or an inability to understand speech

◆ Sudden severe headaches for no apparent reason

◆ Unexplained dizziness, balance problems, or sudden falls

The more of these symptoms a person has, the greater the likelihood of a stroke or—if the symptoms appear only briefly—a TIA.

If you or someone you know exhibits any of these signs, don't delay. Call your local emergency number or get the person to an emergency room as quickly as possible.

Tendinitis and Bursitis

When you do something over and over again, you expect your body to get used to it. You don't expect it to rebel.

But that's more or less what happens when you develop tendinitis or bursitis. By performing some repetitive motion—swatting tennis balls, weeding your garden, or painting the rooms of your home—you can irritate and inflame tendons or small fluid-filled sacs called bursae. And that hurts.

Medically, tendinitis and bursitis are two distinct conditions. But they affect the same body parts, and they are treated in very similar ways.

Both involve inflammation. That's your body's natural response to an injury. When you see the redness and swelling characteristic of inflammation, you know that your immune system is working hard to help you heal. But severe or prolonged inflammation can do more harm than good. In the case of tendinitis or bursitis, it causes sharp, achy, often burning pain in the affected body part. Here's how each condition develops.

SIMPLE SOLUTIONS
1. Exercise
2. Herbal Medicine
3. Home Remedies
4. Over-the-Counter Drugs
5. Massage
6. Aromatherapy
7. Homeopathy
8. Chinese Medicine
9. Medical Measures

Tendinitis. Tendons are the fibrous, elastic bands that connect your muscles to your bones. If a tendon somehow becomes injured, it can partially tear. And that causes inflammation and pain.

You develop tendinitis not because your tendons are weak or abnormal but because the muscles that support them are out of shape. When your muscles can't handle their workload, your tendons become stressed. And that makes them vulnerable to tearing.

Bursitis. As your tendons slide across bone, they are lubricated by your bursae. Your bursae protect your tendons from damage. If you repeatedly move a body part in a certain way, your bursae have to keep relubricating the tendons in that area. Over time, this can cause the bursae to become inflamed. That's bursitis. Along with the inflammation, you can count on pain. And you may find that you can't move the joint as much as you could in the past.

The best way to avoid tendinitis and bursitis is to get in shape. The stronger your muscles, the lower your risk of injuring a tendon or bursa. Be sure to include some sort of resistance training in your exercise routine. Or consider joining a health club, where you can combine aerobic exercise with resistance training.

If you already have tendinitis or bursitis, you may be able to relieve your pain and speed your recovery with a combination of natural remedies, alternative remedies, and over-the-counter drugs. (Many of these remedies also work for sprains.) Here's what works, according to the experts.

BEST CHOICES

Exercise

Change your ways. To prevent a repeat episode of tendinitis or bursitis, you'll need to pinpoint the activity that first caused problems. Then change the way you perform that activity. You may want to consult with a personal trainer, physical therapist, or sports-medicine physician, who can help you adjust your form and technique so that you're not overusing the joint that's in trouble.

Gradually add intensity. Tendinitis and bursitis often set in when you suddenly increase the intensity of your workout—say, extending your daily walks from 1 mile to 5 miles or playing tennis for 2 hours instead of ½ hour. Make small, gradual changes as you move toward a higher level of activity.

Herbal Medicine

Bet on willow bark. Drinking willow bark tea may help relieve the pain of tendinitis and bursitis, says James A. Duke, Ph.D. To make the tea, simmer about 2 teaspoons of powdered bark in 1 cup of boiling water for 10 minutes. Then strain and allow to cool. Drink two or three cupfuls of tea a day.

Feel better with bromelain. An enzyme found in pineapple, bromelain has anti-inflammatory properties. Research has shown that it can help heal musculoskeletal injuries, including tendinitis and bursitis, says Alan Gaby, M.D.

If you want to try bromelain yourself, Joseph Pizzorno Jr., N.D., recommends taking 450 milligrams of the enzyme before each meal. Or you can simply eat lots of pineapple, as Dr. Duke does when he's nursing an injury.

Heal faster with hawthorn. Hawthorn contains compounds that help stabilize the protein called collagen. This protein reinforces the structure of tendons, so they heal faster and are less vulnerable to reinjury.

Until your tendinitis subsides, Dr. Pizzorno recommends taking 2 teaspoons of standardized hawthorn tincture three times a day. You can take hawthorn for 3 to 4 weeks.

Home Remedies

At first, treat your injury with RICE. RICE stands for rest, ice, compression, and elevation. These four measures are considered standard first-aid for tendinitis and bursitis, says Steven Subotnick, D.P.M., a sports-medicine specialist in San Leandro, California, and author of *Sports and Exercise Injuries*. (For a description of the RICE treatment for sprains, see page 580. The treatment for tendinitis and bursitis is the same.)

Later, add some heat. Once the swelling from bursitis or tendinitis has started to subside, you may want to switch from cold treatments to heat. Soak the injured body part in warm to tolerably hot water, use a heated gel pack, or take contrast baths.

For a contrast bath, soak the injury site first in hot water for 5 minutes, then in cold water for 30 seconds. Repeat for three to five cycles.

Over-the-Counter Drugs

Pick the right product. To relieve the pain and inflammation of tendinitis or bursitis, take aspirin or ibuprofen instead of acetaminophen. While acetaminophen can also ease pain, it has no anti-inflammatory action.

If aspirin bothers your stomach, look for enteric-coated tablets or capsules that dissolve in your intestines rather than in your stomach.

OTHER GOOD CHOICES

Massage

Stimulate your circulation. Once your pain has subsided, gently massage the injured body part for 10 minutes twice a day. This enhances blood flow through the injury site, which supports the healing process, Dr. Subotnick says.

Aromatherapy

Try a scented massage. Certain essential oils can help treat musculoskeletal injuries, including tendinitis and bursitis. Kathi Keville and Mindy Green, coauthors of *Aromatherapy: A Complete Guide to the Healing Art*, suggest making your own massage lotion or oil from a blend of essential oils: To 2 ounces of unscented skin lotion or vegetable oil, add 6 drops of helichrysum, 4 drops of marjoram, 4 drops of birch, 3 drops of chamomile, 3 drops of lavender, 3 drops of ginger, and 2 drops of juniper. Rub in the scented lotion or oil as part of your self-massage.

Homeopathy

Maximize relief with a microdose medicine. For tendinitis and bursitis, Dr. Subotnick suggests trying one of the following homeopathic medicines. Choose the one that most closely matches your symptoms.

- Arnica, if your injured body part feels achy and sore
- Sulfuricum acidum, if Arnica doesn't help within 2 hours
- Ruta graveolens, if you feel stiff and sore
- Rhus toxicodendron, if you feel better with heat treatment and motion

Take the medicine in the 6th, 12th, or 30th potency—four pellets four times a day. You can buy homeopathic medicines in many health food stores.

Chinese Medicine

Unblock Blood. To treat tendinitis and bursitis, Chinese physicians recommend alternating ice and heat treatments right from the onset of pain.

In addition, Efrem Korngold, O.M.D., L.Ac., prescribes herbs such as clematis root, gentian root, chaenomeles fruit, and dried ginger. He also prescribes herbs that "open channels" and get Blood moving, including cinnamon twig, peppermint oil, camphor, and red pepper.

Visit an acupuncturist. Research has shown acupuncture to be an effective treatment for tendinitis and bursitis. During an acupuncture session, which points are stimulated depends on which body part is injured. For example, if you have tennis elbow, your acupuncturist is likely to insert needles in the opposite elbow and burn moxa (mugwort) over the affected elbow. This technique, called moxibustion, is intended to draw out Wind, Damp, and Cold and to activate Blood, Dr. Korngold explains.

Look into cupping and bleeding. Acupuncturists sometimes use two other techniques to draw out Wind, Cold, and Damp. One, called cupping, involves burning alcohol-soaked cotton in small jars. When the flames die out, the practitioner places a jar mouth-down over the affected body part. Because the fire has reduced the air pressure in the jar, some of your skin gets sucked up inside.

The other technique, called bleeding, involves only tiny pinpricks, which draw out only a minute amount of blood. Just like acupuncture and moxibustion, cupping and bleeding should be administered only by qualified Chinese medicine doctors.

MEDICAL MEASURES

For an especially severe case of tendinitis or bursitis, your doctor may inject the inflamed area with corticosteroids and an anesthetic. This combination provides rapid relief, but the effects are only temporary. Some physicians are willing to reinject corticosteroids many times, but some research suggests that steroids weaken tendons and impede healing.

There is another treatment option for severe bursitis. To reduce swelling, your doctor may use a syringe to draw off the excess fluid in the affected bursa.

If you experience recurrent knee, ankle, or foot problems, consult a podiatrist. You may have a foot abnormality that can easily be corrected with custom shoe inserts, called orthotics.

RED FLAGS

Call your doctor if your pain persists or gets worse after 2 weeks of home care or if the affected body part appears discolored or deformed. Your doctor will probably take x-rays to rule out a fracture, then prescribe a short course of a nonsteroidal anti-inflammatory drug (NSAID). You may also be referred to a physical therapist.

Also, consult your doctor promptly if your joint pain is accompanied by fever, chills, or night sweats or is near a break in your skin. You may have an infection.

Ulcers

Simply stated, an ulcer is an open wound. Ulcers can occur inside the mouth, on the skin, or elsewhere on the body. But when people say "ulcers," they're almost always referring to sores either in the stomach (called gastric ulcers) or at the junction of the stomach and small intestine (duodenal ulcers). Collectively, these are known as peptic ulcers—*peptic* meaning digestive.

The pain associated with ulcers is caused by stomach acid, which is very caustic. "If you were to put stomach acid on your skin, you'd get a very nasty burn," says Anne Simons, M.D.

Normally, the acid doesn't burn your stomach, because the stomach cells secrete thick mucus that creates a protective barrier. The cells also produce a natural antacid that provides a chemical shield against damage.

If either of these protective mechanisms fails, the acid can easily burn your stomach cells. This is how an ulcer forms—and it also accounts for the pain that an ulcer causes.

Ulcer pain tends to be worst between meals and at night, when your stomach is empty. When your stomach is full, the acid can work on breaking down food rather than gnawing at stomach cells.

SIMPLE SOLUTIONS
1. Nutrition
2. Supplements
3. Elimination Diet
4. Visualization
5. Herbal Medicine
6. Home Remedies
7. Homeopathy
8. Chinese Medicine
9. Ayurvedic Medicine
10. Over-the-Counter Drugs
11. Medical Measures

But pain isn't the only symptom of ulcers. These sores can also produce nausea, vomiting, a bloated feeling after meals, and black, tarry, foul-smelling stools.

Ulcers were one of the first conditions attributed to stress. Doctors believed that stress stimulated the release of excess stomach acid, which in turn burned holes in the stomach's mucous lining. Then in the early 1980s, two Australian doctors proposed that most ulcers result not from stress but from bacteria called *Helicobacter pylori*. The doctors arrived at this conclusion after noticing that the majority of people with ulcers have *H. pylori* in their stomach tissue.

The bacteria are able to survive inside the stomach because, just like stomach cells, they produce their own antacid. With long, swishing tails to power their progress, the bacteria burrow through the stomach's mucous lining and into the cells underneath.

"It seems *H. pylori* must be present for ulcers to develop," says Alan P. Brauer, M.D. "But the infection by itself isn't sufficient to cause ulcers."

In other words, some other factor must create the conditions necessary for *H. pylori* to do their dirty work. Once again, the primary suspect is stress. And the stress-ulcer connection is supported by the findings of several studies, including one sponsored by the Centers for Disease Control and Prevention (CDC) in Atlanta.

If you think that you have an ulcer, but you haven't been officially diagnosed, your first step is to see your doctor. Your doctor can test you for *H. pylori* infection using what's called a urea breath test.

For *H. pylori* ulcers, the treatment of choice is a drug regimen that features antibiotics. But recently, many mainstream and alternative practitioners have begun to endorse a blended approach that uses a combination of alternative therapies, home remedies, and over-the-counter drugs to complement the prescription medications.

BEST CHOICES

Nutrition

Be a bean counter. In 1986, Harvard researchers determined that the fiber in beans was most protective, while the fiber in fruits and vegetables was moderately protective.

But how does *any* fiber prevent ulcers? It slows the rate at which the contents of your stomach empty into the duodenum on their way to your small intestine. The slower your stomach empties, the lower the concentration of stomach acid in your duodenum, the place where most ulcers develop.

Fiber not only prevents ulcers but also helps treat them, says Joseph Pizzorno Jr., N.D. When people with ulcers increase their fiber intakes, they're less likely to get ulcers again.

To increase your fiber intake, fill your plate with whole grains, beans, fruits, and vegetables. Try to get at least 25 grams of fiber a day, the Daily Value.

Add a little heat to your meals. For a long time, mainstream physicians prescribed a bland diet for people with ulcers, believing that spicy foods aggravated the condition. As it turns out, though, hot peppers may actually help heal ulcers. Capsaicin, the compound that gives hot peppers their heat, appears to be particularly beneficial.

"Capsaicin appears to work its magic by stimulating nerves in the stomach wall," say pharmacists Joe Graedon and Teresa Graedon, Ph.D., coauthors of *The People's Pharmacy* books. "This dilates blood vessels and improves blood flow to the stomach wall, which supports healing." To get capsaicin, all you have to do is eat more jalapeños and other hot peppers.

Forget milk. Doctors used to tell people with ulcers to drink lots of milk to neutralize stomach acid. Now doctors know that milk's antacid effects work only briefly, says Melvyn R. Werbach, M.D., assistant clinical professor at the University of California, Los Angeles, School of Medicine. And once those effects wear off, milk actually stimulates acid secretion. While you don't have to give up milk and milk products completely, cutting back is probably a good idea.

Avoid irritating beverages. Coffee, tea, and alcohol also increase stomach acid secretion, Dr. Werbach says.

Eat dinner early. Eating early reduces nighttime stomach acidity, which can help control ulcer pain in the wee hours. In one study, 23 people ate the same breakfast at 7:00 A.M. and the same lunch at noon. Then they ate dinner at either 6:00 or 9:00 P.M. Those who ate early produced less stomach acid during the night than those who ate late.

Supplements

Reinforce the barrier. Naturopaths believe that strengthening the stomach's mucous lining can help deter *H. pylori* from burrowing into it. Supplementation with vitamins A, C, and E and the mineral zinc can "improve stomach integrity," according to naturopath Enrico Liva, N.D., director of the Connecticut Center for Health in Middletown.

For people with ulcers, Dr. Liva recommends taking a daily multivitamin/mineral supplement. He also suggests twice-daily doses of each of the following: 25,000 international units of beta-carotene, which the body converts to vitamin A; 1,000 milligrams of buffered vitamin C; 1,000 milligrams of flaxseed oil, a source of vitamin E; and 15 milligrams of zinc. But talk to your doctor before supplementing with beta-carotene at this level. You can buy all of these supplements in health food stores and many drugstores.

Dr. Duke's Anti-Ulcer Cabbage Soup

Cabbage is rich in glutamine, a compound that helps stimulate the production of protective mucus in your stomach. "Raw cabbage juice is well-documented as having remarkable success in treating ulcers," says Alan Gaby, M.D. In one study, people with ulcers who drank about 1 quart of cabbage juice a day saw their ulcers heal in an average of 10 days.

Unfortunately, cabbage juice tastes pretty bitter. But you can treat yourself to some cabbage soup, using this recipe from James A. Duke, Ph.D.

3 cups water	Ground red pepper
2 cups shredded cabbage	Ginger
1 cup chopped celery	Black pepper
1 cup diced potatoes	Cinnamon
½ cup chopped okra	Cloves
½ cup diced onions	Licorice
½ cup chopped green peppers	

In a soup pot, place the water, cabbage, celery, potatoes, okra, onions, and green peppers. Bring to a boil over high heat. Reduce the heat, cover, and simmer until the vegetables are tender. Season to taste with the red pepper, ginger, black pepper, cinnamon, cloves, and licorice.

Elimination Diet

Cut out the ulcer aggravators. Research has shown that the same elimination diet used to identify food intolerances can also help heal ulcers. People with ulcers tend to be most sensitive to corn, chocolate, cola, sugar, and foods made with white flour. Citrus, peanuts, soy, shellfish, and dairy products have also been linked to ulcers.

An elimination diet is best followed under the supervision of a nutrition-minded doctor.

Visualization

See your ulcer healing. At the University Hospital of South Manchester in England, researchers taught a visualization technique to people with ulcers. The researchers found visualization to be "unequivocally beneficial" in relieving ulcer pain. You can try this therapy on your own by practicing the following exercise, recommended by Gerald N. Epstein, M.D., director of the Academy of Integrative Medicine and Mental Imagery in New York City.

Close your eyes. Slowly inhale and exhale three times. As you continue this slow, relaxed breathing, envision a mermaid with flowing golden hair and a sleek, silvery body and tail. She's swimming rhythmically through your digestive tract, which is calm. Sense her there. Watch her swim to any places where you feel cramping, pain, or any other symptoms. Have her touch those areas and gently massage them until they are healed and you no longer feel discomfort. See her complete her swim through your digestive tract, making sure that everything is in order. When she's done, open your eyes. Repeat this exercise three or four times a day.

Herbal Medicine

Elude pain with licorice. When researchers began analyzing licorice for its ulcer-healing compounds, they identified glycyrrhetinic acid, a potent anti-inflammatory that heals ulcers in both animals and humans.

You can buy chewable tablets of deglycyrrhizinated licorice in health food stores. Take two to four 380-milligram tablets 20 minutes before eating or between meals, advises Seattle naturopath Michael T. Murray, N.D.

Discover a new use for ginger. You may know ginger as an effective remedy for indigestion and motion sickness. But you may not realize that the herb contains 11 compounds with scientifically verified anti-ulcer properties, says James A. Duke, Ph.D.

Home Remedies

Use pain relievers prudently. Both aspirin and ibuprofen belong to the class of medications known as nonsteroidal anti-inflammatory drugs (NSAIDs). These are the most likely to trigger or aggravate ulcers. So if you have an ulcer, you shouldn't take aspirin or ibuprofen, Dr. Simons says. If you've never had an ulcer but the condition runs in your family, you'd be wise to limit your use of these medicines—or better yet, not to use them at all.

Dr. Duke's Anti-Ulcer Fruit Cocktail

Herbal medicines don't just come as teas and tinctures. All of the herbs in this recipe—and the fruits, for that matter—contain compounds that help prevent and treat ulcers, says James A. Duke, Ph.D. There are no quantities for any of the ingredients, so you can make as much or as little as you like.

Bananas
Pineapple, fresh or canned
Blueberries, fresh, frozen,
   or canned

Ground cinnamon
Ground cloves
Ground ginger
Honey (optional)

Cut the bananas and pineapple into bite-size chunks. Place them in a bowl. Add the blueberries. Season to taste with the cinnamon, cloves, ginger, and honey (if using).

Stop smoking. When you smoke, your stomach empties faster, which exposes your duodenum to high concentrations of stomach acid, Dr. Pizzorno says. Smoking also impairs the production of natural antacids in the stomach.

OTHER GOOD CHOICES

Homeopathy

Let a little medicine do a lot of good. A number of homeopathic medicines have been proven effective as ulcer treatments, according to homeopath Dana Ullman. Among the medicines he prescribes are Argentum nitricum, Arsenicum album, Hydrastis, Kali bichromicum, Kali carbonicum, Lycopodium, Mercurius, Nux vomica, Phosphorus, and Pulsatilla. To find out which of these best suits your symptoms, consult a homeopath.

Chinese Medicine

Support your Stomach and Spleen. Practitioners of Chinese medicine attribute ulcers to a weak, cold Stomach and Spleen, says Efrem Korngold, O.M.D., L.Ac. For people with ulcers, he usually prescribes the herbs coptis, which has anti-inflammatory properties, and ginger and erodia fruit, which are warming. He may also recommend a Chinese medicine called Yunnan Bai Yao.

Score points against pain. Acupuncture does such a good job of treating ulcers that it has won the endorsement of the United Nations World Health Organization. But if you prefer a self-care approach, acupressure may work just as well. Apply steady, penetrating finger pressure to each of the following points for 3 minutes.

◆ Conception Vessel 12, located halfway between the end of your breastbone and your navel on the midline of your abdomen

◆ Stomach 36, located four finger-widths below your kneecap and one finger-width toward the outside of your shinbone

◆ Pericardium 6, located in the middle of your inner wrist, 2½ finger-widths above the wrist crease

Ayurvedic Medicine

Rein in Pitta. In Ayurveda, ulcers result from an excess of Pitta dosha, explains John Douillard, D.C., a chiropractor who practices Ayurvedic medicine at the Invincible Life Spa in Boulder, Colorado. Excess Vata dosha may be a factor, too.

To treat ulcers, Dr. Douillard recommends a Pitta-pacifying diet of fresh, well-cooked vegetables and barley water tea. To make the tea, boil 2 cups of barley in 6 cups of water until only 4 cups of liquid remain. Drink three cupfuls of tea each day. Refrigerate any leftover tea and reheat as necessary.

An Ayurvedic ulcer prescription may include licorice, ginger, cloves, cinnamon, and black pepper. For dosage information, consult an Ayurvedic physician.

Over-the-Counter Drugs

Block your discomfort. The H_2 blockers—a group of pharmaceuticals that includes Tagamet, Zantac, Axid, and Pepcid—reduce stomach acid secretion. The nonprescription formulations are used primarily to treat indigestion and heartburn, but they can help relieve ulcer symptoms, too. Follow the package directions for proper dosage.

Control the acid. Antacids such as Tums and Rolaids don't cure ulcers,

Dr. Simons says. But they do help neutralize stomach acid, which can temporarily relieve ulcer pain. Follow the package directions for proper dosage.

MEDICAL MEASURES

Mainstream M.D.'s treat *H. pylori* ulcers by prescribing a combination of antibiotics; bismuth, such as Pepto-Bismol; and drugs that suppress stomach acid secretion, such as omeprazole (Prilosec).

If your doctor gives you antibiotics, take the full prescription. Don't stop just because your pain subsides. The absence of pain doesn't mean that all of the bacteria have been killed. Those that survive can continue to multiply, and eventually the pain comes back. Also, these bacteria are more likely to be resistant to antibiotics, which makes them more difficult to eliminate.

RED FLAGS

If you have an ulcer and you experience the sudden onset of intense, unrelenting abdominal pain, call your local emergency number or have someone take you to the nearest emergency room without delay. This may be a sign that the contents of your stomach are spilling into your abdominal cavity. If so, you'll need immediate surgery.

Also, see your doctor if your stools appear black, red, or bloody or if you're vomiting what looks like blood or coffee grounds. This may mean that your ulcer is bleeding.

Urinary Tract Infection

A urinary tract infection goes by many names: UTI, bladder infection, cystitis. No matter what you call it, it can make you feel miserable.

When you have a urinary tract infection, you're constantly running to the bathroom because of a persistent urge to void. Then when you go, you don't produce much urine, but you experience intense pain and burning nonetheless. Your urine may appear pinkish, a sign of blood. And you may develop a fever, along with pain in your lower abdomen.

Urinary tract infections are usually caused by the intestinal bacteria *Escherichia coli*. These bugs are necessary for digestion, but if they find their way into your bladder and grow there, you get a UTI.

How do *E. coli* travel from point A to point B? They get incorporated into your stool, and when you move your bowels, some of the bacteria remain around your anus. From there, they get transported to your urethra, usually by careless wiping or vigorous or careless sex. Then they work their way into your bladder.

SIMPLE SOLUTIONS
1. Nutrition
2. Supplements
3. Herbal Medicine
4. Home Remedies
5. Relaxation Therapies
6. Homeopathy
7. Chinese Medicine
8. Ayurvedic Medicine
9. Naturopathy
10. Medical Measures

Depending on the study, *E. coli* are responsible for 50 to 90 percent of UTIs. But several other intestinal microorganisms, including staphylococcus, can cause UTIs, too.

Both men and women get UTIs, but women are at much greater risk. A woman's urethral and anal openings are closer together than a man's, so bacteria can easily migrate from one opening to the other. Also, a woman's urethra is considerably shorter than a man's, so bacteria don't have to travel far to infect the bladder.

Anything that puts pressure on the bladder increases the likelihood of a UTI, which is why many women get the infections during pregnancy. In addition, women may become more prone to UTIs after menopause, as the urethra and bladder become more fragile.

About half of all women develop at least one UTI during their lifetimes, and millions suffer maddeningly frequent recurrent infections.

The good news is that most UTIs respond well to home treatment. Only the most persistent infections require medical intervention. Here's what the experts say can help.

BEST CHOICES

Nutrition

Restore balance with yogurt. The bacteria that cause UTIs may get out of hand because you don't have enough beneficial (probiotic) bacteria to keep them in balance. One way to increase the population is to eat yogurt containing live cultures of *Lactobacillus acidophilus* and other beneficial bacteria, says Anne Simons, M.D. Look for the words "live cultures" on yogurt labels.

Supplements

Buy bacteria in capsules. If you're not fond of yogurt, you can buy *L. acidophilus* and other beneficial bacteria in supplement form. Most of these products require refrigeration. One that doesn't is PB8, says Christiane Northrup, M.D., founder of the Women to Women health center in Yarmouth, Maine, and past president of the American Holistic Medical Association.

Fight infection with C. Vitamin C can help prevent UTIs, Dr. Northrup says. She recommends taking 1,000 to 2,000 milligrams a day. And if you tend to get UTIs after sex, you can take an additional 1,000 milligrams before intercourse and 1,000 milligrams after.

Herbal Medicine

Consider the cranberry cure. Cranberries have an age-old reputation as a treatment for urinary problems. While the berries definitely seem to help, scientists have had a hard time figuring out why. The latest theory is that cranberries prevent and treat UTIs not by killing bacteria but by stopping them from attaching to the bladder wall.

If you suffer from recurrent UTIs, Dr. Northrup recommends drinking 8 ounces of cranberry juice a day as a preventive. But be aware that commercial cranberry juice is actually "cranberry juice cocktail"—a little juice with lots of added sugar. If you don't want all that sugar, Dr. Northrup suggests taking a concentrated cranberry extract in pill form. CranActin is a popular brand. Follow the label directions for proper dosage.

Bear up better with bearberry. Bearberry is the common name of the medicinal herb uva-ursi. "Uva-ursi contains a urinary antiseptic called arbutin," says Joseph Pizzorno Jr., N.D. Arbutin is particularly effective against the *E. coli* bacteria that usually cause UTIs.

According to Dr. Pizzorno, uva-ursi seems to produce the best results when taken as a tea. Add 2 teaspoons of the herb to 1 cup of boiled water and steep for 10 minutes. Strain. Drink three cupfuls of the tea per day.

Dr. Northrup says that uva-ursi also works well when taken as a tincture. She recommends one dropperful of tincture in water three times a day.

Keep your eye on echinacea. Also known as coneflower, echinacea stimulates the immune system. "There's a great deal of research showing that the herb's immune-boosting effects help the body fight bacterial infections such as UTIs," says James A. Duke, Ph.D. He recommends taking a teaspoon of tincture three times a day, mixed into water or juice.

Feel golden with goldenseal. "Goldenseal is one of the most effective herbal antibiotics," Dr. Pizzorno says. "It's particularly effective against *E. coli* and other bacteria that cause UTIs." He recommends taking 1 to 1½ teaspoons of tincture three times a day. If you're a woman and your UTIs seem to come on after sex, Dr. Pizzorno suggests rinsing your labia and urethral opening with a solution of 2 teaspoons of goldenseal and 1 cup of water after intercourse.

Minimize discomfort with marshmallow. Naturopath Jill Stansbury, N.D., chairperson of the botanical medicine department at the National College of Naturopathic Medicine in Portland, Oregon, suggests drinking marshmallow tea at the first sign of a UTI. Marshmallow contains a soothing fiber called mucilage that relieves pain, reduces inflammation, and promotes healing of the bladder—often quite quickly. To make marshmallow tea, gently boil 1 teaspoon of chopped marshmallow root in 1 cup of water for 10 to 15 minutes. Strain out the plant material and allow the tea to cool. Drink up to three cupfuls a day.

Interstitial Cystitis: Pain That Doesn't Go Away

Interstitial cystitis causes symptoms similar to a urinary tract infection (UTI): a frequent urge to urinate, pain upon urination, nighttime urination, and sometimes blood in the urine. But unlike a UTI, interstitial cystitis is not caused by an infection, says Anne Simons, M.D. It's a chronic pain problem.

Mainstream M.D.'s treat interstitial cystitis with bladder distention (overfilling with water), oral pain relievers, and drugs delivered by catheter directly to the bladder. The following strategies may also help.

Don't badger your bladder. Caffeinated beverages, alcohol, and nicotine in cigarettes can irritate your bladder. Avoid these substances to see whether your symptoms improve, suggests Christiane Northrup, M.D., founder of the Women to Women health center in Yarmouth, Maine, and past president of the American Holistic Medical Association.

Get relief through relaxation. If you have interstitial cystitis, you may feel tense and anxious, which only aggravates your pain. Regular practice of a relaxation technique such as meditation, visualization, biofeedback, yoga, or tai chi may provide relief from your symptoms.

Seek support. The Interstitial Cystitis Association provides information and support services for women with this condition. You can write to the association at 51 Monroe Street, Suite 1402, Rockville, MD 20850-2408.

Home Remedies

Prevent infections with yogurt suppositories. Dr. Northrup suggests dipping a stiff tampon, such as the O.B. brand, in live-culture yogurt and inserting it in your vagina for a few hours. In one study, 27 women with recurrent UTIs who used *L. acidophilus* vaginal suppositories reported significantly fewer infections.

Drink lots of *agua*. At the first twinge of infection, Dr. Pizzorno says, start drinking lots of water—up to 10 glasses (8-ounce size) a day. You may be able to flush the bacteria out of your bladder before they become established enough to cause a full-blown infection.

Eliminate irritants. Some substances can irritate your urinary tract. The list includes spicy foods, caffeinated beverages, alcohol, and nicotine in cigarettes. If you're prone to UTIs and you consume any of these substances, abstain for a while and see whether you notice any change in the frequency and severity of your infections.

Go when you gotta. Studies of women with recurrent UTIs show that they tend to hold their urine for extended periods, Dr. Simons says. If you feel the urge to urinate, go. In fact, even if you don't feel the urge, go every hour or two anyway.

Wipe from front to back. When you go to the bathroom, always wipe away from your urethra. Wiping in the other direction, from back to front, moves bacteria from your anus to within striking distance of your urethra.

Be sanitary. During menstruation, change tampons or sanitary napkins often, Dr. Simons says. Blood is an excellent medium for bacterial growth.

Dress in cotton. Wear underpants made from cotton, which is less irritating than synthetic materials. Avoid leotards and other tight-fitting garments, which may help move bacteria toward the urethra.

Make love gently. Many women develop UTIs after making love unusually enthusiastically or frequently. Back when premarital sex was less common than it is today, so many new brides developed UTIs that the condition was dubbed honeymoon cystitis. "If you're prone to UTIs, make love gently and consider using a commercial lubricant," Dr. Simons says. "Vigorous sex can irritate your urethra and increase the risk of moving anal bacteria into it."

Keep it clean. Another reason why honeymoon cystitis was so common was that many newlyweds were uninformed about sexual hygiene. "Nothing that touches a woman's anal area should come in contact with her vagina," says Sacramento, California, sex and marital therapist Louanne Cole-Weston, Ph.D. "Keep track of where fingers and any sex toys have been."

Head for the bathroom afterward. "Be sure to empty your bladder after intercourse," Dr. Simons says. "Urinating helps flush out any bacteria before they have a chance to cause infection."

Consider the contraception connection. Compared with women who use other forms of birth control, those who use diaphragms are more susceptible to UTIs. For a long time, doctors believed that the diaphragm rim was to blame. When the rim presses against the urethra, it causes irritation, which increases the risk of infection. Now research suggests that the spermicide used with diaphragms plays a role in UTIs, too.

Don't stop using birth control, advises Andrew T. Weil, M.D., director of the program in integrative medicine at the University of Arizona College of Medicine in Tucson. But if you use a diaphragm, you may want to consider other contraceptive options.

OTHER GOOD CHOICES

Relaxation Therapies

For relief, relax. "Stress and tension aggravate the discomfort of a UTI and impair your immune system's ability to fight the infection," says Martin L. Rossman, M.D. "Deep relaxation shouldn't be considered a primary treatment, but it's a useful, immune-boosting adjunct." He recommends regular practice of any relaxation technique that appeals to you: deep breathing, meditation, visualization, massage, yoga, or tai chi.

Homeopathy

Ask a homeopath for help. Homeopaths recommend an array of medicines for UTIs, depending on a person's individual symptoms. Among the medicines commonly prescribed are Apis, Berberis, Cantharis, Mercurius, Nux vomica, Pulsatilla, Sarsaparilla, and Staphysagria, says homeopath Dana Ullman. To find out which of these medicines might work best for you, consult a homeopath.

Chinese Medicine

Turn down Heat. Practitioners of Chinese medicine attribute UTIs to the stagnation of qi in the Bladder. "The stagnation creates Heat, which obstructs qi and makes the urinary tract vulnerable to external attack," says Efrem Korngold, O.M.D., L.Ac.

To treat UTIs, Dr. Korngold prescribes several herbal formulas. One formula, called Qian Lie Xian Wan, contains a combination of licorice root, astragalus root, peony root, and other herbs. Another formula, Yao Zhi Gui Ling Gao, is made from a mixture of licorice, rehmannia root, lonicera flowers, and other herbs and animal parts.

Vulvadynia: When Love Hurts

The classic symptom of vulvadynia is pain—possibly severe pain—during intercourse. But women who have the condition may experience pain, burning, or stinging at other times as well. These symptoms might easily be mistaken for a urinary tract infection (UTI).

Vulvadynia is completely different from a UTI, however, says Christiane Northrup, M.D., founder of the Women to Women health center in Yarmouth, Maine, and past president of the American Holistic Medical Association. It is neither a bacterial infection nor a viral infection. Rather, it's a chronic pain problem.

There is no quick fix for this mysterious ailment. But if you have vulvadynia, the following strategies may help relieve some of your symptoms.

Eliminate oxalate. Many foods contain high levels of calcium oxalate, a chemical that gets into your urine and can irritate your vulva. High-oxalate foods to avoid include strawberries, celery, rhubarb, spinach, and chocolate. But be patient: You may be on a low-oxalate diet for 3 to 6 months before you notice any improvement.

Count on calcium citrate. Supplements of calcium citrate can help lower the levels of oxalate in your body. Dr. Northrup recommends a product called Citracal, which contains 200 milligrams of calcium and 750 milligrams of citrate per tablet. "Take two tablets an hour before meals," she advises.

Solicit support. The National Vulvadynia Association provides information and support services for women with vulvadynia. Write to the organization at P. O. Box 4491, Silver Spring, MD 20914-4491.

Make your point against pain. You may get some relief from your UTI symptoms with acupressure, says Michael Reed Gach, founder and director of the Acupressure Institute. He suggests applying steady, penetrating finger pressure for 3 minutes to each of the following points.

◆ Spleen 6, located four finger-widths above your inner anklebone on the back inner border of your shinbone

◆ Liver 8, located on your inner leg at the end of your knee crease

If your symptoms don't improve, consider consulting an acupuncturist. Sometimes professional needle stimulation helps when finger pressure doesn't.

Ayurvedic Medicine

Put out your fire. Ayurvedic physicians view UTI as a condition of excess Pitta, or fire, says David Frawley, O.M.D. To treat a UTI, he recommends an anti-Pitta approach: lots of cranberry juice, pomegranate juice, and coconut milk; no spices, alcohol, or members of the nightshade family (especially tomatoes but also potatoes and eggplant, among others).

He also prescribes Ayurvedic herbs, especially sandalwood, which he calls a natural urinary antiseptic. Other helpful herbs include coriander, marshmallow, fennel, lemongrass, gotu kola, punarnava, and shilajit.

Naturopathy

Douse discomfort with water. Heat helps relieve the discomfort of a UTI, Dr. Simons says. She suggests taking tolerably hot baths or applying a heating pad to your lower abdomen.

Or try alternating hot and cold baths, advises Tori Hudson, N.D., professor of gynecology at the National College of Naturopathic Medicine in Portland, Oregon. First, sit in a tolerably hot bath for up to 5 minutes, then sit in a basin of cold water for 30 seconds. Repeat this sequence three times, finishing with the cold water. Alternating hot and cold compresses on your pelvic area produces similar benefits, she adds.

MEDICAL MEASURES

If you see your doctor about your UTI, you'll probably be asked to produce a urine sample. If the sample contains bacteria, you'll be given an antibiotic. Be sure to take the entire prescription, even if your symptoms subside sooner, Dr. Simons says. Otherwise, some of the bacteria may linger in your urinary tract, leading to another infection that's harder to treat.

If you tend to develop vaginal yeast infections after taking antibiotics, Dr. Simons suggests asking your physician to prescribe a yeast medication—just in case.

If you're prone to recurrent UTIs, Dr. Simons recommends keeping some phenazopyridine (Pyridium) on hand. It's a urinary pain reliever that helps minimize the burning sensation that accompanies a UTI. Phenazopyridine is available by prescription only. Ask your doctor for enough to see you through several UTIs, Dr. Simons says. Just don't use it for more than 24 hours without consulting your physician to see if you need antibiotics. Also, be aware that phenazopyridine turns your urine bright orange.

RED FLAGS

Some mainstream M.D.'s prescribe sulfa antibiotics to treat UTIs. If you're African-American, you don't want to take these drugs until you've been tested for a hereditary deficiency of an enzyme called G6PD. About 10 percent of African-Americans have this deficiency and should not take sulfa drugs. If you are G6PD-deficient, your doctor can prescribe other antibiotics.

Left untreated, a UTI can move from your bladder into your kidneys, causing infection there (acute pyelonephritis). Usually, the first symptom is pain on one or both sides of your midback, where your kidneys are located. As the infection progresses, other symptoms may develop, including fever, chills, nausea and vomiting, and difficult and painful urination. If you experience any of these, see your doctor right away. A kidney infection is a potentially serious condition. It usually responds to treatment with antibiotics but often requires hospitalization.

Varicose Veins

The word *varicose* comes from the Latin *varix*, meaning "twisted." The name fits: Varicose veins certainly appear twisted as they spread across your legs. The veins also become enlarged, or dilated.

You get varicose veins when the valves in the veins near the surface of your legs stop working properly. These valves have a tough job. They must move blood all the way up your legs, against the pull of gravity, until it reaches your heart. To do this, the valves rely on your leg muscles.

As you move, your leg muscles contract, pushing blood up through your leg veins. The valves lining the veins open up like tiny gates to allow the blood through. Then they snap shut to prevent blood from rushing back down to your feet. If a valve fails to close properly, blood pools in the vein, causing it to stretch. Eventually, it bulges toward the surface of the skin. This is what's known as a varicosity.

SIMPLE SOLUTIONS
1. Nutrition
2. Supplements
3. Exercise
4. Herbal Medicine
5. Home Remedies
6. Homeopathy
7. Chinese Medicine
8. Medical Measures

Technically, any vein in your body can become varicose. But the most vulnerable veins are located in your legs as well as around your anus. When an anal vein becomes varicose, it's called a hemorrhoid.

Varicose veins appear bluish or gray in color. They cause painful aching and swelling. If left untreated, they tend to get worse over time.

An estimated 80 million Americans have varicose veins. The condition is four times more common among women than among men. In most women, varicose veins first appear after age 50. But if you have a family history of them, they can appear much earlier—even in your twenties.

Besides gender, other factors can increase your risk of varicose veins. In fact, anything that impairs the movement of blood up your legs can make you more vulnerable. For example, if you're overweight, those extra pounds can compress your veins so that blood has a harder time passing through. The same is true if you're a mom-to-be—although varicose veins that develop during pregnancy usually go away on their own after delivery.

Another contributor to the formation of varicose veins is the overproduction of lysosomal enzymes. These enzymes break down the "cement" that holds your veins together. As a result, veins become enlarged, swollen, and twisted. Certain people are simply genetically predisposed to producing more lysosomal enzymes than normal.

While varicose veins usually aren't serious from a health standpoint, they can be painful and unsightly. Most people who get them want to make them go away—and the sooner, the better. Mainstream medical procedures work quickly, but they can't stop new varicose veins from forming. To do that, you need to follow a blended approach to treatment that includes some or all of the measures that follow.

BEST CHOICES

Nutrition

Fight fibrin flavorfully. Fibrin is a substance that's naturally produced by your body. It gets deposited around varicose veins, causing the lumpy skin associated with the condition. According to Joseph Pizzorno Jr., N.D., garlic, onions, and ground red pepper contain compounds that help break down fibrin. To increase your intake of these foods, simply use them in your cooking.

Supplements

Help your veins with bromelain. An enzyme found in pineapple, bromelain is able to break down fibrin. If you want to try bromelain for your varicose veins, you can buy the enzyme in supplement form in health food stores and some drugstores. Take 500 milligrams three times a day, before meals, Dr. Pizzorno advises.

Exercise

Use your legs. Your leg muscles push blood through your leg veins up to your heart. If you sit or stand for long periods, those muscles don't contract much—and you're more likely to develop varicose veins. So move around as much as possible, says Alan P. Brauer, M.D. If you have a desk job or a job that requires you to stand in one place for long periods of time, use your break time to exercise your leg muscles.

Step lively. Walking is excellent exercise for people with varicose veins, says Anne Simons, M.D. It not only gets your blood moving but also helps you shed the extra pounds that contribute to varicose veins. She recommends walking at a moderate to brisk pace for 30 to 60 minutes every day.

Herbal Medicine

Get help from gotu kola. Its name sounds a lot like the famous cola. In fact, gotu kola has nothing to do with soft drinks. The herb has shown tremendous promise as a treatment for a condition called venous in-sufficiency, in which varicosities develop within the deep veins of the legs. Venous insufficiency is much more serious than varicose veins. But gotu kola can help both conditions, Dr. Pizzorno says. The herb works by reinforcing the "cement" that holds your veins and valves together, so they work more efficiently.

Many European studies have demonstrated that gotu kola is an effective treatment for venous insufficiency. In one study, French researchers gave 94 people with venous insufficiency either 60 milligrams or 120 milligrams of gotu kola or a placebo (a fake pill) every day. After 2 months, the people taking the placebo showed no changes in leg swelling or discomfort. But the people taking gotu kola did, with those on the larger dose reporting the greatest im-provement.

Gotu kola extract capsules are available in health food and some drug-stores. Follow the package directions.

Horse around with horse chestnut. Horse chestnut seeds have a long history as a folk remedy for varicose veins. The seeds contain a compound called aescin, which strengthens the walls of your veins and increases their elasticity. This, in turn, supports healthy blood flow.

Commission E, the German expert panel that evaluates the safety and ef-fectiveness of herbal medicines, endorses horse chestnut extract as a treatment for varicose veins. Horse chestnut extract is not widely available in the United States. If you have access to the herb, use only a standardized extract and follow package directions.

Sweep away problems with butcher's broom. Butcher's broom, a shrubby herb that's native to the Mediterranean region, is another time-honored treatment for varicose veins. To test the herb's effectiveness, Italian researchers recruited 40 people with varicose veins and evaluated their symptoms of leg pain, swelling, and itching. Then each participant began taking either a preparation containing butcher's broom extract and vitamin C or a placebo three times a day. After 2 months, those who took the herbal preparation experienced significant improvement in their symptoms, and without side effects.

The people in the study were given 16.5 milligrams of butcher's broom extract and 50 milligrams of vitamin C every day. Generally, butcher's broom comes in higher doses in health food stores and drugstores. Follow the package directions.

Treat your veins "berry" well. Bilberries, also known as European blueberries, are rich in antioxidant compounds called anthocyanosides. These compounds strengthen the walls of your veins and reduce the production of lysosomal enzymes, which contribute to varicose veins. Several European studies have shown that bilberry extract improves circulation through the veins and decreases the discomfort of varicosities.

Naturopath Donald Brown, N.D., professor of herbal medicine at Bastyr University in Kenmore, Washington, recommends taking 80 to 160 milligrams of bilberry extract three times a day. Or if you prefer, eat lots of cherries, blackberries, and blueberries. These fruits contain the same antioxidant compounds as bilberries, so they may help treat and prevent varicose veins.

Home Remedies

Elevate your legs. To minimize the discomfort of varicose veins, sit with your legs raised above the level of your heart. This supports blood flow from your legs back to your heart.

Slip on supportive stockings. Wearing support hose can alleviate much of the discomfort of varicose veins. "The hose compress varicosities, so less blood pools in those veins," says Alan Gaby, M.D. Put on your hose first thing in the morning—ideally, before you even get out of bed.

Give high heels the heave-ho. High-heeled shoes and cowboy-style high-heeled boots put tremendous stress on your calves—exactly what you don't need when you have varicose veins. Instead, wear sensible, comfortable flats, advises family practitioner Dudley Phillips, M.D., of Darlington, Maryland.

OTHER GOOD CHOICES

Homeopathy

Consider a combination. Homeopath Dana Ullman generally recommends Ledum palustre.

Homeopath Andrew Lockie, M.D., author of *The Family Guide to Homeopathy*, also suggests Carbo vegetabilis, Ferrum metallicum, Hamamelis, and Pulsatilla. To find out which of these medicines works best for you, consult a homeopath.

Chinese Medicine

Reinforce qi. Practitioners of Chinese medicine attribute varicose veins to a deficiency of qi brought on by overwork—that is, too much standing. This leads to a collapse of your veins. "The Lung organ network draws Blood back to the Heart," explains Efrem Korngold, O.M.D., L.Ac. "But with weakened qi, the Lung can't do its job. In addition, the Spleen is responsible for the integrity of your veins, so it needs strengthening, too."

To treat varicose veins, Dr. Korngold prescribes herbs that strengthen qi as well as the Lung and Spleen. These herbs include astragalus root, licorice root, angelica (dang gui), black cohosh root, bupleurum root, and citrus peel.

Put on the pressure. To relieve the discomfort of varicose veins, try acupressure. Simply apply steady, penetrating finger pressure to each of the following points for 3 minutes.

◆ Lung 9, located on the thumb side of your inner forearm in the hollow between the wrist bone and wrist crease

◆ Spleen 6, located four finger-widths above your inner anklebone on the back inner border of your shinbone

If pressing the above points doesn't improve your symptoms, you may want to consult a certified acupuncturist. Sometimes professional needle stimulation can help even when finger pressure doesn't.

MEDICAL MEASURES

If you're bothered by the appearance of your varicose veins, or if home treatment doesn't relieve your pain, you can have the veins reduced or removed with one of several medical procedures.

Small spider veins can often be treated with laser therapy. They can also be treated nonsurgically by injection therapy, or sclerotherapy. In this procedure, your doctor injects a combination of fatty acids and salt water into the affected area. The solution causes the veins to collapse. The same method works well with small varicose veins.

The standard surgical treatment for varicose veins, called mini-phlebectomy or stripping, involves the complete removal of the affected veins. The surgeon makes several incisions, inserts a wire hook, pulls out the veins, and wraps the area in tight bandages. For this procedure, recovery time varies but can last up to several weeks.

After any of these mainstream treatments, doctors generally recommend walking several miles a day. Walking stimulates circulation and the growth of new, healthy veins.

RED FLAGS

Varicose veins raise your risk of phlebitis, a condition in which veins become painfully inflamed. Untreated, phlebitis can progress to thrombophlebitis, in which blood clots form in the affected vein. If a clot develops in a deep vein, a piece of it may break off and travel to your lungs—a potentially life-threatening situation. For this reason, if you experience painful swelling in either leg and the swelling doesn't go away when you elevate your leg, consult your doctor without delay.

Warts

If warts have a good side, it's that they often go away on their own . . . after a while. But the question is, where did they come from in the first place?

Warts are viral infections caused by the approximately 70 different strains of human papillomavirus, or HPV. According to Bernard A. Cohen, M.D., associate professor of dermatology at Johns Hopkins University School of Medicine in Baltimore, HPV is everywhere. This may explain why warts affect some nine million Americans every year.

The wart virus spreads from person to person by direct contact. It usually enters the skin through a cut, crack, or scratch, then incubates for 2 to 6 months before developing into the characteristic lump. If you pick or scratch at the lump before touching broken skin elsewhere on your body, you can transfer the virus to the new site. That's how you get multiple warts.

SIMPLE SOLUTIONS
1. Visualization
2. Herbal Medicine
3. Home Remedies
4. Over-the-Counter Drugs
5. Chinese Medicine
6. Medical Measures

Warts themselves usually appear as grayish, cauliflower-textured growths. They can be as tiny as a pinhead or considerably larger. They usually erupt on the fingers, though they can show up just about anywhere.

Folk remedies for warts abound. There are a couple of reasons for this. Since warts go away by themselves over time, a particular remedy could get credit for what is really nothing more than nature taking its course. Second, and perhaps more important, any remedy can have what experts call a placebo effect. In other words, if you believe that whatever you're doing works, it *will* work—even if there's no scientific reason that it should.

The placebo effect is one of many things that can boost immune function, says Andrew T. Weil, M.D., director of the program in integrative medicine at the University of Arizona College of Medicine in Tucson. And ultimately, it's your immune system that defeats the wart virus and prevents warts from coming back.

Even without treatment, about one-third of garden-variety warts disappear within 6 months. Some linger for as long as 5 years. For a small and probably frustrated proportion of the population, warts go away and come back repeatedly throughout life.

Of course, even 6 months is a long time to live with a wart. To make yours disappear sooner, try one or more of the following blended-medicine remedies.

BEST CHOICES

Visualization

Will your wart away. The first modern scientific demonstration of the mind's ability to direct immune system activity toward the elimination of warts took place in 1973 at Massachusetts General Hospital in Boston. Owen Surman, M.D., a psychiatrist at the hospital, hypnotized people with warts. He instructed them to try as hard as they could to will the warts out of existence. After five weekly hypnosis sessions, 53 percent of the study participants were wart-free.

You can tap into the healing power of the mind-body connection yourself, through visualization. Try this exercise developed by Gerald N. Epstein, M.D., director of the Academy of Integrated Medicine and Mental Imagery in New York City: Close your eyes and take three deep breaths. Envision yourself at the edge of a stream. Picture your warts as some part of your body, such as an arm or a leg. Imagine removing that part, turning it inside out, and washing it thoroughly in the stream. See the part's waste products as gray strands being carried away by the current. Once the part is clean, envision hanging it in the sun to dry. Picture it healing from the inside out. When the part is dry, reattach it to your body. Notice that your warts are gone. Open your eyes.

Dr. Epstein recommends practicing this exercise for 3 minutes three times a day over the course of 21 days.

Herbal Medicine

Reach for echinacea. An immune system stimulant, echinacea helps fight viral infections, including those that cause warts. You'll find echinacea in tea, capsule, and tincture form in health food stores. Whichever product you choose, follow the package directions for proper dosage.

Plantar Warts: Trouble under Foot

Plantar is the medical term for the bottom surface of the foot. Not so coincidentally, that's where plantar warts appear.

Like other types of warts, plantar warts are caused by strains of the human papillomavirus. The virus likes to hang around on public shower floors and on the walkways bordering swimming pools, hot tubs, and saunas—places where people tend to walk barefoot.

What makes plantar warts unique is that they grow inward. Rather than lumps, they're hard, flat growths. You know when you have one: You feel as though you're walking with a pebble in your shoe.

To help get rid of a plantar wart and prevent it from coming back, heed this expert-recommended advice.

Give your dogs a bath. Anne Simons, M.D., swears by the following home remedy: Add 2 tablespoons of mild laundry detergent to ½ gallon of warm water. Soak the affected foot for 10 minutes. Cut out a square of wart-removing salicylic acid plaster (sold in drugstores) and place it over the wart. Cover the plaster with an adhesive bandage.

Two days later, remove the plaster. Vigorously brush the wart using a toothbrush moistened with soap and water. If the wart hasn't gone away, repeat the procedure. Continue until the wart disappears.

Go shod to the shower. Wear flip-flops or plastic sandals when you're around locker rooms, pools, and hot tubs, advises New York City podiatrist Suzanne M. Levine, D.P.M. This simple measure will reduce your chances of picking up the wart virus—or passing it to someone else.

Bite back with birch bark. The Chinese, Scandinavians, and Native Americans have all used birch bark as a remedy for warts, according to James A. Duke, Ph.D. The herb contains salicylic acid, the active ingredient in over-the-counter wart-removal products. Birch bark also contains betulin and betulinic acid, two compounds with antiviral action.

To use birch bark, moisten a small piece of the bark and apply it over the wart. Hold the bark in place with medical tape. Leave it on for 24 hours, then get a fresh piece of bark and repeat. Continue until the wart goes away.

Genital Warts: A Very Private Problem

Since the 1980s, genital warts have been the nation's most prevalent sexually transmitted disease. In studies of cervical tissue, about one-half of adult American women show evidence of infection, says Christiane Northrup, M.D., founder of the Women to Women health center in Yarmouth, Maine, and past president of the American Holistic Medical Association. About 30 percent of sexually active women develop noticeable warts.

The strains of human papillomavirus that cause genital warts spread only through sexual contact. People can be infected for months, even years, before they show any symptoms. It's only when the immune system can no longer keep the virus in check that warts begin to appear. This often happens during a period of stress or illness, when immune function becomes compromised.

In women, genital warts can produce a burning sensation or a noticeable change in the pattern of vaginal discharge. Men who are infected may experience bleeding or discharge or may feel the need to urinate more frequently. If you have these symptoms, see a doctor, who will be able to diagnose internal or external warts.

While genital warts sometimes clear up by themselves, they're generally quite persistent. In women, genital warts should be treated and monitored by a physician because they're associated with an increased risk of cervical cancer.

Home Remedies

Play kitchen chemist. In a pinch, you can make your own wart remover by crushing an aspirin and mixing the powder with a little water, says Anne Simons, M.D. Apply the paste directly to the wart, then cover with a bandage for a day or so. Be careful not to apply it to skin that has an open wound.

Hands off! Never pick or scratch at a wart. That's how the wart virus finds its way to other parts of your body.

Over-the-Counter Drugs

Let a remover do the work. Wart-removal products come in liquid, gel, and plaster form. According to Dr. Simons, plasters are preferable because they stay on the wart best. But try different products and choose the one you like. Be sure to follow the label directions.

OTHER GOOD CHOICES

Chinese Medicine

Rally the healers. "You want to draw Blood and qi to your warts, to strengthen your body to fight the growths," explains Efrem Korngold, O.M.D., L.Ac. He most often recommends two approaches to his patients: moxa and bleeding. Moxa is mugwort, the plant traditionally burned on acupuncture needles to boost their effectiveness. Dr. Korngold waves a stick of burning moxa over the warts, a technique that the Chinese believe focuses Blood and qi.

Bleeding, as performed by a doctor of oriental medicine, is intended to draw Blood and qi to the site of the wart, enabling your body to overcome the viral infection. But, of course, it takes a doctor of oriental medicine to do this properly.

Seek an acupuncturist's assistance. Acupuncture is also an effective treatment for warts, Dr. Korngold says. Which acupuncture points are stimulated depends on where your wart is located.

MEDICAL MEASURES

For especially persistent warts, mainstream M.D.'s rely on an array of treatment options. They may apply powerful compounds to dissolve the warts. They may try freezing the growths with dry ice or liquid nitrogen or burning the growths using one of two procedures, called electrocautery and loop electrode excision. They may even resort to laser surgery or interferon, a powerful drug that stimulates the immune system. With any of these treatments, there's still a chance that the warts will return.

Wounds

A hard, knee-first landing on a sidewalk. A too-close encounter between a finger and a bagel knife. A shin banging against the corner of a coffee table.

They're the sorts of everyday mishaps that can leave your skin bruised or bleeding. While they're painful, they're seldom serious. They can usually be treated at home, the place where 80 percent of all minor wounds occur. For these sorts of injuries, you can count on blended medicine to help you heal.

For more severe wounds—including large, deep cuts and punctures; scrapes that cover large areas; and some second-degree and all third-degree burns—you need emergency medical care. Once you've been treated, you can use blended medicine to speed healing and minimize scarring.

Your skin has two layers: the epidermis and the dermis. The epidermis is the skin you see, the thin layer that's directly exposed to the environment. Your epidermis is constantly shedding cells, explains Anne Simons, M.D. They are replaced by new cells from the underlying dermis. Riding piggyback on the epidermis are millions of bacteria and other microorganisms that ordinarily cause no problems but that might cause infection if you experience a wound.

SIMPLE SOLUTIONS
1. Nutrition
2. Supplements
3. Relaxation Therapies
4. Herbal Medicine
5. Home Remedies
6. Over-the-Counter Drugs
7. Aromatherapy
8. Homeopathy
9. Chinese Medicine
10. Ayurvedic Medicine
11. Medical Measures

Beneath the epidermis is the dermis, which has a rich supply of blood. It also contains lots of collagen, the protein that forms the connective tissue that holds your skin together and gives it elasticity. And it has lots of nerve endings, which is why even minor wounds can hurt so badly.

Shortly after an injury to your dermis, your immune system goes to work to close the wound and kill any microorganisms that get inside. Blood vessels around the wound expand, and extra blood rushes to the site. This extra blood cleanses the wound. It also carries a small army of white blood cells that attack any microorganisms that might cause infection. This process causes redness, inflammation, and swelling around the wound. Meanwhile, the cells injured by the wound die, but before they expire, they release a protein that triggers blood clotting and eventually forms a scab to close the wound.

After about 24 hours, other white blood cells arrive at the wound site and release chemical growth factors. These proteins stimulate the creation of new skin cells, new capillaries, and new collagen, explains Alan P. Brauer, M.D. The complete regeneration of new skin takes from several days to 3 weeks, depending on the severity of the wound.

Sometimes the healing process is less than perfect, and collagen forms where there should be skin cells. This produces a scar. Most people want to prevent scarring for cosmetic reasons. But there's also a sound medical reason to do so: Scar tissue is weaker than well-formed skin, so it's more vulnerable to future injury.

When a wound gets infected, any pain and inflammation persists or gets worse. After a few days, a creamy whitish yellow fluid may ooze from the scab. That's pus. It's made up of dead bacteria and white blood cells as well as debris from the battle between the two.

For years, doctors advised leaving minor wounds exposed to the air to encourage drying and scab formation. Then research showed that leaving wounds uncovered actually dehydrates them and delays their healing. In light of this finding, doctors now recommend covering wounds with moist dressings.

There are other measures that can help heal you faster with minimal scarring. Here's what the experts recommend.

BEST CHOICES

Nutrition

Cut back on fat. If you eat a high-fat diet, your wounds heal more slowly and are more likely to leave scars, says Melvyn R. Werbach, M.D., assistant clinical professor at the University of California, Los Angeles, School of Medicine. Dietary fat impairs the movement of the white blood cells that fight infection and initiate production of new skin cells, capillaries, and collagen. What's more, a high-fat diet tends to be low in vitamins C and E and the mineral zinc, nutrients crucial to healing.

The easiest way to lower your fat intake is to minimize your consumption of meats, dairy products, snack foods, and desserts. Replace these foods with naturally nutritious, low-fat grains, legumes, fruits, and vegetables—the staples of a healthful diet.

Supplements

Stimulate healing with C. Studies dating back to the 1930s show that low blood levels of vitamin C slow wound healing. More recent research agrees. In one study, British researchers gave 20 people with bedsores standard medical care plus 500 milligrams of vitamin C or a placebo (a fake pill) twice a day. After a month, the sores shrank by an average of 84 percent among those taking vitamin C, compared with 43 percent among those taking the placebo.

For a large wound or burn, clinical nutritionist Shari Lieberman, Ph.D., suggests taking 5,000 to 10,000 milligrams of vitamin C a day while you heal. For a minor wound, 2,000 milligrams a day is sufficient.

Increase your intake of E. "Several studies have shown that vitamin E promotes wound healing and reduces scarring," Dr. Lieberman says. She recommends taking 400 international units (IU) of vitamin E a day until your wound heals. If a scab has already formed, try puncturing a vitamin E capsule and squeezing the oil inside it directly onto the wound.

Add zinc to the mix. Zinc is one of several nutrients that boost the immune system. Dr. Lieberman cites one study involving hospital patients who were mildly deficient in zinc and healing slowly. When these people were given zinc supplements, they began to heal more quickly. Dr. Lieberman recommends taking 30 to 50 milligrams of zinc a day while your wound heals. Doses over 30 milligrams per day, however, must be taken under a doctor's supervision.

Relaxation Therapies

Control stress. When you're under stress, your immune system doesn't function as well as it should. As a result, wounds take longer to heal. That's what researchers at the Ohio State University College of Medicine found in a study of 26 women, half of whom had the stressful responsibility of caring for a spouse with Alzheimer's disease. The researchers gave minor puncture wounds to all of the women, then treated the wounds with hydrogen peroxide. As the researchers monitored the wounds, they noticed that the caregivers took significantly longer to heal than the non-caregivers—49 days versus 39.

Studies like this one suggest that managing stress is essential to wound healing. You can choose from any of a number of stress-relieving relaxation techniques, from meditation and visualization to tai chi and yoga.

Herbal Medicine

Make aloe your ally. The fleshy leaves of the aloe plant contain a gel that's well-known as a treatment for minor burns. But it can help heal cuts and other minor wounds, too.

Researchers have identified many reasons why aloe gel stimulates wound healing. It has antibacterial, antifungal, and antiviral properties that keep wounds from becoming infected. It's an immune stimulant. It has some anti-inflammatory action. It stimulates collagen production and skin regeneration. And it contains vitamins C and E and the mineral zinc, nutrients that speed wound healing.

You've probably seen aloe gel in your drugstore, often with the sunscreen products. At least one study suggests that commercial gel loses its wound-healing ability and actually slows the healing process. Instead, Dr. Simons suggests keeping a potted aloe plant in your kitchen, where most cuts and burns occur. That way, you'll have fresh gel handy whenever you need it. Just snip off a leaf, slit it open, and scoop out the gel.

Keep in mind that aloe should be used only on minor, superficial wounds. It isn't appropriate for deep wounds. In fact, one study showed that the gel delays the healing of such wounds.

Rub on gotu kola. In India and Indonesia, gotu kola has been used for centuries to help heal wounds. Research has shown that the herb contains compounds responsible for stimulating collagen production.

Some health food stores carry gotu kola salve. If you can find it, apply it to your wound according to the package directions. Otherwise, you can make a compress by soaking a small towel in gotu kola tea. To make the tea, add 2 teaspoons of dried leaves to 1 cup of boiled water, steep, and strain. Pour the tea into a bowl big enough to soak a small towel. Fold the towel and apply it over the wound, leaving it in place until it dries out. Then resoak and reapply the compress, repeating the process a total of three times.

Treat wounds with tea tree. When British explorer James Cook first arrived in Australia in 1777, he found the native Aborigines treating skin infections with the crushed leaves of the tea tree. Modern science has since discovered that the oil in tea tree leaves is a powerful antiseptic. "I have personally used tea tree oil as an antiseptic on wounds, and I can attest to its value," says James A.

Bruises: Black and Blue and Sore All Over

Bruises are patches of discoloration that appear anywhere on your skin. They occur when a fall or blow doesn't break your skin but damages the tiny blood vessels, called capillaries, beneath it. The capillaries leak blood, which collects under your skin.

Initially, bruises have a red-purple hue. But as your body reabsorbs the blood pigments, they turn green, yellow, and brown. They disappear completely within 10 to 14 days. If you sustain a bruise, here's what to do.

Apply ice as soon as possible. Ice helps reduce any pain and swelling, says Anne Simons, M.D. To make a cold pack, throw a few ice cubes in a plastic bag, then wrap the bag in a cloth. Apply the pack to the bruise for 20 minutes, then take it off for 10 minutes before reapplying. Never put ice directly on your skin, as it may cause frostbite.

Then add warmth. Once the bleeding beneath your skin has stopped—usually within 24 hours—switch from cold packs to warm compresses, Dr. Simons says. The warmth opens your blood vessels, which helps speed the reabsorption of the blood that created the bruise.

Increase C. Vitamin C is crucial to the production of collagen, a protein that gives blood vessels their structural integrity. Studies by Sheldon V. Pollack, M.D., associate professor of medicine in the dermatology division at Duke University School of Medicine in Durham, North Carolina, show that people who bruise easily tend to have low blood levels of vitamin C. Dr. Pollack suggests taking 500 milligrams of the vitamin three times a day.

Bank on bromelain. An enzyme found in pineapple, bromelain has anti-inflammatory properties that can help relieve the swelling associated with a bruise. You can buy bromelain supplements in health food stores. Take 400 milligrams before each meal. Or do what James A. Duke, Ph.D., does when he gets a bruise: Eat lots of pineapple.

Duke, Ph.D. "It's as good as any nonherbal antiseptic—alcohol, iodine, or hydrogen peroxide."

Look for 100 percent tea tree oil in health food stores. Apply the oil with a cotton ball or cotton swab twice a day.

Find comfort in comfrey. Comfrey contains a compound called allantoin that helps heal wounds. Dr. Duke suggests applying fresh, washed, crushed leaves directly to a wound or making a paste from powdered leaves and water. In addition, some health food stores carry skin-care products that contain comfrey. Look for the herb on labels.

Be aware that comfrey is appropriate only for external use and only for superficial (not deep) wounds. It should never be ingested, as it contains compounds that can cause liver damage.

Count on calendula. Commission E, the German expert panel that evaluates the safety and effectiveness of medicinal herbs, has endorsed calendula as a treatment for wounds. The herb promotes healing by stimulating the growth of new skin and blood vessels and reducing inflammation.

Most health food stores sell skin creams made with calendula. If you find such a cream, use it according to the package directions. Otherwise, you can make an herbal compress by soaking a small towel in calendula tea. To prepare the tea, add 1 to 2 teaspoons of dried calendula flowers or tincture to 1 cup of boiled water, then steep until cool. If you use dried flowers, strain the tea before making your compress. Apply the compress a total of three times, allowing it to dry out before resoaking it.

Keep chamomile close by. Chamomile is much more than a calming beverage tea. The oils in the herb not only have anti-inflammatory and antibacterial properties but also promote skin regeneration. That's why Commission E recommends chamomile as a wound treatment. You can make a compress by soaking a small towel in chamomile tea. To prepare the tea, add 3 teaspoons of chamomile flowers to 1 cup of boiled water, steep until cool, then strain out the plant material. Apply the compress a total of three times, allowing it to dry out before resoaking it.

Home Remedies

To stop bleeding, apply pressure. In most cases, minor wounds stop bleeding spontaneously. If yours doesn't, apply direct pressure until it does. For a puncture wound, allow bleeding to continue for a few minutes to flush out any infection-causing microorganisms.

Get in a lather. Carefully clean your wound with soap and water, Dr. Simons says. Remove any remaining dirt and foreign matter, then disinfect it with hydrogen peroxide. For a puncture wound, soak the injured area in comfortably hot water for 15 minutes every few hours, continuing for several days. This helps prevent infection.

Keep it under wraps. To speed healing and prevent scarring, the American Pharmaceutical Association recommends covering your wound with a moist dressing. Drugstores carry all shapes and sizes of bandages. Once you select one, moisten it with water, aloe gel, honey, or an antiseptic or antibacterial ointment. (There's more on the healing properties of honey below.) Change the bandage once or twice a day.

Cool down a burn. If you have a minor burn, run cold water over it, advises William P. Burdick, M.D., associate professor of emergency medicine at the Medical College of Pennsylvania in Philadelphia. Or use an ice pack: Place a few ice cubes in a plastic bag, wrap the bag in a towel, and apply it directly to the burn. Leave it on for 20 minutes, then take it off for 10 minutes before reapplying.

Put yourself in a sticky situation. Egyptian medical papyruses dating back more than 3,000 years recommend covering wounds with honey. More modern research has shown that honey has potent antibacterial properties.

Honey works best when it's sterilized, as most store-bought brands are. If you can't find the sterilized variety, Richard A. Knutson, M.D., an orthopedic surgeon at Kings Daughter's Hospital in Greenville, Mississippi, suggests substituting a paste made from granulated sugar and water. Generally, sugar is sterile, and like honey, it helps prevent infection and speed healing.

Don't break blisters. As tempted as you may be to pop a blister, don't do it. It only raises your risk of infection. If a blister ruptures on its own, wash it with soap and water. Then put antibiotic ointment on a piece of gauze and bandage the blister. Change the dressing and wash the wound once a day until it heals.

Be wary of bagels. More people cut themselves while slicing bagels than any other food. "The problem is that you have two very unstable points of contact: the bagel in your hand and the knife against the bagel," says Mark Smith, M.D., an emergency physician at Washington Hospital Center in Washington, D.C. "One slip, and you slice your fingers or palm."

To cut a bagel without cutting yourself, Dr. Smith suggests holding it from the top with your thumb and index finger forming an inverted U. Place the knife inside the U and cut from the top down. Or invest in a bagel slicer, a kitchen gadget that cuts bagels safely. You can probably find one in a kitchen supply store, department store, or housewares catalog.

Over-the-Counter Drugs

Raise the ante against infection. By applying an antiseptic ointment to a wound, you largely eliminate the risk of infection. In fact, the combination of soap, water, and antiseptics reduces the likelihood of infection to less than 2 percent. Several antiseptic ingredients have been approved by the Food and Drug Administration, including alcohol, iodine, povidone-iodine, hydrogen peroxide, and phenol. Look for a product containing one of these ingredients and use it according to the package directions.

Battle bacteria right away. A dab of an antibiotic ointment containing bacitracin, neomycin, or polymixin may help prevent infection, Dr. Simons says. But for the ointment to work, you must apply it within the first few hours after sustaining a wound.

Put an end to pain. For pain and inflammation, take aspirin or ibuprofen. Acetaminophen relieves pain but not inflammation. If aspirin or ibuprofen upsets your stomach, Dr. Simons suggests trying an enteric-coated product, which will break down in your intestines rather than in your stomach. If you have a history of ulcers or you're a woman who is pregnant, you shouldn't take aspirin or ibuprofen. Ask your doctor for a recommendation.

OTHER GOOD CHOICES

Aromatherapy

Rely on lavender. In the 1920s, French fragrance chemist Rene-Maurice Gattefosse was in his laboratory blending essential oils when a sudden explosion burned his arm. Frantic with pain, he plunged his arm into the nearest cold liquid, which happened to be a bowl of lavender oil. His pain subsided immediately, and his burn healed remarkably quickly, with minimal discomfort and no scarring. Gattefosse's experience led him to devote his life to studying the healing properties of essential oils. In 1937, he published *Aromatherapie*, coining the term now used to describe the healing art based on aromatic plant oils.

To treat a burn, Kathi Keville and Mindy Green, coauthors of *Aromatherapy: A Complete Guide to the Healing Art*, suggest placing a few drops of lavender essential oil directly on the injured skin. You can buy essential oils in health food stores and bath and body shops.

Bee Stings: A Bug's Revenge

As tiny as they are, bees sure cause their share of misery. Tick one off, and it may respond by injecting a stinger full of venom into your skin. The venom causes not only pain but also redness, swelling, and itching. The following measures can provide welcome relief.

Scrape out the stinger. If the bee has left its stinger in your skin, don't try to pull it out, says Anne Simons, M.D. Pulling squeezes the attached venom sac, sending more venom into your skin. Instead, scrape out the stinger with a sterilized knife or a credit card. Then wash the area with soap and water.

Put your discomfort on ice. To control the pain and swelling of a bee sting, apply an ice pack to the affected area. Place a few ice cubes in a plastic bag, wrap the bag in a towel, and apply it directly to the sting. Leave it on for 20 minutes, then take it off for 10 minutes before reapplying.

Take a pain reliever. Aspirin and ibuprofen can help control pain and inflammation after a bee sting, Dr. Simons says. Acetaminophen can relieve pain but does nothing for inflammation. If aspirin or ibuprofen upsets your stomach, look for an enteric-coated version. These pills break down in your intestines, so they won't irritate your stomach. If you have a history of ulcers or you're a woman who is pregnant, you shouldn't take aspirin or ibuprofen. Ask your doctor for a recommendation.

Homeopathy

Seek aid from Arnica. The homeopathic medicine Arnica is often the first choice among homeopaths for treating any wound.

Other medicines can help, too, says homeopath Dana Ullman. They include Calendula, Graphites, Hypericum, Silicea, and Urtica dioica. Check with a homeopath to find out which medicine works best for your particular type of wound.

Chinese Medicine

Get your Blood circulating. Practitioners of Chinese medicine view wounds as "rents in the fabric," says Efrem Korngold, O.M.D., L.Ac. "You want to stimulate the circulation of Blood to promote tissue repair."

Try a little tenderizer. Most meat tenderizers contain either papain, an enzyme in papaya, or bromelain, an enzyme in pineapple. Both of these compounds break down the proteins in insect venoms, says Elson Haas, M.D., director of the Preventive Medical Center of Marin in San Rafael, California. In this way, they help reduce the inflammation associated with a bee sting.

To use the tenderizer, mix it with a little water to make a paste. Then apply it directly to the affected area.

Be alert to anaphylaxis. Anaphylaxis is a relatively uncommon but potentially life-threatening allergic reaction to bee stings and other types of insect bites. Symptoms usually develop within 30 minutes of a sting and include nausea and vomiting, abdominal cramps, rapid heart rate, wheezing and difficulty breathing, hives, dizziness, and agitation. If not treated, the person may lose consciousness. That's why emergency medical care is vital.

If you're at risk for anaphylaxis, you should carry an "epi kit" with you at all times. You'll need to get one from your doctor. The kit contains a syringe filled with epinephrine. At the first sign of anaphylaxis, you inject the epinephrine into your thigh. Immediately afterward, call your emergency medical number or have someone take you to the nearest emergency room without delay.

In China, one of the most frequently prescribed treatments for wounds is Yunnan Bai Yao, which means white powder from the Yunnan province. Its main ingredient is pseudoginseng, which promotes circulation of Blood and helps stop bleeding. "You put the preparation right on your wound," Dr. Korngold says.

Heal with needles. Dr. Korngold also recommends acupuncture as a treatment for wounds. You should receive acupuncture only from a trained acupuncturist. Which points are stimulated depends on where the wound is located.

Ayurvedic Medicine

Turn to turmeric. To treat minor wounds, David Frawley, O.M.D., recommends topical applications of aloe, calendula, and comfrey. These are the

Lyme Disease: Transmitted by Ticks

In 1975, health officials identified cases of an arthritis-like condition among children in Old Lyme, Connecticut. The officials dubbed the ailment Lyme disease. Since then, Lyme disease has been reported from coast to coast but is most common in the New England states as well as in New York, Pennsylvania, Wisconsin, and Minnesota.

Lyme disease is caused by a microorganism that lives in the digestive tracts of three species of deer ticks. If you get bitten by one of these ticks, you may get infected.

At first, Lyme disease may cause no symptoms. But eventually, you develop a circular red rash around the site of the bite. Sometimes the rash has a bull's-eye appearance, a red center within a clear area that's bordered by a red ring. The rash may be painful or cause a burning sensation. Even without treatment, the rash goes away within a few weeks. But you develop other, flulike symptoms: headache, fever, chills, muscle and joint aches, and an overall ill feeling.

If Lyme disease isn't treated early on, it can become quite serious. Over months and sometimes years, you may experience episodes of severe joint pain, fatigue, and insomnia. You may also experience nervous system disorders: severe headaches, Bell's palsy (a temporary paralysis of the facial muscles), weakness in the limbs, and loss of coordination. Occasionally, Lyme disease causes irregular heartbeat.

What can you do to avoid Lyme disease? If you notice that a tick has burrowed into your skin, remove it immediately, but carefully. Douse the bug with rubbing alcohol to help loosen its grip, then gently ease it out with tweezers, advises Herbert Luscombe, M.D., professor emeritus of dermatology at Jefferson Medical College of Thomas Jefferson University in Philadelphia.

Once you've removed the tick, dab the affected area with antibiotic ointment. Then monitor your skin for the telltale rash. If one develops, consult your doctor right away. Physicians treat Lyme disease with antibiotics, notably doxycycline (Vibramycin).

same herbs prescribed by Western herbalists. Dr. Frawley also suggests using turmeric topically (in a salve) and internally (1 teaspoon three times a day, mixed with honey). Turmeric has antiseptic properties.

MEDICAL MEASURES

Wounds naturally cause pain, tenderness, redness, and swelling. As your wound begins to heal, these symptoms should subside. If they persist or become worse, your wound is probably infected.

You can treat a minor infection at home by washing the wound with soap and water, soaking it in warm water, and coating it with antibiotic ointment. But if pain, tenderness, redness, and swelling persist—and especially if the wound begins to ooze pus—you need professional medical care. Your doctor may prescribe warm-water soaks or antibiotics.

A deep cut or puncture wound can lead to tetanus, a potentially fatal bacterial infection. If you have a dirty wound and you haven't gotten a tetanus booster in the past 5 years, now is the time. Even if you have a clean, minor wound, you should schedule an appointment for a tetanus shot.

RED FLAGS

If you experience any of the following, see your doctor right away.

◆ A cut that doesn't stop bleeding or that has jagged edges that don't come together

◆ A wound that contains dirt or other foreign material that you cannot remove

◆ A large, deep cut or large burn on your face, hands, feet, or genitals

◆ A burn that produces extensive blistering

◆ A blister that's more than 1 inch in diameter

◆ A human or animal bite that breaks your skin

◆ A wound that develops signs of infection: increased pain, swelling, tenderness, redness, red streaks, or pus

◆ A wound that doesn't get noticeably better within 2 weeks, despite home care

Yeast Infection

A re you *sure* that you have a yeast infection?

True, the condition is quite common. Some 75 percent of women develop at least one yeast infection in their lives. And 40 percent experience multiple infections.

Still, what you suspect is a yeast infection may not actually be one. After all, vaginal discharge—indicated by a whitish or yellowish stain in your underwear—is perfectly normal, says Christiane Northrup, M.D., founder of the Women to Women health center in Yarmouth, Maine, and past president of the American Holistic Medical Association. Your cervix and vagina shed cells constantly. These cells mix with cervical mucus, producing discharge.

But a yeast infection, or Candida vaginitis, is different. It produces a thick, cottage-cheese-like discharge, along with redness in the vaginal area and mild to severe itching. There are no urinary symptoms, as you would have with a bladder infection.

SIMPLE SOLUTIONS
1. Nutrition
2. Supplements
3. Herbal Medicine
4. Home Remedies
5. Over-the-Counter Drugs
6. Visualization
7. Homeopathy
8. Chinese Medicine
9. Ayurvedic Medicine
10. Medical Measures

If this is your first encounter with a suspected yeast infection, see your doctor for a proper diagnosis. You don't want to start treating a condition that you may not have. But if your doctor confirms your suspicions, try blended medicine for fast, effective relief.

Yeast infections are caused by the common fungus *Candida albicans*. It isn't an invading germ, like a cold virus, says Marjorie Crandall, Ph.D., a former yeast infection sufferer who now runs Yeast Consulting Services in Torrance, California. *C. albicans* lives in your vagina, along with a host of other microorganisms. If something causes your vaginal environment to change, *C. albicans* may reproduce rampantly, way beyond normal limits. That's when you wind up with a yeast infection.

Many factors can alter your vaginal environment in ways that favor *C. albicans* overgrowth. You're more at risk shortly before menstruation. And you're setting up a yeast-friendly situation if you have frequent intercourse, wear tight clothing (you need airflow), eat a high-sugar diet, or come under a lot of stress. Other factors that can cause yeast to multiply are vaginal irritants such as feminine hygiene sprays, antibiotics, corticosteroid drugs, and birth control pills. Your risk is also raised if you are pregnant or have diabetes that isn't kept under control.

As uncomfortable and annoying as they can be, yeast infections are seldom serious. But they may cause problems if they keep coming back again and again, which is what happens in about 5 percent of women. According to William G. Crook, M.D., author of the groundbreaking book *The Yeast Connection Handbook*, recurrent yeast infections can move beyond the vagina into the digestive tract. This condition, which Dr. Crook called chronic candidiasis, can lead to headaches, fatigue, rashes, depression, food sensitivities, and a host of other ailments.

Chronic candidiasis is very controversial. While most alternative practitioners consider it a major health problem, many mainstream physicians doubt that it exists. For women, it certainly provides incentive for bringing a quick end to yeast infections—and keeping the infections from coming back. That's where a blended approach can help.

BEST CHOICES

Nutrition

Kiss sweets goodbye. You can't avoid sugar completely. After all, your body converts carbohydrates into sugars—and you need carbohydrates as part of a healthful diet. But you can reduce your risk of yeast infection by avoiding sugary foods such as candies, cakes, cookies, and sodas. Joseph Pizzorno Jr., N.D., also suggests avoiding fruit juices, honey, maple syrup, dairy products, and foods high in molds such as cheeses, dried fruits, peanuts, and alcoholic beverages.

Go for yogurt. Some research has shown that yogurt helps prevent yeast infections. For one study, Eileen Hilton, M.D., president and chief executive officer of Biomedical Research Alliance of New York in Great Neck, recruited

11 women who had at least three yeast infections during the previous 6 months. Dr. Hilton instructed the women to eat a cup of live-culture yogurt a day. *Live culture* means that the yogurt contains the good bacteria *Lactobacillus acidophilus*. During the next 6 months, the women averaged less than one yeast infection.

Supplements

Find friendly bacteria in a capsule. If you don't care for yogurt, most health food stores carry supplements of *L. acidophilus* and other probiotic bacteria. Most of these supplements require refrigeration. Dr. Northrup recommends PB8, a brand that does not. Take according to the directions on the label.

Maximize your immunity with a multi. To keep your immune system in top infection-fighting form, Dr. Pizzorno recommends taking a daily multivitamin/mineral supplement.

Herbal Medicine

Get your garlic. Many medicinal herbs contain antifungal compounds, says James A. Duke, Ph.D. Chief among these herbs is garlic, which boasts a potent antifungal called allicin.

To treat a yeast infection, Paul Reilly, N.D., adjunct instructor at Bastyr University in Kenmore, Washington, and a naturopathic doctor in Tacoma, recommends eating several cloves to a bulb of raw crushed or chopped garlic a day.

As another option, Dr. Duke suggests stirring a teaspoon of fresh garlic juice into a few tablespoons of yogurt. Soak a tampon in the mixture, then insert the tampon as usual and leave it in for a few hours. Repeat twice a day for as long as your symptoms persist.

Be generous with berberine. A powerful antifungal compound found in goldenseal, barberry, and Oregon grape, berberine fights yeast infections in two ways. First, it revs up macrophages, special white blood cells that gobble yeast. Second, it stimulates other components of the immune system to defeat the infection.

To treat a yeast infection, Dr. Pizzorno recommends taking goldenseal or barberry—1½ teaspoons of tincture or ½ teaspoon of extract three times a day. You can buy both forms of the herbs in most health food stores.

Benefit from echinacea. Echinacea is a daisylike plant native to the Great Plains. Its flower and root juice have powerful immune-stimulating effects, especially for treating yeast infections. In one study, German researchers

Routine Douching? Don't!

Although a vinegar or yogurt douche every now and then may help treat yeast infections, routine douching for what TV commercials call "that clean, fresh feeling" is not a good idea, says Johns Hopkins University gynecologist Jean R. Anderson, M.D.

Considerable evidence shows that regular douching raises the risk of pelvic inflammatory disease (PID), a serious and potentially life-threatening infection of the reproductive organs.

The fact is, the vagina is a self-cleansing organ. Cervical mucus and other natural secretions that lubricate the vagina also keep it clean, making douching unnecessary.

tested echinacea extract that was given by injection or taken orally. Both were beneficial.

Look for echinacea tincture in health food stores. Take 1 teaspoon three times a day, mixed with water or juice.

Eat, drink, and be healed. The popular beverage herb chamomile and several common spices, including ginger, cinnamon, thyme, and rosemary, also contain antifungal compounds. If you're bothered by recurrent yeast infections, Dr. Duke suggests drinking lots of chamomile tea and adding liberal amounts of the antifungal spices to your cooking. To make chamomile tea, add 1 to 2 teaspoons of the herb to 1 cup of boiled water. Steep for 10 minutes, then strain.

Home Remedies

Try a vinegar douche. At the first sign of a yeast infection, Anne Simons, M.D., suggests douching with a mild solution of 2 tablespoons of vinegar and 1 quart of water. Repeat the treatment three times a day for a week, then twice a day for another week. Vinegar is a weak acid that can restore your vaginal pH to a more normal level.

But don't get in the habit of douching every day as a preventive measure. Done routinely, douching increases the risk of pelvic inflammatory disease, a serious infection of the reproductive organs. And when you do douche as suggested above, don't squirt the douche into your vagina. Let it just flow in, since squirting may also increase your risk of pelvic inflammatory disease.

Bacterial Vaginosis: A Bigger Problem

Bacterial vaginosis (BV) is similar to yeast infection in that both conditions are caused by an upset in the balance of organisms that normally live in your vagina. BV is sometimes called gardnerella, after one type of vaginal bacteria, but it can be caused by other bugs as well.

While BV is less widely known than yeast infection, it's actually more common. It accounts for about 50 percent of all vaginal infections, compared with 25 percent for yeast infection.

BV causes a fishy-smelling discharge and gray or yellowish vaginal secretions. Some women also experience vaginal itching, cramping, pain on urination, lower-back pain, and discomfort during intercourse. If you suspect that you have BV, see your doctor.

Avoid irritants. "Any chemical that irritates sensitive vaginal tissue may trigger a yeast infection," Dr. Crandall says. She suggests avoiding bath oils, bubble baths, and scented soaps and toilet paper.

"Tampons may also dry out vaginal tissue and cause irritation," Dr. Simons says. "If recurrent yeast infections are a problem for you, consider switching to pads for a while. That may help."

Wear white cotton underwear. White underwear has no dyes to irritate vaginal tissue. And cotton breathes, which helps maintain a healthy vaginal environment.

Wash it wisely. To kill yeast, Dr. Crandall suggests presoaking underwear in chlorine bleach and unscented detergent. Then machine-wash, using unscented detergent.

Take a break from sex. For most women, the discomfort caused by a yeast infection is enough to dampen any urge to engage in intercourse. But even if you can have sex comfortably, don't, Dr. Crandall says. "Your partner may pick up your infection, then pass it back to you."

For the same reason, don't have oral-genital sex either.

Reconsider your contraception. Oral contraceptives and spermicides can change your vaginal pH in ways that promote *C. albicans* overgrowth. "You may experience fewer infections if you switch to condoms or a diaphragm," Dr. Crandall says.

Over-the-Counter Drugs

Let cream be your cure. According to the American Pharmaceutical Association, over-the-counter antifungal vaginal creams effectively treat 85 to 90 percent of yeast infections. These creams contain one of four active ingredients approved by the Food and Drug Administration: clotrimazole (GyneLotrimin), miconazole (Monistat-7), butoconazole (Femstat), or tioconazole (Vagistat-1). Whichever of these products you choose, use it according to the package directions. Chances are you won't experience any side effects, although itching and burning are possible.

OTHER GOOD CHOICES

Visualization

See and smell vanilla. To achieve deep relaxation, Gerald N. Epstein, M.D., director of the Academy of Integrative Medicine and Mental Imagery in New York City, recommends the following visualization exercise: Close your eyes and take three deep breaths. Imagine yourself entering a beautiful orchid that smells of vanilla. Inhale the vanilla. See vanilla beans. Gather some of the beans in your hand and take them with you as you leave the orchid and enter your vagina. Survey your vaginal wall, looking for areas of yeast overgrowth. Using a golden brush that you carry in your other hand, brush away the yeast until none is left. Plant the vanilla beans in the areas where the yeast grew. See beautiful white orchids growing from your vaginal wall. Watch the petals unfold and release the fragrance of vanilla as your vagina heals perfectly. Now leave your vagina, take three deep breaths, and open your eyes.

Dr. Epstein suggests practicing this visualization three times a day—in the morning, at twilight, and before bed—for 21 days.

Homeopathy

Try a symptom-specific prescription. To treat yeast infections, homeopaths rely on a number of medicines, including Arsenicum album, Chamomilla, Graphites, Sulfur, and Candida (the yeast organism itself). Which of these works best for you depends on your individual symptoms, says homeopath Dana Ullman. For a recommendation, consult a homeopath.

Trichomonas: Fight Back with Vinegar

Trichomoniasis, better known as trich, is most common among young women. Two-thirds of those who get it are under age 30, although it's sometimes diagnosed in menopausal women, too.

The infection is caused by a single-celled microorganism called *Trichomonas vaginalis*. While some women experience no symptoms, trich usually produces a foul-smelling, frothy discharge, along with vaginal itching and pelvic pain.

Your doctor can easily diagnose trichomoniasis by examining your discharge under a microscope. The infection requires professional treatment.

Chinese Medicine

Use herbs to cool Heat and dry Damp. Practitioners of Chinese medicine attribute yeast infections to the accumulation of Heat and Damp in the vagina. "The Heat and Damp cause stagnation of qi and make the area vulnerable to external attack," explains Efrem Korngold, O.M.D., L.Ac.

To treat yeast infections, Dr. Korngold prescribes several herbal formulas. One such formula is Long Dan Xie Gan Wan, which contains a combination of Chinese angelica (dang gui), bupleurum root, rehmannia root, gardenia fruit, licorice root, and several other herbs.

Flex your fingers. To treat a yeast infection, you may want to try acupressure. Michael Reed Gach, founder and director of the Acupressure Institute, suggests applying steady, penetrating finger pressure for 3 minutes to each of the following points.

◆ Spleen 6, located four finger-widths above your inner anklebone on the back inner border of your shinbone

◆ Liver 8, located on your inner leg at the end of your knee crease

Ayurvedic Medicine

Enhance your digestion. Ayurvedic physicians view yeast infection as a "weakness of digestive fire" caused by a high-sugar diet, antibiotics, poor immune function, and "the general toxic state of the environment," says David Frawley, O.M.D. To treat a yeast infection, he recommends eating three to five cloves of garlic a day while avoiding sugar, dairy products, breads, and fruit. He also prescribes immune-boosting herbs such as ginseng, astragalus, bala, ashwagandha, and kapikacchu.

MEDICAL MEASURES

Mainstream M.D.'s treat yeast infections with prescription-strength versions of the antifungal vaginal creams described earlier. If you experience recurrent yeast infections and need to take an antibiotic for a bacterial infection, Dr. Crandall advises asking your doctor for yeast-treating medication at the same time.

RED FLAGS

If you experience recurrent yeast infections, you may have high blood sugar and not know it. High blood sugar may mean diabetes or a prediabetic condition. "Women with recurrent yeast infections should be tested for diabetes," Dr. Simons advises.

Resources

Guidelines for Safe Use

Vitamins, Minerals, and Other Supplements

Although reports of toxicity from vitamins, minerals, and other supplements are rare, toxic reactions do happen. This guide is designed to help you use supplements safely. The doses mentioned below are not recommendations; rather, they are the levels at which harmful side effects can occur. Some people may experience problems at significantly lower levels, however.

For best absorption and minimal stomach irritation, take supplements with a meal. If you have a serious chronic illness that requires continual medical supervision, always talk to your doctor before self-treating. Even if you're perfectly healthy, always tell your doctor which supplements you're taking. This way, if you need medication for any reason, your doctor can factor in your supplements and avoid dangerous drug combinations.

If you are pregnant, nursing, or attempting to conceive, do not supplement without the supervision of your doctor.

Supplement	Safe Use Guidelines and Possible Side Effects
Beta-carotene	Doses above 15 milligrams seem to have no benefit and should only be taken under medical supervision. Smokers in one study who received doses of 30 milligrams had an increased risk of lung cancer.
Bromelain	May cause nausea, vomiting, diarrhea, skin rash, and heavy menstrual bleeding; may increase the risk of bleeding in people taking aspirin or anticoagulants (blood thinners). Do not take if you are allergic to pineapple.
Calcium	Doses above 2,500 mg must be taken under medical supervision. Some natural sources of calcium, such as bonemeal and dolomite, may be contaminated with lead.
Carnitine (also known as L-carnitine)	Like other amino acids, carnitine should be taken only with a qualified health professional's guidance. The use of individual amino acids in large doses is considered experimental, and the long-term effects on health are unknown.
Coenzyme Q_{10}	May cause a slight decrease in the effectiveness of blood thinners in some people.
Fish oil	Increases bleeding time, possibly resulting in nosebleeds and easy bruising, and may cause upset stomach. Do not take if you have a bleeding disorder or uncontrolled high blood pressure, if you take anticoagulants (blood thinners) or use aspirin regularly, or if you're al-

Supplement | Safe Use Guidelines and Possible Side Effects

Supplement	Safe Use Guidelines and Possible Side Effects
	lergic to any kind of fish. Take fish oil, not fish-liver oil, which is high in vitamins A and D and is toxic in high amounts. People with diabetes should not take fish oil because of its high fat content.
Folic acid	Doses above 1,000 mcg must be taken under medical supervision. Excess folic acid can cause progressive nerve damage in individuals with vitamin B_{12} deficiency. Levels of more than 400 mcg can mask vitamin B_{12} deficiencies.
Iron	Doses above 25 mg must be taken under medical supervision.
Magnesium	Supplemental magnesium may cause diarrhea in some people. Also, people with heart or kidney problems should check with their doctors before taking supplemental magnesium.
Melatonin	Causes drowsiness, so take only at bedtime; never take before driving. Do not use if you have an autoimmune disease. Consult your doctor before using if you're on a prescription medication; interactions, though rare, do occur.
Niacin	Daily doses of more than 35 mg may cause flushing, itching, and other side effects and should be taken only under medical supervision.
Omega-3 fatty acid	See entry for fish oil.
Potassium	No need to supplement unless prescribed. Potassium may be prescribed if the patient has chronic diarrhea, laxative abuse, prolonged vomiting, high blood pressure, or metabolic disturbances such as diabetic acidosis.
Pyridoxine	See entry for vitamin B_6.
Selenium	Daily doses of more than 200 mcg may cause hair and nail loss, dizziness, nausea, a garlic odor on the breath and skin, and a metallic taste in the mouth. Doses above 200 mcg must be taken under medical supervision.
Vitamin A	Taking more than 10,000 IU a day may cause vomiting, fatigue, dizziness, and blurred vision. Doses above 10,000 IU must be taken under medical supervision.
Vitamin B_6 (pyridoxine)	Daily doses of more than 100 mg may cause nerve damage, resulting in a tingling sensation in the fingers and toes. Other possible side effects include pain, numbness and weakness in the limbs, depression, and fatigue. Doses above 200 mcg should be taken only under medical supervision.
Vitamin C	Daily doses of more than 1,000 mg may cause diarrhea.

Supplement	Safe Use Guidelines and Possible Side Effects
Vitamin D	Doses above 1,000 IU may cause headache, excessive thirst, and loss of appetite. Daily doses of more than 2,000 IU (50 mcg) may cause headache, fatigue, nausea, diarrhea, and loss of appetite. Doses above 2,000 IU must be taken only under medical supervision.
Vitamin E	Daily doses of more than 400 IU may cause headache, nausea, diarrhea, and fainting, so do not supplement at this level without talking to your doctor first. Although vitamin E is generally sold in doses of 400 IU, one small study showed a possible risk of hemorrhagic stroke in dosages higher than 200 IU. Consult your doctor if you are at a high risk for stroke. If you take blood-thinning medication or aspirin, consult your doctor before taking vitamin E.
Zinc	Daily doses of more than 30 mg may cause nausea and vomiting. Doses above 30 mg should be taken only under medical supervision.

Herbs and Their Compounds

While herbal home remedies are generally safe and cause few, if any, side effects, herbalists are quick to caution that botanical medicines should be used cautiously—and knowledgeably.

Foremost, if you are under a doctor's care for any health condition or are taking any medication, do not take any herb or alter your medication regimen without your doctor knowing about it. Do not administer herbs to children without consulting a physician. Also, if you are pregnant, do not self-treat with any natural remedy without the consent of your obstetrician or midwife. The same goes for nursing mothers and women trying to conceive. Some herbs may cause adverse reactions if you are allergy-prone, have a major health condition, take prescription medication, take an herb for too long, take too much, or use the herb improperly.

The guidelines in this chart are intended for adults only and usually refer to internal use. Be aware that some herbs may cause a skin reaction when used topically. If you are applying an herb for the first time, it is always wise to do a patch test. Apply a small amount to your skin and observe it for 24 hours to make sure that you aren't sensitive. If redness or a rash occurs, discontinue use.

Before you try the remedies in this book, check these safety guidelines, based on the American Herbal Products Association's *Botanical Safety Handbook*—a recognized source of herb safety information—and on the advice of experienced herbal healers. Then you can enjoy the world of herbal healing with confidence.

Herb or Compound	Safe Use Guidelines and Possible Side Effects
African star grass	May cause a drug interaction with some oxytocin drugs.
Aloe	Do not ingest the dried leaf, as it is a habit-forming laxative. Do not use gel externally on any surgical incision because it may delay wound healing.
Angelica	Use sparingly and only for short periods of time. Increases sun sensitivity.
Arnica	Do not use on broken skin.
Basil	Do not take large amounts (several cups a day) for extended periods.
Birch bark	Do not take birch bark if you need to avoid aspirin; its active ingredient, salicin, is related to aspirin.
Blackberry leaves	Considered safe.
Black cohosh	Avoid using this herb if you have heart disease or if you're taking medication for high blood pressure. Do not use for more than 6 months.
Black (or brown) mustard	When used as a plaster, mustard is likely to cause tearing in the eyes and local redness to the skin, with severe irritation in some cases. Apply olive oil after you are done. The plaster may aggravate symptoms in those with chronic pulmonary disease and should be used cautiously. Do not apply to mucous membranes or eyes. Never inhale mustard oil.
Buchu	Do not use if you have kidney disease. Also, do not use as a diet aid.
Bugleweed	Do not use if you have thyroid disease.
Butcher's broom	Avoid using with blood pressure medications, alpha blockers (medications typically used for prostate enlargement), and MAO inhibitors.
Chamomile	When ingested, this herb can cause rare but severe allergic reactions, especially in people with known ragweed allergy. Those allergic to closely related plants, such as aster and chrysanthemum, should drink the tea with caution. Chamomile contains coumarin, an anticoagulant. It should be used with caution by people who have blood-clotting disorders or who are on anticoagulant medications.
Chasteberry	May counteract the effectiveness of birth control pills. Some supplements may contain licorice or Siberian ginseng, which can elevate blood pressure. Read product labels carefully if you have high blood pressure.
Curcumin	See entry for turmeric.
Dandelion	If you have gallbladder disease, do not use dandelion root preparations without medical approval. Do not use as a diet aid.

Herb or Compound	Safe Use Guidelines and Possible Side Effects
Devil's claw	Do not use if you have gastric or duodenal ulcers. Avoid if you have a history of peptic ulcers or are taking medication for a heart rhythm disorder. Consult your physician before using to treat gallstones.
Dill seed	This herb contains high levels of sodium, so avoid it if you're on a low-sodium diet. People with an allergic tendency toward spices should avoid using this herb since it's likely to cause a reaction.
Echinacea	This herb is an immune system stimulant and should not be used by anyone with a chronic immune or autoimmune disease. Avoid using in conjunction with drugs that are toxic to the liver, such as anabolic steroids, amiodarone, methotrexate, and ketoconazole, as it may worsen liver damage. Do not use if you're allergic to closely related plants such as ragweed, asters and chrysanthemums.
Elecampane	Simply handling this herb may trigger allergic reactions in people who are prone to them, producing symptoms similar to those associated with poison ivy.
Ephedra	Do not self-administer this herb. Use it only under the guidance of a qualified health practitioner.
Eucalyptus	Do not use if you have an inflammatory disease of the bile ducts or gastrointestinal tract or severe liver disease. May cause nausea, vomiting, and diarrhea in doses larger than 4 grams a day.
Fennel	Do not use medicinally for more than 6 weeks without the supervision of a qualified herbalist.
Feverfew	When chewed, the fresh leaves can cause mouth sores in some people.
Garlic	Do not use if you are taking anticoagulant drugs or if you're about to have surgery, since it thins the blood and may increase bleeding. Do not use if you are taking hypoglycemic drugs.
Ginger/ gingerroot	If you have gallstones, do not take therapeutic amounts of the dried root or powder without the guidance of a qualified practitioner. Ginger may increase bile secretion.
Ginkgo	Do not use with antidepressant MAO inhibitor drugs such as phenelzine sulfate or tranylcypromine, with aspirin or other non-steroidal anti-inflammatory medications, or with blood-thinning medications such as warfarin. The concentrated extract can cause dermatitis, diarrhea, and vomiting in doses larger than 240 mg.
Ginseng	May cause irritability if taken with caffeine or other stimulants. Do not use if you have high blood pressure.

Herb or Compound	Safe Use Guidelines and Possible Side Effects
Goldenrod	Do not use if you have a chronic kidney disorder.
Goldenseal	Chronic use can decrease the absorption of vitamin B_{12}, thereby leading to deficiency. Do not use if you have high blood pressure.
Gotu kola	Do not use with medications for diabetes or high blood pressure.
Guggulsterone	See caution for mukul myrrh.
Hawthorn	If you have a cardiovascular condition, do not take hawthorn regularly for more than a few weeks without medical supervision. You may require lower doses of other medications, such as blood pressure drugs. Likewise, if you have low blood pressure caused by heart valve problems, do not take hawthorn without medical supervision.
Hops	Do not use if you're prone to depression. Rarely, hops can cause skin rashes, so handle the fresh and dried forms carefully.
Horse chestnut	May interfere with the action of other drugs, especially blood thinners such as warfarin. May irritate the gastrointestinal tract.
Kaffir potato	May intensify the effects of medications for asthma or high blood pressure, with negative results. Do not use unless you're under medical supervision.
Kelp	If you have high blood pressure or heart problems, use only once a day or less. Do not use if you have hyperthyroidism. Take with adequate liquid. Long-term use is not recommended.
Licorice	Do not use if you have diabetes; high blood pressure; heart rhythm abnormalities; cardiovascular, liver, or kidney disorders; or low potassium levels. Do not use daily for more than 4 to 6 weeks because overuse can lead to water retention, high blood pressure caused by potassium loss, or impaired heart and kidney function. Do not take with blood pressure, diuretic, corticosteroid, antiarrhythmic, or antihistamine medications. Do not take the deglycyrrhizinated licorice (DGL) form more than three times a week without the supervision of a qualified health professional.
Marshmallow	May slow the absorption of medications taken at the same time.
Meadowsweet	Do not use if you need to avoid aspirin. The herb's active ingredient, salicin, is related to aspirin.
Milk thistle (silymarin)	Consult a physician before using this herb. Its effects may make monitoring the effectiveness of other liver medicines more difficult. You may need periodic liver function tests while taking the herb.

Herb or Compound	Safe Use Guidelines and Possible Side Effects
Mint	May possibly worsen symptoms of heartburn in people with this problem. May cause allergic reactions.
Mukul myrrh (guggulsterone)	Rarely, may trigger diarrhea, restlessness, apprehension, or hiccups.
Nettle	May worsen allergy symptoms in people who have them. Take only one dose a day for the first few days.
Nutmeg	Do not use therapeutic amounts without a trained practitioner. Safe when used as a spice.
Parsley	Not appropriate for people with kidney disease; large amounts—on the order of several cups a day—can increase urine flow. Safe as a garnish or ingredient in food.
Peppermint	May relax the muscle at the lower end of the esophagus, increasing the likelihood of stomach acid sloshing into the esophagus and causing heartburn. Use the herb cautiously if you are prone to acid reflux either after meals or at night while in bed.
Psyllium seed	Do not use if you have a bowel obstruction. Take 1 hour after other drugs. Take with at least 8 ounces of water.
Pygeum	May cause nausea and stomach pain.
Raspberry leaf	If you have diabetes, talk to your doctor before using this herb since it may alter blood sugar levels.
Rhubarb	Do not use if you have an intestinal obstruction, abdominal pain of unknown origin, or any inflammatory condition of the intestines (such as appendicitis, colitis, or irritable bowel syndrome). If you have a history of kidney stones, use with caution. Do not use for more than 8 to 10 days.
Rosemary	May cause excessive menstrual bleeding in therapeutic amounts. Considered safe when used as a spice.
Sage	In therapeutic amounts, can increase the sedative side effects of drugs. Do not use if you're hypoglycemic or undergoing anticonvulsant therapy. Safe when used as a spice.
St. John's wort	Avoid using with alcohol, over-the-counter cold medications, or prescribed antidepressants. May cause photosensitivity, so avoid overexposure to direct sunlight. May cause high blood pressure when taken with ephedra compounds. Do not attempt to use this herb as a treatment for clinical depression.
Sarsaparilla	If you are taking any prescription medication, talk to a qualified health practitioner before using this herb. It may speed your body's elimina-

Herb or Compound	Safe Use Guidelines and Possible Side Effects
	tion of the medication, thereby requiring an increase in the effective dose.
Saw palmetto	If using to treat an enlarged prostate, consult your doctor first.
Shepherd's purse	Avoid while taking high blood pressure medications, medicines that alter heart rate such as beta-blockers, calcium channel blockers, or digitalis medicines. Avoid if taking sedatives or any medicines that alter cognitive function. Also, don't take this herb if you have heart disease, lung disease, or a history of kidney stones.
Silymarin	See caution for milk thistle.
Tea	Fermented black tea is not recommended for excessive or long-term use because it can stimulate the nervous system.
Turmeric	Do not use if you have excessive stomach acid, ulcers, gallstones, or bile duct obstruction or if you're taking anticoagulant medications, immune system suppressants, or nonsteroidal anti-inflammatory drugs such as ibuprofen. Do not use as a treatment for acute gallstone attacks. (Curcumin, a compound in turmeric, is safe as a preventive for gallstones.) May induce miscarriage in pregnant women. May cause stomach ulcers with prolonged use.
Uva-ursi	Do not use for more than 2 weeks without the supervision of a qualified herbalist. Do not use if you have kidney disease, because the tannins it contains can cause further kidney damage. Tannins can also irritate the stomach. Do not use as a diet aid.
Valerian	Do not use with sleep-enhancing or mood-regulating medications, because it may intensify their effects. May cause heart palpitations and nervousness in sensitive individuals. If such stimulant action occurs, discontinue use.
Wild cherry bark	Not for long-term use. Do not exceed recommended dose.
Willow bark	Do not use if you are allergic to aspirin. May trigger asthma or allergies. May cause gastrointestinal bleeding, liver dysfunction, blood-clotting disorders, kidney damage, or anaphylactic reactions. Do not use if you are taking a blood-thinning medication such as warfarin, because the herb's active ingredient is related to aspirin. Avoid using the herb with anticoagulants, diuretics, blood pressure drugs, and anti-inflammatory medications, especially aspirin. May interact with barbiturates or sedatives such as aprobarbital or alprazolam. Can cause stomach irritation when consumed with alcohol.
Witch hazel	Do not use internally.

Essential Oils

Essential oils are inhaled or applied topically to the skin, but with few exceptions, they're never taken internally.

Of the most common essential oils, lavender, tea tree, lemon, sandalwood, and rose can be used undiluted. The rest should be diluted in a carrier base—which can be an oil (such as almond), cream, or gel—before being applied to the skin.

Many essential oils may cause irritation or allergic reactions in people with sensitive skin. Before applying any new oil to your skin, always do a patch test. Put a few drops on the back of your wrist. Wait for an hour or more. If irritation or redness occurs, wash the area with cold water. In the future, use half of the amount of oil or avoid the oil altogether.

Do not use essential oils at home for serious medical problems.

During pregnancy, do not use essential oils unless they're approved by your doctor. Essential oils are not appropriate for children of any age.

Store essential oils in dark bottles, away from light and heat and out of the reach of children and pets.

Essential Oil	Safe Use Guidelines and Possible Side Effects
Birch	Do not use for more than 2 weeks without the guidance of a qualified practitioner.
Clove bud	Do not use for more than 2 weeks without the guidance of a qualified practitioner because of potential toxicity. Do not use more than 3 drops in the bath. Can be used undiluted for tooth pain.
Ginger	Avoid direct sunlight while using this oil, because it can cause skin sensitivity.
Juniper	Do not use for more than 2 weeks without the guidance of a qualified practitioner, because of potential toxicity. Do not use if you have kidney disease.
Lavender	Can be used undiluted, but keep it away from your eyes.
Peppermint	Do not use at the same time as homeopathic medicines. Can be used internally, with this caveat: It may lead to stomach upset in sensitive individuals. If you have gallbladder or liver disease, do not use without medical supervision.
Ravensara	Do not use for more than 2 weeks without the guidance of a qualified practitioner because it may be habit-forming.

How to Find What You Need

When you go looking for a mainstream doctor—whether a family physician or a specialist—you probably talk to friends or medical professionals whom you can trust to give you sound advice. The same principle applies if you're seeking a practitioner of alternative or complementary medicine. But the search may be somewhat more difficult.

Of course, you may already have an integrative or complementary medicine clinic in your area that can provide you with all the resources you need for blended medicine consultation and treatment. In addition, the resources in this section can provide you with further guidance.

Skilled Professionals

Acupuncture and Chinese Medicine

An estimated 10,000 acupuncturists and Chinese medicine physicians currently practice in the United States. Since 1982, the National Certification Commission for Acupuncture and Oriental Medicine (NCCAOM) has established three certification programs in acupuncture, Chinese herbology, and oriental bodywork.

To become certified, acupuncturists must pass the NCCAOM exam, which includes acupuncture theory as well as clean needle technique. To take the exam, candidates must meet national standards of education or complete a 4,000-hour apprenticeship with an experienced acupuncturist in no less than 3 years. If trained abroad, they must meet equivalency requirements. The NCCAOM certification is used in every state (and the District of Columbia) except for California and Nevada, which have their own examinations.

In addition, an estimated 5,000 American doctors (M.D.'s and D.O.'s) include acupuncture in their practices. Most are family practitioners, anesthesiologists, orthopedists, or pain specialists who have met the training requirements of the American Academy of Medical Acupuncture.

The following states license acupuncturists: Alaska (licensed acupuncturist, L.Ac.), Arizona (L.Ac.), Arkansas (doctor of oriental medicine, D.O.M.), California (L.Ac.), Colorado (registered acupuncturist, R.Ac.), Connecticut (acupuncturist, Ac.), District of Columbia (Ac.), Florida (certified acupuncturist, C.A., acupuncture physician, A.P.), Hawaii (L.Ac.), Idaho (L.Ac.), Illinois (Ac.), Indiana (L.Ac.), Iowa (R.Ac.), Louisiana (acupuncture assistant, Ac.A.), Maine (L.Ac.), Maryland (L.Ac.), Massachusetts (licensed acupuncturist, Lic.Ac.), Minnesota (L.Ac.), Missouri, (L.Ac.), Montana (C.A.), Nevada (D.O.M.), New Hampshire (L.Ac. Lic.Ac.), New Jersey (C.A.), New Mexico (D.O.M.), New York (L.Ac., or C.A. if the practitioner is an M.D., D.O., or dentist), North Carolina (L.Ac., Ac.), Oregon (L.Ac.), Pennsylvania (Ac.), Rhode Island (doctor of acupuncture, D.Ac.), South Carolina (Ac.), Texas (L.Ac., Lic.Ac.), Utah (Ac.), Vermont (L.Ac., Lic.Ac.), Virginia (L.Ac., Lic.Ac.), Washington (L.Ac.), West Virginia (L.Ac.), and Wisconsin (Ac.).

All states also allow M.D.'s and D.O.'s to practice acupuncture. Fourteen states plus the District of Columbia require M.D.'s and D.O.'s to be specifically trained in acupuncture to practice it: Florida, Georgia, Hawaii, Louisiana, Maryland, Montana, Nevada, New Jersey, New York, Ohio, Pennsylvania, Tennessee, Virginia, and West Virginia. The 36 other states do not require proof of training for M.D.'s and D.O.'s to practice acupuncture.

The following organizations can provide referrals to certified acupuncturists, many of whom also practice Chinese medicine.

The American Academy of Medical Acupuncture (AAMA) has a membership of 1,800 M.D.'s and D.O.'s who offer acupuncture treatment in their practices. For referrals to AAMA members in your area, contact the AAMA at 5820 Wilshire Boulevard, Suite 500, Los Angeles, CA 90036-4500.

The National Acupuncture and Oriental Medicine Alliance distributes a biannual updated guide called *Acupuncture and Oriental Medicine Laws.* For ordering information, contact the Alliance at 14637 Starr Road SE, Olalla, WA 98359-8554. There is a charge for the guide. There is no fee for referrals.

The National Certification Commission for Acupuncture and Oriental Medicine (NCCAOM) is located at 11 Canal Center Plaza, Suite 300, Alexandria, VA 22314-1595. A small fee is charged for referrals.

Ayurveda

Currently, there is no U.S. certification program for Ayurvedic physicians. At India's 200 Ayurvedic medical schools, it takes 5 or 6 years to earn a bachelor of Ayurvedic medicine and surgery (B.A.M.S.). U.S. training programs are considerably shorter (8 months to 4 years), but most U.S. programs limit enrollment to licensed health professionals (M.D.'s, N.D.'s, R.N.'s, or chiropractors) who already have considerable medical knowledge. Most training programs in the United States will make referrals to their graduates. Training programs include the following:

The American Institute of Vedic Studies is a program directed by the prominent Ayurvedic physician and author David Frawley, O.M.D. The address is P. O. Box 8357, Santa Fe, NM 87504-8357.

The Ayurvedic Institute is a training program directed by prominent Ayurvedic physician and author Vasant Lad, B.A.M.S., M.A.Sc., former professor of medicine at the Pune University College of Ayurvedic Medicine in Pune, India, and medical director of the Ayurvedic hospital there. The address is P. O. Box 23445, Albuquerque, NM 87192-1445.

Bastyr University, the nation's leading school of naturopathic medicine, also offers training in Ayurvedic medicine. The address is 14500 Juanita Drive NE, Kenmore, WA 98028-4966.

Maharishi College of Vedic Medicine trains M.D.'s and other health professionals in Maharishi Vedic medicine, including Ayurvedic. The address is 2721 Arizona Street NE, Albuquerque, NM 87110-3330.

The College of Maharishi Vedic Medicine provides training to nonhealth professionals. It is part of Maharishi University of Management in Fairfield, Iowa.

The Raj Maharishi Ayurveda Health Center maintains a list of practitioners around the country and sells Ayurvedic herbs and other products. The address is 1734 Jasmine Avenue, Fairfield, IA 52556-9005.

Biofeedback

The Association for Applied Psychophysiology and Biofeedback (AAPB) includes more than 2,000 members who teach and conduct research in biofeedback. The AAPB also began the Biofeedback Certification Institute of America, which certifies biofeedback therapists. For a list of certified biofeedback therapists in your area, send a self-addressed, stamped envelope to 10200 West 44th Avenue, Suite 304, Wheat Ridge, CO 80033-2840.

Bodywork

The following are a number of organizations that represent the various disciplines of bodywork.

The Aston Training Center can be contacted at P. O. Box 3568, Incline Village, NV 89450-3568.

Bonnie Prudden Pain Erasure can be reached at P. O. Box 65240, Tucson, AZ 85728-5240.

Feldenkrais Resources is located at 830 Bancroft Way, Suite 112, Berkeley, CA 94710-2246.

American Society for the Alexander Technique is located in the Enterprise Travel Building, 401 East Market Street, Charlottesville, VA 22902-5264.

The Rolf Institute provides referrals to certified practitioners, plus sells books and videos about Rolfing. The address is 205 Canyon Boulevard, Boulder, CO 80302-4920.

Trager Institute is located at 21 Locust Avenue, Mill Valley, CA 94941-2805.

Hellerwork International, L.L.C., can be contacted at 406 Berry Street, Mount Shasta, CA 96067-2548.

Chiropractic

To be licensed, chiropractors must pass two certification exams, a national test given by the National Board of Chiropractic Examiners and, depending on the state requirement, an exam given by the state's licensing board. To find out the specific licensing requirements in your state, contact your state's licensing board.

Most chiropractors approach the body as a whole. Some seek additional training to specialize in radiology, orthopedics, neurology, or sports injuries, however.

Chiropractors are not required to belong to professional organizations, and no single organization represents all of the nation's chiropractors. But if you want referrals, the following organizations can be helpful.

The American Chiropractic Association is the largest chiropractic organization in the United States. The association works closely with independent state associations in every state. The address is 1701 Clarendon Boulevard, Arlington, VA 22209-2721.

The International Chiropractic Association, founded in 1926 by B. J. Palmer, is the oldest chiropractic organization. The address is 1110 North Glebe Road, Suite 1000, Arlington, VA 22201-5765.

The American Osteopathic Association (AOA) can refer you to an osteopath in your area. The address is 142 East Ontario Street, Chicago, IL 60611-2864.

The American Academy of Osteopathy is a 1,700-member subgroup of practitioners within the AOA who frequently use osteopathic manipulation in their practices. For information, write to 3500 DePauw Boulevard, Suite 1080, Indianapolis, IN 46268-1136.

The Association for Network Chiropractic is located at 444 North Main Street, Longmont, CO 80501-5535.

The Federation of Straight Chiropractors is located at 642 Broad Street, Clifton, NJ 07013-1615.

The World Chiropractic Alliance is located at 2950 North Dobson Road, Suite 1, Chandler, AZ 85224-1819.

Complementary and Holistic Therapies

A number of organizations provide listings of medical professionals and practitioners who use some or all of the therapies of blended medicine. For general listings, contact the following.

The Alternative Medicine Yellow Pages lists more than 16,000 practitioners of complementary therapies around the country, including many M.D.'s and D.O.'s. It's published by Future Medicine Publishing, 1640 Tiburon Boulevard, Tiburon, CA 94920-2523.

American Holistic Health Association is a national clearinghouse of information about complementary therapies and practitioners. Its address is P. O. Box 17400, Anaheim, CA 92817-7400.

The American Holistic Medical Association represents M.D.'s and D.O.'s who combine mainstream medicine with complementary therapies. The organization publishes the *National Referral Directory of Holistic Practitioners*. The address is 6728 Old McLean Village Drive, McLean, VA 22101-3951.

The American Holistic Nurses Association is an organization for nurses who have a particular interest in complementary therapies. Its address is P. O. Box 2130, Flagstaff, AZ 86003-2130.

Herbal Medicine

Most herbalists practice as acupuncturists, naturopaths, or Chinese medicine physicians, but some train through one of the nation's several dozen herbal schools, correspondence courses, or apprenticeship programs. All are listed in the American Herbalist Guild's (AHG) *Directory of Herbal Education Programs*. These training programs can refer you to graduates who practice herbalism.

In addition, the AHG has created its own designation, "professional member." To qualify, candidates must have completed 4 years of herbal practice beyond formal training, be recommended by three professional members, and demonstrate competence in working with both medicinal herbs and clients. The guild makes referrals to its 100 professional members.

To obtain a copy of *The American Herbalist Guild's Directory of Herbal Education Programs*, write to the AHG at P. O. Box 70, Roosevelt, UT 84066-0070.

Homeopathy

Most U.S. homeopaths are licensed to practice some other health profession and also practice homeopathy, so their ranks include M.D.'s, D.O.'s, N.D.'s, acupuncturists, chiropractors, and nurses. Homeopathic Educational Services and the National Center for Homeopathy sell a directory of licensed health professionals around the United States who also practice homeopathy. (Not all qualified homeopaths are listed in the directory, however.)

Skilled homeopaths have been certified by one of three organizations.

The American Board of Homeotherapeutics certifies M.D.'s and D.O.'s who practice homeopathy. The address is 801 North Fairfax Street, Suite 306, Alexandria, VA 22314-1757.

The Homeopathic Academy of Naturopathic Physicians certifies naturopathic homeopaths and offers referrals. The address is 12132 SE Foster Place, Portland, OR 97266-4983.

The North American Society of Homeopaths is located at 1122 East Pike Street, Suite 1122, Seattle, WA 98122-3916.

Other resources include:

Homeopathic Educational Services, which is owned and operated by well-known homeopath and author Dana Ullman, can provide homeopathic books, medicines, and other resources. For a free catalog, write to 2124 Kittredge Street, Berkeley, CA 94704-1436.

The National Center for Homeopathy is a nonprofit organization that promotes homeopathy, sponsors a training program and study groups around the country, and publishes a magazine called *Homeopathy Today*. Write to 801 North Fairfax Street, Suite 306, Alexandria, VA 22314-1757.

Massage

The **American Massage Therapy Association (AMTA)** provides referrals to certified massage therapists and certified massage schools around the country. The address is 820 Davis Street, Suite 100, Evanston, IL 60201-4444.

Associated Bodywork and Massage Professionals (ABMP) provides referrals to members around the country. The address is 28677 Buffalo Park Road, Evergreen, CO 80439-7347.

Meditation and Visualization

The **Academy for Guided Imagery**, established by visualization pioneer Martin Rossman, M.D., trains health professionals to use imagery in healing. For information, send a stamped, self-addressed envelope to P. O. Box 2070, Mill Valley, CA 94942-2070.

The **Society for Clinical and Experimental Hypnosis** is a professional organization that can refer you to member hypnotherapists around the country. Send a stamped, self-addressed envelope to 2201 Haeder Road, Suite 1, Pullman, WA 99163-8619.

The **American Society of Clinical Hypnosis** also provides referrals. Send a stamped, self-addressed envelope to 33 West Grand Avenue, Suite 402, Chicago, IL 60610-4306.

Music Therapy

The **American Association for Music Therapy** provides information about music therapy and referrals to training programs and therapists. The address is 8455 Colesville Road, Suite 1000, Silver Spring, MD 20910-3392.

Naturopathy

Naturopaths are currently licensed to practice in 11 states (Alaska, Arizona, Connecticut, Hawaii, Maine, Montana, New Hampshire, Oregon, Utah, Vermont, and Washington), the Commonwealth of Puerto Rico, and five Canadian provinces (Alberta, British Columbia, Manitoba, Ontario, and Saskatchewan). Licensing criteria differ, but an increasing number of states and provinces have adopted a standard exam, the Naturopathic Physician Licensing Exam (NPLEX), as part of their credentialing requirements.

Elsewhere, naturopaths practice under other medical credentials. Often, they are qualified as acupuncturists, chiropractors, or clinical nutritionists.

The American Association of Naturopathic Physicians (AANP) maintains a complete list of licensed naturopaths. Though membership is not a requirement to be on their list, the association is open to practitioners who have completed training at any of the four schools. About 1,500 naturopaths, physicians, and naturopath medical students are members.

To find a naturopath near you, consult the following organizations.

The **American Association of Naturopathic Physicians** publishes a membership directory for a fee. Send inquiries to the AANP, 601 Valley Street, Suite 105, Seattle, WA 98109-4229.

The **Canadian Naturopathic Association (CNA)** makes referrals to naturopathic doctors in Canada. Contact the CNA at 4174 Dundas Street West, Suite 303, Etobicoke, Ontario, Canada M8X 1X3.

The **Homeopathic Academy of Naturopathic Physicians** certifies naturopathic homeopaths. The address is 12132 SE Foster Place, Portland, OR 97266-4983.

Nutrition

The American Dietetic Association (ADA) makes referrals to registered dietitians around the country. The organization also has a staff of registered dietitians (R.D.'s) who answer nutrition-related questions. Contact the ADA at 216 West Jackson Boulevard, Suite 800, Chicago, IL 60606-6995.

Social Support

The American Self-Help Clearinghouse is a New Jersey–based organization that focuses primarily on self-help groups in that state. For information, contact American Self-Help Clearinghouse, 25 Pocono Road, Denville, NJ 07834-2954.

The National Institute for Relationship Enhancement (RE) provides information about weekend workshops. Write to 4400 East-West Highway, Suite 28, Bethesda, MD 20814-4501.

Premarital Personal and Relationship Evaluation (PREPARE) provides referrals to premarital and marriage counselors near you. The address is P. O. Box 190, Minneapolis, MN 55440-0190.

Practical Application of Intimate Relationship Skills (PAIRS) is located at 318 Indian Terrace, Suite 158, Weston, FL 33326-2996.

Prevention and Relationship Enhancement Program (PREP) can send information about 1-day or weekend workshops. Write to PREP at P. O. Box 102530, Denver, CO 80250-2530.

Walking Programs

The Prevention Walking Club has more than 15,000 members. If you join, you get a bimonthly newsletter, information about the annual walker's convention and fantastic walking vacations, and other benefits. Contact the club at 33 East Minor Street, Emmaus, PA 18098-0099.

Creative Walking, Inc. (CWI) is an organization started by Rob Sweetgall to train education, corporate, and health-care specialists to support walking programs in schools, corporations, hospitals, and communities. Since 1985, CWI has helped more than 1,000 clients develop walking programs. Write to the organization at P. O. Box 50296, Clayton, MO 63105-5296.

Health-Care Products

You can find many of the herbs, supplements, and other health-care products recommended in this book in your local drugstore or health food store. If specific products are unavailable, however, you may be able to obtain them from the following sources.

Biofeedback Equipment

The leading manufacturer is Thought Technology of Montreal. The company markets Galvanic Skin Response devices, plus a dozen programs that combine them with visualization audiotapes for specific personal goals: athletic improvement, stress management, insomnia relief, smoking cessation, weight loss, pain control, overcoming fear of flying, improved sexual function, breathing for health, taking tests, speaking in public, and chemical dependency. Contact Thought Technology at 2180 Belgrave Avenue, Montreal, Quebec, Canada H4A 2L8

Essential Oils

Aroma-Vera offers more than 100 essential oils, plus a large variety of aromatic soaps, candles, bath and massage oils, and hair- and skin-care products. You can order a free catalog from 5901 Rodeo Road, Los Angeles, CA 90016-4319.

Leydet Aromatics offers about 150 essential oils, one of the largest selections available in the United States. Contact them at P. O. Box 2354, Fair Oaks, CA 95628-2354.

Santa Fe Botanical Fragrances carries approximately 75 essential oils. Request a free catalog from P. O. Box 282, Santa Fe, NM 87504-0282.

Herbs

If you can't find medicinal herbs in your area, you can order them from Nature's Herbs. This mail-order company markets 350 kinds of herbs by mail. For a free catalog, write to 47444 Kato Road, Freemont, CA 94538-7319.

Meditation Tapes and Videos

For a series of audiocassettes from Herbert Benson, M.D., of the Mind/Body Medical Institute, request a free catalog from the Mind/Body Medical Institute, 110 Francis Street, Suite 1A, Boston, MA 02215-5501. Dr. Benson teaches the relaxation response and other deep relaxation techniques.

Meditation audiotapes can also be ordered from Jon Kabat-Zinn, Ph.D., and are available from Stress Reduction Tapes, P. O. Box 547, Lexington, MA 02420-0005.

Visualization tapes can be ordered from the Imagery Store at the Academy for Guided Imagery. In addition to basic relaxation tapes, Martin L. Rossman, M.D., and pain specialist David Bressler, Ph.D., offer a variety of relaxation and visualization tapes for specific health and behavior problems, including "Mind-Controlled Anesthesia for Systemic Pain," "Restful Sleep," and "Forgiveness in Healing." The address is P. O. Box 2070, Mill Valley, CA 94942-2070.

Another source of visualization tapes is Source Cassette Learning System. In addition to basic relaxation tapes, psychiatrist Emmett Miller, M.D., a pioneer in visualization cassettes, offers tapes for specific health and behavior problems, among them: "Smoke No More," "The Sleep Tape," "Imagine Yourself Slim," "Letting Go of Stress," "Freeing Yourself from Fear," "Successful Surgery and Recovery," "Power Vision," and "The Source Meditation." Contact Source Cassette Learning System, 131 East Placer Street, P. O. Box 6028, Auburn, CA 95603-5241.

Self-Massage

The SelfCare Catalog offers many massage and self-massage items. For the catalog, write to 2000 Powell Street, Suite 1350, Emeryville, CA 94608-4700.

For an introduction to Swedish and shiatsu massage techniques, you can order "Massage Your Mate," a 92-minute color VHS cassette. Rebecca Klinger, a licensed massage therapist in New York, is your guide through this excellent introduction to massage. Despite its title, this isn't just for spouses. It can be ordered from V.I.E.W. Video, 34 East 23rd Street, New York, NY 10010-4499.

Another video introduction to massage is "Massage for Health," a 70-minute color VHS cassette by Shari Belafonte-Harper (Harry Belafonte's daughter). The video presents a relaxing combination of Swedish and shiatsu techniques. A 40-page booklet accompanies the video. You can order this video from most video stores, or you can purchase it from an online outlet.

Tai Chi Videos

Terry Dunn's Tai Chi for Health color videos teach the Yang form of tai chi. They are available for order at most video stores, or you can purchase them from an online outlet.

For videos about tai chi, qigong, and the martial arts, contact Wayfarer Publications at P. O. Box 39938, Los Angeles, CA 90039-0938.

Bibliographic Note

In researching *Blended Medicine*, I used 1,973 sources, including 116 books, 219 interviews, 1,136 medical journal articles, and 502 other sources—mostly medical trade publications, consumer health magazines, *The New York Times*, and materials published by organizations such as the National Institutes of Health and the American Heart Association. Unfortunately, there is not room for all the references in this book. But the complete, 74-page bibliography is available. If you would like a copy, please send a check or money order for $10.00 (for reproduction, postage, and handling) to Self-Care Associates, P. O. Box 460066, San Francisco, CA 94146-0066. Please allow 3 weeks for delivery.

Degrees in Mainstream and Alternative Medicine

Many of the experts cited in this book have professional degrees other than M.D.'s, Ph.D.'s, or R.N.'s. These designations are granted by a variety of schools, boards, and associations, usually after completion of certain educational or training requirements. The following list highlights some of the more common degrees in mainstream and alternative medicine, along with the qualifications for each.

A.H.G. (American Herbalist Guild) Indicates professional membership in the American Herbalist Guild, a nonprofit organization. At least 4 years of experience working with clients in the field of herbal medicine and peer review of credentials is required. Professional members are recognized with the title Herbalist, A.H.G. (or A.H.G. for short). There are two other categories of membership in this organization: General members are individuals working toward professional status, and supporting members are organizations or individuals who support the Guild.

B.A.M.S. (Bachelor of Ayurvedic Medicine and Surgery) Indian college degree that is equivalent to an M.D. but in Ayurvedic medicine; requires 4 years of graduate studies. There are no state-recognized certification exams or titles in the United States. Most Ayurvedic practitioners have either an N.D. or an M.D. degree and practice under that title.

D.Ac. (Diplomate of Acupuncture) Indicates that the acupuncturist has passed an exam given by the National Commission for the Certification of Acupuncturists.

D.C. (Doctor of Chiropractic) Professionals with this degree are graduates of 4-year chiropractic medical colleges (following a minimum of 2 years of college in a pre-medical or science curriculum) and are licensed in all 50 states according to standards set by the Council of Chiropractic Education and the Federation of Chiropractic Licensing Boards. They may not perform surgery or prescribe drugs. Chiropractic is based on the idea that the human body has an innate self-healing ability and seeks balance. Chiropractic treatment consists of manipulation of the vertebral column and the extremities.

D.D.S. (Doctor of Dental Surgery) Indicates the successful completion of a 4-year dental program by an accredited college or university. Before people can start practicing dentistry, they are required to take a state board examination in order to obtain a license. Dentists care for teeth by helping to prevent tooth decay, periodontal disease, and other oral disorders. Equivalent to D.M.D. (Doctor of Medical Dentistry).

D.N.Sc. (Doctor of Nursing Science) Indicates graduation from an approved 5- to 7-year doctoral program of nursing science.

D.O. (Doctor of Osteopathy) A professional using this designation has received an undergraduate degree, completed 4 years of basic medical education, and passed a state licensing examination. A D.O. can choose to practice in a specialty area of medicine after completing a residency program (typically 2 to 6 years of additional training). Osteopathic physicians focus on preventive health care and receive special training in the musculoskeletal system.

D.O.M. (Doctor of Oriental Medicine) Licensure title used by some states; same as O.M.D. (Oriental Medicine Doctor).

D.P.M. (Doctor of Podiatric Medicine) Indicates graduation from an approved 4-year program of podiatric medical education, following at least 2 years of preprofessional college study. Podiatrists are examined and licensed by a state's medical board. They diagnose, treat, perform surgery, and prescribe drugs for any disease, injury, deformity, or other condition of the foot.

Dr.P.H. (Doctor of Public Health) Indicates graduation from an approved program of public health education; the length of the program may vary. Generally, doctors in public health design, conduct, assess, and apply scientific research to critical issues affecting the health of populations and on the effectiveness and efficiency of health-care delivery organizations and systems.

Ed.D. (Doctor of Education) Indicates the completion of a 5- to 7-year doctoral program in education from an accredited university or college.

L.Ac. (Licensed Acupuncturist) Indicates a state license or a diploma from a European school. Synonymous with C.A, Lic.Ac., R.Ac., Ac., A.P., and Ac.A.

M.A.Sc. (Master of Ayurvedic Science) Indian college degree that requires 3 years of postgraduate studies, including an internship of 2 years. This is in addition to the 4 years of graduate work necessary to earn a B.A.M.S.

M.B. (Bachelor of Medicine) Conferred after satisfactory completion of a medical school program in Great Britain. The typical curriculum covers 5 years. The M.D. degree is given only after further study.

N.D. (Naturopathic Doctor) N.D. licensure laws require a resident pre-med course of at least 4 years and 4,000 hours of study at a college recognized by the state examining board. N.D.'s are considered the general practitioners of the natural healing world.

O.D. (Doctor of Optometry) This health-care provider is qualified to examine the eyes and related structures in order to identify abnormalities. Optometrists may prescribe eyeglasses and other visual aids but cannot prescribe drugs or perform surgery. Four years of optometry school post-baccalaureate are required for this degree.

O.M.D. (Oriental Medicine Doctor) Indicates some additional training beyond state licensure to practice acupuncture. It also is sometimes taken by professionals who have graduated from traditional Chinese or Korean medicine programs in China but who are not M.D.'s in the United States. If you are considering treatment from someone who calls himself an O.M.D., note if he also uses the initials C.A., L.Ac., Lic.Ac., R.Ac., or Ac., all of which usually indicate state licensure or qualification.

P.E.D. (Physical Education Doctorate) Similar to a Ph.D. in physical education, except with less emphasis on research.

Pharm.D. (Doctor of Pharmacy) Indicates graduation from an approved 6-year professional program of pharmaceutical sciences. Generally, doctors in pharmacy are responsible for the distribution of medications. They are trained to ensure the most appropriate drug therapy outcomes. A Pharm.D. degree is different from a P.D. degree, which is an honorary title.

R.D. (Registered Dietitian) R.D.'s are food and nutrition experts who have completed a minimum of a bachelor's degree at a U.S.-accredited university or college and have passed a national examination. They also must have completed a 6- to 12-month practice program at a health-care facility, community agency, or a food service corporation.

Sc.D. (Doctor of Science) Indicates a person who has completed a doctorate-level program of study. Sc.D. degrees are awarded by a select group of universities and colleges. In most cases, it is equivalent to a Ph.D. and covers a broad range of fields.

About the Author

Medical journalist Michael Castleman, M.A., has been called "one of the top health writers in the country" (*Library Journal*). A graduate of the University of California, Berkeley, Graduate School of Journalism, he has written about both mainstream medicine and complementary therapies since 1972.

His nine other health books have more than 2 million copies in print, among them: *Nature's Cures, The Healing Herbs, An Aspirin a Day), Before You Call the Doctor* (with Anne Simons, M.D., and Bobbie Hasselbring), and *Cold Cures.*

Castleman has contributed articles on health, medicine, fitness, nutrition, and sexuality to an enormous number of publications, among them: *The New York Times, Prevention, Reader's Digest, Family Circle, New Woman, Redbook, Self, Glamour, American Health for Women, Psychology Today, Parenting, Mademoiselle, Men's Health, Men's Fitness, Men's Journal, Modern Maturity, Natural Health, Your Health, Healthy Living, Walking, Herb Quarterly, Herb Companion, Herbs for Health, Sierra, Mother Jones, Utne Reader, The Nation,* and *Playboy.* He also contributes to several consumer health Web sites, among them: Diabetes.com, Depression.com, Alzheimer's.com, and PlanetRx.com.

Castleman has won numerous journalism awards and has taught medical writing at the University of California, Berkeley, Graduate School of Journalism.

He lives in San Francisco.

Index

Underscored page references indicate boxed text and tables.

Curcumin
  safety guidelines for, 662
  for treating
    gallstones, 302
    osteoarthritis, 502
Curing Pills, for diarrhea, 247
Cystitis. *See also* Urinary tract infection
  interstitial, 619
Cysts, ovarian, 272

Dairy avoidance, for colds, 195
Dandelion
  for hepatitis, 361
  safety guidelines for, 662
DASH diet, for high blood pressure, 365
Dead Sea minerals, for psoriasis, 554
Dead Sea Psoriasis Clinic, 554
Decoctions, 89
Decongestants, for treating
  incontinence, 404–5
  sinus infection, 576–77
Deep breathing, for stress, 588
Deep-tissue manipulation, 72
Depression, 219–30
  factors contributing to, 219–21
  forms of, 219
  insomnia from, 429
  postpartum, 224
  red flags concerning, 230
  seasonal, 226–27
  signs of, 220
  treating, with
    acupressure, 228–29
    acupuncture, 228
    alcohol avoidance, 226
    antidepressants, 229–30
    brahmi, 229
    bright-light therapy, 226–27, 227
    B vitamins, 221–22
    caffeine, 226
    Chinese herbs, 228
    citrus oil, 227
    electroconvulsive therapy, 230
    exercise, 222
    ginkgo, 225
    homeopathy, 228
    L-tryptophan, 222
    massage, 223
    music therapy, 80, 223
    psychotherapy, 230
    relaxation therapies, 222–23
    social support, 223–25
    St. John's wort, 225

Devil's claw
  for back pain, 150
  safety guidelines for, 663
Diabetes, 231–41
  effect of modern culture on, 233
  exercise safety with, 236–37
  red flags concerning, 241
  treating, with
    acupressure, 239–40
    alcohol avoidance, 238–39
    antioxidants, 233
    Ayurvedic medicine, 240
    bilberry, 238
    biofeedback, 237
    borage oil, 234–35
    Chinese herbs, 239
    chromium, 234
    evening primrose oil, 234–35
    exercise, 235
    fenugreek, 237–38
    fiber, 233
    garlic, 238
    ginseng, 238
    low-fat diet, 232–33
    magnesium, 234
    onions, 238
    prescription drugs, 240
    relaxation therapies, 235–36
    soy products, 234
    tea, 238
    visualization, 236–37
    vitamin E, 234
    weight control, 238
    yoga, 235
    zinc, 234
  types of, 231–32
  yeast infections with, 655
Diabetic neuropathy, capsaicin cream for, 239
Diabetic retinopathy, bilberries for, 238
Diarrhea, 242–48
  causes of, 242
  red flags concerning, 248
  traveler's, preventing, 244–45
  treating, with
    acupressure, 247–48
    carob, 245
    Curing Pills, 247
    diet, 243
    elimination diet, 247
    goldenseal, 245, 246
    homeopathy, 246
    home remedies, 246